Defender of the Public Interest:

The General Accounting Office, 1921-1966

Roger R. Trask

The U.S. General Accounting Office
Washington, D.C.

About the Author

Roger R. Trask received his Ph.D in history at the Pennsylvania State University in 1959. He then taught in succession between 1959 and 1980 at Upsala College, Thiel College, Macalester College, and the University of South Florida. He served as chief historian of the U.S. Nuclear Regulatory Commission (1977-1978), deputy historian in the Office of the Secretary of Defense (1980-1987), and chief historian of the U.S. General Accounting Office (1987-1993).

Among his publications are *The United States Response to Turkish Nationalism and Reform, 1914-1939*, (1971), *The Secretaries of Defense: A Brief History, 1947-1985* (1985), *GAO History, 1921-1991* (1991), *A Bibliography of United States-Latin American Relations Since 1810* (co-editor, 1968), as well as many articles and essays in scholarly journals and anthologies.

He is a past president of the Society for History in the Federal Government. Since 1993 he has been working as an independent historian.

Library of Congress Cataloging-in-Publication Data

Trask, Roger R.
    Defender of the public interest: the General Accounting Office,
    1921-1966 / Roger R. Trask.
        p.   cm.
    Includes bibliographical references and index.
    ISBN 0-16-048728-5 (hard cover. alk. paper)
    1. United States. General Accounting Office—History. I. United
States. General Accounting Office. II. Title.
HJ9802.T728   1996
359.0072'3—dc20   96-43135
                                                             CIP

Published by the U.S. General Accounting Office, Washington, D.C., 1996

ISBN #0-16-048728-5

For sale by the U.S. Government Printing Office, Superintendent of
Documents, Stock #020-000-00271-9

To the officials and staff of GAO, past and present, and to my close friends and colleagues in the Society for History in the Federal Government

Table of Contents

List of Photographs

Foreword

Shortly after becoming comptroller general in 1981, I determined that the General Accounting Office should have a formal history program. Even though it would be a modest effort, I wanted to create the program because I had learned earlier in my career as a partner at Arthur Andersen and Co. and as assistant secretary of the navy for financial management that maintaining an institutional history is a very useful tool for those who manage large organizations. One can deal with contemporary problems more effectively and plan more intelligently for the future if one understands the lessons of the past.

After appointing an advisory panel and studying existing history programs in the Senate and House of Representatives, as well as in other federal agencies, I launched GAO's history program in 1987. The office of the historian began conducting oral interviews with past GAO leaders, preparing historical background studies related to current issues, briefing new evaluators on GAO history, offering advice on records management questions, maintaining a small museum room, assisting GAO's divisions and offices on historical questions, and responding to external inquiries about GAO's history.

Another of its tasks was to research and write a history of GAO. The present volume, a very detailed history of the agency from its founding in 1921 through the career of the fourth comptroller general in 1966, is solidly based on original documentary materials. I believe it will prove to be of great value in the ongoing work of GAO in terms of the Office's organization, management, training programs, and other areas.

GAO personnel, especially new evaluators, will profit from the book because it puts into context the work they do and the processes they use in preparing reports. Members of Congress, the primary customers of GAO's audits, evaluations, and investigations, will gain insight in understanding GAO's role within the legislative branch of government. Just as important, this history should serve to inform and educate outsiders—historians, political scientists, journalists, and students of public administration, among others—about the role of the General

Accounting Office in the federal system of government. Finally, this book should help to acquaint the general public with the unique role GAO plays in defending the public interest, not only by helping to prevent waste, fraud, abuse, and mismanagement, but also in promoting better management of federal programs.

Charles A. Bowsher
Comptroller General
of the United States
1981-1996

Preface

My primary objective in preparing this book is to make available a detailed history of the U. S. General Accounting Office during its first four and one-half decades, from 1921 to 1966. Scholarly writing on GAO's history has not been extensive, and no one previously had prepared a comprehensive account based essentially on documentary materials. Frederick C. Mosher's study, *The GAO: The Quest for Accountability in American Government* (1979), which covers some major aspects of GAO's history to the late 1970s, is useful. Drawing more extensively on original documents, my book provides wider scope and more detail for researchers and others interested in the development of this important institution.

Although accounts of GAO's work, reflecting the reports it issues on a wide variety of subjects, appear almost daily in the nation's newspapers and in other media, the public knows little about the origins, the evolution, and the current activities of the organization. Even in the academic world, among historians, political scientists, and others who write and teach about the U.S. government, there is a surprising lack of knowledge of and attention to the work of this very important legislative agency. I do not recall ever mentioning GAO during my own teaching in institutions of higher education over a period of many years before I joined the federal service permanently in 1980, even though I taught extensively about U.S. government and politics. Within the federal government, there are officials and staff in various agencies whose knowledge of GAO is insufficient. Numerous times I have encountered individuals, including fellow historians, who confused GAO with the General Services Administration or thought that I worked at the "Government" Accounting Office. If this book can serve as the detailed record often needed by the GAO staff and if it helps to educate officials in the U. S. government, especially members of Congress and their staffs, historians and academics in other disciplines, auditors and accountants in the private and public sectors, GAO's counterparts in the International Organization of Supreme Audit Institutions, and the public, my efforts will have been richly rewarded.

This book is the result of eight years of detailed work in the documentary materials described in appendix I, "Essay on Sources." For the most part, these sources have not been used previously by any scholar working on GAO's history. I completed much of the research between 1987 and 1993, when I served as chief historian of GAO. I undertook some specific areas of research in response to requests for historical background studies from GAO's head, the comptroller general of the United States.

Both during my tenure as GAO's chief historian and since my retirement at the end of 1993, I have received enthusiastic support and encouragement from Comptroller General Charles A. Bowsher and other officials and staff of the GAO, as well as many persons outside GAO. The members of the Comptroller General's History Program Advisory Committee—Brig. Gen. Edwin H. Simmons (ret.) (former director of the Marine Corps Historical Center), Robert M. Warner (former archivist of the United States and professor, University of Michigan), Norman A. Graebner (professor emeritus of history, University of Virginia), Richard A. Baker (historian of the U.S. Senate), and Theodore C. Barreaux (an original member of the committee and later an ex officio member, when he joined GAO as special counselor to the comptroller general)—have provided far-reaching support, encouragement, and expert counsel over the years, both to this project and to the GAO History Program in general.

I also wish to acknowledge the support of three officials responsible for the GAO History Program, both during my tenure as chief historian and subsequently: 1987–1992, Werner Grosshans, assistant comptroller general for policy; 1992–1993, Milton J. Socolar, special assistant to the comptroller general; and 1994–1996, Brian P. Crowley, assistant comptroller general for policy.

I have profited greatly from suggestions made by many reviewers who read the chapters of the book as I drafted them during 1994 and 1995: Charles A. Bowsher; Frank C. Conahan, former assistant comptroller general for national security and international affairs; J. Dexter Peach, assistant comptroller general for planning and reporting; Brian P. Crowley; Henry Eschwege, former assistant comptroller general for planning and reporting; Harry S. Havens, former assistant comptroller general; Donald J. Horan, former assistant comptroller general for planning and reporting; Milton J. Socolar; J. Samuel Walker, historian, U.S. Nuclear Regulatory Commission; George T. Mazuzan, historian, National Science Foundation; Richard A. Baker; Robert M. Warner; Edwin H. Simmons; Norman A. Graebner; and Elizabeth Poel and Maarja Krusten, GAO History Program.

I wish to extend special thanks to the individuals who performed a final review of the manuscript before publication: GAO General Counsel Robert Murphy; Brian P. Crowley; and former Comptroller General Elmer B. Staats (1966-1981).

I owe to Elizabeth Poel, associate historian, and Maarja Krusten, staff historian, a great deal for their contributions to this book. Ms. Poel, with her special knowledge of GAO records, especially the A- and B- files and the

Decisions and Letters series, was instrumental in locating critical research materials. She also did extensive research on GAO's annual testimony during budget hearings of the House Appropriations Committee from fiscal years 1922 through 1966. Ms. Krusten identified other valuable research materials in the various collections in the GAO History Program Archives. She also located the photographs included in this book and did some of the research for chapter 1. Both Ms. Poel and Ms. Krusten collaborated on the research for chapter 7, concerning GAO's efforts between 1921 and 1951 to acquire a new headquarters building. Finally, both of them responded promptly and with good humor to my many requests for documents and other information during 1994 and 1995, when I was writing the book at my home, 70 miles distant from GAO headquarters in Washington.

During the early months of 1996 when I was revising the manuscript, Ms. Krusten put up with my sudden and frequent queries for documents and other information and responded cheerfully and quickly. She worked after hours, both in her office and at home, to facilitate both the completion of the final manuscript and the process within GAO to prepare it for printing. She deserves high credit for everything she did to make this book a reality.

I also wish to acknowledge the expert help provided by Vicki L. Gullixon, executive assistant to the assistant comptroller general for policy (until September 1995); her successor, Sylvia Posten; and Carroll Anne Mrozek of the office of the assistant comptroller general for operations. James O. Benone, assistant director in the Office of Policy, ably coordinated the arrangements for review and final preparation of the manuscript for publication. His support of the GAO History Program over the years is greatly appreciated.

The staff of GAO's Office of Information Management and Communications played a critical role in bringing this book to publication and distributing it. I wish to thank Delaney Branch, customer service representative, who skillfully coordinated the publishing process; Orlando Boston, lead visual information specialist, and Armetha Liles and Karen Burke, visual information specialists, for their expert design and typesetting services; and Diane I. Reinke. Mrs. Reinke is a skillful editor who reviewed most of the publications of the GAO History Program over the years, including the extensive draft of this book. With a keen eye and a swift pencil, she improved the manuscript in countless ways. She also coordinated the publication process within GAO for most of the History Program's publications. I also am grateful to Thomas Kneeland, the Operations Manager in GAO's publishing unit, and Wanda Okoro, senior printing procurement specialist, for ably coordinating the book's printing with the Government Printing Office, and to the GAO distribution staff for their efficient services.

Finally, I wish to recognize the contributions of my wife, Dorothy B. Trask. Most important of all, she tolerated the fact that I was buried in my study for many months during the writing process. She also made many useful syntactic and editorial suggestions and did some of the word processing on the manuscript. In the process, she probably learned more about the General Accounting Office than she cared to know.

Although I wrote this book under the auspices of and with the support of the General Accounting Office, I am solely responsible for its contents and conclusions.

Roger R. Trask

Abbreviations

AAA	Agricultural Adjustment Administration
AAPS	Accounting and Auditing Policy Staff
ADP	automatic data processing
AEC	Atomic Energy Commission
AICPA	American Institute of Certified Public Accountants
AID	Agency for International Development
BIA	Bureau of Indian Affairs
BOB	Bureau of the Budget
CAAD	Civil Accounting and Auditing Division
CAD	Corporation Audits Division
CCC	Commodity Credit Corporation
CFA	Commission of Fine Arts
CIA	Central Intelligence Agency
CPA	certified public accountant
DAAD	Defense Accounting and Auditing Division
DMPA	Defense Materials Procurement Agency
DOD	Department of Defense
EB	European Branch
ECA	Economic Cooperation Administration
EDP	electronic data processing
FAS	Foreign Agricultural Service
FDIC	Federal Deposit Insurance Corporation
FEB	Far East Branch
FGAA	Federal Government Accountants Association
FMC	Federal Maritime Commission
FOD	Field Operations Division
GAO	General Accounting Office
GPO	Government Printing Office
GSA	General Services Administration
ICA	International Cooperation Administration
IG	Inspector General
INTOSAI	International Organization of Supreme Audit Institutions
IOD	International Operations Division
JAIP	Joint Accounting Improvement Program
JFMIP	Joint Financial Management Improvement Program
NAACP	National Association for the Advancement of Colored People
NASA	National Aeronautics and Space Administration
NCPPC	National Capital Parks and Planning Commission
NME	National Military Establishment

OAS	Office of Administrative Services
OCG	Office of the Comptroller General
OGC	Office of the General Counsel
OI	Office of Investigations
OLL	Office of Legislative Liaison
OSM	Office of Staff Management
PWA	Public Works Administration
RFC	Reconstruction Finance Corporation
RG	Record Group
RIF	reduction-in-force
TVA	Tennessee Valley Authority
USAREUR	U.S. Army, Europe
VA	Veterans Administration

Introduction

Between 1921 and 1965, four men held the position of comptroller general of the United States. With one exception, they served long terms, at least over ten years, and one served a full 15-year term. During this 44-year period, the General Accounting Office underwent vast changes. The agency that began operating in 1921 differed significantly from the one existing in 1965—not only in formal organization but also in the kinds of work it did; in how it accomplished that work; in staff size, composition, and professionalism; and in its relationships with the legislative and executive branches of the government. Especially after World War II, change was the order of the day at GAO.

Although GAO's work, from the beginning, reflected the contributions of its staff, the comptrollers general played a central role in carrying out the main mission of the organization. One vital factor in the pivotal role of the comptroller general was the statutory 15-year term assigned to the position. A term of this length gave each comptroller general time to fashion the agency in the image he preferred. There was ample opportunity for centralized leadership at the top of the organization. The three comptrollers general who served during most of the period from 1921 to 1965 were strong individuals who had their own ideas about organization and deep interest in determining how the Office should carry out its basic mission. The history of GAO cannot be told without close attention to the role of the comptrollers general, while at the same time recognizing the significance of the staff, which did the line work on a day-to-day basis.

Another important factor in promoting change in GAO was the evolving national and international scene. The focus of the Office's work through the years from 1921 to 1965 reflected events occurring at home and abroad. Congress passed the Budget and Accounting Act, 1921, in part to correct problems in the U.S. government's financial system that became obvious during and after the war. The first comptroller general, John Raymond McCarl (1921-1936), entered office in the aftermath of World War I. During the 1920s, reflecting the nation's preoccupation with business at home, GAO concentrated on the government's financial affairs. With the stock market crash of 1929 and Franklin D. Roosevelt's rise to the presidency in 1933, GAO became involved in auditing the many New Deal domestic programs that operated during the 1930s. The depression and the nation's effort to beat it became important determinants of GAO's work agenda.

During his term, McCarl worked hard to establish the independence of GAO from the executive branch, as the Budget and Accounting Act intended, and to support the role of Congress as the branch of government responsible for the nation's financial soundness. He insisted that decisions of GAO were final and that executive branch agencies were not free to ignore or reject them. Gradually opposition to McCarl and GAO developed, leading to attempts, which peaked in the late 1930s, to change GAO's role or even to abolish the agency. Although Congress considered several proposals along these lines, it ultimately rejected them all.

With the coming of World War II in Europe in 1939 and U.S. involvement in the conflict in 1941, GAO's work emphasis shifted to the tremendous task of auditing war programs and activities. Influenced by its war work, GAO determined that some of its traditional ways of doing things were outmoded or unnecessary and began to make important changes as the war ended. Comptroller General Lindsay C. Warren (1940–1954) provided strong leadership in initiating these changes.

Soon after the war, GAO began to audit government corporations, on the basis of a law passed late in 1945. Warren brought in many professional accountants to do this work; the methods and the programs they developed led by 1949 to a broadened, more-comprehensive approach to GAO's audits in the government as a whole. At the same time, Warren placed new emphasis on accounting systems work—the development and the installation of modern accounting systems in government agencies and the general improvement of the federal government's financial management system.

During the latter 1940s, the nation returned to what was supposed to be a peacetime economy but, at the same time, remained inextricably involved in external affairs. The onset of the Cold War, with the United States and the Soviet Union heading two economic, political, and ideological poles, helped move GAO extensively into audits of defense and international programs. The Korean War, fought between 1950 and 1953, accelerated this change. The establishment in 1952 of GAO's first overseas branch, in Europe, with headquarters in Paris, reflected the increasing importance of U.S. interests abroad.

Comptroller General Joseph Campbell (1954–1965) put further emphasis on the professionalization of GAO's staff by instituting new recruitment and training programs. Civil audit work expanded, out of both GAO's Washington headquarters and an extensive regional office system, created by Warren in 1952. During Campbell's term, the role of the United States in international affairs— foreign military and economic aid programs; maintenance of military forces in many overseas locations; and increased spending to develop new weapon systems, such as ballistic missiles and nuclear submarines—led to increasing attention to defense and international activities. Overseas work continued to expand; in 1956, GAO established a Far East Branch, with headquarters in Tokyo.

During this period, GAO gave special emphasis to audits of defense contracts, both at Department of Defense (DOD) installations and at contractor sites. The number of such audit reports expanded gradually under Campbell, and they became increasingly critical and hard-hitting. In 1965, opposition to these audits by defense contractors and the Department of Defense led to a series of hearings chaired by Rep. Chet Holifield (D—California). GAO, DOD, and defense contractors all underwent serious criticism during these hearings. The ultimate result in GAO was the decision to change the Office's approach to defense contract audits and in effect to diminish their number. Thus the controversy ended. The retirement of Comptroller General Campbell at the same time marked the end of an era in GAO's history.

GAO did not exist in its own private world—it was a product of its times, and as the times changed, so did GAO. The comptrollers general after 1940 presided over these changes and, in fact, initiated most of them. By 1966, as GAO embarked on a new era under the leadership of a new comptroller general, its position as the "Defender of the Public Interest" had been clearly and firmly established and the foundations for further change and progress in the Office had been solidly built.

This book is organized chronologically and topically. It begins with two chapters that trace the development of accounting and auditing in the United States from the American Revolution to 1921 and the passage of the Budget and Accounting Act in 1921. The next three chapters introduce the four comptrollers general who served between 1921 and 1965—with discussion of their backgrounds, personal and management styles, congressional relationships, and organizational changes under each of them. Chapter 6 surveys the evolution of GAO's budget and staff between 1921 and 1966, and chapter 7 presents the history of GAO's efforts, ultimately successful in 1951, to acquire a headquarters building in Washington.

The 13 subsequent chapters—8-20—discuss GAO's operations and activities between 1921 and 1966. Chapters 8-10 cover the McCarl period and that of his immediate successors, Acting Comptroller General Richard N. Elliott (1936-1939) and Comptroller General Fred H. Brown (1939-1940). Chapters 11-15 cover Warren's term, and chapters 16-20 discuss GAO's work under Campbell. Chapter 21 presents conclusions and observations about the history of GAO from 1921 to 1966.

The appendixes provide a variety of information: the sources used to prepare this book; the text of Title III of the Budget and Accounting Act, 1921; information on the GAO Seal; statistics on GAO personnel, appropriations, and reports to Congress; a list of top GAO officials; and key organization charts. Readers will find it useful to read appendix I, "Essay on Sources," before proceeding to the text of this book.

CHAPTER 1

Accounting and Auditing from the American Revolution to 1921

The Budget and Accounting Act, which created the General Accounting Office (GAO) in 1921, was the product of a historical process that began in England in the seventeenth century and lasted through the American colonial period into the nineteenth century. The framers of the act had historical traditions and developments of at least three centuries in mind as they crafted the legislation between 1919 and 1921. The passage of the law was in part the culmination of a movement to ensure that the nation's auditing officers were independent of executive control. This movement grew out of more than a century of experience with the U.S. financial management system.

English and Colonial Backgrounds

The origins of the U.S. financial system can be found in England. Between 1603 and 1689, during the reigns of James I and Charles I, the Commonwealth period and the Restoration, respectively, some basic English principles and procedures of government finance emerged. Raising of public revenue came to be the exclusive province of the House of Commons; Commons appropriated money for specific purposes; members of Parliament, serving as ministers in charge of government agencies, supervised the spending of appropriated funds; and a group headed by the minority party was responsible for making sure that public spending was covered exclusively by appropriations.[1]

These principles and practices spread to the British colonies in North America and were well-established by the middle of the eighteenth century. Fear of executive power, demonstrated by opposition to colonial governors, especially in lower houses of colonial legislatures, was widespread. The British government imposed taxes and other restrictive measures on the colonies after the end of the French and Indian War in 1763, partly to pay the costs of that war. The colonists

---

[1]Testimony of O. R. McGuire, August 12, 1937, in *Reorganization of the Government Agencies*, Hearings before the Senate Select Committee on Government Organization, 75th Cong., 1st sess. (Washington: U.S. Government Printing Office, 1937), 367-71. Hereafter cited as *Reorganization of the Government Agencies*. McGuire was a GAO lawyer at the time of his testimony.

resisted, raising cries of taxation without representation and taking more direct action, such as refusal to pay the stamp taxes imposed in 1765 and the dumping of taxed tea in Boston harbor in 1773. A very important cause of the American Revolution (1775-1783) was the alleged tyranny of the British king and the efforts of Parliament to levy what colonial leaders considered illegal taxes. Among the important issues at stake were the principles of public finance developed previously in England.[2]

Finance in the United States, 1775-1789

As the thirteen former colonies, states after the Declaration of Independence in 1776, drafted new constitutions, they incorporated provisions reflecting traditional English financial practices, as well as the practices of colonial legislatures. These state constitutions generally provided for legislative control of the raising and the spending of public money, origination of money bills in lower legislative houses, treasurers appointed by legislatures to hold and dispense state funds on the basis of signed warrants (authorizations to pay money for a specific purpose), and the auditing and the settlement of public accounts on authority of the lower houses of legislatures.[3]

The governments of the United States after the break with England—the two Continental Congresses (1774-1781) and the Congress under the Articles of Confederation (1781-1789)—used state institutions and practices as models for a national system of public finance. This meant reserving financial control in Congress, particularly through use of congressional committees or officials. With the tyranny of the king of England in mind, the governments of the 1770s and 1780s were chary of executive power embodied in a central government. During this period, much experimentation occurred and repeated changes took place in public financial systems intended to provide for a proper accounting of public funds.[4]

On July 29, 1775, the First Continental Congress appointed two "Treasurers of the United Colonies" to handle funds received through bills of credit issued by Congress. Less than two months later, on September 25, 1775, Congress estab-

---

[2]See Frederick C. Mosher, *The GAO: The Quest for Accountability in American Government* (Boulder, CO: Westview Press, 1979), 18-19 (hereafter cited as Mosher, *GAO*). See also Merrill Jensen, *The Founding of a Nation: The History of the American Revolution, 1763-1776* (New York: Oxford University Press, 1968).

[3]Mosher, *GAO*, 18-20; and McGuire testimony in *Reorganization of the Government Agencies*, 372. For general histories of the period between 1776 and 1789, see E. James Ferguson, *The Power of the Purse: A History of American Public Finance, 1776-1790* (Chapel Hill, NC: University of North Carolina Press, 1961); Merrill Jensen, *The New Nation: A History of the United States During the Confederation, 1781-1789* (New York: Alfred A. Knopf, 1950); and Richard B. Morris, *The Forging of the Union, 1781-1789* (New York: Harper & Row, 1987).

[4]Harvey C. Mansfield, Sr., *The Comptroller General: A Study in the Law and Practice of Financial Administration* (New Haven, CT: Yale University Press, 1939), 24 (hereafter cited as Mansfield, *Comptroller General*).

lished a Committee on Accounts to examine and report on claims against the government before payment.

During the next several years, the system changed frequently. In February 1776, Congress established a committee of five members, the Committee of Finance, to oversee treasury affairs and two months later created the Treasury Office of Accounts, headed by an auditor general. This office was responsible to the Committee of Finance, by then called the Treasury Board. In July 1776, the Office of Accounts took over the work of the Committee on Accounts set up in September 1775. In March 1777, Congress appointed three commissioners of claims responsible for the accounting function and, in August 1778, established a new congressional Committee on Finance to report periodically on the state of the nation's finances.[5]

On September 26, 1778, Congress reorganized the whole system by creating the offices of comptroller, auditor, treasurer, and six commissioners of accounts, abolishing the Treasury Office of Accounts and making the Treasury Board the general supervisor of the new officers and the liaison between them and Congress. This arrangement provided a model for the system adopted by the new U.S. government in the Treasury Act of 1789 and, in the view of J. R. McCarl, the first comptroller general of the United States, the model for GAO. "The history and functions of this office originated in an Ordinance of September 26, 1778, of the Continental Congress," McCarl wrote to a member of the House of Representatives in 1928. Congress's motives included a desire to speed up the conduct of public business; to improve the accountability of persons handling public funds; and to give Congress better information about expenditures, sources of public revenue, and the public debt.[6]

Congress made another major change on July 30, 1779, by abolishing the Treasury Board and establishing the Board of Treasury with five commissioners—two members of Congress and three outsiders with financial experience. The act also eliminated the comptroller's office, retained the other offices established in September 1778, and added six auditors to settle Army claims and accounts. The Board of Treasury, rather than Congress as a whole, was to receive appeals of Treasury officer decisions. By placing responsibility for the nation's

---

[5]For surveys of these matters, see Darrell H. Smith, *The General Accounting Office: Its History, Activities and Organization* (Baltimore: The Johns Hopkins Press, 1927), 1-3 (hereafter cited as Smith, *General Accounting Office*); Mansfield, *Comptroller General*, 24-25; Mosher, *GAO*, 20-21; and Richard Maycock, "History of Government Accounting," a paper written by a GAO official around 1948, copy in GAO History Program Archives, 2-3 (hereafter cited as Maycock, "History of Government Accounting.")

[6]Smith, *General Accounting Office*, 3; letter, J. R. McCarl to Rep. LaFayette L. Patterson, December 19, 1928, 88 MS 738 in *Decisions and Letters* of the comptroller general, GAO Records (see appendix I for a description of this source); and Maycock, "History of Government Accounting," 3.

two-house Congress, providing two senators for each state and representation based on population in the House.

Sections 7 through 10 of article I of the Constitution gave the federal government broad fiscal powers, providing a basis for the subsequent development of a national financial system. Section 7 provided that all revenue bills originate in the House of Representatives. Section 8 authorized Congress to lay and collect taxes, duties, imports, and excises; to pay debts; to borrow money; to coin money and fix its value; and to raise and support military forces, with appropriations for that purpose limited to a term of two years. Section 9 prohibited direct taxes "unless in Proportion to the Census or Enumeration herein before directed to be taken," as well as duties on exports from a state. This section also provided that money was to be drawn from the Treasury only on the basis of appropriations made by law. Section 10 prohibited the states from coining money, emitting bills of credit, making anything but gold and silver coin legal tender, and laying import and export duties without the consent of Congress.

These provisions had their sources in the heritage and the experiences of Americans: From the British and colonial past came the principles that money measures were to originate in the lower house of the legislature and that money could not be spent unless legally appropriated, and from the revolutionary and immediate postrevolutionary experience came recognition that the government needed the powers to tax and to borrow and coin money and had the responsibility to account for public receipts and expenditures. The Constitution provided general principles for the financial system but left it to Congress to devise the details.

The Treasury Act of 1789

Shortly after Congress convened in 1789, it began considering bills to establish departments to handle three major concerns—defense, foreign affairs, and finance. Laws creating the War Department and the State Department, passed in the summer of 1789, were short and general, leaving specific organizational details for the executive branch to work out.

Congress acted differently in the case of the Treasury Department; it passed a law intended to bind the department more closely to the legislative branch than to the executive branch. Leonard D. White, a distinguished historian of U.S. public administration, observed that "at no point was suspicion of government more definitely written into law and practice than in the management of federal finance."[13] This suspicion had its origins in the prerevolutionary experience with British financial practices in the colonies. Thus there was extended debate on various features of the Treasury Act, and the result was a law full of details and specifics. The clear intention of Congress was to maintain control of money, although within a decade, congressional authority had eroded somewhat.

Among the issues in the 1789 debate was whether the Treasury Department should have a single head or be run by a board, reminiscent of the committee approach that prevailed between 1775 and 1789. James Madison of Virginia, a leader of the first Congress, argued for a single secretary, and that approach became part of the law, with the secretary appointed by the president but responsible to Congress in a variety of ways.[14]

A second issue was whether the secretary should "digest and prepare" financial plans and programs for the House of Representatives or "report" them. The former terminology prevailed, reflecting fear that if the secretary "reported" financial plans, he might be interfering with the House's prerogative to originate money bills.[15]

Another question dealt with the term of office of the comptroller of the treasury, one of the statutory officials proposed for the new department. Debate on this question also raised the issue of the president's power to remove officials. Madison preferred a set term for the comptroller, who he believed would carry out a mixture of executive and judicial functions. Congress failed to support Madison's position, leaving the comptroller to serve at the president's discretion, as was the case with other executive officials.[16]

The Treasury Act (1 Stat. 65), signed on September 2, 1789, enumerated the powers and the duties of the Treasury Department. The department was to digest and prepare plans for the management of the revenue and for support of public credit; prepare and submit revenue and spending estimates; superintend revenue collection; prepare forms for keeping and stating accounts and making returns; grant warrants for money to be issued by the Treasury; service the sale of public lands; report, in person or in writing, on matters Congress referred to the Treasury or pertinent to the department; perform services as directed relating to government finances; superintend the adjustment and the preservation of public accounts;

---

[13]Leonard D. White, *The Federalists: A Study in Administrative History, 1789-1801* (New York: The Macmillan Company, 1948; New York: Free Press, paperback edition, 1965), 323 (hereafter cited as White, *Federalists*).

[14]Mansfield, *Comptroller General*, 27; and Smith, *General Accounting Office*, 13.

[15]Mansfield, *Comptroller General*, 27; and White, *Federalists*, 118.

[16]Mansfield, *Comptroller General*, 28.

handle prosecution of delinquent revenue officers; and receive, keep, and disburse the nation's money.[17]

The Treasury Act provided for several departmental officials—secretary, comptroller, auditor, treasurer, and register—to be appointed by the president and confirmed by the Senate. All had specific duties and were in effect checks on one another. Representative Abraham Baldwin of Georgia stated during debate on the Treasury Act that he did not favor placing unlimited authority in the secretary of the treasury. As reported in the *Annals of Congress*, "He hoped to see proper checks provided; a Comptroller, Auditors, Register, and Treasurer. He would not suffer the Secretary to touch a farthing of the public money beyond his salary. The settling of accounts should be in the Auditors and Comptroller; the registering them to be in another officer, and the cash in the hands of one unconnected with either."[18]

The secretary of the treasury was responsible for managing the department. The treasurer was to receive and be custodian of government funds and disburse them on the basis of warrants initiated by the secretary, countersigned by the comptroller, and recorded by the register. The auditor was to receive public accounts, certify account balances after examination (audit), and transmit accounts with supporting documents to the comptroller for final decision. The register was to keep accounts of public receipts and expenditures and of debts of or due the United States. He was also to receive from the comptroller and preserve finally adjusted accounts, to record all warrants for Treasury receipt or payment of money, and to transmit to the secretary copies of adjusted account balance certificates.[19]

The comptroller's duties included overseeing the adjustment and the preservation of public accounts, examining the auditor's settled accounts and certifying the balances to the register, countersigning all warrants drawn by the secretary of the treasury, and providing to the secretary forms for collecting the public revenue and the manner of keeping and stating accounts in the offices responsible for them.[20] The comptroller was a very important official, who ranked second to the secretary and in fact had powers independent of him.

Alexander Hamilton, the first secretary of the treasury, advised President George Washington on qualities desirable for the comptroller: "It is of the greatest

[17]White, *Federalists*, 120.
[18]Quoted in Mansfield, *Comptroller General*, note #15, 28-29.
[19]Maycock, "History of Government Accounting," 5-6.
[20]Ibid., 6.

importance to the proper conducting the business of the Treasury Department that the Comptroller should be a man of the following description: of strong sense, of clear discernment, sound judgment, indefatigable industry, firmness, and prompt decision of temper; possessing a comprehensive knowledge of accounts, and of course good principles."[21]

Federalist Financial Administration

The 1789 law did not spell out in great detail how the comptroller was to carry on his duties, including that of guaranteeing that money would not be withdrawn from the Treasury except in accordance with the law. Leonard White's comment suggests the scope of the comptroller's influence: "This duty compelled him to state for what purposes and according to what restrictions the law permitted money to be drawn, and to establish the forms of proof that money had been properly used. These were matters of the widest discretion, taking a quasi-judicial form."[22]

Gradually the comptroller acquired other duties, not specified in the original law. In 1792, he became supervisor of the collection of import and tonnage duties by delegation from the secretary of the treasury and, in 1793, superintendent of shipping. The succession in 1795 of the incumbent comptroller, Oliver Wolcott, as secretary of the treasury emphasized the importance of the comptroller's position.[23]

Hamilton was a strong secretary, though he was not greatly interested in administrative detail. He fashioned a comprehensive financial plan—the creation of a national bank, the funding of the national debt, and the assumption of state debts—which did much to help the United States overcome some of the major domestic and international problems that afflicted the nation in the aftermath of the Revolution in the 1780s. He made the Treasury Department the premier federal agency and played a key role before his retirement in 1795 in the administration of George Washington. In listing the accomplishments of the Federalists, the party of Washington and Hamilton, Leonard White included "the formation of a fiscal system that ensured the proper use of and accounting for public funds." By 1801, the Treasury Department employed more than half of all federal civilian employees—78 in

---

[21]White, *Federalists*, 345.
[22]Ibid., 450.
[23]Ibid., 122, 345.

headquarters and 1,615 in field locations.[24] Hamilton's system, carried on by his successor, Wolcott, was highly centralized in the executive branch.

The Jeffersonians and the Law of 1817

The election to the presidency in 1800 of Thomas Jefferson, the Democratic-Republican candidate, brought to power a leader and a party with somewhat different views on financial management. While Hamilton and the Federalists had favored lump sum appropriations for government departments, Jefferson and his colleagues, including Secretary of the Treasury Albert Gallatin, preferred specificity in appropriations. Congress supported this approach, and detailed appropriations, specifying the purposes for which funds were to be spent, became the rule. In 1802, the House of Representatives expanded the role of the Ways and Means Committee to include handling appropriations bills. In 1809, Jefferson signed a law (2 Stat. 535, March 3, 1809) requiring that warrants drawn on the treasurer indicate the appropriation being charged and state that appropriations were to be spent only for the specific objects that the law provided. These changes enhanced congressional controls over appropriations and put into place a legislative budget process that lasted until 1921.[25]

The financial problem that caused the most trouble for the Jeffersonians was the slowness in settling accounts, which the crisis of the War of 1812 greatly intensified. To some degree, the origins of the problem dated to the Federalist period, especially to acts that created separate accountants for the War Department in 1792 and the Navy Department in 1798. The laws permitted these financial officers to settle accounts in their respective departments. In the latter 1790s, the postmaster general gained authority to use postal receipts to pay departmental operating expenses and to settle departmental accounts. These changes whittled away at the principle of centralization of responsibility for accountability in the Treasury Department, written into the Treasury Act of 1789. Furthermore, many government departments began administrative checking of their own accounts, as a way to control spending of appropriated funds. This all added up to examination of accounts by disbursing agents, departmental accountants, the Treasury auditor, and the Treasury comptroller. The result was a growing backlog in accounts settlement and delay in final payments to government creditors.[26]

The War of 1812 with England further strained the system, leading to a House study of the problem in 1816 and a Senate resolution requiring four department

---

[24]Ibid., 123, 512.

[25]Paul Studenski, *Financial History of the United States* (New York: McGraw-Hill, 1963), 71-72; and Mansfield, *Comptroller General*, 31-33.

[26]Mansfield, *Comptroller General*, 43-45.

secretaries (War, Navy, State, and Treasury) to study, and make recommendations relating to, executive organization and procedures. The secretaries eventually recommended that responsibility for settling accounts be centered in the Treasury Department, as originally intended in the Treasury Act of 1789.[27]

The secretaries' report led to the adoption of a reform law (3 Stat. 366, March 3, 1817) making several changes aimed at concentrating accounts settlement in the Treasury Department and increasing the department's officials to accomplish this task promptly. The act abolished the accountants' positions in the War and Navy departments, retained the original auditor position, and created four new auditor positions and a second comptroller in the Treasury Department to handle the additional workload expected as a result of the reorganization.

The first auditor was to audit Treasury Department accounts and accounts of all other departments not assigned to another auditor; the second and third auditors were responsible for War Department accounts; the fourth auditor, for Navy Department accounts; and the fifth auditor handled accounts of the State Department, Indian affairs, and the Post Office (until 1836, when a sixth auditor position was created to handle postal accounts). The original comptroller (the "first comptroller") was to receive reports from the first and fifth auditors on accounts for the Treasury Department and other civil departments. The second comptroller received reports for the War and Navy departments from the second, third, and fourth auditors.[28]

While the new organization permitted more prompt and orderly settlement of accounts, the expansion of the number of auditors and comptrollers lowered their status and prestige. Under the new system, the original comptroller and the auditor had to share auditing and settlement responsibilities with five other officials. As Harvey C. Mansfield points out, only the president; the vice president; and the secretaries of the Treasury, State, and War outranked the comptroller whose position was created by the 1789 law. After passage of the 1817 statute, Mansfield observed, "the Comptrollers took their places among the ranks of bureau chiefs."[29]

1829-1865: Jacksonian Finance and the Civil War

Although there was progress in eliminating the backlog of settlements after passage of the 1817 law, the problem did not disappear completely, and

[27]Ibid., 45-46; Leonard D. White, *The Jeffersonians: A Study in Administrative History, 1801-1829* (New York: The Macmillan Company, 1951; New York: Free Press paperback edition, 1965), 165-66, 171-72 (hereafter cited as White, *Jeffersonians*); Smith, *General Accounting Office*, 23-24; and Mosher, *GAO*, 31.

[28]Mosher, *GAO*, 31-32; Mansfield, *Comptroller General*, 46-47; White, *Jeffersonians*, 173-74; and Smith, *General Accounting Office*, 24-27.

[29]Mansfield, *Comptroller General*, 47-48; and Mosher, *GAO*, 31-32.

in the 1830s and 1840s, delays still occurred. Other financial issues caused differences between Congress and the executive branch. For example, Congress preferred specific and thoroughly justified budget estimates from the executive departments, while the latter preferred generalities and less congressional control. The same division existed over appropriations; the executive branch preferred lump sums, while Congress wished to make appropriations under specific heads. Congress favored restrictions on transferring funds from one appropriation head to another, while the executive branch wanted discretionary power in this area. Another problem was overspending by agencies followed by requests for deficiency appropriations.[30] As Leonard White wrote, "Congress was thus engaged, during the Jackson years, in a long battle to realize its full control of federal expenditures. . . . The executive branch . . . found means, where necessary or useful, to avoid or to evade many of the fiscal limitations that Congress deemed it proper to impose."[31]

Another issue arose during the presidency of Martin Van Buren (1837-1841) over the relationship between the comptrollers and auditors on the one hand and the secretary of the treasury on the other. A man disappointed with a decision of the first auditor on his claim requested Secretary of the Treasury Levi Woodbury (1834-1841) to reexamine his case. When Woodbury asked the auditor to provide information, the auditor complied but gave the secretary his views on the proper relations between the two officials. The auditor felt that he had the duty to reach his own decisions in cases of this sort, with the comptroller having the power to revise the decision on appeal. He rejected a role for the secretary, saying that "in ordinary cases . . . falling within the general provisions of the law establishing the accounting offices of the department, I regard the decision of the Comptroller in the construction of the laws relating to accounts as having the same force and obligation upon the Auditor as the decision of a superior court has upon an inferior one." Secretary Woodbury did not contest the auditor's position, and neither did his successors.[32]

Between 1817 and the end of the Civil War, there were a few changes in administrative organization for financial affairs but no significant changes in substance. Positions for a solicitor, responsible for investigating delinquent fiscal officers, and a commissioner of the customs were established in 1830 and 1849, respectively, in the Treasury Department. The new commissioner assumed the duties of the first comptroller relating to customs receipts and accounts of cus-

---

[30]Leonard D. White, *The Jacksonians: A Study in Administrative History, 1829-1861* (New York: The Macmillan Company, 1954; New York: Free Press paperback edition, 1965), 125-38 (hereafter cited as White, *Jacksonians*).

[31]Ibid., 141.

[32]Ibid., 167.

toms officers, in effect serving as a third comptroller. In 1855, Congress established a Court of Claims to hear and report on claims based on alleged violation of contracts, after the second comptroller noted that the number of such claims was substantial and was increasing.[33]

The Civil War, like the War of 1812, placed new demands and intolerable strains on the nation's accounting system. In order not to impede military operations, field officers received advances of funds, but routine accounting and subsequent settlement of accounts could not take place under these conditions. Settlement after the war ended was almost impossible—in many cases the necessary records either were never prepared or were lost or destroyed during the fighting. According to Mansfield, "Accounting control in the accepted sense was for the time being physically impossible."[34] The war also led to lack of enforcement of legal limitations on executive discretion in spending. The distinctions between different objects of appropriation broke down somewhat in practice, and officials transferred funds at will without concern for their original purposes.[35]

Financial Affairs, 1865-1914

In 1868, Congress approved a law (15 Stat. 54, March 30, 1868) that clarified the relationship of the comptrollers to heads of executive departments. The law said that the 1817 act "shall not be construed to authorize the heads of departments to change or modify the balances that may be certified to them by the commissioner of customs or the comptroller of the treasury, but that such balances, when stated by the auditor and properly certified by the comptroller . . . shall be taken and considered as final and conclusive upon the executive branch of the government, and be subject to revision only by Congress or the proper courts."[36]

In the background of the 1868 law was a controversy over payment of Civil War claims. When such claims came in, the War Department normally examined them first. The War Department quartermaster's office decided that many of the claims were inflated or unfounded and either reduced or rejected them. When the cases went to the auditor and the comptroller for settlement, these officials often raised the amounts due in favor of the claimants. The Treasury paid settlements by warrants drawn against departmental requisitions. But when the quartermaster's office disagreed with the increased settlement amounts, it refused to draw the requisitions for an amount differ-

---

[33]Ibid., 165; Smith, *General Accounting Office*, 34-35; and Mansfield, *Comptroller General*, 55.

[34]Mansfield, *Comptroller General*, 55-56 (quote on 56).

[35]Leonard D. White, *The Republican Era: A Study in Administrative History, 1869-1901* (New York: The Macmillan Company, 1958; New York: Free Press paperback edition, 1965), 58 (hereafter cited as White, *Republican Era*).

[36]Quoted in Mansfield, *Comptroller General*, 57.

ent from its original decision. The claimants, suffering from this procedure, took their problems to Congress, which passed the 1868 law. The statute made clear that decisions of Treasury accounting officers were final.[37]

In the latter part of the nineteenth century, there were various congressional studies of executive branch operations, all initiated by Congress—the Patterson Committee (1869-1871), the Boutwell Committee (1875-1876), the Cockrell Committee (1887-1889), and the Dockery-Cockrell Commission (1893-1895).

Little resulted from the work of the first three groups, but the Dockery-Cockrell Commission's recommendations led to major legislation in 1894.[38] Congress established the commission after Secretary of the Treasury Charles Foster recommended reforms in the methods of disbursing federal funds and examining, settling, and adjudicating public accounts. Foster proposed establishing, among other things, an office of the comptroller general or chief comptroller of the treasury. He also advocated appointment of a nonpartisan commission to examine the functioning of the executive departments, with special attention to methods of disbursement and the settlement of public accounts.[39]

Legislation approved on March 3, 1893, authorized formation of the Dockery-Cockrell Commission. The commission included three senators and three representatives, with Rep. Alexander M. Dockery (D—Missouri) as chairman. Francis M. Cockrell (D—Missouri) was one of the members from the Senate. The commission employed several accounting experts and issued a series of reports and recommendations, urging economy and focusing mainly on government organization and practice for accounting and fiscal control. Its work ultimately resulted in the Dockery Act (28 Stat. 162), signed on July 31, 1894.[40]

The Dockery Act, mandating major changes in federal accounting and auditing organization and practices, was the first major legislation on those subjects since 1817. A report accompanying the bill in the Senate in 1894 spelled out its purpose: "It is clear that the present mode of settling accounts does not answer

---

[37]Ibid., 57-58; and Mosher, *GAO*, 32.

[38]Mosher, *GAO*, 32; and White, *Republican Era*, 84-85.

[39]Maycock, "History of Government Accounting," 9; Smith, *General Accounting Office*, 41; and U.S. Senate, Staff of the Committee on Government Operations, *Financial Management in the Federal Government*, 87th Cong., 1st Sess., Senate Document No. 11 (Washington: U.S. Government Printing Office, 1961), 4 (hereafter cited as Senate, *Financial Management,* 1961).

[40]Smith, *General Accounting Office*, 41-42; White, *Republican Era*, 89-91; Senate, *Financial Management,* 1961, 4-6; and Maycock, "History of Government Accounting," 9-11. See also Oscar Kraines, "The Dockery-Cockrell Commission, 1893-1895," *Western Political Quarterly* 7, no. 3 (September 1954): 417-62.

Members of the Dockery-Cockrell Commission, 1893-1896. Seated, left to right: Sen. James K. Jones, Sen. Francis M. Cockrell, Rep. James D. Richardson, Rep. Alexander M. Dockery. Standing, left to right: Thomas P. Cleaves and James C. Courts, clerks of the Senate and House Committees on Appropriations. Source: Senate History Office.

the demands of public justice or economy; and it is also clear that the divided responsibility does not protect the Government."[41]

The principal terms of the law were as follows:

- One comptroller of the treasury replaced the first and second comptrollers and the commissioner of customs. The legislation also authorized an assistant comptroller of the treasury. The comptroller of the treasury would no longer routinely examine settlements by the auditors but would examine them on appeal. The comptroller would also render advance decisions on the legality of proposed payments when requested to do so by disbursing officers or department heads, with his decisions binding. The comptroller was also to countersign warrants and prescribe the forms for keeping and rendering public accounts.

- The six auditor positions remained, with their responsibilities expanded, including final settlement of accounts, and their jurisdictions clarified. The first audi-

---

[41]Quoted in Smith, *General Accounting Office*, 45.

tor was responsible for the Treasury Department; the second, the War Department; the third, the Interior Department; the fourth, the Navy Department; the fifth, the State Department and other departments; and the sixth, the Post Office Department. The auditors' settlements of accounts were final except on appeal.

- A Division of Bookkeeping and Warrants in the Treasury Department, replacing the Division of Warrants, Estimates, and Appropriations, was to maintain the government appropriation accounts, previously kept by the register and the second, third, and fourth auditors. The register position was retained, with duties assigned by the secretary of the treasury, but the position had little importance after 1894.

- The appropriate auditor's office had to approve department requisitions for advances to disbursing officers, who were required to submit accounts within ten days for monthly accounts and twenty days for quarterly accounts. The departments had twenty days to examine monthly accounts and sixty days for quarterly accounts. If this schedule lagged, the auditors had power to disapprove requisitions for advances.[42]

The Dockery Act established the system that existed until passage of the Budget and Accounting Act of 1921. Harvey Mansfield's analysis of the comptroller's duties shows the importance of the position:

> In summary, the new Comptroller was established as an executive officer with centralized responsibility for the settlement of all public accounts. But his jurisdiction was appellate and supervisory; the Auditors carried the work to completion unless someone was dissatisfied. The Comptroller was sufficiently separated in fact from the departments, including the Treasury, to act impartially in interpreting the laws. At the same time, the legal reservations of power in the Secretary and the President were enough to prevent his abusing his authority.[43]

The Movement for Change, 1894-1918

Between 1894 and the end of World War I in 1918, the stage was set for major changes in the U.S. financial management system. The Dockery Act's revised plan for accounting and auditing was an improvement over the ear-

---

[42]28 Stat. 162; Mosher, *GAO*, 33-34; Mansfield, *Comptroller General*, 60-63; Senate, *Financial Management*, 1961, 5-6; Smith, *General Accounting Office*, 45-46; and Maycock, "History of Government Accounting," 11-12.

[43]Mansfield, *Comptroller General*, 64.

lier arrangement, yet it had problems. Referring to the system as it existed through the nineteenth century and up to the passage of the Budget and Accounting Act, 1921, Frederick C. Mosher made several points: It emphasized "legality, accuracy, and regularity" and rarely concerned itself with "efficiency, wisdom, or effectiveness of expenditures"; it was "detailed," even down to a penny; it was "duplicative"—with transactions reviewed by a disbursing officer, a departmental examiner, and a Treasury auditor, and necessitated the keeping of multiple but not identical records; it was "highly centralized" organizationally and geographically—most accounts had to be transmitted to Treasury auditors for review in Washington; it was "unprofessional"—the comptrollers, the auditors, and their staffs usually had little training or experience; and Treasury Department decisions were legally final for the executive branch, with appeals to the courts and Congress possible.[44]

After passage of the Dockery Act, and especially with the emergence of the Progressive Era of the early twentieth century, with its emphasis on governmental reforms in the interest of economy and efficiency at the local, state, and national levels, financial management systems attracted more and more attention. An ultimate result of this reform movement was the Budget and Accounting Act, 1921. Especially important in the background of this law was interest in an executive budget—the initiation and the recommendation to Congress of a national budget by the president assisted by officials responsible to him. Eventually associated with the effort to institute an executive budget system was the idea of examination of executive branch financial transactions by an auditing agency responsible to Congress. Mosher observes that "this idea was a latecomer, added probably to gain congressional support as a counterbalance to the granting of powers and staff to the president for initiating the budget."[45]

Unlike the movement that led to the Dockery Act, the leadership in the national budget campaign centered in the executive branch, especially between 1901 and 1913, during the presidencies of Theodore Roosevelt and William Howard Taft. In 1905, Roosevelt appointed the Commission on Department Methods chaired by Charles H. Keep, assistant secretary of the treasury, to investigate and report on changes leading to economy and effectiveness in the executive branch. Between 1905 and 1909, the Keep Commission issued numerous reports with recommendations, some of which could be initiated by executive order and some requiring legislation.

---

[44]Mosher, *GAO*, 39.

[45]Frederick C. Mosher, *A Tale of Two Agencies: A Comparative Analysis of the General Accounting Office and the Office of Management and Budget* (Baton Rouge: Louisiana State University Press, 1984), 26 (hereafter cited as Mosher, *Tale of Two Agencies*).

One of the commission's reports, in January 1907, recommended installation of a double entry bookkeeping system in the Treasury Department's Division of Bookkeeping and Warrants.[46] The Treasury Department accepted this recommendation, and Congress provided funding to implement it. By definition, "double entry bookkeeping" is debiting a transaction amount to one account and crediting it to another. Under the new Treasury system, it meant keeping a detailed ledger of appropriations and expenditures. One author has observed: "The idea of the double-entry system had much to recommend it. It provided the means whereby the Secretary of the Treasury, the officer who advanced money to disbursing officers, could be kept informed of what happened to the moneys advanced. It was an automatic check on the auditors, whose decisions resulted in substantial sums being disbursed from the Treasury."[47]

In 1911, President William Howard Taft, who, like Roosevelt, was interested in government reform, appointed the Commission on Economy and Efficiency. Frederick A. Cleveland chaired this congressionally authorized commission. He had been a professor of finance at both the University of Pennsylvania and New York University and had headed the Bureaus of Municipal Research in Philadelphia and New York City.

His colleagues on the commission included, among others, William F. Willoughby, who had earlier served as treasurer of Puerto Rico and assistant director of the census and later became director of the influential Institute of Government Research in Washington (later named the Brookings Institution); Walter W. Warwick, previously an official of the Treasury Department and auditor of the government of the Panama Canal Zone and later (1915) comptroller of the treasury; and Frank J. Goodenow, a professor of law at Columbia University and a member of commissions dealing with the charter of the city of New York and New York finance and taxation.[48]

The Cleveland Commission issued more than 20 reports and made three major recommendations relating to the government accounting system: development of a national budget system, consolidation of the Treasury auditing offices into a single organization, and installation of a uniform accounting system in administrative agencies. Little resulted immediately from the commission's proposals, even though they had the support of President Taft, who specifically recommended to Congress in 1912 that it create a national budget system. Taft provided a model by submitting a fiscal year 1914 budget to Congress. Congress took no action,

---

[46]Mosher, *GAO*, 34-35; and Maycock, "History of Government Accounting," 13-14.

[47]Maycock, "History of Government Accounting," 14-15.

[48]Margaret L. Macfarlane and Judith Hatter, "Personalities Contributing to the Enactment of the Budget and Accounting Act, 1921," *GAO Review* (fall 1971): 57-59.

and Taft lost the presidency in the election of 1912 to Woodrow Wilson. The Cleveland Commission, however, had made the most thorough study up to that time of the government's organization and procedures, and its proposals were "the seed that grew and eventually blossomed as the Budget and Accounting Act of 1921."[49]

President Wilson also was interested in the various reform proposals, including the concept of a national budget, but his own domestic agenda gave higher priority to other matters, and after 1914, World War I precluded much attention by the White House to reform issues. During the 1916 presidential campaign, both the Democratic and Republican platforms supported budget reform, with the Republicans the stronger of the two parties on the issue.[50]

Participation of the United States in World War I actually made more urgent the development of a national budget system and related changes in accounting and auditing organizations and processes. The war forced a vast expansion of administrative offices and resulted in major increases in federal spending, taxes, and the public debt. The national budget movement, with the goals of economy and efficiency, grew much stronger during this period. Between 1915 and 1918, when Congress began looking ahead to budget and accounting legislation, 15 states considered the question of financial reform. During this period Illinois and Maryland adopted an executive budget system; nine other states adopted some features of such systems, and three states had budget reforms under consideration. Also by 1918, 49 countries had national budget systems with features similar to what was being proposed for the United States, including, among others, Germany, Great Britain, Japan, Mexico, the Netherlands, Panama, Russia, Spain, Sweden, Switzerland, Venezuela, the Dominican Republic, and Italy.[51]

The congressional elections of 1918 resulted in Republican control of both the House and the Senate. Both parties favored national budget and accounting legislation, but the Republican position was stronger than the Democratic stand. With the Republicans in power in Congress, the likelihood of such legislation's being introduced and passed was greater.[52]

Conclusions

The preceding brief history of the origins and the implemention of the U.S. financial system from the colonial period through the early twentieth

---

[49]Mosher, *GAO*, 35-36 (quote on 36); and Maycock, "History of Government Accounting," 18-20.

[50]Mosher, *GAO*, 45-47

[51]Plan for a National Budget System, by Charles Wallace Collins, submitted by Rep. Medill McCormick, H. Doc. 1006, 65th Cong., 2d Sess. (Washington: GPO, 1918), 15, 23.

[52]Maycock, "History of Government Accounting," 20-21; and Mansfield, *Comptroller General*, 64-65.

century is intended to provide both an understanding of why the system was adopted and how it operated in practice. The new states and the national government after the Declaration of Independence built their initial fiscal systems on both a historical British model and fear of centralization of authority, such as the British government tried to install in the colonies in the middle of the eighteenth century. But when the loose confederation of states embodied in the nation's first constitution, the Articles of Confederation, failed to ensure the continued independence of the United States, delegates at a special convention drafted a new constitution in 1787, which strengthened the central government at the expense of the states. The Constitution included numerous sections relating to public finance. One of the new government's first laws, the Treasury Act of 1789, established the Treasury Department with a group of officials to manage the nation's financial system. Although Congress wrote in controls, the executive branch received the power to operate the system.

With changes and refinements, the 1789 system lasted until 1921. The stresses of war—the American Revolution itself and later the War of 1812 and the Civil War—revealed flaws and deficiencies that Congress tried to remedy with major laws passed in 1817 and 1868. In the Dockery Act of 1894, Congress reformed the system again, creating the structure, centering in the Ofice of the Comptroller of the Treasury, that still existed in 1919.

In that year, again motivated by financial problems exacerbated by U.S. participation in World War I, Congress began to discuss further changes as an adjunct to a strong movement in favor of a national executive budget. The result was the Budget and Accounting Act, 1921, which created the United States General Accounting Office. The sections in the Budget and Accounting Act spelling out GAO's functions represented an effort by the legislative branch to reassert the principle of legislative control of government spending as expressed in legislative appropriations and an audit of expenditures independent of the executive branch.

Auditors of War Department records at the Treasury Department, 1920.

CHAPTER 2

GAO's Charter: The Budget and Accounting Act of 1921

Introduction

The Budget and Accounting Act, 1921, evolved from bills introduced in Congress during the fall of 1919. By that time, given the strong support that had developed for both creation of an executive budget system and independent audit of administrative expenditures, introduction of budget and accounting legislation was no surprise. The inadequacies of the nation's financial system, demonstrated by the World War I experience, and the wartime buildup of a substantial national debt provided further impetus. The Republican Party, which gained control of both houses of Congress in 1919, advocated budget reform, as did the Democratic Party and other groups, including the influential Institute for Government Research (later the Brookings Institution), located in Washington.[1]

During the summer of 1919, both houses of Congress created select committees on the budget. Sen. J. Medill McCormick (R—Illinois), who as a member of the House of Representatives had introduced budget reform legislation in 1918, became chairman of the Senate committee. McCormick, a journalist and one-time owner of the *Chicago Daily Tribune*, served one term in the House before his election to the Senate in 1918. Rep. James W. Good (R—Iowa), a lawyer who served in the House from 1909 to 1921, chaired the House committee.[2]

---

[1]Frederick C. Mosher, *The GAO: The Quest for Accountability in American Government* (Boulder, CO: Westview Press, 1979), 47 (hereafter cited as Mosher, *GAO*).

[2]*Biographical Directory of the United States Congress, 1774-1989, Bicentennial Edition*, 100th Cong., 2d Sess., S. Doc. 100-34 (Washington: GPO, 1989), 1072 (Good), and 1453-54 (McCormick) (hereafter cited as *Biographical Directory*); Mosher, *GAO*, 47; Staff of the Senate Committee on Government Operations, *Financial Management in the Federal Government*, 87th Cong., 1st Sess., S. Doc. 11 (Washington: GPO, 1961), 298 (hereafter cited as Senate, *Financial Management,* 1961); and Frederick C. Mosher, *A Tale of Two Agencies: A Comparative Analysis of the General Accounting Office and the Office of Management and Budget* (Baton Rouge: Louisiana State University Press, 1984), 27 (hereafter cited as Mosher, *Tale of Two Agencies*).

House Hearings, 1919

Good's committee held hearings on establishment of a national budget system in late September and early October 1919. Although these hearings preceded the introduction of the House bill, they brought out ideas and approaches to budgeting and accounting debated later when both houses considered specific legislation. William F. Willoughby, director of the Institute for Government Research, credited by several sources as being a primary author of the Budget and Accounting Act, gave a lengthy statement early in the hearings. He traced the history of the office of the comptroller and auditor general of Great Britain. The comptroller and auditor general, Willoughby explained, essentially had the legal status and the tenure of a judicial official; his duty was to audit and report cases of uneconomical administration, inefficiency, or improper conduct. "This duty," Willoughby observed, "he exercises fearlessly."

Willoughby regarded the establishment of a similar office in the United States as a necessary component of a federal budgetary plan. "No organ that grants funds," Willoughby explained, "has fulfilled its obligation until it follows up and sees that the orders that it has given have been carried out." Such an office would "inform Congress of how its orders have been executed" and "give Congress as complete a report of the way its agent, the administration, has carried out orders given to it as possible." Willoughby also recommended that Congress create a committee of public accounts, which would receive, study, and take action on reports from the comptroller and auditor general.[3]

Charles W. Collins, a Washington lawyer, pointed out the central problem with the existing office of comptroller of the treasury: "The whole business is under the executive branch of the Government, and the executive is in the situation of auditing his own accounts, which is contrary to good finance." As Collins put it, "an audit is an examination from the outside to determine whether the disbursing office has been faithful; and that only can be done by an absolutely independent officer."[4] Walter W. Warwick, the comptroller of the treasury, made clear that he felt that auditing done by the executive branch was wrong. Putting the auditing duties into a new comptroller's office responsible to Congress would solve the problem. He argued that the present functions of the comptroller and the six auditors should

---

[3]*National Budget System*, Hearings before the House Select Committee on the Budget, 66th Cong., 1st Sess. (Washington: GPO, 1919), 63, 97-98 (hereafter cited as *National Budget System*).
[4]Ibid., 228.

be combined under one official. He added that one of the benefits would be the issuance of an annual statement of government receipts and expenditures.[5]

Several witnesses offered opinions on how the new comptroller should be appointed—whether by the Congress or the president. Frank J. Goodenow, the president of The Johns Hopkins University, thought that it would be preferable to have the comptroller appointed by the legislative branch but thought that such an appointment was not authorized under the U.S. Constitution. If he was to be an officer of the U.S. government, his appointment would have to follow the formula prescribed by the Constitution—appointment by the president. Goodenow suggested that the comptroller's tenure be similar to that of Supreme Court justices.[6]

Francis Oakey, a certified public accountant, who at the time served as a consulting accountant for the federal Bureau of Efficiency, felt that the comptroller should be responsible for auditing, prescribing accounting methods, and investigating and reporting to Congress both on executive branch budget estimates and on his investigations into whether congressionally authorized financial programs were being carried out properly. Rep. Good observed in response to Oakey that a comptroller appointed by Congress might be subject to political pressures emanating from that body. As Good put it, "If he is to tell some other official of the Government what he can do and what he can not do, he must be an official of the United States."[7]

Other prominent witnesses at the hearing were Secretary of the Treasury Carter Glass, former Secretary of War (1911-1913) Henry L. Stimson, and Assistant Secretary of the Navy Franklin D. Roosevelt. Glass argued that the auditor should remain in the Treasury Department but that Congress should provide more funds to broaden the scope of the audit and increase the auditing staff "so that there may be covered also the question whether expenditures have been made efficiently, economically, and without duplication."[8]

Stimson thought that the United States should have an official patterned after Great Britain's comptroller and auditor general; this person should concentrate on a postaudit. "I do not think that that man ought to be given duties which would tend toward making him share executive functions. . . . In other words, I do not think he should have the responsibility of saying

---

[5]Ibid., 238-41, 244, 252.
[6]Ibid., 348-49.
[7]Ibid., 438-39, 441.
[8]Ibid., 491.

beforehand whether sums would be expended. That would simply mean the creation of a little subexecutive, a little subpresident, controlling the department." Stimson envisioned the new auditor as independent of the comptroller of the treasury and one who reported problems to Congress, but he did not describe him as a legislative official.[9]

Roosevelt favored the creation of a uniform accounting program to accompany the new budget system. He thought that locating the audit organization in the legislative branch would raise a question of the prerogatives of the legislative and executive branches—"as to how far the legislative branch should go in assisting in the conduct of affairs of the administrative branch." Creating a budget system under the president together with reformation of the accounting system "would give Congress all the facts, in simple terms, that average laymen, as all of us are, could understand."[10]

Representative Good's position that the new comptroller general or auditor should be appointed by the president was particularly significant, given his position as chairman of the House Select Committee. Responding to Rep. James A. Frear (R—Wisconsin), who said that he did not think it mattered where the auditor was located "provided you can rely on his report," Good said: "If he is to pass on the legality of the expenditures by the various spending departments, he would have to be an officer of the United States, and not an officer of the House of Representatives." Good suggested that when the control of Congress shifted to another party, the new leadership would change the auditor. Frear said appointing the auditor for a stated term would eliminate this possibility.[11]

House Debate and Passage, October 1919

The general airing of issues relating to the executive budget system and an independent audit organization in the House Select Committee prepared the ground for consideration of specific legislation on the issues. Between October 17 and October 21, 1919, the House of Representatives debated H.R. 9783, the budget and accounting bill introduced by Good's select committee. Although the bill's provision for an executive budget system was the more significant initiative, the debate made clear that an effective audit system independent of the executive branch was also a matter of considerable importance.

---

[9]Ibid., 644-45.
[10]Ibid., 656-57, 665.
[11]Ibid., 690-92.

In opening the debate, Good noted that the British Parliament in 1866 passed the Exchequer and Audit Departments Act, creating the office of comptroller and auditor with broad powers to audit and investigate government expenditures. The bill before the House, Good explained, would set up what he called the accounting department with functions similar to those of the British comptroller and auditor general.[12] He spoke at length about Congress's inability to control appropriations after approving them and detailed the problems he saw in abdicating that control to the executive branch. Serious criticism from the existing auditors or the comptroller of the treasury was not possible; these officials "can not be expected long to hold their positions if they should criticize wastefulness, extravagance, or inefficiency in any of the executive departments."[13]

The accounting department would make possible a "practical business policy" in the conduct of the nation's fiscal affairs. The comptroller general, Good predicted, "will become the real guardian of the Treasury of the United States. He will become one of the most powerful and useful Government officials. . . ." An independent audit will have three benefits: providing Congress with information on spending in government agencies, serving as a check on the president and subordinate officials in preparation of the budget, and requiring cabinet officials to become thoroughly familiar with all aspects of their departments and make each one realize his responsibility "for the waste and extravagant use of public funds appropriated for the use of his department."[14] To the applause of his colleagues, Good concluded his introductory speech as follows:

> The proposed legislation is of total importance to the people of the United States. . . . In my opinion this legislation is solidly founded upon sound business principles, and its adoption will mark the beginning of a new era in the financial history of the United States. Once enacted, this legislation will need no defender. The saving it will effect will speak more loudly than words can tell of its real worth. As Burke put the old Latin law, it will "give us a system of economy, which is itself a great revenue."[15]

---

[12]*Congressional Record* (hereafter cited as *Cong. Rec.*), 66th Cong., 1st Sess., 1919, 58, pt. 7: 7084-85.

[13]Ibid., 7085.

[14]Ibid., 7085-86.

[15]Ibid., 7086.

Because there was bipartisan support for the general objectives of the proposed legislation, the House debate centered on specific issues. For example, many members of the House stressed the need for economy in government and the contributions a bureau of the budget and a new accounting and auditing office would make toward economy. Rep. Adolphus P. Nelson (R—Wisconsin) asserted that the budget and accounting bill was one of the most important bills to come before Congress in a quarter of a century. "The independent audits provided for in this bill are . . . of tremendous importance, . . . and will help us to eliminate the tremendous waste and extravagance which are so liable to creep in under a system of expenditures such as our Government has had in the past."[16] Rep. William E. Andrews (R—Nebraska), who had served as an auditor in the Treasury Department (1897-1915), described the proposal for an accounting department as "a foundation for the largest measure of economy that can be realized under this bill." The department could "gather the facts and submit them."[17] Lucian W. Parrish (D—Texas) observed that the critical issue before Congress was "the economic expenditure of public money."[18]

George S. Graham (R—Pennsylvania) offered an amendment to the bill, subsequently passed, which required the comptroller general to report to Congress on every expenditure or contract made by a department head in excess of appropriations. As Graham put it, "this amendment is intended to effectuate the very purpose and object of the budget system. A budget system is intended to have the Government of the United States live carefully and economically within its estimated revenues."[19]

The original bill required the comptroller general to investigate the "receipt" and the "disbursement" of public funds. Rep. Robert Luce (R—Massachusetts) proposed to add the word "application" to receipt and disbursement, to require the comptroller general to indicate how the funds were used. The House rejected the amendment after Rep. Good argued that the original wording covered application of funds: "the comptroller general would not be worth his salt if he believed that moneys were used for a specific use not provided for in the appropriation and did not report it to Congress and hold that an expenditure under it could not be made at all. If he failed to do it he would be removable from office."[20]

---

[16]Ibid., 7295-96.

[17]Ibid., 7198-99.

[18]Ibid., 7204.

[19]Ibid., 7291.

[20]Ibid., 7291, 7293. When Luce offered the same amendment to a later version of this bill in 1921, it passed. See also Ellsworth H. Morse, Jr., "The Application of Public Funds," *GAO Review* (summer 1971): 20-25.

Another subject of discussion involved the provisions for appointment, removal, and tenure of the comptroller general. Given the general conclusion that auditing of administrative agencies ought to be done by an authority outside the executive branch, the challenge was to devise an appointment and removal process that would preserve congressional prerogatives and remove the comptroller general's office from politics. Good's original bill provided for appointment of the comptroller general and the assistant comptroller general by the president and confirmation by the Senate. The bill did not specify a definite term of office but provided for mandatory retirement of both officials at age 70. Their removal from office, only on grounds of inefficiency, neglect of duty, or malfeasance in office, would be done by a concurrent resolution of both houses of Congress; no role for the president in the removal process was specified.[21]

The substance of the debate focused on the question of whether the proposed removal process was proper and whether it would prevent the president from removing an official he had appointed. The wording of the Select Committee bill designated the comptroller general an officer of the United States but ensured his independence of the executive branch after appointment and confirmation. Rep. Simeon D. Fess (R—Ohio) noted that "the power to appoint has always been interpreted to carry with it the power of removal, unless in the appointment there was some inhibition written in the law."[22] This introduced a concept that later was to play a crucial role in the fate of the bill.

Rep. Henry W. Temple (R—Pennsylvania) saw the concurrent resolution as a way of giving the Congress control of the audit, "not through the power of appointment, but through the power of removal. It seems to me that the whole plan goes back to the scheme of the Constitution of the United States. It restores something of the power that Congress formerly had and ought to have, but which in practice has been largely taken over by the Executive."[23]

On the other hand, Rep. James B. "Champ" Clark (D—Missouri), a former speaker of the House, offered an amendment according the president the power to remove the comptroller general when he wished. Martin B. Madden (R—Illinois) opposed the amendment, arguing that it would make the office a "political football." "The man who is comptroller general should be the instrument of the people, provided for by the Congress, and if you adopt

---

[21]*Cong. Rec.*, 66th Cong., 1st Sess., 1919, 58, pt. 7: 7088, 7274.

[22]Ibid., 7136.

[23]Ibid., 7211.

the amendment . . . you destroy every vestige of the people's right to supervise and survey the expenditure of their own money." Ultimately the House rejected Clark's amendment and the provision for removal by concurrent resolution stood.[24]

The House acted on the bill on October 21, 1919, after thorough debate. The final tally was 285 in favor, 3 opposed, and 143 not voting.[25]   The bill then went on to the special Senate committee on the budget, which held hearings on H.R. 9783 in December 1919 and January 1920.

Senate Hearings, 1919-1920

The Senate hearings concentrated mainly on the question of a national budget, but there was frequent discussion of the need for a related accounting and auditing system. Several of the witnesses who had testified at the House hearings appeared again at the Senate hearings, most conspicuously W. L. Willoughby. Giving the president the task of formulating and submitting a budget would "enormously increase his power," Willoughby observed, both within and outside the government. As this occurs, "control should be correspondingly strengthened" by establishing an accounting organization reporting directly to Congress.[26]

Another prominent witness was Nicholas Murray Butler, president of Columbia University. Butler suggested that there be three sets of provisions in budget legislation: one set on preparation and submission of the budget, one set on requiring cabinet heads to explain budget matters on the floor of Congress, and one set on "an independent audit of all Government expenditures, not only as to the correctness of their form but as to their propriety . . . ." He preferred a "public auditor" instead of a comptroller general. He proposed that each house establish a committee on public audit, chaired by a member of the minority party in the legislature. "Care must be taken," Butler observed, "not to let the public audit develop into a source of purely political

[24]Ibid., 7276-77, 7281. A joint resolution does not differ greatly from a bill. Both houses of Congress must approve a joint resolution and the president must sign it. A joint resolution has the force of law. Joint resolutions usually deal with limited matters. A concurrent resolution, which does not have the force of law, requires the approval of both houses but not the president's signature. Congress uses concurrent resolutions to make or amend rules pertaining to both houses or to express the joint position of Congress on a particular issue. See Roger H. Davidson, ed., *Congress and Its Members*, 2d edition (Washington: Congressional Quarterly, Inc., 1985), 268.

[25]*Cong. Rec.*, 66th Cong., 1st Sess., 1919, 58, pt. 7: 7297.

[26]*National Budget*, Hearings before the Committee on Consideration of a National Budget, United States Senate, 66th Cong., 2d Sess. (Washington: GPO, 1920), 36.

criticism and attack. It should be strictly a business office to inform the Congress as to whether the moneys that had been appropriated had been expended not only in accordance with law, but wisely and well."[27]

Several times during the hearing, the idea came up that reforming the accounting and auditing system would be a complicated business and that it might be wise to handle those issues in separate legislation. Senator McCormick expressed this view. "What we need for Congress," he said, "is a comptroller general with real powers, but the subject is so vast . . . that I shrink from making a slapdash proposition until we can have hearings on that subject and that alone. . . ."[28] McCormick did not restate this suggestion when the Senate later considered the budget and accounting bill.

Senate Debate and Passage, April-May 1920

On April 29, 1920, Sen. Reed Smoot (R—Utah), called up for Senate consideration H.R. 9783, explaining that the Senate special budget committee had recommended striking out the entire text of the House bill after the enacting clause and substituting a new text developed by the Senate committee. The Senate bill established a budget bureau in the Treasury Department instead of in the president's office as in the House bill and specified details about the development of the budget and its submission to Congress. The bill created a "general accounting office," independent of the executive departments, to be headed by a comptroller general and three assistant comptrollers general, each serving a five-year term, removable only for cause. The first assistant comptroller general was to be the chief auditor, responsible for settling accounts; the second was to prescribe forms for keeping and rendering accounts; and the third was to keep accounts. The bill also provided for a three-member board of appeals, including a chairman (known as the solicitor, nominated by the president and approved by the Senate) and the second and third assistant comptrollers general. The board of appeals was to review decisions of the first assistant comptroller general and make decisions on payments when requested by agency heads and disbursing officers.[29]

In its report on H.R. 9783, the Senate Select Committee stated that it was "in entire harmony with the principle given expression in the House bill that an independent audit is an essential part of any budget program. . . ." While

---

[27]Ibid., 72, 74.
[28]Ibid., 154.
[29]*Cong. Rec.*, 66th Cong., 2d Sess., 1920, 59, pt. 6: 6278-80.

noting that the House bill transferred the duties, the functions, and the staff of the comptroller of the treasury and the six auditors, the Senate committee said that the bill should "accomplish a concentration of authority over all Federal accounting activities." Thus the committee added terms giving the general accounting office a key role in prescribing and supervising accounting methods and examining accounts and claims and overall control of the federal government's accounting procedures. Appealing to history, the committee said that the proposed system "practically follows the specifications laid down by Alexander Hamilton," the first secretary of the treasury.[30]

A statement by Sen. Walter E. Edge (R—New Jersey) early in the Senate debate provided the rationale for legislation that was not really controversial. Edge felt that adoption of the bill, providing for a "businesslike budget" and a general accounting office, would help solve problems "responsible for the unrest in the country." He observed, "Today the great spirit of unrest, while it can be traced of course to many causes, fundamentally, I believe, is based on . . . a realization upon the part of all classes of people, rich and poor alike, that the Government is not administered economically and that the public is receiving but a small proportion in results for the amount of money they are paying the Government."[31]

Sen. William H. King (D—Utah) gave a thoughtful speech about the bill, noting that there was little opposition to it. He stressed the need for both economy in government and better financial management. While assuming that it would not pass, King proposed a substitute bill in the form of an amendment, stating that he hoped the expected conference committee would consider its terms. King proposed creating, in place of the bureau of the budget in the Treasury Department, a "bureau of estimates" because making estimates was to be the primary duty of the office. He suggested placing the general accounting office, headed by a "comptroller of accounts," in the Treasury Department rather than giving it independent status. King argued that the title comptroller general "is rather too big and overwhelming. The office created deals with the accounts, and the chief official of this organization is the comptroller of accounts. It seems to me that the term is misleading if he is named the comptroller general of the United States." Putting both the bureau of estimates and the general accounting office in the Treasury Department "will make for greater efficiency and facility of administration."[32]

---

[30]Ibid., 6350-53.
[31]Ibid., 6349.
[32]Ibid., 6389-93.

The Treasury Department building in 1920. Source: Washingtoniana Division, D.C. Public Library.

The proposal ignored a crucial argument for creating a general accounting office, that it would conduct an independent audit as an organization not responsible for the actual spending of the government funds it audited. On May 1, 1920, after rejecting King's amendment, the Senate passed the budget and auditing act by voice vote.[33]

Final Congressional Action on the Bill, 1920

A few days later both the House and the Senate agreed to establish a conference committee to reconcile differences between the two bills. Representatives Good, Madden, Philip P. Campbell (R—Kansas), Joseph W. Byrns (D—Tennessee), and John N. Garner (D—Texas) were appointed conferees for the House; designated conferees for the Senate were Senators McCormick, Smoot, Andrieus A. Jones (D—New Mexico), Henry W. Keyes (R—New Hampshire), and Furnifold M. Simmons (D—North Carolina).[34]

Good and McCormick presented the conference committee's report to their respective bodies on May 26, 1920.[35] When McCormick explained the conference committee's final bill the next day, he suggested that there were only minor changes to the Senate bill. But actually McCormick glossed over the fact that Title III, which created the general accounting office, looked more like the House version than the Senate's. The conference committee dropped the Senate provision for three assistant comptrollers general. McCormick explained that the House conferees thought that having three assistants to the comptroller general would too rigidly departmentalize the general accounting office. "They held that especially it would inhibit an effort to rid the department of about 20 per cent of the employees now engaged in the work for which the comptroller general would be responsible," according to McCormick. He also noted that the conference group had deleted the Senate's provisions for a board of appeals.[36]

When Senator King raised the question of the right of the general accounting office to examine departments to secure efficiency, Senator Simmons responded that in the final bill "the accounting department has the right to make investigations to enlighten itself with reference to expenditures, and that for that purpose they may call for the books of every bureau, department, or establishment of the Government." After a very short discussion on May 27, the Senate agreed by a voice vote to the conference report.[37]

---

[33]Ibid., 6393, 6395.
[34]Ibid., 6480; pt. 7: 6502.
[35]Ibid., pt. 8: 7660, 7708; the text of the conference committee report is on 7660-63.
[36]Ibid., 7721.
[37]Ibid., 7722.

Representative Good brought up the conference committee report in the House on May 29, 1920. He stated that the conferees had agreed unanimously to the report and that the final bill was a combination of the original House and Senate bills. But he added, "In principle . . . it maintains the provisions of the House bill." He described the general accounting office as an independent establishment "that will be to the appropriations made by Congress what the Supreme Court is to the construction of laws that are enacted by Congress." The general accounting office would report to the appropriate committees of Congress and the president when it found waste, inefficiency, and duplication in executive agencies. "With that system of checks and balances it is believed this great overlapping of activities, this duplication that exists in every department of the Government, will cease, and that the Government of the United States will be placed upon a business basis, and that we will then administer the greatest business in all the world, the business of the United States, upon the same principles that govern the business men in the conduct of their affairs."[38]

The only hitch in the House debate was the result of complaints by Rep. Gilbert N. Haugen (R—Iowa) about the budget provisions of the bill. He argued that a similar system had not worked in England, contributing to serious financial problems there. Although he spoke at length, Haugen did not attract much support, and when he finished, the House agreed to the conference report. The bill went to the president for his approval on June 2, 1920.[39]

President Wilson's Veto

On June 4, 1920, President Woodrow Wilson vetoed H.R. 9783. He said he had taken the action with "the greatest regret" because he was entirely sympathetic with the objectives of the bill. The problem was the provision in Section 303 providing for removal of the comptroller general and the assistant comptroller general by concurrent resolution of the House and Senate. For the president, an expert on constitutional law, it was a constitutional issue:

> The effect of this is to prevent the removal of these officers
> for any cause except either by impeachment or a concurrent
> resolution of Congress. It has, I think, always been the ac-
> cepted construction of the Constitution that the power to ap-
> point officers of this kind carries with it, as an incident, the

[38]Ibid., 7942, 7947, 7949.
[39]Ibid., 7949-56, 8281.

power to remove. I am convinced that the Congress is without constitutional power to limit the appointing power and its incident, the power of removal derived from the Constitution.

Wilson noted that he had acted quickly with the hope that Congress could "remedy this defect" before its scheduled adjournment on June 5.[40]

Congressional Response to the President's Veto

Representative Good expressed regret that the president had vetoed the bill and added, "I can not arrive at any conclusion other than that the legal advice he had received as to the constitutional powers of Congress in this respect is, indeed, faulty." He pointed out that the Supreme Court had never decided a case involving the issue at stake, but he observed, "I think it may be stated as a general rule that the power given to the President to appoint an officer carries with it the inherent power of removal, unless that inherent right or incidental right is taken away by the statute itself." Later, when questioned about his statement, Good withdrew the word "inherent" but continued to speak about an incidental right.[41]

The House debated at length the substance of Wilson's veto message; Good continued to argue that Congress had the right to restrict the president's power to remove officials he had appointed. But when the House voted on a motion to overrule the veto, the tally was 178 yes, 103 no, and 145 not voting. Because the resolution did not get two-thirds approval, it failed and the House sustained the president's veto.[42]

Good was determined to get budget and accounting legislation enacted. On June 5, 1920, he introduced H.R. 14441, which was identical to the vetoed bill except for a new provision vesting the powers of appointment and removal of the comptroller general in the Supreme Court, not requiring confirmation by the Senate.[43] Good's objective in this odd proposal was to

---

[40]Ibid., 8609-10. See also Mosher, *GAO*, 54-55; Margaret L. Macfarlane, "The Day President Wilson Vetoed the Budget and Accounting Bill," *GAO Review* (fall 1968): 57-60; and Senate, *Financial Management*, 1961, 9-10. The removal power issue has had a contentious history and led to, among other things, the impeachment of President Andrew Johnson in 1867. See Louis Fisher, *Constitutional Conflicts Between Congress and the President* (Lawrence: University Press of Kansas, 1991); James Hart, *The American Presidency in Action* (New York: MacMillan Co., 1948); and Donald C. Bacon, Roger H. Davidson, and Morton Keller, eds., *Encyclopedia of the U.S. Congress* (New York: Simon & Schuster, 1995), 3: 1711.

[41]Ibid., 8610.

[42]Ibid., 8610-14.

[43]Ibid., 8647-49.

ensure the independence of the comptroller general from the executive branch. His suggestion attracted very little support in the House and some very pointed opposition, especially from Democratic members.

Rep. Warren Gard (D—Ohio) described the proposal as an affront to the president and as a scheme that would "make impossible the proper performance of the manifold provisions of the budget." Rep. Andrew J. Montague (D Virginia) stated that the power to appoint and remove the comptroller general was an executive or an administrative function inappropriate to the Supreme Court and predicted that the Court would refuse to do it, "knowing that such a declination is the only safe path it may pursue to preserve its judicial ermine free from the soil and taint of partisan politics." Rep. Otis T. Wingo (D—Arkansas) complained that Good was trying to ram his proposal through the House. "It strikes me," Wingo said, to the applause of his colleagues, "as so outrageous to drag the Supreme Court . . . into an effort, which I think is a mean, petty, partisan effort, to slap the President . . . in the face, that I shall not stand for it. It is an outrageous performance."[44]

Good then proposed amending the bill to give to the president the power to appoint the comptroller general and the assistant comptroller general with the advice and the consent of the Senate, with no mention of the removal process. Even this, the usual way to make such appointments, evoked some opposition. Rep. Benjamin G. Humphreys (D—Mississippi) believed that making the comptroller general responsible to the executive branch would eliminate the possibility of an effective independent audit. Humphreys thought that the amendment "takes 90 per cent of the merit and virtue out of the budget legislation." Eventually the House passed Good's bill, including the provision for appointment of the comptroller general, and sent it immediately to the Senate.[45]

The Senate took up the bill at the request of Senator Smoot, who urged instant passage while the House was still in session. Various issues came up during a long and rambling debate. Sen. James A. Reed (D—Missouri), who opposed the bill, thought that Congress would be abdicating its power and giving in to the executive if it approved the plan. Reed exclaimed, "The Executive! We hear nothing but 'the Executive.' There seems to be an impression that the only department of this Government that functions is the

---

[44]Ibid., 8650-52.
[45]Ibid., 8652-57.

Executive." The Senate never voted on H.R. 14441 because of the lengthy and inconclusive debate. At 4:00 p.m. on June 5, 1920, at the predetermined time, the vice president declared the Senate adjourned.[46]

The Bill Reintroduced and Debated, 1921

In November 1920, the Republican candidate, Warren G. Harding, defeated the Democratic nominee, James M. Cox. Shortly after the 67th Congress convened in March 1921, the Republicans, who controlled both houses, reintroduced the budget and accounting legislation. Senator McCormick introduced S. 1084, the Budget and Accounting Act, 1921, in the Senate on April 25, 1921. A very short debate on the bill took place the next day. McCormick compared the bill with the one that President Wilson had vetoed in 1920. McCormick pointed out that other than a few changes in the section dealing with the proposed bureau of the budget, the major change provided for appointment of the comptroller general by the president for a period of seven years, removable by joint resolution of Congress. A joint resolution, unlike a concurrent resolution, required the president's signature, thus giving him a role in the process. McCormick explained that he had sought legal advice and that his advisers had told him the joint resolution approach was acceptable.[47]

A brief discussion took place about the proposed salaries of $9,000 for the assistant director of the bureau of the budget and $7,500 for the assistant comptroller general. Eventually the Senate agreed to an amendment putting the salary of both officials at $7,500 and then passed the bill.[48]

S. 1084 came before the House on May 3, 1921. While technically considering the Senate bill during lengthy debates on both May 3 and May 5, the House really discussed H.R. 30, its own version of budget and accounting legislation. Rep. Good again was the floor leader and played a major role in the debate. He explained the respective roles of the director of the bureau of the budget and the comptroller general and the need for an official to represent the interests of Congress. The comptroller general, he said, would sit with the Committee on Appropriations, give Congress the information it needed, and correct any erroneous information provided by the bureau of the budget. "In this way," Good said, "the facts will come before Congress in a way that we may eliminate duplications wherever we

---

[46]Ibid., 8625-44.
[47]*Cong. Rec.*, 67th Cong., 1st Sess., 1921, 61, pt. 1: 595, 657-59.
[48]Ibid., 659-62.

find them, and where we find there is an excess of employees they can be eliminated, and the service will not be injured by an injudicious cut in the appropriation."[49]

Good spoke at length on the question of appointment and removal of the comptroller general. He pointed out that the current House bill contained a clause like the one Wilson had vetoed in 1920, providing for removal of the comptroller general by concurrent resolution. Good said that the proposed law should not allow the president to remove the comptroller general at will because if that was the case, he would not be an effective watchdog over the executive branch. "We create here an independent office that will be a real, live thing for Congress and a great improvement over the present plan. I have no hesitancy in saying that if this provision [removal by concurrent resolution] shall become a law, we will receive as much if not more substantial benefit, more economy through the fearless administration of the general accounting office than we may expect to secure through the budget itself."[50]

Good presented a rather convoluted explanation of the effects of a concurrent resolution. He referred to Article II, Section 2, of the Constitution, which gave the president the power to appoint ambassadors, public ministers and consuls, Supreme Court justices, and other officers established by law and stated that "the Congress may by law vest the appointment of such inferior officers, as they think proper, in the President alone, in the courts of law, or in the heads of departments." Good argued that the officers created in the bill, including the comptroller general, were "inferior" officers and asserted that if the Supreme Court had to rule on their removal, it would say that if Congress had created the offices, fixed the pay, and specified causes of removal, Congress had the power, independent of the appointing power, in this case the president, to remove them. Good added, "And if we have no power to do that, then I say to you that we will not be able to create this great office that is to serve as an arm of the Congress in its efforts to save, by economy, untold millions of dollars."[51]

But then Good distinguished between two kinds of concurrent resolutions, those that do not have the effect of law (such as inviting a visitor to address a house of Congress) and those that do. The comptroller general, he said, was a semijudicial officer; "I can not conceive how we could construe this provision of the Constitution to mean that we could dismiss the comptroller general or the assistant comptroller general without passing a resolu-

---

[49]Ibid., 980-82.
[50]Ibid., 983.
[51]Ibid., 982-83.

tion that required the signature of the President." Thus Good seemed to be saying that Congress had the power to remove an officer appointed by the president if he was an inferior officer but that in the case of the comptroller general, Congress should not remove him unless the president agreed. Actually, what Good proposed had the same effect as a joint resolution of Congress, which required the president's signature. Good's argument also meant that the president did not have the power to remove the comptroller general on his own initiative. The House accepted Good's position, after rejecting an amendment offered by Rep. Richard W. Parker (R—New Jersey) to delete the concurrent resolution proposal and give the president the power to remove the comptroller general.[52]

There was also discussion of the length of tenure for the comptroller general, precipitated by an amendment put forward by Rep. Paul B. Johnson (D—Mississippi) to limit the comptroller general's term to seven years. Good countered by pointing out that the comptroller general's tenure lasted only to age 70 and emphasizing that if the Congress was not satisfied with his work, Congress had the power to remove him for cause by concurrent resolution. Other opponents of the amendment argued that a seven-year term would subject the comptroller general to politics and deprive him of his independence, problems that would be avoided with a longer term. The House overwhelmingly rejected the amendment.[53]

Representative Luce of Massachusetts, as in 1919, proposed an amendment to add the word "application" to Section 312 of the bill, authorizing the comptroller general to investigate all matters relating to the receipt and the disbursement of public funds. Luce emphasized the need for the comptroller general to constantly search for economy in government. His amendment was designed "to make it sure that the comptroller general shall concern himself not simply with taking in and paying out money from an accountant's point of view, but that he shall also concern himself with the question as to whether it is economically and efficiently applied." Good said he had no objection to the amendment and it passed.[54] The provision took on added significance in later years, especially after World War II, when GAO expanded its work in the direction of program evaluation.

On May 5, 1921, the House passed S. 1084 after substituting the text of the House bill as amended for the Senate version. The tally was 344 yes votes, 9 no votes, and 76 not voting. The House also agreed to request a

---

[52]Ibid., pt. 2: 1083-84.

[53]Ibid., 1079-83.

[54]Ibid., 1090; Morse, "The Application of Public Funds," 20-25; and Mosher, *Tale of Two Agencies*, 32.

conference committee with the Senate, and the speaker appointed to the committee the same representatives who had served in 1920 on the earlier bill—Good, Campbell, Madden, Byrns, and Garner. The next day the vice president appointed the Senate conferees—McCormick, George H. Moses (R—New Hampshire), and Oscar W. Underwood (D—Alabama).[55]

On May 26, without debate, the Senate agreed to the conference report.[56] The House took up the report on May 27. Garner described the bill: "The bill as reported by the conferees is the House bill, with a little sprinkling of Senate principle in it, and a little of the quibbling of the Senate. Outside of this it is the 'Jim' Good original bill of the Sixty-sixth Congress."[57]

One of the most contentious issues between the House and Senate conferees, causing what Good described as "a very serious argument," was the tenure of the comptroller general and procedures for removing him from office. The Senate bill provided for seven-year terms for the comptroller general and the assistant comptroller general, removable for cause by joint resolution. The House provided for the two officials to hold office during good behavior, retire at age 70, and be removable for cause by concurrent be resolution. The conference committee had agreed to 15-year terms for the comptroller general and the assistant comptroller general and removal for cause by joint resolution. Representative Byrns, explaining this provision to the House, said it "relieves him [the comptroller general] from any sense of responsibility or dependency upon the Executive, and he can and will exercise that independence which is so necessary if he is to function as this law contemplates that he shall."

Referring to House acceptance of the Senate's decision allowing removal of the comptroller general by joint resolution, Good contended that there had never been a clear distinction between concurrent and joint resolutions. As he put it, "My understanding of a concurrent resolution is that if it has the effect of law it must be signed by the President. The name offered to a resolution of this kind does not determine its status." To remove any question about whether the president's consent was required, the House conferees agreed to the term "joint resolution," which definitely required the

---

[55]Ibid., 1091-93, 1122.

[56]Ibid., 1783; the text of the conference report is on 1783-86.

[57]Ibid., 1850, 1857.

president's signature.[58]   When the House voted on the conference report, there were 335 yes votes and 3 no votes; 92 did not vote. President Harding signed the bill on June 10, 1921.[59]

Terms and Analysis of the Budget and Accounting Act, 1921

Title I of the law specified that it was to be cited as the "Budget and Accounting Act, 1921."[60] Title II provided details on the process of development of the annual budget, its transmission to Congress, and the creation of the Bureau of the Budget in the Treasury Department. The sections establishing the General Accounting Office and detailing its functions appeared in Title III.[61]

The law created GAO; abolished the offices of comptroller and assistant comptroller of the treasury and the six Treasury Department auditors; and transferred to GAO their powers, duties, staff, and property. Removal of two GAO statutory officers, the comptroller general and the assistant comptroller general, who were to hold office for terms of 15 years, would be done by joint resolution when Congress determined that they were incapacitated or guilty of neglect of duty, malfeasance in office, felony, or moral turpitude.

The law provided that balances certified by the comptroller general "shall be final and conclusive upon the executive branch of the government." GAO was to adjust and settle all claims by or against the U.S. government as well as all government accounts. The comptroller general was given the duty to prescribe all forms, systems, and procedures for administrative appropriation and fund accounting and for administrative examination of the accounts of fiscal officers and claims against the United States. Section 312 of Title III contained a key provision: "The Comptroller General shall investigate . . . all matters relating to the receipt, disbursement, and application of public funds. . . ." He was to report to Congress regularly and to the president when requested on GAO's work. He was to make investigations and reports as ordered by either house of Congress or a committee and "direct assistants from his office to furnish the committee such aid and information as it may request." Another section directed government agencies to furnish to the

---

[58]Ibid., 1854-56.

[59]Ibid., 1858-59, 1932, 1940; ibid., pt. 3: 2500. Good resigned from Congress on June 15, 1921, and then practiced law in Chicago. He became secretary of war under President Herbert C. Hoover on March 5, 1929, and served until his sudden death in Washington on November 18, 1929. He died of septicemia (blood poisoning) following an emergency apendectomy. See *Biographical Directory*, 1072; and clipping, *Washington Evening Star*, November 19, 1929, GAO History Program Archives.

[60]Public Law 67-13, 42 Stat. 20. The original printed law was 10 pages long, half of them devoted to GAO.

[61]See Appendix III for the complete text of Title III of the Budget and Accounting Act, 1921.

comptroller general, as required, information on their powers, duties, activities, organization, financial transactions, and methods of business. GAO was to have access to the books and the documentary records of these departments and agencies to secure the necessary information.

In theory, and especially in practice, the Budget and Accounting Act gave GAO exceptionally broad authority. Several later laws, all passed after 1944, clarified or expanded GAO's role and powers. But the original law provided not only the basis for the office's operations but also a foundation for many new roles, expanded functions, and changes in direction by the office after 1945. The charter granted to GAO by Congress in 1921 proved broad and flexible enough to sustain the evolution of GAO's work over many years. But the law also provided less detail than necessary in some instances to ensure a smooth operation, especially in the early years.

The terms of the act relating to GAO reflected existing practices in the accounting and auditing field and created a new organization to carry on these practices. The law merged the old offices of the comptroller of the treasury and the six auditors into the General Accounting Office but made no significant changes in the way GAO was to conduct the business of these offices. GAO "shall be independent of the executive departments," according to the law, but the statute did not specify that the office was part of the legislative branch. An assistant comptroller general was provided for, but the law left the definition of this official's duties almost entirely up to the comptroller general.

The provisions for appointment and removal of the comptroller general and the assistant comptroller general left unresolved practical and constitutional questions that contributed to continuing controversy about GAO in the years after 1921. W. F. Willoughby wrote in 1927 that the final procedure for removing the comptroller general, a joint resolution signed by the president, "in no way met the objections of President Wilson," who could not accept any limitation on the president's right to remove an officer he had appointed. Willoughby thought that the removal provisions had one major effect, to make it difficult to remove the comptroller general and the assistant comptroller general because removal would require the consent of both houses of Congress as well as the president. "So far as the act now in force is concerned, Congress achieved its purpose of making these officers completely independent of the executive power."[62]

---

[62]W. F. Willoughby, *The Legal Status and Functions of the General Accounting Office of the National Government* (Baltimore: The Johns Hopkins Press, 1927), 10.

A later well-known critic of GAO, Harvey C. Mansfield, Sr., wrote in an influential book in 1939 that Congress had established GAO

> mainly in response to a theory rather than a condition. The theory was that Congress needed an officer, responsible to it alone, to check upon the application of public funds in accordance with appropriations. The need was thought to be a proper correlative of the need which Congress was brought to see of drastic changes in the methods of estimating and appropriating. The nature of the need was not analyzed, nor was there any general realization of the practical differences between a checkup for the purpose of reporting, in order that Congress might legislate more intelligently, and a checkup for the purpose of exerting direct administrative controls. The two purposes were not distinguished.[63]

Mansfield's suggestion that Congress did not concern itself enough with the provisions relating to GAO seems questionable, given the extensive attention paid to GAO during congressional hearings and debates on the bill in 1919, 1920, and 1921. Perhaps Mansfield meant that Congress did not understand when it passed the bill exactly what GAO's role would turn out to be. But his main concern was the mixture of legislative and executive functions granted to GAO by the law.

Lucius Wilmerding, Jr., a scholar whose professional writings focused on aspects of the history of financial management in the United States, commented in a 1943 book on the Budget and Accounting Act and the role of GAO. Although he referred frequently to the British system of audit as a model for the United States, Wilmerding argued that the act was not really patterned on the Exchequer and Audit Departments Act of 1866. It was this law to which Willoughby, Good, and others referred as Congress put together the Budget and Accounting Act between 1919 and 1921. Wilmerding asserted that Willoughby was wrong, "that there is nothing but a formal, perhaps only a nominal, correspondence between the Comptroller General and his supposed analogue." Wilmerding added: "The plain fact is that the Comptroller General audits the accounts on behalf of himself alone." While the British auditor audited for Parliament, GAO's audits were related to settlement, Wilmerding stated, and the comptroller general settled accounts without any relationship on the matter with Congress.

---

[63]Harvey C. Mansfield, Sr., *The Comptroller General: A Study in the Law and Practice of Financial Administration* (New Haven: Yale University Press, 1939), 65-66.

In passing the Budget and Accounting Act, Wilmerding contended, Congress replaced the Treasury Department audit with a GAO audit. "That the Comptroller General was expected to act simultaneously as an administrative controller and as a Congressional auditor was not the result of a reasoned determination by Congress after weighing the arguments for and against such a combination of functions. It was something that happened because Congress failed to distinguish between the two functions and so failed to perceive the existence of any difficulty." The passage of the Budget and Accounting Act, Wilmerding observed, "had the important effect of lulling Congress into a feeling of security."[64]

A more recent scholar of public administration, Frederick C. Mosher, viewed the act as resulting from congressional confusion. A model executive budget system, according to Mosher, contains four components: preparation of the budget by the executive; appropriation of funds by the legislature; execution and control by the executive; and postaudit, by the legislature or independently elected officials. "The basic flaw of the 1921 act, according to many students," Mosher wrote, "was its confusion of the third and fourth steps. . . ." GAO was not only made responsible for the postaudit, but played a major role in budget execution and control, more properly, according to the model, an executive function. The framers of the Budget and Accounting Act "visualized the GAO as the closing arc of the budgetary loop since it would report back to Congress what had happened to its appropriations."

That could not happen, Mosher argued, because Congress had no committee designated to receive and act on GAO reports. And even if such a committee had existed, the comptroller general could not provide effective reports; "his postaudits were meaningless" because he rendered advance decisions and did preaudits on some transactions. As Mosher wrote, "The mixture of current controls with postaudit accountability was an indigestible combination, both in theory and in practice."

Mosher contends that the architects of the Budget and Accounting Act did not study and understand the duties of the comptroller of the treasury and the six auditors, "some of which were plainly incompatible with an independent postaudit." The transfer of these duties to GAO "made little sense in terms of realizing the concept of an executive budget system."[65]

---

[64]Lucius Wilmerding, Jr., *The Spending Power: A History of the Efforts of Congress to Control Expenditures* (New Haven: Yale University Press, 1943), 252-59, 283, 285.

[65]The preceding three paragraphs are based on Mosher, *Tale of Two Agencies*, 33-34.

Mansfield, Wilmerding, and Mosher based their criticisms of GAO's powers as incorporated in the Budget and Accounting Act on governmental theory, but to a significant extent, the problems that emerged in the relationships between GAO and the executive branch between 1921 and 1945 were not the result of theoretical problems. They originated more directly in the personality and the actions of the first comptroller general, John Raymond McCarl. The Budget and Accounting Act, flawed or not, withstood the test of time with remarkable strength and without serious alteration, either by court decision or amendment by Congress. As GAO began to operate in 1921, the law provided a firm foundation for the office.

John R. McCarl, Comptroller General, 1921-1936.

CHAPTER 3

Establishing the Foundations:
John Raymond McCarl, 1921-1936,
and Fred H. Brown, 1939-1940

McCarl's Appointment

On June 27, 1921, President Warren G. Harding nominated John Raymond McCarl to be the first comptroller general of the United States. Two days later, the Senate confirmed the nomination.[1] McCarl, born in Iowa on November 27, 1879, was educated in public schools and received a law degree from the University of Nebraska in 1903. He then served as a member of a law firm in McCook, Nebraska, from 1903 to 1914.

As a young lawyer, McCarl was a progressive Republican. This political orientation led him to Washington to become secretary to Senator George W. Norris, a well-known progressive Republican leader, also from McCook. McCarl held this position from 1914 to 1918. He suddenly resigned from Norris's staff in the summer of 1918 when it appeared that Norris, first elected to the Senate in 1912, would be denied renomination by Nebraska Republicans because of his opposition to U.S. involvement in World War I in 1917. McCarl went to work for Sen. Simeon D. Fess (R—Ohio) as executive secretary of the Republican Congressional Campaign Committee, which Fess headed. According to Richard Lowitt, a Norris biographer, "McCarl sought to salvage something for himself by leaving Norris at a critical juncture in his (Norris's) career." Norris, according to Lowitt, was extremely disappointed with McCarl's departure.[2] In any case McCarl was well-placed politically during the 1918 congressional campaign, which resulted in Republican control of both houses of Congress, and the presidential campaign of 1920, leading to the Republican Harding's capture of the presidency.[3]

---

[1]*Congressional Record* (hereafter cited as *Cong. Rec.*), 67th Cong. 1st Sess., 1921, 59, pt. 4: 3079, 3202.

[2]Richard Lowitt, *George W. Norris: The Persistence of a Progressive, 1913-1933* (Urbana, IL; Chicago; and London: University of Illinois Press, 1971), 96 (hereafter cited as Lowitt, *George W. Norris*).

[3]*Who Was Who in America*, vol. 1, *1897-1942* (Chicago; Marquis Who's Who, 1962), 798; Frederick C. Mosher, *The GAO: The Quest for Accountability in American Government* (Boulder, CO, Westview Press, 1979), 67-68 (hereafter cited as Mosher, *GAO*); and Obituary, "J. R. McCarl Dead; Ex-U.S. Controller," *New York Times*, August 3, 1940.

McCarl reportedly advised President Harding on possible candidates for the new position of comptroller general before getting the appointment himself.[4] Richard Lowitt suggests that Senator Fess was responsible for McCarl's selection.[5]   There was some speculation that Walter W. Warwick, the incumbent comptroller of the treasury (1915-1921), would get the position; earlier, during consideration of the Budget and Accounting Act, 1921, he had recommended creation of an official independent of the Treasury Department. But he was not a Republican.[6] As a Washington newspaper observed just before McCarl's appointment, "This is the best patronage job that has ever been at the disposal of any President—with the single exception of appointments to the Supreme Court of the United States." The paper added, in reference to Warwick, "it is not likely that the present administration would be willing to stand before the people of the country as admitting that to get an efficient controller general they had to take a democrat."[7]

McCarl's appointment was largely political. Although he was a lawyer, his background and professional career included no special preparation for the position of comptroller general. He lacked experience in accounting and government financial management. But once installed in office, he took firm control of GAO and, over the next 15 years, led its development as an organization that functioned with official impartiality, independent of control by either the executive or the legislative branches of the government. Because of both the stands he took in decisions and opinions and the independent powers he asserted for himself and GAO, McCarl became very controversial. He created GAO's image and style during its early years, and he fought stubbornly to establish and maintain the role he envisioned for the agency. His previous affiliation with the Republicans did not prevent him from taking stands disliked by his former political colleagues, both in Congress and the executive branch.[8]

Personal Style and Approach to Management

There is little information available about McCarl's personal life and habits. During his 15 years as comptroller general, he acquired the reputation of being obstinately independent and harsh in some of his decisions. His frequent refusal

---

[4]Mosher, *GAO*, 68; Harvey C. Mansfield, *The Comptroller General: A Study in the Law and Practice of Financial Administration* (New Haven: Yale University Press, 1939), 71 (hereafter cited as Mansfield, *Comptroller General*).

[5]Lowitt, *George W. Norris*, 139.

[6]Mansfield, *Comptroller General*, 70.

[7]*Washington Sunday Star*, June 26, 1921, quoted in "J. R. McCarl—Some Glimpses of the First Comptroller General," *GAO Review* (summer 1971): 46-47.

[8]See Mosher, *GAO*, 66-68, for comments on McCarl's role and influence.

to go along with spending proposals of executive agencies and the White House made him unpopular and soundly disliked in some circles.[9] As the columnist Drew Pearson observed about McCarl in 1933, "beneath his friendly, pleasant-faced exterior is a tendency to be as hard-headed as a Missouri mule. According to Justice McCoy of the District of Columbia Supreme Court, only ice water runs in his veins—which a lot of people are inclined to believe, especially after looking over the long list of his economy decisions." A writer in a national magazine described McCarl as "short, stocky, fond of Windsor ties and golf."[10]

The scholar Harvey Mansfield, who in 1939 published a book very critical of GAO, made these observations:

> Comptroller General McCarl was a man of crusading zeal who
> espoused the simple faith of pre-war midwestern progressivism
> —a creed that found equally abhorrent the privileged corruption
> of the Harding administration and the social welfare programs of
> the Roosevelt administration. He brought to his office abundant
> energy but little training in administration, law, or accounting that
> would equip him for his tasks.[11]

The Pension Building, GAO headquarters from 1926-1951, during the late 1920s.

---

[9]See chapters 7, 8, and 9, especially chapter 9.

[10]Drew Pearson, "Watchdog of the Budget," *Scribner's Magazine*, February 1933, quoted in *GAO Review* (summer 1971): 47; and excerpt from *Review of Reviews* (May 1935), quoted in ibid., 48. See also Mosher's characterization of McCarl in *GAO*, 68.

[11]Mansfield, *Comptroller General*, 71.

McCarl presided over GAO with little personal contact with the staff other than his closest assistants, office heads, and division chiefs. One reason for McCarl's limited contact was that the staff, which grew from about 1,700 in 1921 to 4,400 in 1936, was scattered about Washington in many different buildings, even after 1926 when GAO's headquarters moved from the Treasury Building to the Pension Building.[12]

McCarl demanded integrity, accuracy, and efficiency from his staff, as illustrated by some of the personnel rules he issued. One of the earliest general regulations, issued during McCarl's first year in office, warned GAO staff against gambling:

> It is rumored that certain employees of the General Accounting Office occasionally engage in gambling during office hours. While no convincing proof has been furnished, the nature of the charge is so serious that it is deemed necessary to inform all concerned that gambling, or aiding gambling, in any form by an employee of the General Accounting Office at any time on premises under the control of the General Accounting Office will not be tolerated and any person so offending will be promptly dismissed.

This regulation did not solve the problem to McCarl's complete satisfaction, because he issued a similar one in 1926.[13]

Work hours and other aspects of staff members' days were strictly regulated, including the ringing of bells to mark starting and quitting times and the lunch period.[14] A 1925 bulletin gives some sense of McCarl's determination to regiment his staff: the workday extended from 9:00 a.m. to 4:30 p.m., with time out for luncheon from 12:30 p.m. to 1:00 p.m. The bulletin went on: "Clerks and employees will not be permitted to visit each other or to receive visits during office hours, except on official business, and then only with the knowledge and concurrence of their immediate official superiors. Frequenting or loitering in the corridors of the buildings will not be permitted." The comptroller general, the bulletin added, would take "suitable action" if the watchman informed him of employees leaving their buildings before 12:30 p.m. or 4:30 p.m.[15]

---

[12]See chapter 7 for information on GAO's housing problems.

[13]General Regulations No. 2, May 6, 1922, and General Regulations No. 49, January 23, 1926, GAO Records.

[14]Mosher, *GAO*, 71.

[15]Bulletin No. 6, February 4, 1925, GAO Records.

After several years in office, McCarl thought more of his staff and relaxed some of the rules of behavior and work. In his 1927 annual report, he wrote that "enthusiasm has been the keynote of service in the General Accounting Office. The personnel of the office has during the year been alert, capable, and industrious." McCarl added that he believed that the improvement in morale was due "to a lessening of control by restrictive regulations, and a broadening of individual trust and responsibility."[16] In his annual report two years later, McCarl waxed eloquent about his staff:

> Generally it may be said that the spirit of the personnel of the General Accounting Office is that of friendly cooperation, initiative, alertness for the betterment of accounting or other conditions, in whatever byways or channels activities lead; devising, suggesting, and applying, whenever and wheresoever practicable, improved methods, systems, procedures, and practices for the accomplishment of the maximum of results with the minimum of expenditure, and the perfecting and standardizing of the governmental accounting system as a whole. Out of the accounting "melting pot," as it were, there has developed a unique and many-sided personnel, of necessity equipped and in instant readiness to approach and to cope, with equal thoroughness and equanimity, with any Governmental accounting problem arising, great or trivial, involving millions or pennies.[17]

McCarl spent long hours at the office and kept himself informed about all aspects of GAO's work. His long term and the frequent controversies aroused by GAO reports and decisions made him well-known, if not always respected, in Washington. He had a reputation before becoming comptroller of being devoted to efficiency, and this compulsion affected his management of GAO. He worked extensively on GAO's internal organization for the first five years of his term, to ensure that GAO provided efficient, effective, and economical services.

Organization under McCarl

When GAO came into existence on July 1, 1921, it inherited the organizational structure and the staff of its predecessor agency, the Office of the Comptroller of the Treasury, and the six former Treasury auditing offices. McCarl took over the

---

[16]*Annual Report of the Comptroller General of the United States for the Fiscal Year Ended June 30, 1927* (Washington: GPO, 1927), 71.

[17]*Annual Report of the Comptroller General of the United States for the Fiscal Year Ended June 30, 1929* (Washington: GPO, 1929), 104.

office space of the comptroller of the treasury in the Treasury Building, and the staff, initially numbering 1,708 persons, occupied offices in the Treasury Building and several other structures in Washington.[18] McCarl reported to Congress on GAO's start-up: "We commenced functioning at 9 o'clock sharp [on July 1, 1921], and we have not failed in a single month to make a gain [progress] in each section and division of the establishment."[19]

On GAO's first working day, McCarl issued a bulletin establishing six audit divisions, mirroring offices that had existed in the comptroller of the treasury's office: the Treasury Department, the War Department, the Interior Department, the Navy Department, the State and Other Departments, and the Post Office Department Divisions. The bulletin also contained several other provisions: all correspondence to members or committees of Congress was to be prepared for signature of the comptroller general; all questions in divisions involving an original construction of laws and all requests for reconsideration of GAO settlements of financial officers' accounts were to be referred directly to the comptroller general; and all requests for sick leave or leaves of absence were to be submitted to the office of the comptroller general after consideration by the appropriate division director.[20]

This important bulletin established the initial GAO structure, organized according to specific departments in the executive branch. The provision on congressional correspondence reflected recognition of the importance of maintaining high level control of this critical function. McCarl also quickly established his own final responsibility for statements involving interpretations of law and decisions on settlement reconsiderations. He made clear in the section on leaves of absence and sick leave that he would run a tight ship on personnel matters. The bulletin clearly established the principle of centralized control in the organization.

In another early organizational decision, McCarl established a legal office on July 26, 1921, and appointed Rudolph L. Golze as chief attorney. Golze was a graduate of the University of Pennsylvania Law School. He served before 1921 with the Office of the Comptroller of the Treasury and moved to GAO when it began operations.[21] In 1922, the legal office became the Division of Law and Golze became the solicitor. The creation of this office, staffed by attorneys, reflected the heavy legal content of GAO's work. The Division of Law prepared

---

[18]See chapter 7 for a history of GAO's housing problems.

[19]McCarl testimony, December 19, 1921, *Independent Offices Appropriation Bill, 1923*, Hearings before a Subcommittee of the House Committee on Appropriations, 67th Cong., 2d Sess. (Washington: GPO, 1922), 262.

[20]Bulletin No. 1, July 1, 1921, GAO Records.

[21]"GAO's General Counsels," *GAO Review* (summer 1971): 123.

advance decisions, reviews, and memorandum decisions. Heads of executive agencies were permitted to request advance decisions (on proposed expenditures, for example) and apply for reviews of previous decisions or appeal previous decisions. In 1928, McCarl renamed the Division of Law the Office of the General Counsel and gave Golze the title of general counsel.[22]

In 1922, McCarl expanded GAO's organization by setting up the Bookkeeping Section, the Transportation Division, and an investigations group. The Bookkeeping Section checked and countersigned warrants and examined disbursing officers' accounts. McCarl reported that the section countersigned 134,691 warrants, amounting to $36,275,836,750.37, during fiscal year 1923.[23] The Transportation Division, established by regulation on June 26, 1922, replaced the earlier Transportation Rate Board, which had existed in the Treasury Department. The division's duties were to examine and certify for payment all transportation claims (bills from carriers) received for settlement and to audit transportation payments made by disbursing officers. The division had three sections—Passenger, Freight, and Records.[24]

On October 30, 1922, McCarl established the Investigations Section to make investigations, inspections, reports, and recommendations on matters relating to the receipt, the disbursement, and the application of public funds. Its duties included developing the forms, the systems, and the procedures for executive branch appropriation and fund accounting; examining accounts of fiscal officers and claims against the government; assessing the effectiveness of executive agency examination of accounts and claims and inspecting fiscal officers' accounts; and inspecting and examining documents and matters related to disbursing officers' offices and accounts. The section also was to investigate, and report as requested by the House and Senate and its committees, on matters relating to revenue, appropriations, or expenditures.[25]

Renamed the Office of Investigations in the late 1920s, the unit became the major organization responsible for preparing reports sent to Congress and the executive branch. While the other divisions carried on routine functions from their offices in Washington, the Office of Investigations operated extensively in

---

[22]"GAO's General Counsels," 123; and *Annual Report of the General Accounting Office, 1922*, H. Doc. 482, 67th Cong., 4th Sess., 1922, 2.

[23]*Annual Report of the General Accounting Office, 1923*, H. Doc. 101, 68th Cong., 1st Sess., 1923, 36; and Mosher, *GAO*, 69.

[24]General Regulations No. 8, June 26, 1922, 10 MS 1978 (see Appendix I for information about the manuscript volumes of the Office of the General Counsel and its predecessors); GAO, *Annual Report, 1922*, 12; *Annual Report of the General Accounting Office, 1924*, H. Doc. 484, 68th Cong., 2d Sess., 1924, 19; and David Lodwick and Donald H. Friedman, "The Transportation Division—A Forward Look Over the Past 50 Years," *GAO Review* (summer 1971): 144.

[25]General Regulations No. 11, October 30, 1922, 14 MS 2114; and GAO, *Annual Report, 1923*, 26-27.

the field, looking into alleged fraud, corruption, and misuse of public funds. The chief of investigations became one of GAO's top officials and remained influential until 1956, when the office was abolished.[26]

In April 1923, McCarl simplified GAO's organization by creating the Civil and Military Divisions. The Civil Division took over the duties of the former Treasury Department, Interior Department, and State and Other Departments Divisions, and the Military Division succeeded the War and Navy Department Divisions. At the same time, McCarl established the Check Accounting Division, responsible for proving, reconciling, and adjusting the deposit balances of government fiscal agents and for receiving canceled checks of the government.[27] In December 1923, McCarl set up the Claims Division. Previously each of the separate divisions handled claims work for its areas of jurisdiction. The new Claims Division took over the work of the claims sections of the Military and Civil Divisions.[28] The Transportation and Post Office Department Divisions continued to handle their own claims cases.

Employees of GAO's Check Accounting Division, 1924.

McCarl's creation of the Military and Civil Divisions began a shift to a functional rather than a department-oriented organization. He carried this approach further in September 1926 by consolidating the Military and Civil Divisions into an Audit Division. "The duties of the Audit Division . . . ," McCarl stated in 1927, "are to audit and settle the disbursing accounts of every branch of the Government, except the Post Office Department."[29] Other 1926 changes included elimi-

---

[26]See chapter 17, pp. 419-20.

[27]GAO, *Annual Report, 1923*, 2, 9, 20, 24; Mosher, *GAO*, 69; General Regulations No. 22, March 28, 1923, 19 MS 1486 (establishment of the Civil Division); General Regulations No. 26, May 12, 1923, General Regulations 1-51, vol. I, Set 1, GAO Records (establishment of the Military Division); and General Regulations No. 23, March 28, 1923, 19 MS 1487 (establishment of the Check Accounting Division).

[28]General Regulations No. 33, November 26, 1923, 27 MS 1205; GAO, *Annual Report, 1924*, 4-5; and Eric P. Berezin, "A History of the Claims Division," *GAO Review* (summer 1980): 25-26.

[29]Memorandum, McCarl to chiefs, assistant chiefs, chiefs of sections, Civil and Military Divisions, May 26, 1926, 57 MS 1054a; and GAO, *Annual Report, 1927*, 51.

nation of the Check Accounting Division, to be replaced by a check section in the Audit Division, resulting in a reduction of 16 staff and an annual savings of about $32,000.[30] The Records Division, established to unify recordkeeping in one organization, began operations in 1926. Previously individual divisions and sections filed various records—accounts, claims, contracts, checks, and other materials.[31]

By 1927 McCarl had completed his efforts to reorganize GAO along functional lines. The changes reflected policy decisions he made about how the Office could work most effectively. The emphasis was on tight control of disbursements and meticulous recordkeeping. There was little thought about what GAO might do to improve agency management and programs. The 1927 organization chart showed five operating divisions—Audit, Bookkeeping, Claims, Post Office Department, and Records—under the comptroller general. His immediate office included the assistant comptroller general, assistants to the comptroller general, the chief clerk, the disbursing clerk, the Division of Personnel, the Division of Law, and the Investigations Division.[32] This organization persisted through the remainder of McCarl's term except for one final change in August 1935—the replacement of the Bookkeeping Division and several smaller units with the Accounting and Bookkeeping Division. The new division assumed the functions and the staff of the old Bookkeeping Division as well as responsibility for the settlement of accounts of accountable officers and the adjustment of appropriations and funds.[33]

GAO Relationships with Congress During McCarl's Term

From the beginning, GAO's leadership cultivated special relationships with the legislative branch, although the Budget and Accounting Act, 1921, did not state that GAO was a congressional agency. Section 312 of the law required the comptroller general to report annually to Congress and "to the President when requested by him" on GAO work. McCarl considered GAO a practically autonomous office, and GAO contacts with Congress during his term were somewhat subtle. McCarl held Congress responsible for the financial well-being of the nation, and he envisioned GAO as Congress's agent in carrying out that responsibility. The law did not absolutely prohibit cooperative working relationships with executive branch agencies, but it did state that GAO was independent of the executive agencies. If McCarl's views and predilections had been different, he could have tried to develop GAO as an organization dedicated to assisting the executive branch or, more narrowly, the office of the president. But he chose

---

[30]GAO, *Annual Report, 1927*, 56.

[31]Ibid., 63.

[32]See Appendix IX for the 1927 organization chart.

[33]General Regulations No. 82, August 20, 1935 (effective September 1, 1935), 168 MS 1625.

independence instead. Given the intention of Congress when it passed the Budget and Accounting Act and its continuing attitudes on the question, an effort by McCarl or anyone else in the office of comptroller general to ally in any significant way with the executive branch or the president almost certainly would have been resisted by the legislative branch.

Very early in his term, McCarl spelled out his conception of GAO's status. The Budget and Accounting Act, he said, "makes the General Accounting Office an independent establishment, entirely disconnected from all executive departments, and, as I conceive it, accountable to the Congress for what it does."[34] In 1934, when McCarl received for verification a list of executive agencies, including GAO, from the National Emergency Council, he returned a revised list excluding GAO. He explained that Congress in 1921 created "an agency independent of the Executive Branch and responsible directly to the Congress. . . . Running through the act are provisions directing the office to act as the agent of the Congress for investigating the transactions of the executive departments and establishments, and a reading of the whole act shows that the Congress was convinced there should be for the purposes enumerated . . . an agency removed from control by the Executive Branch and accountable only to the Legislative."[35]

As McCarl encountered difficulties in dealing with executive agencies, he emphasized more and more GAO's ties with Congress and referred to the terms of the Budget and Accounting Act as justification for his position. He did not hesitate to make pointed suggestions to Congress about its own role; he did not assume that GAO's status as a congressional agency precluded such suggestions. As GAO's efforts to impose its decisions and interpretations of law encountered opposition from executive agencies, McCarl repeatedly suggested to Congress that it assert control over the nation's spending. Especially in his annual reports to Congress during the 1920s, McCarl discussed his views on congressional responsibility for the nation's financial resources, the roots of trouble with executive agencies, and the way in which Congress could deal with serious problems in the financial system.

In both 1924 and 1925, McCarl raised concerns about the flouting of GAO's authority, sometimes by court decisions, but especially by executive agencies, which used a far-flung and loosely controlled system of disbursing agents to pay government bills. In his 1925 report, he implicated Congress in the problem, complaining

---

[34]McCarl testimony, December 19, 1921, *Independent Offices Appropriation Bill, 1923*, 237.

[35]Letter, McCarl to the Executive Council [of the National Emergency Council], January 17, 1934, 149 MS 1104.

about "exceptions placed in the statutes permitting fiscal matters to go without check by the General Accounting Office."[36]

In 1926, McCarl began his annual report with a long dissertation entitled "Congressional Control Over Public Money." He noted "a persistent tendency in spending agencies to avoid the control of Government exercised by the Congress through its enactments" and to secure special exceptions from the law. He quoted from Article I, Section 9, of the Constitution: "No money shall be drawn from the Treasury but in consequence of appropriations made by law." What was needed was an agency (GAO) "free from executive or judicial control and responsible only to the Congress." McCarl declared, "A weak accounting system will necessarily mean a weak and ineffectual control in the Congress." Then McCarl brought up what he thought was a most serious problem, the system of disbursing officers. As he put it,

> The most serious difficulties arise when spending agencies elect to act in obligating an appropriation without submitting the doubt as to the availability of the funds proposed to be used for advance decision by the head of the accounting system [the comptroller general]. Such uncooperative procedure often results in unlawful payments by disbursing officers, who under existing system are connected with the interested spending agency.

McCarl explained that as federal spending increased, the responsibility for making disbursements devolved from direct payment by the Treasury, by warrant, to disbursing officers employed by spending agencies, with the permission of Congress "for what reason it is difficult to perceive." He added, "Such an arrangement tends to weaken control by law and to encourage disregard of limitations and directions given therein, and . . . makes most difficult the full accomplishment of the duties imposed by law upon the accounting officers [GAO]." He recommended detaching disbursing officers from the spending agencies and cutting down the number, at the time about 1,000 in the continental United States.

McCarl pointed out that Congress had constitutional responsibility to appropriate and account for public funds and that GAO was its organ for the accounting. In some cases, Congress passed exceptions allowing executive departments to settle claims conclusively under their cognizance, leaving GAO to audit such settlements after payment to determine their mathematical correctness. And Congress occasionally appropriated money not subject to the usual spending and

---

[36]GAO, *Annual Report, 1924*, 1-3; and *Annual Report of the General Accounting Office for the Fiscal Year 1925* (Washington: GPO, 1925), 1.

accounting laws. McCarl referred specifically to legislation creating government corporations. He also noted an instance where District of Columbia courts had authorized the Navy to make payments to a naval officer even though GAO had determined that the officer owed money to the government. The Department of Justice initially refused GAO's request that it apply to the Supreme Court of the United States for a writ of certiorari to review the lower courts' action, and the solicitor general made clear that he thought that the lower courts were correct. Justice did file with the Supreme Court a petition prepared by GAO, but the Court, aware of the solicitor general's opposition, denied it.[37]

McCarl kept up his campaign for reform in his 1927 report. He reiterated his previous comments about money spent without specific congressional authorization. He noted that during 1927, GAO had collected more than $7 million owed the government and that $285 million more was outstanding. This suggested, McCarl wrote, the need for a study of the government disbursing system "with a view to the adoption of a system that will encourage law observance in the use of public funds, reduce to a minimum unauthorized payments, and effect economies . . ." including a reduction in the number of disbursing officers from 1,000 to 50.[38] McCarl also recommended, pending reformation of the disbursing system, that a preaudit procedure, whereby agencies would request advance opinions from the comptroller general on proposed spending, be used.[39]

McCarl discussed his views on the disbursement system and the lack of proper congressional control of public spending almost every year in his annual report and in testimony in Congress on GAO's budget request. In hearings before the House Committee on Appropriations on December 20, 1926, McCarl explained that originally in the United States, the Treasury made payment only on the basis of a warrant drawn by the secretary of the treasury and countersigned by the accounting officer (originally the comptroller of the treasury). This method made possible a preaudit of the proposed payment, ascertaining that it was for a proper claim against the government and that an appropriation existed to cover it. The position of disbursing officer developed in response to the increase in government payments and the need to make them promptly.

---

[37]The above paragraphs on McCarl's 1926 comments are from *Annual Report of the Comptroller General of the United States for the Fiscal Year 1926* (Washington: GPO, 1926), 1-9.

[38]GAO, *Annual Report, 1927*, iii-ix. McCarl used different figures for the number of disbursing officers from time to time. For example, testifying before a House committee on January 26, 1926, McCarl said there were about 2,400 disbursing officers in the continental United States and 300 or 400 abroad. See McCarl's testimony in *Independent Offices Appropriation Bill, 1927*, Hearings before the House Committee on Appropriations, 69th Cong., 1st Sess. (Washington: GPO, 1926), 195.

[39]GAO, *Annual Report, 1927*, 42-43.

At first the Treasury Department used clerks under bond to make payment in the field. Then spending agencies asked Congress to approve use of their own staff to make such payments, saying that the salary costs of these disbursing officers would be less than those of Treasury clerks. McCarl argued that Congress had made a great mistake when it agreed to such requests, which came one by one from the agenices. The result was that the power to obligate an appropriation and the power to spend that money resided in the same person or agency. Furthermore, the disbursing officers owed first allegiance to the agencies employing them rather than to Congress or the accounting officers. What was worse, McCarl observed, was that Congress, through private legislation, encouraged disregard of the law by clearing disbursing officers' records of illegal payments.[40]

Testifying again a year later, McCarl laid out a hypothetical case that illustrated the problems he saw in the disbursing officer system. In McCarl's scenario, Congress appropriated $1 million to purchase white horses. The involved agency head had administrative control of the appropriation, picked the disbursing officer, fixed his bond (perhaps at $5,000), and requisitioned the funds credited to his account (perhaps $500,000). But the agency wanted tractors rather than white horses and approved such a purchase. The disbursing officer could object that the money was not appropriated for tractors but that, if ordered by his superior to pay the bill, he had little choice but to do so. Then the disbursing officer would argue for the payment when later GAO questioned it.

In such a situation, McCarl said, "We [GAO] know the law has been violated, but we are almost helpless." McCarl said the remedy was to reduce the number of disbursing officers and to make each an "absolutely disinterested person," not subject to control by an agency administrative officer. He proposed creating a disbursing officer system with the country divided into about 35 districts; one disbursing officer in each district would be responsible for making government payments. The responsibilities for purchase and payment had to be separated. "This is one of the most important problems before us, because Congress has lost . . . constitutional control over public moneys."[41]

In his 1929 annual report, McCarl called for passage of legislation "to facilitate the prompt and accurate rendition and settlement of accounts." The law would require federal personnel who received federal funds to submit reports to their agencies on such funds at the end of a designated accounting period and

---

[40]*Independent Offices Appropriation Bill, 1928,* Hearings before a Subcommittee of the House Committee on Appropriations, 69th Cong., 2d Sess. (Washington: GPO, 1927), 712-15.

[41]*Independent Offices Appropriation Bill, 1929,* Hearings before a Subcommittee of the House Committee on Appropriations, 70th Cong., 1st Sess. (Washington: GPO, 1928), 237-40.

would require the agencies to transmit the reports to GAO immediately. If the reports were delinquent, GAO should have the power to withhold approval of the agency's requisition of funds from the Treasury.[42] Commenting the next year on the "corrective influence of audit," McCarl suggested that "one of the most important results of an audit is the restraining or corrective influence it exerts upon disbursing agencies," causing them to improve their regulations and instructions to conform to the law and accounting methods.[43]

McCarl was pleased when President Franklin D. Roosevelt issued Executive Order No. 6166 on June 10, 1933, consolidating disbursing functions exclusively in a Division of Disbursement in the Treasury Department. The order transferred disbursing officers attached to various agencies to the Division of Disbursements and had the effect of extensively cutting the number of such officers. The division received authority to establish local offices or delegate its functions to local officers. The order stated: "The Division of Disbursement shall disburse moneys only upon the certification of persons by law duly authorized to incur obligations upon behalf of the United States. The function of accountability for improper certification shall be transferred to such persons, and no disbursing officer shall be held accountable therefor."[44]

Through annual reports and yearly appearances before congressional committees dealing with GAO's budget requests, McCarl presented detailed information about GAO's work and his views on accounting and auditing systems under GAO review. Soon after it opened in 1921, GAO began to send written reports on specific matters to Congress, in the beginning usually in letter form. These reports represented GAO's most important form of contact with Congress. GAO did not begin to tabulate the number of such reports in its annual report until fiscal year 1926. In that year, GAO sent 225 reports to Congress—162 required by law or requested and 63 in the form of suggestions on improving accounting or clarifying language in legislation under consideration and on other matters. In later years the number fluctuated—288 in fiscal year 1930, 320 in 1932, and 100 in 1934. During fiscal year 1936, McCarl's last year in office, GAO sent 203 reports to Congress.[45]

---

[42]GAO, *Annual Report, 1929*, 2-3.

[43]*Annual Report of the Comptroller General of the United States for the Fiscal Year Ended June 30, 1930* (Washington: GPO, 1930), 86.

[44]*Annual Report of the Comptroller General of the United States for the Fiscal Year Ended June 30, 1933* (Washington: GPO, 1933), 16-17. See also *Investigation of Executive Agencies of the Government*, Preliminary Report of the Senate Select Committee to Investigate the Executive Agencies of the Government . . ., 75th Cong., 1st Sess., S. Rept. 1275 (Washington: GPO, 1937), 87. The Brookings Institution prepared this report for the select committee.

[45]See Appendix VII.

Another form of assistance to Congress was the occasional detailing of a GAO staff member to aid a congressional committee, although in the McCarl years, this was not a widely used practice. One early example was the detailing of a staff member from the Post Office Department Division to attend meetings of a committee concerned with the Post Office. When agreeing to this, McCarl instructed the chief of the Post Office Department Division that the staffer should not spend more than one afternoon a week in this duty, his participation had to be general and not interfere with his GAO division work, and he should not act in the committee on behalf of GAO.[46] By 1940 the practice of detailing staff members had grown. During that year, at the request of Congress, GAO sent seven investigators to the Subcommittee on the Works Progress Administration of the House Committee on Appropriations, three investigators to the House Special Committee to Investigate the National Labor Relations Board, and one staff member to a subcommittee of the Senate Committee on Public Lands and Surveys.[47]

By the time McCarl retired in 1936, direct GAO contacts with Congress were generally more extensive than they were in the early years and continued to increase slowly in the next few years. But McCarl's determination to maintain GAO's independence and integrity extended to Congress as well as the executive branch. Not until after 1940, under significantly different leadership, did GAO begin more overt efforts to improve and expand its relationships with Congress.

McCarl's Retirement

McCarl retired at the end of his 15-year term on June 30, 1936. In a farewell letter to GAO officials and staff, McCarl expressed his confidence in their "ability, capacity, and purpose not only to fully maintain the high level of efficiency and effectiveness you have attained by your united and tireless efforts but to move constantly forward." He also commented on the absolute need for "an effective system for accounting control over the uses of public money," which he deemed "essential to the success of our form of government." He showed his concern about the policies of the Roosevelt administration by referring to current pressures on Congress "for broader administrative discretion and wider latitude in the spending of the public moneys." When Congress should decide "to resist such importunings and to reserve control and direction of the uses of the public moneys, it must look to and depend upon the independent accounting system as its only means of exacting obedience to its laws." He exhorted the GAO staff to "be ready for that day. Don't fail the Congress." He added, "You must expect peri-

---

[46]Memorandum, McCarl to chief, Post Office Department Division, May 8, 1922, 9 MS 592.

[47]*Annual Report of the Comptroller General of the United States for the Fiscal Year Ended June 30, 1940* (Washington: GPO, 1941), 60-61.

ods of discouragement as the forces you must constantly combat are powerful and resourceful, and it may appear at times that even the Congress has deserted you, but don't give up—don't even be downhearted—just keep fighting on for law observance and honesty in government. Fortunately, such dismal periods usually induce beneficial reactions so always remember that a resolute and purposeful Congress will seriously need an efficiently functioning accounting system."[48]

During the New Deal period that began in 1933, McCarl avoided direct involvement in partisan politics. But his rulings against various Roosevelt administration spending proposals and his frequently expressed concern that Congress was not vigilant enough about regulating public spending made clear his hostility to New Deal programs. Even before he retired, there was some press speculation that he might be a candidate for the Republican presidential nomination in 1936. An article in *Review of Reviews* in May 1935 reported that McCarl's insistence on a strict interpretation of the law in regard to government spending had brought him into frequent conflict with the Roosevelt administration. The article noted that McCarl had "won a high reputation for ability, integrity, and watchfulness, a record which would be an asset in a campaign where federal extravagance is a prominent issue. Probably no man in Washington is more familiar with the intimate details of the government machinery and the way money is spent."[49]

As soon as he retired, free from the nonpartisan restraints of his office, McCarl spoke out publicly in opposition to the New Deal, saying that he "might take some part in politics." Soon thereafter he visited with Governor Alfred Landon of Kansas, the 1936 Republican nominee for the presidency.[50] In October 1936 McCarl published two articles in the *Saturday Evening Post*, making very critical comments about the Roosevelt administration and the weakness of Congress in agreeing to expensive New Deal programs. What was necessary in 1933, McCarl contended, was "a program of economy and retrenchment," but it did not happen because "Washington fell under the control of a group to be known as, self-styled, the New Dealers. It is this group that is responsible for our present predicament."

McCarl described Congress's "surrender of constitutional responsibilities to the Executive Branch" as "a harrowing experience, one that seemed such a blow at the very foundation of representative government as seriously to endanger our system, as tending dangerously toward dictatorship. . . ." The congressional surrender was so extensive "that there was nothing the accounting officers could do

---

[48]McCarl to officials and staff of the General Accounting Office, June 30, 1936, reprinted in *GAO Review* (fall 1971): 78-79.

[49]Excerpt from *Review of Reviews*, May 1935, reprinted in *GAO Review* (summer 1971): 48. For details on actual GAO operations during the McCarl period, see chapters 8 and 9.

[50]Mansfield, *Comptroller General*, 1.

to avoid the waste and extravagance that was sure to result." McCarl indicted both the executive branch for wasting money on expensive programs and Congress for taking "its responsibilities so lightly as to permit such a thing to happen."[51] Harvey Mansfield, a severe critic of McCarl and a man who was intimately involved in efforts to radically change GAO's role in the 1930s, said McCarl's articles were "intended to be campaign documents" but concluded that they had had little influence.[52]

McCarl's retirement brought forth some evaluations of his service as comptroller general in the public press. The *Saturday Evening Post* praised him for being a "no-man" on excessive public spending. "Many a time powerful political influences were brought to bear upon him to reverse or modify his decisions," the *Post* observed, "but those who went up against him found his rulings as unchangeable as the law of the Medes and Persians."[53] The *St. Louis Post-Dispatch* praised McCarl on his retirement: "Among the welter of Washington's yes-men, he was a forthright, solitary and heartening no-man." The *Baltimore Sun* said that McCarl had "done a great deal to establish Federal accounting on a sound basis" but stated that he had "erred too often on the side of literalism" in his decisions.[54]

Although McCarl expressed interest in becoming involved in Republican politics when he retired, he had no real political base and, other than some writing, did little else in the political arena. After he left GAO, he practiced law in Washington. He suffered a stroke and died in his office on August 2, 1940. In his obituary the *New York Times* reported that in 1939 he had "criticized Congress for abandoning its prerogative to the President, and said the United States was in a worse condition than since the 1929 collapse." McCarl was survived by his wife and two sisters.[55]

The Assistant Comptrollers General during the McCarl Period

The Budget and Accounting Act, 1921, provided for one assistant comptroller general, to be appointed by the president at a salary of $7,500 per year, for a term of 15 years, removable in the same way for the same causes as the comptroller

---

[51]Excerpts from McCarl articles in *Saturday Evening Post*, October 3 and October 17, 1936, reprinted in *GAO Review* (summer 1971): 50-53.

[52]Mansfield, *Comptroller General*, 1. See chapter 10, pp. 236-37, for information on Mansfield's work in the 1930s.

[53]Excerpts from *Saturday Evening Post,* August 8, 1936, reprinted in *GAO Review* (summer 1971): 49-50.

[54]Quoted in *GAO Review* (summer 1971): 49.

[55]"J. R. McCarl Dead; Ex-U.S. Controller," *New York Times* (August 3, 1940).

general. The assistant comptroller general had to retire at age 70. He was to "perform such duties as may be assigned to him by the Comptroller General."[56]

Between 1921 and 1943, two men served in the position of assistant comptroller general, both of them beginning their terms while McCarl was in office. On June 30, 1921, President Harding nominated Lurtin R. Ginn of Indiana to be the first assistant comptroller general, and the Senate confirmed the nomination the same day. Ginn was sworn into office on July 1, 1921, the day GAO began to operate. Previously a career employee in the Treasury Department, he became assistant comptroller of the treasury in 1917. In this position, he supervised the audit of U.S. military spending in Europe during World War I from a branch office of the comptroller of the treasury in Paris.

During the decade he served as assistant comptroller general, Ginn backed up McCarl in various ways. McCarl asked for his advice on some matters, and he acted as comptroller general during McCarl's rare absences. He also served as

Lurtin R. Ginn, Assistant Comptroller General, 1921-1930.

GAO's budget officer. In this capacity, he was responsible for preparing budget estimates, reporting on expenditures, and testifying on budget matters. He wrote regularly to the director of the Bureau of the Budget (BOB), reporting on monthly GAO expenditures and other budget matters.[57] Ginn retired at the statutory retirement age of 70 in 1931.

To replace Ginn, President Herbert C. Hoover nominated Richard Nash Elliott of Indiana. Elliott was born near Connersville, Indiana, on April 25, 1873. He attended public schools and taught school for three years. He then began to study law and gained admittance to the Indiana bar in 1896, when he began to practice law in Connersville. He served as a county attorney, 1897-1906, and as a member of the Indiana House of Representatives and city attorney of Connersville from 1905 to 1909. In 1917, Elliott, a Republican, was elected to fill a congressional vacancy; he was reelected six successive times. He served in the House of Repre-

---

[56]Public Law 67-13, 42 Stat. 20, Title III, Section 302.

[57]For example, see letter, Ginn to Charles G. Dawes, director of BOB, October 15, 1921, 2 MS 713; letter, Ginn to director of BOB, April 8, 1922, 8 MS 528; and letter, Ginn to director of BOB, January 22, 1923, 17 MS 910.

sentatives from June 26, 1917, to March 3, 1931. Elliott was an unsuccessful candidate for reelection in 1930. He entered office as assistant comptroller general on March 6, 1931.[58]

Elliott did not play as important a role as assistant comptroller general under McCarl as had Ginn. James L. Baity, GAO executive officer in the 1930s, handled the budget matters that Ginn had dealt with earlier. Elliott, usually addressed as "Judge Elliott" for reasons that are not clear, commented on his role after six years on the job: "My period of service as Assistant Comptroller General began on March 6, 1931, and I have closely, perhaps for a time somewhat silently, observed things here. In all matters, particularly those having a vast mag-

Richard N. Elliott, Assistant Comptroller General, 1931-1943, and Acting Comptroller General, 1936-1939, 1940.

nitude, perfection is not possible, but I can say major errors here have been rare and such as there may have been probably mainly involve resolving the doubt in the interest of the United States through safeguarding the uses of public moneys."[59] At a hearing in 1937, Elliott noted that when he served under McCarl, "I had nothing to do with the question of making policies, or anything of that kind."[60]

Elliott's most important service to GAO came during two periods when he was acting comptroller general. After McCarl retired on June 30, 1936, almost three years elapsed before President Franklin D. Roosevelt nominated a new comptroller general. Elliott served as acting comptroller general from July 1, 1936, until April 11, 1939, when Fred Herbert Brown became comptroller general.[61] After Brown left office because of ill health in June 1940, Elliott stepped in again as acting comptroller general and held the office until Lindsay C. Warren became the comptroller general on November 1, 1940.

---

[58]*Biographical Directory of the United States Congress, 1774-1989, Bicentennial Edition*, 100th Cong., 2d Sess., S. Doc. 100-34 (Washington: GPO, 1989), 960 (hereafter cited as *Biographical Directory*).

[59]*Annual Report of the Acting Comptroller General of the United States for the Fiscal Year Ended June 30, 1937* (Washington: GPO, 1937), iii.

[60]Elliott testimony on August 11, 1937, *Reorganization of the Government Agencies*, Hearings before the Senate Select Committee on Government Organization . . . , 75th Cong., 1st sess. (Washington: GPO, 1937), 286.

[61]See pp. 68-70.

Elliott retired at age 70 on May 1, 1943. During his last years in office, he served as assistant comptroller general under Warren.[62] During his periods as acting comptroller general, Elliott carried on GAO's routine work quietly, particularly between 1936 and 1939 in the aftermath of a controversial comptroller general and during the time when there were serious efforts, fostered by both the executive branch and elements in Congress, to radically change the organization and the mission of GAO.[63] In GAO's annual report for 1937, Elliott wrote that he thought his duty was "to carry on the business of the office without drastic changes in the procedures that have prevailed for the past 15 years, so as not to in any way affect the freedom of action—either in matters of organization or of procedure—of a Comptroller General when appointed."[64]

As Frederick Mosher has observed, Elliott's tenure as acting comptroller general "must have been a difficult one" for several reasons: he was a Republican, appointed by a Republican president, but served beginning in 1933 with a Democratic-controlled Congress and a Democratic president who hoped to cut GAO's powers. At the same time, GAO was enmeshed in controversies with various executive agencies, such as the Treasury Department and the Tennessee Valley Authority (TVA).[65]

Fred H. Brown, the Second Comptroller General

After McCarl's retirement in 1936, GAO was without a comptroller general for almost three years while President Roosevelt sought a replacement. One factor in the delay was Roosevelt's hope of making radical changes in GAO's organization and mission. This injected an element of uncertainty into GAO's future, which must have caused potential nominees for comptroller general to wonder about the permanence of the position.[66] Roosevelt did offer the position several times to Rep. Lindsay C. Warren of North Carolina, but Warren declined to accept.[67] Finally on March 30, 1939, Roosevelt sent to the Senate the nomination of Fred Brown as comptroller general. On this same date the Reorganization Bill of 1939 passed in Congress, with a clause exempting GAO from the president's reorganization authority. Frederick Mosher suggested that there may have been

---

[62]*Annual Report of the Comptroller General of the United States for the Fiscal Year Ended June 30, 1943* (Washington: GPO, n.d.), iv.

[63]See chapter 10, pp. 235-46.

[64]GAO, *Annual Report, 1937*, iii.

[65]Mosher, *GAO*, 91. See chapter 9, pp. 211-219, for a discussion of the TVA controversy.

[66]See chapter 10, pp. 235-46.

[67]See chapter 10 for information about Roosevelt's reorganization plans and chapter 4, pp. 74-77, for information about his efforts to get Warren to take the appointment.

an agreement between congressional leaders and Roosevelt leading to the ex-
emption and Brown's appointment. On April 3, 1939, Roosevelt signed the Reorganization Act and the Senate confirmed Brown's nomination.[68]

Fred H. Brown, Comptroller General, 1939-1940.

---

[68]Mosher, *GAO*, 91-92.

Brown was born in Ossipee, New Hampshire, on April 12, 1879. He was educated in New Hampshire in the public schools, Dow Academy, and Dartmouth College and received a law degree at Boston University School of Law. In his youth, Brown was an excellent baseball player, on local amateur teams and at Dartmouth College. Later he played minor league ball and a few games as a catcher and a utility infielder for the Boston Braves. After admittance to the bar, he began to practice law in Somersworth, New Hampshire. He then served successively as city solicitor from 1910 to 1914 and mayor of Somersworth from 1914 to 1922; governor of New Hampshire from 1923 to 1924; and member of the New Hampshire Public Service Commission from 1925 to 1933. In 1932, he was elected, as a Democrat, to the U. S. Senate and served from March 4, 1933, to January 3, 1939. In 1938, he lost a reelection campaign for the Senate. Brown's term as comptroller general lasted only from April 11, 1939, until June 19, 1940, when he resigned because of illness.[69]

There is little to record about Brown's term as comptroller general because it was so short. The records show that he carried on the routine business of GAO but had no time to leave any substantial imprint on the organization. His earlier record as a liberal Democrat was extensive, and it suggests that if he had been able to lead GAO for a longer period, he would have left his mark, as did his predecessor and successors, who served long terms. The *New York Times* reported when he died on February 3, 1955, that as governor, he had supported the textile workers of New Hampshire, substantially cut the state debt during his first year in office, and eliminated the debt completely by the end of his term. In the U. S. Senate, he supported Roosevelt's New Deal programs.[70]

Shortly after Brown resigned as comptroller general, President Roosevelt appointed him to be a member of the U. S. Tariff Commission. After serving during 1940-1941, he resigned again because of ill health and returned to Somersworth, New Hampshire, where he lived the rest of his life. The *New York Times* reported that even after retirement, Brown remained a confidante of Roosevelt and his successor, Harry S. Truman, whom Brown had known when he and Truman were colleagues in the Senate.[71]

---

[69]*Biographical Directory*, 681-682; and clipping (obituary), *New York Times*, February 4, 1955, GAO Records.

[70]Clipping (obituary), *New York Times*, February 4, 1955, GAO Records.

[71]Ibid.

Lindsay C. Warren, Comptroller General, 1940-1954.

CHAPTER 4

The Initiator of Change:
Lindsay C. Warren, 1940-1954

Nomination and Background

President Franklin D. Roosevelt nominated Lindsay Carter Warren to be the third comptroller general of the United States on August 1, 1940. On the same day, the Senate unanimously confirmed the nomination.[1] Warren, a prominent Democratic member of the House of Representatives, was born in Washington, Beaufort County, North Carolina, on December 16, 1889. His early education was in local public schools in Washington and at the Bingham School in Asheville, North Carolina. He entered the University of North Carolina as a freshman in 1906 and studied there for two years, but financial problems forced him to withdraw in 1908 and go to work at the First National Bank in Washington, North Carolina. He then returned to the University of North Carolina (1911-1912) to study law. He was admitted to the North Carolina bar in 1912.[2]

Warren's efforts to finance his education at the University of North Carolina led to some interesting fund-raising schemes. A story frequently repeated in the press was that he tried to raise money using a roulette wheel that he had built. Eventually the college dean discovered Warren's efforts. As *Newsweek* recounted the story, "Confiscating the wheel, the dean sternly ordered Warren upon the carpet—then praised him for his display of 'practical mathematics' in concocting a machine on which the customer could not possibly win."[3]

After his admittance to the bar in 1912, Warren began to practice law in Washington, North Carolina, and soon also became the attorney for Beaufort

---

[1]Frederick C. Mosher, *The GAO: The Quest for Accountability in American Government* (Boulder, CO: Westview Press, 1979), 92 (hereafter cited as Mosher, *GAO*).

[2]*Biographical Directory of the United States Congress, 1774-1989, Bicentennial Edition*, 100th Cong., 2d Sess., S. Doc. 100-34 (Washington: GPO, 1989), 2010 (hereafter cited as *Biographical Directory*); Frank H. Weitzel, "Lindsay Carter Warren: Comptroller General of the United States, 1940-1954," *GAO Review* (spring 1977): 1-2; and letter, Warren to Frank O. Ray, March 3, 1949, The Papers of Lindsay C. Warren, Southern Historical Collection, Wilson Library, University of North Carolina at Chapel Hill, Box 12, Folder 431 (hereafter cited as Warren Papers).

[3]Clipping, "From the Capital," *Newsweek*, October 27, 1943, Warren Papers, Scrapbooks, vol. 7.

County, holding that position until 1925. He immediately became active in Democratic politics—chairman of the Beaufort County Democratic executive committee from 1912 to 1925, terms in the North Carolina Senate in 1917 and 1919 (when he was president pro tempore), and in the North Carolina House of Representatives in 1923.[4] In 1924, he was elected to represent the First District of North Carolina in the U.S. House of Representatives. He was reelected between 1926 and 1938 to seven succeeding congresses. Warren was an active and influential congressman, who rose gradually in influence and stature. After Roosevelt's election to the presidency in 1932, he became a staunch but not slavish supporter of the president's New Deal programs.

Warren's assignments in the House included the Committee on Accounts (he was chairman for 10 years), the Committee on Roads, the Committee on Conservation of Wildlife Resources, the Committee on Merchant Marine and Fisheries, the Special Committee to Investigate Campaign Expenditures, and the Committee on Government Organization. He involved himself in various matters before Congress of interest to his home state, such as agriculture, especially matters dealing with cotton, tobacco, peanuts, potatoes, roads, and waterways. He took a special interest in the U.S. Coast Guard, reflecting his origins in the coastal areas of North Carolina and his great love of sport fishing. He secured congressional support for various projects in his district, including the Wright Brothers Memorial at Kill Devil Hills and a beach erosion project from the Virginia-North Carolina line to Ocracoke Inlet. He played an instrumental role in the drafting and the passage of the important Government Reorganization Act of 1939.[5]

Warren's selection as acting majority leader in the House of Representatives in September 1940 testifies to his prominence in that body. When Speaker William B. Bankhead of Alabama died suddenly on September 15, 1940, Democratic Majority Leader Sam Rayburn of Texas moved up to the speaker's position. Warren, already confirmed to become comptroller general, served as acting majority leader for two weeks until the House Democrats elected John W. McCormack of Massachusetts to succeed him.[6]

President Roosevelt began his efforts to persuade Warren to become comptroller general shortly after J. R. McCarl's term expired in the summer of 1936. While Warren was on vacation in North Carolina in August 1936, Sens. Joseph T.

---

[4]*Biographical Directory,* 2010; and Weitzel, "Lindsay Carter Warren," 2.

[5]*Biographical Directory*, 2010; and clipping, *Elizabeth City (NC) Advance*, August 1, 1940, Warren Papers, Scrapbooks, vol. 6.

[6]Weitzel, "Lindsay Carter Warren," 2; and clipping, extension of remarks of Sen. Clyde R. Hoey of North Carolina, in *Congressional Record*, August 29, 1950, A6483-84, clippings file, GAO History Program Archives.

Robinson (D—Arkansas) and James F. Byrnes (D—South Carolina) announced on the White House steps that Warren would be nominated as comptroller general. "It was news to me as the President had never mentioned it to me, nor was I a candidate. A few days later he tendered it to me and I declined."[7]

Warren had actually heard about the possibility of his appointment earlier. He wrote to Roosevelt on August 1, 1936, referring to an article in the *Baltimore Sun* of July 11, 1936, saying that the president would offer him the comptroller general's post. Warren told the president "that if by the remotest chance you have had me under consideration, . . . I do not feel that I could accept such a place if tendered to me. My devotion to my district and my interest in the welfare of North Carolina convinces me that I could be of far greater service both to you and our people by remaining in the Congress." Roosevelt responded that he had been considering Warren, but had decided that it would be best to wait until after the 1936 presidential election before making the nomination. Roosevelt added: "Frankly, I am sorry that you do not want me to consider you, though I can well understand your feeling—for you are still young and with a very bright political future ahead of you. To become Comptroller General would give you a definite tenure for many years but at the same time it is restricting work and after the first year or two would bore me to death."[8]

Again, in 1938, Roosevelt offered Warren appointment as comptroller general, but he declined. He observed in a letter to a North Carolina friend that "this constant talk about me being Comptroller General has been very embarrassing to me and keeps my friends and district stirred up. . . . I am not at all interested and would like to remain in Congress."[9]

When Roosevelt for the third time tendered Warren the appointment as comptroller general during the summer of 1940, Warren was interested and apparently had taken steps to let the president know it. Warren's friend, Rep. John J. Cochran (D—Mississippi), wrote him in late June 1940 that he had talked to Gen. Edwin M. Watson, the president's secretary, about Warren's interest in the position and that Watson had promised to convey the message to the president. Cochran wrote, "I told him I felt you were in a receptive mood but that you would like to discuss the matter with the President in the event he was considering you."[10] In a letter to the president on July 8, 1940, Warren wrote, "I wish to accept this appointment because of your confidence in me and because it offers a genuine

---

[7]Statement initialed "LCW," Warren Papers, Folder 259.

[8]Letter, Warren to Roosevelt, August 1, 1936, ibid., Folder 264; and letter, Roosevelt to Warren, August 5, 1936, ibid., Scrapbooks, vol. 18.

[9]Letter, Warren to Judge John J. Parker, Charlotte, NC, June 15, 1938, Warren Papers, Folder 305-N.

[10]Letter, Cochran to Warren, June 25, 1940, ibid., Folder 359.

opportunity for constructive public service." He asked the president to delay announcement of the appointment until July 31, 1940, saying that publicity before then would prove embarrassing to him. In this same letter, Warren mentioned the serious illness of his son, Lindsay, Jr.[11]

In testimony almost ten years later, Warren claimed that he had been drafted by the president for the office. He mentioned the suggested nominations in 1936 and 1938 and added that Roosevelt offered him the job four times in July 1940. "I accepted the fourth time for very personal reasons after declining the other three."[12] The illness of his son influenced Warren in 1940. As he wrote to a North Carolina acquaintance, "The thing that actuated me more than anything else in leaving Congress was that I was told my boy could not live but a few months. I felt like the world had caved in."[13] To another friend Warren remarked about his son's illness and observed, "I was so distracted at that time that I attribute my acceptance of Comptroller General to his situation."[14] Although Lindsay, Jr., had been diagnosed with a life-threatening illness, he soon recovered, served in the military during World War II, studied law, and was admitted to the bar in 1951.

According to his own testimony, Warren extracted a promise from President Roosevelt at the time he accepted the GAO appointment. He stated in a 1950 hearing that when Roosevelt became president, he "was hostile and bitterly antagonistic to the General Accounting Office" and made various efforts to destroy it. He asserted that after McCarl retired in 1936, GAO "was headless and without leadership, because for 2 years the President had refused to appoint a Comptroller General." Warren ignored during this testimony the fact that Roosevelt had offered him the appointment in 1936 and 1938. Warren added, "It is hard to conceive that I would give up a seat in Congress and accept this position in order to preside over the liquidation of the General Accounting Office. President Roosevelt told me, and he told it to many others, that the very fact that I had

---

[11]Letter, Warren to Watson, July 8, 1940, transmitting Warren letter to Roosevelt, July 8, 1940, ibid., Folder 360.

[12]Warren testimony on February 27, 1950, *To Improve Budgeting, Accounting, and Auditing Methods of the Federal Government,* Hearings before the Senate Committee on Expenditures in the Executive Departments, 81st Cong., 2d sess., on S. 2054 (and amendments) (Washington: GPO, 1950), 49 (hereafter cited as *To Improve Budgeting*).

[13]Letter, Warren to I. H. Morris, Greenville, NC, May 24, 1943, Warren Papers, Folder 391.

[14]Letter, Warren to Judge John McDuffie, Mobile, AL, December 19, 1941, ibid., Folder 386; and letter, Warren to Ashley B. Futrell, Washington, NC, September 21, 1951, ibid., Folder 443.

accepted this appointment was sufficient notice to the Congress and to everyone else that he had dropped his fight."[15]

Warren's appointment generally was favorably received, both in the nation's capital and in his home state. His home town of Washington, North Carolina, honored him a few days before his swearing-in with a parade and speakers, including North Carolina Governor Clyde R. Hoey and U.S. Secretary of Commerce Jesse Jones. Warren's neighbors presented him with a new Buick and Mrs. Warren received a chest of silver.[16] While taking note of Warren's appointment, *Time* magazine described him as follows:

> A bull necked, leathery man's man, he thrives on the frugal, quiet outdoor life of Washington, N.C. ("Little Washington"), where he lives with his wife and three children in a two-story frame house on Main Street. He likes weekend trips to Little Washington; sitting on the rail fence in front of Arthur Mayo's house on Main Street and talking politics with the boys; fishing in old clothes at Kitty Hawk and Hatteras with Postmaster Billy Culpepper and Bruce Etheridge of Manteo and Dudley Bagley of Currituck; winning a little change at poker during the long winter nights (there is an undenied story that he roundly shellacked the President at poker during a weekend trip); motoring around the countryside in his three-year old Buick, talking potato and tobacco crops with his farmer constituents; looking out his windows at flower-festooned boats on the Tar River during the spring tulip festival.[17]

Reporting Warren's swearing-in, the *Washington Post* noted that Warren "has long ranked as one of the President's closest House advisers" and that his becoming comptroller general was welcomed by some federal agency heads who had clashed with Acting Comptroller General Richard N. Elliott and his predecessor, McCarl.[18] Editorial comment around the country generally favored Warren's appointment. For example, the *St. Louis Post-Dispatch*

---

[15]Warren testimony in 1950 quoted in Staff of the Senate Committee on Government Operations, *Financial Management in the Federal Government*, 87th Cong., 1st Sess., S. Doc. 11 (Washington: GPO, 1961), 314-15. See also "Comptroller General Warren Reviews Efforts to Transfer Functions from the General Accounting Office," *GAO Review* (summer 1971): 60-63. For information on efforts during the 1920s and 1930s to abolish or change GAO, see chapter 10, pp. 229-47. For details of Warren's response to the proposals of the first Hoover Commission, which included the above testimony, see chapter 13, pp. 324-27.

[16]Clipping, *The State: A Weekly Survey of North Carolina*, November 2, 1940, Warren Papers, Scrapbooks, vol. 6.

[17]Clipping, *Time*, August 12, 1940, ibid.

[18]Clipping, *Washington Post*, November 2, 1940, ibid.

compared Warren's selection with those of Felix Frankfurter to the Supreme Court and Archibald McLeish as librarian of Congress.[19]

One group that actively opposed Warren's nomination was the National Association for the Advancement of Colored People (NAACP). In fact, the NAACP and other black groups and individuals protested in both 1936 and 1938 when rumors circulated that President Roosevelt intended to appoint Warren as comptroller general. In 1936, Roosevelt received letters of protest from Assistant Secretary Roy Wilkins and Secretary Walter White of the NAACP. Both Wilkins and White referred to Warren's refusal in 1934, as chairman of the House Committee on Accounts, to allow black persons to eat in the House restaurant. White sent the president a copy of a story carried in the October 3, 1936 edition of the *New York Age*, an African-American newspaper, presenting a detailed chronology of the 1934 episode. Wilkins wrote the president that the NAACP "believes that a man who faithfully transplants the customs and prejudices of his local community to the seat of the national government of all the people and enforces those prejudices as the law of the land, does not have the perspective required of a man to fill the office of comptroller general." Roosevelt's secretaries replied politely to both letters, telling Wilkins that his message would be brought to the president's attention and informing White, whose letter arrived later than Wilkins's, that the president had no one in particular under consideration for the post.[20]

White sent similar protests on behalf of the NAACP against Warren's nomination in 1938 and 1940, on both occasions referring to the 1934 controversy over African-Americans being barred from the House restaurant by Warren. In a telegram to Roosevelt in 1940, White claimed that Warren had "an unbroken record of hostility to American Negroes" and urged the president to nominate as comptroller general "a person who is not imbued with anti[-]negro or other prejudices."[21]

The NAACP and other black opposition to Warren did not deter President Roosevelt from going ahead with his nomination. Warren originally planned to be sworn in on October 1, 1940. But shortly before then, he asked the president for a month's delay, pleading the need for more time to wind up his service in the House of Representatives. Roosevelt eventually agreed, although there was some pressure to get Warren sworn in earlier. On

---

[19]Clipping, *St. Louis Post-Dispatch*, August 1, 1940, ibid

[20]Letter, Wilkins to Roosevelt, August 14, 1936; letter, Stephen Early, assistant secretary to the president, to Wilkins, August 27, 1936; letter, White to Roosevelt, October 2, 1936; and letter, Marvin H. McIntyre, assistant secretary to the president, to White, October 30, 1936, all in the Papers of Franklin D. Roosevelt, President's Official File, #500-A, the Roosevelt Library, Hyde Park, New York (hereafter cited as Roosevelt Papers). This file contains numerous other letters and resolutions against Warren's rumored appointment in 1936..

[21]Telegram, White to the president, June 7, 1938, and telegram, White to the president, August 1, 1940, both in ibid.

October 2, 1940, the president received a letter from Secretary of the Interior Harold L. Ickes, expressing apprehension that if Warren did not enter office until November 1, Acting Comptroller General Richard N. Elliott would cause an incident, or a series of incidents, to embarrass the administration. Presumably Ickes's concern related to the fact that Elliott was a former Republican congressman. Roosevelt informed Ickes that he had talked to Warren "and he tells me that he has a definite check on any opinions or actions in the Comptroller General's office. That being so, I think it is safe for him to wait until November 1st. If any problem comes up, let me know."[22]

Personal Aspects of Warren's Term as Comptroller General

Warren served nearly 13-1/2 years of his statutory term of 15 years before retiring in the spring of 1954. His tenure spanned the years of U.S. participation in World War II, the postwar reconversion, the coming of the Cold War, and the Korean conflict. It was also a period, especially after World War II, of strenuous efforts by Warren and others to improve financial management in the federal government. The scope and the pace of GAO's activities increased significantly.

Warren discovered as soon as he took office that he had accepted a tough job. He described his daily routine in a letter to President Roosevelt in 1942:

> I get up every morning at 6-30 A.M. [sic], eat no lunch, never leave the building unless called on official business and get home late. It is a gruelling grind and I have been warned about it, but I find so much here needing my attention that I feel I must keep up the pace for I have no one to share it with. . . .The work of the General Accounting Office has increased over 100% in the last two years, and we think we are playing a vital part in the war effort.[23]

Warren decided not long after he began at GAO that he did not really like the job. The increased activity because of the war effort, health problems, the difficulty of returning to North Carolina as often as he preferred, and nostalgia for the House of Representatives all affected his response to his duties as comptroller general. A year after he took office, he wrote to a friend: "I don't know yet why I am in my present position. I was quite happy in Congress and had been renominated for my ninth term without opposition. The work I am now engaged in

---

[22]Letter, Warren to Roosevelt, September 26, 1940, and memorandum, Roosevelt to Ickes, October 4, 1940, both in ibid. A notation on the latter document refers to Ickes's letter to the president, October 2, 1940.

[23]Letter, Warren to Roosevelt, September 21, 1942, Warren Papers, Folder 389.

is of course foreign to anything I have ever done, and it is most exacting and confining."[24] He fretted when his duties prevented him from returning to North Carolina at Christmas. To one friend he wrote that "I am tied down as though I was in prison. . . . The joy of living is work . . . but I never dreamed that mine would be so confining and exacting." Thanking another friend during the 1942 holiday season for a gift of ducks and a goose, he wrote: "We are spending our second Christmas away from home, and I don't think any of us will ever be happy again until we are back there permanently." He added that he had an "awful and thankless job" but that he was "beginning to like it better."[25]

While Warren often expressed his pride in GAO's accomplishments, he grew cynical about what he learned about the government. In a revealing letter, he vented his feelings to a close friend and former colleague in Congress:

> You say you are sorry you ever served in Congress. Well, I am sorry I was ever Comptroller General. . . . I have now decided that when I was in Congress my knowledge of the Government was almost nil. To see and to know and to evaluate what our Government is, one must be Comptroller General. In this position I see it the few times at its best and most of the time at its worst. I see scheming, plotting and conniving men holding high office who think first forever about themselves and the country last; men who are sitting up late at night trying to circumvent the Congress, and who don't wish their acts audited and checked. I see daily the most unbridled waste and extravagance and a "hell and don't care" attitude on the part of most administrators. I have no power or authority to stop it. I report it to the Congress so much that it is almost a joke, but they don't give a damn and are almost impotent to prevent it anyway. . . . I will admit that what I daily see makes me somewhat cynical, but above all it makes me wish to wash my hands of all of it and fold my tent and leave.[26]

There were personal problems that undoubtedly affected Warren's general attitude toward his work as comptroller general. One was the frequent illnesses he suffered while in office—problems he sometimes blamed on overwork and the pressures of his job. His first bout with high blood pressure occurred early in 1943, and although he recovered after treatment, the problem reoccurred at fre-

---

[24]Letter, Warren to Guy U. Hardy, Canon City, CO, November 28, 1941, ibid., Folder 386.

[25]Letter, Warren to E. G. Flanagan, December 29, 1941, ibid.; and letter, Warren to Joseph P. Knapp, December 23, 1942, ibid., Folder 389.

[26]Letter, Warren to John McDuffie, Mobile, AL, February 21, 1946, ibid., Folder 413.

quent intervals thereafter.[27] In September 1944, he spent a week at the Duke University Hospital. He reported to a friend that the doctors had found nothing organically wrong with him: "They said that my trouble was over-work, worry, lack of proper diet and exercise. I am now trying to remedy all of these things."[28] He spent a few days in Bethesda Naval Hospital in June and July 1946 for an appendectomy.[29]

Warren was back at Bethesda for four weeks early in 1948. On this occasion, the doctors told him that he was overweight and put him on a diet. To his North Carolina friend Dudley Bagley, who served as his executive assistant at GAO between 1940 and 1945, Warren wrote: "I know I will feel much better if I can further reduce my weight. I have got to get off nineteen pounds more between now and July 1st and it is going to be pretty hard to do so." In

GAO employees examining records stored in the Great Hall of the Pension Building. Copyright 1940, The Washington Post. *Reprinted with permission.*

the same letter, he thanked Bagley for sending him a package of sausage, adding "Although I am rationed I am certainly going to enjoy it and appreciate it so much."[30]

Warren's medical problems took him back to Bethesda Naval Hospital for nearly seven weeks in February and March 1951. Again his weight was high and blood pressure elevated; in addition, he had throat surgery, from which he recovered fully. Writing to a friend about his hospital stay, Warren remarked that he "used to smoke 50 cigarettes a day, always waking up in the night to start again," but noted that he stopped smoking abruptly in May 1942. "That was about the time when cigarette companies were paying large sums to get people in the public to expatiate on their product. When they came to me I told them that what I might

---

[27]Letter, Warren to Mr. and Mrs. Harry McMullan, Raleigh, NC, March 17, 1943, ibid., Folder 390; and letter, Warren to Dudley W. Bagley, March 9, 1948, ibid., Folder 426.

[28]Letter, Warren to Sen. J. W. Bailey, September 23, 1944, ibid., Folder 399.

[29]Letter, Warren to President Harry S. Truman, July 1, 1946, ibid., Folder 416; and letter, Warren to H. S. Ward, July 10, 1946, ibid. In the letter to Ward, Warren mentioned that President Truman had visited him for 15 minutes on July 3.

[30]Letter, Warren to Bagley, February 10, 1948, ibid., Folder 425; and letter, Warren to Bagley, March 9, 1948, ibid., Folder 426.

say would ruin them."[31] Warren's next stay in the hospital, for three weeks, began in late December 1952. Again his weight was a problem, and a concurrent sinus condition led to minor surgery again. After his hospital stay, Warren and his wife spent a month in Florida for rest and recuperation. To one of his correspondents he wrote, "There is nothing radically wrong with me except overwork and exhaustion. My Office is not very conducive to keeping one in good health."[32]

Warren concluded, after another two weeks in the hospital in August 1953, that he would sooner or later have to resign as comptroller general. He injured his legs in an accident (the nature of which he did not describe), and he was overweight again. In the hospital, he was put on a strict diet and his doctors advised him to retire. As he wrote to a friend, "Five doctors sat in on me and have urge [sic] me to retire at once or that I might expect the worse [sic]." He indicated in letters to others in the next few months that the doctors continued to recommend his retirement.[33] In late March, 1954, Warren decided to retire after one of his doctors told him his condition had worsened and that he was in bad shape.[34]

Warren had serious medical problems during almost all of his term as comptroller general and spent considerable time in hospitals and additional periods away from the office for recuperation. In addition to blaming his weight problem—Warren readily admitted his love of good food—he and his doctors blamed the heavy workload he carried at GAO and the stress associated with it for his medical problems.

Another factor that perhaps contributed to this stress was his financial situation. When Warren became comptroller general in 1940, his salary was $10,000 per year, although apparently President Roosevelt told him at the time that it would be raised to $15,000. Instead Congress increased the salary to only $12,000. Although not covered for retirement at all when he entered office, a general retirement law for federal employees enacted in 1947 did apply to Warren, but in order for him to get sufficient benefits, he would have had to make a lump sum payment for previous federal service (as of 1949) of $15,000, which he could not afford.[35]

---

[31]Letter, Warren to Louis Graves, Chapel Hill, NC, April 26, 1951, ibid., Folder 441.

[32]Letter, Warren to Gordon Gray, January 7, 1953, ibid., Folder 453; letter, Warren to W. H. Lewark, Kill Devil Hills, NC, January 14, 1953, ibid.; and letter, Warren to R. Bruce Etheridge, Raleigh, NC, January 28, 1953, ibid.

[33]Letter, Warren to F. S. Worthy, Washington, NC, August 25, 1953, ibid., Folder 461 (source of the quotation); and letter, Warren to Herbert Bonner, October 20, 1953, ibid., Folder 463.

[34]Letter, Warren to Dr. T. Lynch Murphy, Salisbury, NC, April 26, 1954, ibid., Folder 475. See pp. 93-95 for information on Warren's retirement on April 30, 1954.

[35]Letter, Warren to McDuffie, July 15, 1949, Warren Papers, Folder 433.

In 1949, Warren was in touch with several friends, including some members of Congress, about the prospects for legislation to provide him with a good federal pension. At the time, Congress was considering pension legislation for federal judges. At Warren's urging, his friend Judge John McDuffie, who earlier (1919-1935) represented Alabama in the House of Representatives, wrote to a current Alabama representative, Samuel F. Hobbs, asking him to work on legislation providing a new retirement plan for the comptroller general. He pointed out that Warren owed "a great deal of money," including a mortgage on his home in Washington, D.C.[36] Nothing came of this effort, but in 1953, Congress did pass legislation providing a new retirement system for the comptroller general.

The law, approved on July 28, 1953, amended Section 303 of the Budget and Accounting Act, 1921. It provided a comptroller general who served at least ten years in office with a lifetime annuity equal to the salary he was receiving at the end of his term, with a reduction of one-fourth of 1 percent for each full month under age 65. If the comptroller general retired on medical disability, he was to receive a full annuity if he had served at least ten years and one-half of a full annuity for service under ten years.[37]

While Congress considered the retirement bill, Warren presented arguments supporting it to the chairman of the House Committee on Government Operations. He pointed out that the length of the comptroller general's term made it impossible for one holding the position to retain other professional ties, but yet it was too short for him to build up a sufficient annuity under the Civil Service Retirement System. A person appointed to the position would be mature and probably at retirement would be beyond the age to seek new employment. Warren added that the type of retirement benefits to be provided should be equated to the nature of the position of comptroller general—the General Accounting Office was a part of the legislative branch, and the comptroller general's position was of a semijudicial nature. During the House debate on the bill, the point was made that the proposed retirement system was similar to that provided for federal judges. Both the Civil Service Commission and the Bureau of the Budget concurred in the terms of the bill.[38] It was under this law that Warren was able to retire because of illness the following year.

The legislative history of the 1953 law discloses two central reasons for creation of a new retirement plan for the comptroller general: (1) Congress viewed

---

[36]Letter, McDuffie to Warren, July 13, 1949, enclosing letter, McDuffie to Hobbs, July 13, 1949, ibid.

[37]Public Law 83-161, 67 Stat. 229.

[38]S. Rept. 594, 83d Cong., 1st Sess., reprinted in *U.S. Code Congressional and Administrative News*, 83d Cong., 1st Sess., vol. I (St. Paul, MN: West Publishing Co., 1953), 2017-18. See also letter, Warren to Rep. Sam Rayburn, July 9, 1953, and letter, Warren to R. L. Harris, Roxboro, NC, July 9, 1953, both in Warren Papers, Folder 460.

the existing benefits as inadequate, possibly deterring in the future qualified persons from accepting appointment as comptroller general, and (2) Congress thought it was necessary, to ensure the complete independence and objectivity of individuals serving as comptroller general, to provide an adequate retirement annuity for the office.

Probably the fact that Warren had employment opportunities from time to time that would have substantially raised his income and given him retirement security intensified his interest in improving his pay and benefits as comptroller general. In 1944, he received an offer of a law partnership in North Carolina.[39] Warren told Sen. Harry F. Byrd in 1946 that he had had an offer of private employment that would have carried a high salary as well as an endowment worth $15,000 a year for life beginning at age 65.[40] His name came up for a federal district judgeship in North Carolina early in 1945, but he told the two North Carolina senators who backed him that because of his current presidential appointment and his "increased responsibilities by reason of the War," he could not consider the appointment. He added that he had made his decision because of passage of the George bill in February 1945, directing GAO to audit government corporations and placing a very important duty in GAO.[41]

Friends and officials in North Carolina pressed Warren as early as 1945 to consider running for governor in 1948. At that time, Warren said that he did not have campaign funds and that he could not make a definite decision on the matter until after the war ended. Within days of the end of the war in August 1945, he wrote to a friend that he was going to seriously consider entering the race. If he did so, he added, he would resign as comptroller general early enough to make an effective campaign.[42] In February, 1946, he explained his current thinking on the matter as well as other job opportunities:

> I have nearly 10 more years of my present term, but it is so arduous that I will never live to fill it out. Financially I stay at zero all the time. I have never had any money or cared any-thing about it, but as I am the only one in our office who is not under retirement, it is high time that I am thinking about the future. If I had known the War would have ended so quick I would have accepted the Federal Judgeship in North Carolina which would

---

[39]Letter, Warren to J. L. Emanuel, October 30, 1944, ibid., Folder 400.

[40]Letter, Warren to Byrd, June 12, 1946, ibid., Folder 415.

[41]Letter, Warren to Sen. Josiah W. Bailey and Clyde R. Hoey, February 23, 1945, ibid., Folder 402; and letter, Warren to McDuffie, March 17, 1945, ibid., Folder 403. See chapter 12 for information on GAO's corporation audits.

[42]Letter, Warren to Judge Richard D. Dixon, Edenton, NC, July 30, 1945, Warren Papers, Folder 405; and letter, Warren to Edwin Gill, Raleigh, NC, August 11, 1945, ibid., Folder 406.

have been ideal, but some of my close friends almost made me think I would have been a War deserter had I gotten out at the time. I have twice been offered employment carrying $25,000 per annum, but I just couldn't afford to have my name associated with such lobbying affairs.[43]

At the end of 1946, Warren decided not to enter the 1948 North Carolina gubernatorial race. "If I was interested," he explained, "I am unable to make the *financial* and *physical* sacrifice that it involves. I was assured of the financial end without embarrassment to me, but my greatest problem was that I could not permit any personal financing for the two years prior to the election, as I have no income, and would have to resign my office within the next two or three months."[44]

At least one North Carolina newspaper, citing his national role as comptroller general, suggested that Warren would make a good running mate for President Truman in 1948. Also the Beaufort County, North Carolina, Board of Commissioners in 1949 urged the governor of North Carolina to appoint him to the U.S. Senate to replace Senator Joseph M. Broughton, who had died in office. Warren told the board that when he became comptroller general, "he gave up all thought of further political office," and added: "I am a candidate for just one thing, and that is to return to Beaufort County to spend the rest of my life in a section and among people whom I love."[45]

Actually, as his personal correspondence clearly shows, Warren maintained a keen interest in the politics of his home state and, on occasion, he worked behind the scenes on state issues. In 1944, for example, he became concerned about the possibility that some Japanese-Americans would be moved to North Carolina. In a confidential letter to a friend in Washington, North Carolina, Warren confided that he had received a letter "from a high source" indicating that someone in Beaufort County had invited the War Relocation Authority "to permanently settle in our county a large colony of Japs." He added, "I can't imagine anything more horrible for our section than a thing of this kind. Of course, there are up here certain ones who would call me Un-American and intolerant for making such a statement, but God spare our section from such a thing. I would have said the same had there not been a war." Warren said that if the rumor proved true, he would work hard to prevent it.[46]

---

[43]Letter, Warren to McDuffie, February 21, 1946, ibid., Folder 413.

[44]Letter, Warren to R. E. Williams, Raleigh, NC, December 26, 1946, ibid., Folder 419.

[45]Clipping, *Durham (NC) Herald*, August 11, 1946, ibid., Scrapbooks, vol. 11; and letter, Warren to Beaufort County Board of Commissioners, March 15, 1949, ibid., Folder 431.

[46]Letter, Warren to W. B. Rodman, Jr., January 7, 1944, ibid., Folder 397.

In 1948, Warren wrote to the attorney for the Orville Wright estate about a permanent location for the historic Wright plane. He noted his earlier authorship in the House of Representatives of the bill to establish the Wright Memorial at Kill Devil Hills in North Carolina and said that he had talked to Orville Wright before his death about the placement of the aircraft. Warren thought that it would be located more suitably in North Carolina than in the Smithsonian Institution in Washington.[47]

Also in 1948, Warren supported privately the candidacy of Charles M. Johnson for governor of North Carolina. Referring to a primary election in North Carolina, Warren wrote to Johnson: "I personally saw to it that sixteen from my office [GAO] went down to vote for you, and they will go again [apparently referring to a run-off primary]. Of course you got many more from this Office that I knew nothing about."[48] Two years later, he wrote Gov. W. Kerr Scott of North Carolina, recommending two men for appointments, one to the North Carolina Supreme Court and the other as attorney general. "I never worry Governors with endorsements," Warren wrote, "and this is merely my thought about two old friends, both of whom I know to be finely qualified."[49] When Warren returned to North Carolina in 1954 after his retirement from GAO, he resumed his involvement in home state politics, even to the point serving two terms in the state senate.[50]

When it came to national politics, Warren was careful not to get involved publicly because of his position as the head of a nonpartisan agency that worked for Congress as a whole. He kept his public speaking, even about GAO, to a minimum, and declined invitations to speak on partisan issues. When the chairman of the speakers' bureau of the Democratic National Committee wrote asking him to make speeches during the 1944 presidential campaign, Warren responded:

> As deeply as I feel about the present campaign, and as much as I would like personally to participate in same, I am sure you will realize that my position is strictly independent and non-political, and nothing more would completely destroy the value of the General Accounting Office than to have its head become involved in partisan politics or political discussion.[51]

Warren was in office more than five years before he made his first public speech as comptroller general. During World War II, GAO's Postal Accounts Division

---

[47]Letter, Warren to Charles H. Funkhouser, Dayton, OH, February 13, 1948, ibid., Folder 425.

[48]Letter, Warren to Johnson, June 8, 1948, ibid., Folder 427.

[49]Letter, Warren to Scott, October 18, 1950, ibid., Folder 438.

[50]See p. 25.

[51]Letter, Warren to Robert Ramspeck, September 11, 1944, Warren Papers, Folder 399.

moved from Washington to Asheville, North Carolina.[52] Warren had promised to speak before the Asheville Chamber of Commerce when he visited the GAO offices there, and he fulfilled this promise in January 1946. The speech generally concerned the federal government, its finances, and its relationships with the states. Warren warned against excessive spending and deficit financing. His speech, which the nation's press reported widely, elicited many favorable editorials and invitations to speak elsewhere.[53] Responding to an invitation to speak before the Missouri Public Expenditure Survey soon after his Asheville appearance, Warren declined, explaining his position as follows:

> Somehow, I have the feeling that I should not be going over the country making speeches. I occupy the only strictly independent office in the Government. It is non-partisan and non-political, and I am answerable not to the Executive, but solely to the Congress. I may be wrong, but I have the idea that if the head of the Office is constantly making speeches, that it will be misunderstood and will do the office no good. I firmly believe that the General Accounting Office is the last remaining bulwark between the taxpayers of the Nation and the illegal expenditures of public funds.[54]

Warren generally held to his rule to severely limit his public speaking, other than in congressional testimony, and if he did appear in such a role, he spoke mainly about GAO and its work.[55]   Warren purposely avoided establishing a public affairs office at GAO and occasionally noted this proudly in congressional testimony.[56]

But as his term wore on, press coverage of GAO and Warren personally did increase—mainly in response to disclosure of important GAO investigations and publication of official reports. Warren did not grant any interviews to the press until February 1952, when one appeared in *U.S. News and World Report*. In this interview, Warren commented on examples of scandal and corruption that had come to GAO's attention during his term.[57] An article about Warren entitled

---

[52]See chapter 11, p. 254.

[53]Letter, Warren to Pickett L. Warren, Chicago, IL, January 16, 1946, Warren Papers, Folder 411; and letter, Warren to McDuffie, February 21, 1946, ibid., Folder 413.

[54]Letter, Warren to Edward Staples, executive director, Missouri Public Expenditure Survey, Jefferson City, MO, February 19, 1946, ibid.

[55]An example was his speech before the Women's National Democratic Club in Washington on February 4, 1952. See text of speech in ibid., Folder 445.

[56]Warren testimony, April 23, 1947, *General Accounting Office Building, No. 4*, Hearings before the Subcommittee on Public Buildings and Grounds, House Committee on Public Works . . ., 80th Cong., 1st Sess. (Washington: GPO, 1947), 2.

[57]Interview of Warren, *U.S. News and World Report*, February 15, 1952, in Warren Papers, Folder 445.

"Watchdog on Washington's Waste," which appeared in the August 1952 edition of *Reader's Digest*, attracted much attention and several letters to Warren. One person in Philadelphia wrote, asking "why have we (the general public at the grass roots level) never heard of you before? We clamor over back fences and office water coolers for good efficient government and then apathetically do nothing because its [sic] such a hopeless and impossible task, trying to convert this huge bureaucratic monster into efficient business."[58]

Congressional Relationships

While Warren's predecessor, J. R. McCarl, maintained somewhat restrained relationships with Congress, Warren made a sustained, conscious effort to expand and improve congressional relationships. His long career in Congress, where he continued to have close ties with old friends, helps to explain this. But he also saw closer relationships with Congress as helping to protect GAO from executive branch efforts to change the Office's role and functions, such as had occurred frequently in the years before 1940.[59] Also, GAO's vastly expanded work during World War II, checking on war expenditures, brought it frequently in touch with congressional committees and Congress as a whole.[60] Central to Warren's thinking was the fact that GAO was an agent of Congress and that its relationship to Congress had to be enhanced.

Although the Budget and Accounting Act, 1921, had described GAO as an agency "independent of the executive departments," the law did not specifically state that GAO was a legislative agency. Congress annually during the war years considered GAO's budget as part of appropriations for independent offices rather than within the congressional budget. Warren welcomed the provision in the Reorganization Act of 1945 (P.L. 263, Dec. 20, 1945) stating that GAO was "a part of the legislative branch of the government." The Reorganization Act, which renewed the president's authority, originally granted in 1939, to reorganize executive agencies, specifically excluded GAO from this authority. Warren had urged such exclusion in testimony on the bill and in correspondence with members of Congress and other officials. The law was very important because it confirmed GAO's status as a legislative agency.[61]

---

[58]Letter, Ritanne R. McDonald to Warren, July 24, 1952, ibid., Folder 448.

[59]See chapter 10, pp. 229-47.

[60]See chapter 11, pp. 249-78.

[61]Mosher, *GAO*, 104-105; letter, Warren to M.S. Eccles, chairman, Federal Reserve Board of Governors, September 25, 1945, 289 MS 1521; and letter, Warren to Carter Manasco, chairman, House Committee on Expenditures in the Executive Departments, June 13, 1945, 286 MS 1001.

In its recommendations on accounting and auditing in 1949, the first Hoover Commission criticized GAO's activities, saying that some of them involved executive functions, and proposed major changes in GAO's work and organization. Warren successfully fought these proposals, arguing that they constituted an unwarranted and illegal attack and emphasizing GAO's status as a congressional agency.[62]

Warren highlighted GAO's success in recovering money illegally expended by government agencies as a measure of the Office's service to Congress and the nation as a whole. GAO estimated that the total amount it had collected from fiscal year 1941 through the middle of fiscal year 1953 was $816,317,328. This amount, GAO pointed out, was more than double the agency's operational costs during the same period.[63] When Warren retired a year later, he noted that GAO collections had increased to a total of $915,000,000 between 1941 and 1954.[64] While Warren regularly reported GAO's collection totals—the return to the Treasury of funds illegally or erroneously spent by the government—he also emphasized the deterrent effects of audits in saving money for the government.

Another measure of GAO's expanding service to Congress was the number of reports issued to Congress and its committees. Statistics for the Warren period show a steady increase, somewhat during World War II but even more so afterwards.[65] Not only did the number of reports increase, but in the latter years of Warren's term, they became more substantive, reflecting GAO's movement into new areas, such as government corporation audits and the "comprehensive audit," which went beyond financial auditing to look at the scope and the effectiveness of government programs.[66]

GAO also assisted Congress during the Warren period by detailing staff to congressional committees. Before Warren's term, GAO had assigned staff to congressional committees only rarely.[67] But Warren was more willing to do so, and by the end of his term, the practice had become common. For example,

---

[62]See chapter 13, pp. 324-27.

[63]Testimony of Warren and other GAO officials, March 5, 1953, *Independent Offices Appropriations for 1954*, Hearings before a Subcommittee of the House Committee on Appropriations, 83d Cong., 1st Sess., pt. 3 (Washington: GPO, 1953), 727; letter, Warren to members of Congress, March 31, 1954, reprinted in *GAO Review* (summer 1981): 7-8; and *Comptroller General of the United States: Annual Report for the Fiscal Year Ended June 30, 1953* (Washington: GPO, n.d.), 37.

[64]Letter, Warren to members of Congress, March 31, 1954, reprinted in *GAO Review* (summer 1981): 7-8.

[65]See appendix VII.

[66]See chapter 12 for information on corporation audits and chapter 13, pp. 321-24, for discussion of the comprehensive audit program.

[67]Testimony of E. W. Bell, chief, Audit Division, and J. L. Baity, budget officer, December 5, 1941, *Hearings on the Independent Offices Appropriation Bill for 1943*, Subcommittee on Independent Offices, House Committee on Appropriations, 77th Cong., 2d Sess. (Washington: GPO, 1942), 72.

Warren noted in March 1953 that 18 GAO staff were working full-time on budget studies for the House Committee on Appropriations and that 16 staff were assisting on a consulting basis.[68]

Warren established the foundations for improving GAO relationships with Congress, and his successors further strengthened them. This is not to say that there had never been problems in GAO-congressional relationships. But on the whole, the ties became stronger as time passed, demonstrated by the increasing scope and volume of GAO's work and its direct contacts with Congress through reports, testimony, and other means. Warren repeatedly reminded Congress of its ties to GAO. In 1954, a few months before his retirement, he observed that it was "important for Congress to remember that the General Accounting Office is your agency. To be worth its salt it must continue always to be independent, nonpartisan, and nonpolitical. To be effective, it must always have your wholehearted support and your vigilant safeguarding of its functions and powers."[69]

Management and Organization under Warren

Warren devoted himself fully to his duties at GAO. He brought into leadership positions men whose contributions to GAO were outstanding, including Frank L. Yates, Frank H. Weitzel, Robert F. Keller, Ted B. Westfall, and Walter F. Frese. Yates, Weitzel, and Keller all were insiders who rose through the ranks. Frese came in from the Treasury Department in 1948 to head a new Accounting Systems Division, and Westfall joined the Corporation Audits Division in 1946, eventually rising to become director of the large Audit Division in 1951. Warren believed that GAO had been "revolutionized" and "reorganized" under his leadership. After two years on the job, he wrote to President Roosevelt about his work:

> I found a floundering institution with no leadership. I am today told on all sides that there has been a better understanding, more cooperation and a more amicable relationship between the departments and agencies and this Office than has ever existed before. I have satisfactorily ironed out bitter disputes that have been pending for 20 years, and although at times the position calls for the exercise of stern qualities, the so-called "chill" of the General Accounting Office has been dissipated.[70]

---

[68]General statement, Warren, March 5, 1953, *Independent Offices Appropriations for 1954*, pt. 3, 726.

[69]Warren statement, January 13, 1954, *Independent Offices Appropriations for 1955*, Hearings before a Subcommittee of the House Committee on Appropriations, 83d Cong., 2d Sess., pt. 1 (Washington: GPO, 1954), 349.

[70]Letter, Warren to Roosevelt, September 21, 1942, Warren Papers, Folder 389.

Warren was a strong manager, who successfully directed the tremendously increased workload that GAO had to carry during World War II as well as the gradual but large downsizing after the war. More importantly, he planned and presided over the initial stages of the transformation of GAO from a voucher-checking agency to one that issued substantive, comprehensive audit reports on federal programs, paying increased attention to economy and efficiency. He moved from the formerly adversarial relationship between GAO and the executive branch to a more cordial one, including some cooperative activities, such as the joint program to improve accounting announced in 1947.[71]

Warren paid close attention to GAO's organization, making piecemeal organizational changes as necessary to cope with the World War II workload, the corporation audits mandated by Congress in 1945, and the financial management work begun under the joint program to improve accounting after 1947. Once the comprehensive audit work started in 1949, Warren planned a major reorganization, which he completed in 1952. Warren's reorganization was a response to the changing focus and nature of GAO's work.[72]

Warren began the process of professionalizing GAO, especially after World War II. GAO's new duties, including corporation audits, comprehensive audits, and financial management work, required more professionally trained staff than was the case when most of the work involved voucher checking and other routine functions. Most of the new professional people who came to GAO after 1945 were trained in accounting and auditing. By the end of Warren's term, the number of GAO staff that had college degrees and professional experience had increased greatly over what it had been when his term began in 1940. Reflecting common attitudes and practices of the era, almost all these professional staff additions were white males. During World War II, the number of women employees increased to the point where they constituted more than 60 percent of the staff at the end of the war, but as the workforce decreased after 1945, men became the majority again. Warren's executive officer testified early in 1945 about the proportion of staff positions occupied by women and added: "Practically any position in the office is available for women, if they can make the grade; that is, they are not stopped because they happen to be women."[73]

---

[71]See chapters 11-15. The comprehensive audit is discussed in detail in chapter 13.

[72]Because organizational change was so directly connected with GAO's work program, a detailed discussion of reorganization actions during Warren's term will be deferred until the work program is discussed. See chapter 14.

[73]Testimony of Dudley W. Bagley, January 18, 1945, *Independent Offices Appropriation Bill for 1946*, Hearings before a Subcommittee on Independent Offices, House Committee on Appropriations, 79th Cong., 1st Sess. (Washington: GPO, 1945), 1122.

While opportunities for women may have expanded because of wartime personnel demands and the scarcity of employable males, these opportunities could not be described as professional. For the most part, women were in lower grades and worked mainly on clerical and secretarial duties.[74]   A factor was that during this period, women rarely pursued accounting and auditing training and few were available to GAO.

About the time he retired, Warren defended GAO's policy of using men in the most important positions. Rep. Edward H. Rees, chairman of the House Committee on Post Office and Civil Service, asked him for a statement on GAO's policy on the use of women in comprehensive audit work. Warren responded that GAO employed only men for such work. This was "not to be considered as a reflection on the ability of women" but rather that "comprehensive audit staff must be available for assignment to all types of audit engagements, including those to which only men can be assigned." Women were not assigned to any comprehensive audit work, Warren explained, because of inadequate hotel accommodations in some locations, objections by some government agencies to the use of women auditors, and observation of inventories which "frequently involve considerable physical activity and exertion on the part of the auditors." He noted that the Bureau of Prisons had asked GAO not to use women auditors at its institutions "because of the effect on the morale and conduct of the inmates." And Warren commented that if women were used on some assignments, "the less desirable assignments would fall to male members of the staff making them dissatisfied and desirous of obtaining other employment."[75]

Not until the 1960s, in another era and under other leadership, did GAO begin to shed some of the old attitudes and deal with equal opportunity questions relating to women and minorities. While Warren was a competent manager, who respected his staff and applauded their achievements, he was a product of his times and reflected prevailing attitudes in the government on the employment of women and minorities.

When the government, responding to worsening relations with the Soviet Union and rising concern about alleged internal communist activity in the United States, established a loyalty program in 1948, Warren set up the Loyalty Board, composed of six high GAO officials. In the order establishing this board, Warren stated that GAO assumed that each employee was loyal to the U.S. government in the absence of contrary evidence. In dealing with matters concerning employee loyalty, GAO would give "fair and impartial consideration." The Loyalty

---

[74]See GAO, *Audit and Legal Services, 1943-1983: A Women's Perspective: Interview with Margaret L. Macfarlane, Geraldine M. Rubar, and Stella B. Shea*, GAO History Program, Oral History Series, GAO/OP-10-OH (Washington: 1990).

[75]Letter, Warren to Edward H. Rees, April 28, 1954, Warren Papers, Folder 476.

Board was to adjudicate loyalty cases, hold hearings, and issue written reports.[76] There is no known evidence that any GAO employees ever came before the Loyalty Board.[77]

Warren's Retirement

The July 1953 law that provided a generous pension to a retiring comptroller general made retirement financially feasible for Warren. Some of his friends advised him to leave office because of his health. Warren wrote to one of them when he left the hospital after a two-week stay in August 1953 that his doctors had urged him to retire. Warren indicated that when he found a new assistant—Assistant Comptroller General Frank L. Yates had died suddenly in office in June 1953—he would consider retiring.[78] Before the end of 1953, press accounts noted the possibility that Warren might leave office because of health problems.[79]

During the summer of 1953, as soon as he realized that he would have to retire, Warren began to think about a successor. By this time, President Eisenhower was in office, ensuring that the new comptroller general would be a Republican. "I don't want to be succeeded by a damn scrub," Warren wrote to a close friend. "The republican politicians are hungry and I am afraid they will not discriminate when it comes to filling my place. I have ruined my health in building up the General Accounting Office from nothing to the greatest agency in the Government, and I want to see it maintained on the same high plane."[80]

Warren already had someone in mind—Rep. W. Sterling Cole (R—New York), who had begun his career in the House of Rep. in 1935. He wrote to Cole on August 4, 1953, saying that he wanted to talk to him about a confidential matter. On his file copy of the letter, Warren wrote: "Wish to see him succeed me as Comptroller General." He wrote to Cole again a week later, after he had talked with him at Bethesda Hospital, where Warren was a patient. "There are 435 Congressmen and 96 Senators. There is *one* Comptroller General free and untrammeled. There will come into full fruition during the next regime the great program that I initiated. . . . The opportunity for leadership and accomplishment is

---

[76]Administrative Order No. 62, "Loyalty Board," May 3, 1948, *Comptroller General's Orders*, vol. 2, GAO Records.

[77]The author found no evidence in GAO records he examined.

[78]Letter, F. S. Worthy, Washington, NC, to Warren, August 18, 1953, and letter, Warren to Worthy, August 25, 1953, both in Warren Papers, Folder 461.

[79]See, for example, clipping, *Raleigh (NC) News and Observer*, November 1, 1953, clippings files, GAO History Program Archives.

[80]Letter, Warren to Worthy, August 25, 1953, ibid., Folder 461.

unlimited."[81] Warren's efforts on Cole's behalf succeeded in establishing him as a candidate for the position of comptroller general.

Even before Warren announced his intention to retire, the press noted that his House Republican colleagues favored Cole for the position. The *Charlotte (NC) News*, reporting on Warren's retirement plans, noted that Cole had been groomed as his successor and that more than 200 of his House colleagues had written to President Eisenhower urging him to appoint Cole.[82] Three days before he left office, Warren wrote again to Cole: "I had rather see you succeed me . . . than any other person in this Country, for you would bring to it all of the noble attributes with which you are so finely en-

Comptroller General Warren arriving at the White House to discuss his request to retire, 1954.

dowed. Your appointment is long overdue, and I trust and pray that it will take place before I leave town."[83]

On March 29, 1954, Warren wrote to President Dwight D. Eisenhower requesting disability retirement effective April 30, 1954, according to the 1953 law. Since he had 13-1/2 years of service as comptroller general, he was eligible for a pension at full salary, $17,500, for life. Eisenhower accepted his decision with regret, thanking him for his outstanding service and cooperation with his administration.[84] Soon Warren was back in Bethesda Naval Hospital for a lengthy stay. From the hospital, he wrote to a friend in the House of Representatives about his

---

[81]Letter, Warren to Cole, August 4, 1953, and letter, Warren to Cole, August 11, 1953, both in ibid. In referring to his "great program," presumably Warren meant the joint accounting improvement program, the comprehensive audit, and other aspects of GAO's activities developed under his leadership.

[82]Letter, Jim Morse, columnist for the *Elmira (NY) Star-Gazette*, to Warren, March 23, 1954, Warren Papers, Folder 466; and clipping, *Charlotte News*, March 31, 1954, clippings files, GAO History Program Archives.

[83]Letter, Warren to Cole, April 27, 1954, Warren Papers, Folder 475. See chapter 5, pp. 101-8, for an account of the appointment of Warren's successor.

[84]Letter, Warren to the president, March 29, 1954, and letter, Eisenhower to Warren, March 31, 1954, GAO History Program Archives.

decision to retire: "I hated very much to get out but the doctors told me it was imperative now."[85]

There was considerable editorial comment on Warren's work at GAO and his retirement. The *Baltimore Evening Sun* observed that Warren was less cantankerous than McCarl had been. Warren, the *Sun* said, "brought to his job . . . an old-fashioned conception of honesty and a rugged capacity to stand up to pressure from others without being offensive. Under his administration, the general accounting office . . . has won a much wider esteem than it had under . . . [McCarl]." The *Washington Star*, reporting Warren's intention to retire, wrote: "Many believe he rates a blue ribbon: Best watchdog in show."[86]

Shortly after he left office on April 30, 1954, Warren and his wife moved back to their family home in Washington, North Carolina. In retirement his health improved. He became active again in North Carolina politics and served terms in the North Carolina Senate in 1959 and 1961. He also served as a director of a local bank. One of his proposals while in the state senate, reflecting his experience as comptroller general, was the creation of a new state officer who would have broad powers over financial matters.[87] Warren died in Washington, North Carolina, at the age of 87 on December 28, 1976.[88]

The Assistant Comptrollers General under Warren

When Warren took office in 1940, the incumbent assistant comptroller general was Richard Nash Elliott, who had held the position since his appointment by President Herbert Hoover in 1931. Until his mandatory retirement at age 70 in 1943, he worked with Warren, who appears to have valued his services.[89] Anticipating Elliott's retirement, Warren suggested a successor, Frank L. Yates, to President Roosevelt almost eight months in advance. Warren described Yates as his "strong right arm" and added that "his appointment would be to the best interest of this Office and of your Administration."[90]

Yates was born in Kablestown, West Virginia, on January 23, 1894. He attended local public schools; Shepherd College in Shepherdstown, West Virginia; and The George Washington University, where he earned a law degree in 1922. He began government service on the staff of the auditor for the War Department

---

[85]Letter, Warren to Rep. James C. Auchincloss, April 14, 1954, Warren Papers, Folder 472.

[86]Clipping, *Baltimore Evening Sun*, April 1, 1954, and clipping, *Washington Star*, April 2, 1954, clippings files, GAO History Program Archives.

[87]Clipping, Norfolk *Virginia-Pilot*, February 25, 1959, clippings files, GAO History Program Archives.

[88]*Biographical Directory*, 2010-11.

[89]See chapter 3, pp. 66-68, for an account of Elliott's service between 1931 and 1940.

[90]Letter, Warren to Roosevelt, September 21, 1942, Warren Papers, Folder 389.

in 1919 and transferred to GAO when it began operations in 1921. Between 1921 and 1943, Yates served as an attorney and as a special assistant to the comptroller general.[91]

There were other contenders for the assistant comptroller general's position in 1943. Luther Patrick, a Democratic representative from Alabama who failed to gain renomination in 1942, sent Roosevelt an application for the job. The White House asked Warren what he thought of the idea. There is no record of Warren's reply, but he must have opposed Patrick, given his strong support for Yates.[92] Also, Attorney General Francis Biddle urged the president to appoint Eric Kohler, a former comptroller of the Tennessee Valley Authority, who in 1943 was with the accounting firm of Arthur Andersen and Company. Biddle told the president that Kohler was "familiar with the problems" of GAO and recommended that he appoint someone "technically qualified to unwind the red tape in the Comptroller's office, and who is loyal to you and to your point of view." Because Roosevelt had already informed Warren that he would appoint Yates, he rejected Biddle's recommendation.[93]

President Roosevelt nominated Yates to be assistant comptroller general on March 16, 1943. After confirmation, he took up his duties on May 1, 1943, for a stated term of 15 years.[94] Yates served until June 29, 1953, when he died suddenly of a heart attack. In expressing his sympathy to Mrs. Yates, Warren wrote: "I loved Frank and was truly devoted to him. I don't believe that two men could have worked together more harmoniously and . . . there was never a major difference between us. I leaned heavily on him because in addition to his knowledge, I knew that he had judgment, fairness and great ability. He was the finest example of a career public servant."[95]

The record shows that Yates played a central role in the conduct of GAO's business between 1943 and 1953. He testified frequently, sometimes alongside Warren and sometimes in his place. He worked especially hard to secure a new headquarters building for GAO, an effort culminating with the opening of the new

---

[91]*Annual Report of the Comptroller General of the United States for the Fiscal Year Ended June 30, 1943* (Washington: GPO, n.d.), iv; clipping, *Washington Star*, March 16, 1943, Warren Papers, Scrapbooks, vol. 7; and *GAO Review* (summer 1971): 5.

[92]Note summarizing Patrick's letter to the president, August 20, 1942, and statement that the president asked Warren for his opinion, in Roosevelt Papers, President's Official File, #500-A.

[93]Memorandum, Biddle to the president, February 11, 1943, and memorandum, Marvin McIntyre, assistant secretary to the president, to Grace Tully, personal secretary to the president, February 13, 1943 (reminding her that the president had earlier agreed with Warren to appoint Yates), both in Roosevelt Papers, President's Official File, #500.

[94]Clipping, *Washington Star*, March 16, 1943, Warren Papers, Scrapbooks, vol. 7; and letter, Warren to Roosevelt, March 17, 1943, ibid., Folder 390.

[95]Letter, Warren to Mrs. Yates, June 29, 1953, ibid., Folder 459; and GAO, *Annual Report*, 1953, v.

structure in 1951.[96] He was a loyal and active supporter of various Warren initiatives, including the audit of government corporations, the joint program to improve accounting, the comprehensive audit, and many others.

After Yates died, Warren immediately launched an effort to persuade President Eisenhower to appoint Frank H. Weitzel as his successor. By this time, as noted earlier, Warren's health was bad and he was already thinking about retiring. Thus he was eager to have the vacancy filled without delay. The day after Yates died, Warren got Weitzel's name to Secretary of the Treasury George Humphrey through Sen. Harry F. Byrd. Humphrey promised to do all he could to press Weitzel's nomination, presumably with the president. Two days later, Warren talked with Eisenhower, who said he had heard of Weitzel. Warren recorded after this meeting, "The President made no promise, but received me cordially and said that generally speaking he believed that the head of a department

Frank L. Yates, Assistant Comptroller General, 1943-1953.

or agency ought to have the man of his choice under him." Warren urged the president to make the appointment at once. Before he saw Eisenhower, Warren talked with the president's assistant, Sherman Adams, who told him that the White House had received several endorsements on behalf of E. L. Fisher, GAO's general counsel, and that Adams had told him Fisher "was putting on quite a campaign." Warren noted in his memo on this conversation, "I thought he [Fisher] was grossly lacking in propriety."[97]

In early October 1953, President Eisenhower did nominate Weitzel to be assistant comptroller general. He took office on an interim appointment on October 12, 1953. His official 15-year term began when the Senate confirmed his nomination on January 18, 1954.[98]

---

[96]See chapter 7, pp. 156-65.

[97]Letter, Sen. Byrd to Warren, June 30, 1953, Warren Papers, Folder 459; and Warren, memorandum for personal files, July 2, 1953, ibid., Folder 460.

[98]E. H. Morse, Jr., "Frank H. Weitzel Retires," *GAO Review* (spring 1969): 63-75; *GAO Review* (summer 1971): 9-12; and *GAO Review* (fall 1973): 66.

Weitzel first came to work at GAO in 1923 at the age of 16 as a messenger in the Claims Division at a salary of $14 per week. He worked intermittently at GAO for the next four years and then began full-time service in 1927. He earned a bachelor's degree from The George Washington University in 1931 and a law degree in 1935. From 1935 to 1942, he was an attorney in the Office of the General Counsel. In 1942, he moved to the Office of the Comptroller General as an adviser on legal, organizational, and procedural problems. Three years later, Warren appointed him assistant to the comptroller general, responsible for legislative and interagency relations. He held this position until he became assistant comptroller general in 1953.[99]

When Warren left on April 30, 1954, Weitzel, after only a few months as assistant comptroller general, became acting comptroller general. He held this post until December 14, 1954, when the new comptroller general, Joseph Campbell, entered office. When Campbell retired at the end of July 1965, Weitzel again became acting comptroller general, serving until March 8, 1966, when Elmer B. Staats became comptroller general. Weitzel retired on January 17, 1969, at the end of his 15-year term.[100]

Except for the period between 1954 and 1965, when Campbell was comptroller general, Weitzel was involved in practically every important GAO activity from the early 1940s until his retirement in 1969.[101] Among his contributions during the Warren period were the key role he played in the passage of the Government Corporation Control Act of 1945; the founding of the Joint Program for Improving Accounting in the Federal Government, 1947-1949; the passage of the Budget and Accounting Act of 1950; and his effective leadership in the interim between comptrollers general in 1954 and 1965-1966.[102]

Warren had long relied on Weitzel, and his appointment as assistant comptroller general in 1953 made it possible for Warren to retire with confidence that GAO would be in good hands until a new comptroller general took office. When Warren left, he expressed his appreciation to Weitzel: "You have outstanding ability, integrity and nobility of character. I have watched your rise with admiration and personal joy. I don't know of anything else to say in leaving you

[99]Morse, "Frank H. Weitzel Retires," 64; GAO, *Management News*, vol. 14, no. 42 (July 27-31, 1987), 7; and "Frank H. Weitzel–Forty Years in the General Accounting Office," *GAO Review* (winter 1967): 61.

[100]Morse, "Frank H. Weitzel Retires," 64-65; and "Frank H. Weitzel–Forty Years in the General Accounting Office," 61.

[101]See chapter 5, pp. 126-29, for information on Weitzel's status during the Campbell period.

[102]Morse, "Frank H. Weitzel Retires," 65-69.

As Comptroller General Warren looked on, Judge James R. Kirkland swore in Frank H. Weitzel as Assistant Comptroller General, October 12, 1953.

except to again express to you my love and affection."[103] During Campbell's term, although Weitzel served as assistant comptroller general for the entire period, his role and duties changed considerably.[104]

---

[103]Letter, Warren to Weitzel, April 29, 1954, Warren Papers, Folder 476.
[104]See chapter 5, pp. 126-29.

Joseph Campbell, Comptroller General, 1954-1965.

CHAPTER 5

Change, Centralization, and Progress: Joseph Campbell, 1954-1965

More than seven months elapsed after Lindsay C. Warren disclosed his intention to retire before President Dwight D. Eisenhower nominated a new comptroller general. The president's choice, announced on November 9, 1954, was Joseph Campbell, at the time a member of the Atomic Energy Commission (AEC). Differences between the House and the Senate on Warren's replacement explain Eisenhower's delay in making the nomination.

By 1954, the tradition had been established that the comptroller general should come out of the congressional arena, as had the first three holders of the office—John R. McCarl, Fred H. Brown, and Warren. By the time Warren announced that he would retire, the House and the Senate, both controlled by the Republican party, had selected their favorites for the position. The House candidate was Representative W. Sterling Cole (R—New York), whom Warren had been promoting behind the scenes for the position since the summer of 1953. The Senate's choice was J. Mark Trice, secretary of the Senate. With the Republican majorities in neither the Senate nor the House willing to compromise, Eisenhower delayed action on the nomination.[1]

During this period, the press, observing that Eisenhower was trying to break the congressional deadlock, mentioned other rumored nominees, including Wilfred J. McNeil, the Department of Defense comptroller; Frank H. Weitzel, the acting comptroller general; and Republican Senator Frederick G. Payne of Maine. Payne actually discussed the appointment with the president but decided that he preferred to remain in the Senate.[2]

---

[1]Clippings, *Washington Evening Star*, April 1 and June 16, 1954, clippings files, GAO History Program Archives; and Frederick C. Mosher, *The GAO: The Quest for Accountability in American Government* (Boulder, CO: Westview Press, 1979), 133-34 (hereafter cited as Mosher, *GAO*).

[2]Mosher, *GAO*, 134; clipping, *Washington Evening Star*, June 16, 1954; clipping, *New York World-Telegram and Sun*, October 16, 1954; and clipping, *Washington Evening Star*, November 6, 1954, all in clippings files, GAO History Program Archives.

Campbell's Background

In November 1954, Eisenhower ended the impasse with the surprise nomination of Campbell, who had not figured in the speculation about possible candidates. Campbell, born in New York City on March 25, 1900, received his early education in New York City public schools. He served briefly in the U.S. Army during World War I. After receiving a bachelor's degree from Columbia University in 1924, he worked in public accounting, first at private firms in New York and then, beginning in 1933, as the head of his own firm. In 1941, he became assistant treasurer of Columbia University. In 1949, Eisenhower, then the president of Columbia, promoted him to vice president and treasurer. In 1953, President Eisenhower selected Campbell for a term on the Atomic Energy Commission.[3]

Eisenhower's intention to nominate him came as a surprise to Campbell. He had decided by September 1954 to resign from the AEC and return to Columbia University. When he spoke to Eisenhower about his plans, the president, without any advance notice, asked him if he would like to be comptroller general. On September 30, 1954, Campbell told the president he would take the nomination.[4]

Campbell's nomination immediately provoked a storm of controversy—there were questions about his qualifications, aspects of his work at the AEC, and his lack of previous connections with Congress. The Democrats, who regained majorities in both houses of Congress in the November 1954 elections, delayed hearings on Campbell's nomination until early 1955, when they would be in control. Impatient with the delay, Eisenhower gave Campbell a recess appointment on December 14, 1954, allowing him to enter office on that date. The president resubmitted his nomination on January 10, 1955.[5]

President Eisenhower received some strong expressions of approval of his nomination of Campbell from the accounting profession. John L. Carey, executive director of the American Institute of Accountants, indicated in a

---

[3]Mosher, *GAO*, 134-35; and biographical data, Joseph Campbell, in file, Clippings CG [Campbell] 1964-1965, GAO History Program Archives.

[4]Senate Committee on Government Operations, *Nomination of Joseph Campbell*, 84th Cong., 1st Sess. (Washington: GPO, 1955), 6-8 (hereafter cited as *Nomination of Joseph Campbell*). William L. Ellis, for a time head of the Office of Investigations under Campbell, recounted a story Campbell had told him and others at a luncheon. Campbell stated that as he was leaving Eisenhower's office after telling him that he wanted to resign from the AEC, the president had asked: "Aren't you an accountant?" and had then offered him the appointment as comptroller general. See GAO, *William L. Ellis: GAO, 1935-1955*, GAO History Program, Oral History Series, GAO/OP-21-OH (Washington: 1991), 28.

[5]Senate Committee on Government Operations, *Financial Management in the Federal Government*, S. Doc. 11, 87th Cong., 1st Sess., vol. I (Washington: GPO, 1961), 321; and clipping, *Washington Post and Times-Herald*, November 10, 1954, clippings files, GAO History Program Archives.

telegram to the president that the institute was "highly gratified" with the nomination, describing Campbell as a "distinguished member of his profession" and eminently qualified. T. Coleman Andrews, commissioner of internal revenue, wrote to Eisenhower to express his pleasure that an accountant had been designated as comptroller general, "after I had seen this office filled by nonaccountants during the entire thirty-three years since it was created and, as a consequence, had seen it operated throughout most of this period as a law factory instead of an auditing office." J. S. Seidman, president of the New York State Society of Certified Public Accountants, expressed to Eisenhower his delight that an accountant would occupy the position of comptroller general. "This custom-tailoring of the man for the job is most reassuring."[6]

Eisenhower learned soon after he announced Campbell's nomination that there would be trouble gaining Senate confirmation. On November 17, 1954, Charles F. Willis, Jr., a White House staff member, informed Sherman Adams, the president's assistant, that the Republican National Committee "does not feel Mr. Campbell will be confirmed as Comptroller General." Willis did not explain the reasons for the committee's view, but by this time, congressional opposition to Campbell had become public.[7] Later Leonard W. Hall, chairman of the Republican National Committee, provided to the president a copy of a letter he had received from Osro Cobb, the U.S. attorney in Little Rock, Arkansas. Cobb discussed a talk he had had with Sen. John L. McClellan (D—Arkansas). McClellan expressed concern over Campbell's nomination and said that he thought that Campbell could not be confirmed. Cobb wrote: "The Senator pointed out that the position of Comptroller General is directly responsible to the Congress and not to the Executive. It was his thinking that if someone with congressional experience were nominated by the President that it would greatly help in obtaining confirmation." Cobb reported that McClellan thought that Sen. Guy Cordon (R—Oregon), recently defeated for reelection, would be a good choice for comptroller general and would be easily confirmed if nominated. McClellan asked Cobb to pass on to Hall the suggestion that Campbell's nomination be withdrawn and Cordon nominated in his place.[8]

---

[6]Telegram, Carey to the president, November 9,1954, Papers of Dwight D. Eisenhower, White House Central Files, General Files, Box 64, Eisenhower Presidential Library, Abilene, KS; letter, Andrews to the president, November 17, 1954, Eisenhower Papers, White House Central Files, Official File, Box 334; and letter, Seidman to the president, November 9, 1954, Eisenhower Papers, White House Central Files, General Files, Box 64. Andrews worked for Comptroller General Warren from 1945 to 1947 as director of the Corporation Audits Division.

[7]Memorandum, Willis to Adams, November 17, 1954, Eisenhower Papers, White House Central Files, Official File, Box 334.

[8]Letter, Cobb to Hall, December 8, 1954, Eisenhower Papers, White House Central Files, GF15-F-Arkansas, Eastern District.

Campbell and the Dixon-Yates Affair

The controversy over the nomination took place in the press and behind the scenes in Congress from the time of Campbell's initial selection until his confirmation several months later. Campbell's involvement in the Dixon-Yates affair was a contentious issue. Some years earlier, the Tennessee Valley Authority (TVA) had agreed to provide the city of Memphis with electric power and had proposed to build a steam power plant in Tennessee to generate the power. The Eisenhower administration, favoring private power interests, proposed that the AEC buy power from private companies and sell it to Memphis.

Edgar H. Dixon, president of the Middle South Utility System, and Eugene A. Yates, chairman of the Southern Company, represented the private utilities involved in the contract. TVA supporters saw the Dixon-Yates contract as a Republican attempt to destroy the agency and argued that the AEC was about to become involved in unauthorized activities. Before the five-member Atomic Energy Commission, the proposal received support only from the chairman, Lewis L. Strauss, and Commissioner Joseph Campbell. The unresolved Dixon-Yates matter brought immediate opposition from some Democrats. Sen. Estes Kefauver (D—Tennessee), a very vocal opponent of the Dixon-Yates contract, said that Campbell's support of it was a "substantial mark of disqualification" and called for an investigation of his record. Rep. Chet E. Holifield (D—California), a leading member of the congressional Joint Committee on Atomic Energy, after referring to the Dixon-Yates affair, described the Campbell nomination as "a travesty on justice."[9]

GAO, headed by Acting Comptroller General Frank H. Weitzel, had issued critical reports on the Dixon-Yates contract. One Washington paper observed: ". . . GAO officials are in a position of having criticized as contrary to the Government's interests provisions of a contract which had been endorsed by their boss-designate."[10]

---

[9]Clippings, *Washington Daily News*, November 9, 1954 (Kefauver quotation), and *Washington Post and Times-Herald*, November 9 and November 10, 1954 (Holifield quotation), all in clippings files, GAO History Program Archives; and Mosher, *GAO*, 160-61. See also Aaron Wildavsky, *Dixon-Yates Controversy: A Study in Power Politics* (New Haven: Yale University Press, 1962).

[10]Clipping, *Washington Star*, November 21, 1954 (quotation) and clipping, *Washington Post and Times-Herald*, November 9, 1954, both in clippings files, GAO History Program Archives. See the comments on GAO's work on Dixon-Yates in GAO, *John P. Abbadessa, 1947-1962*, GAO History Program, Oral History Series, GAO/OP-18-OH (Washington: 1990), 33-37. An example of GAO's Dixon-Yates reports was a report to Representative Holifield entitled *"Dixon-Yates" Proposal to Supply Electrical Energy Under Contract* (B-120188, June 1, 1954).

Nomination Hearings and Confirmation

When the Senate Committee on Government Operations held hearings on Campbell's nomination on February 2 and March 3, 1955, the Dixon-Yates matter and other questions were thoroughly aired. Sen. John L. McClellan, the chairman of the committee, referred to Campbell's numerous connections with businesses and other organizations and wondered if they might constitute conflicts of interest. While Campbell did not agree that he had a conflict-of-interest problem, he provided McClellan with a list of his associations with businesses and other organizations and said that he would resign from all of them.[11]

Some committee members questioned Campbell's lack of legal training, noting that all previous comptrollers general had been lawyers and that the comptroller general had to make many legal decisions. Sen. Henry Jackson (D—Washington), describing the position of comptroller general as a "quasi-judicial office," asked Campbell if his lack of legal training would make it hard for him to sign judicial decisions. Campbell responded that he had often worked with lawyers and that making the final decisions was his re-sponsibility. He added that he could rely on the GAO general counsel's office for legal advice. Campbell also explained that his duties at Columbia University required him to be familiar with decisions of the comptroller gen-eral and with GAO's functions related to government contracting.[12]

In a subsequent letter to McClellan, Campbell separated the comptroller general's functions into five categories—administrative, legal, investigative, accounting, and auditing. He noted that of GAO's total staff of 5,784, 673 were engaged in legal or quasi-legal work and 5,101 were engaged in the other areas. He pointed out that Frank Weitzel, the assistant comptroller general, "is a lawyer of outstanding ability" with 30 years of GAO experi-ence, and he mentioned General Counsel Edwin Lyle Fisher and his staff of more than 100 lawyers.[13]

At the February 2 hearing, Sen. Margaret Chase Smith (R—Maine) op-posed Campbell because he had not been chosen by Congress. Smith said, "the Comptroller General is accountable to Congress. He is an agent of Congress and not an agent of the President, which would mean to me that the choice should come from the Congress rather than the President." Smith

---

[11]*Nomination of Joseph Campbell*, hearing day of February 2, 1955, 8-10, 40 (copy of letter, Campbell to McClellan, February 3, 1955).

[12]Ibid., 6, 15-17.

[13]Ibid., hearing day of March 3, 1955, with letter, Campbell to McClellan, February 8, 1955, 38-39.

also complained because President Eisenhower had not consulted with anyone in Congress about Campbell's nomination.[14]

Sen. Stuart Symington (D—Missouri) questioned Campbell about the
Dixon-Yates contract. Campbell stated that the contract was actually better
than some others the AEC had entered into because it included both an arbi-
tration clause and a ceiling on costs. Symington badgered Campbell about
his reasons for leaving the AEC. Campbell suggested that one reason was
that the AEC general manager, rather than the five commissioners, did most
of the administrative and supervisory work. In his previous work, Campbell
explained, administration and supervision had been his responsibility, and
he preferred it that way. When Symington asked him if he agreed that perhaps the most important function of the comptroller general was to be an
agent of Congress, Campbell answered affirmatively.[15]

Although Campbell spent most of the first day's hearing defending himself, he did receive strong support from Republican Sen. Bourke B.
Hickenlooper of Iowa. Hickenlooper stated that as a member of the Joint
Committee on Atomic Energy, he had known Campbell since 1953. He said
that he had been very impressed with how fast Campbell learned AEC's
work and with Campbell's performance on the commission. "I can only say
to the committee," Hickenlooper added, "that there is no man in government
for whom I have formed a higher opinion. . . . No Commissioner has come
in . . . and has more quickly acquired a grasp of the general situations which
came within his view than Mr. Campbell." Responding to Senator Jackson's
comments about Campbell's lack of legal experience, Hickenlooper said that
he did not think that this would be a problem.[16]

Chairman McClellan submitted for the record a letter he had received
from Maurice H. Stans, president of the American Institute of Accountants.
Stans stressed the importance of having a certified public accountant as comptroller general, noting GAO's work in corporation auditing and the cooperative program to improve accounting in the federal government. Stans strongly
endorsed Campbell, describing him as "eminently qualified" to serve as comptroller general.[17]

---

[14]Ibid., hearing day of February 2, 1955, 14. See also clipping, *Washington Post*, February 3, 1955,
in clippings files, GAO History Program Archives.

[15]*Nomination of Joseph Campbell*, hearing day of February 2, 1955, ibid., 10-18; and clipping, *Washington Post*, February 3, 1955, clippings files, GAO History Program Archives.

[16]*Nomination of Joseph Campbell*, hearing day of February 2, 1955, 21-22.

[17]Ibid., with letter, Stans to McClellan, January 28, 1955, 19-20.

At the hearings on March 3, 1955, Sen. Albert Gore (D—Tennessee), made the major statement. Gore reviewed the legislative history of the Budget and Accounting Act, 1921, to point out that the comptroller general was a creation of Congress. "The General Accounting Office was specifically created by the Congress as its agent, or watchdog . . . ," he observed, adding that the terms of the law were set to ensure the independence of the comptroller general. He referred to "a sort of gentlemen's understanding" that the comptroller general would be chosen on the recommendation of Congress. "Advice and consent with respect to the Comptroller General . . . has never been treated as a mere matter of confirmation. It must not be so treated now."[18]

Gore said that he did not oppose Campbell on partisan or personal grounds or because of the Dixon-Yates affair, although Dixon-Yates "has by no means added luster to his record." Rather, he felt that Campbell lacked the essential background in legal and legislative affairs. Campbell's record, Gore asserted, "is devoid of experiences calculated to steep him in the tradition of the Congress and the urgency for its independence; devoid, too, of experience in interpretation of legislative intent as well as of legal training or judicial review. Not only is the nominee without these essential qualifications, but he comes directly from the Executive, which violates another unwritten law in respect to appointment to the position of Comptroller." Finally, Gore suggested that Congress had been losing power to the executive branch. He observed, "If we are to lose control of the one and only agency delegated by law the responsibility to review the expenditures of funds and the administration of laws in conformity with the intent of Congress, and responsible to the Congress therefor, then the checks and balances between the executive and legislative are seriously endangered."[19]

On March 10, 1955, the Senate Committee on Government Operations voted 8 to 4 to report Campbell's nomination favorably to the Senate.[20] On March 18, 1955, when the Senate debated the nomination, Senator Gore reiterated his previous arguments against Campbell and Senator Kefauver criticized Campbell for his role in the Dixon-Yates affair. Sen. William Langer (R—North Dakota) agreed with Kefauver on Dixon-Yates, saying, "If a man will take orders, as a member of the Atomic Energy Commission, and enter into a contract because he is ordered to do so by the President of the United States, what assurance has this body that he will not act in a similar manner as Comptroller General?" Langer added that while he did not think that

---

[18]Ibid., hearing day of March 3, 1955, 25-26.
[19]Ibid., 27-28, 36.
[20]*Congressional Record*, 84th Cong., 1st Sess., vol. 101, pt. 3, March 10, 1955, 3164.

Campbell was the best-qualified person for the position, he was an outstanding man who would do a good job. Both Senator Hickenlooper and Senator Payne strongly supported Campbell. Ultimately the Senate confirmed him by voice vote, with only about two dozen senators present.[21]

Management Style and Approach

As the top manager in GAO, Campbell was clearly in control. He immersed himself in the various aspects of GAO's work and paid attention to the many minute details of GAO's daily activity. He undertook a major reorganization of GAO within a year of entering office, to clarify divisional responsibilities and to clean up areas he considered to be problems.[22] Commenting on GAO's 35th anniversary in mid-1956, after he had been in office about a year and a half, Campbell wrote:

> A review of the impressive record of accomplishments in the first 35 years suggests a guiding principle for the future. Simply stated, it may be said that continued progress will require us to change as the world around us changes and that leadership will be retained only by those who foresee the necessity for changes and accomplish them in an orderly manner. It is this constant searching for new ideas and means of improving our work which will continue to keep us in the vanguard of our field of endeavor.[23]

Campbell recognized early in his term the need for GAO to evolve in response to the demands of its environment and in terms of the nature and the quality of its work and the capabilities of its management and staff. During his term of more than a decade, he had a profound personal impact on GAO and helped prepare the organization to meet the challenges that were to come after he departed.

The Independence of GAO

One thing that Campbell felt very strongly about and consistently emphasized was the need to safeguard the independence of GAO. To Campbell, independence meant maintaining a strict aloofness from the executive agencies that were the subjects of GAO audits, investigations, and other reports. As Campbell explained it,

---

[21]Ibid., March 18, 1955, 3142-65. See also clipping, *New York Times*, March 19, 1955, in file, Clippings CG [Campbell] 1954-1962, GAO History Program Archives.

[22]For Campbell's reorganization, see chapter 17, pp. 416-20.

[23]Campbell, *Watchdog* (June 1956), reprinted in *GAO Review* (summer 1971): 94-95.

As auditors, our men are just as independent as accountants in public practice. We always have to remember that in matters affecting the many contracts between government and business we are in between the contractor and the agency. A contractor who thinks he has not been treated fairly, or a low bidder who had not been awarded a contract, must feel that he can come to GAO for justice; so we have to be completely independent of the agencies in the executive branch.[24]

During the first year of his term, one newspaper that had raised questions about Campbell's appointment because of his "rubber-stamp record as a member of the Atomic Energy Commission" praised him: "He has been truly independent and has construed the law as he has seen it without regard to the wishes of the administration."[25] John Abbadessa, who came to GAO in 1947 and progressed rapidly to senior management positions under Campbell, commented that "independence has been a byword from the day I walked into GAO. . . . When Joe Campbell showed up, I mean it became almost a religion, emphasized maybe a little bit too much."[26]

Another senior GAO official, Arthur Schoenhaut, noted that after Campbell became comptroller general, it became obvious "that you could not socialize with the agency people. You sure couldn't socialize with any of their contractors." Schoenhaut explained that on one occasion, a GAO audit group at the Bureau of Public Roads, of which he was a part, joined a bowling team at the Bureau. Campbell learned of this and asked Schoenhaut to come to his office. "He asked me whether I wanted a career as a bowler or as an accountant. I told him I wanted to be an accountant. He said, 'Okay, then get your crew out of that bowling league,' which we immediately did."[27]

Attitude Toward Foreign Visitors and Assistance to Foreign Countries

Perhaps Campbell's insistence that GAO maintain its independence determined his attitude toward foreign visitors to GAO and assistance by the Office to foreign countries. Throughout his term, he showed little enthusi-

---

[24]Clipping, "Governmental Accounting," an interview with Joseph Campbell, reprinted in *Journal of Accountancy* (March 1957): 6, in Clippings CG [Campbell] 1954-1962, GAO History Program Archives.

[25]Clipping, *Raleigh (NC) News and Observer*, September 3, 1955, in the Papers of Lindsay C. Warren, Southern Historical Collection, Wilson Library, University of North Carolina at Chapel Hill, Scrapbooks, vol. 17 (hereafter cited as Warren Papers).

[26]GAO, *John P. Abbadessa*, 10.

[27]GAO, *Arthur Schoenhaut*, GAO History Program, Oral History Series, GAO/OP-4-OH (Washington: 1988), 17.

asm for receiving foreign visitors and participating in international accounting and auditing activities. His general approach was that such activities took too much time and did not bring positive results to GAO. For example, when Ellsworth H. Morse, Jr., the director of the Accounting and Auditing Policy Staff, told Campbell in 1957 that he had a request from a man from Formosa to do a six-week internship at GAO, the comptroller general said that he was concerned about GAO's apparent open-door policy for visitors. As Morse noted, "Mr. Campbell's concern is that a considerable amount of high-grade time seems to be going into talking with such visitors."[28]   In response to a request from an International Cooperation Administration (ICA) official for a GAO speaker at an accounting workshop for foreign visitors, Campbell told Morse that he thought that high-grade staff should not take this kind of assignment and that if it was necessary, GS-11s and GS-12s ought to be used.[29]

Campbell was not pleased when he learned from Morse of the visit to GAO of Danielette Jackson, the auditor-general of Liberia, in December 1960. Mrs. Jackson did not meet Campbell, and even Morse did not realize that she was coming until she was already in the GAO Building talking with a policy staff member. Mrs. Jackson was particularly critical of the ICA programs in Liberia and asked about GAO's audit responsibility for these programs.[30]

In July 1961, the auditor general of New South Wales, Australia visited GAO for several days but apparently did not see Campbell. The auditor general did ask Morse if he could have a copy of the GAO *Report Manual*. Morse discussed this request with Campbell and noted in his daily record: "Mr. Campbell indicated no enthusiasm for giving him a copy of the manual and it was agreed not to do anything about it further unless a written request is made."[31]

Campbell also exhibited no interest in the International Organization of Supreme Audit Institutions (INTOSAI). This group, founded in the early 1950s with headquarters in Vienna, Austria, held triennial congresses, the first in Cuba in 1953. Morse discussed with Campbell the possibility of GAO representatives attending the 5th INTOSAI congress, scheduled for 1965. Morse and Campbell agreed that the State Department Bureau of International Conferences ought to determine who from the United States should attend. As Morse recorded, "Mr. Campbell . . . commented that he

---

[28]Entry for February 12, 1957, Morse, *Daily Notes*, 1957-1958. See appendix I for information on Morse's daily notes.

[29]Entries for March 6 and 7, 1957, ibid.

[30]Entry for December 30, 1960, Morse, *Daily Notes*, 1959-1960.

[31]Entry for July 7, 1961, Morse, *Daily Notes*, 1961-1962.

Assistant Comptroller General Weitzel with visiting accountants from Denmark, 1954.

did not think our office ought to have to meet with the foreign representatives on such a matter" and "expressed some reservations about all the time we had to spend on foreign visitors."[32]

Staff Participation in Professional Associations

Campbell's concern about participation of GAO staff in some professional associations, especially the Federal Government Accountants Association (FGAA), was related, at least in part, to his determination to preserve GAO's independence. Although a 1957 policy statement approved by Campbell encouraged GAO staff to join organizations as part of their personal and professional development, participation was acceptable "where the time and effort required involves no conflict with the official duties and responsibilities of General Accounting Office employees."[33]

Campbell's concern with FGAA apparently reflected his conviction that it was not a reputable professional organization, even though many GAO officials belonged to it. Morse recounted a conversation with Campbell about the FGAA:

> He stated that he did not see how we were going to be helped very much and even suggested that such association with FGAA might be a hindrance from the standpoint that employees of other Government agencies who are members of FGAA are less qualified and capable and in the eyes of state board officials all Federal accountants tend to be colored with the same brush. In other words, GAO auditors are likely to be judged by the fact that they are directly associated with other accountants in the Government.[34]

On another occasion, Campbell raised with Morse his concern about the number of GAO officials who made speeches before FGAA chapters. Morse wrote, "Mr. Campbell seems to be thoroughly unimpressed with the nature of any contribution or benefit that the FGAA as an organization can render to us."[35] When Morse told Campbell that he had been invited to speak at an FGAA symposium, "Mr. Campbell stated that he thought that I had too many other things to do to be concerned with speeches before this association."[36] Campbell also worried about the absence of GAO staff from their official

---

[32]Entries for October 23 and November 2, 1964, Morse, *Daily Notes*, 1963-1964.

[33]Entry for May 23, 1957, Morse, *Daily Notes*, 1957-1958.

[34]Entry for December 4, 1957, ibid.

[35]Entry for March 5, 1958, ibid.

[36]Entry for November 19, 1958, ibid.

duties and the cost of their travel when attending FGAA meetings during work hours or travel out of Washington for such functions.[37]

One matter that did cause Campbell to encourage GAO participation in certain other professional associations was his desire to expand the number of certified public accountants (CPA) at GAO. He approved membership in the American Institute of Certified Public Accountants (AICPA) and its local branch in the District of Columbia. Campbell was especially interested in gaining AICPA support for the concept of crediting government service toward the experience required in most states for granting CPA status. Campbell said that it would be a good idea if more GAO staff joined the local institute.[38]

Campbell worked both to increase the number of CPAs at GAO and to persuade individual states to recognize GAO experience as qualifying for the CPA certificate. GAO began a CPA training course for its staff in 1957, and the Office continued to try to persuade states to recognize GAO experience. Campbell reported in 1962 that GAO auditors could obtain the CPA certificate in 34 states on the basis of GAO experience or upon meeting educational requirements.[39]

Relationships with GAO's Divisions and Regions

Campbell's approach to the everyday operations of GAO offices and division was double sided: He expected office and division heads to manage their work without his direct intervention, but he kept himself closely informed about division activity and raised questions when he thought that he needed more information. It was clear to GAO's managers that he was the boss and that if things did not proceed according to his liking, he would intervene. John Abbadessa, who served as director of the Transportation Division and deputy director of the Civil Accounting and Auditing Division (CAAD) under Campbell, observed: "My impression of Mr. Campbell was that he let the division directors do their thing. I think he was satisfied that he had essentially competent people. . . . He made some broad suggestions, but my observation was he didn't tell any of the division directors what to

---

[37]GAO, *Arthur Schoenhaut*, 19.

[38]Ibid., 19; and entries for December 17 and December 23, 1957, and February 4, 1958, Morse, *Daily Notes, 1957-1958*.

[39]Meeting of September 13, 1956, Morse, *Notes of Meetings of the Accounting and Auditing Division Heads, September 1956 through June 1957*. See Appendix I for information on this source. See also testimony of Campbell et al., February 9, 1962, *Independent Offices Appropriations for 1963*, Hearings before a Subcommittee of the House Committee on Appropriations, 87th Cong., 2d Sess., 1962, pt. 2 (Washington: GPO, 1962), 75. See chapter 17, pp. 439-44, for a discussion of training programs during the Campbell period.

do, but he was intensely interested in what went out in reports. If a report was criticized, he wanted to be damn sure it was right."[40] Arthur Schoenhaut, like Abbadessa a deputy director of CAAD, reported that Campbell put individuals he considered best in positions and except for overall policy guidance, let them do the job. "If they didn't do the job, he got rid of them." Both Abbadessa and Schoenhaut noted that Campbell would get involved directly in particular jobs only if there was special congressional interest.[41]

Adolph T. Samuelson, director of CAAD through most of Campbell's term, confirmed that the comptroller general placed responsibility on managers and followed up to make sure that they were carrying out that responsibility. "He did that through his close contact with what was being worked on and with the reports that were going to come out of it. He followed up on reports very religiously in my case, anyway." Samuelson described Campbell as "pretty tough" in his review of Civil Division reports. He would call Samuelson on the "squawk box" to inquire if reports scheduled to be released in a certain month did not appear on time.[42]

The squawk box was a voice intercom system used at GAO to connect Campbell with selected top officials. He called people without warning on the squawk box, seeking information on ongoing work and other matters. J. Kenneth Fasick, who headed the Navy group in the Defense Accounting and Auditing Division, reported that Campbell would call him occasionally about jobs in progress "and you had to know it" when he called. Fasick said that he had devised a flip chart system with information on each ongoing job so that he could get up-to-date data quickly when Campbell called.[43]

Campbell had his favorites among the higher officials- -Robert F. Keller, his general counsel; Ellsworth "Mose" Morse; Abbadessa; and Samuelson, among others. Victor Lowe, who served in both CAAD and the International Division under Campbell, observed that during that period, "the Cabots spoke to the Lodges and the Lodges spoke only to God. . . . [Campbell] didn't have much to do with anybody else except his Division Directors and his General Counsel people."[44] Schoenhaut recounted details of an occasion when he asked Keller to suggest something to Campbell. Keller responded, "you

[40]GAO, *John P. Abbadessa*, 23.

[41]GAO, *Arthur Schoenhaut*, 2.

[42]GAO, *Adolph T. Samuelson, 1946-1975*, GAO History Program, Oral History Series, GAO/OP-11-OH (Washington: 1989), 7-8, 15-16, 18.

[43]GAO, *International Activities, 1959-1981: Interview with James A. Duff, J. Kenneth Fasick, and Charles D. Hylander*, GAO History Program, Oral History Series, GAO/OP-19-OH (Washington: 1991), 27.

[44]GAO, *The Civil Division, 1956-1972: Interview with Gregory J. Ahart, Henry Eschwege, and Victor L. Lowe*, GAO History Program, Oral History Series, GAO/OP-22-OH (Washington: 1992), 120.

don't suggest anything to him. If he asks me, I'll tell him what I think."
Keller added, "You remember that; don't you ever suggest anything to him."[45]

Campbell did appear intimidating to some people, including some of his
top managers. John E. Thornton, long-time director of the Field Operations
Division (FOD), stated: "When you went in to see Joe, you kind of grabbed
your chair a little bit; you felt a little bit ill at ease at times."[46] Thomas E.
Sullivan, director of the Transportation Division for a time under Campbell,
stated that many people were "scared" of Campbell, including himself: "Like
most people, I was scared to death of him, but we did get along well. He
called me into his office from time to time to chat." Explaining why people
were intimidated by Campbell, Sullivan suggested that "Campbell had an
austere Brahmin-like personality, coming out of Columbia University and
the eastern establishment."[47]

Campbell was very much interested in GAO's regional offices and had a
special relationship with the regional managers. He considered them his
direct representatives in the field. He presided over periodic meetings of the
regional managers, both in Washington and at other locations. Thornton,
FOD director, observed that "the field was kind of his pet, in a way. He
never believed everything he heard in Washington; he did not feel that way
about the field."[48] When regional managers visited Washington headquarters individually, they always went in to see Campbell. Walter H. Henson,
who served in the Seattle office and as regional manager at New Orleans
under Campbell, stated that "Mr. Campbell had a very, very detailed and
acute knowledge of the field people."[49]

Beginning in 1956, the heads of headquarters accounting and auditing
divisions began to meet regularly to discuss current important issues.
Campbell usually did not attend these meetings, chaired by Ellsworth Morse,
because he preferred to give the division heads the opportunity to discuss
matters without feeling inhibited by his presence. These meetings, which
Morse summarized for Campbell after they took place, continued through-

[45]GAO, *Arthur Schoenhaut*, 21.

[46]GAO, *John E. Thornton, 1935-1976*, GAO History Program, Oral History Series, GAO/OP-3-OH (Washington: 1988), 90.

[47]GAO, *Transportation Activities, 1946-1975: Interview with Joseph P. Normile, Fred J. Shafer, and Thomas E. Sullivan*, GAO History Program, Oral History Series, GAO/OP-24-OH (Washington: 1992), 35.

[48]GAO, *John Thornton*, 15.

[49]GAO, *Regional Offices and the Field Operations Division: Interview with Francis X. Fee, Walter H. Henson, and Hyman L. Krieger*, GAO History Program, Oral History Series, GAO/OP-15-OH (Washington: 1990), 13, 15.

out the rest of his term.[50] For a time, Campbell hosted a series of luncheons, where a GAO official discussed a particular project that engaged his organization at the moment.[51] Also, Campbell had a large map installed in the executive suite, indicating all locations, at home and abroad, where GAO currently had work under way. He found this map very useful in explaining GAO activities to visitors to his office.[52] He also fostered the development of GAO's two libraries, one for law and one for financial, accounting, and auditing materials. In 1963, these two collections were consolidated into one location in the GAO Building.[53]

Relationships with the GAO Staff

Campbell had a reputation for aloofness among GAO's rank-and-file staff. On occasion, he had a direct impact on their personal and professional lives. For example, he let it be known that he had rules for dress for GAO staff. These rules were not necessarily inconsistent with prevailing practices in the government at the time. For men, sport, colored, and short-sleeved shirts and sports jackets were out; he favored white shirts and suits.[54] If Campbell learned about what he considered improper behavior by a staff member, even outside duty hours, he looked into it and went so far on occasion as to have the person dismissed. One GAO official reported in this regard, "There was no second chance, no drawn-out procedure about it. It was 'bang' and you were fired."[55]

Henry Eschwege, who held supervisory positions in the Civil Division under Campbell, noted that once he had been called in to answer questions about a GS-7 on his staff. According to Eschwege, Campbell "allegedly . . . was very much concerned about people and their personal lives, as well as their conduct on the job. The rumors were probably much embellished compared with what was really going on, but it created a lot of fear amongst us younger staff members about our conduct."[56]

---

[50]Meetings of September 13, 1956, and April 16, 1957, Morse, *Notes of Meetings of the Accounting and Auditing Division Heads, September 1956 through June 1957*; and entry for April 8, 1957, Morse, *Daily Notes, 1957-1958*.

[51]Entry for January 24, 1961, Morse, *Daily Notes*, 1961-1962.

[52]Entry for October 29, 1957, Morse, *Daily Notes*, 1957-1958; and entries for January 9, October 20, and November 6, 1959, Morse, *Daily Notes*, 1959-1960.

[53]Entries for August 19, September 6, and October 23, 1963, Morse, *Daily Notes*, 1963-1964. Later, after Campbell left GAO, the collection was divided again into two separate libraries.

[54]GAO, *Arthur Schoenhaut*, 18; and GAO, *Audit and Legal Services, 1943-1983—a Women's Perspective: Interview with Margaret L. Macfarlane, Geraldine M. Rubar, and Stella B. Shea*, GAO History Program, Oral History Series, GAO/OP-10-OH (Washington: 1990), 26.

[55]GAO, *The Civil Division*, 120; and GAO, *Transportation Activities*, 36.

[56]GAO, *The Civil Division*, 117.

Campbell regularly involved himself in decisions on staff promotions. He sometimes wanted to know how many reports the recommended staff member had gotten out, and he was particularly preoccupied with prospective promotees' sick leave records. Often when supervisory officials or even division directors took promotion recommendations to Campbell for his approval, he would want to examine the candidate's sick leave record. Thomas Sullivan, director of the Transportation Division, noted that he had to have Campbell's permission even to promote a staff member in the lower ranks. As Sullivan put it, "We had no latitude at all. He would always bring up . . . what the person's [sick] leave record was."[57] Victor Lowe of the Civil Division observed that when a staff member reached the grade 12 level, "you used to have to write up a recommendation for promotion and make the person look like he or she walked on water before you could get him or her promoted. . . . If that 'J.C.' [Campbell's initials] wasn't on there, it didn't go through, I'll guarantee you."[58]

Another thing that bothered Campbell was the departure of staff whom he valued for positions in other organizations. One example was Walter F. Frese, who headed the Accounting Systems Division between 1948 and 1956. In 1956, Frese informed Campbell that he had been offered a professorship at Harvard University; indicated that he wanted to take it; and suggested arranging a time-table, extending over two or three months, for his departure. As stated by another GAO official, "Campbell was reported to have said, 'How about tonight?' and that was the end of that."[59]

A similar case involved John Abbadessa, a Campbell favorite, who received an offer in 1962, after 15 years of GAO service, to be comptroller at the AEC. As a GAO staff member, Abbadessa had worked extensively on AEC audits. Campbell suggested to Abbadessa that the AEC job was not a good one and offered to promote him to GS-18, the top rank at GAO. As Abbadessa reported it, after he told Campbell he had decided to take the AEC job, ". . . I became persona non grata. . . . When he figured out that I was serious, he wanted me out of here 'yesterday.'"[60] There was a party for Abbadessa when he left, attended by about 200 people. Because of Campbell's attitude, the party had to be arranged without publicity and most of GAO's top officials, who knew Abbadessa well, did not attend. One who did was Arthur Schoenhaut, a close associate of Abbadessa in the Civil Divi-

[57]GAO, *Transportation Activities*, 36. For other evidence on this topic, see GAO, *Defense-Related Audits,* 43; GAO, *Policy Guidance, 1963-1986: Interview with Donald J. Horan, Eugene L. Pahl, and Allen R. Voss*, GAO History Program, Oral History Series, GAO/OP-23-OH (Washington: 1992), 18; and entries for June 19 and July 1, 1958, Morse, *Daily Notes, 1957-1958.*

[58]GAO, *The Civil Division*, 122.

[59]Ibid., 10.

[60]GAO, *John P. Abbadessa*, 47.

GAO employees at work in GAO's headquarters building during Campbell's tenure.

sion. "If you left GAO under Campbell," Schoenhaut observed, "you were considered stupid, unless he wanted you to leave."[61]

Campbell did make an effort to welcome new staff to GAO. Donald J. Horan, who joined GAO as an auditor in 1955, recalled that the comptroller general tried to meet new staff personally during their first year in the office and occasionally entertained them in his home in Georgetown.[62] Campbell also visited the training sessions attended by new staff.

Congressional Relations

Campbell enjoyed good relations with Congress throughout most of his term. The experience of the confirmation hearings themselves, where there was much discussion of GAO's independence from the executive branch and its statutory ties to Congress, could not help impressing on Campbell the importance of close relations with the legislative body. For almost all of Campbell's term, the Democrats controlled both houses of Congress, while Campbell was a Republican, appointed by a Republican president.[63] He worked hard to sustain and improve GAO's relationships with Congress.

Testifying early in his term, Campbell emphasized GAO's intention to serve Congress. After observing that Congress was turning more and more to GAO "as its independent facility for obtaining impartial analysis and appraisal of financial and administrative problems involved in legislation . . . ," Campbell stated that he and GAO had the responsibility "to render as much service as possible to the Congress and its committees in the form of reports and assistance. I understand this function was greatly developed by my esteemed predecessor. It is my intention to continue to emphasize and develop this phase of the work."[64]

At this hearing, the question of timeliness of GAO reports to Congress came up. Robert L. Long, director of audits at GAO, said that GAO was trying to get its reports to Congress delivered in time to be of use. "I do not think any of us are satisfied, yet, that we are as current as we would like to be and as we intend to be, in getting the information up to Congress," Long added.[65]

---

[61]Ibid., 46-48; and GAO, *Arthur Schoenhaut*, 55-56.

[62]Horan statement to the author, November 1995.

[63]Mosher, *GAO*, 137.

[64]Testimony of Campbell and others, February 22, 1955, *Independent Offices Appropriations for 1956*, Hearings before a Subcommittee of the House Committee on Appropriations, 84th Cong., 1st Sess., pt. 1 (Washington: GPO, 1955), 723-24.

[65]Long testimony, February 22, 1955, ibid., 788.

During testimony in subsequent years, Campbell invariably mentioned the continuing expansion of GAO's service to Congress. In 1962, he stated, "In planning our programs, we take into consideration the known needs and desires of the Congress. We feel that the effectiveness of our congressional service is continually improving and the steady increase in the utilization of our services is evidence of our progress."[66] While the number of congressional requests for reports gradually increased during the Campbell years, the bulk of GAO's work was generated either by standing laws or was self-initiated. In 1961, Campbell estimated that GAO did 5 percent or 6 percent of its work at the direct request of Congress. In 1964, he told a House committee that "substantially all of our program is by our own choosing. We do have increasing interest and suggestions from Congress both from the legislative committees, and the Appropriations committees, but our program generally is our own program." He added that GAO's own program happened "to agree pretty much with the ideas of the committees."[67] (By the early 1990s, more than 80 percent of GAO's work was at the request of Congress).

Early in his term, Campbell formalized the organizational structure responsible for direct GAO contacts with Congress. He established the Office of Legislative Liaison (OLL) in 1956 "in order to bring about an even closer relationship between the Congress and the General Accounting Office." Campbell charged OLL with the responsibility for keeping congressional committees current on information emanating from GAO work and ascertaining committee interests so that they could be reflected in GAO's work program.[68] Before 1956, GAO's legislative liaison activities were the responsibility of a small staff of assistants, usually lawyers, in the immediate office of the comptroller general, including for many years Robert F. Keller. After Campbell appointed Keller as general counsel, Keller took the legislative liaison function with him to the Office of the General Counsel.[69]

GAO under Campbell measured its assistance to Congress in terms of quantitative accomplishments—reports issued to Congress and its committees, investigations undertaken, testimony given, other work completed, and

---

[66]Campbell testimony, February 9, 1962, *Independent Offices Appropriations for 1963*, pt. 2, 15.

[67]Campbell testimony, March 15, 1961, *Independent Offices Appropriations for 1961*, Hearings before a Subcommittee of the House Committee on Appropriations, 86th Cong., 2d Sess., pt. 1 (Washington: GPO, 1960), 313; and Campbell testimony, February 6, 1964, *Legislative Branch Appropriations for 1965*, Hearings before a Subcommittee of the House Committee on Appropriations, 88th Cong., 2d Sess. (Washington: GPO, 1964), 24.

[68]*Annual Report of the Comptroller General of the United States for the Fiscal Year Ending June 30, 1957* (Washington: GPO, 1957), 9.

[69]Entry for December 5, 1956, Morse, *Daily Notes*, 1956; and Roger L. Sperry, Timothy D. Desmond, Kathi F. McGraw, and Barbara Schmitt, *GAO 1966-1981: An Administrative History* (Washington: GAO, 1981), 28. In the 1970s, OLL was renamed the Office of Congressional Relations.

money saved by the federal government. Campbell reported statistics on these activities in each of his annual reports. To cite an example, the annual report for fiscal year 1962 listed these accomplishments: refunds, collections, and measurable savings of nearly $162,875,000, a return of four to one over the amount spent to achieve these savings; 766 examinations, reviews, and audits at 411 plants and offices of defense contractors and at 96 plants and offices of civil agency contractors; 459 reviews at 1,359 civil agency locations; 152 reviews at 611 military installations; audits of 4.5 million bills of lading for freight shipments and 2.3 million transportation requests for passenger travel; 4,487 legal decisions and related matters; 822 legislative and legal reports to committees and members of Congress; 133 reports to the director, Bureau of the Budget, on proposed, pending, or enrolled bills and on legal questions; settlement of 15,097 general claims against the United States, certifying $50,617,957 for payment; settlement of 57,247 claims by the United States, collecting $6,233,491; 271 reports on audits or investigations to congressional sources (130 of them on civil agencies, 138 on the Department of Defense, and three on both); 548 reports to officials of various agencies; and assignment of 158 GAO staff to congressional committees.[70]

Among the special ways that GAO increased its assistance to Congress under Campbell was the detailing of staff upon request to congressional committees, a practice that had been used in earlier years. Assistant Comptroller General Weitzel testified in 1961 that GAO's loan of staff to congressional committees was much larger than it had been and added, "we have completely changed our approach so that we are trying to put the needs and the interests of Congress first in all of our audit and investigative work."[71]

During fiscal year 1957, GAO detailed 107 staff for varying periods of time to three Senate committees, four House committees, and one joint committee. The largest number—61 accountants, investigators, and stenographers—worked for the Senate Permanent Subcommittee on Investigations. Seventeen staff went to the House Committee on Appropriations. Salaries and travel expenses for these 107 staff totaled $198,209. GAO received reimbursement from the committees of $15,190, leaving a net cost to GAO of $183,019.[72] Six years later, the number of detailees had increased significantly. GAO assigned 181 staff to five Senate committees, seven House committees, and two joint committees—155 accountants, 16 investigators, and ten others. The largest numbers still went to the Senate Permanent Sub-

[70]*Annual Report of the Comptroller General of the United States for the Fiscal Year Ended June 30, 1962* (Washington: GPO, 1962), 1.

[71]Weitzel, testimony, March 15, 1961, *Independent Offices Appropriations for 1961*, pt. 1, 314.

[72]GAO, *Annual Report 1957*, 260.

committee on Investigations and the House Appropriations Committee. The net expenditure by GAO for these staff was $484,090 for the year.[73] The detailees varied in rank, but the committees preferred-higher graded people. GAO generally accommodated them, even though on occasion a committee asked a detailee to perform duties that could be accomplished by a lower-graded staffer. GAO tried to work with the committees to develop detailee work programs and grade levels.[74]

Campbell was especially interested in providing comments to Congress on proposed legislation. The Office of the General Counsel coordinated the development of comments, with input from the Defense and Civil divisions and the Accounting and Auditing Policy Staff.[75] Campbell remarked in his 1961 annual report on the importance of bill comments; during 1961, GAO furnished 610 reports on bills at the request of committees. "We included in our reports," Campbell wrote, "recommendations for major legislative changes, as well as suggestions for perfecting or clarifying the provisions of bills to achieve increased economy or efficiency in public expenditures and to protect the interests of the Government."[76]

In 1964 testimony, Campbell said that GAO averaged 600 to 700 bill reports per session in response to committee requests and frequently made unsolicited comments on pending legislation of interest to GAO. At the same hearing, General Counsel Keller explained that GAO often became involved in developing legislation on an informal basis. "Our people work with the committee staffs in the drafting of legislation to get as many problems worked out as we can before the legislation is presented to the committee and before its consideration by the House and Senate."[77]

GAO also testified on pending legislation before congressional committees. This practice developed gradually over the years; Campbell's predecessor, Lindsay Warren, testified only infrequently, but during the Campbell years, GAO presented its views more often. Campbell appeared on occasion, and other top officials, including Keller and Weitzel, helped carry the

[73]*Annual Report of the Comptroller General of the United States for the Fiscal Year Ended June 30, 1963* (Washington: GPO, 1963), 298.

[74]Entry for meeting of November 12, 1957, Morse, *Notes of Meetings of the Accounting and Auditing Division Heads, July 1957 through June 1958*; and Campbell testimony, February 26, 1957, *Independent Offices Appropriations for 1958*, Hearings before a Subcommittee of the House Committee on Appropriations, 85th Cong., 1st Sess., pt. 2 (Washington: GPO, 1957), 1968.

[75]Entry for March 15, 1956, Morse, *Daily Notes*, 1956; and entries for November 20 and 27, 1957, in Morse, *Daily Notes*, 1957-1958.

[76]*Annual Report of the Comptroller General of the United States for the Fiscal Year Ended June 30, 1961* (Washington: GPO, 1961), 17-19.

[77]Campbell and Keller testimony, February 6, 1964, *Legislative Branch Appropriations for 1965*, 19.

testimony load. Each year, usually in February, Campbell and other GAO representatives testified on GAO's annual budget request; these sessions, in fact, amounted to a detailed review of the past year's activities and plans for the coming year. Other testimony was given periodically. During the first session of the 87th Congress in fiscal year 1961, for example, GAO testified 28 times before 21 committees and subcommittees.[78]

Congressional Evaluation of Campbell and GAO

Except for two notable exceptions, the so-called "zinc stink" in 1955 and the Holifield hearings in 1965, Campbell enjoyed smooth relationships with Congress.[79] Rep. Albert Thomas (D—Texas), who for several years chaired the subcommittee of the House Appropriations Committee that dealt with GAO's budget, regularly complimented Campbell on GAO's work. In February 1957, when Campbell and other GAO officials appeared before his subcommittee, Thomas said:

> I don't know of any agency of Government that the Congress feels any closer to than the General Accounting Office. Certainly there is good reason for that. It is set up to do a particular job. It is more or less an arm of Congress. Congress feels whenever it wants exact information, the cold facts without bias or prejudice, that type of information where the chips will fall where they may, we can always depend upon the reports and investigations and the invaluable help of the General Accounting Office. Mr. Campbell, you have certainly done a fine job. This committee and the Congress are proud of you. You have brought further closeness between the Congress and the General Accounting Office.[80]

It will be recalled that Sen. Albert Gore spoke at length in opposition to Campbell at his confirmation hearings in 1955. At a 1958 hearing involving GAO officials, Gore said:

> I think this might be an appropriate place for me to eat a little crow about Mr. Campbell. I opposed his confirmation sincerely, entertaining doubts about his qualifications and his

---

[78]For an example of annual budget testimony, see testimony of Campbell, Weitzel, et al., March 15, 1961, *Independent Offices Appropriations for 1962*, Hearings before a Subcommittee of the House Committee on Appropriations, 87th Cong., 1st Sess., pt. 1 (Washington: GPO, 1961), 302ff. See also GAO, *Annual Report, 1961*, 3.

[79]For information on the zinc stink, see chapter 17, pp. 411-14; for information on the Holifield hearings, see chapter 20, pp. 505-12.

[80]Thomas statement, February 26 , 1957, *Independent Offices Appropriations for 1958*, pt. 2, 1930.

capacity to be a good Comptroller General. I am glad to say and to acknowledge that his record proves my apprehension without foundation. . . . You understand it is only upon rare occasions when a Senator ever admits he is wrong about anything. But I have been so pleased with the diligence and dedication of Mr. Campbell that I have been thinking that at some appropriate time I should make this statement. . . .[81]

Campbell continued the expansion and the improvement of GAO relationships with Congress that Comptroller General Warren had begun. He did this by being responsive to congressional requests to GAO for assistance in various ways, by trying to run GAO efficiently and economically, and by improving the scope and the quality of GAO's work. Although not a product of Congress as had been McCarl, Brown, and Warren, once Campbell became comptroller general, he recognized the importance of close relations between GAO and Congress and worked hard to maintain and improve them. The difficult Holifield hearings at the end of his term were a low point in GAO-congressional relations, and Campbell left under a cloud of criticism. Campbell had neither the personality nor the interest to work as closely with Congress as had Warren. His concern about maintaining independence from the executive branch extended, although to a lesser degree, to Congress. But during his term, GAO's identification as a congressional agency and the extent of its service to Congress expanded.

Campbell's Retirement

At the end of June 1965, Campbell decided to retire on disability. At the time, he was a patient in Georgetown University Hospital, suffering from rheumatoid arthritis. Arthur Schoenhaut, who visited him in the hospital, commented later that Campbell "was a mess, a total physical wreck. The doctor had told him that if he wanted to live, he had to stop working. . . ." When Ellsworth Morse visited him at the hospital on July 1, 1965, the day after disclosure of his impending retirement, he noted that Campbell "discussed briefly the principal considerations that led to his decision not to continue in office," but Morse did not reveal the nature of those considerations.[82]

---

[81]Clipping from *Highway Cost Estimates*, Hearing before a Subcommittee of the Senate Committee on Public Works, 85th Cong., 2d Sess., August 12, 13, and 15, 1958, in Clippings CG [Campbell] 1954-1962, GAO History Program Archives.

[82]GAO, *Arthur Schoenhaut*, 41; and entries for June 30 and July 1, 1965, Morse, *Daily Notes*, 1965-1966.

It was known that Campbell had health problems, but there was still some speculation about the real reasons for his departure, most of it related to the current Holifield hearings.[83] Representative Chet Holifield, when asked years later if he thought that Campbell's retirement was related to the Holifield hearings, said "there should have been concern on his part" but did not conclude directly that the hearings were a major factor. Arthur Schoenhaut believed that "the Holifield hearings had nothing to do with his retirement, unless it brought on the onslaught of severe rheumatoid arthritis." Schoenhaut also said that Campbell told him that Holifield was not out to harm GAO and that he was a good friend of the office.[84] When he learned of Campbell's intention to retire, Holifield emphasized that he and his subcommittee, then holding hearings on GAO, "recognizes the need and importance" of GAO and that they wanted the office "to be stronger, not weaker" and "more effective, not less effective." He praised Campbell as "an outstanding public servant" who "has rendered a fine service to the Congress, the executive branch, and the taxpayers of this country."[85]

Although there was speculation in GAO at the time that the pressure of the Holifield hearings caused Campbell to resign, there is no hard evidence to support this speculation. There is no basis for concluding that factors other than his health forced Campbell's retirement.[86]

Press comment at the time of Campbell's retirement was generally complimentary to him. The *Chicago Sun-Times* observed that Campbell's departure "is sad news for the American taxpayer" and expressed the hope that President Lyndon B. Johnson "will choose a man who will continue to administer the GAO with the same zeal for the taxpayer's rights as did Campbell." The *Albuquerque Tribune* wrote, "If LBJ can find another like Campbell— tough, inquisitive, independent—that's the man to name. This is no job for a hack or a pliable politician." The *Richmond News-Leader* said that Campbell's exit "represents a great loss to the taxpayers" and that Campbell "has di-

---

[83]See entry for November 8, 1961, mentioning "a very serious operation" Campbell had had several weeks earlier, Morse, *Daily Notes*, 1961-1962. See chapter 20, pp. 505-12, for a discussion of the Holifield hearings.

[84]GAO, *Chet Holifield*, GAO/OP-5-OH, GAO History Program, Oral History Series, (Washington: 1988), 14; and GAO, *Arthur Schoenhaut*, 41.

[85]*Comptroller General Reports to Congress on Audits of Defense Contracts*, Hearings before a Subcommittee of the House Committee on Government Operations, 89th Cong., 1st Sess. (Washington: GPO, 1965), 573-74. See also clipping, *Cong. Record*, 9th Cong., 1st Sess., July 7, 1965, 15174-75; and Morse, *Daily Notes*, 1965-1966.

[86]Roger R. Trask, "Joseph Campbell's Resignation as Comptroller General of the United States," typescript paper, February 7, 1989, GAO History Program Archives. See also Mosher, *GAO*, 166, n. 45.

rected his agency's functions in a manner beyond reproach, without regard for the particular party in power."[87]

These press comments were consistent with commentary that appeared during Campbell's term. In 1958, the *Washington Daily News* described Campbell as "a warm-voiced, solidly constructed man with a sailing enthusiast's deep sunburn and the vigor that comes from wielding a squash racket against often youthful competition three or four times a week. . . . Certainly it would be a mistake to think of Joseph Campbell as something less than a fighter." An article in the *National Observer* in 1963, entitled "An Energetic Scot, and How He Keeps Tabs on Federal Government," said that Campbell and his staff "wage week-in, week-out guerilla warfare against waste and mismanagement" in the U.S. government. "Because his staff is so small, his quarry so large, the distinguished-looking Scot mixes the icy objectivity of a certified public accountant with the dashing tactics of a John Singleton Mosby to accomplish his ends."[88]

Because of his illness, Campbell's departure from GAO was very quiet. The only formal observance was a luncheon in his honor held in the comptroller general's dining room on October 20, 1965, hosted by Acting Comptroller General Weitzel. Among the small group present were Morse, Samuelson, Keller, Thornton, and other top division and staff office heads who had served under Campbell.[89] After his retirement, Campbell's health improved and he lived for almost 19 more years. Eventually he and Mrs. Campbell settled in Sarasota, Florida, where he died at the age of 84 on June 21, 1984. He was buried in Cooperstown, New York.[90]

Assistant Comptroller General Frank H. Weitzel

Frank Weitzel was the only person who served as assistant comptroller general during Campbell's tenure. Appointed by President Eisenhower on Comptroller General Warren's recommendation, his official 15-year term began in January 1954, 11 months before Campbell took office, and extended to January 1969, almost five years after Campbell left. By law, he was the top assistant to the comptroller general, but under Campbell his du-

---

[87]Clipping, *Chicago Sun-Times*, July 6, 1965, and clipping, *Albuquerque Tribune*, both in Clippings CG [Campbell] 1964-1965, GAO History Program Archives; and clipping, *Richmond News-Leader*, July 23, 1965, Morse, *Daily Notes*, 1965-1966.

[88]Clipping, Bruce Biossat, "Solid, Competent Man," *Washington Daily News*, November 25, 1958, in Clippings, CG [Campbell] 1954-1962, GAO History Program Archives; article in *National Observer*, November 18, 1963, copy in Legislative Digest Unit files, Box 38, Folder 18, #2, "Remarks," GAO History Program Archives.

[89]Entry for October 20, 1965, Morse, *Daily Notes*, 1965-1966.

[90]GAO, *Management News*, vol. 11, no. 41 (June 26, 1984), 3.

Frank H. Weitzel, Assistant Comptroller General, 1953-1969; Acting Comptroller General, 1954, 1965-1966.

ties and powers were limited. The precise reasons for the poor relationship between Campbell and Weitzel are not certain, but it is clear from the comments of officials serving at GAO at the time that Campbell froze Weitzel out of most substantive matters. Some speculated that the root of the trouble was that Campbell would have preferred to choose his own top assistant rather than finding him in office, serving a term that had almost 15 years left, when he arrived. If Campbell had served his full term, Weitzel would have been assistant comptroller general for all but 11 months of that term.[91]

Some observers thought the Dixon-Yates affair had caused the rift because of Weitzel's involvement, as acting comptroller general in 1954, with GAO reports critical of the AEC's role in the matter. Arthur Schoenhaut reported that as soon as Campbell had entered office, he examined GAO's Dixon-Yates workpapers and that even though he could see why GAO had reported as it had, "he never forgave Weitzel for testifying against the Commission at public hearings. The relationship [between Campbell and Weitzel] went downhill from there on." Schoenhaut recounted a personal experience that suggested Campbell's hostility to Weitzel. When Schoenhaut was deputy director of the Civil Division, Weitzel occasionally asked him to do something for him; Schoenhaut completed the work and then went to Weitzel's office, next to Campbell's, to discuss the matter with him. After a while, Adolph Samuelson, director of the Civil Division, advised Schoenhaut to quit doing things for Weitzel and to stop visiting him. According to Schoenhaut, Samuelson said to him, "Every time you do something or go in there, a record of your visit is made available to Mr. Campbell, and I don't know how to tell you to stop helping Weitzel but you stop or you won't be around here very long." Schoenhaut stated that a messenger who sat outside the offices of Weitzel and Campbell recorded the names of Weitzel's visitors and the length of the visits and provided the information to Campbell.[92]

John Abbadessa said, on the basis of personal observation, that relations between Weitzel and Campbell were tense. "He [Weitzel] was . . . almost put in a corner and there were strained relations. When I saw the two of them together, they were always polite to each other. You never heard a harsh word. . . . But I think Frank was hurt." Abbadessa acknowledged that a lot of people at GAO thought that the cause of the rift was the Dixon-Yates affair, but he questioned this reasoning, noting that he was as much involved in the GAO reports on Dixon-Yates as Weitzel, but nevertheless became "a fair-haired boy of Campbell."[93]

For whatever reason, Weitzel's scope of activity at GAO was circumscribed under Campbell, and although he had the title, he did not completely

---

[91]GAO, *Arthur Schoenhaut*, 19. Schoenhaut stated that the breakdown between Campbell and Weitzel may have occurred because Campbell had not selected Weitzel as assistant comptroller general. See also GAO, *Audit and Legal Services*, 29, for similar comments by Geraldine Rubar, an attorney in the Office of the General Counsel during Campbell's term, and GAO, *John Abbadessa*, 37-38, for additional comments.

[92]GAO, *Arthur Schoenhaut*, 20.

[93]GAO, *John Abbadessa*, 37-38.

fill the role of assistant comptroller general. He did testify before congressional committees, where he was well-known even before Campbell became comptroller general, sometimes accompanying Campbell to hearings and sometimes testifying without him. Campbell assigned him responsibility for the European Branch, and the director of the branch reported to Weitzel until 1963, when Campbell established the International Operations Division. Weitzel also had responsibility for decisions on transportation questions made by GAO.

As soon as Campbell retired in the summer of 1965, Weitzel became acting comptroller general and served effectively in that position until Elmer B. Staats became comptroller general in March 1966. Staats relied on Weitzel and restored him to full duties as assistant comptroller general. Weitzel served until his term expired in January 1969. After he retired, he lived in Washington until his death in July 1987.

GAO employees in the Great Hall of the Pension Building during the late 1920s.

CHAPTER 6

Evolution of the Budget and Staff, 1921-1966

Between 1921 and 1966, the organization and work of the General Accounting Office (GAO) were affected by several factors, including GAO's mandate in the Budget and Accounting Act, 1921, and subsequent legislation; the objectives of each comptroller general; changes in government programs; and major national and international developments. The financing and the staffing of GAO during this period of four and one-half decades required close attention by the agency's leadership and Congress. Between 1921 and 1966, GAO's staff size ranged from 1,708 (July 1, 1921) to a peak of 14,904 (the spring of 1946) to 4,148 (June 30, 1966). During the same period, GAO's appropriated budget increased gradually from $2,019,550 (fiscal year 1922) to $47,435,000 (fiscal year 1966).[1]

Budgeting and Staffing, 1921-1940

GAO's basic budget for fiscal year 1922 amounted to a little over $2 million, transferred from existing Treasury Department appropriations intended to finance activities and staff moved to GAO from Treasury in 1921. In addition, the transfer of staff by the Post Office Department when GAO took over the postal audit added over $892,000 to the budget. Other funds from a deficiency appropriation gave GAO a total budget of more than $3,442,000 for fiscal year 1922.[2]

GAO's first opportunity to deal directly with Congress on the budget occurred in December 1921 hearings when the Office asked for an increase for fiscal year 1923 of more than $300,000 over the funds available for fiscal year 1922. Comptroller General J. R. McCarl testified that GAO needed the extra money to clear up a backlog of work (he called it "graveyard stuff") inherited from the old Trea-

---

[1]See appendix V for number of GAO personnel, 1921-1966, and appendix VI for GAO appropriations, 1921-1966.

[2]For fiscal year 1922, existing records are spotty and inconsistent, but the amount given here appears to be reasonably accurate. See letter, Assistant Comptroller General Lurtin R. Ginn to director, Bureau of the Budget, March 27, 1922, 7 MS 1744; and testimony of J. R. McCarl, December 20, 1926, *Independent Offices Appropriation Bill, 1928*, Hearing before a Subcommittee of the House Committee on Appropriations, 69th Cong., 2d Sess. (Washington: GPO, 1927), 715.

sury offices and to accomplish other tasks assigned to GAO in the 1921 law. McCarl also wanted funds to pay for four top officials at $6,000 each, as the 1921 act allowed, and to increase salaries for some other GAO accountants. He noted that there was only one top-level assistant and that the workload was excessive. He and Assistant Comptroller General Lurtin R. Ginn, McCarl pointed out, sometimes worked on Sundays, holidays, and evenings to get the work done. McCarl said that GAO could not pay its best accountants more than $1,800 while they could move to the Internal Revenue Bureau and get $2,500 or $3,000. He suggested that his accountants get as much as those in other federal agencies or "you should cut down on the other fellows in the matter of the salaries that they pay . . . . If you are going to keep high-grade men in the general accounting office, you have got to pay them as much as they can obtain in other departments and establishments."[3] McCarl thus introduced a theme that he returned to at annual appropriation hearings for several years—the need for additional qualified staff. Congress ultimately appropriated $3,922,418 to cover GAO's operations during fiscal year 1923, including an increase of over $500,000 in salaries.[4]

In these early years, GAO submitted budget estimates to BOB, which determined the final figure recommended to Congress. The basis for this procedure was Section 306 of the Budget and Accounting Act, which provided that "all laws relating generally to the administration of the departments and establishments shall, so far as applicable, govern the General Accounting Office." For budgetary purposes, both the executive branch and BOB in particular classified GAO as an independent agency. BOB reviewed and changed GAO's budget estimates. It did this until the Reorganization Act of 1945 declared GAO to be a part of the legislative branch. Congress included GAO's budget in the independent offices appropriations bill until the mid-1960s. According to the 1921 act, GAO was independent of the executive branch but, in some matters, including budget, there was little distinction. This suggests that GAO's statutory connections with Congress in the early years were tenuous.[5]

On occasion, BOB's processing of GAO budget figures resulted in requests to Congress lower than what GAO thought was essential. For example, GAO's original request for fiscal year 1925 was $4,140,688; BOB reduced the amount to

[3]McCarl testimony, December 19, 1921, *Independent Offices Appropriation Bill, 1923*, Hearings before a Subcommittee of the House Committee on Appropriations, 67th Cong., 2d Sess. (Washington: GPO, 1922), 249-50.

[4]Memorandum, Ginn to W. W. Matthews, Bureau of the Budget (BOB), July 19, 1923, 23 MS 606.

[5]See Frederick C. Mosher, *A Tale of Two Agencies: A Comparative Analysis of the General Accounting Office and the Office of Management and Budget* (Baton Rouge and London: Louisiana State University Press, 1984), 166-67. As Mosher points out, the Civil Service Commission had jurisdiction over the GAO personnel system until passage of the GAO Personnel Act of 1980 (P.L. 96-191), which put GAO in control of its personnel system. For information on the Reorganization Act of 1945, see chapter 4, p. 88.

$3,869,312 (to which GAO initially acquiesced) and then attached a further reduction of more than $144,000, much of it in the salary category, bringing the recommended budget down to $3,725,000. McCarl wrote a strong letter of protest to the BOB director and later testified that BOB had acted arbitrarily. To Director H. M. Lord of BOB, McCarl wrote: "For the most part the work . . . [GAO] must do under the law is not of its making—but it must be done and should be done most correctly and promptly. There results loss not saving by causing the final audit and settlement of accounts to be unreasonably delayed. The work cannot be done promptly and correctly without adequate personnel."[6] Later GAO asked for a supplemental estimate from BOB of more than $90,000, citing the extra auditing work imposed on GAO by enactment of legislation providing adjusted compensation for World War I veterans. GAO's appropriation for fiscal year 1925 was $3,724,612, about what BOB preferred.[7]

On later occasions, GAO had similar problems with BOB estimates. For fiscal year 1930, GAO gave BOB a preliminary figure of $4,338,560. BOB reduced the request to $4,105,000. McCarl responded with a letter claiming that his original request was more than $16,000 low, and he submitted a new request for $4,355,000—his original number plus $16,440. He explained that recently authorized executive branch activities, new duties imposed on GAO by statute, and salary increases to staff authorized by job reclassification supported his new estimate. He pointed out that GAO "was created to function on behalf of the Congress. Indeed, one of its principal duties is that of enforcing for the Congress its laws in relation to fiscal matters. That it was to be removed from every form of control by the executive branch" was provided in Sections 301 and 304 of the Budget and Accounting Act, 1921. "The independence, the effectiveness, and the promptness of the General Accounting Office may be controlled just as emphatically and as conclusively by reducing the number of its employees below the minimum needed, or by denying the remainder, the salaries they are clearly entitled to . . . , thus rendering employees disgruntled and dissatisfied. . . ." He argued that requiring GAO to follow BOB estimates "would defeat its necessary and stipulated independence from the executive branch." Ultimately Congress appropriated $4,092,000, somewhat less than McCarl had requested.[8] Congress did not appear impressed with McCarl's complaints about the role of the BOB. GAO appropriations in these years were approximately what BOB recommended.

[6]Letter, McCarl to Lord, October 19, 1923, 26 MS 807; and McCarl testimony, February 23, 1924, *Independent Offices Appropriation Bill, 1925*, Hearings before a Subcommittee of the House Committee on Appropriations, 68th Cong., 1st Sess. (Washington: GPO, 1924), 187-88.

[7]Letter, Ginn to Lord, May 23, 1924, 33 MS 885.

[8]Letter, McCarl to the director, BOB, September 15, 1928, reprinted in testimony by Ginn and J. L. Baity, January 4, 1929, *Independent Offices Appropriation Bill for 1930*, Hearings before a Subcommittee of the House Committee on Appropriations, 70th Cong., 2d Sess. (Washington: GPO, 1929), 332-35.

GAO, like other federal agencies, faced considerable pressure to reduce its budget during the Great Depression of the 1930s. McCarl felt, as he pointed out to the chairman of the House Appropriations Committee late in 1931, that GAO needed additional expert staff to monitor the use of public funds but would keep its fiscal year 1933 estimate below actual needs in order to do its share in accomplishing government economies. He did suggest, "in view of the vast number of competent and deserving men and women seriously in need of employment to provide a livelihood," that Congress immediately establish a special fund to allow GAO to hire at least 100 persons through the end of the current fiscal year 1932. "No better means of aiding the unemployed—and obtaining beneficial results at the same time—has occurred to me."[9]

The Economy Acts of 1932 and 1933 and efforts to cut the costs of the federal government created substantial extra work for GAO. Agency heads and their disbursing officers flooded GAO with requests for decisions on the terms of the Economy Acts, most of them affecting personnel. McCarl pointed out that the laws, in addition to decisions, increased GAO's work "in formulating accounting procedures, as well as in connection with the audit of accounts to determine that the many changes in basic statutes have been complied with by the various administrative offices."[10] When James L. Baity, the GAO executive officer, testified on the fiscal year 1934 budget, he pointed out that the Office's work had increased more than 21 percent over the previous year. Baity said that any reduction in GAO's staff, whose salaries had been cut like those of other federal workers by the Economy Act of 1932, would force GAO to fall further behind, causing potential losses to the government many times greater than GAO's annual appropriations.[11]

Congress cut GAO's funds for 1934 by almost $1 million compared with those for 1933, necessitating a reduction-in-force (RIF) of 175 staff by July 1, 1933. Further complicating the situation was passage of the National Industrial Recovery Act (June 1933), which among other things created the Public Works Administration (PWA) to undertake major federal projects, with an initial

---

[9]Letter, McCarl to Will R. Wood, December 3, 1931, reprinted in testimony of James L. Baity, GAO executive officer, February 8, 1932, *Independent Offices Appropriation Bill for 1933*, Hearings before a Subcommittee of the House Committee on Appropriations, 72d Cong., 1st Sess. (Washington: GPO, 1932), 236. The position of executive officer, responsible for administration in the Office of the Comptroller General, existed from the beginning of McCarl's term until 1953, when Comptroller General Lindsay C. Warren established the Office of Administrative Services. Baity held the position from 1921 until 1944. When Assistant Comptroller General Lurtin R. Ginn retired in 1931, McCarl added to Baity's duties the important role of budget officer.

[10]*Annual Report of the Comptroller General of the United States for the Fiscal Year Ended June 30, 1933* (Washington: GPO, 1933), 17.

[11]Baity testimony, January 6, 1933, *Independent Offices Appropriation Bill for 1934*, Hearings before a Subcommittee of the House Committee on Appropriations, 72d Cong., 2d Sess. (Washington: GPO, 1933), 282-83.

appropriation of more than $3 billion. GAO received an allocation of $506,000 from PWA, available until June 30, 1935, to cover the Office's extra work related to PWA, but these funds were not authorized to be used to deal with the work backlog or regular ongoing functions. McCarl said that GAO, despite these problems, would continue striving to do the best possible job it could under trying circumstances.[12]

Throughout the rest of the 1930s, GAO's work continued to increase, in a period of tightness in the federal budget. By the end of 1934, activities funded by emergency appropriations for both regular and emergency agencies had doubled GAO's workload. Legal questions, requiring attention by the Office of the General Counsel as well as the comptroller general personally, had increased greatly; GAO asked for funds for 15 new lawyers. Investigations work, involving examination of the uses of public funds, and the development of accounting procedures and forms for administrative agencies had similarly increased; GAO requested more investigators. The work of the Claims Division had expanded rapidly because of claims resulting from the emergency activities, and the work of the Audit Division had ballooned, both in volume and complexity. GAO did some preaudit work (determining the legality and the accuracy of proposed expenditures before actual payment), especially in the field, but funding did not permit an adequate program. The number of checks received for reconciliation by the Check Section of the Audit Division increased from about 31 million in fiscal year 1933 to 100 million in fiscal year 1934. At the end of that year, GAO had on hand about 90 million checks in unreconciled accounts. The number of postal money orders that GAO had to audit increased by 12 percent from fiscal year 1933 to fiscal year 1934, amounting to 196 million, and the Office anticipated the same or greater rates of increase in the next two fiscal years. For fiscal year 1936, GAO expected to receive 18 million paid postal savings certificates for audit.[13]

This situation prevailed for the rest of the decade. Testifying on GAO's budget needs in December 1935, Baity said that GAO was "absolutely overwhelmed with work, the volume of which far exceeds what we anticipated, and for the next few years we will have work that will require a vast number of employees and more space than we now occupy."[14]

---

[12]Baity testimony, December 5, 1933, *Independent Offices Appropriation Bill for 1935*, Hearings before a Subcommittee of the House Committee on Appropriations, 73d Cong., 2d Sess. (Washington: GPO, 1934), 155-56.

[13]Testimony of Baity and others, December 13, 1934, *Independent Offices Appropriation Bill for 1936*, Hearings before a Subcommittee of the House Committee on Appropriations, 74th Cong., 1st Sess. (Washington: GPO, 1935), 287-89.

[14]Baity testimony, December 3, 1935, *Independent Offices Appropriation Bill for 1937*, Hearings before a Subcommittee of the House Committee on Appropriations, 74th Cong., 2d Sess. (Washington: GPO, 1936), 262.

The budget between 1929 and 1940 increased from $3,820,000 to $10,531,540, about a 275-percent jump, but not enough to meet the agency's stated needs. GAO received substantial allotments of emergency relief funds beginning in 1933. These funds were specifically allocated to pay for GAO's work on emergency programs. For example, GAO's regular appropriation for fiscal year 1940 was $5,306,540, but it also received $5,225,000 in emergency funds, adding up to a total of $10,531,540.[15]

GAO's staff size also increased significantly. On June 30, 1929, a few months before the stock market crash, GAO's staff numbered 1,961. Even with the expanding workload, especially with the creation of the New Deal programs, GAO had only 2,758 staff on June 30, 1935. A year later there were 4,401, and 5,195 by June 30, 1940. Thus over the 11-year period between 1929 and 1940, the staff had increased over 260 percent, but not nearly enough to handle the existing volume of work.[16]

Budgeting and Staffing, 1940-1954

During Comptroller General Lindsay C. Warren's term from 1940 to 1954, GAO went through three distinct periods that greatly affected the size of its budget and staff. The war, which began in Europe in 1939, led eventually to a rearmament effort in the United States. By the time Warren entered office in November 1940, rearmament costs had already had a major impact on the nation's budget. For the next five years, and especially after the United States entered the conflict in December 1941, GAO's major challenge was to cope with the vastly increasing workload caused by the war effort. The budget skyrocketed, as did the number of staff.

The second period began shortly after the war ended in August 1945. Although still facing a tremendous backlog of work and new functions, GAO's budget and staff began to shrink, especially the staff. A third period began with the outbreak of the Korean conflict in June 1950; once again GAO's task increased because of the war effort and the impact of new approaches the agency adopted toward audits and government financial management.

---

[15]Baity testimony, December 6, 1939, *Independent Offices Appropriation for 1941*, Hearings before a Subcommittee of the House Committee on Appropriations, 76th Cong., 3d Sess. (Washington: GPO, 1940), 229.

[16]See appendixes V and VI for tables on number of GAO personnel and GAO appropriations, respectively.

GAO staff at work in the Pension Building. Copyright 1940, The Washington Post. *Reprinted with permission.*

Warren's first budget request, for fiscal year 1942, reflected the initial impact of the defense effort as well as continuing work on Depression programs. For fiscal year 1941, the regular GAO appropriation was $5,306,540 and its emergency allotment, contained in the Emergency Relief Act of 1941, was $5.6 million, making a total of $10,906,540. For fiscal year 1942, Warren requested an appropriation of $10,763,880. He added that GAO would later submit estimates for emergency work (for Depression programs) of over $1 million if there was no emergency relief bill for 1942, such as had been passed for previous years. Although GAO requested about the same amount for fiscal year 1942 as it received in 1941, most of the money, rather than half as earlier, would be for GAO's regular work, including the added burden from the preparedness effort.[17]

Warren emphasized to the House Appropriations Committee the profound impact of the nation's defense effort on GAO: "The unprecedented amounts which have recently been appropriated principally for preparedness and national defense will bring the work of the General Accounting Office to an all-time high mark." He described the specific impact on various GAO divi-

---

[17]Warren statement presented in Baity testimony, December 10, 1940, *Independent Offices Appropriation Bill for 1942*, Hearings before a Subcommittee of the House Committee on Appropriations, 77th Cong., 1st Sess., pt. 1 (Washington: GPO, 1941), 138-39.

sions. The Accounting and Bookkeeping Division, affected the most of any division, had experienced an increase in warrants, requisitions, and other documents and had had to establish and maintain many additional accounts. The Audit Division's volume would increase greatly because of contract payments, military pay and allowances, civilian pay and travel, purchases, communications, and other expenses. The Claims Division would have to handle vast increases in claims for pay and allowances, as well as freight and passenger transportation claims—"all incident to the National Defense program." The Reconciliation and Clearance Division, the Office of the General Counsel, and the Investigations Office would experience similar work expansion.[18]

Ultimately Congress appropriated what GAO requested for fiscal year 1942; the House Appropriations Committee, in recommending the amount, stated that "the vast burden placed upon this Office by the expansion of Government activities including the ever-increasing defense program fully justifies the increases allowed for the next fiscal year."[19]

A year later, in December 1941, when GAO presented its budget request for fiscal year 1943, the increasing impact of the defense effort was evident. GAO requested $16,936,490, the amount approved by the Bureau of the Budget, of which $16,326,490 was for salaries for a much-expanded staff. In testimony, Baity, using Warren's prepared statement, explained that GAO expected additional funds—$2,450,000 from lend-lease appropriations to pay for GAO's work in that area and $823,000 in relief emergency appropriations to cover audits of relief work in 1943. These funds, if appropriated, would total over $20 million.[20]

In his budget statement, Warren referred to the "herculean task" facing the GAO in fiscal year 1943—"a duty that has never before been in any way equaled and which is almost overwhelming to contemplate." He again summarized the impact of the war work on each of GAO's major divisions and their needs for increased staff. The Audit Division, for example, would need an increased appropriation of over $4 million to handle an estimated 38 million

---

[18]Ibid., 139.

[19]*Independent Offices Appropriation Bill, 1942*, Rept. 15, January 29, 1941, 77th Cong., 1st Sess. (Washington: GPO, 1941), 14; and Public Law 77-28, approved April 5, 1941. The final amount GAO received for fiscal year 1942 was actually over $12 million, reflecting supplemental funds added later.

[20]Warren statement presented in Baity testimony, December 5, 1941, *Independent Offices Appropriation Bill for 1943*, Hearings before a Subcommittee of the House Committee on Appropriations, 77th Cong., 2d Sess. (Washington: GPO, 1942), 58-59. The Lend-Lease Act, signed by President Franklin D. Roosevelt in March, 1941, was a program created initially to lend goods to Great Britain and later to many other allies to sustain the war effort; repayment in goods and services was to be made after the war. In describing his plan for lend-lease, Roosevelt said that the United States had to "be the great arsenal of democracy." The initial appropriation for the program was $7 billion. For an account of the development of lend-lease, see James MacGregor Burns, *Roosevelt: The Soldier of Freedom* (New York: Harcourt Brace Jovanovich, Inc., 1970), 25-29, 43-49.

vouchers in 1943, covering construction of plants, fortifications, and vessels; the manufacture of planes, tanks, guns, and ammunition; and the purchase of military supplies and equipment. Eventually Congress provided essentially what GAO requested for fiscal year 1943.[21]

The budget patterns established for GAO in the early years of World War II continued through the end of the war and beyond. Each year there was a substantial increase in GAO's appropriations, mainly to pay for additional staff. For fiscal year 1944, GAO requested and got more than $26 million, all but about $880,000 for staff salaries. Warren pointed out to the House Appropriations Committee that GAO's request for increased salary funds would have been greater "but for the fact that it will be extremely difficult to provide sufficient competent help and adequate office space" for a greater force. He also noted that the total federal expenditure with which GAO had to deal in fiscal year 1944 would be about $85 billion "and will double and triple many classes of work" for GAO. Warren mentioned a new expense, the establishment by GAO of field stations around the country to audit spending on cost-plus-a-fixed-fee contracts with defense industries.[22]

For fiscal year 1945, GAO requested and received an increase of $12 million, again mainly for staff salaries, for a total of over $38 million. GAO's original request to the Bureau of the Budget was for about $44 million; BOB cut it and GAO then formally requested the reduced amount in appropriation hearings—the usual pattern for these years.[23]

Reflecting the fact that the war was winding down, for fiscal year 1946 GAO asked for over $4 million less than it had received for 1945. Warren personally presented GAO's request before the House Appropriations Committee in January 1945, the first time he testified at appropriations hearings. Warren reminded the committee that this was his first appearance before them. "Heretofore, I understood the head of the Office did not appear, and it certainly was through no lack of interest on my part that I did not come [previously]. . . ."[24] Congress appropriated just less than $34 million as

---

[21]Warren statement presented in Baity testimony, December 5, 1941, *Independent Offices Appropriation Bill for 1943*, 59-61; and Public Law 77-630, 56 Stat. 1257, approved June 27, 1942.

[22]Warren statement presented in Baity testimony, January 12, 1943, *Independent Office Appropriation Bill for 1944*, Hearings before a Subcommittee of the House Committee on Appropriations, 78th Cong., 1st Sess. (Washington: GPO, 1943), 257-59; and Public Law 78-90, approved June 26, 1943.

[23]Testimony of Dudley W. Bagley, assistant to the comptroller general and budget officer, December 14, 1943, *Independent Offices Appropriation Bill for 1945*, Hearings before a Subcommittee of the House Committee on Appropriations, 78th Cong., 2d Sess. (Washington: GPO, 1944), 799-800; and Public Law 78-358, 58 Stat. 361, approved June 27, 1944.

[24]Warren testimony, January 18, 1945, *Independent Offices Appropriation Bill for 1946*, Hearings before a Subcommittee of the House Committee on Appropriations, 79th Cong., 1st Sess. (Washington: GAO, 1945), 1114, 1120.

GAO requested; later, through supplemental appropriations and transfers to GAO, the total funds available were several million dollars more; thus GAO's budget did not decline in the year after the war ended.[25]

While GAO's spending went from about $10.5 million in fiscal year 1940 to about $38.5 million in fiscal year 1945, the staff jumped from 5,195 (reflecting an increase of over 3,000 during the Depression years) to almost 14,000. The staff continued to expand for eight months after the war ended, reaching an all-time high of 14,904 in April 1946.[26] Of the 14,034 staff GAO reported on board in December 1945, 7,713 worked in headquarters offices in Washington and 6,321 in field and branch offices around the country, most of them engaged in defense plant and military pay and expense audits.[27]

GAO requested and received over $40 million to operate during fiscal year 1947. In explaining its request, GAO pointed to the large backlog of work from the wartime period and its hope to bring its audits up-to-date. The work areas most in arrears were the settlement of fiscal officers' accounts, reconciliation of disbursing officers' depositary accounts, and especially the audit of transportation vouchers.[28]

The appropriation of $40 million for GAO's operations in fiscal year 1947 was the highest amount the Office received for any one fiscal year between 1922 and 1960. In 1960, Congress provided $41.8 million, and thereafter funding increased each fiscal year into the early 1990s.[29] Warren consciously tried to keep his budget to a minimum and emphasized the return on the government's investment in GAO. Testifying in April 1947, he stated that for every dollar GAO spent in salaries, it collected and deposited in the Treasury three dollars through its audits, collections, and reviews of transportation bills. He estimated that GAO's collections for 1946 totaled $112 million. He stressed the importance of indirect savings—"the wrongful and unlawful payments of all kinds that surely would be made if we were not there, like a policeman on his beat, to put a stop to it. Upon that basis I submit that no office of the Government accomplished so

---

[25]Public Law 79-49, approved May 3,1945; and *Annual Report of the Comptroller General of the United States for the Fiscal Year Ended June 30, 1946* (Washington: GPO, n.d.), 46.

[26]See appendix V for table on number of personnel.

[27]Bagley testimony, December 10, 1945, *Independent Offices Appropriation Bill for 1947*, Hearings before a Subcommittee of the House Committee on Appropriations, 79th Cong., 2d Sess. (Washington: GPO, 1946), 420. See chapter 11 for a detailed account of GAO's work during World War II.

[28]GAO budget estimates justification, in the record of hearing on December 10, 1945, *Independent Offices Appropriation Bill for 1947*, 414-15; and Public Law 79-334, approved March 26, 1946. See chapter 11 for details of the wartime and postwar transportation audits.

[29]See appendix VI for table on GAO appropriations.

much for the taxpayer on so little outlay."[30]   He returned to this theme repeatedly in subsequent years. At his last appropriations hearing, in January 1954, less than four months before his retirement, Warren estimated that during his term, GAO had recovered and returned to the Treasury nearly $900 million.[31]

When making his budget requests for several years following World War II, Warren emphasized the need to eliminate the wartime backlog of work and catch up on GAO's regular duties. He told the House Appropriations Committee in December 1947 that he expected that all phases of GAO's work would be brought up-to-date in the next fiscal year (1949), and early in 1949, he confirmed that this goal had been met except for the transportation audit.[32]

During the immediate years after the war, GAO's workload changed somewhat because of decisions to discontinue the routine auditing of millions of vouchers each year and to undertake what GAO called the "comprehensive audit." The new audit approach emphasized going beyond a mere checking of spending against appropriations to look at program effectiveness and results. GAO also began in 1945 a new program to audit government corporations and, in collaboration with the Treasury Department and the Bureau of the Budget, developed a plan to improve accounting in the federal government. The emergence of the Cold War by 1947 and the outbreak of the Korean conflict in 1950 necessitated increasing attention to the audit of defense expenditures as well as economic and military aid.[33]

During these years, salaries were still the main budget item, but much of the staff redirected their efforts to new approaches or new tasks. GAO's regular appropriations fluctuated from $36,517,000 for fiscal year 1948 to $31,981,000 in fiscal year 1954, Warren's last year in office.[34] While appropriations dropped about 12 percent during this period, the size of the staff also fell rapidly. It dropped from a peak of almost 15,000 in April 1946 to

---

[30]Warren testimony, April 9, 1947, *Independent Offices Appropriation Bill for 1948*, Hearings before a Subcommittee of the House Committee on Appropriations, 80th Cong., 1st Sess., pt. 1 (Washington: GPO, 1947), 20.

[31]Warren testimony, January 13, 1954, *Independent Offices Appropriations for 1955*, Hearings before a Subcommittee of the House Committee on Appropriations, 83d Cong., 2d Sess., pt. 1 (Washington: GPO, 1954), 348.

[32]Warren testimony, December 11, 1947, *Independent Offices Appropriation Bill for 1949*, Hearings before a Subcommittee of the House Committee on Appropriations, 80th Cong., 2d Sess. (Washington: GPO, 1948), 92; and Warren testimony, February 9, 1949, *Independent Offices Appropriation Bill for 1950*, Hearings before a Subcommittee of the House Committee on Appropriations, 81st Cong., 1st Sess., vol. 1 (Washington: GPO, 1949), 965.

[33]See chapters 12, 13, 14, and 15 for detailed accounts of these and other changes.

[34]See appendix VI for table on GAO appropriations.

10,695 a little more than a year later; 8,919 on June 30, 1949; and 5,913 on June 30, 1954.[35]

Warren thought that the federal government was generally too large, and he wanted GAO to set an example by cutting staff when possible. He dismissed temporary wartime staff as soon as he could after the war and used formal reductions-in-force to cut many others. RIFs were still taking place as late as 1952. Warren reported that 386 staff received RIF notices in February 1952—54 received outright separation notices and 332 received offers of lower-graded positions in GAO, which if taken would displace lower-graded staff who would have to leave. Warren explained to the chairman of a Senate committee: "I yield to no man in my heartfelt sympathy with the plight of the individual employees affected by the reduction. Yet, I know of no earthly justification for keeping on the payroll . . . in their present grades employees who are not needed. . . . If we are not to be able to separate . . . employees not needed, then we are squarely up against this issue: Is it possible under any conditions to reduce the size of our Federal establishment, or of any single agency in it?"[36]

At the same time, changes in GAO's work program, including corporation audits, federal financial management activities, and comprehensive audits, required recruiting highly trained and experienced professional staff. Personnel that were more highly skilled plus higher salaries due generally to postwar inflation and government personnel policy led to relatively stable personnel costs even though the number of staff declined. Assistant Comptroller General Frank L. Yates told Congress in 1951 that if GAO had retained its staff at 1946 levels, it would be requesting almost $62 million for salaries rather than half as much.[37]

Budgeting and Staffing, 1954-1965

Under Comptroller General Joseph Campbell, the swings in budget and staffing were less drastic than under Warren. The GAO budget increased gradually by about 50 percent during Campbell's term between 1954 and 1965, and the staff declined slowly, from nearly 6,000 on board when Warren left to a little over 4,000 when Campbell's term ended in 1965.

---

[35]See appendix V for table on number of personnel.

[36]Warren testimony, February 9, 1949, *Independent Offices Appropriation Bill for 1950*, 964 (on RIFs); and letter, Warren to Sen. Olin B. Johnston, chairman, Senate Committee on the Post Office and Civil Service, February 27, 1952, B-108242.

[37]Warren testimony, January 27, 1950, *Independent Offices Appropriation for 1951*, Hearings before a Subcommittee of the House Committee on Appropriations, 81st Cong., 2d Sess., pt. 1 (Washington: GPO, 1950), 857 (on hiring professional staff); and Yates testimony, March 13, 1951, *Independent Offices Appropriations for 1952*, Hearings before a Subcommittee of the House Committee on Appropriations, 82d Cong., 1st Sess., pt. 1 (Washington: GPO, 1951), 1476. See chapters 12-14 for information on changes in the composition of the staff under Warren.

During the Campbell years, several factors determined the levels of GAO's budget and staff. In 1955-1956, Campbell undertook a substantial reorganization that concentrated audit activity in two large divisions. At the same time, GAO established both an ambitious recruiting program to bring college-trained accountants to the staff and a broad training program to upgrade their knowledge and skills.[38] Fieldwork expanded, both through overseas offices in Europe and Asia and a more-formalized regional office system. The travel budget grew to accommodate the costs of staff working in the field and traveling to regional offices from Washington.[39] Periodic statutory salary increases and some inflation also affected the budget, as did GAO's efforts to introduce new electronic data processing techniques (EDP) to audit work.

The funds appropriated by Congress during Campbell's tenure usually were close to the amounts GAO requested. The budget ranged from a little less than $32 million for fiscal year 1955, in effect when Campbell joined GAO, to nearly $47 million in fiscal year 1965, his last full year in office. This increase, about 47 percent, was modest given the expanding scope and extent of GAO's audit work and other activities. GAO's staff decreased during this decade (June 30, 1955, to June 30, 1965) by about 1,500 positions. The cost of staff salaries during Campbell's last year in office still represented the lion's share of the budget, giving some indication as to how individual staff salaries increased, to a significant degree because of the rising professional qualifications of GAO's audit staff. In addition, salaries and wages throughout the nation's economy, as well as in government, were rising to compensate for inflation.

Campbell's general approach was to appear personally at annual appropriations hearings. Usually accompanying him were Assistant Comptroller General Frank Weitzel; Robert Keller, who served as Campbell's assistant until 1958 and general counsel thereafter; and Lawrence Powers, another assistant and later director of the Defense Accounting and Auditing Division (DAAD). Occasionally other division directors and staff office heads attended. Campbell usually read a lengthy prepared statement on the budget request, justifying the amount and summarizing in detail the work and the accomplishments of GAO's various divisions. The appropriations hearings in fact amounted to an annual report on the past year's activities and a projection of GAO's work in the coming year. Campbell usually ended his formal statement by emphasizing the extent and the importance of GAO assistance to Congress. Typically the Appropriations Committee received Campbell well, and while on occasion there was some adjustment of the requested amount through committee deliberations, Campbell got about what he wanted.[40]

---

[38]For details of Campbell's reorganization and the recruiting and training programs, see chapter 17.

[39]See chapter 18, pp. 451-61.

[40]For a detailed discussion of Campbell's congressional relationships, see chapter 5, pp. 119-24.

Campbell used the hearings to highlight particular needs and problems. At his first appearance as comptroller general before the House Appropriations Committee in February 1955, he told the legislators that GAO's "most serious problem is the recruitment of qualified auditors. . . . We need several hundred additional top flight auditors if we are to adequately carry out our duties and responsibilities." At this same hearing, Campbell stressed the overseas activities of GAO, particularly the work of the European Branch, noting especially the branch's examination of the offshore procurement program under the Mutual Defense Assistance Act.[41]

In testimony a year later on the fiscal year 1957 budget request, Campbell explained his reorganization plan, headed by creation of the Civil Accounting and Auditing Division (CAAD) and the Defense Accounting and Auditing Division. He again emphasized the shortage of qualified auditors but explained the efforts GAO was making to expand recruiting of professional staff and train them once they were on board.[42]

For fiscal year 1957, Campbell requested $34,581,000. Of this amount, $31,860,000 would pay the salaries of an estimated staff of 5,863 and $2,721,000 would cover other expenses. Congress ultimately approved a budget of $34 million, more than 98 percent of what GAO had requested.[43]

When he presented GAO's budget request for fiscal year 1958, Campbell emphasized GAO's accounting, auditing, and investigative work in the Department of Defense (DOD) and the military departments. The defense effort included reviewing and evaluating the military assistance program, procurement, supply management, defense contracting, and military installations. At this same session, Campbell noted GAO's work in encouraging adoption of EDP systems in government agencies, including the Treasury Department. "In addition to actively participating in some of these developments, we have undertaken a governmentwide survey of present and planned use of electronic data processing systems, with the objective of determining the extent of progress which has been made and the effect on financial management processes of the Federal Government."[44]

---

[41]Campbell testimony, February 22, 1955, *Independent Offices Appropriations for 1956*, Hearings before a Subcommittee of the House Committee on Appropriations, 84th Cong., 1st Sess. (Washington: GPO, 1955), 718, 723.

[42]Campbell testimony, February 10, 1956, *Independent Offices Appropriations for 1957*, Hearings before a Subcommittee of the House Committee on Appropriations, 84th Cong., 2d Sess., pt. 2 (Washington: GPO, 1956), 1338-39.

[43]Chart included with Campbell testimony, February 10, 1956, ibid., 1349. See also appendix VI for table on GAO appropriations.

[44]Campbell testimony, February 26, 1957, *Independent Offices Appropriations for 1958*, Hearings before a Subcommittee of the House Committee on Appropriations, 85th Cong., 1st Sess., pt. 2 (Washington: GPO, 1957), 1925-26, 1927-28.

In the later years of his term, Campbell provided many examples of on-going GAO work as part of his annual budget justification. Illustrative is his testimony of February 1963 on the fiscal year 1964 budget request. For CAAD, Campbell described several jobs—audits of the National Aeronautics and Space Administration and the Agency for International Development, a report on crude helium procurement by the Bureau of Mines, a review of mail processing, and a report on automated data processing equipment in the General Services Administration. Examples of DAAD job subjects Campbell discussed were procurement of aircraft tires, vehicle maintenance operations, DOD stock funds, uneconomical procurement of aircraft engine bearings, reenlistment of undesirable military personnel, DOD's use of excess and surplus property, and leased line communication facilities. In this testimony, Campbell also provided details on the work of the European and Far East branches as well as summaries of the activities of the Office of the General Counsel, the Claims group, and the Transportation Division.[45]

In what turned out to be his last budget hearing, in February 1965, Campbell requested $46.9 million for fiscal year 1966, an amount equal to GAO's 1965 appropriation. He noted that as in other recent years, there would be net staff reductions of 63 positions—113 nonprofessional positions would be cut and 50 accountants would be added. Campbell stated that in the past decade, GAO's total staff had been reduced by 26 percent but that the auditing staff had increased by about 60 percent. For fiscal year 1966, about 48 percent of the audit effort would be on defense programs, 42 percent on civil programs, and 10 percent on international programs.[46]

In his 1965 testimony, Campbell also stressed the financial benefits to the government resulting from GAO's work. He reported collections of $27,166,000 for fiscal year 1964, including over $10 million resulting from the transportation audits, nearly $6.5 million in claims, and almost $6 million through work in DOD and the military departments. He stated that GAO had calculated measurable benefits to the government through its work other than direct collections during 1964 at $294,323,000, bringing a total financial benefit for the year of $321,489,000. Cash collections during his term, from fiscal year 1955 through fiscal year 1964, totaled $498,896,000.[47]

---

[45]Campbell testimony, February 25, 1963, *Independent Offices Appropriations for 1964*, Hearing before a Subcommittee of the House Committee on Appropriations, 88th Cong., 1st Sess., pt. 2 (Washington: GPO, 1963), 139-65.

[46]Campbell testimony, February 18, 1965, *Independent Offices Appropriations for 1966*, Hearings before a Subcommittee of the House Committee on Appropriations, 89th Cong., 1st Sess., pt. 1 (Washington: GPO, 1965), 424-25, 427.

[47]Ibid., 431-32.

Budgeting and Staffing, 1921-1966: Perspectives

For the first four decades of its history, the General Accounting Office generally received from Congress the support it needed. Slow but steady change in
GAO's internal organization and the scope and the character of its work proceeded essentially as the comptrollers general and other top management officials
thought necessary. There were some difficult times in the 1920s and 1930s, stemming from executive branch concerns over some aspects of GAO's work, leading
to proposals to change or even abolish the organization.[48]

Congress resisted such pressures. When the United States became enmeshed
in World War II, causing a tremendous increase in GAO's workload, Congress
provided the funding to support an expanded organization that reached a size of
almost 15,000. Once the conflict was over, as wartime tasks diminished, Comptroller General Warren took the initiative in cutting the staff back to its prewar
size. The budget, after reaching over $40 million in fiscal year 1947, declined
gradually over the next decade and did not top the 1947 figure until fiscal year
1960, after which it increased by small amounts each year. All the comptrollers
general between 1921 and 1965, given GAO's mandate to monitor government
expenditures in accordance with statutory appropriations, practiced economy in
running their own organization. As previously noted, a high percentage of the
annual budget paid staff salaries and the staff size fluctuated depending on GAO's
workload—with the World War II period the most graphic example.

[48]For details see chapter 10, pp. 229-47.

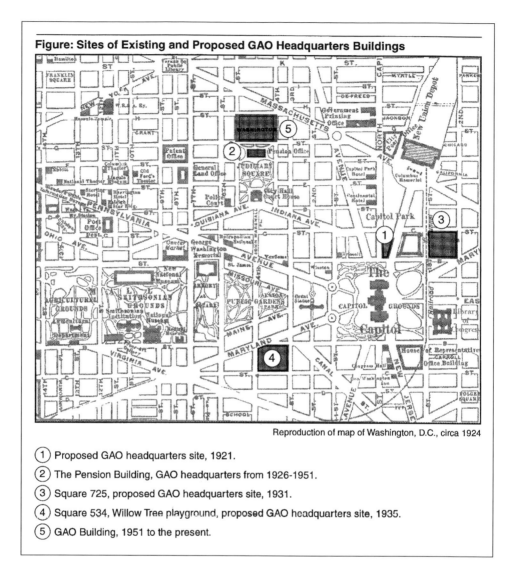

Figure: Sites of Existing and Proposed GAO Headquarters Buildings

Reproduction of map of Washington, D.C., circa 1924

① Proposed GAO headquarters site, 1921.

② The Pension Building, GAO headquarters from 1926-1951.

③ Square 725, proposed GAO headquarters site, 1931.

④ Square 534, Willow Tree playground, proposed GAO headquarters site, 1935.

⑤ GAO Building, 1951 to the present.

CHAPTER 7

GAO's Quest for a Headquarters Building, 1921-1951

From its beginning in 1921, the General Accounting Office (GAO) faced a serious problem in housing its staff, initially just over 1,700 persons. The problem persisted until 1951, when GAO moved into a new building large enough to consolidate its Washington headquarters operations.[1]

When GAO began operations on July 1, 1921, the comptroller general and his principal assistants occupied offices previously assigned to the comptroller of the treasury in the main Treasury Building. Other GAO staff had quarters in several buildings in the District of Columbia. From the beginning, GAO's workforce was decentralized because of lack of a headquarters building.

Early Efforts, 1921-1935

In GAO's first annual report (1922), Comptroller General J. R. McCarl wrote that "the supreme need of the General Accounting Office at the present time is a building which will house its entire personnel . . . and its records." Dispersion of staff and records in 20 buildings, McCarl observed, led to unsatisfactory administration, higher overhead expenses, duplication of work and effort, and reduced output.[2] As early as December 1921, a bill came up in Congress to provide GAO with a building of its own—designating a site on Capitol Hill, bounded by B Street NE (now Constitution Avenue), Delaware Avenue NE, C Street NE, and North Capitol Street. The bill proposed to create a commission, including the comptroller general, to plan a fireproof building, architecturally harmonious with the Senate Office Building (now the Russell Building) on the adjoining square.[3]

---

[1]For a somewhat more detailed account than appears here, see Roger R. Trask, Maarja Krusten, and Elizabeth E. Poel, "Buildings in GAO's History, 1921-1991" (GAO History Program, typescript paper, 1991), GAO History Program Archives.

[2]*Annual Report of the General Accounting Office, 1922* (Washington: GPO, 1922), 16.

[3]H.R. 9288, 67th Cong., 2d Sess., December 5, 1921, copy filed in Record Group (RG) 66, Records of the Commission of Fine Arts, Project Files, Folder: GAO Building, Box 67, in National Archives, Washington (hereafter cited as *CFA Records*).

McCarl presented his arguments for the building at a hearing in January 1922. He maintained that consolidating GAO in one place would save money in rental costs and increase efficiency. He thought also that GAO auditors should be separated from the executive agencies they were auditing. The proposed site was on high ground, permitting construction of basements and subbasements for storage of records. McCarl also saw as an advantage of the site that "it brings us in closer contact with Congress and gives us less intimate contact with the departments." Speaking to the Congress, he said, "we are your child, and we want to do the job just as well as you want it done."[4]

The bill did not get far in Congress. This was due at least in part to opposition from the federal Commission of Fine Arts. The commission did not approve placing the GAO building on Capitol Hill and recommended that the matter be referred officially to it for a report.[5] There is no record of any further congressional action on the bill.

After this initial setback, McCarl did not give up the fight. Almost every year thereafter, he wrote in his annual report about GAO's need for a building, and he worked in other ways to achieve his objective. Even after GAO received new space for its central offices in the Pension Building in 1926,[6] McCarl continued his campaign. Writing in 1926 to Sen. Reed Smoot (R—Utah), chairman of the Public Buildings Commission, he said that GAO's move to the Pension Building would help but would not solve the problem. "Certainly there is no Government activity more in need of a home for its entire office than is this office." McCarl suggested a site on the south side of Pennsylvania Avenue between 12th and 13th Streets NW that the Commission of Fine Arts had proposed in 1921.[7]

Pressure on GAO from the Treasury Department to vacate the space it occupied in the Treasury Building complicated McCarl's work and made more urgent his efforts to secure a headquarters building.[8] In 1925, concurrently with a proposal to move the Pension Bureau to the Department of the Interior Building, the

[4]*Public Buildings and Grounds, No. 13,* Hearings before the House Committee on Public Buildings and Grounds on H.R. 9288, Fixing Site and Creating Commission to Have Plans and Estimates Prepared for General Accounting Office Building, 67th Cong., 2d Sess., January 27, 1922 (Washington: GPO, 1922), 3-10.

[5]Minutes of the meeting held in New York City, December 13, 1921, 4-5, RG 66, Microfilm Copy of the Minutes of the Commission of Fine Arts, Microfilm No. M1148, Roll 2, National Archives, Washington, D.C. (hereafter cited as *CFA Minutes* (Microfilm)).

[6]See pp. 150-51.

[7]Letter, McCarl to Smoot, July 26, 1926, *CFA Records*, Box 67.

[8]Letter, Secretary of the Treasury Andrew W. Mellon to Smoot, December 30, 1925, RG 6, Records of the Department of the Treasury, Office of the Secretary, General Correspondence 1917-1932, Space Requirements (Office) 1922-1932, Box 150 (hereafter cited as *Treasury Records, Space Requirements*).

Commission of Fine Arts, with McCarl's agreement, considered relocating GAO's main offices in the Pension Building, located along G Street NW between 4th and 5th Streets. This large red brick building was constructed in the 1880s for the Pension Bureau. Between 1885 and 1909, presidential inaugural balls were held in the enormous great hall on its main floor.[9] Although there were proposals to move various other agencies to the Pension Building, GAO eventually got possession of the space. The first GAO offices transferred in June 1926, and McCarl moved in three months later. The new quarters still did not accommodate all GAO's staff, leaving many in other buildings in Washington.[10]

While the Pension Building, after 1926 sometimes called the GAO Building, served as GAO headquarters, the Office's efforts to get a larger new building continued. In January 1931, Rep. Richard N. Elliott (R—Indiana) (later assistant comptroller general under McCarl) introduced a bill to provide for acquiring a site and planning for a new GAO building to be located on Square 725, bounded by 1st, B, 2nd, and C Streets NE, just west of the Senate Office Building, at a cost of $950,000.[11] Like the 1921 proposal, this one encountered congressional opposition. One problem was the presence on a portion of the square of the home of the National Women's Party (now called the Sewall-Belmont House). Some members of the Commission of Fine Arts opposed razing the historic building, one of the oldest in Washington.[12]

The Pension Building Remodeling Plan, 1935

The expansion of GAO's audit effort during the New Deal raised anew the question of a new building. By January 1934, the Commission of Fine Arts began to consider remodeling and expanding the Pension Building to better accommodate GAO. J. F. deSibour, a Washington architect working for the supervising architect's office in the Treasury Department, drew plans providing for new wings on the east and west ends, altering the building's elevated roof structure, and resurfacing its brick exterior walls with stone.[13] Remodeled along classical lines, the building would have been more consistent with other federal buildings in Washington and in Judiciary Square, where it stood. The chairman of the Fine Arts Commission wrote that deSibour's plan was "a satisfactory solution of the problem of transforming into a building of appropriate monumental character a building

---

[9]*Washington Evening Star*, December 29, 1925.

[10]*Washington Evening Star*, June 28 and September 9, 1926.

[11]H.R. 16245, 71st Cong., 3d Sess., January 16, 1931, copy in *CFA Records*, Box 67. This square later became the location of the Dirksen and Hart Senate Office Buildings.

[12]Letter, Benjamin W. Morris, member, Commission of Fine Arts, to Charles Moore, chairman, January 26, 1931, *CFA Records*, Box 67; and letter, Moore to Morris, January 27, 1931, ibid.

[13]Minutes of the meeting of the Commission of Fine Arts, January 18-19, 1934, Washington, D.C., *CFA Minutes* (Microfilm), Roll 5.

The Great Hall of the Pension Building, as it appeared in the late 1920s.

which during its entire lifetime has been ridiculed both by the public and by the architectural profession." He also characterized the Pension Building as "one of the three or four eyesores of the city."[14]

In June 1935, the House of Representatives passed a bill providing $2 million out of a planned total of $4.7 million to undertake the Pension Building project. On July 23, 1935, the Senate amended the bill to authorize construction of a new building for GAO on Square 725, the site of the National Women's Party home, for $11,150,000, rather than remodeling the Pension Building. A long debate ensued in the Senate the next day when that body reconsidered its action. Overnight, leaders of the National Women's Party had lobbied hard against the plan for Square 725 and enlisted Sen. Hiram W. Johnson (R—California) in their cause. Johnson lived directly across B Street from the site.

In the debate, Johnson criticized McCarl for initially favoring the Pension Building project and later switching his support to the Capitol Hill site. Sen. Carl

Proposal for remodeling the Pension Building, 1934. Source: Washingtoniana Division, D.C. Public Library.

Hayden (D—Arizona), who favored the Capitol Hill location, explained that one reason for McCarl's switch was the protest of some justices on the District of Columbia Supreme Court, who argued that the Pension Building site was needed for eventual construction of a new court building, consistent with long-standing plans for Judiciary Square. McCarl told a Senate committee that he had agreed to the plan for the Pension Building because it looked better at the time than anything else that had been offered. Hayden suggested two advantages to the Capitol Hill site: First, it was on a hill, permitting a deep basement; second, "the General Accounting Office is an arm of the Congress. It is a special offspring of Con-

---

[14]Letter, Moore to Egerton Swartwout, March 29, 1934, *CFA Records*, Box 67.

gress, designed to see that the various executive departments and independent agencies . . . obey the will of the Congress and that they do not make expenditures not authorized by law. The nearer we can keep that office as a separate and distinct organization from the executive departments and the independent agencies the better it will be for all concerned."

Several others took part in the heated debate, including Sen. Robert R. Reynolds (D—North Carolina), who opposed building on Capitol Hill. As Reynolds put it, "the only single person who would benefit by the construction of the building proposed here would be the architect, in order that he might rear to the heavens a great monument to himself for those of the centuries to come to feast their eyes upon and say, 'That building was designed by Mr. Whoosis.'"[15]

Eventually the Senate reversed itself, and both houses agreed in August 1935 to remodel the Pension Building for GAO's use at a total cost of $4.7 million, with an initial $2 million appropriated to begin the project. Congress took this step even though a law approved on May 6, 1935, authorized the commissioners of the District of Columbia to borrow money from the Public Works Administration to construct several new court buildings in Judiciary Square. Because of this law, the National Capital Park and Planning Commission (NCPPC), which played a role in approval of new federal buildings in Washington, withdrew its previous endorsement of the plan to remodel the Pension Building.[16]

Alternate Proposals, 1935-1939

Because of the proposal to build court buildings in Judiciary Square and other objections, the August 1935 law was not the final word.[17] Alternate proposals for a GAO building surfaced immediately, including Square 635 at the southwest corner of the Capitol grounds; space on the north side of Pennsylvania Avenue between 3d and 4-1/2 Streets NW; and Square 534, between B, C, 4-1/2, and 3d Streets SW. (At the time, there were two B Streets in Washington. The one bordering the Mall on the north became Constitution Avenue, and the one on the southern border of the Mall became Independence Avenue). Square 534, the Willow Tree playground, had the largest usable area and gained the support of

[15]Debate of July 24, 1935, *Cong. Record*, 74th Cong., 1st Sess., vol. 79, pt. 11, 11769-75. Also see news coverage in *Washington Post*, July 25, 1935.

[16]RG 328, Records of NCPPC, Planning Files 545-15-80, GAO Building, Box 40, in National Archives, Washington, D.C. (hereafter cited as *NCPPC Records*).

[17]See *Washington Star*, August 9, 1935, for an article describing the disappointment of D.C. officials with the decision to remodel the Pension Building because it would interfere with their plan to build a new D.C. Supreme Court Building on the site.

GAO officials, including McCarl.[18] NCPPC officials demonstrated on quickly prepared drawings that a building there, including a basement and five floors above ground, with 103,500 square feet of usable space per floor, would provide more than enough room for GAO staff and files.[19]

NCPPC chairman Frederic A. Delano lobbied with President Roosevelt against the Pension Building project and in favor of the Willow Tree site, informing the White House that "completing the acquisition of this square would clean up one of the worst and most historic slum neighborhoods in Washington."[20] In the period before World War II, 4-1/2 Street, described as "obnoxious" by the local black civic association, was the border between segregated white and black sections of southwest Washington. From 1900 until an urban renewal effort cleared the area between 1954 and 1960, the southwest section contained low-income housing and notorious alley slums. Willow Tree playground stood on the site of Willow Tree Alley, a block that so symbolized the worst of the slums that there was a campaign to tear down its dwellings in 1913.[21] Chairman Charles Moore of the Commission of Fine Arts supported Delano's position. He informed the president that the Pension Building remodeling would ruin plans for Judiciary Square and that the Pension Building site should be used for a D.C. Supreme Court building.[22]

Notwithstanding the authorizing legislation, remodeling of the Pension Building did not begin in 1935. GAO announced late in that year that a remodeled Pension Building would not be large enough to accommodate the agency, explaining that with the increases in spending on relief and public works programs and the creation of new agencies, GAO's staff and space needs were expanding. The space planned for the Pension Building "would be wholly inadequate for the needs of the General Accounting Office now and at any time in the future."[23]

------

[18]Memorandum, John Nolen, director of planning, NCPPC, to Arno B. Cammerer, director, NCPPC, July 25, 1935, *NCPPC Records*, Delano Office Files, Box 5; letter, Cammerer to Sen. Carl Hayden, July 27, 1935, ibid., Box 28; and memorandum, T. S. Settle, secretary of the NCPPC, to Frederic A. Delano, chairman, NCPPC, and Cammerer, July 30, 1935, ibid.

[19]Memorandum, Nolen to Cammerer, July 31, 1935, ibid., Box 5.

[20]Letter, Delano to Marvin H. McIntyre (secretary to President Roosevelt), August 7, 1935, ibid., Box 28; memorandum, Roosevelt to Delano, August 20, 1935, ibid., Box 5; and letter, Settle to McIntyre, August 22, 1935, ibid.

[21]For a description of the development after 1900 of a segregated southwest section of the city, see Keith Melder, "Southwest Washington: Where History Stopped," in Kathryn Schneider Smith, ed., *Washington at Home: An Illustrated History of Neighborhoods in the Nation's Capital* (Northridge, CA: Windsor Publications, 1988), 65-75. For a detailed account of the alley slums, see James Borchert, *Alley Life in Washington: Family, Community, Religion, and Folklife in the City, 1850-1970* (Chicago: University of Illinois Press, 1982).

[22]Telegram, Moore (in Maine) to the Commission of Fine Arts, Washington, August 21, 1935, *NCPPC Records*, Delano Office Files, Box 5; and letter, Moore (in Maine) to Delano, August 22, 1935, ibid.

[23]Letter, Baity to Adm. C. J. Peoples, director of procurement, Treasury Department, November 8, 1935, RG 121, Records of the Public Buildings Service, General Correspondence 1910-1939, Folder: GAO Building, Box 2947, National Archives, Suitland, MD (hereafter cited as *PBS Records*).

Between 1936 and 1939, there was frequent discussion of GAO's need for a building and consideration of several sites, including the previously proposed Willow Tree playground and a location in the southwest quadrant of Washington. A 1936 proposal coupled the Pension Building remodeling project with construction of a records storage building for GAO on Square 518, directly across G Street from the Pension Building, between 4th and 5th Streets NW. This was the first known suggestion that Square 518 be used as a site for a GAO building.[24] During this period, GAO officials continued their campaign for a building. In 1937, Acting Comptroller General Richard N. Elliott described conditions in 12 buildings GAO occupied in Washington "and as far away as Alexandria, Va." He wrote, "Some of the buildings are poorly heated and lighted, with little or no ventilation, necessitating the use of hand flashlights for light, and men have to work in lumber jackets, heavy shoes, and mittens in winter to keep comfortable."[25] Two years later, Comptroller General Fred H. Brown wrote to W. E. Reynolds, the commissioner of public buildings, that he was "astounded" at the housing conditions he encountered at GAO. GAO, he observed, would never reach the desired levels of efficiency and effectiveness until it was consolidated and adequately housed.[26]

Because of concerns about congestion in the Northwest section of the city, planning agencies recommended to GAO and other federal agencies seeking space that they consider construction on sites in the southwest quadrant. In October 1939, the NCPPC noted that "as to the General Accounting Office Building, the Public Buildings Administration feels that it would be a mistake to undertake further construction in the Northwest Rectangle area, although the General Accounting Office has indicated that that is the area where they desire to be located."[27]

Selection of a Site and Delay in Construction, 1939-1945

Shortly thereafter, Reynolds reported to Brown that his office had submitted budget estimates for constructing a GAO building on Square 518 at a cost of

---

[24]For information on these proposals, see letter, J. H. deSibour to Procurement Division, Public Works Branch, Treasury Department, February 28, 1936, *PBS Records*, Box 2947; memorandum, Settle to Delano, January 6, 1936, *NCPPC Records*, Delano Office Files, Box 5; letter, Peoples to James P. Buchanan, chairman, House Appropriations Committee, April 27, 1936, *PBS Records*, Box 2947; First Deficiency Appropriations Bill, Fiscal Year 1936, 74th Cong., 2d Sess., H. Rept. 2591, May 7, 1936, 12; extract from minutes of the 114th meeting of NCPPC, December 18-19, 1936, *NCPPC Records*, Box 40; letter, Peoples to Cammerer (now director, National Parks Service), December 9, 1936, *PBS Records*, Box 2947; letter, Harold L. Ickes (secretary of the Interior) to secretary of the Treasury, December 31, 1936, ibid.; letter, Ickes to Peoples, March 6, 1937, ibid.; and extracts from the minutes of the 120th meeting of NCPPC, July 28-29, 1937, *NCPPC Records*, Box 40.

[25]*Annual Report of the Acting Comptroller General of the United States for the Fiscal Year Ended June 30, 1937* (Washington: GPO, 1937), 107.

[26]Letter, Brown to the commissioner of public buildings, Federal Works Agency, November 2, 1939, *PBS Records*, Box 2947; and *Annual Report of the Comptroller General of the United States for the Fiscal Year Ended June 30, 1939 (Washington: GPO, 1939), iii.*

[27]Extract from minutes of NCPPC meeting, October 19-20, 1939, *NCPPC Records*, Box 40.

Design for a proposed new GAO Building on Square 518, 1941.
Source: National Archives.

$9,850,000. Reynolds described a six-story building with a gross floor area of 1,070,000 square feet and 665,000 square feet of usable space.[28] By October 1940, Congress had authorized $9,850,000 for acquiring a site on Square 518 and construction there of a building for GAO. The balance of the $2 million appropriated in 1935 for remodeling the Pension Building and an additional $5 million appropriated early in 1941 made a total of nearly $7 million available for the project.[29]

In January 1941, both the Commission of Fine Arts and the NCPPC began considering preliminary plans for the new building. The original sketches showed a "fishbone" type building of six floors with a central section and a series of flanking wings. Because St. Mary's Catholic Church occupied the property at the northwest corner of Square 518 at 5th and H Streets NW, the proposed limestone-faced building measured 640 feet on G Street and only 400 feet on H Street.[30]

Issues raised during this and subsequent meetings involving the NCPPC and the Fine Arts Commission included the height of the building, the 600-foot colon-

[28]Letter, Reynolds to the comptroller general, December 27, 1939, *PBS Records*, Box 2947.

[29]First Supplemental Civil Functions Appropriation Act, 1941, October 9, 1940, Public Law 812; and Independent Offices Appropriation Act of 1942, April 5, 1941, Public Law 28.

[30]Extracts from the minutes of the 157th meeting of the NCPPC, January 16-17, 1941, *NCPPC Records*, Planning Files 545-15-80, Box 40; minutes of the meeting of the Commission of Fine Arts, January 23, 1941, *CFA Minutes* (Microfilm), Roll 7; and Short and Ford Architects, *Historic Structure Report and Preservation Manual for the General Accounting Office*, Final Report (Princeton, NJ: Short and Ford, 1990), 12 (hereafter cited as Short and Ford, *Historic Structure Report*).

Future site of the GAO Building, 1941. Source: National Archives.

nade proposed for the G Street side of the building, the exterior facing (limestone or brick?), and space for an interior parking garage.[31] While these discussions proceeded, work went ahead rapidly to prepare Square 518 for construction of the building. Most of the structures fronting on G, H, 4th, 5th, and G Place NW (a street bisecting Square 518 from 4th to 5th Streets) were three-story brick or frame row houses, some of them containing small stores. There were stables, garages, and yards along the rear lot lines. Two brick warehouses stood on the north side of G Place, and an electric substation was on the south side of G Place. A large parking lot lay at the northeast corner of the block, at 4th and H Streets.[32]

The commissioners of the District of Columbia closed and vacated that portion of G Place NW that extended from 4th Street toward 5th Street to the point in the square where the church property started so that the vacated area could become part of the GAO site. The government acquired title to the rest of the site

---

[31]Extract from minutes of the 158th meeting of the NCPPC, February 20-21, 1941, *NCPPC Records*, Planning Files 545-15-80, Box 40; minutes of the meeting of the Commission of Fine Arts, February 28, 1941, *CFA Minutes* (Microfilm), Roll 7; Short and Ford, *Historic Structure Report*, 12; and letter, Delano to Louis Simon (supervising architect), March 10, 1941, *NCPPC Records*, Delano Office Files, Box 5.

[32]Short and Ford, *Historic Structure Report*, 13.

by purchase from the individual owners, and the District Court ordered all occupants of the block except for St. Mary's Church to vacate by October 15, 1941.[33]

The government awarded a contract to Jeffress-Dyer, Inc., to construct the building, and excavation began. Shortly after the United States entered World War II in December 1941, the work stopped; the necessary government priorities for construction materials, including reinforcing steel, could not be obtained. Eventually the government canceled the contract with Jeffress-Dyer, and throughout the war, all that remained on the building site was a deep hole.[34]

After cancellation of the major construction job, the Public Buildings Commission proposed, in succession, to put up on the site a semipermanent building of 560,000 square feet and a temporary building of 368,000 square feet but failed again to obtain priorities for construc-

One of a series of condemnation photographs of Square 518 taken in November 1941. Source: National Archives.

tion materials. In the meantime, GAO's need for space continued to expand as the war forced a rapid increase in its workload. It occupied 1,009,099 square feet of space on June 30, 1941; 1,288,839 square feet in 19 buildings on June 30, 1943; and 1,335,125 square feet in 20 buildings on June 30, 1944. Comptroller General Lindsay C. Warren reported that on the latter date, 4,577 of GAO's 11,992 employees were working outside Washington, including the entire Postal Accounts Division, which moved to Asheville, North Carolina, for the duration of the war. Warren emphasized the space problem in his annual report for fiscal year 1942: "The providing of a mere shelter in which to house the incoming records—about 92 tons a month at the close of the fiscal year—has become a serious day-to-day problem." The next year, he noted the value of these records on which the government had to rely to adjudicate claims and emphasized their historical value.

---

[33]Letter, John M. Carmody, administrator, Federal Works Agency, to the NCPPC, March 26, 1941, *NCPPC Records*, Planning Files 545-15-80, Box 40; and Short and Ford, *Historic Structure Report*, 13-14, summarizing an article in *Washington Evening Star*, September 17, 1941.

[34]Reynolds testimony, October 19, 1945, *Construction of Public Buildings*, Hearings before the House Committee on Public Buildings and Grounds, 79th Cong., 1st Sess., on H.R. 4276, A Bill to Provide for the Construction of Public Buildings (Washington: GPO, 1945), 96 (hereafter cited as *Construction of Public Buildings, 1945*).

World War II halted construction of a new GAO Building (1) across the street from the Pension Building (2). Source: Washingtoniana Division, D.C. Public Library.

They "are filed or stored largely on temporary wooden shelves, unprotected from dust, insects, and rodents, in buildings beset with fire and water hazards."[35]

While the war stopped construction, discussion of GAO's housing needs continued. By mid-1944, GAO's staff had expanded to nearly 12,000, with over 15,000 expected by 1945. Assistant Comptroller General Frank Yates stated at an NCPPC meeting in June 1944 that the staff would not fall below 10,000 for the next 10 to 15 years. GAO expressed the view that both the site selected for the GAO building and the planned structure itself would be too small. In response, the NCPPC approved a recommendation to allow expansion of the GAO building site to both the east (across 4th Street) and to the west (across 5th Street).[36] At a meeting almost a year later, because of opposition to this proposal, an NCPPC official suggested reexamination of the question of where to locate a new GAO

---

[35]*Annual Report of the Comptroller General of the United States for the Fiscal Year Ended June 30, 1942* (GAO, typescript, 1942), 21-22; *Annual Report of the Comptroller General of the United States for the Fiscal Year Ended June 30, 1943* (Washington: GPO, n.d.), 11, 12; and *Annual Report of the Comptroller General for the Fiscal Year Ended June 30, 1944* (Washington: GPO, n.d.), 9-10.

[36]Extract from minutes of the 196th meeting of the NCPPC, June 22-23, 1944, *NCPPC Records*, Planning Files 545-15-80, Box 40.

building.[37] As World War II approached its end, there was still debate about the suitability of the chosen site.

Postwar Planning for the GAO Building, 1945-1949

A bill introduced in the House of Representatives in October 1945 suggested where and how much space GAO should get by authorizing the Federal Works Administrator to construct an additional building for GAO in Square 529 to the east across 4th Street from Square 518 and a tunnel to connect it to the building authorized in 1941, at a total cost of $18.9 million for the two buildings.[38] Yates testified at length in support of the bill. Comments on the Pension Building, still GAO's headquarters, strengthened his case. Rep. Fritz G. Lanham, chairman of the committee holding hearings, observed that the Pension Building was not suited to GAO's needs and added: "Years ago it was described by some wag as three red barns, one on top of another." Yates said that GAO had "great respect for landmarks, especially historical ones," but added, "our feeling about the [Pension] building is that it does not do its modern job very well, and does not even speak its history very eloquently."[39]

The House of Representatives did not take conclusive action on this bill and two similar ones introduced in 1946. In September 1946, both the NCPPC and the Commission of Fine Arts discussed a new plan for the GAO building. Commissioner Reynolds of the PBA presented preliminary sketches of a block building of eight stories, with the top two floors set back. The ground area would be 211,900 square feet, covering 76 percent of the available site. The gross space would be 1,922,300 square feet, with 1.2 million square feet of usable space. Reynolds noted that this type of building would provide much more basement parking space, addressing one of the earlier concerns. With a block structure, the core of the building could be used for files and the periphery, where natural light would be available through windows, for offices. As Reynolds explained, "We hope to overcome the effects of claustrophobia by having, in the rather large open spaces, low partitions so that you can see the daylight and landscape, which apparently the doctors say is all that is needed."

Reynolds stated that if the St. Mary's Church property could be acquired, the site would accommodate a seven-story building large enough to meet GAO's needs. He later told the Commission of Fine Arts that negotiations were under way with church authorities, but he did not exude confidence that the talks would succeed. He explained that the grandfathers and fathers of the present genera-

[37]Extract from minutes of the 206th meeting of the NCPPC, May 17-18, 1945, ibid.
[38]H.R. 4276, introduced October 3, 1945, in *Construction of Public Buildings, 1945*, 12.
[39]Yates's testimony and Lanham's comments are in *Construction of Public Buildings, 1945*, 39-47.

tion of members had been baptized at the church and that the church felt that it was important to hold noon services to accommodate downtown workers.[40]

As of 1946, this was an important consideration for city planners. Although Square 518 presently is in the Chinatown section of Washington, the neighborhood was home to ethnic German businessmen from the 1860s until well after World

St. Mary's Church viewed from the GAO Building excavation site (circa 1946).
Source: Washingtoniana Division, D.C. Public Library.

War II. Some local historians believe that land at 5th and G Streets was donated for construction of a church in order to attract more Germans to the neighborhood during the latter part of the nineteenth century. St. Mary's heard confessions in German as late as 1961. Only with the destruction for redevelopment in 1931 of a Chinatown then located at 4th and Pennsylvania Avenue NW did Chinese merchants begin to move into the neighborhood near Square 518.[41]

---

[40]Extract from minutes of the 220th meeting of the NCPPC, September 19-20, 1946, *NCPPC Records*, Planning Files 545-15-80, Box 40; and record (minutes) of a meeting of the Commission of Fine Arts, October 4, 1946, *CFA Records*, Box 66.

[41]Alison K. Hoagland, "7th Street Downtown: An Evolving Commercial Neighborhood," in *Washington at Home: An Illustrated History of Neighborhoods in the Nation's Capital*, 49-53.

When the NCPPC met in October 1946, its main concern was the projected building's height of 137 feet. This was much more than the 90 feet allowed on surrounding squares. Stating that government policy should be predicated on the assumption that the church property would be acquired in a few years, the commission approved a seven-story structure rather than eight. Use of the property for church purposes "will become increasingly untenable" because of continuing changes in the neighborhood and the effects of construction of the GAO building.[42]

During this period, Warren continued an active campaign for a GAO building. In January 1947, he wrote to Rep. Howard Buffet (R—Nebraska), responding to his request for information on the status of GAO audits. Warren reported that work on military and naval audits, which had been heavy during the war, was "acceptably current," with audits being completed four to eight months after payment. He expected GAO to be current on audits of civil agency accounts by the end of June 1948. Warren said that he was "convinced that one of the paramount needs of the General Accounting Office for its most efficient functioning is a building designed to meet the nature of its work and sufficiently large to house its Washington activities under one roof."[43]

Early in 1947, H.R. 3030 was introduced in the House of Representatives. The bill authorized the Federal Works Administration, over a period of three years, to construct on Square 518 a building of 1,880,000 gross square feet. At hearings on this bill, Warren summarized the by now familiar information about the scattering of GAO offices, the poor conditions in them, and the amounts of money GAO recovered each year for the government. "We are the agent of Congress," he said, "and we now think it is high time that the Congress looks after its child, at least so far as giving us proper housing is concerned."[44] Yates also spoke extensively about GAO's building needs, emphasizing the rent and maintenance costs of housing GAO in 21 different buildings in 1947. Yates now estimated that GAO's staff would be about 9,000 by 1950, down from earlier estimates, with 8,000 expected to work in the new building and 1,000 in the field.[45]

There was much discussion about the need for storage space for voluminous GAO records. Yates made clear that GAO was getting rid of excess files; in the last three years, GAO had ground up and sold as wastepaper over 18 million

---

[42]Extract from minutes of the October 17-18, 1946, meeting of the NCPPC, *NCPPC Records*, Planning Files 545-15-80, Box 40; and letter, U. S. Grant III (chairman, NCPPC) to Reynolds, October 30, 1946, ibid.

[43]Letter, Warren to Buffet, January 29, 1947, in Legislative Digest Unit Subject Files, Folder 13.b.1, Box 44, GAO History Program Archives.

[44]Text of H.R. 3030 in *GAO Building*, Hearings before the Subcommittee on Public Buildings and Grounds of the House Committee on Public Works, 80th Cong., 1st Sess. . . . (Washington: GPO, 1947), 1-4.

[45]Yates testimony on April 23 and April 24, 1947, ibid., 6-7, 9, 13, 16.

pounds of records, earning $254,407.84 for the U.S. Treasury. Yates pointed out that GAO had explored the possibility of microfilming records, but he said that storing paper records was cheaper and that there was only one company in the United States capable of handling the massive microfilming job GAO records would entail.[46]

In late July 1947, H.R. 4068, authorizing construction of a GAO building, passed but the Senate took no action on it. Nevertheless, planning for the building continued during the year.[47] A Senate bill introduced early in 1948 proposed the construction of a GAO building on Square 518 for $22.5 million, less funds already appropriated.[48] Yates commented on the general plan for the building: It would not be a monumental type of building nor

> has the General Accounting Office ever desired such a building. For such a costly structure would not accord with our conception of economy in Government spending nor would it be in harmony with the role of the Office in the Government. We wish a building as economically constructed as due regard for practical construction considerations and use requirements will permit and of sufficient size to permit the consolidation of all activities of the Office in one place by the time the building can be made ready for occupancy.[49]

Discussion at the hearing disclosed that St. Mary's Church was still worried about efforts to acquire its property on Square 518. Reynolds of PBA indicated that there would be no attempt to buy the property unless the church wanted to sell. As Reynolds put it, "We would not think of condemning that property," and Yates added that GAO foresaw no future need that would require acquisition of the space.[50]

Eventually both houses passed the bill and the president approved it on May 19, 1948. The law authorized construction of a building on Square 518 at a total cost not to exceed $22,850,000. The figure was set, even though cost estimates were at $26 million on the assumption that construction costs would decrease. Because this did not happen, Congress passed supplementary legislation in 1949

---

[46]Yates testimony, April 24, 1947, ibid., 25, 27, 28-30.

[47]*Annual Report of the Comptroller General of the United States for the Fiscal Year Ended June 30, 1947* (Washington: GPO, n.d.), 2.

[48]*GAO Building, Federal Court Building, District of Columbia*, Hearings before a Subcommittee of the Senate Committee on Public Works, 80th Cong., 2d Sess., on S. 1634 (H.R. 4068) . . . . (Washington: GPO, 1948), 1-2 (hereafter cited as *Hearings, GAO Building, 1948*).

[49]Yates testimony, February 4, 1948, *Hearings, GAO Building, 1948*, 10-15.

[50]Yates testimony, February 5, 1948, ibid., 5-6; and Short and Ford, *Historic Structure Report*, 15.

increasing the authorization to $25.4 million. On February 25, 1949, the government issued a contract to John McShain, Inc., Builders, of Philadelphia for $21,635,500, an amount not including the cost of elevators and escalators. McShain was the principal builder of the Pentagon between 1941 and 1943.[51]

Construction and Plan of the Building

By the summer of 1949, the McShain Company had begun construction of the building. The General Services Administration (GSA), a new agency that subsumed the PBA in 1949, was responsible for overseeing the work, which progressed rapidly with no serious problems. Even though the building was not yet completed, the first GAO occupants, including Comptroller General Warren, moved in in early 1951.[52] In explaining this early move, Warren told the GAO staff that "It will not be long before we can settle down in our permanent quarters and enjoy the many modern facilities that our new home will provide." In the same letter, he complained about areas of the new building that had been "soiled and even defaced" because of both the move into the building and the "carelessness and thoughtlessness of some of our own employees." He urged GAO staff to take care of the new facilities.[53]

A recent historic structure report on the GAO Building describes in detail its architectural characteristics and other features. The building is an example of the Art Moderne style of the period between 1930 and 1950, sometimes called Depression Modern. It is a massive block building, with its dimensions determined by the portion of Square 518 available for its construction. The exterior of the seven-story building is faced with limestone above a polished granite base. The building appears like "a solid block set squarely on the ground" and "the walls rise sheer and unadorned." Triple windows set in aluminum frames "reinforce the horizontal lines of the design."[54]

Inside the building, the lobbies on each floor on the G and H Street sides and the connecting corridors have marble wainscoting and terrazzo floors. Only these

---

[51]Letter, Warren to Sen. Dennis Chavez, chairman, Senate Committee on Public Works, in GAO, Office of the General Counsel, *Legislative History, Public Law 81-10*, 5; Short and Ford, *Historic Structure Report*, 4; S. 713, 81st Cong., 1st Sess., January 31, 1949, in *CFA Records*, Project Files, Box 66; S. Rept. 37, 81st Cong., 1st Sess., *Amending Public Law 533 of the Eightieth Congress Authorizing the Construction of a Building for the General Accounting Office on Square 518 in the District of Columbia*, February 7, 1949, in *CFA Records*, Project Files, Box 66; and extract from minutes of the 244th meeting of the NCPPC, March 17-18, 1949, *NCPPC Records*, Planning Files 545-15-80, Box 40. See Alfred Goldberg, *The Pentagon: The First Fifty Years* (Washington: Historical Office, Office of the Secretary of Defense, 1992).

[52]Short and Ford, *Historic Structure Report*, 4, 14; and *Washington Daily News*, November 22, 1950, clipping in *Legislative History, Public Law 81-10*, 73.

[53]Letter, Warren to employees in the new building, April 6, 1951, *Legislative History, Public Law 81-10*, 64.

[54]Short and Ford, *Historic Structure Report*, 2.

Construction of the GAO Building, 1950. Source: National Archives.

lobbies, corridors, and the executive suite and other areas on the seventh floor "received any kind of detail and finishes that can be said to have any distinctive architectural quality. The remainder of the spaces throughout the building can only be described as typical office interiors of their period." But the GAO Building "is an important example of a building type." Office buildings constructed in Washington earlier had either interior courts or a series of wings branching out from an interior spine (like the structure planned for GAO in 1941) in order to provide light and air. Two important technological developments before World War II made it possible to build a block structure—air-conditioning and fluorescent lighting. Although a few earlier government buildings, including the Pentagon and the National Archives, were air-conditioned, the GAO Building, at the time of its completion, was the largest air-conditioned structure in the District of Columbia and second in size in the United States to the Pentagon. Also, while not an innovation, the flat concrete slab construction was an important technological feature of the building design. The thick concrete floors allowed heavy loads anywhere in the building, accommodating the large volume of records GAO normally kept.[55]

The executive suite was in the southeast corner of the building on the seventh floor. Originally, the suite had a series of rooms running from east to west beginning in the southeast corner with the comptroller general's public office, a large reception and secretarial room, and the comptroller general's private office. Run-

---

[55]Ibid., 31-32.

ning north along a private corridor, beginning next to the comptroller general's public office, was the office of the secretary to the assistant comptroller general, the office of the assistant comptroller general, a large conference room, the office of the executive officer, and the office of the assistant executive officer. Other spaces to the west of the private corridor included a files room, a kitchen, and a private dining room. There were two interesting features of the comptroller general's public office: a fireplace centered on the west wall, faced with alberene soapstone, and a distinctive clock, 12 inches in diameter, its works placed behind the paneled wall, with the hands and numerals mounted directly on the paneling.[56]

Works of Art in the Building

Although the building itself was relatively plain inside and out, its planners and designers anticipated the installation of several works of art. The January 1949 model for the building showed sculptural pieces at the southwest (5th and G Streets NW) and southeast (4th and G Streets NW) corners. When the Commission of Fine Arts considered this plan, it eliminated these works and decided that land-scaping for the building should carry around these corners.[57]

Three other sculptural elements were in the original plans: reliefs carved in granite on both sides of the main entrances on G and H Streets and a series of aluminum panels on and near the elevator doors in the lobbies near the entrances on G and H Streets. The Commission of Fine Arts selected the sculptors to do these works by October 1949—Joseph Kiselewski for the G Street sculpture, Lee Lawrie for the H Street sculpture, and Heinz Warneke for the aluminum panels in the elevator lobbies.[58]

Joseph Kiselewski, born in Minnesota in 1901, studied at the Minneapolis School of Art, the National Academy of Design, and the Beaux-Arts Institute of Design and abroad at the American Academy in Rome and the Academy Julian in Paris.[59] His $24,500 contract with the Public Buildings Service required him to design and prepare models for the G Street reliefs and to supervise both the roughing

---

[56]Ibid., 70-71. There were several identical clocks in other rooms of the executive suite.

[57]Short and Ford, *Historic Structure Report*, 17-18; and minutes of the Commission of Fine Arts, January 10, 1949, *CFA Minutes* (Microfilm), Roll 9.

[58]Minutes of the meeting of the Commission of Fine Arts, June 29, 1949, *CFA Records*, Project Files, Folder: GAO Building, Box 66; and office memorandum, S. G. Wetzel to A. S. Thorn (supervising architect, Public Buildings Service, GSA), October 3, 1949, *CFA Records*, Central Files, Folder: GAO Sculpture, Box 46.

[59]Glenn B. Opitz, ed., *Dictionary of American Sculptors* (Poughkeepsie, NY: Apollo, 1984), 219; and Joseph Kiselewski, "From Farmboy to Sculptor: An Autobiography," *National Sculpture Review*, vol. 28 (winter 1979-1980): 16-19, 27.

out and the finish carving of the sculpture. Several stonecutters carved the panels, completing their work in the spring of 1952.[60]

The stonecutters carved Kiselewski's bas-relief panels, each nine feet high and 15 feet long, in polished red granite, a band of which ran completely around the building at ground level. Titled "American Professional Workers and American Laborers," the panels show professional people at work on the left of the G Street entrance and laborers on the right and contain a total of 30 figures.[61] Asked a quarter century after he completed his work to explain his design for the panels, Kiselewski responded: "To some degree, I kept it simple in style so that there would be less of a problem for the carvers who had to work with very dense red granite. . . . If I had done otherwise, the cost of the carving would have been enormous. Also the relief was only about two inches. At the same time, I kept it simple to conform or adapt to the building."[62]

Lee Lawrie was born in Germany in 1877 and came to the United States as an infant. He studied under the prominent sculptors Philip Martigny and Augustus Saint-Gaudens in New York and earned a fine arts degree at Yale University, where he taught sculpture from 1908 to 1918.[63] Kiselewski worked and studied with him for several years in the 1920s in New York. Like Kiselewski, Lawrie created full-scale models for the two panels intended for the H Street entrance. The models portrayed American trade, industry, religion, education, science, and the security of the family. Stonecarvers never executed these panels because of a lack of funds.[64] Lawrie's and Kiselewski's models are still in GAO's possession.

Heinz Warneke was born in Germany and came to the United States in 1925. He taught sculpture at the Corcoran School of Art and George Washington University in Washington. He designed eight large panels—representing the spirit of laws, freedom of religion, freedom of speech, liberty, justice, internal development, national ideology, and national security—and eight small panels—labeled sunlight, rain, snow, wind, hydrography, energy-matter, geology, and astronomy. Four copies of the large bas-relief panels and 16 copies of the small panels were made in

---

[60]Thorn to Kiselewski, December 7, 1949; P. S. Hart (acting supervising architect, Public Buildings Service, GSA) to Kiselewski, January 5, 1950; Thorn to Kiselewski, April 17 and October 2, 1950; copies in the Papers of Joseph Kiselewski, Archives of American Art, Washington, D.C.

[61]James M. Goode, *The Outdoor Sculpture of Washington, D.C.: A Comprehensive Historical Guide* (Washington: Smithsonian Institution Press, 1974), 232. Also see Joseph S. Rosapepe, "Works of Art at GAO," *GAO Review*, vol. 13, Issue 2 (spring 1978): 28-31.

[62]Interview with Kiselewski by George Gurney, January 16, 1978, typescript, 6, provided by George Gurney, National Museum of American Art, Smithsonian Institution.

[63]Obituary, *Washington Evening Star*, January 24, 1963.

[64]Goode, *Outdoor Sculpture of Washington*, 232; Short and Ford, *Historic Structure Report*, 18-19; and Rosapepe, "Works of Art at GAO," 31.

shiny aluminum. Each door in the 16 sets of double doors on the elevators in the first floor lobbies on G and H Streets received a large panel, and the small panels were mounted in vertical rows of four to frame each side of each pair of doors. Installation of the aluminum panels was completed in November 1951; Warneke received $7,400 for his work.[65]

The 1949 building plans included a proposal to install mural paintings in various locations. Early drawings for the building specified wall space for murals in two locations in the comptroller general's suite. Four other murals initially proposed for the two first floor public lobbies were not commissioned because of a shortage of funds.[66] The Commission of Fine Arts and the PBA eventually selected artists for the murals in the comptroller general's suite: Mitchell Jamieson to do the mural in the large conference room and John Chapman Lewis to do the second mural.[67]

Mitchell Jamieson was born in Maryland in 1915. He studied in Washington at the Abbott School of Fine and Commercial Arts and the Corcoran School of Art and later in Mexico City and Italy. During his career, he taught art in Florida; Virginia; Texas; and Washington, D.C., and at the University of Maryland. Among his works were watercolor scenes of the Roosevelt estate at Hyde Park, New York, on commission from President and Mrs. Franklin D. Roosevelt. He was also noted for his works of wartime art with the Navy Combat Art Program between 1942 and 1946.[68]

Before doing his mural, titled *Historic Dare County*, Jamieson visited the area in North Carolina depicted in the painting, Comptroller General Warren's home territory.[69] When the Commission of Fine Arts inspected the finished 15' x 7'5" mural, done in oils, Warren listed its contents with great pleasure: the restored Fort Raleigh, the cradle of Virginia Dare (about which Warren said, "I wish so much the artist had put a baby in the cradle as I suggested"), a tree with the word *Croatan* carved on it, the Atlantic Ocean in a storm, the Dare County Courthouse, Kill Devil Hills and the Wright memorial, the Oregon Inlet Coast Guard Station, the Wright Brothers' first flight and plane, a fisherman's cottage

---

[65]Short and Ford, *Historic Structure Report*, 19; Rosapepe, "Works of Art at GAO," 31; and minutes of the meeting of the Commission of Fine Arts, January 6, 1950, *CFA Records*, Box 66.

[66]Short and Ford, *Historic Structure Report*, 19; minutes of the meeting of the Commission of Fine Arts, June 25, 1951, *CFA Minutes* (Microfilm), Roll 9.

[67]Minutes of the Commission of Fine Arts, with attached exhibit E, "Discussion of Murals for General Accounting Office," December 12, 1952, *CFA Records*, Box 46.

[68]"Mitchell Jamieson," in Peter H. Falk, ed., *Who Was Who in American Art* (Madison, CT: Sound View Press, 1985), 312; and obituary, *Washington Post*, February 6, 1976.

[69]Minutes of the Commission of Fine Arts, April 13, 1953, *CFA Minutes* (Microfilm), Roll 10.

with net hung out to dry, driftwood, shells on the beach, the Pea Island Snow Goose Refuge, the calm ocean with a wreck on the beach, the wreck of another ship, Jockey's Ridge and sand dunes, Pamlico Sound and fish houses and boats, the Cape Hatteras Lighthouse, and sea oats and willets on the beach. In the lower right-hand corner of the mural was a bottle washed up on the beach, with the artist's name on it, probably based on the well-known Irish whiskey with a similar name, Jameson. Jamieson received $3,500 for his work. The mural was mounted in the conference room, now named the Warren Room, where it remains at present.[70]

John Chapman Lewis was born in Washington, D.C., in 1920, of parents who hailed from the North Carolina coastal area. He attended the Corcoran School of Art and later studied in New York City. After World War II service in the Navy, he taught art at the Corcoran School and at other Washington area institutions.[71] As he had done with the Jamieson mural, Warren exercised considerable influence in determining the composition of Lewis's work. Lewis visited Warren, who gave him a general idea of what he thought the mural should depict, and showed him a photograph of women working in tulip-growing fields in Warren's home area of North Carolina. On this basis, as well as a visit to the site in North Carolina, Lewis prepared a preliminary drawing and later painted the large 10'6" x 7'5" mural in his home studio. He received a payment of $1,875 for his work. Lewis's *Tulip Culture* was mounted on a wall in the comptroller general's private office.[72]

Warren described the painting when the Commission of Fine Arts inspected it at the time of its completion in January 1954:

> This is believed to be the largest tulip field in the United States, in my county of Beaufort in North Carolina, comprising 22 acres. When the Dutch lost thousands of bulbs by flood, we sent 14,000 tulip bulbs to Holland. The green field in the background of the tulips is intended to indicate that the tulips have been picked. Mr. Lewis went to Beaufort County to talk with the people. The three persons depicted are personally known to me. The tulip

---

[70]"Dare County Coastline and History Depicted Lavishly in General Accounting Office," *Coastland (NC) Times*, January 1, 1954, clipping in the Papers of Lindsay C. Warren, Wilson Library, Southern Historical Collection, the University of North Carolina at Chapel Hill; Short and Ford, *Historic Structure Report*, 20; and letter, David E. Finley to Reynolds, December 19, 1953, *CFA Records*, Central Files, Box 46.

[71]Minutes of the meetings of the Commission of Fine Arts, December 12, 1952, and February 3, 1953, *CFA Records*, Central Files, Box 46.

[72]GAO, *John Chapman Lewis*, GAO History Program, Oral History Series (typescript, 1991), 5-17; and Short and Ford, *Historic Structure Report*, 20.

field represents reclaimed swamp land. The marketing of tulips has become a great industry there.[73]

Dedication, 1951

The builder completed the GAO Building on schedule in mid-1951, and a formal cornerstone-laying and dedication ceremony took place before a large crowd on September 11, 1951. The U.S. Air Force Band played, and the chaplains of the Senate and the House offered prayers. Assistant Comptroller General Yates, who had worked so hard for many years to get the building, presided. Commissioner Reynolds of the Public Buildings Service delivered brief remarks. He said that the building ". . . has the best lighting, heating, air-conditioning, and vertical transportation of any modern government building in Washington. Yet with all these advantages—and very importantly—it cost, considering price changes, less per square foot to build than any of them and will cost less per square foot to operate."[74]

Comptroller General Warren delivered a major address, speaking not only about the building but also about the history of GAO and its work. While the building was expensive, Warren acknowledged, GAO collected enough money in any five-month period to pay that cost.[75] Following Warren's remarks, President Harry S. Truman, who on at least one occasion had inspected construction progress on the building during one of his famous morning walks, laid the cornerstone and delivered an address. He began by saying that many people in government considered GAO "a bugaboo that keeps them from doing what they want to do" and that many people outside the government considered GAO "a dry and boring subject." He added, "But the General Accounting Office is neither a bugaboo nor a bore. It is a vital part of our Government. Its work is of great benefit to all of us. The people who run the General Accounting Office certainly deserve these new and better quarters." He congratulated GAO for handling "the biggest auditing job in the history of mankind" and described the joint accounting program involv-

---

[73]Minutes of the meeting of the Commission of Fine Arts, January 28, 1954, *CFA Records*, Central Files, Box 46. Lewis's mural hung where it was installed between 1954 and 1973. It was apparently not appreciated by everyone and was removed from the wall in 1973, rolled on a cylinder, and sent to the National Museum of American Art for storage. In 1990, Comptroller General Charles A. Bowsher decided that it should be returned to the GAO Building. In 1991, after restoration, *Tulip Culture* was rehung in the GAO Auditorium.

[74]Reynolds speech, September 11, 1951, copy in GAO History Program Archives.

[75]Warren speech, September 11, 1951, copy in GAO History Program Archives.

Dedication of the GAO Building, September 11, 1951.

ing GAO, the Treasury Department, and the Bureau of the Budget as one of the Office's outstanding achievements under Warren's leadership.[76]

The dedication of the GAO Building marked an important occasion for GAO staff and the culmination of an effort that began 30 years earlier. Ironically, by the time the new building was finished, it was not entirely suitable for GAO. The old GAO was essentially a voucher-checking organization that conducted most of its business from offices in Washington, dealing with a mountain of vouchers and other financial documents. In both the original 1941 plan for the building and the postwar revisions, its designers envisioned the need for large file space. Therefore, the building, when completed in 1951, had enclosed offices with windows along the outer walls, but with much of the inner space unpartitioned. By this time, GAO, under Warren's leadership, was moving away from the old voucher-checking tasks toward what he called the comprehensive audit. This approach called for much of GAO's audit activity to take place at sites in the agencies under audit in Washington, the field, and abroad. The almost overwhelming need for file space, a part of GAO's past, no longer existed. So GAO had a building too large

---

[76]Copy of the original text of President Truman's speech, with handwritten insertions of the president, as delivered on September 11, 1951, provided by the Harry S. Truman Library, Independence, MO, in GAO History Program Archives. Part of Truman's speech, in which he defended his tax and spending policies, provoked partisan criticism from his political opponents. See *Cong. Record*, 82d Cong., 1st Sess., vol. 97, pt. 15, appendix, September 25, 1951, A5854-55.

President Harry S. Truman laying the cornerstone of the GAO Building, September 11, 1951.

for its 1951 needs, when many of its staff worked outside Washington, and with its internal structure designed for the past rather than for the present.

GAO was pleased to have the new building, but there were some nostalgic expressions about the Pension Building that GAO had occupied for 25 years. The GAO employee newspaper, the *Watchdog*, carried this item early in 1951:

> Now about this new building we've moved into—we don't wish to appear ungrateful or unappreciative of all the money and effort expended to give us a splendid modern mausoleum, but our heart remains in the old building across the street. We miss the archways and balconies, the reflecting pool which appeared in the hall outside our door after a heavy rain, the pigeons which used to blunder through the skylight and cruise above their captive audience, the lonely gargoyle above the elevator on the third floor, and the dry dusty fountain on the main floor over which the roof should have leaked but didn't. Yes, we even miss the fluttery Zazu Pitts quality of the elevators. Now we have air-conditioning, fluorescent lights, and floors which don't creak but we have

lost our quaintness and our charm. And we have a sneaking suspicion that no inaugural ball will ever be held in *this* building.[77]

Conclusion

Much change came to GAO between 1921 and the mid-1960s. GAO's increasingly professional program and staff and its new building symbolized after 1951 the Office's emergence as an agency of expanding importance and significance in the federal government. During this period, GAO became more identified with Congress and its leaders worked hard to cultivate closer and wider relationships with the legislative branch. By its willingness to give GAO sufficient funding and staff and, ultimately, an imposing new building, Congress signaled its recognition of GAO's contributions and its support for the Office.

---

[77]*Watchdog*, vol. 9, no. 2 (February 1951), 8.

CHAPTER 8

GAO Operations, 1921-1940: Decisions, Claims, Accounting Systems, and Contracts

The first two decades of GAO's existence were very important in setting the organization's image, style, and operational methods. Comptroller General J. R. McCarl left a profound mark on GAO; impressions of his exercise of both personal prerogatives and organizational powers formed the basis for the Office's early reputation. That reputation was controversial, to say the least.

McCarl and his immediate successors, Acting Comptroller General Richard N. Elliott and Comptroller General Fred H. Brown, looked to the Budget and Accounting Act, 1921, as the source of GAO's jurisdiction and authority and as a mandate for its work program. McCarl applied a broad and flexible interpretation of the act in arriving at his understanding of GAO's powers and jurisdiction.[1]

GAO's Organization for Legal Work

During these early years, much of GAO's work had a high legal content. McCarl was a lawyer, but he determined his legal approach not by that fact but by his interpretation of the nature of the duties assigned to GAO by the Budget and Accounting Act. Many of these duties GAO inherited from its predecessors, the comptroller of the treasury and the six auditors. One of McCarl's earliest organizational steps was establishment in July 1921 of a legal department under a chief attorney, who presided over a staff of attorneys. In 1922, this office became the Division of Law, headed by the solicitor. In 1928, McCarl renamed the Division of Law the Office of the General Counsel (OGC) and changed the solicitor's title to general counsel.

Rudolph L. Golze, chosen by McCarl as solicitor in 1921, headed the Division of Law and the Office of the General Counsel until 1939, when

---

[1] See chapter 2 for a legislative history of the Budget and Accounting Act, 1921, and an explanation and an analysis of the law. See appendix III for the text of the law.

John C. McFarland succeeded him. Golze, a graduate of the University of Pennsylvania Law School, practiced law privately for a time in Philadelphia and then entered government service, working in Panama and with the Office of the Comptroller of the Treasury. McFarland, trained at the National University Law School, later a part of George Washington University, also worked as an attorney with the comptroller's office and transferred to GAO as a senior attorney in 1921. The fact that initially the head of the legal office was the third- ranking official in GAO, serving as acting comptroller general in the absence of the comptroller general and the assistant comptroller general, testifies to his importance in the organization.[2]

GAO attorneys in the Pension Building. Copyright 1940, The Washington Post. *Reprinted with permission.*

McCarl emphasized the importance of legal work in GAO in his 1926 annual report. He wanted to dispel the common impression that GAO's work

[2]"GAO's General Counsels," *GAO Review* (summer 1971): 123-27; office memorandum, Chief Clerk John K. Willis, March 27, 1928, 79 MS 1273; and *Annual Report of the Comptroller General of the United States for the Fiscal Year Ended June 30, 1928* (Washington: GPO, 1928), 35-36.

was mainly accounting. Rather, "the question whether any particular expenditure or collection is in accordance with law is the principal function of the General Accounting Office." "It staggers the imagination," he added, "to consider the variety and complexity of legal questions which arise during the course of a year in the conduct of the business of the United States requiring the disbursement of public funds."[3]

In a 1933 report on GAO, McCarl emphasized the many functions involving legal work. This required, McCarl wrote, "a group of specially and highly trained lawyers—lawyers who, through wide and long experience have acquired an intimate knowledge of the Government's almost innumerable activities and the methods and matters peculiar to each. If there exists 'career' work in the Government it is to be found in the law work of the General Accounting Office."[4]

McCarl's reference to career work provides insight into the central role the lawyers in OGC played during these years. Other than the top managers, they were the only highly trained people in GAO, with college degrees and professional experience. Besides the OGC attorneys, there were staff trained in the law, working elsewhere in the Office, but not necessarily on legal matters. For example, numerous staff working in the claims area were lawyers, but they were not assigned to OGC and they did not necessarily perform duties requiring legal training. OGC in fact was the most influential organization in GAO, other than the Office of the Comptroller General, until after World War II. Thereafter, as GAO moved into audits of government corporations, comprehensive audits of agency programs, and new financial management work, the audit divisions rose in influence.

Decisions of the Comptroller General

One of the most important legal functions of the comptroller general was to decide on the legality of proposed or actual federal expenditures. Government disbursing officers or agency heads could request him to issue a decision or an opinion, and he could render decisions as part of the audit process if questions arose or problems appeared. The Budget and Accounting Act, 1921, did not delineate this power specifically, but the law stated, in Section 304, that all statutory powers and duties of the comptroller of the

---

[3]*Annual Report of the Comptroller General of the United States for the Fiscal Year Ended June 30, 1926* (Washington: GPO, 1926), 16-17. See also *Annual Report of the Comptroller General of the United States for the Fiscal Year Ended June 30, 1927* (Washington: GPO, 1927), 38-42, for a summary of the work of the Division of Law.

[4]Letter, McCarl to the president of the Senate, April 6, 1933, "Functions of the General Accounting Office," S. Doc. 16, 73d Cong., 1st Sess. (Washington: GPO, 1933), 3. McCarl sent an identical letter to the president of the United States.

treasury and the six auditors were to be vested in and imposed upon GAO. The Dockery Act (1894) authorized the comptroller of the treasury to render decisions, and section 304 passed this power to the comptroller general.[5]

McCarl extensively exercised his power to make decisions. His decisions covered all manner of questions relating to the disbursement of public money. In making some of his decisions, McCarl explained and asserted his understanding of GAO's jurisdiction.[6] His jurisdictional decisions aroused controversy with the attorney general and other agency heads. Disputes over McCarl's decisions, both within and outside the government, contributed to the perception, especially in the executive branch, that he was an arbitrary official who had exceeded his authority and violated the constitutional principle of separation of powers.[7]

McCarl's very first decision resulted from a question posed by the secretary of war about payment of enlistment and reenlistment bonuses by the Army. Section 27 of the Army Reorganization Act (approved June 4, 1920) authorized the payment of such bonuses, but the Army Appropriations Act (approved June 30, 1921) repealed the bonus provision. The secretary of war questioned whether the Army was authorized to pay the bonus to men who enlisted or reenlisted before June 30, 1921, but had not yet received payment. McCarl ruled that the 1921 law did not affect rights to the bonus for soldiers who enlisted or reenlisted between June 4, 1920, and June 29, 1921.[8]

Another early decision illustrated two points—(1) that McCarl interpreted the law as requiring him to render decisions on matters involving small amounts of money and (2) that he was willing to be flexible in his application of the law. A 1922 case involved an expenditure of $10.09 for purchase of envelopes from a private supplier by the warden of Leavenworth Penitentiary, a federal prison in Kansas. Routine settlement of the prison's accounts in March 1922 had resulted in disallowance of the expenditure; the warden then asked McCarl to review the settlement. The statute in question, enacted in 1906, required the postmaster general to contract for the purchase of all envelopes needed by federal agencies. In his decision, McCarl noted the warden's statement that the envelopes were to be used for correspondence

---

[5]See chapter 1, pp. 14-16, for terms of the Dockery Act, and appendix III for text of the Budget and Accounting Act, 1921.

[6]GAO published leading decisions in monthly pamphlets and in a cumulative annual volume, *Decisions of the Comptroller General of the United States*. This compilation replaced *Decisions of the Comptroller of the Treasury*. See GAO, *Annual Report, 1926*, 67-68.

[7]See chapter 10 for a detailed discussion of this point.

[8]Letter, McCarl to the secretary of war, July 5, 1921, 1 Comp. Gen. 1; also found in 1 MS 1.

with paroled prisoners—plain envelopes, to avoid the possibility of publicly identifying the recipients as former prisoners. McCarl concluded that the purchase violated the 1906 law, but previous, similar purchases had apparently not been questioned. Thus he allowed the payment of $10.09 but asked that the prison comply with the law in the future.[9]

Twice in 1924, McCarl made decisions related to the activities of Gen. John J. Pershing, the commander of the American Expeditionary Force in Europe during World War I and later Army chief of staff. On August 2, 1923, President Warren G. Harding died in San Francisco after a western speaking trip and a vacation in Alaska. General Pershing and his aide, Maj. George C. Marshall, who coincidentally were in San Francisco at the time on official travel, received orders from the Army adjutant general to accompany Harding's body on a funeral train from San Francisco to Washington. On the train, Pershing occupied a drawing room and Marshall, half of a parlor car compartment. For this trip, each officer received $152.90 for the mileage traveled. In addition, Pershing received $111 for his drawing room costs and Marshall, $44.25 for his compartment. McCarl had to decide whether these reimbursements were legal. He decided that they were not. Neither the law governing regular Army travel nor the Deficiency Act of April 2, 1924, appropriating money for expenses incurred because of Harding's illness and death, allowed them to be reimbursed for sleeping or parlor car accommodations. McCarl ruled that Pershing, the most prominent U.S. general during World War I, and Marshall, later to be chief of staff of the Army during World War II, would have to refund the amounts they had received for their Pullman accommodations on this trip.[10]

In September 1924, the secretary of war asked McCarl to decide whether General Pershing, who was about to retire, would in retirement be entitled to the pay and the allowances he was receiving as an active officer. As McCarl explained in his decision, Pershing held the special title of "general of the Armies of the United States," a title that had been used from time to time since 1799, held in the past by officers such as Gens. Philip H. Sheridan, William T. Sherman, and Ulysses S. Grant. The title was exclusive, granted only to outstanding military leaders, one at a time and only in special circumstances. McCarl also cited an 1882 law stating that the general of the Army shall be retired at full pay and allowances. He ruled that under this law, Pershing was entitled in his retirement to the pay and allowances he was receiving at the end of his active service.[11]

---

[9]Letter, McCarl to A. V. Anderson, warden, Leavenworth Penitentiary, Leavenworth, KS, July 12, 1922, 11 MS 529.

[10]McCarl decision, unaddressed, August 8, 1924, 36 MS 279.

[11]Letter, McCarl to the secretary of war, September 20, 1924, 4 Comp. Gen. 317.

Early in his term, McCarl began to use decisions to establish the authority and the jurisdiction of the General Accounting Office. A May 1923 decision, which Harvey C. Mansfield, Sr., a scholar who in the 1930s became a severe critic of GAO, described as McCarl's "declaration of independence," was especially significant.[12] The case at issue, relating to the powers of the U.S. Employees' Compensation Commission, led to a direct confrontation between the comptroller general and the attorney general. McCarl had issued a formal decision on January 29, 1923, denying the commission authority to pay certain awards from public funds in conflict with the 1916 law that established it. The commission had paid the awards in question to public employees for medical care for diseases they had contracted. McCarl had ruled that he would allow previous payments because the commission had been making them for some time, but he cut off awards made after June 30, 1923. Congress then considered legislation allowing such awards in the future but did not pass it, except that in a law of March 4, 1923, it permitted the awards to be made until March 1, 1924.

On May 16, 1923, the acting attorney general issued an opinion stating, in regard to the awards, that the "Employees' Compensation Commission has the power by virtue of the act under which it was created [1916] to construe the terms of said act, and that any construction so rendered is final and beyond interference by other governmental officials." McCarl, in a decision addressed to the president of the United States, described the acting attorney general's opinion as "advisory" and lacking "the force of a judicial determination." He argued that Congress, by passing the March 1923 law, had "recognized the determinative effect" of his decision and described the law as "the most recent expression of the only authority to which there lies an appeal from the decision of this office." The heart of McCarl's decision, his "declaration of independence," was as follows:

> To hold that in the examination of the commission's accounts this office may not refuse credit for payments made in violation of the law would be to disregard the clear intent of the law, make ineffectual the provision that the action of this office "shall be final and conclusive upon the executive branch of the Government," abandon all pretense of accountability for public funds, and destroy a sound accounting procedure that has been built up through the experience of more than a century.

---

[12]Harvey C. Mansfield, Sr., *The Comptroller General: A Study in the Law and Practice of Financial Administration* (New Haven: Yale University Press, 1939), 76.

McCarl added that he was always pleased to consider the views of other government agencies, "but I may not accept the opinion of any official, inclusive of the Attorney General, as controlling of my duty under the law."[13] McCarl had made his point clearly, but the fact remained that, other than his power to disallow payments, he could not enforce his views with complete effect.

An important decision in 1935 also illustrated McCarl's determination to explain and assert GAO's jurisdiction. The specific case involved the Navy's contention that a naval officer named Bullard, who was detached from duty and ordered to his home to await retirement orders, was involved in a permanent change of station and therefore was eligible to receive payment for his wife's expenses in traveling to their home. This question came up in a whole series of instances over a period of more than a decade. McCarl quoted the definition of "permanent station" as it appeared in a 1920 law—that it was a "shore station or the home yard of the vessel to which the person concerned may be ordered." Despite this clear definition, the Navy allowed payment for travel to officers' homes, as in the Bullard case.

As McCarl pointed out in his decision, contained in a letter to the secretary of the navy, the Supreme Court in *United States v. Phisterer*, 94 U.S. 219, had ruled that "the home of an officer to which he is ordered is not a military station." But Bullard brought suit in the Court of Claims after GAO disallowed the claim for payment of his wife's travel expenses. The Court of Claims, in *Bullard v. United States*, 66 Ct. Cls. 264, overruled GAO's disallowance. McCarl argued that the Court of Claims was aware of the attorney general's views in opposition to GAO's disallowance, views that McCarl considered adverse to the federal government. The *Bullard* decision, McCarl contended, was invalid because it had ignored the Supreme Court's decision in the *Phisterer* case. After this decision, the secretary of the navy informed McCarl that he had directed that the "Attorney General's opinions and the decisions of the Court of Claims be followed hereafter."

In his letter to the secretary of the navy, McCarl warned him of the seriousness of his stand and reminded him, quoting the Budget and Accounting Act, that balances in disbursing accounts certified by GAO are "final and conclusive on the executive branch of the Government." McCarl acknowledged that the attorney general had the statutory right to give opinions on questions of law but that such opinions "are merely advisory and necessarily so else an Attorney General could become effectively dominant in the affairs of all departments." If GAO accepted decisions made by the attorney gen-

---

[13]McCarl to the president, May 29, 1923, 2 Comp. Gen. 784.

eral or other agency heads on the legality of expenditures, the result would be "to undo all that the Congress did in separating the accounting officers from the influence and domination of the Executive branch."

McCarl also pointed out that if executive agencies believed that GAO had improperly restricted the use of appropriations, "the proper and orderly procedure, and the only procedure showing a proper degree of respect for the authority of the Congress, is to apply to the Congress for clarification of the law." He said "it is beyond understanding" why the Navy Department had not taken this route in the present case. He concluded by stating that GAO would no longer try to help the Navy Department resolve such issues, as it had in the past, and held that all future payments such as in the Bullard case would be disallowed.[14]

One additional example from the thousands of decisions issued by McCarl during his 15-year term will suffice to illustrate their subjects and range. Again, this case gave McCarl an opportunity to assert GAO's jurisdiction. In June 1934, the assistant commissioner of the General Land Office in the Interior Department requested GAO to return to the Land Office the original lease for recreational land signed by the federal government and a New Mexico county. The assistant commissioner stated that "the original signed copy of this lease is a necessary part of the public land records, and as such may not lawfully be removed from the General Land Office." McCarl pointed out in his reply, addressed to the secretary of the interior, that the law, including Section 304 of the Budget and Accounting Act, required that original copies of all government contracts be filed with GAO. GAO was not authorized to waive this requirement, even in cases such as this, where a General Land Office regulation conflicted. McCarl suggested that if the Land Office needed a copy, it make a photostatic copy. He concluded by asking the secretary to instruct Department of the Interior employees accordingly.[15]

The issuing of decisions and opinions was an important function assigned to the comptroller general by the Budget and Accounting Act and one that McCarl took seriously and exercised widely. His decisions, perhaps more than anything else, enabled McCarl to establish GAO's role in the government as a watchdog of the Treasury. Some decisions, especially those in which he asserted GAO's authority over executive agencies, including the Department of Justice, caused considerable controversy and provided one basis for efforts in the 1920s and 1930s to change GAO's functions or even to abolish the Office.[16] GAO's Office of the General Counsel prepared these

---

[14]Letter, McCarl to the secretary of the navy, February 27, 1935, 14 Comp. Gen. 648.

[15]Letter, McCarl to the secretary of the interior, August 1, 1934, 14 Comp. Gen. 89.

[16]See chapter 10 for a detailed account of these efforts.

decisions and opinions, in close collaboration with McCarl, who obviously was a strong influence in their drafting. After McCarl's term, his successors continued to issue decisions and opinions, but they tended to be less contentious and assertive and thus attracted less public notice. But they remained a significant function of the comptroller general.

Claims

Another important GAO function requiring extensive legal work was handling claims. Section 305 of the Budget and Accounting Act provided that GAO settle and adjust all claims by and against the U.S. government, a function that earlier was the responsibility of the comptroller of the treasury. Section 307 empowered the comptroller general to provide for payment, through agency disbursing officers, of accounts and claims it settled. When GAO began operations in 1921, the six original divisions handled claims work in their respective areas. In the special area of transportation, responsibility for claims work resided between 1921 and 1922 in the Transportation Rate Board, a Treasury Department organization transferred to GAO, and then in the Transportation Division, created in 1922.[17] When the new Military and Civil divisions began operating in the spring of 1923, they took over claims work in their jurisdictions.[18]

Late in 1923, McCarl decided, in an effort to achieve efficiency and uniformity of procedure, to establish a separate Claims Division to handle most of the claims work. The new organization took over the claims job of the Civil and Military divisions, while the Transportation and Post Office Department divisions continued to handle claims in their areas of responsibility. When established in 1923, the Claims Division had 160 staff.[19] Another reorganization to handle claims became effective on July 1, 1926, when McCarl consolidated the existing Claims and Transportation divisions into the Claims Division. The new division handled all claims except postal claims. Previously the Claims and Transportation divisions were located in separate buildings in Washington. GAO's move to the Pension Building in the summer of 1926 made possible the merger of the organizations.[20]

---

[17]*Annual Report of the General Accounting Office, 1922*, H. Doc. 482, 67th Cong., 4th Sess. (letter, McCarl to speaker of the House, December 4, 1922), 3-10. See pp. 188-91 for detailed information about transportation claims.

[18]*Annual Report of the General Accounting Office, 1923*, H. Doc. 101, 68th Cong., 1st Sess. (letter, McCarl to speaker of the House, December 3, 1923), 2, 20.

[19]General Regulations No. 33, November 26, 1923, 27 MS 1205; Circular No. 15, November 26, 1923, 27 MS 1206; *Annual Report of the General Accounting Office, 1924*, H. Doc. 484, 68th Cong., 2d Sess. (letter, McCarl to the speaker of the House, December 1, 1924), 12-13.

[20]Memorandum, McCarl to chiefs, assistant chiefs, and chiefs of sections, Claims and Transportation divisions, June 5, 1926, 58 MS 216.

There were many different kinds of claims. Claims *against* the United States, many raising complex legal questions, came to GAO both from federal agency administrative officers and directly from claimants. Among these claims were those arising out of contracts let by the government; transportation claims; claims by sureties, when a surety, or a guarantor, had to complete the work of a defaulting contractor; claims from the military services, the Coast Guard, the Coast and Geodetic Survey, and the U.S. Public Health Service in such areas as dependents' allowances, travel allowances, and medical treatment; and a broad category of miscellaneous claims, involving check forgery, foreign currency exchange, salaries, travel expenses, refunds, fraud, and many other things.[21]

When claims arose, the relevant agency examined the matter, reported the facts, and made a settlement recommendation. Then a GAO claims examiner analyzed the claim and reached a conclusion that constituted a tentative settlement. Next, a GAO examiner with legal training reviewed the tentative settlement independently. If a question remained about the proper action, the case went up to a section head or the chief of the Claims Division, who had authority to make a final decision on behalf of the comptroller general. Certain claims required instruction from the comptroller general before settlement—cases concerning original construction of the law, interpretation of indefinite contracts, ambiguous regulations or executive orders, and the alteration or the reformation of contracts. Also, the Claims Division referred to the comptroller general cases in which the action to be taken was not clear.[22] In the latter two categories of cases, OGC became involved.

Many claims *by* the United States dealt with money due the government, including assessments, fees, duties, imposts, taxes, fines, penalties, and forfeitures; charges for permits, privileges, and licenses; rents and royalties; interest, foreign currency exchange, and dividends; sales of property and services; repayment of loans; costs and damages due to delay and default under contracts; and recoveries of duplicate, illegal, and improper payments.[23] Agencies responsible for the activity involved in a claim had initial responsibility to make collection. If this effort failed, the case moved to GAO, which examined the matter as it did in settling claims against the United States.

Shortly after GAO began operations in 1921, McCarl established a collections unit, later attached to the Claims Division, which recorded all claims

---

[21]*Annual Report of the Comptroller General of the United States for the Fiscal Year Ended June 30, 1939* (Washington: GPO, 1939), 29-30.

[22]Ibid., 27-28.

[23]Ibid., 25.

reported to GAO and worked to collect money from persons indebted to the
United States. In 1923, GAO began to compile a "debtors' index," listing the
names of debtors and amounts owed. At this time, McCarl wrote to all federal agencies informing them about the index and requesting that they provide names and amounts of debtors known to them. McCarl explained that
GAO would clear claims settlements against this central index, thereby stop-
ping proposed payments to debtors and applying their awards to the indebtedness. McCarl asked agency heads to report collections so that the index
could be kept current.[24]

When GAO failed to collect through setoffs based on the debtors' index
or by other means, it referred the claim to the attorney general for collection,
at first without suit and later by court action if necessary, on the basis of
evidence provided by GAO.[25] For example, GAO reported that during fiscal
year 1926, it sent to the Department of Justice 181 cases involving indebtedness to the government of $3,445,765. McCarl noted, when testifying to this
fact, that GAO was "now cooperating splendidly with the Department of
Justice and hopes to get some fine results." But he added, "Please do not get
the idea that we want anybody to pay who does not owe; and any time that
an apparent debtor can convince us that he does not owe, we are just as
happy to write off the charge as we are to put the money into the Treasury if
he owes it." A few years later, he described GAO's role in claims "in the
status of a poor man's court, the place where the claimant may come without
fear or favor, without counsel and in his own way present his claim in so far
as it may involve the payment out of moneys of the United States."[26]

McCarl had special concerns about claims that GAO judged legitimate
but could not be paid through existing appropriations. Closely related was
the fact that some of this class of claims were not submitted to GAO but
instead went straight to the courts or by special petition to Congress. In
1927, McCarl proposed legislation to authorize GAO to report to Congress
on claims it thought justified but for which an appropriation did not exist.
"With such an arrangement," McCarl observed, "it is believed there will be a
growing tendency on the part of citizens having meritorious claims . . . to
submit them to the General Accounting Office for investigation and consid-

---

[24]See GAO, *Annual Report, 1924*, 5, for McCarl's description of the collection unit. For further
information on the debtors' index, see GAO, *Annual Report, 1939*, 25.

[25]Ibid.

[26]McCarl testimony, December 20, 1926, *Independent Offices Appropriation Bill, 1928*, Hearings before
a Subcommittee of the House Committee on Appropriations, 69th Cong., 2d Sess. (Washington: GPO,
1927), 729; and *Annual Report of the Comptroller General of the United States for the Fiscal Year Ended
June 30, 1933* (Washington: GPO, 1933), iii.

eration before resorting to expensive litigation or importuning Members of Congress to support private legislation providing relief."[27]

In April 1928, shortly after McCarl's testimony, Congress passed a bill embodying his proposal. In response to a letter from President Calvin Coolidge seeking advice on whether he should sign the bill, McCarl urged the president to do so. The new law would help GAO settle claims against the United States and "its primary benefit will be to the claimants and the public generally."[28] The president approved the legislation.

The volume of claims GAO received and settled fluctuated from year to year during the 1920s and 1930s, with an upward trend, as shown in table 8.1.

The significant increase in claims received and settled in the late 1930s was due to the impact of various New Deal emergency activities of the Roosevelt administration, as well as the creation of new permanent agencies, such as the Tennessee Valley Authority. Acting Comptroller General Elliott reported in 1937 that the magnitude of the expanded claims work became apparent by 1935, necessitating the hiring of more claims examiners and clerical and stenographic staff. Elliott mentioned the Agricultural Adjustment Act (approved May 12, 1933) and the National Industrial Recovery Act (approved June 16, 1933) as examples of New Deal legislation that had led to many new claims. The Agricultural Adjustment Act created several programs to assist farmers. These programs were to be financed by a "processing tax" collected from food and fiber processors. Early in 1936, in the case of the *United States v. Butler*, the Supreme Court declared the processing tax unconstitutional. This resulted in many claims by the United States against government contractors that had included the cost of the processing tax in their bids but did not have to pay the tax after the *Butler* decision. The government thus had claims against contractors that had received contract payments before the court acted, seeking to recover the processing tax allowances. Elliott also pointed out that the vast number of persons on relief had led to additional claims related to pay, forgery, and other causes.[29]

---

[27]McCarl testimony, December 20, 1927, *Independent Offices Appropriation Bill, 1929*, Hearings before a Subcommittee of the House Committee on Appropriations, 70th Cong., 1st Sess. (Washington: GPO, 1928), 234-35; and GAO, *Annual Report, 1927*, 10-11 (source of the quote).

[28]Letter, McCarl to Rep. William Williamson, chairman, House Committee on Expenditures in the Executive Departments, January 24, 1928, 77 MS 908 (comments on the bill, H.R. 9583); and letter, McCarl to the president, April 10, 1928, 80 MS 511.

[29]*Annual Report of the Acting Comptroller General of the United States for the Fiscal Year Ended June 30, 1937* (Washington: GPO, 1937), 95-98. For information about the Agricultural Adjustment Act, the National Industrial Recovery Act, and the *Butler* decision, see Arthur M. Schlesinger, Jr., *The Age of Roosevelt: The Coming of the New Deal* (Boston: Houghton Mifflin Co., 1959), 27-176, and Schlesinger, *The Age of Roosevelt: The Politics of Upheaval* (Boston: Houghton Mifflin Co., 1960), 470-74.

Table 8.1: Claims Received and Settled by GAO's Claims Division (1925-1940)

Fiscal year	Claims received	Claims settled
1925	69,146	71,737
1926	60,388	54,085
1927	188,672	197,917
1928	203,642	205,203
1929	244,623	244,277
1930	232,389	234,468
1931	275,029	268,270
1932	282,668	283,876
1933	252,322	256,236
1934	207,153	198,655
1935	289,291	278,832
1936	387,261	373,820
1937	479,853	473,959
1938	511,232	529,982
1939	441,693	445,264
1940	473,559	466,694

Source: GAO Annual Reports, 1925-1940. GAO had some unsettled claims on hand at the start of each fiscal year; thus the total settled could be higher than the total received in a given fiscal year. The big jump in claims received and settled between 1926 and 1927 was due to the merger in 1926 of the Claims and Transportation divisions. Previously GAO reported each division's claims activity separately.

In his annual report for fiscal year 1939, Comptroller General Fred H. Brown commented on the expansion of claims activity. He noted that during fiscal year 1939, the federal government issued 152 million checks, of which 23,285 were the subject of claims. Irregularities cited by Brown included checks drawn and cashed with fictitious names, forged endorsements, and checks negotiated either by unauthorized relatives or after the deaths of payees. Such cases led to GAO investigations, in some instances Secret Service investigations, and frequently the institution of recovery proceedings by the Treasury Department.[30] In summary, as federal activities increased in the 1930s because of anti-Depression measures, the number of claims escalated accordingly, significantly affecting GAO's workload.

---

[30]GAO, *Annual Report, 1939*, 26.

Two particular groups of claims, relating to transportation and American Indians, deserve special mention. GAO handled charges for government-contracted transportation as claims, even though they were really bills submitted by carriers for payment. Through the Transportation Rate Board (1921-1922), the Transportation Division (1922-1926), and the Claims Division (1926-1948), GAO audited transportation charges. Before 1923, the government agency using private carriers for transport of goods or persons usually made transportation payments, after examining the bills, directly to the carriers. GAO's role in this early period was to do an audit after payment. During the first year of McCarl's term, GAO discovered in audits that the government was losing significant amounts of money through overcharges by carriers. McCarl informed the director of the Bureau of the Budget that in a five-month period ending in January 1922, the Transportation Rate Board had identified $675,234 in overcharges on freight bills. To justify his request for a supplemental appropriation to hire additional staff to handle transportation audits and claims, McCarl explained the complexity of determining the proper rates to be charged for shipments. He also stated: "I am strongly of the opinion that transportation accounts and claims, passenger, freight, and express, should not be paid by disbursing officers of the Government, but should be transmitted to the General Accounting Office for audit before payment and for payment by check of the Treasurer of the United States." McCarl said that if Congress appropriated funds for additional staff, he would ask for issuance of an executive order by the president putting the above suggestion into effect.[31]

Instead of accomplishing his preaudit plan by an executive order, McCarl issued a general regulation on his own authority. He directed that effective January 1, 1923, all claims (bills) of common carriers, after examination in the relevant federal agency, be forwarded to GAO for preaudit, direct settlement, and payment by Treasury check. In explaining the procedure, which GAO had used previously for some small agencies, McCarl stressed the extra work and expense involved in recovering overpayments to carriers. He noted the difficulty agencies had in determining accurate transportation charges, due in part to the complexities of transportation rates and classifications. Agencies would still examine transportation bills but would then forward them to GAO before payment.[32]

---

[31]Letter, McCarl to Charles G. Dawes, director, BOB, February 10, 1922, 6 MS 645.

[32]Letter, McCarl to U.S. Civil Service Commission, December 4, 1922, explaining General Regulations No. 13, November 25, 1922, 16 MS 102; GAO, *Annual Report, 1923*, 4-5; and David Lodwick and Donald H. Friedman, "The Transportation Division—A Forward Look Over the Past 50 Years," *GAO Review* (summer 1971): 145.

GAO sent the proposed preaudit plan to affected agencies for comment, and all agencies responded favorably except the Navy Department, which did not state its position until after the regulation became effective. McCarl reported that "it was admitted by the War Department that it had abandoned the hopeless task of determining the correct amounts and was relying on the General Accounting Office to make proper adjustments in future accounts, and it was known that a similar condition existed in the Navy Department."

Nevertheless, after the new system began, the War Department, like the Navy Department, refused to comply and submitted the matter to the attorney general. His opinion was that the War Department was not permitted to give up the authority to disburse its own funds and that in effect the comptroller general did not have authority to stop War Department disbursing officers from making payments. On the basis of this opinion, the War Department and several other agencies refused to follow the GAO regulation.[33] By January 1926, as McCarl testified in Congress, all civil agencies except Justice, Agriculture, and Labor were complying with the regulation. He reported that direct transportation payments by War and Navy had resulted in large overpayments that had to be recovered after GAO audits.[34]

In the face of this dilemma, GAO could do little to enforce its regulation on transportation payments. It could bring legal action only through the Department of Justice, which was responsible for the ruling causing the problem with the War and Navy departments. GAO had authority to take the extreme steps of disallowing payments made by the noncomplying agencies or refusing to approve requisitions for further funds to departmental certifying officers, but the Office chose not to do so.[35]

GAO's annual report for fiscal year 1939 analyzed transportation claims work in detail. This analysis noted that the War, Navy, and Justice departments were still paying transportation charges after internal examination through disbursing officers and then sending the vouchers to GAO for postaudit. Comptroller General Brown observed that such examination of transportation vouchers required these departments to maintain, at significant expense, rate schedule files and rate clerk staffs. He pointed out that during fiscal year 1939, GAO postaudited 306,269 such vouchers for payments of $40,214,042. GAO disallowed $372,413 as overpayments. "Of

---

[33]GAO, *Annual Report, 1923*, 4-5.

[34]McCarl statement, January 26, 1926, *Independent Offices Appropriation Bill, 1927*, Hearings before the House Committee on Appropriations, 69th Cong., 1st Sess. (Washington: GPO, 1926), 191-92.

[35]Mosher, *The GAO: The Quest for Accountability in American Government* (Boulder, CO: Westview Press, 1979), 82 (hereafter cited as Mosher, *GAO*).

course a large part of this money may eventually be recovered and restored to the Treasury," Brown wrote, "but there will be involved certain expenses of recovery and loss of the use of the money."[36]

In this same report, GAO stated that U.S. property moved by rail, water, air, and motor vehicles was generally subject to the rates, the rules, and the practices that applied to transport of private property. But there were some exceptions, especially for railroads that in the 19th century received land grants from the U.S. government. These railroads were permitted to charge the United States only 50 percent of the fares or rates charged the public for transportation over the granted lands. In theory, this meant that the government was paying the full cost, partly in land and partly in cash. Also, some non-land-grant carriers voluntarily filed land-grant equalization agreements, accepting the same payments (50 percent) that the land-grant carriers received. Although this system reduced the government's transportation costs for these carriers, it complicated the calculation of rates and required considerable expertise on the part of rate examiners in GAO and in agencies with such staff.[37]

In addition to postauditing the more than $40 million in transportation vouchers mentioned above, GAO, during fiscal year 1939, preaudited 304,662 vouchers covering charges of $15,524,752, disallowing $138,150 of this amount. The volume of transportation audit work expanded in the 1930s for the same reasons as did general claims work—the addition of New Deal programs run by emergency and permanent agencies, such as the Civilian Conservation Corps, the Works Progress Administration, the Federal Emergency Relief Administration, the War Department, the Agriculture Department, and many others.[38]

The Transportation Act of 1940, passed to handle the increased government transportation activity as the nation undertook a defense preparedness program, forced GAO to change its system. This law, in order to expedite payments to carriers, provided for payment of transportation charges directly by the using government agency, with a postaudit by GAO. Thus the preaudit system GAO developed in the 1920s and 1930s became a casualty of the preparedness and war efforts. GAO considered this law to be unnecessary, the source of tremendous overcharges during the wartime period, and the

[36]GAO, *Annual Report, 1939*, 37.
[37]Ibid., 35.
[38]Ibid., 37, 38-39.

cause of an enormous postaudit task for the Office both during and after the war.[39]

Dealing with the long-standing claims of American Indians was a particularly onerous and difficult task for GAO. Acts of Congress passed in the early 1920s gave the Court of Claims jurisdiction over the claims against the United States, estimated at up to $1 billion, of various Indian nations and tribes based on treaties between the United States and the Indians, some dating back to the 1820s. Under the laws, GAO had to search old records in its possession to determine what previous payments had been made under the terms of the treaties. GAO sent the information it had compiled to the Court of Claims, which determined the amount of settlements with the tribes.[40]

Examples of the Indian tribes involved in these claims during the 1920s and the 1930s were the Iowa, Osage, Sioux, Cherokee, Blackfeet, Nez Perce, and Delaware; there were numerous others. GAO handled this work through an Indian tribal claims section of the Audit Division. In 1926, McCarl testified that GAO at that time had 88 staff assigned to Indian claims. By mid-1927, he reported that the Office had completed and transmitted to the Department of Justice three Indian claims reports, involving claims of $1,192,850, and that 12 other reports were in progress, involving over $376 million in claims. Investigation of 20 other cases involving a total of $211 million was yet to be started by GAO. McCarl described the task as analyzing the claims petitions; digesting the treaties, the agreements, and the laws relevant to the petitions; searching for information in reports of the commissioner of Indian Affairs, U.S. statutes, and reports of U.S. receipts and expenditures and appropriations digests; and then putting together reports for transmittal to the Department of Justice.[41]

In 1933, McCarl reported that GAO had forwarded reports on 18 Indian tribal claims petitions and had received eight additional petitions. He also noted that GAO's cost to compile reports on 12 petitions disposed of by the Court of Claims was $164,615 while the amount of savings to the government (amount of original claims less settlement amounts) was more than $14

---

[39]See chapter 11, pp. 266-73, for a discussion of transportation audits during and after World War II.

[40]Letter, Assistant Comptroller General Lurtin R. Ginn to H. M. Lord, director, BOB, February 21, 1924, 30 MS 620; and McCarl and Ginn testimony, February 23, 1924, *Independent Offices Appropriation Bill, 1925*, Hearings before a Subcommittee of the House Committee on Appropriations, 68th Cong., 1st Sess. (Washington: GPO, 1924), 193-95.

[41]McCarl testimony, December 20, 1926, *Independent Offices Appropriation Bill, 1928*, Hearings before a Subcommittee of the House Committee on Appropriations, 69th Cong., 2d Sess. (Washington: GPO, 1927), 731; and GAO, *Annual Report, 1927*, 81-83.

million. The "thoroughness and effectiveness" of GAO's reports contributed to these significant savings.[42]

In October 1936, GAO filed its last Indian claims report on the cases it
began to investigate in 1925. During this 11-year period, GAO received
claims amounting to over $878 million. It prepared reports on 103 cases,
totaling 33,937 text pages. To illustrate the nature and the complexity of the
Indian claims work, GAO's annual report in 1939 described action on a claims
petition of the Delaware Tribe filed in May 1927. By agreement in December 1843, the Delawares ceded to the Wyandotte Indians 39 sections of land
in Kansas. The Wyandottes were to pay the Delawares $6,080 in 1844 and
$4,000 annually for ten years; payments were to be completed by January 1,
1855. The Delawares argued that they had received the initial payment of
$6,080 but not the additional $40,000. Thus their claim against the United
States was for $40,000 plus interest. In checking the records of the U.S.
Indian agent in charge of these tribes, GAO found an 1851 receipt showing
that the Wyandottes had paid the Delawares in full. On the basis of GAO's
report, the Court of Claims dismissed the Delaware petition in 1930. The
decision saved the United States, according to GAO, $190,684, constituting
the $40,000 original amount plus 5 percent interest between 1855 and 1930.[43]

By the late 1930s, GAO had resumed its Indian claims work as a result of
new laws providing for consideration of additional Indian claims, including
13 petitions filed in 1938 with the Court of Claims by the Menominee Tribe.
These claims, amounting to $9,860,477, made it necessary for GAO to check
all records dating from an 1854 treaty to 1939.[44]

Clearly the claims work that the law required GAO to do was a major
activity in the 1920s and 1930s. Involving large sums of money, this undoubtedly tedious task required painstaking research and investigation in a
large volume of records and other evidence. GAO's decisions on general
and transportation claims were final unless appealed to the Court of Claims
or private petition to Congress. On Indian claims, GAO acted as an investi-
gatory agency, doing prodigious research in old treaties, financial records,
and other documents. GAO's claims work ultimately saved the federal government a large amount of money. As McCarl and his successors pointed
out, however, the claims process centered in GAO gave claimants an arena
where they could ask for an impartial judgment, based on hard evidence and
existing statutory and case law, with a certain humaneness of approach. Af-

---

[42]GAO, *Annual Report, 1933*, 24-25.
[43]GAO, *Annual Report, 1939*, 46-49.
[44]Ibid., 46, 49.

ter 1940, GAO continued to handle claims but the process became more prominent internally and the number of staff involved declined significantly. Especially after World War II, as GAO entered a new phase, which emphasized more professionally oriented audits and reports, claims became a less obvious aspect of GAO's program.

Accounting Systems Work

Section 309 of the Budget and Accounting Act, 1921, stated: "The Comptroller General shall prescribe the forms, systems, and procedure for administrative appropriation and fund accounting in the several departments and establishments, and for the administrative examination of fiscal officers' accounts and claims against the United States." Comptroller General McCarl interpreted Section 309 broadly. He emphasized particularly accounting systems work. The effort had two major parts—prescribing a uniform accounting system for federal agencies and developing standard forms for governmentwide use. McCarl and his immediate successors made some headway in this work, but progress was slow and spotty. There was resistance to it, contributing to controversy about GAO's role and jurisdiction, especially in the 1930s.

Uniform Accounting System

Between 1921 and 1927, GAO worked slowly to develop a uniform accounting system. McCarl testified as early as December 1921, six months after GAO began operations, that he was thinking about how GAO would do the work and speculated that it might occupy at least part of the time of 85 staff members.[45] In his annual report for fiscal year 1924, McCarl described "considerable progress" on a uniform departmental appropriation accounting system, but noted two big problems: the excessive number of both government disbursing agents and appropriations.[46] On July 10, 1926, GAO issued Circular No. 27, advising federal agencies that the Office had formulated a uniform accounting system and standard accounting forms. An appendix to the circular, released on April 1, 1927, explained details of the accounting system, which provided for four general account classes: appropriations; trust funds and special deposits; transitory accounts for stores, service, and equipment; and collection and deposit of amounts due the government.[47]

---

[45]McCarl testimony, December 19, 1921, *Independent Offices Appropriation Bill, 1923*, Hearings before a Subcommittee of the House Committee on Appropriations, 67th Cong., 2d Sess. (Washington: GPO, 1922), 249.

[46]GAO, *Annual Report, 1924*, 9-10.

[47]GAO, *Annual Report, 1927*, 26; and letter, Comptroller General Lindsay C. Warren to Rep. Robert T. Secrist, December 20, 1940, 232 MS 1353 (explains Circular No. 27 and the appendix).

The issuance of Circular No. 27 did not mean that all agencies would immediately install the prescribed system. McCarl pointed out late in 1926 that GAO's approach was not to agencies as a whole but to separate bureaus in them. McCarl observed, "We must take up each unit in the light of its problems and can help them most by working out a modern system in harmony with other like work and by providing a more efficient administrative control." McCarl mentioned systems work already under way in the Bureau of Mines; the Reclamation Service; the Indian Service; the General Land Office; and units of the Agriculture, Commerce, and Justice departments.[48] In mid-1927, he noted that during fiscal year 1927, GAO helped install 55 uniform accounting systems, including 13 in the Interior Department and 23 in the Treasury Department. McCarl added that GAO was urging agencies to use modern bookkeeping machines rather than the old pen-and-ink methods; one great advantage was that these machines could indicate the status of accounts from day to day.[49]

McCarl commented in detail on progress in uniform accounting in his annual report for 1929. He noted that GAO had provided for development of cost accounting and had cooperated with some agencies in preparing such systems. He estimated that the uniform system for administrative appropriation and fund accounting had been installed in about 40 percent of all government bureaus. In this same report, McCarl recommended that Congress consider legislation making changes that would bring "large economies and improvements in the accounting work" of the federal government.

His proposals included establishment of a disbursing fund for each agency, including all funds appropriated for individual agency use; consolidation for single agencies of multiple appropriations that sometimes allowed spending for similar purposes; provision of working capital funds for each governmental industrial enterprise and rules for their disbursement, reimbursement in accordance with commercial practice, and accounting for all transactions to GAO; and reduction in the number of disbursing officers to a level sufficient to care for government business "economically and efficiently."[50]

In 1937, Acting Comptroller General Richard N. Elliott surveyed GAO's progress in prescribing uniform accounting procedures for the government. He noted that in 1936, GAO issued a revised system of symbols (numbers)

---

[48]McCarl testimony, December 20, 1926, *Independent Offices Appropriation Bill, 1928*, 722.

[49]GAO, *Annual Report, 1927*, 29, 65.

[50]*Annual Report of the Comptroller General of the United States for the Fiscal Year Ended June 30, 1929* (Washington: GPO, 1929), 13-16.

and titles for appropriation and receipt accounts. While most government units cooperated in adopting the new system, the Treasury Department refused to do so, forcing many government administrative offices to provide both the old and new symbols on accounting documents. Elliott reported that the Treasury Department had not explained its reasons for lack of cooperation. The episode was an example of the problems GAO encountered in trying to establish an accounting system. "Under existing law," Elliott observed, "it [GAO] may prescribe but no power is given to enforce compliance with prescribed procedures."[51]

At the heart of GAO's problem with the uniform accounting system, Elliott reported, was "the question raised in some administrative quarters of whether the law directing the Comptroller General . . . to prescribe the forms, systems, and procedure for administrative appropriation and fund accounting comprehended the prescription of an accounting system for the Government as a whole." Elliott recommended adding to the listing of organizations designated "departments" and "establishments" in Section 2 of the Budget and Accounting Act the word "corporation," reflecting the fact that many government corporations were not subject to GAO audits and other measures, including the uniform accounting system. He also recommended amending section 309 of the Budget and Accounting Act to state that agency appropriations should not be made available for expenditure or spent "whenever there is substantial failure to install and maintain systems of accounting and procedures relating to the receipt, deposit, application, or expenditure of public, quasi-public, trust, or corporate funds, prescribed pursuant to this section."[52]

Elliott repeated and expanded his complaints against the Treasury Department in a letter to the chairman of the House Committee on Expenditures in the Executive Departments. He recounted the history of GAO's work on symbols for accounts. The Office had issued its first symbols for appropriation accounts in 1925 and for receipt accounts in 1928. Elliott explained that GAO issued the new system of symbols and titles for accounts in June 1936 because of the great increase in the number of accounts in the executive branch and changes in audit procedures. Except for Treasury, agencies had cooperated fully with GAO in installing and implementing the new system, Elliott reported. He ended his letter by emphasizing Congress's juris-

---

[51]GAO, *Annual Report, 1937*, 2-3.
[52]Ibid., 1-2, 12.

diction over the raising and the spending of revenue and suggested that Congress carefully guard the manner of keeping government financial records.[53]

Elliott's criticism of the Treasury Department elicited a very hostile response from Secretary of the Treasury Henry Morgenthau, Jr., in a long letter to the chairman of the House Committee on Expenditures in the Executive Departments. "It is my belief," Morgenthau wrote, ". . . that the criticism of the Acting Comptroller General is without merit and that it is merely an incident in a continuing effort of the General Accounting Office to assume duties not entrusted to it by law, and to assert authority neither expressly granted by law, nor properly deducible by implication from the law." As for the new symbols, Morgenthau argued that GAO had exceeded its authority in issuing them, that they had been issued abruptly without consultation with Treasury, and that the old symbols worked well.

Morgenthau complained that the comptroller general, in pursuing his role as "watchdog of the Treasury," had "conceived his function to be that of snapping at the heels of the administrative officers of the Government, and undertaking to hamper them in the faithful performance of their duties rather than cooperate with them to render more efficient service." He argued that Elliott, in proposing changes to the Budget and Accounting Act, was seeking "a most amazing grant of power." If enacted, Elliott's proposals would "make a very czar of the Comptroller General. . . ." He would become the government's most powerful administrative officer. "The inability of the Acting Comptroller General to visualize the implications of his proposal is . . . a more serious reflection on his capacity to undertake such a responsibility than any criticism of him which anyone else might voice," Morgenthau concluded.[54] This controversy occurred at a time when GAO was being criticized from other quarters and when Congress was considering proposals that, if enacted, would have substantially changed GAO's roles and functions.[55]

Accounting Forms

As with the uniform accounting system, GAO moved slowly to implement its mandate to prescribe accounting forms. In general, this meant working with individual agencies in developing specific forms relevant to their operations, as well as issuing standard forms for functions common to all

---

[53]Letter, Elliott to Congress, January 3, 1938, reprinted in *Congressional Record*, 75th Cong., 3d Sess., January 11, 1938, appendix, vol. 83, pt. 9: 118-19.

[54]Letter, Morgenthau to John J. Cochran, ibid., 119-21.

[55]See chapter 10 for a detailed discussion of this point. The proposals were not enacted.

government agencies. In July 1922, McCarl formed an Advisory Committee
on Fiscal Accounting Forms and Procedure. He invited 17 agencies to assign representatives to the committee, including the Treasury and Justice
departments, but not the Bureau of the Budget. The committee's mandate
was to study and revise accounting forms. The assistant comptroller general, Lurtin R. Ginn, chaired the committee. McCarl's purpose was to get the
views, the advice, and the cooperation of executive agencies in developing
and adopting the forms. The advisory committee met frequently in 1922
and 1923.

At the first meeting, on October 5, 1922, Ginn explained McCarl's wish
to reduce the number of accounting forms and simplify procedures. He
announced that GAO had already reduced the number of forms used in account audits and that the comptroller general wanted to know agency views
regarding revised accounting forms and procedures. At this meeting, the
Advisory Committee established subcommittees to work on various kinds of
forms, such as schedules of collections and disbursements, funds requisition, purchasing orders and vouchers, payroll forms, transportation vouchers, and appropriations transfers. GAO records show that numerous forms
adopted by GAO for government use resulted from the work of the Advisory
Committee.[56] This committee is an interesting attempt by McCarl to cooperate, early in his term, with executive agencies. There is little evidence of
similar activities in the later years of his tenure.

GAO's work on forms development and approval, both on standard accounting forms and agency-specific forms, continued routinely through the
1920s and 1930s. The volume of work picked up in the mid-1930s because
of the creation of many emergency agencies and the general increase in
government activity to combat the Depression. GAO carried out forms work,
without any serious controversy with executive branch agencies, as an adjunct to its audit work; the approved standard forms, common to all agencies, facilitated the application of uniform audit procedures across the government.

---

[56]See, for example, letter, McCarl to the chairman, Interstate Commerce Commission, July 11, 1922,
11 MS 440 (identical letters went to 16 other agencies, indicating formation of the Advisory Committee); H. A. Harding, secretary, minutes of the first meeting of the Advisory Committee, October 5,
1922, 14 MS 248A; letter, Ginn to Herbert S. Ward, Agriculture Department, March 22, 1923,
transmitting minutes of the sixth meeting of the Advisory Committee and copies of reports and draft
forms, 19 MS 1184; and letter, Ginn to George W. Love, Labor Department, July 7, 1923, transmitting
minutes of the tenth meeting of the Advisory Committee and report on disbursing officers' forms and
revised purchase voucher forms, 23 MS 106. GAO records indicate that the Advisory Committee met
frequently in 1922 and 1923, but evidence of later meetings, if any, has not been found.

In his 1979 study of GAO, Frederick Mosher presents a mixed picture of GAO's work on accounting systems and forms. One criticism he cites, from unidentified sources, was that GAO "prescribed forms and procedures geared to reconciling agency systems with GAO accounts, which meant that they were of little use for purposes of agency management or to the Treasury Department or the Bureau of the Budget." He also notes that studies of government accounting after 1945, including those by the Hoover Commissions (1949 and 1955), concluded that there were still serious problems with federal accounting. As for GAO, Mosher concludes for the period through World War II that "there is little evidence that the GAO provided effective leadership in the reform and modernization of accounting for the government as a whole" before the end of World War II.[57]

Settlement of Accounts

Another duty of GAO, carried over from the Office of the Comptroller of the Treasury and the six Treasury auditors by Section 304 of the Budget and Accounting Act, was settlement of the accounts of disbursing and collecting officers. GAO had to verify that an officer's periodic statement of receipts and disbursements was correct. Reported receipts had to correspond with paid agency requisitions for funds filed with GAO, collections were to be supported by verified and approved collections schedules, and disbursements had to be properly documented. If an officer's statement of receipts and disbursements proved accurate, GAO issued a settlement certificate to the officer and to the administrative head of the agency to which the disbursements or the receipts pertained.[58]

When GAO's voucher audit resulted in discovery of illegal or otherwise improper payments by a disbursing officer, that officer and his agency received a notice of exception. By law, disbursing officers were personally liable for improper payments of government funds. Usually, but not always, the agency administrator and the disbursing officer responded promptly to GAO's notice of exception, and most questions were resolved before final settlement of the accounts.[59]

McCarl regularly submitted to Congress a report on government officers who were delinquent in their accounts. The report included the reasons for the delinquencies, stated whether the delinquencies had been waived, and

[57]Mosher, *GAO*, 79.
[58]GAO, *Annual Report, 1939*, 22-24.
[59]Ibid., 21-22.

stated the names of officers who were still indebted to the government after final account settlement.[60]

Contracts and Bid Protests

Section 312(c) of the Budget and Accounting Act, 1921, required the comptroller general to "specifically report to Congress every expenditure or contract made by any department or establishment in any year in violation of laws." Federal law required agencies issuing contracts to file them with GAO, which examined them for errors or legal defects. If GAO discovered problems, the contracting agencies were informed, in many cases in time to correct the contracts before any payments under them had been made. As McCarl reported in 1928, "illegal payments are thus avoided and the Government saved the expense of recovering moneys so paid and the loss of the full amount and expense incident to recovery if recovery can not be effected."[61]

The volume of contracts received, examined, and filed by GAO during the McCarl period increased gradually as federal activity expanded, especially in the 1930s. GAO received about 102,000 federal contracts in 1928. Five years later, during fiscal year 1933, the number was 602,413; for fiscal year 1934, 847,373.[62] Thus the examination and the filing of federal contracts, a substantial task from the start for GAO, assumed much larger proportions and required the commitment of more and more staff as the years passed.

A specific example of contract work was GAO's objection in 1928 to the purchase of automobiles by the Merchant Fleet Corporation. McCarl informed the chairman of the U.S. Shipping Board, responsible for the Merchant Fleet Corporation, that the automobile purchases violated a 1914 law that prohibited the use of appropriations by any government agency to buy "motor-propelled passenger-carrying vehicles" unless the purchases were specifically authorized by law. The Shipping Board chairman argued that the Merchant Fleet Corporation as a government corporation was not subject to this law. McCarl rejected this view and informed the chairman that in accordance with Section 312(c) of the Budget and Accounting Act, he would report the matter to Congress.[63]

---

[60]See, for example, letter, McCarl to president of the Senate, January 2, 1928, A-13027 (an identical letter went to the speaker of the House).

[61]GAO, *Annual Report, 1928*, 16.

[62]Ibid.; and GAO, *Annual Report, 1934*, 51.

[63]Letter, McCarl to the chairman, U.S. Shipping Board, September 28, 1928, 85 MS 992.

Another example was GAO's objection to the purchase of coal by the Lighthouse Service of the Department of Commerce in excess of amounts specified in written contracts. Two 1927 contracts were involved. Under one of the contracts, the Lighthouse Service ordered 2,000 bushels of coal but accepted delivery of 5,290 bushels, more than 160 percent in excess; under the other instance, the Lighthouse Service ordered 5,000 bushels and accepted 6,485, an excess of about 30 percent. McCarl pointed out to the secretary of commerce that the excess purchases constituted procedures in violation of statutes requiring advertising and competition in bids. McCarl stated that a reasonable excess, say 10 percent, might be allowed because the contracts stated "about" 2,000 and 5,000 bushels of coal but that an excess of 160 percent was not allowed. McCarl advised the secretary to take action to stop such practices. If this was done, McCarl indicated, he would not report the contracts to Congress, though required to do so under Section 312(c).[64]

Handling questions about the legality of actions by federal purchasing and contracting officers in preparing specifications, advertising for bids, and awarding contracts was also part of GAO's contract work. During fiscal year 1939, for example, GAO received and considered 457 such cases—283 from agency heads, 23 from disbursing officers, and 151 from bidders. The contract questions varied, but over 300 concerned whether bids could be changed or corrected on matters affecting price, withdrawn because of alleged errors, or modified in terms and conditions.[65] Questions raised by bidders, including some that lost in the competition for specific contracts, were in fact bid protests. When contract questions came to GAO, the comptroller general had to examine the questions raised and issue decisions.

Conclusions

This chapter considers several important aspects of GAO's work in the first two decades of its existence. Much of this work involved applying statutes, including the Budget and Accounting Act, 1921, and rendering decisions based on these statutes. During this period, reflecting the extent to which McCarl, Elliott, and Brown relied on statutory law to guide GAO's operations, the Office of the General Counsel played a large and central role. This was true especially in regard to comptroller general decisions and opinions, claims, and contract work, but it was true also in regard to the other aspects of GAO's work discussed here. These duties involved painstaking detail, occupying many of the lower-level staff as well as top officials.

---

[64]Letter, McCarl to the secretary of commerce, October 1, 1928, 86 MS 86.

[65]Letter, Elliott to the solicitor general, Department of Justice, March 5, 1940, 223 MS 375.

GAO's work on decisions, claims, contracts, and accounting systems brought the Office into direct regular contact with executive branch agencies. On occasion, especially when GAO expected them to do things they preferred not to do or thought that the law did not require or when their actions were overruled or revised, these agencies were not happy with GAO. In many other instances, they recognized the value of GAO's assistance to them. Questions regarding GAO's legal right to operate as it did arose often, even sometimes to the point where agencies, for example, the Department of Justice, refused to follow GAO's decisions and regulations. Since GAO believed that it had statutory authority to operate as it did, the Office usually stood its ground on such issues. But in many cases, it did not have enforcement power, and this meant that some flouting of GAO's rules and decisions stood. Opposition to GAO built up in the 1920s and 1930, leading to concerted efforts to alter GAO's role by the late 1930s.[66]

There is little evidence that GAO tried to work much in the 1920s and 1930s toward settlement of serious problems with executive branch agencies, such as the Department of Justice and the Treasury Department. Nor did these agencies approach GAO in a cooperative manner. When differences arose between the comptroller general and the attorney general, each official staked out his position and showed little interest in compromise. When disputes arose between GAO and an executive agency, an impasse usually resulted. The comptroller general could insist that his decision was final, as the Budget and Accounting Act, 1921, stated, but it was difficult for him to enforce his decision without active support from Congress or acquiescence on the part of the involved agency. McCarl believed strongly in GAO's independent authority, and he showed no interest in compromising that authority in efforts to settle problems with the executive branch. GAO's relationships with that branch were adversarial. McCarl repeatedly urged Congress to be more vigilant in controlling spending, but he made few efforts to help executive agencies promote improvement and progress in the federal government.

---

[66]See the discussion of this subject in chapter 10.

CHAPTER 9

GAO Operations, 1921-1940:
Audits, Investigations, and Reports

The Budget and Accounting Act, 1921, was the source of the comptroller general's auditing authority. Section 304 of the law transferred to him all the powers and the duties of the comptrollers of the Treasury and the six auditors; several other sections further established his auditing duties. Section 312(a) granted broad powers: "The Comptroller General shall investigate, at the seat of government or elsewhere, all matters relating to the receipt, disbursement, and application of public funds. . . ." Section 312(b) directed him to "make such investigations and reports as shall be ordered by either House of Congress or by any committee of either House having jurisdiction over revenue, appropriations, or expenditures." This section also stated that the comptroller general should, at a committee request, "direct assistants from his office to furnish the committee such aid and information as it may request."[1]

The Audit Division and Its Work

Throughout the terms of J. R. McCarl and his immediate successors, the Audit Division and the Office of Investigations had most of the responsibility for carrying out GAO's audit duties. The Audit Division was to audit and settle the disbursing accounts of executive branch agencies, except the Post Office Department, which was the responsibility of GAO's Post Office Department Division.[2] Reflecting the early emphasis on financial auditing, the initial organization of the Audit Division was complex, with specialized sections for receiving and computing, contract vouchers, civilian pay, military pay, the Veterans' Bureau, accounting, checks, audit review, and Indian tribal claims. A miscellaneous section did audits of areas not otherwise covered, such as accounts of consular and foreign service officers and internal revenue tax refunds.[3]

---

[1]Public Law 67-13, 42 Stat. 20.

[2]*Annual Report of the Comptroller General of the United States for the Fiscal Year Ended June 30, 1927* (Washington: GPO, 1927), 51. See pp. 221-23, for information about Post Office audits.

[3]GAO, *Annual Report, 1927*, 52-53.

For McCarl, the central objective of GAO's audit work was to ensure strict observance and enforcement of the laws relating to government spending. He believed that Congress, in passing the Budget and Accounting Act, expected that executive branch spending would be audited extensively. GAO was helping to establish "the congressional control over appropriations that the law and the Constitution clearly contemplate. . . ." After Congress appropriated money, GAO's duty was to see that there were no violations of the congressional purpose as embodied in appropriations legislation. McCarl recognized resistance to GAO's efforts to intensify the audit but thought that in time federal agencies, which had developed lax procedures and methods, would better understand GAO's responsibilities and the audit would become easier.[4]

McCarl thought that the audit's value could not be based solely on the amount of money saved or recovered by the government because of the audit. "The greatest results flowing from the audit," he testified in 1926, "are to be found in the unpaid accounts and claims, a large percentage of which are never pressed by those claiming. It is the deterrent effect of the audit on wrongdoing that illustrates best its importance and its value in dollars and cents is impossible of estimation."[5] He suggested that 80 percent of the benefit of an audit "ought to come from the knowledge of the fact that it is going to happen. That is what keeps people straight, the knowledge that a full and complete accounting is going to be exacted."[6]

During the McCarl period, the bulk of GAO's audit work was voucher checking. A voucher was a standard or a special form recording information needed by both agency administrative and disbursing officers and GAO to determine the legality, the propriety, and the accuracy of an expenditure. Each voucher and supporting documents included information on the agency concerned, the appropriation to be charged, the date of obligation of the expenditure, a description of the article purchased or the service received, evidence both that the goods or services were approved for purchase and had been actually received, approval by an appropriate agency official, the name of the involved disbursing officer, and the method of payment. On the basis of a voucher, after agency administrative certification and approval, a disbursing officer made payment. Disbursing officers and agency heads were permitted to ask the comptroller general for advance

---

[4]McCarl testimony, January 26, 1926, *Independent Offices Appropriation Bill, 1927*, Hearings before the House Committee on Appropriations, 69th Cong., 1st Sess. (Washington: GPO, 1926), 187-88.

[5]Ibid., 189.

[6]McCarl testimony, December 20, 1926, *Independent Offices Appropriation Bill, 1928*, Hearings before a Subcommittee of the House Committee on Appropriations, 69th Cong., 2d Sess. (Washington: GPO, 1927), 725.

decisions on proposed payments; the decisions governed the accounts' audit and settlement.[7] Under this voucher-checking process, executive branch agencies sent vouchers relative to their operations to GAO for checking. As the volume of government work expanded, especially in the 1930s, the number of vouchers GAO received increased accordingly. During World War II, the volume became almost insurmountable.[8]

McCarl actually preferred the preaudit system, which he thought was more efficient and economical in the long run. Under the preaudit procedure, an agency sent the voucher for a proposed expenditure to GAO for audit before payment. Once GAO had examined the voucher and certified the amount for payment, the agency disbursing officer could make payment with the assurance that the transaction would clear routinely when the paid voucher went back to GAO for final settlement. The law did not require preaudit, but permitted it. McCarl recognized that GAO would need additional staff to expand preaudit work, but he thought that ultimately the government would save money. Agencies would avoid the internal expense of adjusting payments, and the government would be free of the cost of collecting money erroneously paid out. Of course, GAO had to complete preaudits promptly so that agencies could make disbursements without undue delay.[9]

GAO's preaudit work expanded gradually during the 1920s and 1930s. By 1927, GAO was preauditing all Veterans' Bureau payments and did some preauditing for the Agriculture and Navy Departments. By 1930, GAO did some selective preauditing in most of the major departments and in some independent agencies, including, for example, the Civil Service Commission and the Interstate Commerce Commission.[10] Later in the 1930s, as the New Deal emergency programs caused an expansion of federal activity, GAO expanded preaudit work in the field

---

[7]*Annual Report of the Comptroller General of the United States for the Fiscal Year Ended June 30, 1939* (Washington: GPO, 1939), 5-7.

[8]See chapter 11, pp. 251-52, for detailed information on this point.

[9]For information on the preaudit, see McCarl testimony, December 20, 1927, *Independent Offices Appropriation Bill, 1929*, Hearings before a Subcommittee of the House Committee on Appropriations, 70th Cong., 1st Sess. (Washington: GPO, 1928), 256-57; letter, McCarl to Rep. William R. Wood, November 27, 1929, included in testimony of James L. Baity, GAO executive officer, January 10, 1930, *Independent Offices Appropriation Bill for 1931*, Hearings before a Subcommittee of the House Committee on Appropriations, 71st Cong., 2nd Sess. (Washington: GPO, 1930), 144-45, 150, 153; and Baity testimony, February 8, 1932, *Independent Offices Appropriation Bill for 1933*, Hearings before a Subcommittee of the House Committee on Appropriations, 72d Cong., 1st Sess. (Washington: GPO, 1932), 237.

[10]McCarl testimony, December 20, 1927, *Independent Offices Appropriation Bill, 1929*, 240; and Baity testimony, January 10, 1930, *Independent Offices Appropriation Bill for 1930*, Hearings before a Subcommittee of the House Committee on Appropriations, 70th Cong., 2d Sess. (Washington: GPO, 1929), 148.

but the volume of work and the Office's limited budgets precluded a large increase in the activity.[11]

While McCarl favored the preaudit, GAO virtually abandoned it within a few years of the end of his term. The tremendous expansion of government expenditures accompanying the national defense and war efforts after 1939 vastly increased GAO's workload. Even if the Office had maintained its interest in preaudit, continuing or expanding it during the war would have been impossible. There were valid arguments against preaudits, including costs of the process in personnel and the paperwork involved. There was also the problem of delay in making valid payments, caused by the insertion of the preaudit procedure between preparation of a voucher and actual payment. These efficiency considerations would have become more pronounced if GAO had tried to use the preaudit during the war.

The Office of Investigations

The Office of Investigations did a significant part of GAO's audit work during the 1920s and 1930s, as well as specific investigations into alleged financial fraud. McCarl established the Investigations Section on October 30, 1922, to make "investigations, examinations, inspections, reports and recommendations" regarding the receipt, the disbursement, and the application of public funds. Included among the matters to be examined by the new unit were "the forms, systems, and procedures for administrative appropriation and fund accounting, and for the administrative examination of fiscal officers' accounts and claims against the United States; . . . the adequacy and effectiveness of administrative examination of accounts and claims; . . . the adequacy and effectiveness of departmental inspection of the offices and accounts of fiscal officers; . . . [and]; . . . inspection and examination of books, papers, and other matters relating to the office or accounts of disbursing officers."

The section was also to do investigations and reports ordered by either house of Congress or its committees or requested by the president and other work as ordered by the comptroller general. A chief investigator headed the section, which included a staff of investigators, attorneys, accountants, and clerks. The chief investigator was to submit for approval by the comptroller general or the assistant comptroller general all initiatory actions in investigations, examinations, and in-

---

[11]Baity testimony, December 13, 1934, *Independent Offices Appropriation Bill for 1936*, Hearings before a Subcommittee of the House Committee on Appropriations, 74th Cong., 1st Sess. (Washington: GPO, 1935), 288; and Baity testimony, December 3, 1935, *Independent Offices Appropriation Bill for 1937*, Hearings before a Subcommittee of the House Committee on Appropriations, 74th Cong., 2d Sess. (Washington: GPO, 1936), 236.

spections, and he was to submit all reports and recommendations based on the section's work to the comptroller general through the assistant comptroller general.[12]

The list of the duties of the Investigations Section, later called the Office of Investigations,[13] makes clear that it was to work, like the Audit Division, in those areas of activity assigned to GAO by the Budget and Accounting Act. When McCarl asked the House Appropriations Committee late in 1922 to provide extra funds to support the Investigations Section, he justified his request in terms of helping Congress to "find out a little more about what is really going on. . . ." He said that he had discovered after he became comptroller general that GAO's audits of customs collections were inadequate. The Investigations Section could help eliminate this problem. He also said that there were problems with the audits of both internal revenue receipts and disbursements and the District of Columbia government. McCarl said that he and Assistant Comptroller General Lurtin R. Ginn were working "to organize an investigative force that will be capable enough, big enough, brainy enough, and shrewd enough to get at the bottom of these problems and solve them."[14]

In 1927, McCarl listed investigations of several areas undertaken by the Investigations Section: the Office of the Alien Property Custodian, at the request of the president;[15] the administration of St. Elizabeth's Hospital in Washington, at the request of the House; coal prices in the District of Columbia, at the request of the Senate Committee on the District; and suggestions for improvements relating to installation of a uniform accounting system for national parks.[16]

In 1937, the chief of investigations, S. B. Tulloss, described the work of his office at a Senate hearing: "We do very little real investigating. Our work relates primarily to audit functions." His emphasis was really on accounting systems work—the design and the installation of accounting systems in agencies. "One of

---

[12]General Regulations No. 11, "Establishment of Investigations Section, General Accounting Office," October 30, 1922, 14 MS 2114.

[13]No source has been found to indicate a precise date for the change, but by the late 1920s, GAO documents referred to the investigations group as the Office of Investigations.

[14]McCarl testimony, December 14, 1922, *Independent Offices Appropriation Bill, 1924,* Hearings before a Subcommittee of the House Committee on Appropriations, 67th Cong., 4th Sess. (Washington: GPO, 1923), 101-3.

[15]Such requests from the president were rare. The Budget and Accounting Act, Section 312(a), said that GAO was to report to the president, when requested by him, as well as to Congress, on, among other things, "matters relating to the receipt disbursement, and application of public funds. . . ." In mentioning this report on the Alien Property Custodian in congressional testimony McCarl said that he thought that the work "was justified as a matter of cooperation." The secret report went to the president on November 15, 1926. See McCarl testimony, December 20, 1926, *Independent Offices Appropriation Bill, 1928,* 720-21.

[16]GAO, *Annual Report, 1927,* 22.

the functions of investigation," he said, "is not only to survey the administrative procedure and set up the books, but to examine those books, examine the accounts and records of the accountable offices and of the administrative officers, in the field."[17] Tulloss's remarks make clear that before 1940, the Office of Investigations and the Audit Division worked on essentially the same things. By the 1930s, many Office of Investigations staff did inspections and examinations in the field rather than exclusively in Washington but their work, like that of the Audit Division, was essentially to audit government financial transactions. If investigative work led to the discovery of violations of the law, GAO reported the information to the agency involved and the Department of Justice. McCarl noted in 1932 that GAO's disclosure of criminal activity was incidental to the performance of its duty to ensure the proper accounting of public funds.[18]

Audit of Government Corporations

One of the most difficult audit problems GAO faced in the 1920s and 1930s was dealing with government corporations. The Panama Railway Company, acquired by the U.S. government in 1904, was the earliest government corporation. The government created others during World War I, the Depression, and the New Deal period. Government corporations, established to handle specific tasks, many of them commercial, were usually wholly or partially self-financed and thus not subject to the annual appropriations process. This removed them from normal congressional controls related to budgets and expenditures applied to regular government agencies.

McCarl often complained about government corporations. In 1926, for example, he objected to bills proposing to create government corporations or other agencies and authorizing them to spend public funds without accounting further to Congress through GAO and in some instances authorizing them to audit themselves.[19] But a major reason for the corporate form was to enable the organization to use commercial methods and avoid the normal accountability to Congress. According to one scholar writing in 1939, ". . . the chief reason for using the corporate form of organization has been to secure a greater operating freedom than the usual fiscal procedures permit."[20]

---

[17]Tulloss testimony, August 11, 1937, *Reorganization of the Government Agencies*, Hearings before the Senate Select Committee on Government Organization on S. 2700. . . . (Washington: GPO, 1937), 316, in GAO History Program Archives, Legislative Digest Unit files, Box 38.

[18]Letter, McCarl to Rep. John J. Cochran, chairman of the House Committee on Expenditures in the Executive Departments, April 16, 1932, 128 MS 988.

[19]*Annual Report of the Comptroller General of the United States for the Fiscal Year Ended June 30, 1926* (Washington: GPO, 1926), 1-7.

[20]Harvey C. Mansfield, Sr., *The Comptroller General: A Study in the Law and Practice of Financial Administration* (New Haven: Yale University Press, 1939), 11.

McCarl thought that Congress, in establishing corporations, "surrenders its legislative control over accounting for public money" and observed that it was wrong to allow government corporations "to account to themselves for their usage of public money."[21] In 1932, for example, Congress created the Reconstruction Finance Corporation (RFC), with an authorization of $2 billion and an initial appropriation of $500 million. McCarl complained to Congress that the law contained no provision for an independent audit by GAO. He reported that GAO had tried to apply its general jurisdiction to $50 million that Congress had allocated to the secretary of agriculture to make loans or advances to farmers from RFC's $500 million appropriation. The secretary rejected an audit role for GAO in this instance; he chose to follow a February 1932 opinion of the attorney general stating that the Department of Agriculture was not subject to a GAO audit of the $50 million. McCarl wrote to the secretary that the attorney general had no power to make decisions on Agriculture's accountability for government funds. "His opinions are advisory only and if in this matter his view is accepted and adopted by you it must be taken as your own. The responsibility is yours—not his."[22]

GAO regularly provided a list to Congress of government agencies not submitting accounts to the Office for audits. The 1935 list contained 23 organizations, including the Federal Deposit Insurance Corporation, the Home Owners Loan Corporation, the Inland Waterways Corporation, the Federal Farm Mortgage Corporation, the Panama Railway Company, the Panama Steamship Company, the Reconstruction Finance Corporation, and the Tennessee Valley Associated Cooperatives.[23]

The Maritime Commission Audit

GAO audited some government corporations; the determining factor was the wording of legislation creating and regulating the individual corporation. An organization that GAO did audit was the Emergency Fleet Corporation (later renamed the Merchant Fleet Corporation).[24] An 1918 law assigned to the secretary of the treasury responsibility for audit of the corporation. GAO was unsure when it

---

[21]*Annual Report of the Comptroller General of the United States for the Fiscal Year Ended June 30, 1928* (Washington: GPO, 1928), 12.

[22]*Annual Report of the Comptroller General of the United States for the Fiscal Year Ended June 30, 1932* (Washington, GPO, 1932), 14-17.

[23]Included in Baity testimony, December 3, 1935, *Independent Offices Appropriation Bill for 1937*, 264-65.

[24]The Shipping Act of 1916 created the Shipping Board, under which existed the Emergency Fleet Corporation, established to organize and coordinate U.S. shipping during World War I. The Merchant Marine Act of 1936 replaced the Shipping Board with the U.S. Maritime Commission. See Lane C. Kendall, "Federal Maritime Commission (FMC)," in Donald R. Whitnah, ed., *Government Agencies* (Westport, CT: Greenwood Press, 1983), 229-33.

began operations in 1921 whether this function had been transferred to it; to clarify the matter, an act of March 20, 1922, assigned the audit to GAO.[25] One problem was that the law did not provide the extra funds GAO thought it needed to pay additional staff to do this work, and Congress for several years failed to act on GAO's request for funding. GAO officials explained to Congress that a complete audit of the Emergency Fleet Corporation was impossible because the 1922 law authorized the Office only to audit its accounts according to commercial usage. Another problem was that GAO did not have the power to enforce its findings; the corporation operated on funds collected from shippers rather than from appropriated funds. Thus GAO had no effective way to disallow erroneous payments as it had with regular government agencies. The Emergency Fleet Corporation had its own force of auditors, but GAO thought that it was improper for an organization to audit itself without some outside verification. Furthermore, the corporation had offices all over the world. McCarl would have preferred a full audit but explained that he had neither the staff nor the authority to conduct one.[26] GAO had the power, when it identified problems in the Fleet Corporation audit, to notify the chairman of the Shipping Board and the president of the corporation but had no effective authority to ensure improvement.[27]

Even after passage of the 1936 Merchant Marine Act, which replaced the Shipping Board with the U.S. Maritime Commission, GAO continued to experience difficulties in conducting its audit. The Maritime Commission took the position that GAO was not authorized to disallow payments when the Commission determined that a disbursement was necessary. Both Acting Comptroller General Richard N. Elliott (1936-1939) and Comptroller General Fred H. Brown (1939-1940) engaged in a continuing dialog with the Maritime Commission over GAO's jurisdiction. The Commission argued that if GAO disputed an expenditure, its recourse was to report the matter to Congress, in accordance with section 207 of the Merchant Marine Act.

---

[25]*Annual Report of the General Accounting Office, 1922,* (letter, McCarl to speaker of the House, December 4, 1922), H. Doc. 482, 67th Cong. 4th Sess.; letter, Assistant Comptroller General Lurtin R. Ginn to Mr. Gilbert, undersecretary of the treasury, November 15, 1921, 3 MS 699; General Regulations No. 9, "Rules and Regulations for Auditing the Financial Transactions of the United States Shipping Board Emergency Fleet Corporation," July 12, 1922, General Regulations 1-51, vol. 1, GAO Records.

[26]McCarl and Ginn testimony, June 12, 1922, *Third Deficiency Appropriation Bill, 1922,* Hearings before a Subcommittee of the House Committee on Appropriations, 67th Cong., 2d Sess. (Washington: GPO, 1922), 68-76; McCarl and Ginn testimony, February 1923, *Third Deficiency Appropriation Bill, 1923,* Hearing before a Subcommittee of the House Committee on Appropriations, 67th Cong., 4th Sess. (Washington: GPO, 1923), 727-31; and McCarl testimony, December 20, 1926, *Independent Office Appropriation Bill, 1928,* 724-25.

[27]Testimony of Ginn and Baity, January 4, 1929, *Independent Offices Appropriation Bill for 1930,* 340; and letter, McCarl to chairman, U.S. Shipping Board, July 30, 1928, 83 MS 1107.

Brown explained GAO's position in a 1939 letter to the chairman of the Maritime Commission. Section 207, he pointed out, said that GAO should audit the financial transactions of the Maritime Commission, according to approved commercial practice, as did the 1922 act. Section 207 had a proviso to the audit authority: ". . . That it shall be recognized that, because of the business activities authorized by this Act, the accounting officers shall allow credit for all expenditures shown to be necessary because of the nature of such authorized activities, notwithstanding any existing statutory provision to the contrary." The Maritime Commission justified its expenditures, even if GAO objected to them, on the basis of this proviso.

Comptroller General Brown argued that Congress's intention in section 207 was that the Maritime Commission submit statements justifying expenditures. If these statements were acceptable to GAO auditors, there would be no disallowance of the expenditure. Brown wrote to the Maritime Commission chairman, "clearly the Congress did not contemplate that the Commission would make a showing to itself but would rather make a showing to one to be convinced . . . ," meaning GAO. Brown indicated that GAO would continue to take exception to spending it considered illegal or irregular.[28]

The Maritime Commission audit continued to be a problem for GAO through the World War II period. After the war, when GAO acquired broad legislative authority to audit all government corporations, the Maritime Commission audit turned out to be a major activity that attracted much congressional and public attention.[29]

The GAO-TVA Dispute

A controversy with the Tennessee Valley Authority (TVA) in the 1930s and early 1940s further illustrated the problems GAO had in trying to audit government corporations. This dispute attracted considerable attention at a time when GAO was undergoing strong executive branch and congressional scrutiny. Created by the Tennessee Valley Authority Act (approved May 18, 1933), major TVA programs included navigation facilities on the Tennessee River, flood control, agricultural development, and the generation and the distribution of electricity, along with a number of important secondary programs, including recreation and conservation.[30]

---

[28]Letter, Brown to chairman, Maritime Commission, September 16, 1939, 217 MS 780.

[29]For information on the postwar Maritime Commission audit, see chapter 12, pp. 300-306.

[30]See Paul K. Conkin, "Tennessee Valley Authority (TVA)," in Donald R. Whitnah, ed., *Government Agencies* (Westport, CT: Greenwood Press, 1983), 497-504, for a short, informative history of TVA.

Section 9(b) of the TVA Act authorized the comptroller general to audit TVA transactions at least once each fiscal year. GAO was to have full access to TVA records. TVA was to reimburse GAO for any expenses it incurred for the audit. Section 9(b) also required the comptroller general to report to the president and Congress on transactions or conditions found by him to be in conflict with the powers or the duties entrusted to the corporation by law.[31]

GAO encountered serious problems in conducting its audit, in general because TVA claimed that as a government corporation it was not subject to the kind of audit GAO normally performed of government agencies. Following internal disputes in TVA not related to the GAO audit, President Franklin D. Roosevelt in 1938 dismissed Arthur E. Morgan, the chairman of the TVA board of directors. On April 4, 1938, Congress created a Joint Committee on the Tennessee Valley Authority to investigate the administration of the TVA Act and, among other difficulties, GAO's audit problems at TVA.[32] The Joint Committee's chairman was Senator Alvin Victor ("Vic") Donahey (D—Ohio); five other senators, including Fred H. Brown (later the comptroller general), and four representatives were members. The Joint Committee held a long series of hearings between May 25 and December 21, 1938—about half of them in Knoxville, Tennessee, and the rest in Washington.[33]

GAO testified for four consecutive days, November 28 through December 1, 1938. Chief of Investigations Tulloss was GAO's principal witness because the TVA audit was the responsibility of the Office of Investigations. Acting Comptroller General Elliott attended the hearings on November 28, and three other GAO staff assisted with the testimony. The major questioners for the Joint Committee were Francis Biddle, its general counsel, and Representative Charles A. Wolverton (R—New Jersey). Biddle, later attorney general of the United States (1941-1945), was frequently adversarial in his questioning, while Wolverton, interested in improving GAO-TVA relationships, was supportive of GAO.

---

[31]The Tennessee Valley Authority Act of 1933, 48 Stat. 63, Section 9(b), is printed in *Annual Report of the Comptroller General of the United States for the Fiscal Year Ended June 30, 1933* (Washington: GPO 1933), 18. See Richard E. Brown, *The GAO: Untapped Source of Congressional Power* (Knoxville: University of Tennessee Press, 1970), 18-25, for a brief account of the GAO-TVA controversy. Brown considers later GAO-TVA relations on 26-56. See also David E. Lilienthal, *The Journals of David E. Lilienthal*, vol. I, *The TVA Years, 1939-1945* (New York: Harper and Row, 1964), and C. Herman Pritchett, *The Tennessee Valley Authority: A Study in Public Administration* (Chapel Hill: University of North Carolina Press, 1943).

[32]Conkin, "Tennessee Valley Authority," 500-501; and Robert W. Coren, Mary Rephlo, David Kepley, and Charles South, eds., *Guide to the Records of the United States Senate at the National Archives: 1789-1989, Bicentennial Edition* (Washington: National Archives and Records Administration, 1989), 238.

[33]*Investigation of the Tennessee Valley Authority*, Hearings before the Joint Committee on the Investigation of the Tennessee Valley Authority, 75th Cong., 3d sess., 14 pts. (Washington: GPO, 1939).

On his first day of testimony, Tulloss read into the record a long statement by Elliott, prepared in advance at Biddle's request. Elliott provided a detailed account of GAO's relations with TVA from 1933 to 1938. In discussing GAO-TVA problems, Elliott referred extensively to letters exchanged between the two agencies. Elliott stated that TVA's interference with the GAO audit centered on the TVA treasurer's refusal to submit accounts and the failure of the TVA treasurer and the treasurer of the United States to forward paid checks to GAO, though both actions were required by law.

Besides relying on its general audit authority granted in section 9(b) of the TVA Act, GAO relied on the Deficiency Appropriation Act of June 26, 1934, which empowered GAO to "examine and settle claims and to audit and settle the accounts of receipts and expenditures of governmental agencies, including governmental corporations created after March 3, 1933." To implement these laws, GAO asked TVA in June 1934 to file with GAO monthly accounts and supporting papers for receipts and expenditures for audit and settlement and to file contracts so that vouchers representing payments on them could be audited on receipt by GAO. TVA declined to do this, arguing that the TVA Act, in setting up TVA as a corporation, recognized that it could not operate effectively if regular GAO audit procedures applied. TVA also balked at GAO's requirement that TVA's receipts of funds be deposited in the Treasury of the United States—a requirement, GAO stated, that was "fundamental in safe accounting."

Another problem, from GAO's point of view, was a TVA procedure allowing the authority's purchasing agents to make unit purchases of materials, stores, equipment, machinery, and supplies costing less than $500 without competitive bidding. TVA's principal argument was that Congress, in creating TVA, intended to give it the flexibility of a private corporation and that thus it was not subject to the statutes that normally applied to government agencies, including the one governing the competitive bidding process.

After the signing on August 31, 1935, of a law amending the TVA Act of 1933 to clarify TVA financial practices, GAO became even more insistent that TVA follow standard rules relating to audit, deposit of funds, and competitive bidding. Another law, the Second Deficiency Appropriation Act (approved August 12, 1935), created the Tennessee Valley Authority Fund, into which all TVA funds, including receipts, were to be deposited. Withdrawals from the fund were to be made only by accountable warrants. On the basis of this law, GAO insisted that TVA render its accounts monthly for an audit that would take place in GAO offices in Washington. TVA objected to this, partly because GAO had earlier agreed to a full audit in TVA offices. Beginning with passage of the new law in 1935, GAO decided that a proper audit, backed by regular renditions of accounts and supportive documents, could be done only in Washington.

TVA continued to contest GAO's interpretation and application of the TVA Act and the 1935 legislation. In a letter to GAO in October 1935, TVA stated: "We are advised by counsel that the amendments have made no substantial change in the provisions of the act relating to the nature and to the scope of the audit except to make clearer the limits upon your responsibility, and that the action of Congress . . . was based upon a recognition of the distinction between the Authority, as an independent corporate entity, and the regular departments and establishments of the Government." GAO's audit authority, TVA maintained, was limited to a postaudit and report and did not include the power to settle and adjust accounts.

In a January 1936 letter to the comptroller general, TVA summarized its views on the issues with GAO: (1) The TVA Act contemplates a GAO audit at TVA offices, and if TVA sends its accounts to Washington for audit, it "is for the sole purpose of meeting the convenience of your office for the time being;" (2) GAO's function under the TVA Act is to do a field audit at TVA and to report thereafter to the president and Congress any illegal transactions "and does not include the power to make allowances or disallowances of credits or in any sense to settle and adjust our accounts"; (3) the documents TVA sends to GAO to support its accounts are corporate papers and should be returned to TVA upon completion of the audit; and (4) the TVA treasurer is an officer of the corporation responsible to the corporation, and he is not accountable to GAO.[34]

Although TVA by 1938 was sending accounts and supporting papers to GAO for audit, the differences between the two organizations continued to impede an effective audit, and in GAO's view, TVA was still violating the laws governing its operations and GAO's duties. When TVA officials, including Eric Kohler, the authority's comptroller, testified in January 1939, there was a lengthy discussion of GAO-TVA problems. Rep. Everett M. Dirksen (R—Illinois) questioned Kohler, a well-known accountant who became TVA's comptroller in 1938, about an article in a Washington newspaper quoting extensively a paper Kohler had written on GAO-TVA relations. Kohler was quoted as criticizing GAO severely because of its insistence on having original documents supporting transactions. He contended that these documents should remain with the disbursing agency (in this case, TVA) and be audited in the field rather than in Washington. "The long-distance office audit of the G.A.O., requiring as it does tremendous quantities of correspondence with accountable fiscal agents, should be completely abandoned," according to Kohler. The published article quoted Kohler as also saying that the comptroller general should stop issuing opinions. Such opinions, he felt, were an exercise of improper power by a "purely investigative agency." Kohler also stated that what

---

[34]The above account of GAO-TVA problems is drawn from a letter, Elliott to Donahey, November 22, 1938, in *Investigation of the Tennessee Valley Authority*, pt. 10, 4411-35.

he called "adequate bookkeeping records" prepared by a governmental unit should be sufficient basis for an audit. Dirksen argued that such records would not necessarily reveal everything needed for a thorough audit, and he cited several examples to illustrate his point. Kohler concluded that individual government agencies should handle their own accounting. He stated that "the function of postaudit should be put into the hands of an auditor-general and staff who are accountants responsible primarily to the Congress."[35]

By late 1939, TVA and GAO were getting along fairly well.[36] By this time TVA had agreed to submit to GAO current accounts, supporting schedules, paid checks, and financial statements. In return, GAO would audit vouchers covering financial transactions at TVA offices.[37] While the TVA audit was current, Chief of Investigations Tulloss explained that GAO still was not doing the audit in the manner preferred by TVA. "The T.V.A. seems to desire an audit based upon what would normally be made by a firm of accountants. . . . We make an independent audit and therefore make it strictly in accordance with the law and not . . . with any agreement that would be reached between the party whose accounts are being audited and the auditors."[38] Actually, during this period, TVA contracted with the public accounting firm of Lybrand, Ross Brothers and Montgomery to do a commercial audit, described by Kohler "as a general audit, corresponding to the type of audit made by public accountants for business enterprises." TVA paid Lybrand $40,000 for this audit for fiscal year 1938 and $25,000 for fiscal year 1939.[39]

While GAO-TVA relations improved somewhat during Fred Brown's short term as comptroller general, the basic differences between the two organizations remained. Significantly, as soon as Lindsay C. Warren's nomination as comptroller general became known, Kohler and James P. Pope, TVA director, asked to see him to discuss GAO-TVA relationships.[40] On November 23, 1940, less than a month after Warren entered office, Pope sent him a letter outlining TVA's position

---

[35]Kohler testimony, January 24, 1939, *Independent Offices Appropriation Bill for 1940*, Hearings before the Subcommittee on Independent Offices of the House Committee on Appropriations, 76th Cong., 1st Sess. (Washington: GPO, 1939), 1696-1702. The paper containing Kohler's views was entitled "Personal Views of Eric Kohler, T.V.A. Comptroller, Notes on Reorganization of Federal Fiscal Administration."

[36]Tulloss testimony, December 6, 1939, *Independent Offices Appropriation Bill for 1941*, Hearings before the Subcommittee on Independent Offices of the House Committee on Appropriations, 76th Cong., 3d Sess. (Washington: GPO, 1940), 236.

[37]Memorandum, Comptroller General Brown to chief, Audit Division, June 29, 1939, 214 MS 2116.

[38]Tulloss testimony, December 6, 1939, *Independent Offices Appropriation Bill for 1941*, 236.

[39]Testimony of Kohler and Paul W. Ager, TVA chief budget officer, December 8, 1939, ibid., 1696-97.

[40]Letter, Pope and Kohler to Warren, August 2, 1940, The Papers of Lindsay C. Warren, Southern Historical Collection, Wilson Library, University of North Carolina at Chapel Hill, Folder 362.

and making several recommendations for GAO action.[41] The letter indicated that Pope wanted the long-standing controversy settled according to TVA wishes. Pope sent with his letter a document entitled "Statement of Tennessee Valley Authority on Problems Involved in the Relationship between the Authority and the General Accounting Office." The statement covered the nature of GAO's jurisdiction over TVA, GAO's exceptions to TVA expenditures, and TVA's recommendations to settle outstanding issues.

As for GAO's jurisdiction, TVA argued that section 9(b) of the TVA Act of 1933 made no reference to applying GAO's settlement and adjustment procedures to TVA and stated only that GAO would audit TVA transactions. Furthermore, the intended audit was to be a commercial type done by trained auditors who would review accounts and procedures and develop a financial statement in the usual balance sheet form. TVA needed this kind of audit and used public accountants to provide them. In contrast, GAO's audits examined the technical legality of individual expenditures on the basis of the comptroller general's interpretation of the law. Section 9(b), TVA contended, required GAO to do a commercial audit that did not substitute the auditor's judgment for that of management.

TVA's statement noted that GAO's exceptions of TVA expenditures amounting to $6,737,646, covering the fiscal years 1934-1939, were outstanding.[42] GAO's exceptions, according to TVA, fell into three categories: those based on differences of opinion on the legality of disbursements, those based on differences in judgment of facts, and those GAO claimed to be based on inadequate supportive papers. TVA noted that GAO had withdrawn the majority of the exceptions after the authority provided additional information but that the process had increased TVA's paperwork burden, resulting in increased costs and less efficiency. TVA referred specifically to certificates of settlement GAO presented to the authority for the period from July 1933 through June 30, 1934, totaling $31,565.95, which GAO expected TVA to collect from the affected disbursing officers.

The TVA statement made two recommendations designed to settle the controversy along lines preferred by TVA. First, "The General Accounting Office

[41]Pope's letter to Warren is quoted in a letter, Warren to chairman, Board of Directors, TVA, December 21, 1940, 232 MS 1452.

[42]This amount is stated in the TVA letter of November 23, 1940; it also appears in testimony of Gordon R. Clapp, TVA general manager, January 7, 1941, *Independent Offices Appropriation Bill for 1942*, Hearings before the Subcommittee on Independent Offices, House Committee on Appropriations, 77th Cong., 1st Sess. (Washington: GPO, 1941), 564. Clapp's statistics disclosed that for fiscal years 1934-1939, GAO took 21,927 exceptions amounting to $25,405,441.64, it released 13,999 exceptions worth $18,667,795.11, and 7,928 exceptions totaling $6,737,646.53 remained outstanding.

should discontinue the exception procedure as applied to the Authority, recall its representatives now in Knoxville reviewing transactions for the fiscal year 1941, and withdraw the request for collection of the amounts involved in the Certificates of Settlement for the period ending June 30, 1934." Secondly, "The Comptroller General should appoint a firm of certified public accountants of national reputation to make an annual audit of the accounts of the Authority, the expense of the audit to be borne by the Authority."

If GAO insisted "on continuing the application of its exception procedure," TVA had some suggestions on ways to improve relations between the two organizations: GAO should expedite its decisions on exceptions to which TVA had replied and give TVA a chance to restate its position on items GAO plans to disallow; GAO should "recast" its reports on TVA for the period 1933-1940 "in the interests of accuracy," eliminating exceptions already withdrawn and ensuring that financial statements, if included, were compatible in form with statements published by TVA; and TVA and GAO representatives should review the final report to remove as many classes of exceptions as possible, and then GAO should not take future exceptions on the classes removed.

In his reply, Warren clearly rejected TVA's arguments. After reviewing the controversy about whether TVA was subject to the Budget and Accounting Act, 1921, Warren wrote: "I cannot say that I find the views of my predecessors in this office on this point without substantial support or that they went further than appears to be justified in resolving the doubt in harmony with the basic legislative policy of holding public officers to a strict accountability for the use of public money entrusted to them." While some corporations are expressly exempt from GAO audits, the TVA Act does not expressly exempt TVA from such audits. "It is difficult to conclude," Warren wrote, "that the Congress without express mention intended to leave to the directors of the Tennessee Valley Authority the expenditure of hundreds of millions of public money free of the restraints of general law governing spending and accountability." Warren pointed out that TVA had followed the regular budgetary procedure under Title II of the Budget and Accounting Act in requesting, justifying, and obtaining appropriations. It would be incongruous, Warren observed, to regard TVA as an agency when obtaining appropriations but not when accounting for disposition of appropriations. Warren concluded that TVA was not exempt from the Budget and Accounting Act.

Warren held that TVA would have to resume the submission of disbursing and collection accounts supported by original vouchers and other evidence for examination and settlement by GAO. Upon TVA request, GAO's settlements would be reviewed under Warren's personal supervision, rather than having vouchers examined and exemptions raised during periodic field audits. He also stated that, as required by statute, TVA should deposit contracts promptly with GAO.[43]

The meaning of Warren's letter to the TVA chairman was clear: He rejected all TVA's arguments about the nonapplicability of the Budget and Accounting Act, asserted that TVA was subject to GAO's audit and settlement procedures, and instructed TVA on how to comply with the law. David E. Lilienthal, vice-chairman of the TVA Board of Directors, responded to Warren's position. He noted that Warren's stand was identical with McCarl's and that it departed from the relationship TVA had tentatively established with GAO through discussions with Comptroller General Brown. The central question, Lilienthal contended, was the intent of Congress in the TVA Act of 1933. He argued that GAO's position was inconsistent with this act; if TVA acquiesced in GAO's procedures, the TVA Board would be avoiding its responsibility. The TVA Board would follow the advice of its counsel, that GAO's jurisdiction was set by section 9(b) of the TVA act; extension of this jurisdiction would be beyond the law. TVA, Lilienthal stated, believed that the controversy could be settled only by a ruling of the attorney general, and a request for ruling would be transmitted to him through the secretary of the treasury.[44]

Warren reacted to Lilienthal's letter by requesting congressional legislation to settle the controversy. In letters to the Senate and the House, Warren summarized the issues in contention between GAO and TVA. He explained that he had two alternatives—to permit TVA to withdraw large sums of money indefinitely from the Treasury, for which no accounting would be rendered, or to hold TVA fiscal officers delinquent in the rendition of their accounts, requiring GAO to withhold approval of further Treasury advances to TVA. He said that he hesitated to do this because there was room for doubt in interpretation of the applicable law and because the TVA directors believed that they would be avoiding their legal responsibility if they rendered their accounts. Also such action, leaving TVA without funds, would jeopardize normal operations and national defense activities.

Warren argued that it was necessary to amend section 9(b) of the TVA act to settle the dispute. He submitted the texts of two possible amendments: One would exempt TVA from accounting to or rendering accounts to GAO; the other would require TVA to do so, in accordance with the Budget and Accounting Act. Warren acknowledged that over the past few years, there had been charges that GAO's close scrutiny of TVA spending reflected GAO prejudice against TVA.

---

[43]The above account of the GAO-TVA controversy is based on a letter, Warren to the chairman, Board of Directors, TVA, December 21, 1940, 232 MS 1452. This 29-page letter includes the text of the letter, Pope to Warren, November 23, 1940.

[44]Letter, Lilienthal to Warren, February 12, 1941, 238 MS 4.

Warren contended that such charges never seemed to merit serious consideration but that even if there was a basis for the charge in the past, no basis existed at present. Warren said that he appreciated the importance of TVA's work but that he strongly believed in the need for uniform and complete accountability by all government agencies.[45]

A bill introduced in the House of Representatives two days after Warren requested clarifying legislation became law on November 21, 1941. The law amended section 9(b) of the TVA act to make clear that TVA was to render its accounts of receipts and disbursements for adjustment and settlement by GAO according to section 305 of the Budget and Accounting Act. But the law did authorize TVA to make such expenditures and enter into contracts and other agreements as it deemed necessary. Finally, the law stated that "the General Accounting Office, in the settlement of the accounts . . . shall not disallow credit for, nor withhold funds because of, any expenditure which the Board shall determine to have been necessary to carry out the provisions" of the TVA act.[46]

This law, a compromise between the basic positions of the two agencies, essentially ended the controversy in a way acceptable to both sides. The dispute illustrated the problem of accountability of government corporations. In contesting the issues with TVA, GAO gained a forum for expressing its views, not only on TVA but also on government corporations in general. The November 1941 law was a stepping-stone to comprehensive legislation in 1945, strongly supported by Warren, which made all government corporations subject to annual GAO audit.[47]

Agriculture Programs Audits

Agents of the Office of Investigations did some financial audits in field offices of executive agencies in the 1920s. But the New Deal programs beginning in 1933 in agriculture and other areas really were responsible for GAO's moving some of its audit work out of Washington headquarters and into the field. Under the Agricultural Adjustment Act of May 12, 1933, the Department of Agriculture undertook numerous programs, through the Agricultural Adjustment Administration (AAA), to provide relief to farmers. As these programs developed, the Department of Agriculture called on GAO to audit AAA payments in a way that would foster the success of the programs. While Comptroller General McCarl

---

[45]Letter, Warren to president of the Senate, June 2, 1941, 238 MS 1. An identical letter went to the speaker of the House. See also GAO press release, June 2, 1941, Warren Papers, Folder 382, and Warren's summary of the GAO-TVA controversy in *Annual Report of the Comptroller General of the United States for the Fiscal Year Ended June 30, 1942* (Washington: GAO typescript, [1942], 11-12.

[46]Public Law 306, 55 Stat. 775, approved November 21, 1941.

[47]See chapter 12, pp. 279-83.

was not adverse to accommodating the needs of the Department of Agriculture and later other agencies, he was unwilling to bend GAO's standard procedures to do so. For example, in August 1933, the administrator of the AAA informed McCarl that his agency needed auditors immediately in stockyards areas to audit accounts in settlement of payments owed to meat packers for hogs purchased by them for the Department of Agriculture. To audit the accounts before payment, which had to be made to packers daily, AAA requested GAO to detail six auditors, specified by name, to supervise an audit staff assembled by AAA.[48]

McCarl, concluding that AAA wanted "an administrative scrutiny of the vouchers in question before payment," an examination usually done by the administrative agency involved, as distinct from a preaudit, said that GAO was not authorized to do so. It would be improper for GAO staff to examine administratively vouchers that would later be settled finally by GAO. McCarl also said that GAO was "woefully short of personnel" and that the men requested were "qualified for much more important work." He suggested that instead GAO preaudit the vouchers at three or four sites outside Washington. The preaudit would determine the legality and the accuracy of the proposed payments and would ensure that they would be approved at the time of final GAO audit.[49] GAO did not accommodate the Department of Agriculture in this instance.

A few months later, Agriculture submitted to GAO accounting certificates covering disbursement of more than $137,000 by a government finance officer in Chicago in August 1933 to firms slaughtering and processing hogs. McCarl responded that the documents submitted were insufficient and that they must be accompanied by the contracts covering the purchases and the original vouchers. Agriculture eventually consented to provide the vouchers but said that it could not provide rental and benefit contracts because it had only single copies and needed to retain them until payment was made over a two-year period. The secretary of agriculture asked McCarl to "not press the matter of submission of the rental and benefit contracts until such time as this Department has completed its work on them." McCarl continued to insist that the original contracts be submitted and that until they were received, GAO would have to withhold approval of payments made under them.

This impasse continued for several years. GAO officials provided statistics to Congress in December 1937 showing that for the 1933-1937 period, AAA made about 26 million rental and benefit payments, only 1 million of which GAO

---

[48]Letter, Charles J. Brand, co-administrator, Agricultural Adjustment Administration, to comptroller general, undated but received by GAO on August 24, 1933, A-44002, #1.

[49]Letter, McCarl to the secretary of agriculture, August 24, 1933, ibid.; and letter, acting secretary of agriculture to the comptroller general, August 31, 1933, ibid.

had audited. GAO estimated the value of the unaudited payments at $1,281,723,478.[50]

Notwithstanding these problems, GAO gradually expanded its field audits of New Deal agricultural programs after 1933. By 1939, the Office was doing field preaudits of payments under various Department of Agriculture adjustment programs at 22 locations in the Midwest and the West and preauditing programs in the northeast and east-central regions of the nation in Washington.[51] GAO's first field audit office opened in October 1934 in Lexington, Kentucky, to preaudit payments to farmers under AAA's Tobacco Production Adjustment Program. The office closed three months later when the work in Lexington was completed. Later in 1935, GAO established ten field offices in the South to preaudit payments under the Cotton Price Adjustment Program, an effort that continued into the 1940s.[52]

The Postal Audit

The Budget and Accounting Act, 1921, created a Bureau of Accounts in the Post Office Department to take over the administrative examination of postal service accounts and vouchers previously done by the auditor for the Post Office Department. The officers and the staff of the pre-1921 auditor's office were transferred to the Bureau of Accounts, unlike the personnel of the five other auditors' offices, who moved to GAO in 1921.[53] The law separated the functions of administrative examination, to be performed by Post Office Department staff, from the audit, to be performed by GAO. To implement the new law, GAO and the Post Office Department agreed on a division of the staff of the auditor for the Post Office Department—534 clerks transferred to GAO in April 1922 and 31 remained with the Post Office Bureau of Accounts.[54]

GAO's Post Office audit in the 1920s and 1930s involved a large volume of routine work that increased gradually over the years, requiring a corresponding increase in staff. The main duties of the Post Office Department Division (re-

---

[50]Letter, Secretary of Agriculture Henry A. Wallace to the comptroller general, October 14, 1933, A-44002, #1; letter, McCarl to the secretary of agriculture, October 30, 1933, ibid.; letter, Wallace to McCarl, February 13, 1934, A-44002, #2; letter, McCarl to the secretary of agriculture, March 16, 1934, ibid.; and testimony of Baity, Tulloss, and others, December 7, 1937, *Independent Offices Appropriation Bill for 1939*, Hearings before a Subcommittee of the House Committee on Appropriations, 75th Cong., 2d sess. (Washington: GPO, 1937), 531-32.

[51]GAO, *Annual Report, 1939*, 54.

[52]J. Philip Horan, "The First Field Audits by GAO," *GAO Review* (fall 1971): 74-77.

[53]See Section 304, Budget and Accounting Act, 1921, Public Law 67-13, 42 Stat. 20.

[54]Memorandum, McCarl, unaddressed, April 15, 1922, 8 MS 1064; and letter, McCarl to the U.S. Civil Service Commission, May 12, 1922, 9 MS 905.

named the Postal Accounts Division in July 1939) were the audits of postal money orders, postal savings certificates, and postmasters' accounts. It also handled post office claims for such things as lost parcel post items and audited the accounts of the foreign mail service.[55]

GAO's postal accounts staff. Copyright 1940, The Washington Post. *Reprinted with permission.*

In testimony in December 1934, GAO representatives described the postal audit work and its increasing volume. They estimated that by the end of fiscal year 1935, GAO would handle about 10,000 claims of and against former post-masters. Both the number of postal savings depositors and the number of postal money orders purchased had increased greatly. In fiscal year 1934, records for over 196 million postal money orders had been received for audit, an increase

[55]Testimony of Baity and others, December 7, 1937, *Independent Offices Appropriation Bill for 1939*, 533; and General Regulations No. 90, June 30, 1939, 214 MS 2278.

over 1933 of 12 percent, and the increases would be the same or higher in the next two fiscal years. For 1936, GAO expected to receive for audit records in support of 18 million paid postal savings certificate.[56]

GAO did much of the postal audit work by electrical machines. McCarl explained in 1923 that GAO used card perforators, tabulators, and assorters in the audit of postal money orders, requiring the services of 300 operatives and clerks.[57]

Topical Audit Reports

While most of GAO's audit work in the 1920s and 1930s involved what could be described as compliance auditing—checking vouchers for accuracy and legality, settling disbursing officers' accounts, and similar operations—GAO did produce some topical reports, mostly at the request of Congress or its committees. They were the forerunners of the modern "blue cover" reports. One example is a GAO report in 1930 about Department of Agriculture expenditures in an effort to eradicate the Mediterranean fruit fly in Florida. GAO's follow-up work relating to this report extended to the end of the 1940s.

During 1929 and 1930, the Department of Agriculture collaborated with the state of Florida in an effort to control an infestation of the Mediterranean fruit fly, which threatened the state's citrus industry. This work resulted in claims for damages to property and charges of illegal payments. At the request of Rep. William R. Wood (R—Indiana) in March 1930, GAO investigated the activities of the Department of Agriculture in the campaign against the fruit fly. McCarl reported to Wood the results of the audit, which paid particular attention to property accounting, personnel, and general expenditures. He reported that the Department of Agriculture office at Orlando, Florida, had developed a satisfactory property record for such things as motor vehicles, pumps, sprayers, and cabinets and that the office's purchasing methods were acceptable except for the frequent waiving of the required period for bid advertisements on the grounds of emergency.

In regard to personnel employment and compensation payments, GAO's audit showed no problems except for a proposed payment to members of the Florida National Guard, which enforced a Mediterranean fruit fly quarantine line in Florida. There was a proposal to pay the National Guard for this work with federal funds. When GAO examined the proposed Guard payroll in March 1930, before payment was made, it declared that the payments would be illegal because the Guard members were on active duty in the service of the state and thus were not autho-

---

[56]Testimony of Baity and others, December 13, 1934, *Independent Offices Appropriation Bill for 1936*, 287-88.

[57]Letter, McCarl to the postmaster general, February 20, 1923, 18 MS 1050.

rized to be paid with federal funds. Generally, GAO found that federal expenditures in Florida during the campaign were in accordance with the law and accepted practices, although some discrepancies showed up relating to signatures on vouchers and checks and some small duplicate payments were found.

McCarl also reported that GAO had examined claims filed with the Department of Agriculture for such things as destruction of fruits and vegetables; poisoning of animals, fowl, and bees; damage from spraying; and other problems. Agriculture officials in Florida, McCarl reported, thought that the claims figures were much inflated and that some of the claims could not be attributed to the fruit fly eradication campaign.[58]

Controversy over the fruit fly campaign continued for at least two decades, mainly on the matter of claims against the United States for damages sustained by persons in Florida. In 1938, Congress created a Mediterranean Fruit Fly Board, appointed by the secretary of agriculture, to investigate losses suffered by farmers and growers in Florida and to produce a report, for information only, on these losses.[59]

In June 1939, after the board issued its report, Sen. Charles O. Andrews (D—Florida) and Rep. James H. Peterson (D—Florida) drafted a bill authorizing the comptroller general to appoint a three-member committee to determine damages due each claimant, such damages to be certified by the comptroller general as final. Andrews, who had talked previously with Comptroller General Brown about the matter, requested his views on the proposed arrangement.[60] Brown's main objection was that the proposal made GAO responsible for appointing the committee without giving GAO power to control its operations or review its work. He concluded that he would rather not be responsible for appointing the group under such circumstances. He suggested that instead the Department of Agriculture investigate the claims and present its findings to GAO. GAO would then report to Congress after reviewing the findings. He concluded by saying that if GAO was given any responsibility in the matter, it should have authority to examine the findings on claims for legal sufficiency before any were paid.[61]

Later in 1939 Andrews and Sen. Claude D. Pepper (D—Florida) introduced a joint resolution providing for payment of the Mediterranean fruit fly claims. Referring to the report of the Board appointed in 1938, the draft resolution autho-

---

[58]Letter, McCarl to Wood, May 17, 1930, with attached report, "Memorandum of investigation March, 1930, financial transactions, Mediterranean Fruit Fly in Florida," May 17, 1930.

[59]Public Law 535, 52 Stat. 436, approved May 23, 1938.

[60]Letter, Andrews to Brown, June 24, 1939, B-4602.

[61]Letter, Brown to Andrews, June 29, 1939, B-4602.

rized the comptroller general to determine, and certify for payment by the Treasury, of the indemnity due claimants for losses and damages suffered during the eradication campaign in 1929 and 1930. Brown advised the chairman of the Senate Committee on Claims that in his opinion "the United States is neither legally nor equitably responsible for the losses and damages in question and that they should not be assumed by the Federal Government." He argued that any damages to citrus fruit or other property in Florida had occurred entirely under state authority. The federal government aided the state of Florida in this matter and should not be held responsible for local losses. Also, since the eradication campaign took place ten years earlier, any attempt to verify the claims would have to rely on "the self-serving statements of thousands of individual claimants." If it was decided that the United States should pay such claims, it would be best if the Department of Agriculture determined the facts in individual cases and then forwarded the supporting papers and recommendations to GAO for settlement if funds had been appropriated to pay the claims.[62]

This matter carried on without a settlement for many more years. The Senate Committee on Claims held extensive hearings on the issue in 1940.[63] In 1947, similar bills were introduced in the House and the Senate to provide $10 million for payment of claims and expenses in the Mediterranean fruit fly case. Comptroller General Warren analyzed the bills in detail, quoting extensively from GAO's 1939 arguments and reiterating them. He recommended against approval of the bills.[64] As late as 1949, Sen. Pepper and his colleague, Sen. Spessard L. Holland (D—Florida), introduced legislation providing for payment of the claims.[65] The Mediterranean fruit fly controversy is an interesting case study showing GAO's detailed work on a matter referred to it by Congress, occupying GAO's attention for at least two decades.

Another topical report dealt with indebtedness of the U. S. government to the state of North Carolina for claims against the United States and claims by the United States against North Carolina. In January 1928, the Senate passed a resolution directing the comptroller general to account for and report on the in-

---

[62]S.J. Res. 177, July 26, 1939, 76th Cong., 1st Sess., copy in B-4602; letter, Brown to chairman, Senate Committee on Claims, November 21, 1939, B-4602; and letter, Brown to Rep. Andrew J. Kennedy, chairman, House Committee on Claims, December 2, 1939, B-4602 (comments on H.R. 7382, identical to S.J. Res. 177). Congress did not pass this resolution.

[63]*Mediterranean Fruit Fly*, Hearings before the Senate Committee on Claims, February 29, 1940, 76th Cong., 3d Sess. (Washington: GPO, 1940); and *Losses Sustained by Growers Incident to Federal Campaign for the Eradication of the Mediterranean Fruit Fly in Florida*, Hearings before the Senate Committee on Claims, December, 1940, 76th Cong., 3d Sess. (Washington: GPO, 1940).

[64]Letter, Warren to Sen. Alexander Wiley, chairman, Senate Judiciary Committee, February 28, 1947, 306 MS 2400.

[65]Memorandum, J. Darlington Denit, chief, Accounting and Bookkeeping Division, to Warren, February 15, 1949, commenting on S. 164, introduced by Pepper and Holland, January 5, 1949, B-4602. Congress did not act on this bill, and no evidence has been located that it ever passed any legislation on this matter.

debtedness of North Carolina to the United States on bonds issued between 1856 and 1859 and on claims of North Carolina against the United States for money advanced during the War of 1812 and for cotton seized in 1865 and 1866. In its report in February 1928, GAO determined that North Carolina owed the United States $146,140, representing principal of $58,000 plus interest on state bonds. GAO also calculated that the United States owed North Carolina $167,339.88 (principal and interest) for loans to the United States during the War of 1812 and $96,835.81 for the cotton seized during and after the Civil War—$42,532.54 principal and $54,303.27 interest. The difference between the $264,175.69 the United States owed to North Carolina and the $146,140 North Carolina owed to the United States as of February 29, 1928, was $118.035.69. In determining this settlement amount, GAO had to consider previous work on the War of 1812 loans done by GAO in 1923 and to search existing records on the bonds issued by North Carolina, the 1812 loans, and the cotton seizures.[66]

Conclusions

During a hearing of the House Committee on Appropriations in 1926, Rep. William R. Wood observed: "The intent of the law creating the General Accounting Office was that there should be some liaison between the Congress and the executive branches of the Government, so that Congress would know that its intentions were being carried out and that the money was being spent for the purposes for which it was appropriated." Comptroller General McCarl, who very much agreed with Wood, added: "And also to see that the Government is receiving all that the law contemplated it should receive."[67]

These comments suggest a theme for interpreting GAO's audit and investigative activities in the 1920s and 1930s. During these two decades, the Office's workload, large at the start, grew significantly, reflecting the effects of the Depression, the New Deal programs, and the defense effort that began at the end of the period. This work was the main responsibility of the Audit Division and the Office of Investigations. McCarl and his immediate successor, Acting Comptroller General Elliott, stuck to their interpretation of the letter of the law in their insistence on GAO's audit prerogatives and the finality of GAO's conclusions. This seeming inflexibility on GAO's part at times created an atmosphere of hostility; the attorney general, the secretary of the treasury, the chairman of the Tennessee Valley Authority, and others jousted with GAO about jurisdiction and powers. The problem cannot be blamed exclusively on GAO. Agencies typically do not like auditors, particularly when they raise critical questions. Also, some agencies, Justice, for example, tested GAO's audit authority in the Office's early years.

---

[66]The report is a letter, McCarl to the president of the Senate, February 6, 1928, 78 MS 198.
[67]McCarl testimony, January 26, 1926, *Independent Offices Appropriation Bill, 1927*, 192.

Neither McCarl nor Elliott was willing to cede ground to these opponents. Lindsay Warren, after entering office in late 1940, did not repudiate the positions taken by his predecessors, as demonstrated in the case of TVA, but appeared more willing to discuss differences with executive branch agencies and work toward accommodation. In the case of TVA, he ultimately asked Congress to pass legislation clarifying the issues under debate, and Congress quickly did so.

GAO took on some new challenges in audit work during the 1930s, most specifically extending its audit from Washington headquarters into the field, to check widespread agricultural programs and other emergency programs of the New Deal. This experience was to prove valuable during World War II, when thousands of GAO staff labored in the field, and after the war, when a formal system of regional and overseas offices emerged in GAO.

Audits of government corporations, such as described in this chapter for the Maritime Commission and TVA, became an important aspect of the audit operation in the 1930s. GAO learned from this experience and, in the early 1940s, repeatedly urged Congress to develop legislation bringing all government corporations under GAO audit. Congress passed such legislation in 1945.[68]

Frederick Mosher, an earlier student of GAO, wrote: "The GAO of the 1920s, 1930s, and war years of the 1940s can be best described as a prodigious paper mill and an enormous warehouse of paper. . . . On receipt of these documents, the GAO recorded and checked them, sometimes returned or otherwise responded to them, and stored them."[69] It is true that GAO was inundated with paper records that it required agencies to provide to facilitate its audit work. But one should not conclude from Mosher's statement that nothing valuable resulted from GAO's audit work during this period. In spite of GAO's penchant for what its critics called "red tape," its audit activity did accomplish much—in encouraging government agencies to account for their activities to ensure that the law, including appropriations, governed these activities and in recovering money that otherwise would have been lost to the government.

As already suggested, GAO's audit and other activities generated much criticism and hostility on the part of the executive branch. Soon after its creation in 1921, proposals to abolish GAO began to emanate from the executive branch. Questions about GAO's jurisdiction were frequent, and the relevance of constitutional principles, including separation of powers, caused debate.

---

[68]See chapter 12, pp. 279-83.

[69]Frederick C. Mosher, *The GAO: The Quest for Accountability in American Government* (Boulder, CO: Westview Press, 1979), 72.

CHAPTER 10

GAO—A Controversial Watchdog, 1921-1940

The Pension Building, GAO headquarters, 1940. Source: National Archives.

During its first two decades, the General Accounting Office (GAO) became a very controversial institution within the federal government. Much of the controversy can be traced to the position GAO assumed as the watchdog of the nation's money under J. R. McCarl, the first comptroller general. As already noted, McCarl held to a very strict construction of GAO's powers as set forth in the Budget and Accounting Act, 1921. His role in this regard was crucial. GAO was to help Congress ensure that the executive branch spent appropriated funds as Congress intended, or at least as he understood congressional intent. He was determined to enforce GAO's mandate in Section 304 of the Budget and Accounting Act—that "the balances certified by the Comptroller General shall be final and conclusive upon the executive branch of the Government."

Had McCarl chosen to see GAO's powers and role differently, he might have tried to lead the Office down a different path. The Budget and Accounting Act said that GAO "shall be independent of the executive departments." It did not specify that GAO was an instrument of Congress, although assuming that the Office had this status could be justified by studying the legislative history of the law. The president appointed the comptroller general and he could request reports from GAO. These provisions gave McCarl a basis for closer relationships with the White House and the executive branch. McCarl did not choose this route, and there is no evidence that he even considered it. If he had tried such a course, Congress probably would have objected.

There were, as already explained, various disputes with the executive branch—with the attorney general, the secretary of war, the Treasury Department, and government corporations, including the Tennessee Valley Authority and the Merchant Fleet Corporation. McCarl personally, and GAO as an institution, gained an unfavorable reputation in the eyes of the executive branch. Harvey C. Mansfield, Sr., in a very critical study of GAO published in 1939, described McCarl as "a man of crusading zeal" who "brought to his office abundant energy but little training in administration, law, or accounting that would equip him for his tasks." Mansfield contended that "the strengthening and expansion of his controlling powers" was McCarl's guiding principle.[1]

Proposals for Change Under Harding

It is not surprising that proposals to change the Budget and Accounting Act surfaced soon after GAO began its work in 1921. By 1923, the president had changed his mind on both GAO and the Bureau of the Budget (BOB), undoubtedly reflecting his own and his advisers' views on early experience with the two organizations. The changes proposed for GAO and BOB were part of a broader plan to reorganize the executive branch, including the placing of the Army and the Navy in a Department of National Defense; the transfer of nonfiscal functions, such as those performed by the Public Health Service and the Coast Guard, from the Treasury Department; the renaming of the Post Office Department as the Department of Communications; the establishment of a Department of Education and Welfare; and the placing of

---

[1]Harvey C. Mansfield, Sr., *The Comptroller General: A Study in the Law and Practice of Financial Administration* (New Haven: Yale University Press, 1939), 71, 145 (hereafter cited as Mansfield, *Comptroller General*). See pp. 236-37, for a detailed summary of Mansfield's views on GAO.

existing independent agencies, except those quasi-judicial in character, under a cabinet-level department.

On February 13, 1923, Harding submitted his proposals for executive branch reorganization to the Joint Committee on the Reorganization of the Administrative Branch of the Government (established in late 1920), with little explanation or rationale. He proposed detaching the Bureau of the Budget from the Treasury Department and making it an independent establishment and transferring GAO to the Treasury Department. The effect of these proposals was to repudiate the basic rationale for enacting Title II of the Budget and Accounting Act less than two years earlier.[2]

Harding stated that his reorganization plan had the cabinet's sanction "with few exceptions, notably that of coordinating all agencies of national defense." When hearings on reorganization took place in January 1924, Secretary of the Treasury Andrew W. Mellon was the only cabinet member to testify. He opposed the Harding proposals on both GAO and BOB, arguing that GAO should remain independent and that BOB should stay in the Treasury Department.[3] By this time, President Harding was dead and his successor, Calvin Coolidge, was not sympathetic to his reorganization plans. GAO and BOB were less than two years old, and neither had compiled a record of experience sufficient to justify the conclusion that they were ill-conceived. In addition, Harding's plan simply ignored the lengthy arguments between 1919 and 1921 in favor of an independent audit organization such as GAO.

Eventually, the Joint Committee reported a modified plan of reorganization, but Congress failed to act on bills accompanying the report.[4] President Coolidge expressed support for GAO and BOB in his annual message to Congress in December 1925: "The purpose of maintaining the Budget Director and the Comptroller General is to secure economy and efficiency in government expenditure. No better method has been devised for the accomplishment of that end. These offices can not be administered in all the various details without making some errors both of fact and judgment. But the important consideration remains that these are the instrumentalities of the Congress and that no other plan has ever been adopted which was so successful in promoting economy and efficiency."[5]

---

[2]The Harding proposals are in *Reorganization of the Executive Departments*, S. Doc. 302, February 13, 1923, 67th Cong., 4th Sess. (Washington: GPO, 1923), 1-5.

[3]See Frederick C. Mosher, *The GAO: The Quest for Accountability in American Government* (Boulder, CO: Westview Press, 1979), 86 (hereafter cited as Mosher, *GAO*).

[4]Discussed in Select Committee on Government Organization, *Government Organization*, S. Rep. 1236, August 16, 1937, 75th Cong., 1st Sess., 5-6 (hereafter cited as Select Committee, *Government Organization*). See also Mansfield, *Comptroller General*, 279.

[5]Mosher, *GAO*, 100, n. 51. The president's annual message is printed in *Congressional Record*, 69th Cong., 1st Sess., vol. 67, pt. 1, 458.

The Willoughby Study of GAO

In 1927 the first substantial study of GAO operations appeared. Its author was W. F. Willoughby, the director of the Institute of Government Research, later renamed the Brookings Institution.[6] Willoughby described in detail the work of GAO and how the Office functioned. He covered such things as the use of warrants, settlement and adjustment of claims, the prescription of accounting forms and systems, contract work, and the work of disbursing officers. He delineated the issues raised by the establishment of GAO:

> The establishment of this office has raised issues that vitally affect the whole system of administration of public affairs. They involve such fundamental issues as the relationship between the legislative and executive branches of the government, the powers and duties of all executive officers, including the President himself, the conclusiveness of administrative determinations on the rights of persons believing their rights to be violated to appeal to the courts for redress, the location of final authority in the construing of the public law governing the organizations and work of the executive departments; and the determination of the service that shall be responsible for the performance of certain categories of work having to do with the orderly administration of the financial affairs of the government.[7]

Willoughby recommended numerous steps "to put this most important agency [GAO] of the government upon a satisfactory basis." He argued for recognition by executive branch administrative officers of GAO's special status and "its desirability from the standpoint of the general interests of the government. With such a recognition, much of the present antagonism to the work of that office should disappear and be replaced by a spirit of cooperation." Specifically, he advocated making GAO the government's central accounting office, to develop a modern system of central accounts classifying receipts according to their sources; completing a standard accounting system for the operating services; developing a smaller workable system of appropriation categories consistent with agency operating and accounting requirements; legislatively determining whether the comptroller general or the attorney general would be responsible for the meaning of laws under which claims against the government arose; changing the status of disbursing officers, making them officers of the Treasury Department, with

---

[6]Willoughby testified in hearings on the Budget and Accounting Act in 1919 and helped develop the law's terms. See chapter 2, pp. 24, 30.

[7]W. F. Willoughby, *The Legal Status and Functions of the General Accounting Office of the National Government* (Baltimore: The Johns Hopkins Press, 1927), 2 (hereafter cited as Willoughby, *General Accounting Office*).

some exceptions for the Army and the Navy; and codifying the law on government accounting and reporting.[8]

Willoughby urged Congress to create a congressional committee on public accounts. "The most fundamental feature of the General Accounting Office," he wrote, "is that it is an instrumentality set up by Congress . . . [to] control the administration from the standpoint of assuring itself that there is rigid compliance with all of its orders in respect to the collection, custody, and disbursement of public funds . . . ." Willoughby spoke of "grave issues" between GAO and executive branch agencies. A committee on public accounts would give Congress a means to check on GAO's performance and provide GAO with a mechanism to bring matters to congressional attention. Without such a committee, Willoughby contended, the United States would lose "much of the advantages anticipated from the creation of the independent office of Comptroller General."[9]

Willoughby was a recognized scholar of government with much stature. His book presented a dispassionate analysis of GAO operations and described the disagreements that had arisen between GAO and the executive branch. The detailed descriptions of GAO's work and recommendations for improvement were available for study during subsequent debate about organizational change involving GAO. Willoughby recognized a number of problems relating to GAO's operations and functions that required clarification, but he concluded that GAO was a needed institution of government and that it should continue to exist.

Hoover's Reorganization Proposals

President Herbert C. Hoover (1929-1933) obviously did not share Willoughby's views on GAO. He proposed major changes that would have circumscribed important functions assigned to the Office in the Budget and Accounting Act. Title IV of the Economy Act of June 30, 1932, authorized the president to consolidate or transfer functions of executive agencies, effective in 60 days unless disapproved by either house.

On December 9, 1932, Hoover submitted to Congress 11 executive orders to reorganize the executive branch. One of them proposed to transfer two groups of GAO powers—the design, the prescription, and the installation of accounting forms, systems, and procedures and the administrative examination of fiscal officers' accounts and claims against the United States—

---

[8]Ibid., 173-78.
[9]Ibid., 139-44.

to the BOB. In his message to Congress, Hoover argued that "it is not . . . a proper function of an establishment created primarily for the purpose of auditing Government accounts [GAO] to make the necessary studies and to develop and prescribe accounting systems involving the entire field of Government accounting." It was also improper for GAO to prescribe the procedure for, and determine the effectiveness of, administrative examination of accounts. "Accounting is an essential element of effective administration, and it should be developed with the primary objective of serving this purpose."[10]

The House Committee on Expenditures in the Executive Departments held hearings on the Hoover proposals. J. Clawson Roop, the director of the Bureau of the Budget, explained Hoover's proposals in detail but, according to the House report on his testimony, "could not show the committee where any economy would result." Roop also observed in response to a question that it would not be wise to adopt the reorganization proposals of an outgoing president just before a new chief executive (Franklin D. Roosevelt) entered office. The House report pointed out that the Economy Act limited the president's reorganization authority to executive branch agencies, yet he had made proposals on GAO, "an agency specially created to function independent of the executive branch and on behalf of Congress." "What is proposed," the report argued, ". . . would defeat the very purpose of existing law, as it would break down the means of obtaining a uniform accounting system throughout the Government by dividing the work between two agencies, the General Accounting Office, where matters relating to accounting belong, and the Bureau of the Budget—anything but an accounting agency." The House report recommended rejection of Hoover's reorganization orders. The House passed the resolution of disapproval on January 19, 1933.[11]

In November 1932, a month before Hoover submitted his reorganization plans, the Democratic candidate, Franklin D. Roosevelt, defeated Hoover for the presidency, and the Democrats gained control of both houses of Congress. Hoover's lame-duck reorganization proposals stood little chance of passage, whatever their merits. But as Frederick C. Mosher has pointed out, Hoover had put forward the basic doctrine that "the keeping of accounts and the conduct of financial

[10]Message from the President of the United States Transmitting a Message to Group, Coordinate, and Consolidate Executive and Administrative Agencies of the Government, As Nearly As Maybe, According to Major Purposes, H. Doc. 493, December 9, 1932, 72d Cong., 2d Sess. (Washington: GPO, 1932); and Staff of the Senate Committee on Government Operations, *Financial Management in the Federal Government*, S. Doc. 11, 87th Cong., 1st Sess., vol. I (Washington: GPO, 1961), 11-12 (hereafter cited as *Financial Management*, 1961).

[11]*Executive Orders Grouping, Coordinating, and Consolidating Certain Executive and Administrative Agencies of the Government*, H. Rept. 1833, January 9, 1933, 72d Cong., 2d Sess., 1-5; and Mosher, *GAO*, 87-88.

operations should be an exclusively administrative responsibility" under BOB.[12]   When new proposals to alter GAO's functions came up later in the decade, there was further discussion of this basic doctrine.

Efforts to Change GAO During the Roosevelt Administration

The most concerted effort to alter GAO's status and functions occurred during the first two terms of Franklin Roosevelt. Roosevelt was very much interested in reorganizing the executive branch. The attention he paid to GAO seems to be mainly within this context rather than reflecting deep hostility to the Office itself. In 1936, he had an opportunity to select a new comptroller general when McCarl retired. He tried then and several times in later years to interest Lindsay C. Warren (D—North Carolina), a prominent member of the House of Representatives, in the position. If Roosevelt had been intent on sabotaging GAO, it is unlikely that he would have urged Warren, who served as chairman of the House Committee on Accounts between 1931 and 1940, to become comptroller general. Indeed, Roosevelt's repeated efforts to persuade Warren to take the job suggest that he wanted a strong and qualified leader for GAO. Probably he expected Warren, a consistent supporter of the New Deal, to be more cooperative with the executive branch.[13]

Early in 1936, two initiatives on government reorganization began. On January 9, 1936, Sen. Harry F. Byrd (D—Virginia) introduced a resolution to create a Senate Select Committee to Investigate the Executive Agencies of the Government. The committee was to study government units "with a view to determining whether the activities of any such agency conflict with or overlap the activities of any other such agency and whether in the interest of simplification, efficiency, and economy, any of such agencies should be coordinated with other agencies or abolished or the personnel thereof reduced." The Senate agreed to Byrd's proposal on February 24, 1936.[14]

On March 22, 1936, President Roosevelt created the Committee on Administrative Management, chaired by Louis Brownlow, a well-known expert on public administration. Brownlow had experience in journalism and had served as a government administrator and as an adviser to presidents. The other members of the Brownlow Committee, as it came to be called, were Charles E. Merriam and Luther H. Gulick. Merriam, a long-time professor of political science at the University of Chicago, had written widely on politics and democracy. Gulick, the president of the New York Bureau of Municipal

---

[12]Mosher, *GAO*, 87.

[13]See chapter 4, pp. 74-77.

[14]S.R. 217, 74th Cong., 2d Sess.; and *Financial Management*, 1961, 18.

Research, was a prominent authority on public administration and finance. Like that of the Senate Select Committee, the Brownlow Committee's mandate was to study the organization of executive agencies, emphasizing the problems of administrative management.[15]   Both committees studied the entire executive branch; their consideration of GAO's functions was in the context of the impact of its work within that branch.

On January 12, 1937, President Roosevelt transmitted to Congress the Brownlow Committee's report, supplemented by nine separate studies of federal administrative management. Roosevelt commented that the committee's program was "adequate, reasonable, and practical" and provided a basis for "immediate action."[16]

Among the supplemental studies was a confidential memorandum by Harvey C. Mansfield, Sr., entitled "The General Accounting Office." Mansfield began by stating that the Budget and Accounting Act, 1921, "created a new problem of administration and administrative law"—"the failure to distinguish between audit and control." Mansfield defined an audit as a "report upon the fidelity and legality of fiscal transactions" by an independent officer to a body which could hold spending officers accountable. Control, "the power to pass on expenditures and prevent their being made" was normally the responsibility of executive management. The problem was that the Budget and Accounting Act "took the unusual step of vesting both audit and control powers in the hands of an independent officer."[17]

After a lengthy analysis of how GAO exercised control—through settlement of accounts, preaudit, postaudit, prescription of accounting forms and procedures, processing of claims, control of documents, and other means— Mansfield discussed "the irresponsibility of the General Accounting Office." The comptroller general, Mansfield claimed, was not responsible to anyone—not to the executive, the courts, or even Congress. He complained that the comptroller general was not making the reports to Congress that the Budget and Accounting Act required. On the basis of a 1932 economy law, which authorized agency heads to stop printing annual reports, he had not issued printed annual reports since 1933.[18] Special reports issued by GAO since 1921, Mansfield

---

[15]*Financial Management*, 1961, 13.

[16]*Reorganization of the Executive Departments*, Message from the President of the United States Transmitting a Report on Reorganization of the Executive Departments of the Government, 75th Cong., 1st Sess., S. Doc. 8, January 12, 1937 (Washington: GPO, 1937) (hereafter cited as *Brownlow Report*).

[17]Harvey C. Mansfield, Sr., "The General Accounting Office," submitted to the President's Committee on Administrative Management, undated, typescript (88 pages), 1 (hereafter cited as Mansfield, "General Accounting Office"), GAO History Program Archives.

[18]GAO's annual reports for fiscal years 1934, 1935, 1936, and 1938 were prepared in typescript and kept on file for public inspection at GAO headquarters.

stated, had not all been regularly published and Congress had not paid proper attention to them. "Administrative action by the Comptroller General has been substituted for reports to Congress. In place of the constitutional division of authority over financial matters between Congress and the Executive, a third authority has been introduced which impairs the responsibility of the other two," Mansfield asserted.[19]

The consequences of GAO's actions were "the divorce of responsibility and authority, arbitrary and technical decisions, delay, and the want of any adequate central system of accounts for control purposes."[20] Mansfield concluded with several recommendations for change:

• Shift the power to settle accounts and claims to the Treasury Department. Refer questions of jurisdiction between Treasury and others to the attorney general or to the president for action by executive order.

• Transfer the prescribing of administrative forms and accounting methods to the Treasury Department.

• Change the name of the comptroller general to "auditor general," and designate GAO as the "General Auditing Office" or "Office of the Auditor General."

• Abandon the "archaic" system of warrants, and replace it with Treasury orders providing evidence of advances and transfers on account of annual appropriations, approved by the secretary of the treasury with copies to the auditor general.

• Establish a congressional Joint Committee on Public Accounts, which "is indispensable if Congress is to enforce proper accountability for the execution of the budget."[21]

---

[19]Mansfield, "General Accounting Office," 58-64.

[20]Ibid., 65-74.

[21]Ibid., 83-88. Mansfield published a book in 1939, *The Comptroller General, A Study in the Law and Practice of Financial Administration*, which must have grown out of his Brownlow Committee work. The book was a detailed, harsh attack on McCarl and GAO. Mansfield reached three main conclusions about GAO: (1) ". . . Congress has not gotten from the Comptroller General what it looked for when the Budget and Accounting Act was passed, nor what any governing body, public or private, is entitled to expect from an auditor." (2) ". . . the General Accounting Office has developed into a powerful institution irresponsibly free, in practice, from either the legal or the democratic controls that apply to virtually every other governmental establishment. A finality attaches to most of its acts that is little disturbed by the theoretical possibilities of judicial review or relief legislation. It can be a law to itself." Mansfield added that GAO "compensates for the want of a clear statutory objective by substituting policies of its own, in which self-perpetuation and self-aggrandizement, nourished in the conviction of self-righteousness, take precedence." (3) "The General Accounting Office has imposed nearly intolerable conditions on the conduct of all operating establishments within its control." Mansfield, *Comptroller General*, 274-75.

The influence on the Brownlow Committee of Mansfield's paper is clear. The committee identified four major problems in the fiscal management area: inadequate staffing in BOB; authority of the comptroller general over claims settlement, final determination of the uses of appropriations, and the prescription of accounting systems; absence of an independent and prompt audit, enabling Congress to hold the executive branch strictly accountable; and failure to develop and install a modern system of accounts and records.[22] The Brownlow Report adopted Mansfield's distinction between control and audit and his other criticisms of the comptroller general. The system put in place by the comptroller general "deprives the President of essential power needed to discharge his major executive responsibility" and "deprives the Congress of a really independent audit and review of the fiscal affairs of the Government."

The Brownlow Report also raised a question of constitutional principle: "The removal from the Executive of the final authority to determine the use of appropriations, conditions of employment, the letting of contracts, and the control over administrative decisions, as well as the prescribing of accounting procedures and the vesting of such authority in an officer independent of direct responsibility to the President for his acts, is clearly in violation of the constitutional principle of the division of authority between the Legislative and Executive Branches of the Government."[23]

The Brownlow Committee's specific recommendations relating to GAO also generally followed Mansfield's prescriptions:

- Transfer to the secretary of the Treasury authority to prescribe and supervise accounting systems.

- Transfer to the Treasury Department the settlement and the adjustment of claims by and against the U. S. government.

- Authorize the attorney general to render opinions on jurisdictional questions between Treasury and other agencies upon request of agency heads or the secretary of the treasury; the attorney general's opinion was to be final and binding.

- Change the titles of "comptroller general" and "assistant comptroller general" to "auditor general" and "assistant auditor general" and GAO to "General Auditing Office."

---

[22]*Brownlow Report*, 33. See also *Financial Management*, 1961, 13.
[23]*Brownlow Report*, 42-43.

- Authorize and require the auditor general to send auditors to sites in the District of Columbia and in the field to audit accounts.

- Authorize the auditor general to report account exceptions to Congress through designated committees if he and the secretary of the Treasury fail to agree on exceptions.[24]

While the Brownlow Committee pursued its study in 1936, the Senate's Select Committee to Investigate the Executive Agencies of the Government also moved forward. In collaboration with the House Committee on Organization and the President's Committee on Administrative Management, the Select Committee contracted with the Brookings Institution for a functional and fact-finding survey of government agencies. The Senate Select Committee published the Brookings report, which contained more than 500,000 words and about 1,000 pages, in August 1937.[25] The report thoroughly described and analyzed the organization of the executive branch and included recommendations for reorganization. Chapter III, which covered federal financial administration, dealt in detail with GAO, the Treasury Department, and BOB. In particular, the Brookings report discussed the relationship between GAO and BOB functions and duties.

Regarding the Budget and Accounting Act, the Brookings authors defined two types of "financial audit"—"one with a view to verifying the accuracy, regularity, and legality of the financial acts of administrative officers; the other with a view to measuring their effectiveness." In the act, Congress established the GAO and BOB to exercise these two types of control. In practice after 1921, confusion over the functions of the comptroller general had arisen; "the Comptroller General . . . has come to be regarded by many as an administrative officer as well as a final auditor" and "as auditor he reviews acts of administrative officers to determine their legality." The Brookings report concluded that the Budget and Accounting Act made "proper provision for the organization of officers charged with the final audit and settlement of accounts." "Developing the potentialities of the system contemplated by the Budget and Accounting Act" was the solution to the current problems, according to Brookings.[26]

---

[24]Ibid., 46-48. See also *Financial Management*, 1961, 15-17, and Lucius Wilmerding, Jr., *The Spending Power: A History of Efforts to Control Expenditures* (New Haven: Yale University Press, 1943), 295-98.

[25]Senate Select Committee to Investigate the Executive Agencies of the Government, *Investigation of Executive Agencies of the Government*, 75th Cong., 1st Sess., S. Rept. 1275, August 16, 1937 (Washington: GPO, 1937). The Brookings transmittal letter to the Senate Select Committee, signed by Harold G. Moulton, president of Brookings, indicated that the total cost of the report was $59,270, paid as follows: the Senate Select Committee, $18,200; the House Committee on Organization, $10,000; the President's Committee on Administrative Management, $10,000; and the Brookings Institution itself, $21,070, including $9,434 contributed by Marshall Field. See pp. v-vi of the Brookings report.

[26]*Investigation of Executive Agencies of the Government*, 67-68, 162.

The report identified the failure of the nation's budgetary system to give the president the proper means to centralize budgetary and administrative management as one of several fundamental defects in the financial administrative system. Brookings specifically recommended that BOB's structure and organization be improved and that it be removed from the Treasury Department and given independent status under the president.[27] To solve the other problems Brookings identified in the system—the failure to ensure complete congressional control of the collection, the custody, and the disbursement of public funds; the lack of current government financial statements; and unnecessary delay in payment of obligations and final settlement of accounts—Brookings made several recommendations:

- Change GAO's name to "Office of Audit and Settlement"; its primary function would be "to review the financial acts of administrative officers for legality, accuracy, and regularity as the basis of final audit and settlement of their accounts." Also, require the Office to give Congress an annual report on the audit and a detailed government financial statement.

- Change the comptroller general's title to "auditor general".

- Establish a three-member Board of Audit and Settlement with staggered terms of 12 years "if it is desired to safeguard against the possible arbitrary decisions of a single individual."

- Establish an interagency committee to concur jointly on matters affecting the functions of BOB and the Office of Audit and Settlement "to give formal recognition to the community of interests which exist" between the two organizations and to avert friction between them.

- Establish a field preauditing service in the Office of Audit and Settlement to cut delays in certifying vouchers to disbursing officers for payment, prevent cumulative suspensions and disallowances, and expedite payment and settlement of claims and accounts.

- Consider establishing an interagency committee involving BOB, the Treasury Department, and the Office of Audit and Settlement to consider cooperative projects and ensure the "proper integration of activity and authority" among the three agencies.

---

[27]Ibid., 167-69.

- Require the Office of Audit and Settlement and the Treasury Department to agree on replacement of the existing Treasury system of accounting by a simplified system enabling the Treasurer of the United States to produce a statement of the current balance of unexpended appropriated funds "in interests of economy and efficiency."[28]

The Brookings report's recommendations on GAO did not represent a wholesale departure from the system devised in the Budget and Accounting Act, but rather were designed to fix a somewhat flawed system. Unlike the Brownlow group, Brookings was not hostile to GAO and recognized that problems related to the Office's operations were problems of a financial system that included the Treasury Department and BOB as well as GAO. Brookings thought that cooperative interagency committees involving GAO, Treasury, and BOB would help resolve some problems of the financial system.

During 1937 and 1938, several bills on reorganization came up in the House and the Senate. Some reflected the harsh position of the Brownlow Committee, resulting in radical proposals to change GAO and transfer many of its important functions to the executive branch. Others followed the more- moderate recommendations of the Brookings Institution. Among those who introduced bills were Senators Byrd, Joseph T. Robinson (D—Arkansas), and James F. Byrnes (D—South Carolina) and Representatives Lindsay C. Warren (D—North Carolina) and Frederick M. Vinson (D—Kentucky).

A bill introduced by Senator Robinson in 1937, S. 2700, proposed to transfer to BOB all GAO's functions as delineated in the Budget and Accounting Act, 1921, except those in Section 312(b) giving the comptroller general the power to "make such investigations and reports as shall be ordered by either House of Congress or by any committee of either House having jurisdiction over revenue, appropriations, or expenditures" and to assign GAO staff on request to furnish aid and information to congressional committees. The bill vested the 312(b) function in an auditor general at the head of a General Auditing Office, which would have the additional duty of auditing public accounts after payment but before settlement by the Bureau of the Budget.

In response to the bill, Acting Comptroller General Richard N. Elliott wrote to Robinson that he thought that transferring most of GAO's functions to BOB would not provide a more economical, efficient, or expeditious pro-

---

[28]Ibid., 167-74. See also *Financial Management*, 1961, 18-19; and Mosher, *GAO*, 89-90.

cess for handling claims or for adjusting and settling accounts than already existed. Elliott added: "The question as to whether the interests of the Government in other respects can best be served by having such functions performed in an independent agency answerable to the Congress or in a Bureau of the Treasury Department . . . involves a matter of policy on which I express no opinion."[29]

In testimony in August 1937, Elliott expressed general approval of the way GAO had been operating since 1921, but then added: "I do not mean by that this is probably all that it should be, nor that the General Accounting Office has been able to function in all the years in such a manner that it suited everybody. . . . So far as I have been able to see, it has functioned just about the way it was intended to function, and, so far as I am concerned, I want to be put down squarely behind the General Accounting Office, continuing it under the existing law as it is."[30]

S. 2700 did not pass, but Senator Byrnes introduced a later version, S. 3331, in January 1938. Title I of Byrnes's bill provided procedures for the president to issue executive orders reorganizing the executive branch but excluded reorganization action in regard to the General Auditing Office, proposed in the bill to replace GAO. The auditor general, to be appointed by a new Joint Committee on Public Accounts, would audit the receipts and the expenditures of the government and report to Congress on March 1 on the audit for the preceding year. As in the earlier bill, the auditor general would conduct investigations and issue reports as requested by either house of Congress or by the Joint Committee on Public Accounts. The proposed legislation limited the new office's powers to those specified therein, "and nothing contained in this title shall be construed to authorize the General Auditing Office to revise the settlements of public accounts made by the Bureau of the Budget, or to direct the manner in which the functions vested in the Bureau of the Budget by this title shall be exercised."[31]

S. 3331, the Reorganization Act of 1938, passed the Senate. When it reached the House, that body's Select Committee on Government Organization struck out the text of the Senate bill and substituted a new text. The House bill retained GAO and the comptroller general but dropped the existing provision for a 15-year term and provided for appointment of the comptroller general by the president. GAO was to retain the function of settling and adjusting accounts and

---

[29]Letter, Robinson to acting comptroller general, June 24, 1937, A-87280; letter, Elliott to Robinson, June 30, 1937, ibid. Elliott's letter appears also in *Reorganization of the Government Agencies*, Hearings before the Senate Select Committee on Government Organizations on S. 2700 . . . . , 75th Cong., 1st Sess. (Washington: GPO, 1937), 281-84.

[30]Elliott testimony, August 11, 1937, *Reorganization of the Government Agencies*, 285.

[31]S. 3331, "An Act to provide for reorganizing agencies of the Government, extending the classified civil service, establishing a General Auditing Office and a Department of Welfare, and for other purposes," 75th Cong., 3d Sess.

claims but was denied the power to revise actions of other government officers under powers vested in them by law to make findings of fact or decisions in their own agencies. The attorney general would be authorized to render opinions on the jurisdiction and the authority of GAO regarding settlement of accounts or claims; his opinion would be final and conclusive. The bill transferred from GAO to the secretary of the Treasury the prescription and the supervision of accounting forms and systems.

The most striking innovation in the House bill was creation *within GAO* of the Office of the Auditor General, to be headed by the auditor general of the United States, appointed by the president for a 15-year term, removable by joint resolution of Congress. The auditor general was to audit all expenditures after payment but before settlement and adjustment by GAO of accountable officers' accounts. The findings of the auditor general were to be final and conclusive upon GAO in settling and adjusting accounts except in cases of review by GAO or conflict with an advance decision of the comptroller general. When the auditor general disagreed with a settlement and adjustment action or an advance decision of the comptroller general, he was to report his disagreement to Congress, but he was denied the right to revise settlements and adjustments and advance decisions of the comptroller general. Finally, the auditor general would have the power to conduct investigations and issue reports requested by Congress. The effect of the proposal was to transfer GAO's Audit Division, including its staff, to the new Office of the Auditor General.[32]

The House Select Committee said that its purpose in this bill was "to segregate the functions of settlement and adjustment under one officer and the functions of reviewing and criticizing such settlements and adjustments and reporting them to Congress in another officer and thus provide the Congress with an independent audit." The committee argued that in passing the Budget and Accounting Act, Congress thought that it was establishing a system where the comptroller general would report to it illegal or improper expenditures. "It is well known that this has not resulted," the committee held, because the law vested the comptroller general with executive control functions, placing him "in the anomalous position of being required to settle and adjust accounts and claims and then to report to the Congress his criticisms of his own settlements and adjustments."[33] This rather complicated version of S. 3331 did not pass and eventually the proposed legislation died.

---

[32]House Select Committee on Government Organization, *Government Organization*, H. Rept. 2033, March 30, 1938, 75th Cong., 3d Sess. (Washington: GPO, 1938), 1-6.
[33]Ibid., 19-20.

One issue raised during congressional consideration of reorganization legislation was the constitutionality of GAO. A 1938 House Select Committee on Government Organization committee print considered this issue in detail. The unidentified author argued that the provision in the Budget and Accounting Act that gave Congress the right to remove the comptroller general was unconstitutional because it was "an infringement of the President's executive power of removal."[34]

Two decisions of the Supreme Court were part of the evidence presented in the print. The first was *Myers v. United States*, 272 U.S. 52 (1926), involving Frank S. Myers, a postmaster appointed by President Woodrow Wilson in 1917 under an 1876 law providing four-year terms for postmasters unless removed earlier by the president with the consent of the Senate. When Wilson removed him without involving the Senate, Myers sued in the Court of Claims. After the decision went against him there, he appealed to the Supreme Court. In a majority opinion discussing the president's removal power, Chief Justice William Howard Taft affirmed the removal of Myers. Taft relied heavily on a debate in the First Congress (1789) resulting in a decision to make the secretary of state removable without Senate consent. Taft concluded that the president's removal power, even extending to executive officers below cabinet level, was an inherent component of executive prerogative. The implication was that officials like members of independent federal commissions and the comptroller general, where conditions of removal had been set by Congress, could be removed independently by the president.[35] If the *Myers* decision had been applied in practical terms to GAO, presumably the provision in the Budget and Accounting Act, 1921, specifying the process for removal of the comptroller general, providing for removal only for cause based upon a joint resolution of Congress, would have been held unconstitutional.

The second case was *Humphrey's Executor v. United States*, 295 U.S. 602 (1935), involving the 1933 removal of Humphrey, a member of the Federal Trade Commission, by President Franklin D. Roosevelt. Although Humphrey soon died, his executor sued in the Court of Claims to recover his salary from the time of his removal until his death four months later, based on the argument that his removal was illegal. The court's decision was that Humphrey's

---

[34]*Constitutionality of the General Accounting Office*, a monograph submitted to the House Select Committee on Government Organization, 75th Cong., 3d Sess., Revised Committee Print (Washington: GPO, 1938), 1.

[35]*Constitutionality of the General Accounting Office*, 2-3; and Alfred H. Kelly and Winfred A. Harbison, *The American Constitution: Its Origins and Development* (New York: W. W. Norton and Company, 1963), 714-17.

removal was a violation of law because Congress in establishing the Federal Trade Commission (1914) intended it to be independent of the president. The court did not apply the *Myers* decision, arguing that it applied to subordinate executive officers in agencies responsible to the president and not to officials of agencies like the Federal Trade Commission.[36]

The author of the committee print argued that the Humphrey decision did not apply to GAO because it applied only to agencies "wholly disconnected from the executive branch of the Government." GAO, however, had executive functions "to make certain that the provisions of appropriation acts or of general laws governing the expenditure or deposit of public funds are properly executed. In accomplishing this purpose the General Accounting Office not only participates directly in the execution of those laws, but also takes care that they are faithfully executed."[37]

Ultimately, these constitutional arguments and others used in support of the various reorganization bills did not persuade a majority of both houses of Congress to pass such legislation in 1937 and 1938. In fact, the failure of reorganization plans to pass Congress in 1938 was a serious defeat for President Roosevelt. Coming in the immediate aftermath of his failed effort in 1937 to persuade Congress to increase the size of the Supreme Court, which had invalidated some key New Deal laws, his reorganization plans raised opposition in Congress right from the beginning.[38] Opponents of the plan, both in and out of Congress, saw it as a "dictator bill" just as they had seen the court reform proposals in 1937. Even Roosevelt's willingness in the spring of 1938 to make concessions to satisfy congressional objections to aspects of the reorganization plan failed to get it through the House of Representatives.[39]

Congress did pass a reorganization bill that the president signed on April 3, 1939. The law gave the president certain powers, extending to January 1941, to reorganize the executive branch through executive orders. Representative Lindsay C. Warren of North Carolina, later the comptroller general of the United States, was the author of the House bill that became the Reorganization Act of 1939. The law specifically excluded GAO and a number of other agencies from the reorganization authority of the president.[40] Warren

---

[36]*Constitutionality of the General Accounting Office*, 3-4; and Kelly and Harbison, *The American Constitution*, 743.

[37]*Constitutionality of the General Accounting Office*, 4-5, 13-14.

[38]For a detailed account of the so-called court-packing plan, see James MacGregor Burns, *Roosevelt: The Lion and the Fox* (New York: Harcourt, Brace & World, Inc., 1956), 293-315.

[39]Ibid., 344-46.

[40]53 Stat. 36, approved April 3, 1939.

explained his role in a letter written a few years later from his office at GAO: "You may also recall that I personally wrote the Reorganization Bill which later became a law and before it was introduced, I told the President and members of the House that I would have nothing whatever to do with it if any attempt was made to impair the General Accounting Office. The Bill became a law, mainly because of this. I never dreamed at the time that I would ever be down here."[41]

Conclusion

Although there were repeated efforts to alter or abolish GAO between 1921 and 1940, there were no changes to the Budget and Accounting Act, 1921, during that period. The very fact, however, that Republican Presidents Harding and Hoover and Democratic President Roosevelt favored changing GAO's role testified to the fact that some of the Office's actions were controversial. Questions about GAO's constitutionality, and particularly about breaching of the principle of separation of powers, arose during these years. Whenever reorganization proposals affecting GAO came up, as they did in 1923, 1932, and in the late 1930s, there were substantial disagreements in Congress about the proper roles of the legislative and executive branches in the operation of the nation's financial management system. Politics played a part also—Harding died in 1923 and his successor did not favor his reorganization plan; Hoover lost an election in 1932 and his plan died in the lame-duck period; and Roosevelt's various political problems in 1937 and 1938, including his Supreme Court reform scheme, helped defeat his reorganization efforts.

GAO escaped these attacks unscathed in formal organization and legislative mandate. Probably Congress, in ultimately deciding not to allow changes in GAO's status, became more protective of the Office and identified it more closely as a legislative agency. But GAO's reputation, already bad in some circles of the government because of the Office's stubborn insistence that its rules and procedures be followed to the letter, suffered further. The problems associated with GAO and identified particularly by its detractors in the 1920s and the 1930s, many of them real, remained to be solved. Clearly the nation's financial management system had serious problems. Its major components—GAO, BOB, and the Treasury Department—generally did not work together and occasionally, especially in the case of GAO and Treasury, had open squabbles. GAO's top leaders of the period—McCarl, Acting Comptroller General Elliott, and Brown—did little or nothing to work toward a solution of these serious issues.

---

[41]Letter, Warren to Rep. Charles A. Plumley, December 19, 1943, Papers of Lindsay C. Warren, Southern Historical Collection, Wilson Library, University of North Carolina at Chapel Hill, Folder 389.

The coming of Lindsay C. Warren to the office of comptroller general in 1940 marked a turning point in GAO's history. As a prominent Democratic leader in the House of Representatives, he was well-equipped to work with Congress to achieve change. He had been a strong supporter of President Roosevelt and the New Deal. Thus he had influence in the White House. He was not committed irrevocably to the patterns of operation and procedures GAO had used in the past.

Warren first had to cope with the tremendously increased workload heaped on GAO as a result of World War II. That occupied most of his time and attention for the first five years of his term. After 1945, he was free to turn to other things—including many of the issues that had been raised between 1921 and 1940 on GAO's roles and missions. Unlike his predecessors, Warren was willing to confront and resolve these issues.

CHAPTER 11

The Test of War, 1941-1945

By the time Lindsay C. Warren became comptroller general of the United States on November 1, 1940, the General Accounting Office (GAO) had already begun to feel the impact of World War II, which began in September 1939. President Franklin D. Roosevelt, facing isolationist sentiment in the United States, cautiously led the country on a course favoring the European Allies, especially Great Britain. His program included revising existing neutrality laws to allow the United States to sell munitions and raw materials abroad on a cash-and-carry basis. In September 1940, Roosevelt agreed to a deal with England; in return for long-term leases on British naval and air bases in the Western Hemisphere, he transferred 50 World War I-vintage destroyers to Britain.

Also in September 1940, with Warren providing leadership as a member of the House of Representatives, Congress approved a draft law to build up the U.S. armed forces. Just a few days after Warren moved to GAO, Roosevelt won election to his third term as president. By the end of the year, he had proposed the Lend-Lease program, to lend defense materials to countries whose security the president declared vital to the United States. Congress approved the Lend-Lease proposal in March 1941.[1] The United States formally entered the war late in 1941, after months of deteriorating relations between the United States and Japan, culminating with Japan's sudden attack at Pearl Harbor on December 7.[2]

Impact of the War on GAO

As the U.S. national defense effort gradually took form in the late 1930s and 1940, GAO began to feel its impact on the Office's staff and budget. Government efforts to modernize and expand the armed forces, the emer-

---

[1] For a survey of this period, culminating with passage of the Lend-Lease Act, see James MacGregor Burns, *Roosevelt: The Soldier of Freedom* (New York: Harcourt Brace Jovanovich, Inc., 1970), 3-49.

[2] An account of the developing crisis with Japan in 1941 appears in ibid., 78-83, 132-67.

gence of a defense industry to produce military weapons and equipment, and eventually programs such as Lend-Lease necessitated a large extension of GAO's audit efforts. GAO's budget skyrocketed during the war, increasing from $10,906,540 for fiscal year 1941 to more than $38 million for fiscal year 1945, the last full year of the war. The number of staff increased rapidly from 5,195 on June 30, 1940, to a peak of 14,904 in April 1946.[3]

In 1941, Warren noted that the government's national defense program, along with legislative changes in procurement practices and procedures and large increases in appropriations and spending, had already affected the volume and the complexity of GAO's work. He reported that the defense effort had increased account audits and made it necessary for GAO to help train accounting staff in federal agencies for procurement and administrative accounting work in the field. GAO began sending staff out to assist both contracting officers and contractors. Warren stated that GAO would require proper accounting for government expenditures while assisting the defense effort in every way possible.[4]

"The war has affected directly or indirectly practically every branch of the work performed by the General Accounting Office," Warren reported in 1942. "Decisions with respect to war expenditures; the prompt and careful audit of such expenditures; the approval or prescribing of forms, systems and procedures for the use of war agencies; the settlement of claims of war contractors and from members of the armed forces or their families; the audit of war bond and stamp accounts" were duties that "called for the exercise of strenuous and unusual efforts."[5]

Warren observed in his 1944 report that "no such report submitted since the establishment of the office has covered a period of heavier demands upon its capacities, or of greater accomplishments by its personnel under adverse working conditions." He noted that war programs spending increased from $72 billion in fiscal year 1943 to $87 billion in fiscal year 1944. During the same period, the number of vouchers GAO received for audit rose from 26 million to 61 million. As the government's spending broadened, so did GAO's workload.[6]

[3]See chapter 6 for a detailed discussion of GAO's budget and staffing levels during World War II.

[4]*Annual Report of the Comptroller General of the United States for the Fiscal Year Ended June 30, 1941* (Washington: GPO, 1942), 89-92.

[5]*Annual Report of the Comptroller General of the United States for the Fiscal Year Ended June 30, 1942* (Washington: GAO typescript, 1942), 103.

[6]*Annual Report of the Comptroller General for the Fiscal Year Ended June 30, 1944* (Washington: GPO, 1944), ii, 70.

Warren worried about waste and fraud during the war and was determined that GAO would remain vigilant in guarding against such abuses. He made this clear in a letter to President Roosevelt in May 1942: "We are making every effort . . . to see that no illegal contract or payment escapes detection here . . . . I have proceeded on the conviction that the audit of war contract expenditures must be completed and the results shown as promptly as possible after the expenditures are made if the results are to be fully beneficial. The timely detection of improper expenditures will serve to prevent the repetition of the mistakes, sometimes costly ones."[7]

Warren made his position on wartime audits clear in a letter to his general counsel shortly after the United States became involved in the war. He wanted to be sure that GAO did not delay the war effort by technical objections or unreasonable requirements but was "unwilling to see the doors opened wide and proper accounting and auditing broken down. . . . It is of course too much to hope that vast sums can be expended without fraud or scandal. Already certain phases of the Defense Program is [sic] beginning to 'smell to high heaven.' When the inevitable aftermath comes, I do not wish it said that the General Accounting Office contributed in any way in relaxing on such an audit as we are required and expected to make."[8] To an old friend Warren wrote that he had taken "frank and bold positions" in regard to government spending even though he suffered pressure and unpopularity. "Duplication, waste and extravagance is [sic] rampant. There has been some fraud and some dishonesty but there remains to be seen how far that may go."[9]

GAO's World War II work was for the most part a substantial expansion of what the Office routinely did before 1940—voucher audits, processing claims, review of contracts, settlement of accounts, prescription of forms and accounting systems, issuance of opinions and decisions, and investigations. The auditing of war contracts and of disbursements of the War and Navy departments were the most pressing parts of the wartime effort. There was no time during the war to change approaches to work or to undertake new efforts unrelated to the war effort. Fiscal year 1944 work statistics testify to the massive volume of effort required of GAO. During 1944, GAO received the accounts of 44,000 fiscal officers, 62 million vouchers, and 3-1/2 million contracts; processed 72,000 warrants and requisitions; and au-

---

[7]Letter, Warren to Roosevelt, May 19, 1942, Papers of Franklin D. Roosevelt, Roosevelt Presidential Library, Hyde Park, NY, GF 500, Box #1, Folder: Comptroller General, 1941-1945 (hereafter ctied as Roosevelt Papers).

[8]Letter, Warren to General Counsel, January 19, 1942, The Papers of Lindsay C. Warren, Southern Historical Collection, Wilson Library, University of North Carolina at Chapel Hill, Folder 387 (hereafter cited as Warren Papers).

[9]Letter, Warren to Judge John J. McDuffie, April 20, 1943, ibid., Folder 391.

dited and reconciled nearly 300 million government checks issued during the year. The Office also received 294,000 claims, 136,000 of which were military and naval; rendered 7,000 decisions; and collected nearly $40 million in government receipts.[10] GAO could not keep current with its work during the war years, necessitating catch-up operations that extended on some tasks for several years after the war's end. For example, GAO reported that it had on hand 35 million unaudited vouchers at the end of fiscal year 1945.[11]

Organization for Wartime Auditing

One feature of GAO's wartime work was a vast expansion of site audits. During the 1930s, GAO had begun some field audit operations, especially in the agricultural sector. In January 1942, GAO established a Field Auditing Unit within the Audit Division to perform audits at field offices or other installations of government agencies and at contractor facilities.[12] GAO found field audits especially necessary because of the widespread use during the war of cost-plus-a-fixed-fee contracts with defense industries. Warren explained that Congress approved use of this type of contract "to avoid . . . the high cost of lump sum contracts entered into under uncertainty as to actual cost of performance, and . . . the dangers inherent in the cost-plus-a-percentage-of-cost system of contracting." Warren added that while cost-plus-a-fixed-fee contracts cut down the extravagance and abuse accompanying other types, they were "not a perfect or wholly provident contractual arrangement for the Government and . . . careful supervision of such contracts is essential to protect the Government."[13]

In August 1942, Warren established the War Contract Project Audit Section in the Audit Division to handle field audits of cost-plus-a-fixed-fee contracts. The order established five project zones—Western, North Central, South Central, Southeast, and Northeast—and a sixth zone, Great Lakes, was added in 1944.[14] As part of the War Contract Project Audit Section, many GAO staff audited cost-plus contracts at locations all over the United

---

[10]Warren testimony, January 18, 1945, *Independent Offices Appropriation Bill for 1946*, Hearings before the Subcommittee on Independent Offices, House Committee on Appropriations, 79th Cong., 1st Sess. (Washington: GPO, 1945), 1118-19.

[11]*Annual Report of the Comptroller General of the United States for the Fiscal Year Ended June 30, 1945* (Washington: GPO, n.d.), 54.

[12]Office Order No. 13, January 20, 1942, 245 MS 1529A.

[13]GAO *Annual Report, 1942*, 106. For an extended discussion of GAO audits of war contracts and war contract termination activities, see pp. 255-64. Also see Ellsworth H. Morse, Jr., "Site Audits of War Contracts in World War II," *GAO Review* (fall 1977): 49-51.

[14]Office Order No. 29, August 18, 1942, and Office Order No. 29, Supplement No. 11, February 19, 1944, Comptroller General's Orders, vol. I, GAO Records.

States. In mid-1945, just before the end of the war, GAO audited war expenditures in 276 localities, and as late as mid-1947, such audits continued at almost 200 places. During fiscal year 1943, GAO examined 1,098,211 cost-plus contracts, and GAO examined 917,384 the following year.[15]

During the war, GAO established several special field offices to audit Army and Navy expenditures. Responding to a request from Secretary of War Henry L. Stimson, Warren issued an order in July 1943 establishing Army Audit Branches in Chicago, Atlanta, Los Angeles, and New York. These offices, all operating by October 1, 1943, were to exist for the war's duration and up to one year thereafter. Each branch included subdivisions of three headquarters organizations—the Audit, Reconciliation and Clearance, and Personnel divisions.[16]

Shortly after GAO set up the Army Audit Branches, Secretary of the Navy Frank Knox suggested establishment of a Navy Audit Branch in Cleveland, Ohio, where GAO at the time audited Navy pay and current accounts. Warren issued an order creating the Navy Audit Branch in June 1944, organized like the Army branches.[17] GAO anticipated that the new branches would enable it to keep the war audit current in the field and Washington staff to bring the audits done there to reasonably current status. Another anticipated advantage of decentralizing the service audits was the availability of more-qualified personnel in the field than in Washington. These anticipated benefits generally proved to be true.[18]

Shortly after the war ended, GAO established an Army Audit Branch in St. Louis in conjunction with the War Department's placing of a Regional Accounting Office there at the same time.[19] A year later, Warren abolished the Army Audit Branches in Chicago, New York, Atlanta, and Los Angeles, thus consolidating all of GAO's Army audit activity in St. Louis.[20] The de-

---

[15]*Annual Report of the Comptroller General of the United States for the Fiscal Year Ended June 30, 1943* (Washington: GPO, n.d.), 72-73; GAO, *Annual Report, 1944*, 72-73; GAO, *Annual Report, 1945*, 21; and *Annual Report of the Comptroller General of the United States for the Fiscal Year Ended June 30, 1947* (Washington: GPO, n.d.), 18. The War Contract Project Audit Section existed until May 1949, when the Cost Reimbursement Section replaced it. See Office Order No. 82, May 23, 1949, 333 MS 2178.

[16]Office Order No. 41, July 24, 1943, 263 MS 1542A.

[17]Letter, Acting Comptroller General Frank L. Yates to Knox, September 18, 1943, 265 MS 935; and Office Order No. 53, June 3, 1944, 274 MS 279-A.

[18]Letter, Warren to Harold Smith, director of the Bureau of the Budget, October 23, 1944, 278 MS 1568; and testimony of Dudley W. Bagley, assistant to the comptroller general, December 14, 1943, *Independent Offices Appropriation Bill for 1945*, Hearings before the Subcommittee on Independent Offices, House Committee on Appropriations, 78th Cong., 2d Sess. (Washington: GPO, 1944), 800-801.

[19]Office Order No. 69, November 21, 1945, 291 MS 1417a.

[20]Office Order No. 41—Revised, October 29, 1946, 302 MS 1832e.

centralized Army and Navy Audit Branches contributed significantly to GAO's ability to keep almost current on Army and Navy audits during the latter part of the war. They also provided GAO with useful experience in field auditing and organization. Although centralization of operations in Washington was the tradition in GAO, the successful World War II experience with site audits demonstrated some of the advantages of decentralization and planted the seeds for creating a formal regional office system in 1952.[21]

GAO gained additional experience with decentralization as a result of the transfer of the entire Postal Accounts Division, with about 800 staff, to Asheville, North Carolina, in 1943. The move was made because of extremely crowded wartime conditions in Washington and the critical shortage of office space. The Audit Division moved into the offices the Postal Accounts Division had occupied in the Old Post Office Building on Pennsylvania Avenue in Washington, helping to ease GAO's own space problems. While the plan was to return the division to Washington as soon as space became available after the war, the organization remained in Asheville until 1950. In that year, the Post Office Department Financial Control Act transferred responsibility to the Post Office Department for its own administrative accounting, which GAO had been doing for the Post Office since being assigned the responsibility by the Budget and Accounting Act, 1921. The Postal Accounts Division, with 779 staff, transferred to the Post Office Department on November 15, 1950.[22]

Audits of Cost-Plus-a-Fixed-Fee Contracts

By the time the United States entered World War II in December 1941, the impact on GAO of the government's use of cost-plus-a-fixed-fee contracts was already heavy and was to get much heavier in the subsequent war years. Warren calculated that total U.S. war expenditures during fiscal year 1942 were over $26 billion, all of which had to be audited. During that year, the audit of cost-plus contracts "assumed major proportions" for GAO.[23] The next year Warren reported more problems with cost-plus contracts, leading to the suggestion that contractors were overcharging costs to the government. "I have endeavored to make it crystal clear," he wrote, "that the authority of the General Accounting Office to disallow credit in the accounts of

---

[21]See chapter 14, pp. 360-62.

[22]GAO Statement on Postal Accounts Division Move to Asheville, NC, November 4, 1942, Warren Papers, Folder 389; Office Order No. 92, October 13, 1950, 350 MS 852; Office Order No. 92—Revised, "Establishing the Postal Audit Division and Abolishing the Postal Accounts Division," November 1, 1950, 351 MS 1; and testimony of Yates et al., March 13, 1951, *Independent Offices Appropriations for 1952*, Hearings before a Subcommittee of the House Committee on Appropriations, 82d Cong., 1st Sess., pt. 1 (Washington: GPO, 1951), 1478, 1484.

[23]GAO, *Annual Report, 1942*, 109.

disbursing officers does not extend to payments under cost-plus-a-fixed-fee contracts solely on the ground of waste or extravagance, if within the provisions of legally executed contracts and approved by the contracting officers. These officers have been given almost plenary powers under the terms of the contracts." GAO had power to question expenditures in an audit only when they exceeded the amount authorized in a contract or violated the law.[24]

In a March 1944 letter to Sen. James E. Murray (D—Montana), chairman of the War Contracts Subcommittee of the Senate Committee on Military Affairs, Warren explained his views on cost-plus-a-fixed-fee contracts. He said that he understood that Congress had sanctioned this contracting method in the hope of avoiding the high costs of lump sum contracts signed without accurate knowledge of actual costs and the similar risks of cost-plus-a-percentage-of-cost contracts. Cost-plus-a-fixed-fee contracts required the government to assume a certain risk when agreeing to pay actual costs plus a fixed amount, while in theory giving the contractor an incentive for prompt and efficient performance. Warren thought that cost-plus contracts in practice led to waste of public funds because the contractors were overstating the reimbursable costs. He also observed that the system tempted contractors to increase their profits by illegally arranging with suppliers to share the profits from materials bought for use under the contract.

Warren also questioned the broad authority of contracting officers to determine reimbursable costs under the cost-plus contracts, leading to opportunities for collusion and favoritism at government expense. GAO checked each contract to determine that it had been legally entered into and examined each voucher and supporting piece of evidence to verify that payments had been made in accordance with contract provisions and applicable law.[25]

Termination and Settlement of War Contracts

While Warren believed that there was opportunity for fraud related to the cost-plus and other war contracts, GAO did not become aware of the extent of the problem until the latter stages of the war. As Congress in 1943 began to discuss legislation to regulate war contract termination, Warren raised alarms about the roles of government contracting agencies and what GAO's audit powers in contract termination should be. In an internal memorandum in September 1943, Warren described war contract termination as "a mammoth proposition" involving "untold billions." He did not object "to a WPA for war contractors, if the Congress wishes to establish same," but he did not

---

[24]GAO, *Annual Report, 1943*, 68-69.
[25]Letter, Warren to Murray, March 3, 1944, 271 MS 156.

think that it should be done by agreement between executive agencies and the contractors, bypassing GAO in the process. He specifically referred to the War Department and the War Production Board as exercising power through orders and directives in the matter of war contract termination. "We should point out . . . just what they have done and concisely state that it has been done and is being done to circumvent the Congress, and to completely by-pass the General Accounting Office."[26]

Both Warren and War Department representatives explained their views on the war contract termination process and proposed legislation on the matter in hearings of the House Committee on Military Affairs in October 1943. A few weeks earlier, Warren communicated his views to the committee chairman, Rep. Andrew J. May (D—Kentucky). He objected to language in a draft bill that would have granted wide powers to the secretary of war in the termination of War Department contracts, including the right to pay advance or partial payments and make loans to contractors, subcontractors, and suppliers in amounts certified by the contractors as due them for contract termination. Warren thought that any legislation on contract termination must include provisions to protect the interests of the United States. He complained about a "growing tendency" on the part of executive agencies to vest in contracting officers final authority to adjust and settle claims against the United States "in derogation" of GAO's authority and jurisdiction granted by the Budget and Accounting Act, 1921. The intent of the War Department's Procurement Regulation No. 15, Warren contended, was "to make the determination of the contracting officer, as to the amount to be paid the contractor, final and conclusive on the Government, and to provide that such determination is not to be reviewed by the disbursing officer or by the General Accounting Office." Warren added that in regard to cost-plus contracts, contracting officers or their representatives "have certified or approved for payment thousands of items which in no way could be said to be reasonably incident to, or necessary for, the performance of the contract." Legislation on contract termination should ensure a proper audit and review of settlement claims by GAO, Warren argued.[27]

Under Secretary of War Robert P. Patterson was the principal War Department witness in the hearings. He argued against a significant role for GAO in contract termination and maintained that the War Department and other contracting agencies should have the unimpeded right to enter into both contracts and contract termination agreements. He asserted that "the

[26]Memorandum, Warren to general counsel, September 8, 1943, Warren Papers, Scrapbooks, vol. 9.

[27]Letter, Warren to May, September 20, 1943, reprinted in *Authorizing the Secretary of War to Use Funds for Adjustment of Contracts*, Hearings before the House Committee on Military Affairs, 78th Cong., 1st Sess. (Washington: GPO, 1943), pt. 2, 184-89 (hereafter cited as *Adjustment of Contracts*).

speed in finally determining the amount due will materially affect the ability of the contractor to undertake production of other munitions during the war or of peacetime products afterward." Patterson outlined what he considered reasonable principles for prompt settlement: negotiated termination agreements must be final and not subject to reopening "by any independent agency" except in the case of fraud, and the procuring agency would undertake the negotiations.[28]

The War Department's authority to enter into contract termination agreements, Patterson pointed out, was contained in Title II of the First War Powers Act (1941) and Executive Order No. 9001 (1941), issued under this act. The War Powers Act allowed the president to authorize any agency exercising functions related to the war effort "to enter into contracts and into amendments or modifications of contracts . . . and to make advance, progress and other payments thereon, without regard to the provisions of law relating to the making, performance, amendment, or modification of contracts whenever he deems such action would facilitate the prosecution of the war." Executive Order 9001 authorized the War and Navy departments and the U.S. Maritime Commission to "modify or amend or settle claims under contracts heretofore or hereafter made" and to "make advance, progress and other payments upon such contracts . . . whenever, in the judgment of the War Department, the Navy Department, or the United States Maritime Commission respectively the prosecution of the war is thereby facilitated."

Patterson also relied on an opinion of the attorney general, dated August 29, 1942, stating that the language of the First War Powers Act respecting amendments or modifications on contracts "would be largely meaningless if it did not include the power to settle claims and release obligations in favor of or against the United States arising either in connection with the original contract or as a result of a modification or amendment thereof."[29]

Warren rebutted Patterson's testimony and explained GAO's position before the House Military Affairs Committee. He agreed that contract termination was a major economic problem and did not object to advance or partial payments to contractors up to 75 percent of the amount claimed. "If we could then stop . . . and have a speedy but proper audit made to determine what constituted the partial payment and what, if any, is finally due the contractor and settlement be made by the General Accounting Office accordingly . . . ," there would be no problem. "But . . . what is proposed," Warren argued, "and is now actually being done is an arrogant snapping of

---

[28]Patterson testimony, October 15, 1943, *Adjustment of Contracts*, 147-48.
[29]Ibid., 152, 158-59.

fingers in the face of the Congress. . . ." Warren complained about recent War Department regulations implementing the department's plans for contract termination. He warned that the regulations "will permit a grand cover-up" and preclude any opportunity to discover fraud. He also complained about inefficient and incompetent contracting officers who "constantly fraternize with the contractor after working hours—golfing, dining, and wining with them."[30]

Warren summarized 270 cases picked at random from GAO files involving illegal payments to contractors to illustrate the problem with contracting officers. He ended with strong criticism of the War Department: "Its attitude is, to hell with the General Accounting Office or anyone else who dares to challenge an inept and inefficient contracting officer who is dishing out and giving away the property and the money of the United States with reckless abandon. And these are the contracting officers who the War Department insists must have the final and conclusive authority to negotiate contract termination settlements."[31]

Warren admitted that the War Department had authority under the War Powers Act to terminate contracts and make final settlements. But he made clear that he thought that legislation was needed to keep GAO in the picture and not leave the whole process up to the War Department and contracting officers.[32] Under Secretary of War Patterson generally rejected what Warren had said and defended the reputations of his department's contracting officers. His central point was the need to avoid delay in settlements; such delay "will prevent contractors and subcontractors from making commitments for production of other weapons of war with the speed necessary to meet our war needs now or to protect our economy later. If we are to avoid post-war disaster, industry must be able to go forward at once and with certainty to provide civilian jobs for the millions released from the Army and from war work."[33]

In letters to friends after these hearings, Warren defended his criticism of War Department contracting officers. To one acquaintance he wrote that the government was being "robbed and milked" in the contracting process. "I have long since held the opinion," he wrote to another, "that the only ones who have made any sacrifice in this war are those in uniform. The disillu-

---

[30]Warren testimony, October 18, 1943, ibid., 189-90, 193.

[31]Ibid., 194-218; the source of the quote is 218.

[32]Ibid., 220.

[33]Patterson testimony, October 21, 1943, ibid., 251-64; the source of the quote is 262.

sionment that has come over me in my present position is almost complete."[34]
A few months later, as Congress approached the passage of contract termination legislation, Warren railed again against the "shocking waste and extravagance" of war contracts. While most contractors were honest, some were "ratters and chiselers." He also lamented the fact that the Democratic Party, in charge of the federal government, would eventually be accused of "shocking extravagance and scandals."[35] This letter to a Richmond newspaper editor and others to editors elsewhere demonstrated Warren's effort to get his views on the pending legislation to the press while cautioning his correspondents not to cite him as their source of information.[36]

GAO's Work under the Contract Settlement Act of 1944

Despite Warren's strong opposition, Congress passed the Contract Settlement Act of 1944 and the president approved it on July 1, 1944. Warren described this law as "one of the most outstanding examples of legislation ever enacted by Congress in the extent to which it confers administrative authority and freedom from control in the expenditure of public funds."[37] Rather than providing for a GAO audit of proposed contract termination settlements before the government made final payment, the law authorized only a limited audit after payment to determine whether the payment was consistent with the settlement and whether the supporting records warranted a reasonable belief that fraud was involved in the settlement.[38]

In October 1944, Warren issued an order prescribing GAO's functions under the Contract Settlement Act. After the contracting agency and the contractor reached a final settlement agreement and payment was made, GAO's Audit Division would examine settlement records to "determine whether the settlement payments to the war contractor were made in accordance with the settlement." The Audit Division also had power to undertake an investigation as authorized by section 16(c) of the law. If on the basis of this process the Audit Division suspected fraud in the settlement, it was to report the matter to the Committee on Termination Settlements. This committee, established by the law within GAO, with three members appointed by the comptroller general, was to consider the facts and advise the comptroller general on whether the case ought to be referred to the GAO Office of Inves-

---

[34]Letter, Warren to William deB. MacNider, Chapel Hill, NC, October 29, 1943, Warren Papers, folder 394; and letter, Warren to H. S. Ward, Washington, NC, November 5, 1943, ibid., folder 395.

[35]Letter, Warren to Virginius Dabney, ed., *Richmond Times Dispatch*, April 5, 1944, ibid., Folder 398.

[36]See, for example, letter, Warren to Josephus Daniels, the *Raleigh, NC, News & Observer*, May 18, 1944, ibid.

[37]GAO, *Annual Report, 1944*, 4.

[38]Ibid., 4-5; Contract Settlement Act of 1944, Public Law 395, 58 Stat. 649, approved July 1, 1944.

tigations for further action. If the comptroller general directed the Office of Investigations to look into the case, its report would go to the Committee on Termination Settlements, which would advise the comptroller general on whether the record suggested that the settlement was fraudulent. The final step if fraud was suspected was for the comptroller general to prepare reports and recommendations in accordance with section 16(c) for transmittal to the attorney general.

The initial members of the Committee on Termination Settlements were John C. McFarland, GAO general counsel; David Neumann, chief of the Claims Division; and J. C. Nevitt, chief of the Planning and Budget Section.[39]

The war contract termination process, regulated by the 1944 law, lasted until the early 1950s. Warren took every opportunity he could find during these years, in congressional testimony, interviews, and speeches, to criticize the law and emphasize the fraud involved in settlements. In January 1945, he told a House committee that during the preceding fiscal year, GAO examined 3-1/2 million contracts for legality. "[J]ust about all of them are legal. They are so completely wide open, that you can drive a team of horses through all of them, and that is all there is to it. Congress said they could do it." When GAO detected fraud, it reported the matter to the attorney general. "But I tell you now that under the Contract Settlement Act a termination could absolutely be saturated and reeking with fraud and the General Accounting Office would never be able to detect it," Warren testified.[40]

Warren reported annually between 1945 and 1950 to Congress on GAO's work under the Contract Settlement Act. His first report was surprisingly mild compared with his pronounced opposition to the law. He wrote, "To the extent that an examination of these records has been made, the reports received thereon have not warranted a reasonable belief that any settlement was induced by fraud." He noted that it was "highly improbable that fraud will be disclosed in other than a negligible percentage of such cases" because GAO could not examine records until after finalization of settlements.[41] In his second report, he said that "no instance has been found in which the settlement payments to the war contractor were not in accordance with the settlement agreement," but he added that in four settlements, evidence of

---

[39]Office Order No. 57, October 5, 1944, "Prescribing Functions of the General Accounting Office Under the Contract Settlement Act of 1944," B-51662, #1, also in 278 MS 173a; Administrative Order No. 38, October 6, 1944 (appointment of members of the Committee on Termination Settlements), 278 MS 261.

[40]Warren testimony, January 18, 1945, *Independent Offices Appropriation Bill for 1946*, 1136-37.

[41]Letter, Warren to Congress, August 27, 1945, 288 MS 2051.

fraud had been uncovered. He reiterated his conviction that the procedures imposed upon GAO by the Contract Settlement Act made it unlikely that fraud would be found in anything other than a "negligible percentage" of cases.[42]

Before GAO prepared the third report on contract settlement, Warren informed his general counsel that he wanted the document to be "all inclusive" and "in very plain understandable language." The two previous reports he considered to "have been deliberately construed and twisted as giving a complete endorsement by this Office of contract settlements." GAO should make clear in the next report the problems it had had because of existing law in detecting fraud, but nevertheless should point out that some suspected cases of fraud had been reported to the attorney general. Warren also wanted the report to say that GAO, "merely by accident," had learned that some War and Navy Department staff working on contract terminations had subsequently been employed by companies on whose contract termination cases they had worked. The report should also state that the appeals board established under the federal Office of Contract Settlement had allowed settlement claims earlier disallowed by GAO, especially large claims for attorney fees.[43]

During the period when GAO was preparing this report, Assistant Comptroller General Frank L. Yates, in a memorandum to Warren, criticized the draft he had reviewed. He objected that the report complained that Congress in the Contract Settlement Act of 1944, by failing to authorize GAO to audit termination settlements before payment, had interfered with an existing function. Yates pointed out that GAO never had such authority and had made this clear during hearings before passage of the contract termination bill in 1944. Rather, GAO had argued that contract termination agreements were a special case where GAO *should* be given independent audit authority before final settlement. Yates also observed: "This report may come to be regarded as one of the important Government papers—a valuable leaf from the Government's World War II book of experience—to which those assigned the duty of studying plans to avoid the errors of the past will seek access. As such it should be well organized, factual, forthright, informative, objective, show balance and restraint, and devoid of extravagant expression. If these are appropriate standards, the draft seems to fall short of meeting some of them."[44]

---

[42]Letter, Warren to Congress, July 26, 1946, 299 MS 1678.

[43]Memorandum, Warren to the General Counsel, March 27, 1947, B-51662, #2.

[44]Memorandum, FLY [Yates] to Comptroller General, June 2, 1947, B-51662, #2. How much influence Yates's comments had in determining the final wording of the report cannot be determined; the draft Yates reviewed has not been found.

In his third report on contract settlement, in July 1947, Warren reviewed GAO's arguments for an independent audit of proposed settlements before final approval. He observed that GAO's stated role in implementation of the Contract Settlement Act did not amount to much. Nevertheless, between 1944 and 1947 GAO identified 79 termination settlements, involving 107 contracts with 19 contractors, as fraudulent. Warren summarized these cases, including one where a contractor with six termination claims, by overstating or duplicating inventory costs, charging for materials never purchased and plant improvements never made, and claiming other unwarranted costs, had been overpaid $53,711.13. In the 79 cases, the contractors owed the government more than $2 million, although the Department of Justice had not concluded any of the cases. Warren added that there was evidence of 57 other settlements that had been induced by fraud, as well as many overliberal payments to contractors not induced by fraud. Warren concluded his report with the hope that the contract settlement program was drawing to a close. "It is with a feeling of unmixed relief that I contemplate the end of the profligate spending which has characterized its history, and the restoration of proper controls over the expenditure of appropriated funds."[45]

Actually Warren issued three more annual reports on the war contract settlement work. In his 1948 report, he said that by December 31, 1947, GAO had examined 6,701 settlements on 16,072 contracts amounting to $906,893,398.26. Warren stated that 145 of these settlements, involving improper payment of about $4 million, were fraudulent. There were reasonable grounds for believing that 185 additional settlements, involving payments of more than $800,000 to 27 contractors, stemmed from fraud. Warren summarized: One of every 20 settlements and fifty cents of every $100 in settlement payments may have been based on fraud. This, Warren argued, "can be taken only as overwhelming proof of the tremendous—and wholly unnecessary—losses occasioned the Government as a direct result of the failure to provide adequate safeguards in the settlement of terminated war contracts." He strongly recommended the repeal of the Contract Settlement Act of 1944 and urged that experience gained under the act be considered if a need developed in the future for contract termination legislation.[46]

Warren repeated his now familiar complaints in his fifth report in August 1949. He brought previously reported statistics up to date: As of May 31, 1949, GAO had examined 9,195 settlements involving 2,815 contractors, covering termination payments of $1,165,000,000 for 26,484 contracts, subcontracts, and purchase orders. Five percent of the settlements (472), involv-

---

[45]Letter, Warren to Congress, July 10, 1947, 311 MS 780.

[46]Letter, Warren to Congress, February 24, 1948, B-51662, #4.

ing payments of $6,280,000, stemmed from fraud. Of this amount, Warren reported, the Department of Justice recovered only $107,882.02, but he did not blame that department: ". . . the Contract Settlement Act—in providing only for the recovery of payments established as stemming from fraud, instead of effectively preventing such fraudulent payments in the first instance—places the Government in the unenviable position of locking the barn after the horse is stolen."[47]

In May 1950, Warren sent to Congress his sixth and last report on the Contract Settlement Act. The General Services Administration, successor to the Office of Contract Settlement, had reported that only 262 of 324,195 war contracts terminated up to March 31, 1950, remained to be settled. As of April 30, 1950, GAO had examined 9,239 termination contracts involving 2,836 contractors for termination of 26,566 contracts. Warren reported that more than 5 percent of the settlements, 549 to be exact, had involved improper payments totaling more than $20,900,000. Because of the difficulty of proving fraud after passage of so much time, the Department of Justice had recovered only about $200,000 of this amount.

In addition, GAO had identified 684 settlements with overpayments of $4,290,000 not involving fraud. Warren noted the significance of the fact that he had learned of no case where settlement with a contractor involved an underpayment. He said he did not find it pleasant to present the information in this report: "The sole motivating factor is that there may be no possible misunderstanding of the tragic consequences when the Congress releases the reins that control the public purse. . . . Legislation—such as the Contract Settlement Act of 1944—which tends to weaken the jurisdiction of the General Accounting Office, as conferred upon it by the Congress, must of necessity weaken the control of the Congress over public expenditures. . . . The right hand of the Congress—the General Accounting Office—should never again be paralyzed by crippling legislation."[48]

The work in contract termination settlement, as unsatisfactory as it was, was a major World War II concern of GAO, extending for five years after the end of the war. GAO did the best it could in carrying out its limited role, while complaining about serious defects in the Contract Settlement Act. GAO did not report its costs in doing this work, but clearly they were large, given the expenditure of staff time and other overhead. Warren's outspoken criticism of the law and his open expositions of fraud in war contract termination

---

[47]Letter, Warren to Congress, August 1, 1949, 336 MS 9.
[48]Letter, Warren to Congress, May 19, 1950, 345 pt. 2 MS 1582.

agreements attracted attention during a period when there was public concern about the costs of government and other instances of fraud and corruption involving the government.[49]

GAO's Relations with the Truman Committee during the War

On February 10, 1941, Sen. Harry S. Truman (D—Missouri) introduced a resolution to establish a committee to investigate the defense program. Truman's interest in the defense mobilization effort then occurring related to complaints he had received from Missouri contractors that they were not getting a fair share of defense construction contracts. The Senate created the Special Committee to Investigate the National Defense Program, commonly known as the Truman Committee, on March 1, 1941. The committee operated between 1941 and 1948. Truman chaired this committee until he received the nomination for vice president on the Democratic ticket in 1944. He gained a national reputation based on the committees's investigations of the war effort.[50]

GAO cooperated with the Truman Committee in a number of ways during the war, particularly on problems with defense contracts. Because the committee's original budget was only $15,000, making it difficult for Truman to hire many staff, he borrowed personnel from federal agencies to work as investigators and in other positions.[51] Although specific evidence has not been found that Truman borrowed GAO staff in 1941, when the committee began operations, it seems likely, given the existence of the GAO Office of Investigations with a large staff of experienced investigators. Truman Committee personnel lists show that a former GAO employee with investigative experience became associate chief counsel of the committee in March 1941 and that an auditor moved from GAO to the committee staff as a salaried investigator in November 1941. In the fall of 1946, GAO loaned two investigators to the Truman Committee staff.[52]

---

[49]For general histories of the Truman Administration, 1945-1953, see Robert H. Ferrell, *Harry S. Truman: A Life* (Columbia, MO, and London: University of Missouri Press, 1994); Bert Cochran, *Harry Truman and the Crisis Presidency* (New York: Funk & Wagnalls, 1973); David McCullough, *Truman* (New York: Simon & Schuster, 1992); and Alonzo L. Hamby, *Man of the People: A Life of Harry S. Truman* (New York: Oxford University Press, 1995).

[50]For a good survey of the origins and work of the Truman Committee, see Cochran, *Harry Truman and the Crisis Presidency*, 99-115. See also Donald H. Riddle, *The Truman Committee: A Study in Congressional Responsibility* (New Brunswick, NJ: Rutgers University Press, 1964).

[51]Cochran, *Harry Truman and the Crisis Presidency*, 100.

[52]"Personnel of the Senate Committee Investigating the National Defense Program," October 28, 1946, Truman Committee files, The Truman Library, Independence, MO.

There were frequent contacts during the war between Warren and the Truman Committee. On April 24, 1943, Warren wrote to Senator Truman, as well as the chairman of the House Military Affairs Committee, disclosing information about kickbacks paid by four subcontractors to prime defense contractors with cost-plus contracts in the Detroit area. Warren described the problem as involving "payment by firms furnishing services and supplies to prime contractors of gratuities or commissions to employees of the purchasing departments of such prime contractors, and to others, for referring business of the prime contractors to the subcontractors."[53]

The Truman Committee, reacting to Warren's letter, held hearings in Detroit on these apparent kickback cases on May 20-22, 1943. The hearings disclosed the details of the kickbacks on cost-plus contracts and led to the conclusion that the contractors had passed on the kickback costs to the federal government.[54]

On October 5, 1943, Warren proposed to Congress legislation that, in his words, provided for "the elimination of the practice by subcontractors under cost-plus-a-fixed-fee prime contracts of paying fees or kickbacks, or of granting gifts or gratuities to employees of cost-plus-a-fixed-fee prime contractors, or of other subcontractors, for the purpose of securing the award to orders or subcontracts thereunder." The proposed law would authorize the federal government to recover kickback funds. Also it would authorize GAO to require subcontractors to submit their records to GAO to determine whether such improper payments had been made.[55] In response to a request from the Truman Committee's chief counsel, Warren forwarded a copy of his legislative proposal to Truman.[56]

Although it took over two years, Congress eventually passed the legislation Warren proposed—the Anti-Kickback Act of 1946—and Truman, then president of the United States, signed it on March 8, 1946. The law's text, including a provision granting power to GAO to inspect the plants and audit the books and the records of any prime contractor or subcontractor involved in a negotiated contract, departed only slightly from the language Warren proposed in 1943.[57]

[53]Letter, Warren to the chairman, Senate Special Committee to Investigate the National Defense Program, April 24, 1943, B-34055.

[54]Letter, Warren to Congress, October 5, 1943, ibid.

[55]Ibid.

[56]Letter, Warren to Truman, October 14, 1943, B-34055.

[57]Letter, Warren to Rep. James A. O'Leary, chairman, House Committee on Expenditures in the Executive Departments, February 10, 1944, B-34055; letter, Warren to Rep. Carter Manasco, chairman, House Committee on Expenditures in the Executive Departments, January 16, 1945, ibid.; letter, Warren to Sen. Brien McMahon, September 28, 1945, ibid.; and Anti-Kickback Act of 1946, Public Law 319-79, 60 Stat. 37, approved March 8, 1946.

Wartime Transportation Audits

A routine activity of the Claims Division, the audit of government transportation costs, became another major wartime activity of GAO.[58] The central purpose of the Transportation Act of 1940, GAO's authority for conducting transportation audits during World War II, was the expediting of payments to common carriers for transporting people and goods for the government. Before passage of this law, federal agencies that contracted for transportation services by rail, air, trucks, and other means administratively audited bills before payment. As it did with other federal agency payments,
GAO audited transportation costs after the administrative audit and payment.
After enactment of the Transportation Act of 1940, government contracting
agencies paid transportation bills as submitted without examining the rates
charged. The law specified that payment for transportation charges "shall be
made upon presentation of bills therefor, prior to audit or settlement by the
General Accounting Office, but the right is hereby reserved to the United
States Government to deduct the amount of any overpayment to any such
carrier from any amount subsequently found to be due such carrier."[59]

At the time Congress considered the matter, GAO was not invited to testify on the draft legislation and did not officially oppose it, although the
Office was not in favor of parts of it. Warren, still a member of the House of
Representatives at the time, did oppose it.[60] The new law threw the burden
of determining whether proper rates had been charged on GAO. It complicated and expanded GAO's transportation audit at a time when, because of
the national defense and war efforts, the government's transportation bill
was increasing substantially.[61]

The railroad transportation rate structure further complicated GAO's audit task. The federal government made substantial grants of land to railroads
in the latter part of the 19th century to subsidize their development. In return, these so-called land-grant carriers charged only 50 percent of normal
rates to transport government freight and passengers on lines built through

---

[58]See chapter 8, pp. 188-91, for a survey of pre-World War II transportation audit activity.

[59]Text of the law quoted in *Investigation of Procurement and Buildings*, Hearings before the Procurement
and Buildings Subcommittee of the House Committee on Expenditures in the Executive Departments,
80th Cong., 2d Sess. (Washington: GPO, 1948), pt. 7, "General Accounting Office Audit of Wartime
Freight Vouchers," 1028 (hereafter cited as *Investigation of Procurement and Buildings*, pt. 7).

[60]Yates testimony, June 2, 1948, *Investigation of Procurement and Buildings*, pt. 7, 1049-50; and Yates
testimony, March 13, 1951, *Independent Offices Appropriations for 1952*, Hearings before a Subcommittee of the House Committee on Appropriations, 82d Cong., 1st Sess, pt. 1 (Washington: GPO, 1951),
1493.

[61]Yates testimony, December 14, 1943, *Independent Offices Appropriation Bill for 1945*, Hearings before
a Subcommittee on Independent Offices, House Committee on Appropriations, 78th Cong., 2d Sess.
(Washington: GPO, 1944), 826-27.

land-grant areas. Furthermore, to compete effectively, many non-land-grant carriers entered into equalization agreements with the United States, agreeing to accept the same rates charged by land-grant carriers. By fiscal year 1941, when the government spent an estimated $50 million for rail freight and passenger transportation, the land-grant and equalization reductions amounted to between $5 million and $8.5 million. Warren estimated that in fiscal year 1944, the government would pay rail carriers $2 billion, reflecting $200 million for land-grant and equalization deductions, and later he reported that the amount had increased to $300 million in fiscal year 1945.[62] While this system benefited the government, it made difficult GAO's task of determining in an audit the accuracy of the rates charged, particularly in a wartime period when the government's transportation bills grew to immense proportions. The occasional failure of carriers to allow land-grant deductions when setting charges and making errors in calculating the deductions also were problems.[63]

As a result of GAO's freight and passenger transportation audits covering fiscal years 1941-1945, the Office collected $37,528,842 from carriers, representing government overpayments. The amounts collected yearly escalated from $526,510 in fiscal year 1941, before the United States became formally involved in the war, to $23,847,102 in fiscal year 1945. Collections subsequently, in fiscal year 1946 and part of fiscal year 1947, totaled over $85 million, realized mainly from audits of wartime charges just completed in those years.[64]

By the spring of 1947, GAO thought that it was close to clearing up the backlog of wartime transportation audits. On October 1, 1945, GAO, on Warren's orders, had adopted revised audit procedures designed to eliminate the backlog in a reasonable time. A committee of GAO officials had developed the new procedures. Generally they provided for recruiting new staff to help expedite passenger and freight audits; the committee estimated that if the new procedures did not apply, it would take 10 to 12 years to audit transportation payments made through June 30, 1945, without considering of the task of auditing new transportation charges that would accrue during the postwar period. A central feature of the new procedures was that statements of overcharges for transportation would not be issued for amounts under $50. The committee told Warren that "the proposed changes in audit procedures are drastic. Certain losses may be sustained by the Government

---

[62]Letter, Warren to Rep. John J. Cochran, May 15, 1944, B-42019, #1; and letter, Warren to Cochran, November 1, 1945, ibid.

[63]Letter, Warren to Sen. Burton K. Wheeler, chairman, Senate Committee on Interstate Commerce, November 10, 1945, B-44859.

[64]Statistics included in letter, Warren to Rep. Joseph P. O'Hara, January 2, 1947, B-62516.

in connection with the failure to recapture overpayments made in connection with small payments, but the larger sums overpaid will be recaptured and the rate of audit will be considerably accelerated if the proposed changes are adopted." GAO made no public announcement of the new procedures, according to Warren, "because we did not wish the carriers to get the impression that we were revising audit procedures. . . ."[65] As it turned out, adoption of the new audit procedures came back to haunt GAO within two years.

An early indication that GAO faced a serious problem with the accelerated audit was a letter Warren received from Sen. Glen H. Taylor (D—Idaho) in May 1947. Taylor referred to the possibility of large sums owed the government because of excessive charges by railroads during the war and expressed concern about GAO's policy of not processing overpayments of less than $50. Taylor thought that this might involve a substantial amount and asked Warren for an explanation. Warren's brief response said that because of the backlog of unaudited transportation accounts in mid-1945, GAO decided that an accelerated audit was needed to protect the interests of the United States.

An internal memorandum prepared at the time, not provided to Taylor, spelled out the problems GAO had during the war getting qualified rate technicians to carry out the audit. Although several hundred staff received training, their rate of production—the number of audits each rate examiner completed each month—declined significantly compared with prewar standards. The result was a backlog of 7 million unaudited freight transportation vouchers as of June 30, 1945. The memorandum argued that there had been a GAO payroll savings of about $15 million as a result of the accelerated audit because between October 1, 1945, and December 31, 1946, GAO brought the audit up to July 1, 1945. Without the accelerated audit, it would have taken 500 examiners at least 10 years to do the same job, thus the $15 million savings.[66]

In early 1948, there were other congressional inquiries about the accelerated audit, including a pointed letter from Sen. William Langer (R—North Dakota). Langer referred to information he had that in the fall of 1945, GAO hired numerous veterans to train as freight rate examiners, telling them that

[65]Warren testimony, May 20, 1948, *Investigation of Procurement and Buildings*, pt. 7, 947-53; and testimony of A. Banks Thomas, chief, GAO Claims Division, April 7, 1947, *Independent Offices Appropriation Bill for 1948*, Hearings before a Subcommittee of the House Committee on Appropriations, 80th Cong., 1st Sess, pt. 1 (Washington: GPO, 1947), 43.

[66]Letter, Taylor to Warren, May 29, 1947, B-42019, #1; letter, Warren to Taylor, July 11, 1947, B-44859; memorandum, L. E. Noe, chief, Freight Subdivision, Claims Division, "Post audit of Freight Transportation vouchers, Standard audit vs. a visual or *selective* audit, and the $50.00 minimum. For information relating to letter from Senator Glen H. Taylor, dated May 29, 1947," B-42019, #1.

they would have to work at least five years if they took the training and that the audit would take 15 years. Langer also said that he had heard that the $50 minimum standard was the result of pressure on GAO to complete the freight audit within two years. He noted that some persons had estimated the loss to the government as a result of the accelerated audit at $100 million but added that others thought it might be as much as $350 million. Langer asserted that "the interests of the government have been put aside and the only consideration under this policy is to 'complete' the job. Thus far, during 1947 your office has terminated the services of several hundred freight rate examiners indicating that GAO never intended to perform a more thorough audit." He suggested that an investigation of the matter with witnesses under oath would prove his charges and asked Warren to respond at his earliest convenience. In a follow-up letter, Langer told Warren that his source of information was a former GAO employee.[67]

GAO's response to Langer admitted that new staff hired for the freight audit in September and October 1945 had to promise to stay on the job for at least five years and were told that there was a 12- to 15-year backlog of freight vouchers. The progress of the work by fiscal year 1947 made possible substantial staff cuts; to retain these staff would have been a waste of government money. Assistant Comptroller General Yates, who signed this letter, denied that GAO had instituted the accelerated audit under pressure and stated that the Office had developed the procedures to "enable the timely recovery . . . of vast amounts of overpayments." He estimated that the accelerated audit resulted in collection of nearly $250 millon compared with only $24 million during fiscal year 1945. He also reported that GAO currently had under way a review of some audits done under the accelerated procedure to determine whether more-detailed audits were necessary.[68]

After receiving a very critical letter from Rep. George H. Bender (R— Ohio), chairman of the Procurement and Buildings Subcommittee of the House Committee on Expenditures in the Executive Departments, charging that $300 millon to $400 million would ultimately be lost because of the accelerated audit, Warren took defensive action. He refuted Bender's charges but also argued that GAO's intention all along had been to survey the work completed under the accelerated procedures to determine the audit's effectiveness. Warren ordered a complete reaudit of freight transportation vouchers for the period January 1, 1943, to September 30, 1946. In a memorandum written in mid-March 1948, Warren reviewed the circumstances leading to

---

[67]Letter, Langer to Warren, January 29, 1948, B-42019, #1; and letter, Langer to Warren, March 23, 1948, ibid.

[68]Letter, Yates to Langer, February 19, 1948, B-44859.

the accelerated audit and its results, including the collection of nearly $250 million from common carriers. He noted that he had just received the results of the promised reaudit of a representative segment of vouchers subjected to the accelerated audit. This reaudit, Warren reported, showed that government overpayments of $100 million remained to be recovered. Warren explained the problem:

> Audit personnel, due principally to overzealousness on the part of both supervisors and auditors who were making every effort to bring the work to a current status, did not uniformly comply with established audit procedures and policies, left in effect by the accelerated audit program. As a further factor contributing to this result, large numbers of relatively inexperienced employees made many errors without realizing that they were doing so.

He added that many vouchers had been filed without proper audit completion, "subject to recall and correction at the time of the contemplated reexamination." Had he known earlier about these problems, Warren said, he would not have approved the termination of qualified transportation auditors that took place in 1947.[69]

To handle the reaudit of freight vouchers audited between October 1, 1945, and June 30, 1947, Warren established a Reaudit Section in the Claims Division in mid-April 1948. Two weeks later, he detached the transportation audit work from the Claims Division, where it had been since 1926, and created a new Transportation Division, incorporating the Reaudit Section as well as numerous other sections and units. Harrell O. Hoagland, then an assistant general counsel, became head of the new division.[70]

Just as Warren took these steps, Bender's subcommittee held executive session hearings on the matter in April, May, and June 1948. Bender scheduled the hearings partly in response to a letter he had received from Richard T. Mozinski, a GAO freight-rate examiner, in September 1947. In this letter,

---

[69]Letter, Bender to Warren, March 1, 1948, B-42019, #1; letter, Warren to Bender, March 17, 1948, ibid.; and Warren, Memorandum on General Accounting Office Audit of Transportation Payments Made by the United States, March 17, 1948, ibid. (source of the quotation). For a personal account by one of the accelerated audit staff who was terminated, see comments by Geraldine M. Rubar in GAO, *Audit and Legal Services, 1943-1983: A Women's Perspective*, GAO History Program, Oral History Series (GAO-OP-10-OH) (Washington: 1990), 11-13. GAO rehired some of the terminated staff for the reaudit, including Rubar, who later became a lawyer in the Office of the General Counsel.

[70]Office Order No. 39—Revised, Supplement No. 1, April 16, 1948 (establishing the Reaudit Section); Office Order No. 81, "Establishing the Transportation Division," April 30, 1948; and *Annual Report of the Comptroller General of the United States for the Fiscal Year Ended June 30, 1948* (Washington: GPO, n.d.), 4.

Mozinski pointed out that GAO interviewed him and other veterans in September and October 1945 for positions as freight-rate examiner trainees. The training that they needed was available if they agreed to work at least five years, with the suggestion that clearing the voucher audit backlog would take about 15 years. Mozinski stated that "responsible persons" in GAO had been pressured to complete the audit in two years; he did not specify who had exerted the pressure. The ignoring of overcharges less than $50 "as well as that of screening and stamping (without verification of charges) and sending to the files as audited a large percentage of vouchers resulted in the loss to the Government of at least $100,000,000." He added that other estimates set the amount at $250 million. Mozinski reported that 40 veterans (including himself) were to be laid off in October 1947 and that thus far in 1947, several hundred freight-rate examiners had been terminated.[71]

Other GAO staff testifying at the hearings generally backed up Mozinski's complaints. A GAO freight-rate reviewer, asked about morale in the Transportation Division during the accelerated audit and later, said that it had been and continued to be very low. "It is really pathetic. There has been no change in policy, no change in methods. The same boys are still in power, today handling this transportation reaudit work, who were doing the same work during the screening period, starting October 1, 1945. Morale, I would say, is zero and minus."[72]

Henry H. Glassie, counsel of the Procurement and Buildings Subcommittee, did much of the questioning during the hearings of GAO staff and officials. He tended to side with GAO staff who complained about the Office, and he asked provocative questions of high officials, such as Warren and Yates. In detailed testimony, Warren explained the nature of the transportation task during World War II, the problem of getting qualified staff to do the work, and the reason for the accelerated audit. Warren summarized as follows:

> The important things are these: First, that the procedures as proposed and approved by me were sound; second, that the plan was not executed as projected; third, that we recovered a man-sized proportion of the amounts overpaid carriers during a period when such collections as a practical matter were possible; fourth, that I have directed a complete reaudit of all wartime freight payments handled in the accelerated audit;

---

[71]The text of Mozinski's letter is in *Investigation of Procurement and Buildings*, pt. 7, 762-63. His prepared statement at the hearings appears in ibid., 752-53. Fourteen other GAO transportation auditors testified at the hearings. See their testimony in ibid., 763-934.

[72]Testimony of Fay John McCarty, May 20, 1948, ibid., 920.

and finally, that steps have been taken organizationally and procedurally, to insure recovery, wherever possible, of all substantial overpayments to carriers.[73]

The Bender subcommittee's final report was very critical of the accelerated audit but recognized the changes GAO had made in response to criticism and expressed confidence that the reaudit would result in the recovery of substantial additional transportation overcharges. Bender wrote in the report: "I am forced to conclude that the General Accounting Office, often termed the 'watchdog of the Treasury,' fell asleep on the auditing of the Government's transportation bills. Your subcommittee waked the sleeping watchdog. I am pleased to say that at the prodding of the subcommittee the General Accounting Office has shown every disposition to bestir itself and to take prompt measures for the protection of the Government's interest and the recovery of the moneys overpaid."[74]

Bender estimated that in the accelerated audit, GAO had detected only about half of the estimated $700 million overcharges by common carriers in 1943, 1944, and 1945. The overcharges, Bender concluded, had resulted from a carrier-adopted policy to take advantage of the Transportation Act of 1940 to bill at rates higher than the lowest rates available, even though they had had to certify that they were charging the lowest available net rates. Bender said that his subcommittee thought that GAO was right in using the accelerated procedures but that they had been defective. GAO's accelerated audit plan suffered from "ineffective management at the lower supervisory levels," unknown to high GAO officials until the facts came out in the hearings. The overcharges, which the subcommittee felt that the rail carriers could afford to pay, would be recovered by the reaudit currently being conducted by GAO.[75]

The transportation reaudit begun in 1948 proceeded for several years. In January 1950, Warren noted that GAO was making progress but that the reaudit was "a herculean task and still our No. 1 headache."[76] In January 1952, Harrell Hoagland, chief of the Transportation Division, estimated that

---

[73]Warren testimony, May 20, 1948, *Investigation of Procurement and Buildings*, pt. 7, 936. Warren testified on May 20 and 21, 1948. See ibid., 934-1006. For an example of Glassie's role, see ibid., 996-99.

[74]*Investigation of General Accounting Office Audit of Wartime Freight Vouchers*, Eighteenth Intermediate Report of the Committee on Expenditures in the Executive Departments, 80th Cong., 2d Sess., H. Rept. 2457 (Washington: 1948), v.

[75]Ibid., 2-6.

[76]Testimony of Warren and others, January 27, 1950, *Independent Offices Appropriations for 1951*, Hearings before a Subcommittee of the House Committee on Appropriations, 81st Cong., 2d Sess, pt. 1 (Washington: GPO, 1950), 856.

for 1943 and 1944, GAO was collecting about 8 percent of the total transportation bill for those years as a result of the reaudit. The next year, Warren indicated that GAO would complete the reaudit for the 1943-1945 period in early 1956.[77] Exactly how much GAO collected from carriers annually during Warren's term because of the reaudit is difficult to determine, but clearly it was a substantial amount. GAO reported these collections together with collections on audits for current years rather than stating them separately. When GAO finally completed the reaudit in 1961 under Comptroller General Joseph Campbell, it reported detection of overcharges during the years reaudited of $250 million.[78]

GAO Audit of the Manhattan Project

Although it was a carefully guarded secret at the time, GAO, during World War II, audited the accounts of the Manhattan Project, which produced the first atomic bombs. This became publicly known in 1946, when Warren testified in favor of a GAO audit of the accounts of the proposed new Atomic Energy Commission (AEC). Warren told the Senate Special Committee on Atomic Energy in April 1946 that "we were in on the atomic secret from the very beginning" and that GAO had audited the funds of the Manhattan Project, operating under the War Department, throughout the war. Warren said that GAO had audited 100,265 Manhattan Project vouchers worth $1,778,000,000.[79]

During the same hearings, Maj. Gen. Leslie R. Groves praised GAO's wartime audit of the Manhattan Project, which he headed. GAO did everything necessary to protect the security of the undertakings. About the GAO audit, Groves said: ". . . I always had the very strong personal feeling that it was a very desirable thing, because it gives the United States the protection it needs and it also removes, from the officer who is responsible, a tremendous responsibility. It would be a very bad thing . . . to remove these accounts [of AEC] from the control of the Comptroller General." Groves indicated, in response to a question from Sen. Brien McMahon, that GAO had received the documents it needed from the Manhattan Project to make a proper audit but that the comptroller general wanted only what he specifically required

---

[77]Hoagland testimony, January 23, 1952, *Independent Offices Appropriations for 1953*, Hearings before a Subcommittee of the House Committee on Appropriations, 82nd Cong., 2d Sess., pt. 1 (Washington: GPO, 1952), 522; and Warren testimony, March 5, 1953, *Independent Offices Appropriations for 1954*, Hearings before a Subcommittee of the House Committee on Appropriations, 83d Cong., 1st Sess., pt. 3 (Washington: GPO, 1953), 725.

[78]See chapter 18, pp. 469-472.

[79]Warren testimony, April 4, 1946, *Atomic Energy Act of 1946*, Hearings before the Senate Special Committee on Atomic Energy, 79th Cong., 2d Sess., pt. 5 (Washington: GPO, 1946), 500.

for the audit.[80]   Warren thought that Groves's testimony had persuaded the Senate committee to write into the Atomic Energy Act of 1946 authorization for a full GAO audit of AEC.[81]

Another GAO activity related to the Manhattan Project was the approval of several top secret contracts, including two negotiated with E. I. duPont de Nemours and Company. In April 1943, Secretary of War Henry L. Stimson sent to Warren drafts of two contracts with duPont, noting their extreme secrecy and requesting that knowledge of the existence and the provisions of the contracts be limited to Warren and whoever reviewed them in GAO. Noting that the contractor had requested a GAO review of the contracts, Stimson asked Warren to do so. General Groves was involved in this matter as the representative of the War Department and the Manhattan Project.

To emphasize the extreme importance of the contracts involved, Groves gave GAO a copy of a letter to President Roosevelt from Vannevar Bush, director of the Office of Scientific Research and Development, asking him to approve a special project (the atomic bomb work) and to authorize the chief of engineers to enter into contracts necessary to carry on the project. Groves also gave GAO sections of a report on the project, signed by General Groves, that Bush had sent to the president. Bush asked the president to approve contract provisions in which the government agreed that all work would be done at government expense and that the contractor would not be liable for any loss, expense, or damage resulting from the work. He also asked Roosevelt to authorize the chief of engineers to enter into contracts that would cost more than available funds and to pay for them with any funds under his control.[82]

Warren approved all articles of the contract that he had been requested to review, including provisions for reimbursing the contractor, the contractor's agreement to waive profits, and indemnification. Groves reported in his account of the Manhattan Project, published many years later, that an un-named "principal assistant" to Warren had opposed the contract review as contrary to existing GAO procedures but that Warren had summarily overruled him in favor of doing the review. In this account, Groves identified the duPont project as the design, the construction, and the operation of a pluto-

---

[80]Groves testimony, April 8, 1946, ibid., 526-27, 529.

[81]Letter, Warren to R. B. Chandler, publisher of *The Mobile, AL, Press Register*, April 8, 1946, Warren Papers, Folder 414.

[82]Letter, Stimson to Warren, April 10, 1943, B-33801; and letter, Brig. Gen. L. R. Groves to John C. McFarland, GAO general counsel, April 12, 1943, with attachments: letter, Bush to the president, December 16, 1942, and Groves, Report, December 16, 1942, ibid.

nium plant for the atomic bomb project.[83]   In October 1943, at Groves's request, GAO reviewed and approved changes to the two contracts relating to insurance and an employees' benefits fund.[84]

In September 1944, Warren and Yates learned more about the nature of the project GAO had been auditing throughout the war. At that time, Under Secretary of War Robert P. Patterson, Maj. Gen. George J. Richards, and Brig. Gen. Kenneth C. Royall visited Warren and Yates in Warren's office. At this meeting, Patterson and his associates "explained generally the nature and purposes of a War Department program of development and experimentation of the highest urgency and secrecy," Warren recorded. The program under Groves, according to the War Department emissaries, had "reached the point that its secrecy can no longer be safely guarded if disbursements in connection with the program must be made in the usual way."

The War Department representatives specifically asked Warren to approve a plan to advance $12.5 million to Groves from an existing defense appropriation. Groves was to have authority to spend the funds while keeping records that were to be made available for an audit directed by the comptroller general after conferring with Patterson "without endangering the secrecy of the project." Warren and Yates agreed to the plan, which involved clearing a voucher covering the advance of funds in the audit of the accounts of the War Department disbursing officer making the payment. In other words, GAO dispensed with the usual audit for the time being and simplified the process of providing the money to ensure the secrecy of the expenditure.[85]

GAO records on the Manhattan Project audit are sketchy, but enough exist to demonstrate that the Office did the audit. It is unlikely that the auditors conducting the audit knew the reasons for the disbursements, and even Warren was unaware of the project's general nature until meeting with Patterson in September 1944. Warren was proud of GAO's contribution to the war effort, and he frequently referred to the Manhattan Project audit in the postwar years.

---

[83]Leslie R. Groves, *Now It Can Be Told: The Story of the Manhattan Project* (New York: Harper & Brothers, 1962), 38-59. The identity of the "principal assistant" has not been established.

[84]Letter, Groves to McFarland, October 13, 1943, B-33801; and letter, Warren to Groves, October 27, 1943, ibid.

[85]Warren and Yates, confidential memorandum, November 13, 1944, ibid. (an account of the meeting with Patterson et al. on September 27, 1944, and the agreement to advance the funds to Groves).

Conclusion

The task of coping with a massively expanded workload during World War II severely strained GAO's leadership and staff. To the routine audits, investigations, and other duties that were the substance of GAO's prewar activities were added all the war-related jobs, most obviously the audit of wartime procurements. The cost-plus-a-fixed-fee contracts predominately used by the government during the war led to substantial overpayments plus a massive job of contract termination that began as the war drew to a close and extended into the postwar period. Audits of government transportation costs, which increased tremendously during the war and were complicated by the Transportation Act of 1940, further tested GAO.

GAO had to recruit thousands of new staff during a period of severe labor shortages; most of them were untrained and unskilled and required training, mostly on the job, before they could perform satisfactorily. Some experienced staff left, either by enlistment or through the draft, for military service. The staffing of the Office, which increased from slightly over 5,000 in mid-1940 to almost 15,000 in early 1946, was itself a major effort.[86]

Wartime employees of GAO's Claims Division, 1943.

[86]See chapter 6, pp. 136-40.

Wartime employees of GAO's Claims Division, 1943.

All in all, GAO contributed substantially to the war effort. Comptroller General Warren wanted GAO to cooperate to the fullest extent possible, but not at the cost of ignoring the laws regulating GAO's operations or overlooking abuses in spending or record keeping.

There were problems, most obviously GAO's failure to properly audit transportation charges during and just after the war. The practical difficulty of keeping up with the massive inflow of transportation vouchers was an extenuating factor, but it did not justify the stamping of vouchers as audited when that had not been done. There is no evidence that Warren was aware of these problems when they occurred, but as the head of GAO, he bore ultimate responsibility. He and other high GAO officials, and to some extent the congressional committee that investigated the matter, tended to blame lower-level supervisors in the Office for the problem. Once he became aware of the scope of the difficulty, in the face of severe congressional criticism and public complaints from GAO staff, Warren took firm action to correct the Office's earlier failure to do a proper transportation audit. Congress did much to create the transportation problem when it passed the Transportation

Act of 1940. This was one of the more discomfiting periods in GAO history. It detracted somewhat from GAO's otherwise successful effort to contribute to the nation's war effort between 1941 and 1945.

CHAPTER 12

Corporation Audits

The General Accounting Office (GAO), from early in its existence, objected to the exclusion of most government corporations from its auditing jurisdiction. Comptrollers General J. R. McCarl, Fred H. Brown, and Lindsay C. Warren had raised questions about the corporate form of organization and the independence of government corporations from congressional control. GAO believed that all government entities should be subject to its regular audit, in order to enforce financial controls, safeguard the interests of the United States, and especially ensure congressional control of spending. GAO's struggle with the Tennessee Valley Authority (TVA) in the 1930s and early 1940s illustrated the problem.[1]

President Franklin D. Roosevelt issued Executive Order No. 6549 in January 1934, directing that "accounts of all receipts and expenditures by government agencies, including corporations created after March 3, 1933, the accounting procedure for which is not otherwise prescribed by law, shall be rendered to the General Accounting Office . . . for settlement . . . ." Although a step toward financial accountability for government corporations, the order had limited effect because it did not apply to corporations established before 1933. Also, Congress subsequently exempted many new corporations set up to combat the Depression and later to assist in the war effort.[2]

The George Act, February 1945

In one of his early annual reports, Warren suggested that Congress consider legislation "requiring in uniform manner the independent audit and settlement of

---

[1]See chapter 9, pp. 208-19, for a discussion of GAO's views on government corporations and the Office's work on them up to the early 1940s.

[2]Staff of the Senate Committee on Government Operations, *Financial Management in the Federal Government*, S. Doc. 11, 87th Cong., 1st Sess., vol. I (Washington: GPO, 1961), 22 (hereafter cited as *Financial Management,* 1961); and Harvey C. Mansfield, Sr., "The General Accounting Office," undated typescript submitted to the President's Committee on Administrative Management, 48, GAO History Program Archives.

the accounts of Government corporations."[3]   Questions about audits of government corporations came up regularly in GAO's annual appropriations hearings. In December 1943, for example, Assistant Comptroller General Frank L. Yates reported that GAO audited only 15 of the 49 active government corporations. Among those GAO audited were the Commodity Credit Corporation (CCC), the Export-Import Bank, the Home Owners' Loan Corporation, the Smaller War Plants Corporation, and TVA. GAO did not audit, for example, the Federal Deposit Insurance Corporation (FDIC), the Reconstruction Finance Corporation (RFC), or the Inland Waterways Corporation.[4]   GAO had authority to audit the Commodity Credit Corporation beginning on July 1, 1944. Warren considered the law granting this authority to be significant, for one reason because it had resulted from discussions between GAO and the Department of Agriculture, under which the Commodity Credit Corporation operated. He also saw the law as a model for use for other corporations.[5] A few corporations, including those under the jurisdiction of Nelson Rockefeller, the coordinator of Inter-American Affairs, and Cargoes, Inc., under the Foreign Economic Administration, agreed voluntarily to a GAO audit of their accounts.[6]

In January 1945 testimony, Warren provided draft language for legislation subjecting all government corporations to a GAO audit. In an exchange with Rep. Everett M. Dirksen (R—Illinois), who was worried about contracts issued by the Smaller War Plants Corporation, Warren pointed out that Congress had in effect excluded GAO from the audits of many government corporations in laws creating them. Warren admitted that even he, as a member of the House of Representatives, had voted in favor of the individual laws excluding GAO from those audits.[7]

In February 1945, Congress passed the George Act, which authorized GAO to audit the financial transactions of all government corporations in accordance with principles and procedures applicable to commercial corporate transactions. Much of the impetus behind this provision, part of a larger bill, came from a study of government corporations in 1943 and 1944 by the Joint Committee on Reduction of Nonessential Federal Expenditures, headed by Sen. Harry F. Byrd (D—

---

[3]*Annual Report of the Comptroller General of the United States for the Fiscal Year Ended June 30, 1942* (Washington: typescript, GAO, 1942), 9-10.

[4]Yates testimony, December 14, 1943, *Independent Offices Appropriation Bill for 1945*, Hearings before a Subcommittee on Independent Offices, House Committee on Appropriations, 78th Cong., 2d Sess. (Washington: GPO, 1944), 806-8 (includes a chart analyzing congressional, budgetary, and audit control of government corporations as of December 15, 1943, provided by GAO).

[5]*Annual Report of the Comptroller General for the Fiscal Year Ended June 30, 1944* (Washington: GPO, n.d.), 6-7.

[6]Warren reported this in GAO, *Annual Report, 1944*, 7-8.

[7]Warren testimony, January 18, 1945, *Independent Offices Appropriation Bill for 1946*, Hearings before a Subcommittee on Independent Offices, House Committee on Appropriations, 70th Cong., 1st Sess. (Washington: GPO, 1945), 1138-39, 1156.

Virginia). The committee's August 1, 1944, report recommended fiscal control, including GAO audits, of government corporations. The corporation audit provisions of the George Act followed the legislative proposal that Warren had made to Congress earlier.[8]

Warren thought that the George Act was very important. As he pointed out, at that time government corporations had total assets of $29.6 billion and total liabilities of $28.4 billion. He told Congress that GAO's corporation audits "will be a laboratory in which we can develop and test the techniques for providing the Congress with better information as to the use of public funds by these corporate agencies—techniques which experience may prove suitable for application in some degree to the regular Government departments and establishments." Warren conceded that it would be difficult initially for GAO to meet the requirements of the George Act—to prepare annual fiscal year reports for each government corporation for submission to Congress not later than January 15 following the end of the fiscal year the previous June 30.[9]

One measure of how important Warren considered this law was his refusal of an offer of a federal judgeship in North Carolina at the time in part because of passage of the George Act. He described GAO's task of auditing corporations as "a stupendous undertaking, and eventually this office will stand or fall on the kind of job it does." He commented also on the extravagance and the self-interest of government officials and the previous willingness of Congress to pass legislation covering up the actions of these officials. "All of these things have been disturbing to me," Warren wrote, "and why I elected to stay on, and worry myself to death about such things is really beyond me. We just cannot always shape our lives to suit ourselves."[10]

The Government Corporation Control Act, December 1945

The George Act proved to be a preliminary to another law, passed by Congress in December 1945. Bills proposing more-comprehensive audit controls for

---

[8]*Financial Management*, 1961, 22-24; John C. Fenton, "The Corporation Audits Division—Its Legacy to the Seventies," *GAO Review* (summer 1971): 90; letter, Warren to Byrd, January 24, 1945, 281 MS 1557; and Frederick C. Mosher, *The GAO: The Quest for Accountability in American Government* (Boulder, CO: Westview Press, 1979), 106. The George Act was Public Law 79-4, 59 Stat. 5, approved February 24, 1945.

[9]*Annual Report of the Comptroller General of the United States for the Fiscal Year Ended June 30, 1945* (Washington: GPO, n.d.), 3; and Warren testimony, May 15, 1945, *Organization of Congress*, Hearings before the Joint Committee on the Organization of Congress, 79th Cong., 1st Sess., pt. 1 (Washington: GPO, 1945), 531 (source of the quote), 546 (hereafter cited as *Organization of Congress*, 1945.

[10]Letter, Warren to Judge John McDuffie, March 17, 1945, Papers of Lindsay C. Warren, Southern Historical Collection, Wilson Library, University of North Carolina at Chapel Hill, folder 403 (hereafter cited as Warren Papers).

government corporations, reflecting the recommendations of the Byrd Committee, came up in the House and the Senate in the spring and the summer of 1945. In commenting on these bills, Warren emphasized the dangers of unregulated government corporations. In a letter to Rep. Carter Manasco, chairman of the House Committee on Expenditures in the Executive Departments, Warren expressed his fear that if the present trend to create government corporations was not curbed, "we will soon have a government by Government corporations. A large segment of the Government is today operating independently of congressional control and free from accountability to the Executive. Indeed, this thing we call 'Government' has reached such gargantuan proportions that it is sprawled all over the lot."[11]

The Government Corporation Control Act, signed by President Harry S. Truman on December 6, 1945, declared that the policy of Congress was to bring government corporations under annual congressional scrutiny and to provide current financial control of them. Title I listed 41 wholly owned government corporations whose financial transactions GAO was to audit "in accordance with the principles and procedures applicable to commercial corporate transactions and under such rules and regulations as may be prescribed by the Comptroller General of the United States." Corporate accounts to be settled and adjusted by GAO were to be retained in corporate offices where GAO was to conduct the audits. The law guaranteed GAO access to all books, accounts, financial records, and other papers necessary to facilitate the audits.

Audits of each government corporation were to begin with fiscal year 1947, beginning on July 1, 1946. The George Act had required GAO to begin the corporation audits with fiscal year 1945; these audits had been started before passage of the new law. GAO was to submit a report to Congress on each audit, with copies to the president and the secretary of the Treasury, by January 15 following the close of the fiscal year being audited. These reports were to include statements of assets and liabilities, capital, surplus, and deficit; income and expense; sources and application of funds; and comments and information "as may be deemed necessary to keep Congress informed of the operations and financial condition" of the corporation, along with recommendations from the comptroller general on such things as impairment of capital and return of government capital. "The report shall also show specifically any program, expenditure, or other financial transaction or undertaking observed in the course of the audit, which, in the opinion of the Comptroller General, has been carried on or made without authority of law." Title II applied the same audit and reporting provisions to mixed-ownership government corporations, including the Central and Regional Banks for Cooperatives, Federal Land Banks, Federal Home Loan Banks, and FDIC.

---

[11]Letter, Warren to Manasco, June 13, 1945, 286 MS 1001.

Title III specified that GAO would pay expenses of the audits but would be reimbursed by each corporation for the full cost of the audit, such receipts to be deposited by GAO into the U.S. Treasury. GAO was also, during its audits, to use to the extent possible examinations of government corporations done by their supervising administrative agencies. This title also said that henceforth no corporation should be created, organized, or acquired by any federal agency or other corporation except by act of Congress. Furthermore, all wholly owned federal corporations created under the laws of any state, territory, possession of the United States, or the District of Columbia were to cease to exist as agencies or instrumentalities of the United States after June 30, 1948, except for purposes of liquidation, unless Congress reincorporated them.[12]

The Corporation Audits Division, 1945-1952

The George Act and the Government Corporation Control Act required GAO to audit the then-existing 101 corporations financed in whole or in part by the U.S. government. Warren in his annual report for 1945 stated: "I feel that such legislation represents the most forward-looking and outstanding measure in its field since the enactment of the Budget and Accounting Act in 1921."[13] To audit the corporations, GAO created the Corporation Audits Division (CAD) on July 10, 1945. The director of the division was to advise and assist the comptroller general relating to the audits, develop the audit performance rules and regulations that the law required the comptroller general to prescribe, and formulate applicable auditing and accounting procedures. The new division was to audit the accounts and the books and examine the financial transactions of all government corporations covered by the George Act and later the Government Corporation Control Act and to cover other government agencies whose books were to be audited according to principles applicable to commercial transactions. The latter duty was important because it brought to CAD important audits of organizations like the Maritime Commission, which was not a government corporation. With the comptroller general's approval, other GAO divisions were to transfer to CAD all functions corresponding to the new division's mandate.[14]

The two 1945 laws laid a very important new duty on the Office. GAO was not prepared to launch the new effort immediately. The establishment of CAD provided the organizational framework for the task, but leaders and staff had to be recruited outside GAO. While GAO had done some audits of government corpo-

---

[12]The Government Corporation Control Act, Public Law 79-248, 59 Stat. 597, as approved December 6, 1945. See also *Financial Management*, 1961, 23-24.

[13]GAO, *Annual Report, 1945*, 3. See also Elizabeth Poel, "GAO Remembers President Harry S. Truman," *GAO Review* (fall 1984): 14-18, 44.

[14]Office Order No. 67, July 10, 1945, 287 MS 483A. Acting Comptroller General Frank L. Yates signed the order.

rations previously—TVA was a major example—those audits were similar to others GAO generally did before 1945, emphasizing voucher checking and settlement of accounts. Further complicating the picture was the existing audit backlog; the George Act directed that the first corporation audits cover fiscal year 1945, which had already ended.

To direct CAD, Warren brought in T. Coleman Andrews, a well-known leader in public accounting, who headed a firm in Richmond, Virginia. He had been Virginia state auditor of public accounts between 1931 and 1933 and during World War II served in the Marine Corps.[15] GAO recruited other experienced public accountants, including Howard W. Bordner and Irwin S. Decker, the first and second deputy directors of CAD, and Stephen B. Ives, who succeeded Andrews as director of the division in 1947.[16]

Corporation Audits Division officials, 1949. Ted Westfall, fourth from left; Stephen B. Ives, fifth from right.

---

[15]Andrews testimony, December 10, 1945, *Independent Offices Appropriation Bill for 1947*, Hearings before a Subcommittee of the House Committee on Appropriations, 79th Cong., 2d Sess. (Washington: GPO, 1946), 427-28. See also Dale L. Flesher and Tonya K. Flesher, "T. Coleman Andrews and the GAO Corporation Audits Division," *The Government Accountants Journal*, 38, No. 1 (spring 1989): 23-28. See also letter, Warren to Dudley Bagley, June 1, 1945, Warren Papers, folder 405, about Warren's efforts to recruit Andrews. Andrews stayed at GAO until September 1947. In 1953, he became head of the Internal Revenue Service.

[16]Fenton, "The Corporation Audits Division—Its Legacy to the Seventies," 90-94; and Fenton, "Irwin S. Decker—A Career of Service," *GAO Review* (summer 1967): 57-62. See also Ellsworth H. Morse, Jr., "The Government Corporation Control Legislation of 1945," *GAO Review* (fall 1975): 12-13.

Recruiting staff for the new division, especially in the early years, was very difficult. With the war just ending as CAD began operations, professionally trained and experienced public accountants were scarce and were in demand. GAO had to compete with public accounting firms and other private organizations for their services. GAO received advice on its recruiting efforts from members of the American Institute of Accountants and other members of the accounting profession.[17] Acting Comptroller General Yates described the recruiting problem to Sen. Walter George (D—Georgia) a year after the establishment of CAD. Although GAO had the help of the American Institute of Accountants and had been in contact with various educational institutions, the Office had not been able to find enough qualified accountants to do the corporation audits in a timely fashion. Yates pointed out that even public accounting firms were having trouble obtaining sufficient qualified staff.[18]

Warren insisted on building in GAO "the finest aggregation of accounting talent within or without the Government."[19] At the same time GAO tried to recruit experienced professional accountants, it began to recruit new college graduates—at major universities, including, for example, Illinois, Indiana, Michigan, Pennsylvania, Columbia, and Wisconsin.[20] Gradually CAD's staff grew, eventually enabling the division to eliminate the backlog and bring corporation audits to a current status. By June 30, 1948, CAD had 167 professional staff, all men, 54 of whom were certified public accountants (CPAs). A year later, there were 161, including 71 CPAs; on June 30, 1950, there were 210 staff, 88 of them CPAs. In the year ended June 30, 1951, CAD appointed 68 accountants at the GS-5 level, the starting rank for new college graduates, indicating the success by that time of the college recruiting effort.[21]

The Corporate Audits Division began the first corporation audits in October 1945. Andrews reported to the House Appropriations Committee in December that audits were under way at RFC, CCC, TVA, the Virgin Islands Company, FDIC, the Inland Waterways Corporation, and Federal Prison Industries.[22] Andrews explained the differences between a regular GAO audit and a corporation audit. The regular GAO audit of vouchers and supporting documents was an "inquiry into the legality of transactions," normally con-

[17]GAO, *Annual Report, 1945*, 3; and Fenton, "The Corporation Audits Division—Its Legacy to the Seventies," 90-91.

[18]Letter, Yates to George, July 18, 1946, 299 MS 983.

[19]GAO, *Annual Report, 1945*, 3.

[20]Fenton, "The Corporation Audits Division—Its Legacy to the Seventies," 96.

[21]*Annual Report of the Comptroller General of the United States for the Fiscal Year Ended June 30, 1948* (Washington: GPO, n.d.), 30-31; and Fenton, "The Corporation Audits Division—Its Legacy to the Seventies," 96.

[22]Andrews testimony, December 10, 1945, *Independent Offices Appropriations Bill for 1947*, 422.

ducted in GAO offices. Settlement of fiscal officers' accounts was its main purpose. The commercial-type audit used for corporations, Andrews stated, "is a broader and more comprehensive inquiry, embraces the entire field of accounting and necessarily requires for its proper execution personnel whose education and experience afford very comprehensive understanding of commercial, industrial, and financial transactions, organization and management."

These audits usually took place at the offices of the corporation, rather than at GAO. They went beyond the standard voucher audit in that they concerned "the benefits derived from such transactions and the ultimate accounting made." But GAO did not have the power to disallow corporation expenditures that were found to be incorrect or illegal, as it did when settling accounts under the voucher audit. Also, instead of checking every item as in a voucher audit, in corporation audits GAO did test checks, their extent depending upon the degree of internal control maintained by the corporation. The commercial-type audit "establishes whether the corporation's fund of assets at the beginning of the period covered by the audit, plus the assets acquired during the period, were accounted for. It also establishes whether the corporation's liabilities and capital were truly recorded and stated." Andrews defined the ultimate objective of these audits as ascertaining "whether the financial statements of the corporation correctly reflect the corporation's financial condition and results of operations." Also, GAO had to make recommendations on the basis of an audit of a corporation.[23]

By June 30, 1946, GAO had begun auditing the fiscal year 1945 transactions of 97 of the 101 corporations covered by the 1945 laws.[24] Reports to Congress on fiscal year 1945 corporation audits were due no later than January 15, 1946; thus GAO was technically in violation of the law. GAO cited the problems in staffing the division as the reason for the lateness of the reports. A year later, GAO reported that it had sent 17 completed corporation audit reports to Congress and that it expected that corporation audit work would be current by June 30, 1948. Warren explained that the staff shortage "but also in a greater measure . . . the unsatisfactory condition of accounts found in many of the corporations" had delayed the audits.[25] Because of staff shortages, GAO initially contracted with private accounting firms to do a few corporation audits—six audits in fiscal year 1945 and three in fiscal year 1946—but in later years did all the work itself.[26]

---

[23]Ibid., 424.

[24]*Annual Report of the Comptroller General of the United States for the Fiscal Year Ended June 30, 1946* (Washington: GPO, n.d.), 11.

[25]*Annual Report of the Comptroller General of the United States for the Fiscal Year Ended June 30, 1947* (Washington: GPO, n.d.), 13-14.

[26]Andrews testimony, April 9, 1947, *Independent Offices Appropriation Bill for 1948*, Hearings before a Subcommittee of the House Committee on Appropriations, 80th Cong., 1st Sess., pt. 1 (Washington: GPO, 1947), 41.

Gradually the backlog of corporation audits became smaller as CAD's staff grew and the division established its routine. Warren reported in mid-1951 that the backlog had been eliminated completely. By that time, the task had been eased somewhat by the shrinking number of government corporations. Warren noted that for fiscal year 1950, GAO had to audit 64 active government corporations and 8 other agencies (for example the Maritime Commission) that were subject to commercial-type audits.[27] To assist in corporation audits, CAD established field offices in San Francisco, Dallas, New York, and Chicago in 1951. In 1952, these offices became part of a new GAO regional office system.[28]

Corporation Audits: Examples

Tennessee Valley Authority

After settlement by legislation in late 1941 of the dispute over GAO's authority to audit TVA and the nature of that audit, the two agencies got along reasonably well.[29] The passage of the George Act and the Government Corporation Control Act superseded section 9(b) of the 1933 Tennessee Valley Authority Act, which authorized the comptroller general to audit TVA at least once each fiscal year. An amendment to section 9(b) in November 1941 made clear that TVA was to render accounts to GAO for adjustment and settlement but prohibited GAO from disallowing expenditures considered necessary by the TVA Board of Directors.[30] The Government Corporation Control Act continued the latter provision, but GAO had authority to report to Congress any TVA expenditure that it believed improper or illegal.[31]

There were no big problems with GAO's audits of TVA under the Government Corporation Control Act during the remainder of Warren's term. One reason for the lack of serious discord was the high quality of TVA's accounting system. In 1947, T. Coleman Andrews described the system as

---

[27]*Comptroller General of the United States: Annual Report for the Fiscal Year Ended June 30, 1951* (Washington: GPO, n.d.), 21. See also Fenton, "The Corporation Audits Division—Its Legacy to the Seventies," 97.

[28]Fenton, "The Corporation Audits Division—Its Legacy to the Seventies," 108. See chapter 14, pp. 360-62, for information about creation of the regional office system in 1952.

[29]In testimony in 1943, E. W. Bell, chief of GAO's Audit Division, reported that GAO was having no current difficulties with TVA. See Bell testimony, December 14, 1943, *Independent Offices Appropriation Bill for 1945*, 806. For a discussion of the earlier GAO-TVA problems, see chapter 9, pp. 211-19. See Richard E. Brown, *The GAO: Untapped Source of Congressional Power* (Knoxville: University of Tennessee Press, 1970), for a discussion of GAO-TVA relations from the early 1940s through the early 1960s.

[30]See chapter 9, pp. 219.

[31]Testimony of Frank H. Weitzel, assistant to the comptroller general, December 10, 1945, *Independent Offices Appropriation Bill for 1947*, 465.

"probably . . . the finest accounting system in the entire Government and probably one of the best accounting systems in the entire world." In contrast, Andrews thought that the TVA accounting system before 1938 was a "confused mess." TVA considered accounting as "a necessary evil" in the beginning. Andrews credited Eric L. Kohler, who became TVA's comptroller in 1938, for installing the high-quality accounting system.[32]

Issues related to GAO's audits of TVA surfaced from time to time. In late 1945, for instance, David E. Lilienthal, chairman of the TVA Board of Directors, indicated to Warren that TVA wished to be authorized to engage independent public accountants to audit its books as it had done in the late 1930s. Because special interest groups were publicly misrepresenting TVA's power program, the authority wanted to present its financial statements to the public. The TVA board thought that it could better represent itself to the public if it had assurance that the latest policies, procedures, and methods of internal control used in the private sector were available to TVA. Lilienthal requested Warren's support when TVA asked Congress to restore its authority to contract for an independent audit.[33]

Warren pointed out to Lilienthal that Congress had debated the issue of private audits of government corporations before passing the First Deficiency Appropriation Act of 1945 (59 Stat. 81, April 25, 1945). That law had declared that no government corporation funds could be used to pay for a private audit. Furthermore, the George Act had declared that GAO's corporation audits would follow the generally accepted practices and procedures used by public accountants in auditing commercial, industrial, and banking institutions. Warren assured Lilienthal that he was seeking high-caliber public accountants for the Corporation Audits Division and noted the qualifications of Andrews. GAO would be as well-equipped as any public accounting firm to audit TVA. Warren concluded that if his opinion was asked about TVA's proposal to contract for private audits, he would oppose it.[34]

Federal Deposit Insurance Corporation

Section 203 of the Government Corporation Control Act required the comptroller general to make recommendations, when appropriate, for the return to the government of capital provided to individual corporations. In its fiscal year 1945 report on FDIC, GAO recommended retirement of the government's investment in FDIC's capital stock. In 1947, at the time Congress considered legislation to

---

[32]Andrews testimony, April 9, 1947, *Independent Offices Appropriation Bill for 1948*, 39-40.

[33]Letter, Warren to Lilienthal, October 5, 1945, summarizing letter, Lilienthal to Warren, September 8, 1945, 290 MS 460.

[34]Ibid.

accomplish this aim, Warren recommended that the Government Corporation Control Act be amended to provide for continuing the FDIC audit, even though FDIC would not have government funds. He pointed out that FDIC would still be government sponsored, that the president would continue to name FDIC directors, and that the government would be committed to purchasing FDIC's obligations upon request of the board of directors.

In August 1947, Congress passed a law requiring FDIC to return its government funds, in the amount of $289 million, but the law did not provide for continuing the GAO audit. FDIC fully repaid the government on August 30, 1948; thereafter, because FDIC had no government funds, GAO had no statutory authority to audit it. In 1949, however, FDIC voluntarily requested GAO to do an audit for fiscal year 1949. During this audit, FDIC declined to provide GAO access to the records of its Examination Division on the basis of "confidentiality," even though GAO had had access to these records during its previous audits.

In 1950, legislation came before Congress providing for an annual GAO audit of FDIC, as Warren had earlier recommended, even though the corporation had no government funds. Warren was on record as favoring GAO audits of some such corporations as being highly in the public interest. The terms of the bill were almost identical to corresponding sections of the Government Corporation Control Act, but Warren considered certain provisions objectionable because they would qualify GAO's authority to perform a completely independent audit. Eventually, FDIC, GAO, and staff of the Senate Banking and Currency Committee agreed on revisions to the bill to satisfy GAO's objections. The final legislation, signed on September 21, 1950, provided for an unrestricted GAO audit of the FDIC.[35] The FDIC case is an interesting example of continued GAO audit, eventually on a statutory basis, of a corporation that normally would not be subject to auditing on the basis of the Government Corporation Control Act.

The Commodity Credit Corporation

The audits of CCC activities were another example of CAD's work. A 1944 law, authorizing a commercial-type audit, gave GAO its original mandate to audit CCC, a wholly owned government corporation under the Department of Agriculture. It acted for the Department of Agriculture as the administrator of price

---

[35]Fenton, "The Corporation Audits Division—Its Legacy to the Seventies," 101; letter, Warren to Sen. John L. McClellan, chairman, Senate Committee on Expenditures in the Executive Departments, February 10, 1950, 342 MS 684; letter, Warren to Sen. Joseph L. Flanders, May 20, 1947, 309 MS 1455; letter, Warren to Rep. Brent Spence, chairman, House Committee on Banking and Currency, July 10, 1950, 347 MS 379; and letter, Warren to Frederick J. Lawton, director, Bureau of the Budget, September 20, 1950, 348 MS 982.

support programs and extended loans and arranged purchase agreements with farmers who produced commodities under price supports. The Government Corporation Control Act supplanted the 1944 law as the basis for GAO's audits of CCC.[36]

GAO did not issue its report on the first CCC audit until March 1949. This audit, covering activities to June 30, 1945, concluded that CCC had deviated widely from sound accounting practices and had substantial errors and arrearages in its record keeping. Its internal auditing activities and system of internal controls were grossly deficient. GAO's report also disclosed that because of poor records, $350 million of accounts receivable could not be verified and that CCC's grain purchase program was wasteful and lacked proper financial records.[37]

This 1949 report attracted much attention in Congress and created tension between GAO and the Department of Agriculture. Shortly after the report's publication, GAO began a routine annual audit of several CCC midwestern offices, working out of Minneapolis. This audit, directed by Robert L. Rasor of CAD, examined the grain purchase program operated by CCC's Minneapolis office. Eventually the GAO Office of Investigations looked more deeply into CCC's grain purchase activities. In April 1952, GAO issued a detailed report on the matter, which the Senate Committee on Agriculture and Forestry discussed extensively at hearings. Although the committee generally accepted GAO's conclusions, the CCC and the Department of Agriculture continued to disagree with GAO. Rasor, the GAO auditor most involved in this series of events, concluded that GAO's work had eventually resulted in improvement in the CCC's grain purchase procedures and record keeping.

In later years, relationships between GAO and CCC improved. At the time, however, the dispute between GAO and CCC and the Department of Agriculture rose to the level of Comptroller General Warren and the secretary of agriculture. William A. MacArthur, an official of the Grain Branch of the Production and Marketing Administration, for which CCC served as financial agent, was very critical of GAO's reports on the grain purchases: "The GAO never knew what they were doing; they came in wanting to see this paper and that, recommending this and that, criticizing, insinuating—and as always, years after the event . . . . Of course those recommendations that the GAO made about 'procedure' don't mean

[36]Gerald C. Schulsinger and Thomas C. Perry, "Commodity Credit Corporation Audit (1949)," in Erasmus H. Kloman, ed., *Cases in Accountability: The Work of the GAO* (Boulder CO: Westview Press, 1979), 125-26.

[37]Schulsinger and Perry, "Commodity Credit Corporation Audit (1949)," 127-28; and *Audit Report on the Examination of Commodity Credit Corporation*, letter from the comptroller general of the United States transmitting a report on the examination of Commodity Credit Corporation for the period ended June 30, 1945, 81st Cong., 1st Sess., H. Doc. 148 (Washington: GPO, 1949).

a thing. They always want 'procedure' over there so that they can check off what you did like entries on an account book. You can't work that way."[38]

The Reconstruction Finance Corporation

One of the first reports of the Corporation Audits Division dealt with RFC. The report, very critical of RFC and its operations, attracted considerable public attention and led to a series of congressional hearings. GAO's reports on RFC during Warren's tenure provide the basis for a revealing case study of the conduct of corporation audits by GAO and the problems disclosed by these audits. According to one GAO observer, the first RFC report, released in June 1946, established congressional confidence in CAD and confirmed the wisdom of Congress in subjecting government corporations to annual investigation and control.[39]

The Hoover administration created RFC in 1932 to make loans to banks, savings and loan institutions, mortgage companies, credit unions, and railroads. By the 1940s, it was a very large agency. It served as the parent organization of many Depression-fighting agencies and corporations—such as the Home Owners' Loan Corporation and the Federal Farm Mortgage Association—and wartime agencies—including, among many, the Defense Plant Corporation, the Rubber Reserve Company, and the Metals Reserve Company. By 1940, RFC had loaned over $8 billion to various financial institutions and other private businesses and provided many billions more to support defense production during World War II.[40]

From the time of its founding in 1932, RFC was responsible for its own accounting and auditing. In 1943, both Warren and Secretary of Commerce Jesse H. Jones, who headed RFC also, expressed interest in a GAO audit of RFC activities, and their staffs discussed draft legislation to make an audit possible. At the same time, Warren talked to Jonathan Daniels, administrative assistant to President Roosevelt, about the desirability of an audit of RFC. Daniels sent Warren for his comments a draft memorandum to the president recommending a GAO audit. Daniels noted the widespread foreign operations of RFC, citing examples such as the Defense Supplies Corporation, the Metals Reserve Company, the Rubber

---

[38]Schulsinger and Perry, "Commodity Credit Corporation Audit (1949)," 129-32 (quote on 132). An even more-detailed account by Schulsinger, "The Grain Purchase Case," is in *The General Accounting Office: Two Glimpses*, Inter-University Case Program, ICP Case Series: Number 35 (University, AL: University of Alabama Press, 1956).

[39]Fenton, "The Corporation Audits Division—Its Legacy to the Seventies," 98.

[40]For a useful brief history of RFC, see James S. Olson, "Reconstruction Finance Corporation (RFC)," 462-66, in Donald R. Whitnah, ed., *Government Agencies* (Westport, CT: Greenwood Press, 1983). See also Olson, *Herbert Hoover and the Reconstruction Finance Corporation, 1931-1933* (Ames, IA: Iowa State University Press, 1977), and Jesse H. Jones, *Fifty Billion Dollars: My Thirteen Years with the RFC (1932-1945)* (New York: Da Capo Press, 1975 [originally published in 1951]).

Development Corporation, and the U.S. Commercial Company. Daniels wrote to the president, "One day, I am sure, their costly operations abroad will be subject to scrutiny, probably by enemies of the administration. For that and other reasons it seems to me that it would be prudent now to require these corporations to render accounts to the General Accounting Office."[41]

RFC did not become subject to GAO audits until the passage of the George Act and the Government Corporation Control Act in 1945. The RFC audit was among the first started by the Corporation Audits Division when it began its work in the fall of 1945. In June 1946, CAD director Andrews wrote a long letter to the RFC board of directors on GAO's initial effort to audit the corporation for fiscal year 1945. Copies of this letter, characterized by GAO as an interim report, went to the speaker of the House, the president of the Senate, and President Harry S. Truman.

Andrews told the RFC board that CAD, after working on RFC for eight months, could not complete a satisfactory audit for fiscal year 1945 and could not certify the financial statements of RFC companies as of June 30, 1945. "The RFC and its affiliated companies," Andrews wrote, "have not developed an adequate concept of the control of financial and operating responsibilities through accounting." Andrews explained the problems GAO had found in RFC. For example, the balance sheet of the Defense Plant Corporation, an RFC unit, showed an investment of about $7 billion in plant properties as of June 30, 1945, but did not show how much was invested in individual plants or land. The Defense Plant Corporation, GAO contended, had not determined for any of its 2,500 plant projects "that it has a reliable record which reports in identifiable detail the items of property comprising its investments." The interim report included many other examples of problems GAO discovered. GAO concluded that RFC could realize large savings in expense and effort and improve its management effectiveness greatly if it merged all its activities and subsidiaries "into an integrated structure under a single management" and standardized and simplified operating methods, including reporting, record keeping, and accounting practices.

GAO recommended that RFC create the position of controller and "adopt the policy of maintaining proper accounting control over all its activities through reporting and record-keeping procedures which are effective at the locations at which the operating responsibilities are carried out." Finally, GAO recommended

---

[41]Letter, Warren to the secretary of commerce (Jones), May 31, 1943, 261 MS 2200; and letter, Daniels to Warren, June 19, 1943, Warren Papers, Folder 391.

that RFC change its board of directors into a policy-making body and center operating responsibility in an executive group headed by a general manager.[42]

Shortly after receiving the interim report on RFC, the House Committee on Expenditures in the Executive Departments held hearings on it. Along with Andrews, Frank H. Weitzel, assistant to the comptroller general, represented Warren, who was ill at the time. Weitzel discussed the history of RFC, emphasizing its gradual expansion, while Andrews dealt with the details of the RFC report. Andrews observed that "accounting is a responsibility of management." For RFC, "important aspects of accounting not only were faulty but also were deficient, and these conditions have persisted for such a period that we feel that the possibility of serious consequences is substantial." That was why, Andrews explained, Warren felt that it was necessary to inform Congress immediately about the problem. GAO was not saying that RFC had significant losses. Rather, GAO "stated clearly that in some of the most important aspects of the corporation's affairs, the management had not given a satisfactory account of its stewardship and that as to very large amounts of funds the Corporation obviously had 'rendered itself incapable of ever making a satisfactory accounting.'"

The two main groups of problems at RFC concerned defense plants and strategic and critical materials. RFC had generally failed to account for defense plant physical property, and it had never properly accounted for strategic and critical materials. Andrews concluded that RFC's accounting difficulties were the result of "a fundamental weakness in the organization of the corporation—a lack of coordination and integration of accounting responsibility."[43]

RFC representatives defended their organization and contested GAO's conclusions. In its report after the hearing, the committee made several findings. It concluded that RFC accounting for its nonlending activities was inadequate and deficient, as reported by the comptroller general and as confirmed by RFC testimony at the hearings. Accounting was a very important management responsibility, but RFC officials had failed to carry out this duty satisfactorily. A satisfactory audit of RFC affairs was impossible until the corporation's accounting was adequate, accurate, and up-to-date. The committee also concluded that GAO's letter to RFC "was framed with restraint and fairness" and that GAO was trying

---

[42]The above information about the RFC audit is from "Communication from Corporation Audits Division, General Accounting Office, to the Reconstruction Finance Corporation," letter from Comptroller General of the United States Transmitting Copy of a Communication Dated June 17, 1946, from the Corporation Audits Division of the General Accounting Office to the Board of Directors of Reconstruction Finance Corporation, 79th Cong., 2d Sess., H. Doc. 674, copy in B-58302, #1.

[43]Weitzel and Andrews testimony, July 2, 1946, House Committee on Expenditures in the Executive Departments, copies of statements in ibid.

to be "constructively helpful." RFC, the committee said, should accept GAO's aid and recommendations.[44]

Warren's strong conviction on the need to send the interim report to inform Congress about RFC's problems is clear in a letter he wrote to Rep. George H. Bender (R—Ohio). "I shall send no report up to Congress that will not stand up 100%. The interim report on R.F.C. was on my desk a week before it was transmitted, and it was checked and analyzed from every angle. When I had assured myself of its correctness, I knew my duty was very plain that I should send it on up. It is to be regretted that the R.F.C. did not accept it in a spirit of co-operation and set about to remedy the constructive criticisms we made."[45]

Eventually RFC representatives met with GAO officials to discuss the report. John D. Goodloe, general counsel; Henry T. Bodman, a director; and Henry A. Mulligan of RFC met with Warren; Andrews; Weitzel; E. L. Fisher, GAO's general counsel; and others on August 8, 1946. Bodman explained that RFC planned to hire the public accounting firm of Ernst and Ernst to survey RFC's operating and accounting policies and procedures. Warren expressed regret that RFC was proposing in this way "to go over the same ground" covered in GAO's interim report. Andrews felt that since GAO had criticized RFC's accounting and operating procedures and the House Committee had sustained this position, RFC's hiring of Ernst and Ernst might lead to further controversy and would be a waste of RFC funds. The RFC representatives denied that they wanted to use Ernst and Ernst to defend RFC's position; they pledged to cooperate with GAO and said that they would use the firm to implement the Office's recommendations and "to find out the best method of bringing their books into line with accepted accounting principles as set out in the interim report of the Comptroller General."[46] Warren thought that this meeting had been productive and perhaps would lead to good things eventually. He also was pleased when he learned in September 1946 that RFC had created the position of controller, as GAO had recommended.[47]

Ultimately GAO issued its fiscal year 1945 report on RFC in ten parts, the last one released in November 1948. Volume I, a letter from Andrews to Warren, with 104 pages of text plus appendixes, was a report summarizing GAO's findings. When GAO released this letter in mid-June 1947, RFC was due to expire on June 30, 1947. GAO based its recommendations on the assumption that RFC

---

[44]"Report of the House Expenditures Committee on Comptroller General's Interim Report on Audit of RFC," July 31, 1946 (4 pp., mimeographed), copy in ibid.

[45]Letter, Warren to Bender, July 12, 1946, Warren Papers, Folder 416.

[46]Letter, Goodloe to Warren, August 2, 1946, B-58302, #1 (reporting plan to hire Ernst and Ernst); and Weitzel, memorandum for the file, August 8, 1946, ibid. (summarizing the meeting of RFC and GAO officials).

[47]Letter, Warren to Rep. Carter Manasco, September 23, 1946, ibid.

would be extended, as it was. In the report, Andrews reiterated GAO's earlier criticisms of RFC's accounting and reporting procedures. RFC's financial statements were on a cash basis, reporting only transactions that had resulted in the spending or the receipt of cash. The amounts of assets, liabilities, revenues, and expenses had either been omitted or improperly classified in RFC financial statements and were not determinable. Also, RFC generally did not provide for depreciation of its properties or physical loss, destruction, or inventory shrinkage.

GAO also noted the difficulty of understanding RFC's financial statements because of the way RFC kept accounts of its war activities (during the war, RFC had acted as the agent for executive departments and agencies). Also, RFC's internal audits had been defective. GAO could not certify that RFC's financial statements fairly presented the corporation's financial position or the results of its operations as of June 30, 1945.

GAO proposed that RFC be set up as a separate corporation independent of executive agencies. Again GAO recommended that RFC's board of directors be a policy-making and general supervisory body that delegated operational responsibility to a general manager. RFC's war subsidiaries, such as the Rubber Development Corporation and the U.S. Commercial Company, should be liquidated, as well as its loan agency subsidiaries. Congress should consider prohibiting RFC from serving as an intermediary for agencies borrowing from the government. In 1942, GAO pointed out, RFC borrowed more than $1.2 billion from the public, "the purpose and effect of which was to relieve the borrowing requirements of the United States Treasury at a time when the public debt was approaching its statutory limit." RFC should be restricted to borrowing from the Treasury, GAO suggested. Such loans should be made at interest rates equal to those at which the Treasury borrowed the funds so that RFC accounts reflected the full cost to the government of RFC activities.[48]

John D. Goodloe, chairman of RFC in 1947, commended Warren and CAD "for the harmonious and constructive relationship" that existed between the division and the corporation and spoke highly of the personal and professional qualifications of Andrews and others in CAD. But RFC defended itself in hearings and other forums. Goodloe was upset about harsh criticisms of RFC in the press following release of GAO's report. He wrote to Warren in December 1947, "in view of the fact that the press handles anew

---

[48]*Report on Audit of Reconstruction Finance Corporation and Affiliated Corporations*, Letter from the Comptroller General of the United States Transmitting a Report on the Audit . . . for the Fiscal Year Ended June 30, 1945, vol. I, June 11, 1947, H. Doc. 316, 80th Cong., 1st Sess. (Washington: GPO, 1947), copy in ibid.

each volume of the GAO report when filed, I am thankful that it did not consist of more than ten volumes and that by now there remain to be transmitted to the Congress only four more volumes!"[49] Jesse Jones, who in his position as federal loan administrator had headed RFC during World War II, was more direct in his criticism, saying that GAO's charges were "largely unjustified." A Washington newspaper quoted Jones as saying, "During the depression we [RFC] could not have awaited the pleasure of a technical and autocratic GAO. That would have been equally true as to RFC defense and war activities. . . ."[50]

GAO's recommendations on RFC significantly affected legislation (61 Stat. 202) signed on June 30, 1947, extending RFC's life, and RFC's continuing operations. The statute transferred the assets and the liabilities of one of RFC's loan agency subsidiaries, the RFC Mortgage Company, to RFC, and the company itself was soon dissolved. RFC was restricted to borrowing from the U.S. Treasury. Although RFC did not place responsibility for operations in an executive group headed by a general manager, contrary to what GAO had recommended, it did delegate specific responsibilities to the heads of three new units—offices for loans, production, and war activity liquidation—constituting some management improvement. Other acts passed in 1947 and 1948 prohibited RFC from using any of its own or its subsidiaries' money for the benefit of any government agency unless that agency had legal authority and available appropriations to reimburse RFC for funds advanced. RFC made other changes responding to GAO suggestions and recommendations.[51]

In its RFC audit report for fiscal years 1946 and 1947, GAO commended the corporation "for its open-mindedness in considering the recommendations [in the fiscal year 1945 report] and for the aggressive manner in which it has acted in putting the recommendations into effect." GAO made several additional proposals to improve RFC. It noted that RFC, in its lending activities, had had the use of government money at low interest rates or interest free as well as support from other government agencies for some services and employee benefits. RFC's financial statements would provide a fairer statement of the financial results of lending activities if these costs were included. GAO calculated that if this had been done, the reported $46.3 million RFC income in 1946 and 1947 would

---

[49]Letter, Goodloe to Warren, June 17, 1947, ibid.; letter, Goodloe to Rep. George H. Bender, December 5, 1947, B-58302, #2; and letter, Goodloe to Warren, December 23, 1947, ibid.

[50]Clipping, *Washington Evening Star*, January 22, 1948, ibid.

[51]*Report on Audit of Reconstruction Finance Corporation and Subsidiaries*, Letter from the Comptroller General of the United States Transmitting the Report on the Audit . . . for the Fiscal Years Ended June 30, 1946 and 1947 . . ., H. Doc. 468, 81st Cong., 2d Sess. (Washington: GPO, 1950), appendix A, "Recommendations Included in Report on Audit of Reconstruction Finance Corporation and Subsidiaries for the Fiscal Year Ended June 30, 1945, and Actions Taken by the Congress and by the Corporation with Respect Thereto," copy in B-58302, #1.

have been eliminated and 1947 operations alone would have produced a net loss. GAO recommended that Congress pass legislation requiring RFC to pay interest on government investments in its activities and to pay the costs incurred by other agencies for RFC's benefit.

GAO proposed that RFC be financed only by revolving funds appropriated by Congress, "in the interest of financial control by the Congress and simplification of financing methods in the Government." GAO also recommended that RFC money come from interest-bearing advances from revolving funds appropriated in advance for specific purposes. Another recommendation related to RFC's involvement during World War II in building and operating war plants, purchase of critical materials, and other defense programs, as a cost of over $9 billion. These activities, a departure from RFC's original mission to provide loans to private and public enterprises, were "neither necessary nor desirable." GAO recommended that Congress transfer such present activities, or future nonlending activities authorized by Congress, to existing or new agencies concerned primarily with such activities. GAO also recommended that two foreign loans that RFC administered—a 1941 loan to the United Kingdom and Northern Ireland with a balance of over $187 million and a 1947 loan to the Philippines with a balance of $60 million—be transferred to a more-suitable agency, such as the Export-Import Bank.[52]

As in its report for 1945, GAO indicated that "because of the deficiencies in accounting and internal control," it could not say that RFC's financial statements presented fairly the position of RFC and its subsidiaries as of June 30, 1947. GAO did note RFC's actions in correcting deficiencies and improving its accounting system, but the new system had not been in operation long enough to evaluate its effectiveness in this report. GAO stated its belief that "a more prompt and accurate recording and a more effective review of financial transactions is resulting."[53]

GAO's subsequent RFC audit reports showed gradual improvement in the corporation's accounting practices and preparation of financial statements. GAO finally was able to state for the first time, in its report for fiscal year 1950, that RFC's lending activity and nonlending activity financial statements fairly presented its financial position.[54] GAO's reports between 1946 and 1950 continued to make recommendations on RFC's lending and other

---

[52]*Report on Audit of Reconstruction Finance Corporation and Subsidiaries* . . . for the Fiscal Years Ended June 30, 1946 and 1947 . . ., 9-10.

[53]Ibid., 17.

[54]*Report on Audit of Reconstruction Finance Corporation and Its Wholly Owned Subsidiary Federal National Mortgage Association,* Letter from the Comptroller General of the United States Transmitting Report on the Audit . . . for the Fiscal Year Ended June 30, 1950, H. Doc. 125, 82d Cong., 1st Sess. (Washington: GPO, 1951), 15.

activities and its financing. In the report covering fiscal years 1948 and 1949, GAO repeated earlier recommendations that RFC include in its financial statement, among other things, the cost of interest on the government funds it used to "facilitate congressional determination of whether the corporation's lending activities are self-sustaining." GAO noted in this report that it had observed during its audits certain RFC accounting procedures and practices that could be improved. Direct discussions between GAO and the RFC controller's office had resulted in many of GAO's recommendations in this area being put into effect.[55]

In its fiscal year 1950 RFC report, GAO recommended reducing the substantial funds in RFC's possession. It proposed that RFC's $100 million capital stock and $230 millon of retained accumulated net income be paid into the U.S. Treasury. Thereafter RFC's financing would be in the form of interest-bearing advances from a revolving fund appropriated by Congress. If this suggestion was implemented, RFC's retained accumulated income would be reduced to $20 million and any net income over this amount would be paid into the Treasury after the end of each fiscal year. GAO recommended also that RFC transfer the Federal Housing Administration (FHA) and Veterans Administration (VA) mortgages it held, valued at about $100 million, to the Housing and Home Finance Administration, placing in one agency all FHA and VA mortgages held by the government.[56]

One other issue related to the RFC audit during this period was the audit of transportation charges paid by the corporation during World War II. Several RFC subsidiaries, including the Defense Supplies Corporation, the Metal Reserves Company, and the Defense Plant Corporation, typically paid the full rates instead of the lower land-grant rates applicable to the transport in railroad land-grant areas of materials for military and naval use during the war.[57] When later RFC conducted its internal audit of these charges, the proper rate had to be calculated and applied, leading to attempts to collect refunds from the carriers. GAO identified RFC's failure to show the lower land-grant rates in its fiscal year 1945 RFC report and, in subsequent reports, reviewed the slow progress of RFC's effort to recover overpayments.[58]

---

[55]*Report on Audit of Reconstruction Finance Corporation and Its Wholly Owned Subsidiary Federal National Mortgage Corporation*, Letter from the Comptroller General Transmitting the Report on the Audit . . . for the Fiscal Years Ended June 30, 1948 and 1949 . . ., H. Doc. 638, 81st Cong., 2d Sess. (Washington: GPO, 1950), 9-10.

[56]*Report on Audit of Reconstruction Finance Corporation and Its Wholly Owned Subsidiary Federal National Mortgage Association*, Letter from the Comptroller General of the United States Transmitting Report on the Audit . . for the Fiscal Year Ended June 30, 1950, 12.

[57]See chapter 11, pp. 266-73, for a discussion of GAO's work on World War II transportation charges.

[58]Statement by Theodore Herz, assistant director of CAD, before the Subcommittee on Procurement and Buildings, House Committee on Expenditures in the Executive Departments, December 4, 1947, attached to letter, Warren to Sen. George D. Aiken, May 19, 1948, B-58302, #2; and letter, Warren to chairman, RFC board of directors, March 28, 1951, B-58302, #3.

One problem RFC had when auditing its transportation charges after World War II was lack of sufficient staff to calculate the applicable land-grant rates. In 1948, GAO agreed to calculate and provide to RFC a large number of rates for specific shipments; RFC was to reimburse GAO for the cost of this work.[59] Even with this assistance, the RFC transportation audits proceeded very slowly. In early 1951, Warren observed to the RFC chairman that at the current rate, it would take RFC from five to seven more years to complete the World War II transportation audit. He also noted that GAO had information that RFC had decreased considerably the number of staff working on the audit. In response to Warren's request that he be advised on RFC's position on the audit, the RFC chairman reported that the corporation had increased the transportation audit staff and estimated that within one year, all claims would be computed, would be filed with the railroads, and would be in the process of collection.[60]

RFC's corrective efforts did not solve the problem of the lagging transportation audit. The RFC administrator reported in mid-1952 that RFC had recovered $8,774,000 from unclaimed land-grant deductions and estimated that $3.5 to $4 millon remained to be recovered. Two years later, RFC, according to its own calculations, still had claims to be filed amounting to between $4 million and $5 million on a backlog of 150,000 freight bills. At this time, GAO agreed again to help RFC establish the proper rates and land-grant deductions for the RFC claims. RFC itself would prepare and transmit to carriers the claims developed by GAO and process collections.[61]

These events illustrate what sometimes occurred when GAO identified problems in its audits—GAO worked with the audited agencies to find solutions to the problems. In two separate periods, during 1948 and again in 1954, GAO supplied technical assistance and staff time to RFC, on a reimbursable basis, to help the corporation reduce the backlog of World War II transportation claims. To the extent that RFC settled these claims before GAO's own final audit of RFC accounts, GAO's work was simplified and criticism of RFC in its audit reports decreased.[62]

---

[59]Letter, Warren to Goodloe, March 23, 1948, 319 MS 2213; and letter, Warren to Aiken, May 19, 1948, B-58302, #2.

[60]Letter, Warren to the chairman, RFC board of directors, March 28, 1951, B-58302, #3; and letter, W. E. Harber to Warren, April 26, 1951, ibid.

[61]Letter, Harry A. McDonald, RFC administrator, to Warren, July 23, 1952, ibid.; letter, Laurence B. Robbins, assistant to the secretary of the Treasury (on RFC letterhead) to Weitzel, acting comptroller general, July 30, 1954, ibid.; and letter, Weitzel to Robbins, August 6, 1954, ibid.

[62]Congress passed the RFC Liquidation Act in 1953, transferred RFC's loan powers to the Small Business Administration in 1954, and abolished RFC in 1957, after a lifetime of 25 years. See Olson, "Reconstruction Finance Corporation (RFC)," 466.

CAD's Maritime Commission Reports

The history of GAO's first audits of the U.S. Maritime Commission, created in 1936, and of its predecessor, the Shipping Board, has been recounted earlier.[63] During World War II, the Maritime Commission undertook the tremendous task of mobilizing the nation's merchant fleet to transport military personnel and war materials. The amount of money involved in these activities was very large, leading to a heavy audit burden. GAO had to carry the work of auditing the Maritime Commission's wartime activities into the postwar period, as well as cope with the organization's current activities.

In 1947, GAO transferred the Maritime Commission audit from its Audit Division to CAD. The maritime audits were similar to those required under the Government Corporation Control Act—commercial-type audits of the books and the records of the organization.[64] While the Maritime Commission was not a government corporation, in terms of GAO audits it was practically indistinguishable from government corporations. In fact, the Maritime Commission audit was one of the most difficult and widely publicized activities of the Corporation Audits Division. Ted B. Westfall, a public accountant brought into the Corporation Audits Division in 1946, directed GAO's audits of the Maritime Commission.[65] Westfall and other leaders at GAO, including Warren and Frank Weitzel, Warren's assistant at the time, thought that the old voucher-type audit was inadequate and that GAO had to move beyond it to get useful information. Furthermore, Westfall did not think that a commercial-type audit, which he described as a "balance sheet audit in the traditional sense where you certify the financial statements," was what was needed. "That is not the kind of audit the government needs, and that was not the kind of audit I ran over at Maritime." He emphasized investigation and fact-finding and reported serious problems when he was certain he had the facts to back them up.[66]

During World War II, GAO's audits of the Maritime Commission brought some serious problems to light. For example, in August 1942, Warren reported to Congress on a series of transactions between the Maritime Commission and the Waterman Steamship Corporation of Mobile, Alabama. In

---

[63]See chapter 9, pp. 209-11.

[64]Weitzel testimony, December 11, 1947, *Independent Offices Appropriation Bill for 1949*, Hearings before a Subcommittee of the House Committee on Appropriations, 80th Cong., 2d Sess. (Washington: GPO, 1948), 99.

[65]To a large degree because of his work on the Maritime Commission audits, Westfall became director of GAO's large new consolidated Audit Division in 1952, giving him responsibility for more than 3,400 of GAO's total staff of about 6,000. See GAO, *Ted B. Westfall, 1946-1952*, History Program, Oral History Series, GAO/OP-2-OH (Washington: 1988). Westfall left GAO in April 1952 to assume a position at Grace Line, Inc. Later he moved to International Telephone and Telegraph (ITT), where eventually he became executive vice president and director.

[66]GAO, *Ted B. Westfall, 1946-1952*, 8, 22, 31.

June 1940, the commission sold to Waterman five obsolete vessels, all built in 1920, for $596,000, with an option to repurchase the ships at the sale price plus improvements less depreciation. In late 1941 and 1942, the commission bought five other vessels, built in 1919 and 1920, from Waterman at a cost of $3,374,700, instead of exercising its option to repurchase the vessels sold to Waterman in 1940. The company claimed that it had improved the ships sold to the Maritime Commission in the amount of $783,097.32. This amount plus the $596,000 paid for the five other ships amounted to $1,379,097.32; Waterman's profit on the two transactions was $1,995,602.68. Furthermore, GAO reported, Waterman established a construction reserve fund under the Merchant Marine Act of 1936 for this amount, thus avoiding income tax on it "on the theory and apparent promise that said fund would be used in the construction of new vessels for addition to the American merchant marine. . . ." GAO contended that Waterman's profit from the transactions violated the Merchant Marine Act and a 1941 law providing that vessels be acquired at fair and reasonable prices. GAO was also disturbed by the fact that the former general counsel of the Maritime Commission had represented Waterman before the commission in regard to these transactions.[67]

Warren expressed to a House committee chairman concern about the inadequacies of the commission's accounting system in 1946, shortly before GAO issued its 1943 audit report. The report disclosed many accounting errors and operational problems, involving substantial amounts of money. Knowing that Congress recently passed the Reorganization Act of 1945, Warren added that the commission should be the first executive agency to be reorganized and suggested that it be placed under a cabinet officer.[68]

At the same time, Maritime Commission officials decided to install an acceptable accounting system and asked GAO to help. Warren responded positively but suggested to Rep. John H. Cochran, who passed the information on to President Truman, that the Maritime Commission be reorganized and transferred to the Department of Commerce. Warren said that he was impressed with efforts of members of the commission to improve its accounting system but felt that the "only way to insure a permanent improvement in the organization and activities" of the commission was a reorganization under the 1945 reorganization law.[69]

---

[67]Hearing of January 18, 1943, *Independent Offices Appropriation Bill for 1944*, Hearings before a Subcommittee on Independent Offices of the House Committee on Appropriations, 78th Cong., 1st Sess. (Washington: GPO, 1943), 778-87. At this hearing, Rep. Everett M. Dirksen entered into the record GAO's report on the case, dated August 8, 1942. The text of the report is on 779-87.

[68]Letter, Warren to Rep. Schuyler O. Bland, chairman, House Committee on Merchant Marine and Fisheries, February 8, 1946, B-41801, #1.

[69]Letter, Warren to Capt. Edward Macauley, acting chairman, Maritime Commission, March 1, 1946, ibid.; letter, Warren to Cochran, March 15, 1946, ibid.; letter, Cochran to Warren, March 21, 1946, ibid.; and letter, Truman to Cochran, March 19, 1946, ibid. (copy provided to Warren by Cochran).

After Warren formally offered GAO's assistance in installing an accounting system, the commission proposed to set up a committee, including a GAO representative, to develop a system of accounts. GAO declined to participate, partly because the Maritime Commission proposed to include two independent CPAs on the committee. Yates wrote to the commission chairman that the Budget and Accounting Act, 1921, made it the duty of the comptroller general to prescribe accounting systems and that a 1914 law prohibited employing consultants (the two CPAs) in systems installations. Yates reminded the chairman, as Warren did also on occasion, that an accounting system GAO had worked out for the Maritime Commission in 1937 had been ignored by the commission.[70]

After further discussion, GAO and the Maritime Commission established a committee with three representatives from each to analyze and propose a solution to the commission's accounting problems. Subsequently Warren appointed Thomas H. Reavis, Moore Lynn, and Edwin E. Leffler as GAO members of the working committee.[71]

As this committee began its work in late 1946 and early 1947, a House bill proposed to authorize GAO to conduct a special investigation and audit of the accounts of the Maritime Commission and an affiliated agency, the War Shipping Administration,[72] from 1939 to 1947. GAO opposed the bill. Andrews wrote to Warren: "The only comment we have to offer is that if the accounts and financial records generally of these two organizations are as inadequate and inaccurate as we have heard, it is not likely that the Comptroller General or anybody else will be able to come up with the answers that the bill apparently contemplates, no matter how much auditing they might do or how long they might operate on it." Warren, in explaining why he thought the special audit would be undesirable, said that the agencies' records were not available, that it would take 1,000 auditors and accountants 2 years to assemble and review what records could be found, and that "any disclosures of price violations at this time would be of doubtful value." The special audit would cost a great deal, interfere with the current work of the Maritime Commission, and result in little actual recovery by the United States. Warren also stated that the joint GAO-Maritime Commission

---

[70]Letter, Warren to Adm. W. W. Smith, chairman, Maritime Commission, June 20, 1946, ibid.; letter, Smith to Warren, June 26, 1946, ibid.; and letter, Yates to Smith, July 12, 1946, ibid.

[71]"Meeting of Representatives of the House Committee on Merchant Marine and Fisheries, the United States Maritime Commission and the General Accounting Office, October 3, 1946, on Maritime Commission Accounting," ibid.; letter, Weitzel to J. M. Quinn, Maritime Commission, November 1, 1946, ibid.; and memorandum, Warren to Reavis, Lynn, and Leffler, November 1, 1946, ibid.

[72]The War Shipping Administration was established by Executive Order No. 9054, February 7, 1942, to take over the Maritime Commission's functions and duties of purchasing, operating, chartering, and maintaining merchant vessels. See letter, E. W. Bell, chief, GAO Audit Division, to Warren, March 19, 1947, ibid.

committee was making real progress.[73] Ultimately Congress failed to approve the bill.

The GAO-Maritime Commission accounting committee did make progress. In April 1947, it recommended to the Maritime Commission a plan to ensure the internal flow of documents to the commission's Finance Department and suggested that if the commission took immediate action, the new accounting system could be operating fully by July 1, 1947. In September 1947, Warren decided that the joint committee was no longer needed because it had made considerable headway in completing its assignment. Also, Thomas H. Reavis, the lead GAO member of the committee, had recently transferred to the Maritime Commission to head its fiscal accounting branch.[74]

As it turned out, the system was not operational by July 1947. The Maritime Commission explained that because of an agency reduction-in-force, it did not have enough accounting staff to operate the system. In discussing this matter with a House committee, Warren said: ". . . I must confess that 10 years of frustration in our dealings with the Commission in this and many other matters have just about exhausted our patience." Warren also indicated that GAO had considerable confidence in Reavis, the Maritime Commission's new fiscal officer.[75]

At annual appropriation hearings in December 1947, GAO representatives, including Frank Weitzel and Ralph B. Casey, assistant general counsel, discussed several examples of problems discovered in the Maritime Commission audit. Casey's testimony centered on the matter of contract conversion—the changing of the type of contract used to acquire merchant vessels during the war. He used the Maritime Commission's contracts with Froemming Brothers, Inc., as one of his examples. In August 1943, the Maritime Commission and Froemming signed a price-minus-type contract, under which Froemming was to construct ten ships at a fixed cost of $15,930,000 ($1,593,000 per vessel). The contract specified delivery dates for each vessel; the company was to get $200 per day for early deliveries and pay a like penalty for late deliveries. Froemming was to earn a fixed profit of $20,000 per vessel and receive 50 percent of any cost savings under the contract price for each vessel. In February 1944, a second, identical contract pro-

---

[73]Memorandum, Andrews to the comptroller general, January 24, 1947, ibid.; and letter, Warren to Rep. Clare E. Hoffman, chairman, House Committee on Expenditures in the Executive Departments, April 22, 1947, ibid.

[74]Memorandum, Joint M.C.-GAO Accounting Committee to the U.S. Maritime Commission and the comptroller general, April 17, 1947, ibid., #1; and letter, Warren to Rep. Alvin F. Weichel, chairman, House Committee on Merchant Marine and Fisheries, September 3, 1947, ibid.

[75]Warren testimony, December 11, 1947, *Independent Offices Appropriation Bill for 1949*, 120-21.

vided for constructing four more vessels. Now Froemming was to build 14 ships for $22,302,000 and a profit of $280,000.

In December 1944, Froemming and the Maritime Commission replaced the original contracts with a selective-price contract, under which Froemming would build the 14 ships (at the time five had been completed) for $30,800,000 ($2.2 million each). Under this contract, Froemming could earn greater profits on a lower-cost ship than on a more-expensive one. This inverted profits system worked to Froemming's advantage. Froemming was paid a profit of $675,000—$395,000 more than would have been paid under the old contract. GAO also reported that the Maritime Commission had permitted Froemming to "juggle" its cost over the vessels covered by the new contract "so that any saving that might have been recoverable to the Government on a particular vessel was lost, inasmuch as the contractor could apply that saving to another vessel on which his cost exceeded the price selected." The actual cost of constructing the 14 ships was $27,514,495. GAO concluded that if the accounting on this contract had been accurate, the government would have saved $1,187,395. The government's total loss—this amount plus the $395,000 extra profit—was over $1.5 million.

GAO gave the House Appropriations Committee written summaries of the cases Assistant General Counsel Casey had discussed. Casey testified that there was no evidence of illegality or fraud in these contract conversions. Although he did not think the government contract officials' conduct was justifiable, it was not illegal.[76]

GAO's continuing series of reports kept Congress informed of the serious problems of the Maritime Commission and its slowness in making improvements. In April 1948, Sen. George D. Aiken (R—Vermont), chairman of the Senate Committee on Expenditures in the Executive Departments, told Warren that he was disturbed by what he read in GAO's fiscal year 1946 and 1947 reports on the Maritime Commission and War Shipping Administration. "I was shocked to learn," Aiken wrote, "that it was virtually impossible to report on the financial condition and the result of operations of these agencies which are responsible for billions of dollars worth of Government property and funds."[77]

One of the Maritime Commission's problems was its slowness in clearing up a backlog of receivable funds, estimated at $26 million on July 1, 1947. In early 1949, Warren succeeded in fending off a proposal, backed by Rep. Albert Thomas (D—Texas) of the House Appropriations Committee,

---

[76]The account of the Froemming case is in Casey testimony, December 11, 1947, *Independent Offices Appropriation Bill for 1949*, 110-11, and a report submitted for the record, 112. Accounts of other contract conversion cases submitted for the record are on 112-15.

[77]Letter, Aiken to Warren, April 15, 1948, B-41801, #2.

that GAO take over the task of clearing up the receivables backlog. Warren argued that this was properly the work of the Maritime Commission. He added that "shifting the responsibility for administrative failures from where it belongs would tend to encourage repetition of more such failures as soon as the General Accounting Office moved out." Warren also reported that the commission was more cooperative with GAO than in the past and that GAO had recently helped it reorganize its accounting system, which Warren thought should free up some commission staff to work on the receivables problem.[78]

Another contentious issue between the Maritime Commission and GAO involved government subsidies to United States Lines for constructing and selling the superliner SS *United States*. In April 1949, the Maritime Commission contracted with United States Lines to build the ship at a cost of $76,800,000. According to the Merchant Marine Act of 1936, which allowed construction subsidies to U.S.-owned companies calculated on the difference between costs in foreign and domestic shipyards and on features of the vessel designed for "national defense uses," U.S. Lines was to pay about $28 million of the total cost of the SS *United States*. The plan was for the government to turn the vessel over to U.S. Lines for commercial use when it was completed. After the commission and U.S. Lines agreed to the contract, Comptroller General Warren charged that the subsidies and defense allowances in the contract violated the Merchant Marine Act because they were excessive. Warren directed the withholding of about $8.7 million from what was due U.S. Lines as security on the company's indebtedness to the United States. Then the company sued in the Court of Claims to recover the retained money, and the government filed a counterclaim.[79]

Settlement of the controversy over the SS *United States* did not come until 1954. In the meantime, the Maritime Commission was reorganized. In 1950, under Reorganization Plan No. 21, President Truman divided the commission into two new agencies headed by one administrator, the Maritime Administration and the Federal Maritime Board, both located in the Department of Commerce.[80] Warren, the maritime administrator, and the secretary

---

[78]Letter, Warren to Thomas, March 21, 1949, ibid. See also Weitzel testimony, January 27, 1950, *Independent Offices Appropriation for 1951*, Hearings before a Subcommittee of the House Committee on Appropriations, 81st Cong., 2d Sess., pt. 1 (Washington: GPO, 1950), 891-93, for information on the Maritime Commission's progress in collecting receivables. Weitzel testified that the actual amount of receivables was $21,878,000.

[79]See Press Release, Department of Justice, May 18, 1954, copy in Warren Papers, Folder 478, for a summary of the background of the case. See also Frank H. Weitzel, "Lindsay Carter Warren: Comptroller General of the United States, 1940-1954," *GAO Review* (spring 1977): 17-18, for an account of the matter. Although the government withheld $8.7 million from U.S. Lines, Warren frequently used the figure $10 million as owed to the government by U.S. Lines.

[80]See Lane C. Kendall, "Federal Maritime Commission (FMC)," in Donald R. Whitnah, ed., *Government Agencies* (Westport, CT, and London: Greenwood Press, 1983), 232.

of commerce engaged in a public dispute between 1949 and the 1954 settlement. In 1952, when U.S. Lines completed construction of the ship, Secretary of Commerce Charles Sawyer turned it over to the company. When Warren in congressional testimony criticized Sawyer's plan to transfer the ship, Sawyer complained; Warren's statement, he argued, "was obviously for the purpose of creating a public impression that the Comptroller General, a knight in white armor, is defending the taxpayers from some nefarious plot to which I and the Maritime Board are parties." Sawyer also suggested that Warren was trying to scare him into refusing to implement the government's contract with U.S. Lines. Sawyer insisted that the contract was valid and that it was his duty to go ahead with it.[81]

President Truman wrote to the attorney general in June 1952 that transfer of the ship to U.S. Lines did not end the question of what constituted proper payment and soon thereafter directed the secretary of commerce to execute the subsidy agreements with U.S. Lines only if the company agreed to the withholding of $10 million until the attorney general had time to study the matter.[82] Warren wrote to a North Carolina newspaper editor explaining his position: "It is as plain as A, B, C. The ship cost $78 million. The company pays $28 million and the taxpayers $50 million. This office contends that there was a clear overpayment of approximately $10 million, completely excluding national defense features which we are convinced have been grossly overcharged. We contend that it is not a binding contract because the law was almost completely ignored in the making of it, and that the taxpayers of this country should not have to pay this overcharge."[83]

The SS *United States* case dragged on until May 18, 1954, when Attorney General Herbert Brownell, Jr., announced a settlement. U.S. Lines agreed to pay the government an additional $4 million for the ship.[84] On his last day in office, April 30, 1954, Warren had approved the settlement that the attorney general announced 18 days later, even though U.S. Lines paid $6 million less than what he thought the company owed to the government.[85]

Conclusions

The passage of the George Act and the Government Corporation Control Act in 1945 was extremely important to the future of GAO. The laws, in authorizing annual audits of government corporations, provided the first significant mea-

---

[81]Letter, Sawyer to Rep. John F. Shelley, June 20, 1952, copy in Warren Papers, Scrapbooks, vol. 16.

[82]Letter, Warren to Shelley, July 1, 1952, with attachments: letter, Truman to the attorney general, June 20, 1952, and letter, Truman to the secretary of commerce, June 28, 1952, ibid.

[83]Letter, Warren to H. Galt Braxton, Kinston, NC, June 25, 1952, Warren Papers, Folder 447.

[84]Press Release, Department of Justice, May 18, 1954, Warren Papers, Folder 478.

[85]Weitzel, "Lindsay Carter Warren," 18.

sure of congressional control over the more than 100 such organizations existing in 1945. From the beginning, the comptrollers general had recognized that the lack of GAO audit jurisdiction over government corporations had led, in some cases, to poor accounting practices and, most importantly, to the absence of accountability to a higher authority, specifically the Congress. Comptroller General McCarl had first raised pointed complaints about the fiscal practices and the lack of accountability of government corporations in the 1920s. His successors—Acting Comptroller General Richard N. Elliott and Comptrollers General Fred H. Brown and Warren—echoed his indictment. The proliferation of government corporations during the New Deal and World War II along with Warren's influence with Congress, as a prominent former member of the House of Representatives, helped pave the way to government corporation control legislation in 1945. The Government Corporation Control Act not only gave to GAO an important new audit function but also, through the experience of the corporation audits, it was a critical factor in leading to extensive changes in the theory and practice of GAO audits in general.

One result of the corporation audits was the start of an era of professionalization in GAO. Before establishment of the Corporation Audits Division in 1945, the majority of GAO's staff were not highly trained and skilled professionals. Other than the lawyers in the Office of the General Counsel and the leaders of divisions and staff offices, GAO staff were essentially clerks—their work involved checking vouchers or performing other duties that did not require a high degree of technical skill or professional training. The Corporation Audits Division, headed by T. Coleman Andrews, a leader in the national accounting profession, recruited its professional staff, including a large number of CPAs, from public accounting firms, colleges, and universities. Ted Westfall, one of these recruits, who headed the Maritime Commission audits, eventually rose to the top auditing position in GAO.[86]

The nature of corporation audits, which GAO's staff in 1945 were not qualified to undertake, necessitated the recruiting effort. Its impact on GAO over the next two decades was profound; gradually GAO became a professionally oriented organization, staffed mainly by accountants, replacing the earlier conglomeration of clerks.

Also, CAD's work contributed to a movement to improve the structure and the methods of accounting in the federal government. Many of GAO's corporation audits disclosed serious problems in accounting and record keeping in government corporations. Despite earlier efforts by GAO to develop

---

[86]See chapter 14, pp. 343-46.

and prescribe a uniform accounting system for the federal government, the situation after World War II was not much improved. Warren, partially because of his experience with corporation audits—those of the Reconstruction Finance Corporation, for example—assumed leadership by the late 1940s, in cooperation with the executive branch, in a campaign to improve financial management in the federal government.[87]

GAO's experience with corporation audits also definitely affected the Office's approach to audits in general, leading to what Warren termed the "comprehensive audit." GAO departed from the old voucher-checking approach typical of the years before 1945 and moved to site audits concerned with program economy and efficiency, as well as correct financial data. The corporation audits proved to be a laboratory for the new GAO audit approach of the 1950s and beyond.[88]

GAO's corporation audit reports, although at times controversial, enhanced GAO's reputation, with both the public and Congress. The audit reports on the Reconstruction Finance Corporation, the TVA, the Commodity Credit Corporation, and the Maritime Commission, to cite a few examples, caught the attention of Congress, sometimes led to extensive hearings, and brought new respect for GAO in Congress. Although the corporations being audited did not always appreciate GAO's public disclosure and criticism of their activities and financial methods, they sometimes responded by improving their operations and enhancing their effectiveness. Increasing respect for GAO in Congress and improvement in the Office's relations with the executive branch were among the legacies of the Corporation Audits Division.

---

[87]See chapter 13, pp. 312-15, 327-37, for details on the Joint Accounting Improvement Program and other Warren efforts in the area of financial management.

[88]See chapter 13, pp. 321-24, for the development of the comprehensive audit and GAO's revised reporting approach.

GAO's Post-World War II Transformation Under Warren

The end of World War II initiated a new era in the history of the General Accounting Office (GAO). The war brought to GAO a tremendously heavy workload, which the Office found impossible to handle even with an expanded staff. After the war ended, GAO had a large backlog—millions of vouchers, many difficult contract termination cases, and a mountain of unaudited transportation payments. But this backlog did not prevent GAO from undertaking, in the immediate postwar years, far-reaching changes in its audit approach and methods.

GAO—from Comptroller General Lindsay C. Warren to the lower levels of the staff—learned from the wartime experience that its traditional methods were outmoded and in some cases obsolete. Warren, nearing completion of five years as comptroller general, recognized that the end of the war work gave him an opportunity to increase GAO's effectiveness and usefulness and in the process to assist Congress more in ensuring that the nation's money was being spent legally and properly. Congressional testimony by Warren in 1950 confirms his thought that the war's end opened the way for change: "On the day after the surrender of Japan, I called a staff meeting in my office and told them that the No. 1 project in the General Accounting Office from that day on was for a better and sounder accounting system in the Government. . . ."[1]

Warren's leadership of GAO's postwar modernization centered on three initiatives—audits of government corporations, a cooperative program to improve financial management in the federal government, and development of the "comprehensive audit." GAO's audits of government corporations, begun in 1945, required an audit approach different from what was traditional in GAO. GAO hired a new breed of staff for this work, and the Corporation Audits Division became a laboratory for experimentation, not only on

---

[1]Warren testimony, February 27, 1950, *To Improve Budgeting, Accounting, and Auditing Methods of the Federal Government*, Hearings before the Senate Committee on Expenditures in the Executive Departments, 81st Cong., 2d Sess. (Washington: GPO, 1950), 49.

audits of government corporations, but ultimately for audits generally.[2] The comprehensive audit and the cooperative financial management improvement program both were in operation by 1949. In the same period, Congress passed three laws affecting GAO's work—the Federal Property and Administrative Services Act (1949), the Post Office Department Financial Control Act (1950), and the Budget and Accounting Procedures Act (1950). These laws were largely responses to changes GAO either already had made or proposed to make.

Another result of the changes in audit approach and the cooperative financial management program was an extensive reorganization of GAO. By the time Warren left office in the spring of 1954, the new GAO he had fashioned presented many contrasts to the organization J. R. McCarl presided over in the 1920s and 1930s.[3]

GAO's improving relationships with Congress helped Warren manage the transformation. It was important that Warren had served more than 15 years in the House of Representatives before becoming comptroller general and continued to maintain close contact with some of his former colleagues.

In 1945, Congress established a Joint Committee on the Organization of Congress to consider legislative reorganization. In testimony before the Joint Committee, Warren focused on relationships between GAO and Congress and on legislative control of spending. He recommended increased congressional scrutiny of agency budget estimates and reexamination of executive agency exemptions from laws controlling spending. He proposed increased use of GAO on matters relating to spending and application of funds. Warren expressed disappointment that many GAO reports failed to attract the attention of Congress. "If we are interested enough to report," he said, "we should likewise be interested enough in seeing something done about those reports and some have been completely ignored, some have never been considered, and I know of one or two that were given a very generous coat of whitewash." He recommended establishment of a joint committee to receive and act on GAO reports on expenditures, economy, and efficiency.[4]

At this hearing, there was discussion about GAO's position in the government. Rep. Earl C. Michener (R—Michigan) remarked that organization charts published by the Office of War Information showed GAO as part of

---

[2]See chapter 12 for an extended discussion of corporation audits.

[3]See chapter 14 for details of Warren's reorganization.

[4]Warren testimony, May 15, 1945, *Organization of Congress*, Hearings before the Joint Committee on the Organization of Congress, 79th Cong., 1st Sess., pt. 3 (Washington: GPO, 1945), 36, 538 (source of the quote).

the executive branch. Frank H. Weitzel, Warren's assistant, responded: "It is not surprising that they have the information the way they do because . . . after nearly 25 years we still get letters addressed to . . . Treasury Department or War Department or Navy Department or whatever department the claimant or the person happens to be dealing with. In other words, there is still a great deal of confusion in the public mind as to just where the General Accounting Office is in the Government picture."[5]

To clear up this confusion, Congress included in the Reorganization Act of 1945 (approved December 20, 1945) terms that exempted GAO from presidential reorganization plans proposed under the law and described the comptroller general and GAO as "a part of the legislative branch of the Government."[6] Inclusion of this provision was very important; it was the first direct statutory statement of GAO's status as a legislative branch agency.

The main result of the extensive 1945 hearings of the Joint Committee on the Organization of Congress was the Legislative Reorganization Act of 1946. Two provisions related particularly to GAO. First, the House and Senate Committees on Expenditures in the Executive Departments were to receive and examine GAO reports and make recommendations to Congress relevant to them. This provision, an alternative to Warren's proposal of a joint committee, responded to his complaint that Congress often paid little attention to GAO reports. The other provision, Section 206, required the comptroller general to do an "expenditure analysis" of each executive branch agency to "enable Congress to determine whether public funds have been economically and efficiently administered and expended."[7]

Section 206, a potentially important authorization for GAO to look more extensively in its regular audits into the operation of government agencies, again responded to Warren's call for broadened congressional scrutiny. GAO never performed the expenditure analyses. The Office requested a $1 million appropriation for staff and expenses to perform the analyses, but Congress never provided the funds. Nevertheless, the Legislative Reorganization Act of 1946 was an important recognition by Congress of GAO's actual

---

[5]Weitzel testimony, ibid., 534.
[6]Public Law 79-263, 59 Stat. 613.
[7]Public Law 79-601, 60 Stat. 837, approved August 2, 1946.

and potential role in assisting in the economical and efficient administration of public expenditures.[8]

Establishment of the Joint Accounting Improvement Program

In 1947, Warren began working toward one of his principal objectives, a cooperative program to improve accounting and financial management in the federal government. In 1950 testimony, Secretary of the Treasury John W. Snyder stated that his office took the lead early in 1947 to get Treasury, GAO, and the Bureau of the Budget (BOB) together "to start work on a program for the simplification and improvement in our general accounting system. . . . I was delighted to find that I had a strong supporter, or, rather, an equally aggressive advocate for an independent program, in the Comptroller General." At the same hearing, Warren pointed out that this was the first time in history that the heads of the three agencies met for a common purpose. "It is needless to say," Warren observed, "that prior to then there has been distrust and backbiting between the agencies, and the General Accounting Office was just as much to blame as any of them were. All of us were to blame."[9]

Part of the initial impetus for the joint program came from the staff of the Senate Committee on Expenditures in the Executive Departments, which in 1947 undertook a study of federal accounting and reporting systems. The study noted that GAO, Treasury, and BOB required separate reports for agencies, providing essentially identical information. In discussing its study with representatives of the three agencies, the committee staff promoted "a view toward improving the accounting system at all levels of administration and adopting business-type methods, procedures, and forms in order that a single monthly report could be prepared. . . ."[10]

In late 1947, representatives of the committee staff and the three agencies agreed that the agencies would cooperate in a study on improving accounting and reporting in the federal government. This agreement consti-

---

[8]See Roger L. Sperry and Jonathan D. Towers, "Expenditure Analyses by GAO: An Idea Whose Time Had Not Arrived," *GAO Review* (fall 1980): 39-42; Frederick C. Mosher, *The GAO: The Quest for Accountability in American Government* (Boulder, CO: Westview Press, 1979), 104-5 (hereafter cited as Mosher, *GAO*); and testimony of Warren and other GAO officials, April 9, 1947, *Independent Offices Appropriation Bill for 1948*, Hearings before a Subcommittee of the House Committee on Appropriations, 80th Cong., 1st Sess., pt. 1 (Washington: GPO, 1952), 491-92, 523-27.

[9]Snyder and Warren testimony, July 11, 1950, *Budgeting and Accounting Procedures Act of 1950*, Hearings before the House Committee on Expenditures in the Executive Departments, 81st Cong., 2d Sess. (Washington: GPO, 1950), 19, 36.

[10]Staff of the Senate Committee on Government Operations, *Financial Management in the Federal Government*, 87th Cong., 1st Sess., S. Doc. 11 (Washington: GPO, 1961), 37-39 (hereafter cited as *Financial Management*, 1961).

tuted the beginning of the cooperative program, whose formal title was Joint Program for Improving Accounting in the Federal Government, often shortened to Joint Accounting Improvement Program, or JAIP.[11] In 1959, the principals in the program changed the name to Joint Financial Management Improvement Program (JFMIP). Warren, on behalf of himself, James E. Webb (the director of BOB), and Snyder, announced the program to federal agency heads in a letter on October 20, 1948, and requested their cooperation. "This program," Warren wrote, "contemplates the full development of sound accounting within each agency, as a working arm of management, in terms of financial information and control. At the same time it envisions an integrated pattern of accounting and financial reporting for the Government as a whole responsive to executive and legislative needs."[12]

The final step in formally establishing the Joint Accounting Improvement Program was the signature by Warren, Snyder, and Webb on January 6, 1949, of documents stating the program's policies and objectives, work programs, and working arrangements. The results of JAIP, they stated, would be improved management in the executive branch, better information and foundations for congressional action on appropriations and other legislation, and a clearer public picture of federal financial operations and conditions.[13] The three executives took the initiatives leading to the formal establishment of the joint program on their own authority, without a specific legislative mandate. Warren explained his own motives in 1949: "My concern is not based only on my legal responsibility and authority to prescribe certain accounting systems; I am as deeply concerned with the development of proper systems in the agencies as an indispensable adjunct to an effective independent audit for the Congress and as a source of the kinds of information needed by the Congress." He observed that "establishment of the program . . . is widely regarded as one of the most significant contributions in many years to efficiency and economy in the Government." Warren frequently emphasized the

---

[11]Ibid., 40; and Frederic H. Smith, "The Joint Financial Management Improvement Program Is 20 Years Old," *GAO Review* (winter 1969): 81.

[12]Letter, Comptroller General to the heads of all government agencies, October 20, 1948, reprinted in Walter F. Frese, *Early History of the Joint Financial Management Improvement Program* (Washington: JFMIP, 1980), 285-89. This publication is a transcript of interviews with Frese, the former head of GAO's Accounting Systems Division, conducted during the period 1974-1976 by Ellsworth H. Morse, Jr., and Donald C. Kull (hereafter cited as Frese, *Early History of JFMIP*). See letter, Warren to secretary of the Smithsonian Institution, October 20, 1948, 326 MS 2031, for an example of the letter.

[13]Warren, Snyder, and Webb, "Joint Program for Improving Accounting in the Federal Government," January 6, 1949, reprinted in Frese, *Early History of the JFMIP*, 290, 291-312 (pages 291-312 contain attached related documents). Copies of these materials are attached to letter, Warren to Rep. Richard B. Wigglesworth, January 11, 1949, 329 MS 890.

strong support for the program by Congress, executive branch agencies, and President Truman.[14]

Walter F. Frese, Director, Accounting Systems Division, 1948-1956.

Even before formally announcing the joint program, Warren began to make organizational and procedural changes in GAO consistent with its objectives. On January 6, 1948, he established the Accounting Systems Division to spearhead, with the cooperation of BOB and Treasury, the joint program. The division's functions were to study the problems of administrative appropriation and fund accounting and related accounting in the federal government, to inspect and analyze existing systems and those installed later under GAO's authority "to determine . . . [their] effectiveness and appropriateness," to develop and revise accounting systems and procedures, to devise standard account forms for GAO approval, and to advise federal agencies on accounting problems and help the agencies solve them.[15]

Warren appointed Walter F. Frese, a Treasury Department official, to head the new division. Earlier in his career, Frese had taught accounting at the University of Illinois, then moved in 1935 to the Treasury Department, where he worked initially on a system to account for and disburse relief funds.[16] Under Frese, the division's early emphasis was on development, approval, and installation of accounting systems in federal agencies. Frese and his small staff, with strong support from Treasury and BOB, devoted themselves to this task. Frese stressed direct contact with the agencies and efforts to encourage and train them. His

[14]*Comptroller General of the United States: Annual Report for the Fiscal Year Ended June 30, 1949* (Washington: GPO, n.d.), iii-iv; and Warren testimony, February 9, 1949, *Independent Offices Appropriation Bill for 1950*, Hearings before a Subcommittee of the House Committee on Appropriations, 81st Cong., 1st Sess., vol. I (Washington: GPO, 1949), 964.

[15]*Annual Report of the Comptroller General of the United States for the Fiscal Year Ended June 30, 1948* (Washington: GPO, n. d.) iii, 2-3. See also "The Accounting Systems Division," *GAO Review* (summer 1971): 111-14, for a brief history of the division.

[16]"Walter F. Frese, 1906-1987," *Harvard Business School Bulletin* (February 1988), 12-13; letter, Warren to Rep. John Taber, chairman, House Committee on Appropriations, January 8, 1948, Papers of Lindsay C. Warren, Southern Historical Collection, Wilson Library, University of North Carolina at Chapel Hill, Folder 425 (hereafter cited as Warren Papers); and Mosher, *GAO*, 110; 111; 127, n. 22.

approach was positive, highlighting improvements the agencies made rather than pointing out deficiencies, as GAO typically did in its regular audits.[17]

The Frese Plan, 1949

Warren asked Frese to prepare a memorandum on how he thought JAIP would affect GAO's operations and organization and to recommend immediate changes "to adjust the operations of the General Accounting Office to the program and to achieve all possible economies as quickly as possible. . . ." After receiving Frese's memorandum on July 14, 1949, Warren sent copies to his division and office chiefs, asking them to provide recommendations on the document. Recognizing that Frese's proposals were "revolutionary," as several GAO officials later described them, Warren asked them to regard the memorandum as "strictly confidential."[18] The fact that Warren had asked Frese to prepare this document demonstrated both his confidence in him and the importance he assigned to JAIP.

In his memorandum, Frese focused on eliminating or modifying some existing GAO detailed accounting procedures and operations and using improved control and audit procedures concurrently with accounting systems development. This would result in "much needed improvement" in government accounting processes. "The individual operating agencies of the Government," Frese wrote, "are the key points for effectuation of real control over the financial operations of the Government." Frese urged fast action in reorganizing GAO operations; adoption of his recommendations, he said, would enable GAO to cut the costs of its operations and make funds available "for the needed development of more current, useful, meaningful, and effective control and audit methods."[19]

Frese recommended also discontinuing several functions of GAO's Accounting and Bookkeeping Division, including maintaining appropriation ledgers; the expenditure and limitation ledger; receipt ledgers; many subsidiary trust accounts; the General Ledger; and the asset, liability, and other accounts relating to the accounts of the treasurer of the United States. He also proposed eliminating the submission to GAO of advance copies of the schedule of collections and transferring from GAO to the Treasury Department the function of reconciling and matching paid card checks with checks issued.

---

[17]Frese, *Early History of JFMIP*, 239-40.

[18]Memorandum, Warren to chiefs of divisions and offices, July 14, 1949, B-87836.

[19]Memorandum, Frese to the comptroller general, July 14, 1949, ibid.

Frese proposed procedures "in the interest of economy, efficiency, and fiscal control" to implement his recommendations. They included establishing a special group to review Treasury accounting procedures and developing an audit program to replace duplicate accounting processes existing in the Accounting and Book-keeping Division; assigning to the Corporation Audits Division (CAD) the "comprehensive audit" of agencies with business-type activities; rapidly adjusting the Audit Division's procedures to the site audit approach, including evaluation of internal accounting procedures and control, leading "eventually into application of the 'comprehensive audit' concept;" and requesting legislation to authorize discretion in audit procedures of the comptroller general and to permit agencies to retain originals of documents and vouchers.[20]

The responses to Frese's memorandum varied from complete acceptance to hostile rejection. Stephen B. Ives of CAD simply stated that his division concurred "in principle" with Frese's proposals. The chief of the Postal Accounts Division, Gary Campbell, agreed with Frese's recommendations and views but added that there should be a distinction between audits for accounting purposes and audits to determine the legality of transactions. For the latter, Campbell wrote, "a comprehensive voucher audit for the purpose of determining the legality of the transaction should never be sacrificed to the erroneous belief that administrative controls will require such adherence to laws. The only way that fraud can be detected is by going into the details of transactions." E. W. Ballinger, an assistant to Warren, recommended prompt implementation of Frese's suggestions. GAO needed to "radically and quickly revise our thinking and our philosophy of accounting and auditing . . . as well as our work methods, procedures and operating plans. We must also create new and better tools with which to accomplish our work." The Audit Division chief, E. W. Bell, concurred in Frese's plan except for the proposal to assign comprehensive audits of agencies with business-type activities to CAD. He pointed out that his division currently did such audits in several agencies and could extend them to others.[21]

Both A. B. Thomas, chief of the Claims Division, and Harrell O. Hoagland, chief of the Transportation Division, supported Frese's suggestions, saying that they would not adversely affect their units. Hoagland said that he thought that the proposals were revolutionary and that they should receive "serious and mature attention." Thomas said that his division agreed with any program that would carry out JAIP; "it is self-evident," he wrote, "that since the

---

[20]See pp. 321-24, for a discussion of the development and the nature of the comprehensive audit.

[21]Memorandum, Ives to the comptroller general, August 1, 1949, B-87836; memorandum, Campbell to the comptroller general, July 18, 1949, ibid.; memorandum, Ballinger to the comptroller general, July 28, 1949, ibid.; and memorandum, Bell to the comptroller general, July 29, 1949, ibid.

General Accounting Office is the guiding spirit . . . it should serve as a leader in this field."[22]

The opposition to Frese's plan stemmed mainly from four officials who headed operations that would be most affected by the proposed changes. V. J. Kirby, acting director of personnel, worried about the extensive personnel displacements and reassignments that would result from implementation of the plan, especially in the Accounting and Bookkeeping and Reconciliation and Clearance Divisions. The shift to site audits would cause problems for GAO staff with local ties who could not move and others who, "because of personality, appearance, manner, physical handicap, etc." would find site audits difficult.[23]

Stuart B. Tulloss, chief of investigations, justified his opposition in terms of his "duty in safeguarding the principles for which the General Accounting Office was established, and more especially your [the comptroller general's] responsibilities as required under the Budget and Accounting Act, 1921, and other laws relating to control of Federal funds." He thought that implementing Frese's plan would result in the abolition of most of the accounting controls then existing in GAO and replacing them with "spot checks and periodic reviews" of Treasury and other executive agencies.[24]

Vernon R. Durst, chief of the Reconciliation and Clearance Division, thought Frese's proposals were revolutionary; were not based on a complete evaluation of the facts; and were supported by general terms, such as "effectuation of real control" and "more effective and less costly measures," which "leave much to the imagination." He believed that Frese's proposals would return to the Treasury Department the fiscal controls that the Budget and Accounting Act had vested in GAO. Durst questioned especially the proposal to transfer from his own division the function of reconciling and matching paid card checks with checks issued. He contended that Frese did not understand the nature and the purpose of the task. Finally, he questioned whether GAO could do its work—claims settlement, contract settlement, legal decisions, investigations, and other duties—if the necessary records "were scattered to the four corners of the United States, and . . . to the four corners of the world."[25]

The chief of the Accounting and Bookkeeping Division was even more direct in his criticism. J. Darlington Denit described the proposals "as (1) being very definitely and unwisely revolutionary; (2) unduly extravagant in promises; (3) in-

---

[22]Memorandum, Hoagland to the comptroller general, August 2, 1949, ibid.; and memorandum, Thomas to the comptroller general, August 1, 1949, ibid.

[23]Memorandum, Kirby to the comptroller general, July 20, 1949, ibid.

[24]Memorandum, Tulloss to the comptroller general, July 28, 1949, ibid.

[25]Memorandum, Durst to the comptroller general, July 29, 1949, ibid.

accurate in appraising and reporting on some of our present practices and in stating accomplishments under the joint program; (4) undeveloped to an extent which leaves entirely too much to conjecture; (5) taking away from your direct supervision functions essential to the proper performance of your duties; and (6) being incapable of accomplishment under existing law." He accused Frese's Accounting Systems Division of wanting to make changes "regardless of the consequences and regardless of the fact that to do so required not only the side stepping of existing law but the deliberate disregard in some instances of specific statutes." The proposals to shift functions to the Treasury Department, Denit argued, were not necessary to carry out the joint accounting program, would weaken the control and the effectiveness of GAO, and were illegal without specific authorizing legislation.[26]

Denit prepared a second memorandum suggesting that Warren have a plan showing how the Audit Division would accomplish "in an improved fashion, and at lesser cost" its present functions plus others it would be responsible for under Frese's proposals. Denit wrote, "I strongly urge that such a disclosure is most desirable and should be required in order to supply light in many dark places." Denit surveyed previous Warren statements and letters about GAO's role and contended that implementing Frese's proposals would violate them as well as existing law.[27]

These responses to Frese's proposals demonstrated a clear division in the ranks. Part of the support for Frese's plan may have resulted from the reluctance of some division and office chiefs to oppose recommendations they assumed had the comptroller general's backing, although there is no direct evidence supporting this conjecture. It is true that the most vociferous opposition came from division chiefs whose units would lose most in any shift in GAO functions. More to the point, the argument over Frese's plan reflected a fundamental division between the old order and the new order on the question of how GAO ought to operate. Frese, a newcomer with an impressive professional career built up outside GAO, was proposing a substantial change in the Office's work—dropping some traditional tasks and shifting others to the executive branch—just a year or so after he joined the organization. Frese personified the new professionals whom Warren was bringing in—for both the Corporation Audits and Accounting Systems divisions. The thrust under Warren, in the joint accounting program, was cooperation with the executive branch. This was too much for GAO officials such as Tulloss, Denit, and Durst, who had risen to prominence in GAO as directors of the old programs

---

[26]Memorandum, Denit to the comptroller general, August 1, 1949, ibid.
[27]Memorandum, Denit to the comptroller general, August 18, 1949, ibid.

typical of the 1920s and 1930s that Frese thought ought to be discontinued. In that sense, Frese's proposals *were* revolutionary.

Warren considered at length the comments and the suggestions on the Frese plan. Finally, on November 29, 1949, he released a memorandum containing his decisions. For the most part, he approved Frese's proposals. He first stated several general policy decisions: GAO would put government agencies on the comprehensive audit when feasible, advantageous, and permissible; GAO operations "not essential to effective exercise of its audit and control responsibilities" and not specifically required by law will be discontinued as soon as possible; while exercising its control and audit responsibilities, GAO will give constant recognition to evaluation of internal control in the agencies and the Treasury Department "as a basis for considering elimination or modification" of present procedures. Warren also directed all GAO divisions to submit recommendations for legislative changes necessary to carry out the new approach by December 15, 1949.[28]

Warren listed specific actions to be taken as soon as possible:

- On the basis of existing law, appropriation ledgers would continue to be kept, supported by warrants signed by the comptroller general.

- GAO would stop reconciling transcripts of agency appropriation account entries with GAO accounts when agencies reconciled their appropriations accounts with the accounts of the Treasury Department, as required.

- GAO would discontinue receiving agency reports on Standard Form 116 (monthly statement of account balances) and Standard Forms 1117 and 1118 (monthly reports on status of appropriations) as well as the checking and the reconciling of these reports by the Accounting and Bookkeeping Division.

- The Accounting and Bookkeeping Division would stop keeping expenditure and limitation ledgers on an agency basis when site or comprehensive audits had begun in the agency or when the Accounting Systems Division determined that acceptable agency internal accounting procedures for control of obligations and expenditures were effective.

- The Accounting and Bookkeeping Division would continue to maintain receipt accounts for appropriations for the time being but would stop maintaining other receipt accounts.

---

[28]Memorandum, Warren to chiefs of divisions and offices, November 29, 1949, ibid. See pp. 321-24, for definitions and a discussion of the comprehensive audit.

- GAO would drop its regulation requiring agencies to provide advance copies of schedules of collections; the comptroller general would countersign covering documents making the funds available, subject to postaudit.

- When the Accounting Systems Division certified that agency systems and records were satisfactory, the Accounting and Bookkeeping Division would stop maintaining subsidiary trust fund accounts.

- The Accounting and Bookkeeping Division would discontinue the general ledger.

- Until the Accounting Systems Division developed an alternate approach and procedures, the Accounting and Bookkeeping Division would continue to maintain the asset, liability, and other accounts.

- Until the Accounting Systems Division reported further on the matter, a decision on reorganization of operations relating to reconciliation of disbursing officers' checking accounts would be delayed.

Emphasizing that economy was one of his motives, Warren directed GAO's executive officer to "promptly determine the number of people and the amount of funds made available in the various divisions as each of the . . . actions become effective . . . ." The funds thus identified would be available only with his approval.[29]

In another memorandum, Warren stated that his directions should be carried out in "orderly fashion." He assigned responsibility for coordinating implementation of his orders to the Office of Administrative Planning, with participation by the Accounting Systems Division. He appointed Ted B. Westfall, an assistant director in the Corporation Audits Division, to assist part-time with this effort. Westfall was to deal with operations already scheduled to be cut and to review other GAO operations so that the new policies could be implemented promptly and "the full potentialities for economy and improved procedures" could be realized without delay.[30] Warren clarified Westfall's role about a week later. "To avoid the possibility of misunderstanding," he wrote, "I wish you to know that I contemplate an analysis of the operations and organization of the General Accounting Office as a whole." Westfall was to report his findings and recommendations to the heads of the Accounting

[29]Ibid.

[30]Memorandum, Warren to chiefs of divisions and offices, November 29, 1949, ibid. Westfall credited Frese and Frank Weitzel for recommending him to Warren for this role. See GAO, *Ted B. Westfall, 1946-1952*, GAO History Program, Oral History Series, GAO/OP-2-OH (Washington: 1988), 13.

Systems Division and the Office of Administrative Planning. These officials would transmit them to the comptroller general.[31]

The Comprehensive Audit

Concurrently with development of the Joint Accounting Improvement Program, GAO began to shift its audit approach to what came to be termed the comprehensive audit. As was the case with JAIP, the work of the Corporation Audits Division played a significant role in the origins of the comprehensive audit. Westfall claimed that he and Frese originated the name comprehensive audit. The Maritime Commission audit, Westfall said, "was the audit that made it possible for those of us, including Frank Weitzel and Walt Frese and many others who believed that we ought to get away from the old voucher audit . . . [to] get over to . . . what was referred to as a 'site audit.' I think Walt and I created the term 'comprehensive audit' just to give them a term."[32]

In October 1949, Warren announced establishment of the comprehensive audit program. Actually, in his annual report for 1948, most likely written earlier in 1949, Warren gave early notice of his intentions. He mentioned GAO's efforts to expand the number of site audits at locations in Washington and elsewhere where agencies kept accounts and records. He wrote: "The availability at the site of additional documents and other data relating to the financial transactions of an organization, and the opportunity afforded the auditors to familiarize themselves with the facts and circumstances surrounding the transactions, enable the auditor to make a much more comprehensive and effective audit than would otherwise be possible." To handle the work, Warren established a comprehensive audit subdivision in the Audit Division.[33] In July 1950, he shifted responsibility for all comprehensive audits except postal audits to the Corporation Audits Division.[34]

---

[31]Memorandum, Warren to chiefs of divisions and offices, December 5, 1949, B-87836. Warren established the Office of Administrative Planning in 1941; it advised the comptroller general on budget, organizational, and other matters. A 1950 order outlining its functions listed various duties in the categories of administrative planning; budgetary planning; and miscellaneous, including preparing GAO's annual report and doing special studies of technical problems affecting GAO's work. See Office Order No. 5—Revised, December 22, 1950, 352 MS 1228m.

[32]GAO, *Ted B. Westfall, 1946-1952*, 8. See also the comments of John P. Abbadessa, in GAO, *John P. Abbadessa, 1947-1962*, GAO History Program, Oral History Series, GAO/OP-18-OH (Washington: 1990), 11. Abbadessa gave Frese the most credit for originating the comprehensive audit but also credits Westfall, Weitzel, and others in CAD.

[33]GAO, *Annual Report, 1948*, iv; John C. Fenton, "The Corporation Audits Division—Its Legacy to the Seventies," *GAO Review* (summer 1971): 104-5; Warren testimony, January 27, 1950, *Independent Offices Appropriations for 1951*, Hearings before a Subcommittee of the House Committee on Appropriations, 81st Cong., 2d Sess., pt. 1 (Washington: GPO, 1950), 857; and Administrative Order No. 70, October 19, 1949 [instituting the comprehensive audit], attached to memorandum, Warren to chiefs of divisions and offices, November 29, 1949, B-87836.

[34]*Comptroller General of the United States: Annual Report for the Fiscal Year Ended June 30, 1951* (Washington: GPO, n.d.), 22-23.

Warren officially defined the comprehensive audit program in October 1949. The program was "designed to accomplish more effective and comprehensive fiscal and property audits in Federal departments and agencies." GAO's policy would be "to utilize audit processes based upon an evaluation of accounting systems and the effectiveness of related internal checks and controls in the agencies at the site of operations . . . as a basis for the fuller and more effective discharge of its responsibility to the Congress." Warren stated that existing GAO accounting and auditing processes based on central review of agency documents and reports in Washington would be modified or eliminated. Significantly, there was no mention in this document of any plan to look at agency program effectiveness and results as part of the comprehensive audit. The emphasis was on accounting systems and agency internal checks and controls.[35]

Warren's list of comprehensive audit objectives and procedures in 1953 demonstrated how the concept had broadened since his definition of the program in 1949. In 1953, he talked about "evaluating the agency's operations," carrying out authorized activities "efficiently and reasonably," and "the effectiveness of application of public funds." The objectives of the comprehensive audit in 1953 were to determine whether:

> (1) the agency is carrying out only those activities or programs authorized by the Congress and is conducting them in the manner authorized, (2) expenditures are made only in the furtherance of authorized activities and in accordance with applicable laws, regulations, and decisions, (3) the agency collects and accounts properly for all revenues and receipts derived from its activities, (4) the assets of the agency or in its custody are adequately safeguarded and controlled and utilized in an efficient manner, and (5) reports by the agency to the Congress and to the central control agencies disclose fully the nature and scope of activities conducted and provide a proper basis for evaluating the agency's operations. The distinction between a comprehensive audit and a site audit lies solely in the degree to which these objectives are present.

The comprehensive audit procedures included (1) a review of laws and legislative history to ascertain congressional intent on the agency's activities, the way in which they were to be conducted, and the extent of the agency's responsibility and authority; (2) a review of agency policies to see that they conformed to congressional intent and carried out authorized activities efficiently and reasonably; (3) a review of agency internal controls to determine how well they ensured con-

---

[35]Administrative Order No. 70, October 19, 1949.

trol of expenditures, revenue, and assets; ensured accuracy of financial data; promoted operational efficiency; ensured compliance with laws, regulations, and decisions; and conformed to prescribed policy; (4) a review and analysis by activity of revenue, spending, and asset utilization, to evaluate the effectiveness of the application of public funds and the reliability and the completeness of the agency's financial data; (5) an examination of transactions, confirmation of balances, and physical inspection of property to provide assurance that transactions are legal, assets have been correctly accounted for, and the agency's control processes are functioning effectively; and (6) the full explanation of deficiencies discovered and presentation of recommendations for correction to Congress, the agency head, and other interested agencies.[36]

GAO gradually extended the comprehensive audit as its staff size and capabilities permitted. Warren reported to Congress in January 1952 that the program had been applied by then to 31 government units, including some large field installations of the Department of Defense (DOD). He expressed his hope that GAO would have all major operating programs of civilian agencies under comprehensive or other site audits by mid-1953.[37] By the end of the 1950s, the term "comprehensive audit" had fallen into disuse in GAO, although the concepts and the procedures attached to such audits were still pertinent.

Warren's explanation of the objectives and the procedures of comprehensive audits seems clear. Yet GAO staff had difficulty distinguishing between the regular audits they were accustomed to doing and the new approach. John P. Abbadessa, who joined GAO in 1947 and later served as a division deputy director, said that he personally had never seen a definition of the comprehensive audit. "You heard operations audit, you heard program-results audit, but in the final analysis, it became reasonably clear very early that there was a desire to spend less time on financial statement verification. . . . I think what we had is probably an evolving approach . . . which became much more defined as we went along."[38]

Arthur Schoenhaut, another division deputy director, recalled that when he was first assigned to a comprehensive audit, "we had some initial difficulty understanding what was intended. . . . It really was the forerunner to operations audits. . . . I never heard anybody complain about getting away from the rudimentary auditing of the books of the agency and getting down to taking a look at how

[36]*Comptroller General of the United States: Annual Report for the Fiscal Year Ended June 30, 1953* (Washington: GPO, n.d.), 16-18.

[37]Warren testimony, January 23, 1952, *Independent Offices Appropriations for 1953*, Hearings before a Subcommittee of the House Committee on Appropriations, 82d Cong., 2d Sess., pt.1 (Washington: GPO, 1952), 486-87.

[38]GAO, *John P. Abbadessa, 1947-1962*, 13-14.

well the programs were being run, and it didn't matter what it was. . . . You started with the books, but you wound up taking an operation apart to see what went wrong."[39]

Legislation for the New GAO

Almost simultaneously with the inauguration of the joint accounting program and the comprehensive audit, Congress passed three laws that had a substantive impact on GAO's operations—the Federal Property and Administrative Services Act (1949), the Post Office Department Financial Control Act (1950), and the Budget and Accounting Procedures Act (1950).

When Warren announced implementation of the Frese plan, he asked his division and office directors to recommend legislative changes to facilitate the new procedures for federal accounting and the shift to the comprehensive audit. The most important response he received came from Frese himself. He recommended cooperative development with BOB and Treasury of a complete new and modern accounting and auditing law that would "provide the basis for accomplishment of longer range objectives under the [accounting improvement] program." Frese proposed also (1) discontinuing the shipment each year to Washington of millions of paid vouchers for central administrative examination and instead allowing agencies to retain the vouchers at site audit locations; (2) authorizing GAO to stop maintaining appropriation ledgers, which duplicated ledgers kept by the Treasury Department and were inconsistent with the comprehensive audit program; (3) eliminating the use of accountable warrants, "the basic cause of most of the unnecessary, wasteful and time consuming red tape in the central control processes of the Treasury Department, General Accounting Office and their counterparts in the administrative agencies"; and (4) authorizing the secretary of the treasury and the comptroller general to issue regulations leading to modification or elimination of present legal requirements relating to issuance and countersignature of warrants.[40]

The First Hoover Commission

Another stimulus to new financial legislation, especially the Budget and Accounting Procedures Act, was the Commission on Organization of the Executive Branch of the Government, familiarly known as the First Hoover Commission after its chairman, former President Herbert C. Hoover. The commission's

---

[39]GAO, *Arthur Schoenhaut*, GAO History Program, Oral History Series, GAO/OP-4-OH (Washington: 1988), 5.

[40]Memorandum, Frese to the comptroller general, February 7, 1950, B-87836.

main concern was the structural organization of government agencies and their relationships with one another.[41]

When the bill to establish the commission came before Congress in 1947, Warren opposed it. He pointed out to Sen. George D. Aiken that he had a long-standing interest in government reorganization. But the history of reorganization attempts "has shown clearly the ineffectiveness of any legislation which provides merely for investigation and report, without vesting authority in someone to take decisive action placing in operation the changes found necessary." Warren thought that the power to reorganize should be vested in the president; ". . . it will serve no useful purpose to investigate and report again in the expectation that this will ensure reorganization changes being made." Given this past history, Warren thought that passage of the proposed bill would be "a waste of public funds."[42]

Warren was disturbed when he received information before the commission formally reported about its recommendations on federal budgeting and accounting. He wrote to T. Coleman Andrews, former director of the Corporation Audits Division and a member of the commission task force on budgeting and accounting, that he was shocked at the proposals, which included significant changes in GAO's status and assignments. He made a point he reiterated many times, that the law creating the Hoover Commission restricted its jurisdiction to the executive branch; the commission had no authority to make recommendations on GAO's status and functions.[43] A Washington newspaper reported in January 1949 that Warren had described the report on federal accounting as "completely unrealistic" and as prepared by "off-campus professors and advisers." Warren also called attention to the fact that GAO, BOB, and Treasury had recently announced a joint accounting program that had the approval of the president.[44]

In a private letter to a close North Carolina friend, Warren pointed out again that the Hoover Commission was to look at the executive branch, not the legislative branch. "The Commission," Warren wrote, "has no more to do with this Office than the man in the moon." Warren claimed that twice he had "warned President Hoover . . . that his whole report might be discredited if he interfered in matters that he had no jurisdiction over." Warren did not think Hoover intended to attack him personally. Rather, "It is the age old fight to weaken the control of

[41]William E. Pemberton, "Truman and the Hoover Commission," *Whistle Stop*, vol. 19, no. 3 (1991), 2-4; and *Financial Management*, 1961, 51.

[42]Letter, Warren to Aiken, chairman, Senate Committee on Expenditures in the Executive Departments, May 21, 1947, B-50164.

[43]Letter, Warren to Andrews, November 23, 1948, Warren Papers, Folder 429.

[44]Clipping, *Washington Evening Star*, January 20, 1949, clippings files, GAO History Program Archives.

Congress over the purse and to prevent it [from] getting information that it now receives from me, as its agent."[45]

The Hoover Commission issued its budgeting and accounting report on February 24, 1949, incorporating most of what its Task Force on Fiscal, Budgeting, and Accounting Activities had recommended. The commission was very critical of the role GAO played in accounting, which it considered a legitimate function of the executive branch. GAO should be restricted to auditing; for it to continue to serve as both the accountant and the auditor of the government was wrong because in effect GAO was auditing its own accounting work. The task force recommended establishing a central government accounting service in the Treasury Department under the direction of an accountant general. The service would develop accounting systems and procedures, keep accounts for the government, produce financial statements, and maintain a field staff to help other agencies apply accounting principles and issue financial reports prescribed by an accountant general.[46]

The task force also recommended changing the title of comptroller general to auditor general and dropping the name General Accounting Office. The auditor general should be required to broaden the scope of his activities through commercial-type audits, and all audits should be site audits. Auditing of expenditure vouchers should be discontinued except in cases of negligence, fraud, or other reasons requiring detailed examinations. The task force stated that the sending of vouchers and supporting documents to GAO was a tremendous waste of paper and money. GAO had a storage need that was very costly to meet. "We are told that the problem of housing voucher auditors and storing copies of expenditure documents were large and costly considerations in the planning of the new housing facilities recently approved for the General Accounting Office," the task force reported.[47]

The Hoover Commission adopted the recommendations of the task force, but some commission members, most conspicuously Sen. John L. McClellan (D—Arkansas) and former Rep. Carter Manasco (D—Alabama), dissented. They disagreed with the proposal to create an accountant general in the Treasury Department with power to prescribe and enforce accounting procedures. The com-

---

[45]Letter, Warren to F. S. Worthy, Washington, NC, January 27, 1949, Warren Papers, Folder 430.

[46]*Fiscal, Budgeting, and Accounting Systems of Federal Government: A Report with Recommendations*, prepared for the Commission on Organization of the Executive Branch of the Government by John W. Hanes, A. E. Buck, and T. Coleman Andrews, January 1949 (this is the title page title; the cover title is *Task Force Report on Fiscal, Budgeting, and Accounting Activities*, Appendix F), 94-95. Part IV of this publication is the report of the Accounting Policy Committee of the Fiscal, Budgeting, and Accounting Project, T. Coleman Andrews, chairman, 85-110 (hereafter cited as *Hoover Commission*, Appendix F).

[47]*Hoover Commission*, Appendix F, 96-99.

mission was overstepping its jurisdiction and trying to change an agency of Congress. "We do not believe," they wrote, "the Congress will consent to the stripping of its agency of effective authority over accounting systems." If the comptroller general lost his role in prescribing accounting systems, it would make impossible the development of a system needed by GAO for external control and audit and deprive Congress of necessary information on the results of the government's financial operations. "If there is to be any change in basic jurisdiction to prescribe accounting systems, we believe it should be in the direction of strengthening the hand of the Comptroller General." The best hope for improving government accounting was the "down-to-earth work" being done by GAO, BOB, and Treasury in the Joint Accounting Improvement Program. "The joint program will bring benefits desired by all of us."[48]

Another commissioner, James H. Rowe, Jr., agreed in the main with the Hoover Commission's majority proposals but emphasized the need, which he thought the Commission had not put forward effectively, to take control of the accounting system from GAO. Rowe also doubted JAIP's usefulness. He stated that "the present confusion—based on the false concept of the Budget and Accounting Act of 1921 which puts accounting as well as auditing in a legislative agency—is so irreconcilable, and the strain so deep, this voluntary effort will not long endure."[49] Dean Acheson, vice chairman of the Hoover Commission, favored granting the executive branch control over accounting and reporting, not by legislation but rather through JAIP.[50]

The Budget and Accounting Procedures Act of 1950

The fight over the role of GAO figured prominently in the congressional debate on bills designed to transform the Hoover Commission proposals into law. Warren, in congressional testimony and other statements, fought the effort to deprive GAO of accounting functions established by the Budget and Accounting Act, 1921. But he accepted much of what the Commission had recommended for specific improvements in government accounting, as well as the need for government reorganization.

---

[48]McClellan and Manasco reservations, printed in *Budgeting and Accounting*, letter from the chairman, Commission on Organization of the Executive Branch of the Government transmitting its report on "Budgeting and Accounting" in the Executive Branch, H. Doc. 84, February 24, 1949, 81st Cong., 1st Sess. (Washington: GPO, 1949), 47-54 (hereafter cited as Hoover Commission, *Budgeting and Accounting*).

[49]Hoover Commission, *Budgeting and Accounting*, 55-63 (quote on 63).

[50]Ibid., 74.

The first bill to implement the Hoover recommendations was S. 2054, introduced by Sen. Joseph R. McCarthy (R—Wisconsin) on June 13, 1949.[51] This bill's provision to create an accountant general in Treasury, Warren wrote to Senator McClellan, "would transfer to the executive branch a vital and very substantial part of the accounting functions that . . . [GAO] now exercises. . . . [T]his is but one more in a series of attempts through the years to deprive the Congress of a proper measure of control over the financial operations of the executive branch of the Government."[52]

Warren agreed that maintaining accounting systems and producing financial reports were proper functions of the executive branch, that that branch should be able to participate in the development of accounting systems, and that there had to be an audit independent of the executive branch. The deficiency in the Hoover proposals, Warren contended, "lies in the argument that management exclusively must design and supervise its own accounting systems." If the comptroller general lost the power to prescribe accounting systems, auditing would become much more difficult. Federal accounting systems and methods needed improvement; the way to do this was the "cooperative, voluntary, and realistic efforts" inherent in the joint accounting improvement program. GAO, Warren told McClellan, "acts as the right arm of Congress and stands as the last bulwark for the protection of the taxpayer against illegal and extravagant spending. Any weakening of that arm is a weakening of the Congress itself." If there was any relinquishment of Congress's financial controls, it would be only the first step; "once the opening wedge is driven, the attack upon the remaining vestiges of control will be intensified."[53]

When Warren, Weitzel, and Frese testified on S. 2054, they reiterated these arguments.[54] Hoover acknowledged in testimony that GAO as a legislative branch agency was outside his commission's jurisdiction but argued that GAO's methods had to be considered in any discussion of accounting reforms. Accounting reform, Hoover said in reference to JAIP, "needed some more steam and authority than an interdepartmental committee."[55]

Various persons both inside and outside the government supported Warren's position. Frederick J. Lawton, assistant director of BOB, opposed the accountant general plan and argued that JAIP was "basic to the achievement of managerial

[51]*To Improve Budgeting, Accounting, and Auditing Methods of the Federal Government*, 1-2.

[52]Letter, Warren to McClellan, September 23, 1949, 337 MS 1460.

[53]Ibid.

[54]*To Improve Budgeting, Accounting, and Auditing Methods of the Federal Government*, 47-48, 57, 182-85, 202-4, 205-11.

[55]Ibid., 218-31.

improvement throughout the Government and should not be interrupted." Leonard Spacek, head of the prominent accounting firm of Arthur Andersen and Company in Chicago, opposed the Hoover proposals. GAO should prescribe accounting systems and procedures as well as audit under that system, he wrote to Warren, "because a substantial portion of your opinion on auditing results should be your check of the system. Without the responsibility for the adequacy of the accounting system the efficiency of . . . [GAO] would be greatly curtailed and your audit reports would lose a great deal of their significance."[56]

Eventually, the Senate Committee on Expenditures in the Executive Departments failed to act on S. 2054 and both the House and the Senate began considering identical new bills in the summer of 1950. GAO took the lead in drafting this bill, in collaboration with BOB, the Treasury Department, and the staff of the Senate committee.[57] Warren praised it in congressional testimony and stated that "there is no difference between the objectives of the joint accounting program, as written into this bill, and the objectives of the [Hoover] Commission." The bill met all the budgeting, accounting, and auditing objectives of the Commission "in a more realistic and workable way."[58] By early August 1950, the House and the Senate had passed versions of the budget and accounting bill, which went on to a conference committee.

It is interesting to note that some GAO staff opposed the bill. Warren learned the day before the Senate acted that Sen. Patrick A. McCarran (D—Nevada) intended to oppose the bill in a speech actually prepared by J. Darlington Denit, the chief of GAO's Accounting and Bookkeeping Division, who earlier had opposed the Frese plan. He reported this information, received from Senator McClellan, to Assistant Comptroller General Frank Yates, who was on vacation. "I have found," Warren wrote, "that a number of our people were doing all they could to undermine us. . . ." He continued, "I will be talking to you about many things in connection with personnel when you get back."[59]

---

[56]Lawton testimony, February 27, 1950, *To Improve Budgeting, Accounting, and Auditing Methods of the Federal Government*, 33; and letter, Spacek to Warren, March 27, 1950, ibid., 255, and B-87209, #2.

[57]Letter, McClellan to Warren, July 5, 1950, B-87209, #2; letter, Warren to McClellan, July 7, 1950, ibid.; letter, Snyder to Warren, June 26, 1950, ibid.; and testimony of Rep. Frank M. Karsten, July 11, 1950, *Budgeting and Accounting Procedures Act of 1950*, 12-13.

[58]Warren testimony, July 11, 1950, *Budgeting and Accounting Procedures Act of 1950*, 17-18.

[59]Letter, Warren to Yates, August 9, 1950, Warren Papers, Folder 437. It is not clear to whom Warren referred in this letter, but Denit certainly was on his mind. Warren abolished the Accounting and Bookkeeping Division, which Denit headed, on December 31, 1950. Eventually Denit left GAO for a position in another federal agency. Stuart Tulloss, the chief of investigations, who opposed Frese's plan in 1949, retired at the end of that year. Vernon Durst, the chief of the Reconciliation and Clearance Division, who had also criticized the Frese proposal, retained his position until Warren abolished the division in 1952.

After the conference committee completed its work, both houses passed the final bill, the Budget and Accounting Procedures Act of 1950, and President Truman signed it on September 12, 1950. Truman described the new law as "the most important legislation enacted by the Congress in the budget and accounting field since the Budget and Accounting Act, 1921, was passed almost thirty years ago." The president noted that the law embodied the principles and the objectives of the joint accounting program. "This program," Truman said, "has had my indorsement and support from the start."[60] Surrounding Truman as he signed the bill were Warren, Frese, Weitzel, Yates, Secretary of the Treasury Snyder, Director Lawton of BOB, other Treasury and BOB officials, and senators and representatives who had been key figures in getting the bill through Congress.

When he informed the chiefs of GAO divisions about approval of the law, Warren directed: "I shall expect each of you and your staffs to bend every effort, with the utmost cooperation, to see that our plans become a reality and a success, and that the results are no less than anticipated. The transition in our programs is to move forward with dispatch in an orderly and well-defined manner."[61]

Title I, Part II, of the Budget and Accounting Procedures Act of 1950 is sometimes referred to as the Accounting and Auditing Act of 1950. The

President Truman signing the Budget and Accounting Procedures Act of 1950. Walter F. Frese, far left; Frank H. Weitzel, third from left; Comptroller General Warren, standing behind the President; and Rep. William L. Dawson, third from right.

---

[60]White House press release, "Statement by the President," September 12, 1950, copy in B-87209, #2.
[61]Memorandum, Warren to chiefs of all divisions, September 14, 1950, ibid.

law's declaration of policy stated that maintaining accounting systems and producing financial reports on executive agency operations were executive branch responsibilities. Auditing conducted by the comptroller general was to determine how well accounting and financial reporting had fulfilled their purposes, whether financial transactions had been processed in accordance with the law, and whether there was adequate financial control over operations and an effective basis to settle accountable officers' accounts.

The declaration also held that it was the policy of Congress that the comptroller general, the secretary of the Treasury, and the director of BOB "conduct a continuous program for the improvement of accounting and financial reporting in the Government," thus establishing a statutory base for the joint financial improvement program conceived in 1947 by the three officials. Congressional acceptance and approval of the joint program was an important victory for Warren and his associates over proponents of the Hoover Commission's proposals.

Section 112 of the law reconfirmed the comptroller general's duty to prescribe accounting principles and standards for executive agencies, after consulting with the secretary of the Treasury and the director of BOB. GAO was to cooperate with executive agencies in developing accounting systems, approve them as appropriate, and review them from time to time. The secretary of the Treasury was to develop and maintain a system of central accounting and reporting consistent with principles and standards prescribed by the comptroller general.

Section 115 authorized the comptroller general and the secretary of the treasury to make changes in the financial management system when they determined that "existing procedures can be modified in the interest of simplification, improvement, or economy, with sufficient safeguards over the control and accounting for the public funds . . . ." They could issue joint regulations for waiving both the legal requirement that warrants be issued and countersigned in connection with the receipt, the disbursement, or the retention of public funds and the legal requirement that funds be requisitioned and advanced to accountable officers under separate appropriation heads. Also, the joint regulations could allow disbursing agents to pay vouchers by government check under proper safeguards.

Section 116 authorized the comptroller general to discontinue the keeping by GAO of various accounts, including expenditure, receipt, and personal ledger, when he decided that the accounting and internal control systems of executive, legislative, and judicial agencies were effective enough for him to properly perform functions related to the accounts.

Section 117 authorized GAO to audit the financial transactions of executive, legislative, and judicial agencies in accordance with principles, procedures, rules, and regulations prescribed by the comptroller general. When he determined that audits should be done on-site, he could require the involved agencies to retain for up to ten years the accounts, the contracts, the vouchers, and other documents that the law required agencies to submit to GAO. The law permitted this provision to be extended to legislative and to judicial agencies by agreement between the comptroller general and the agencies.[62]

The Budget and Accounting Procedures Act was precisely what Warren wanted, in contrast to the earlier bills that would have adopted the accounting and auditing proposals of the Hoover Commission. The passage of the law gave a statutory foundation for much of what Warren had already initiated in GAO and more broadly in the federal government through the Joint Accounting Improvement Program. The law also had the firm support of GAO's JAIP partners, the Bureau of the Budget, the Treasury Department, and President Truman. The challenge for Warren and GAO was to move ahead with the changes sanctioned by the law, many of them already under way.

The Federal Property and Administrative Services Act

Congress passed two other laws affecting GAO's work during this period, both consistent with recommendations of the Hoover Commission—the Federal Property and Administrative Services Act (1949) and the Post Office Department Financial Control Act (1950). These laws related directly to GAO's objectives in the Joint Accounting Improvement Program and the comprehensive audit.

The Hoover Commission had criticized the high incidence of waste and extravagance in the federal government and recommended that Congress create an office of general services to handle, among other things, supply, records management, and operation of public buildings. In the Federal Property and Administrative Services Act, approved on June 30, 1949, Congress created the General Services Administration (GSA) as a housekeeping agency for the federal government.[63] Two sections of this law pertained to GAO. Section 205(b) directed the comptroller general to prescribe principles and standards of accounting for property, cooperate with the GSA administrator in developing property accounting systems, and approve such systems. Section 206(c) required GAO to audit property accounts and transactions at sites where executive agencies kept their records. This audit "shall include but not necessarily be limited to an evaluation of the

---

[62]This summary of the provisions of the Budget and Accounting Procedures Act of 1950 comes from the text of the law: Public Law 81-784, 64 Stat. 946, approved September 12, 1950.

[63]See William E. Pemberton, "General Services Administration (GSA)," in Donald R. Whitnah, ed., *Government Agencies* (Westport, CT: Greenwood Press, 1983), 268-72.

effectiveness of internal controls and audits and a general audit of the discharge of accountability" for government owned or controlled property.[64]

The terms of this law were consistent with principles and procedures GAO had already subscribed to through JAIP. Until this time, however, GAO did not have audit jurisdiction over federal property. The sections in the Federal Property and Administrative Services Act prescribing a federal property audit by GAO originated in a joint study and report on property control and accounting completed in June 1949 by GAO, Treasury, and BOB.[65] GAO was pleased with the law but recognized that it placed extensive new duties on the Office, requiring well-trained auditors like those in the Corporation Audits Division.

Warren quickly established cordial relations with GSA's first head, Jess Larson, and carefully considered GSA's recommendations on principles and standards for property accounting.[66] Internally, Warren relied on Ted Westfall and Gordon Delk of CAD to develop a plan for implementing GAO functions under the Federal Property and Administrative Services Act. Westfall and Delk recommended that the Accounting Systems, Corporation Audits, and Audit divisions survey all government agencies to determine the extent of work required under the act. The property audits for the time being should be done by two divisions—CAD for agencies with business-type activities and the Audit Division for other agencies. The comprehensive audit approach, covering the accounts of accountable officers as well as property, should be adopted for this work. Trained accountants would be needed.[67]

Warren based his order of October 19, 1949, instituting the comprehensive audit, on the Federal Property and Administrative Services Act and the Budget and Accounting Act, 1921. The order, in part, represented Warren's response to the Westfall-Delk recommendations as well as other factors behind the decision to move to the comprehensive audit.[68] In January 1950, Warren and Larson announced a cooperative working arrangement to improve property management accounting in executive agencies, to be handled as part of JAIP. The GAO-GSA press release pointed out that "this will assure tie-in of the contemplated improvements in accounting for property with the broad objectives of the over-all account-

---

[64]Public Law 152, 66 Stat. 593, approved June 30, 1949.

[65]Warren and Weitzel testimony, January 27, 1950, *Independent Offices Appropriation Bill for 1951*, pt. 1, 871, 881-84; and letter, Jess Larson (GSA administrator) to Warren, July 12, 1949, B-87880.

[66]Letter, Larson to Warren, September 28, 1949, ibid.

[67]Memorandum, Westfall and Delk to the GAO executive officer, September 19, 1949, attached to memorandum, Westfall and Delk to the comptroller general, September 21, 1949, Westfall Survey Records, Box 1, Folder: Westfall Survey Papers, 1951-1952 (contains documents dating from 1949), GAO History Program Archives. Westfall headed a survey of GAO functions, procedures, methods, and organization between 1949 and 1952. See chapter 14, pp. 341-57, for detailed information about this effort.

[68]See pp. 321-24.

ing improvement program. . . ." The agreement included several points: (1) the comptroller general would prescribe property accounting principles and standards developed cooperatively with GSA and other executive agencies; (2) executive agencies were responsible for developing their own accounting systems, including property accounting; and (3) GAO property audits in executive agencies would include evaluation of the effectiveness of property accounting systems and internal controls.[69]

The Federal Property and Administrative Services Act corresponded well to the new directions in which Warren was leading GAO. He was able to relate the activities of JAIP and the comprehensive audit approach to GAO's conduct of property auditing. Implementation of the law strengthened his case for continuing the professionalization of GAO through recruiting trained and experienced accountants. Warren also was able to demonstrate his intention to work cooperatively with executive agencies. The contrast between his cordial cooperation with Jess Larson of GSA and Comptroller General McCarl's relationship with executive agencies in the 1920s and 1930s was striking.

The Post Office Department Financial Control Act, 1950

On August 17, 1950, President Truman approved the Post Office Department Financial Control Act, which transferred to the Post Office Department the administrative accounting and reporting work done by GAO for the department for many years. GAO was to prescribe accounting principles and standards for the Post Office Department, cooperate in development of its accounting system, and do comprehensive site audits of its financial transactions.[70] Warren wrote that this law "did for the Post Office Department what the Budget and Accounting Procedures Act did for the Government as a whole. . . ." He had contributed to the drafting of the law and strongly supported it.[71]

To implement the act, GAO transferred the staff (779), records, equipment, and funds of its Postal Accounts Division, still located in Asheville, North Carolina, to the Post Office Department. To handle GAO's audit of the

---

[69]GAO-GSA Press Release, January 18, 1950, with attachment, "Memorandum Regarding Working Relationship Between General Accounting Office and General Services Administration," signed by Warren and Larson on January 17, 1950, B-87880.

[70]Public Law 81-712, 64 Stat. 460.

[71]*Comptroller General of the United States: Annual Report for the Fiscal Year Ended June 30, 1950* (Washington: GPO, n. d.), 42-48; GAO *Annual Report, 1951,* 2-3; and letter, Warren to Sen. Olin D. Johnston, chairman, Senate Committee on the Post Office and Civil Service, June 4, 1951, 358 MS 185.

department, Warren established a new Postal Audit Division in November 1950.[72] GAO's audit of the department was, as Warren reported, "the largest undertaking in terms of volume of transactions and operating dispersion assigned for comprehensive audit."[73]

To Warren, the act was welcome; it correlated well with the principles and the objectives of both the Joint Accounting Improvement Program and the comprehensive audit. Henceforth the Post Office Department would do its own accounting work, as GAO preferred, and GAO would apply the comprehensive audit approach in auditing the department. The new law was consistent with the direction in which Warren was leading GAO.

The Amendments to the National Security Act, 1949

GAO played an important role in 1949 in development of amendments to the National Security Act. This activity was directly related to the efforts GAO was making to improve federal financial management. The National Security Act of 1947 established the National Military Establishment (NME), headed by the secretary of defense and including the Departments of the Army, the Navy, and the Air Force, as well as the Joint Chiefs of Staff. The law established several other national security agencies—the National Security Council, the Central Intelligence Agency, and the National Security Resources Board.[74]

Early NME operations revealed some defects in the law. James V. Forrestal, the first secretary of defense, recommended changes, as did the Hoover Commission's Committee on National Security Organization. In March 1949, President Truman made specific proposals to Congress for amending the law "to convert the National Military Establishment into an Executive Department . . . to be known as the Department of Defense . . . and to provide the Secretary of Defense with appropriate responsibility and authority. . . ."[75] Within a few months, Congress agreed on legislation amending the National Security Act, and President Truman approved it on August 10, 1949.

---

[72]Office Order No. 92—Revised, "Establishing the Postal Audit Division and Abolishing the Postal Accounts Division," November 1, 1950, 351 MS 1; and Weitzel testimony, March 13, 1951, *Independent Offices Appropriation for 1952*, Hearings before a Subcommittee of the House Committee on Appropriations, pt. 1, 82d Cong., 1st Sess. (Washington: GPO, 1951), 1497-1500.

[73]GAO, *Annual Report, 1951*, 26.

[74]Public Law 80-253, 61 Stat. 495, approved July 26, 1947.

[75]Truman's message of March 5, 1949, is reprinted in Alice C. Cole et al., eds., *The Department of Defense: Documents on Establishment and Organization, 1944-1978* (Washington: Office of the Secretary of Defense, Historical Office, 1978), 77-80.

The law created an executive department, the Department of Defense, to replace the NME. The Departments of the Army, the Navy, and the Air Force became *military* departments, to be administered by their respective secretaries, who lost cabinet status. The secretary of defense received "direction, authority, and control" over DOD, an effort to increase his authority over the whole organization, including the military departments, and the addition of an undersecretary and three assistant secretaries strengthened his office. The law also provided for a designated chairman of the Joint Chiefs of Staff.[76]

GAO's interest in the 1949 amendments centered on the entirely new Title IV, "Promotion of Economy and Efficiency Through Establishment of Uniform Budgetary and Fiscal Procedures and Organization." GAO participated actively in development of the title. Sen. Millard E. Tydings (D—Maryland), chairman of the Senate Committee on Armed Services, introduced a bill amending the National Security Act in March 1949. Later he sent Warren a copy of the draft amendments and a detailed explanation of them. At the same time, the committee's chief clerk communicated with Walter Frese, leading to several conferences involving GAO, Treasury, BOB, NME, and the committee staff. This group proposed changes in the draft amendments, specifically to what became Title IV.

Warren commented in detail on the several provisions in the draft title. He wrote to Tydings that the program proposed in Title IV was of great significance to JAIP. If the amendments were adopted, GAO, BOB, and Treasury would work closely with the new Department of Defense so that the accounting system developed by DOD would respond to the needs of internal management and would be consistent with the accounting principles and standards developed for the federal government.[77]

Title IV created the position of comptroller of the Department of Defense and charged him with supervising and directing the DOD's budget estimates. He was also to establish and supervise the execution of principles, policies, and procedures to be followed in preparing and executing budgets; fiscal, cost, operating, and property accounting; progress and statistical reporting; internal audit; and expending and collecting DOD funds. There was also to be a comptroller in each military department.

Warren considered Title IV to be one of the significant early accomplishments of JAIP.[78] Together with the Federal Property and Administration Services Act,

---

[76]Public Law 81-216, 63 Stat. 578.

[77]Letter, Warren to Tydings, May 4, 1949, 333 MS 416a.

[78]For a documentary history of the 1949 amendments, with commentary, see Cole et al., *The Department of Defense: Documents on Establishment and Organization, 1944-1978*, 61-111.

the Post Office Department Financial Control Act, and the Budget and Accounting Procedures Act, the 1949 amendments symbolized the expanding influence and usefulness of the joint program.

GAO's Transformation

Comptroller General Warren set out consciously at the end of World War II to transform GAO into a modern professional agency, capable of contributing substantially to the efficient and economical operation of the federal government. He concluded that GAO needed to discard many old ideas and approaches to its work and indeed in some cases to give up traditional duties. Through GAO's audits of government corporations, development of JAIP, and adoption of the comprehensive audit, Warren built the framework for GAO's transformation.

The corporation audits program made necessary the professionalization of GAO and served as a model for development of a more far-reaching audit approach that went beyond confirming the legality and the mathematical accuracy of federal financial transactions. Through JAIP and its confirmation in the Budget and Accounting Procedures Act, Warren and his BOB and Treasury partners centered responsibility for accounting in the executive branch, where it belonged, leaving the independent auditing function to GAO, where it belonged. The act, Warren stated, embodied the principles and the objectives of the joint program. The passage of the law, he wrote, gave him "a great deal of personal satisfaction. . . . What has been accomplished so far, during the last three years [1947-1950], is even more than we could have hoped for in the beginning."[79]

Examples of improvements made under the joint program in the Warren era include installation of a revamped accounting system for the Bureau of Reclamation, progress in revision of the accounting system of the Maritime Administration, development of procedures to revise the accounting system of the National Bureau of Standards, development of an accounting system for the General Services Administration, decentralization of accounting functions to field offices in the Bureau of Mines, and revision of accounting systems for the Coast Guard and the Bureau of Engraving and Printing.[80]

After passage of the Budget and Accounting Procedures Act, GAO and Treasury pledged mutual cooperation in implementing the law.[81] Just ten

---

[79]GAO, *Annual Report, 1950*, iii.

[80]Ibid., 18-20.

[81]Letter, Snyder to Warren, October 11, 1950, B-87209, #2; and letter, Warren to Snyder, October 23, 1950, ibid.

days after the president signed the law, GAO and Treasury issued Joint Regulation No. 1, on procedures for handling repayments to appropriations, based on authority provided in the new law. In April 1951, they issued Joint Regulation No. 2, which dealt with procedures for making appropriated funds available for disbursement.[82]

In November 1952, GAO issued the first of a series of Accounting Principles Memorandums entitled "Statement of Accounting Principles and Standards for the Guidance of Executive Agencies of the Federal Government," based on the Budget and Accounting Procedures Act. Warren explained that the purposes of the statement were to provide a flexible framework to fit accounting to the needs of individual organizations, stimulate adherence to the highest standards of accounting and financial reporting, and encourage continued improvement of government financial management. In congressional testimony, he pointed out that "never before have any such overall accounting principles and standards been laid down for the Government. . . . [Their adoption] by the agencies can only result in better accounting and financial reporting through the entire Government."[83] The 1952 statement of accounting principles and standards was the forerunner of GAO's later, more-detailed *Policy and Procedures Manual for Guidance of Federal Agencies.*[84]

The Budget and Accounting Procedures Act was important for another reason: It symbolized the successful effort of GAO to fend off another attempt, reminiscent of those that had been made in the 1920s and 1930s, to alter GAO's role and structure. What the Hoover Commission proposed would, in Warren's view, have interfered with JAIP's purposes and objectives and decreased GAO's ability to audit executive branch agencies effectively. Some good came from the Hoover proposals—including the Federal Property and Administrative Services Act and the Post Office Department Financial Control Act. The first law expanded GAO's audit authority in a legitimate direction; the second relieved GAO of a duty that the Office thought should have been lodged in the Post Office Department much earlier. Warren saw these laws as entirely consistent with the Joint Accounting Improvement Program and the comprehensive audit.

The comprehensive audit represented a new concept of auditing, keyed to the need for oversight of government operations. GAO developed both the concept

[82]Treasury Department-General Accounting Office Joint Regulation No. 1, September 22, 1950, 349 MS 1254a; and Treasury Department-General Accounting Office Joint Regulation No. 2, April 16, 1951, 356 MS 973a.

[83]Warren testimony, March 5, 1953, *Independent Offices Appropriations for 1954*, Hearings before a Subcommittee of the House Committee on Appropriations, 83d Cong., 1st Sess, pt. 3 (Washington: GPO, 1953), 723; and GAO, *Annual Report, 1953*, 58-59.

[84]Mosher, *GAO*, 121-22.

and the techniques required to implement it. The old voucher-checking audit, which Warren worked to discard, had originated in England much earlier. For corporation audits, GAO adapted audit techniques that the public accounting profession in the United States had developed. The comprehensive audit, a GAO innovation, was a very important contribution. It provided the basis as it evolved for the movement of GAO into program evaluation in the late 1960s and beyond.

CHAPTER 14

Reorganization Under Warren for the New GAO

By 1949, the major program changes that Comptroller General Lindsay C. Warren considered necessary to make the General Accounting Office (GAO) a more vital organization had been put in place—the Joint Accounting Improvement Program (JAIP) and the comprehensive audit. As these programs began to operate, Warren recognized the need for organizational changes to ensure effective performance by GAO.

An important factor was Warren's interest in running GAO economically. Among other things, this necessitated substantial staff reductions. After reaching a high of nearly 15,000 employees in early 1946, the staff declined gradually to less than 9,000 in mid-1949.[1] Warren favored further staff cuts to keep GAO's budget under control. Also, GAO's organization and efficiency were matters of congressional interest. For example, in 1952, Congress pressed GAO to establish an overseas office in Europe.[2]

Warren proceeded slowly in making major changes. In November 1949, he commissioned Ted B. Westfall of the Corporation Audits Division to review GAO's operations and organization and make recommendations based on his studies.[3] Warren thus initiated the Westfall Survey, which lasted from 1949 to 1952. Much of Warren's reorganization occurred in 1952, after he had received most of Westfall's reports and recommendations.

The Westfall Survey

As Westfall completed his early survey reports, he submitted them to the comptroller general. After he became director of audits in May 1951, with responsibility for overall planning and programming for audits done by GAO's four audit divisions, he usually circulated the reports informally to division

---

[1] See appendix V.
[2] See pp. 362-64, for discussion of creation of the European Branch in 1952.
[3] See chapter 13, pp. 320-21.

and office heads for internal discussion and, in some cases, reorganization action by the comptroller general.[4]

Report on the Audit Division

Westfall's survey report on the Audit Division, dated September 30, 1950, was one of the first he completed. This division, created in 1926 by combining the Military and Civil Divisions, included various sections with specifically defined duties. In this report, Westfall paid considerable attention to the cost and the efficiency of voucher audits done by the Audit Division—those done centrally in Washington, those done at the military and naval subdivisions in Saint Louis and Cleveland, and those done by the Field Audit Section of the division at sites around the country. Westfall reported that staff in the Cleveland and Saint Louis subdivisions audited about twice as many vouchers per staff-year as the Washington staff and that the subdivision staff costs to examine a contract were only 25 percent as much as those for the Washington staff. Furthermore, collections made by the subdivisions, calculated as a percentage of audit costs, averaged four to five times higher than those made by the Washington division. Westfall criticized the Audit Division for failing to use selective audit techniques rather than auditing every voucher received in an account. He complained that the audits of some classes of vouchers, for example, those on compensation, insurance, and payroll, were "so ineffective as to be practically worthless."

Westfall criticized also the Audit Division's management for failing to correct these problems. He pointed out another organizational weakness—the faulty placement of advisers and assistants in the division's management. The background of these staff suggested that seniority rather than merit was their most important qualification. Westfall discovered that the division used auditors to perform clerical duties. "The management of the Audit Division," the survey report concluded, "does not assume responsibilities commensurate with the position and remuneration received." The report contained 15 specific recommendations for improvement. Some proposed transfer of functions from one section to another—for example, shifting all revenue and receipts audits to the Field Audit Section and the work of the Passenger Travel Unit to the Transportation Division. Another recommendation

---

[4]See *Comptroller General of the United States: Annual Report for the Fiscal Year Ended June 30, 1951* (Washington: GPO, n.d.), 20, for Westfall's appointment as director of audits. See below, pp. 343-46, for a detailed discussion of the origins of the position. Westfall's survey records consist of two boxes held by the GAO History Program Archives. These boxes contain copies of some, probably not all, of the survey reports and, in some cases, related internal correspondence. References hereafter to materials in these boxes are to *Westfall Survey Records* and include the box number, the document title, and the date when given.

proposed "assignment of clean-cut lines of authority and delegation of responsibility at each level of supervision within the Division." Westfall also suggested reorganizing the division on an agency basis, creating a procedures and internal review staff, setting production standards for purposes of qualitative control, and using clerks to perform clerical duties in the voucher audit.[5]

E. W. Bell, the chief of the Audit Division, reacted mildly to the critical tone of Westfall's report. He said that he generally agreed with the major recommendations but thought that "many of the criticisms . . . are neither well-founded nor warranted on the basis of a full and proper evaluation of all the facts, conditions, and surrounding circumstances." Bell noted that some of Westfall's recommendations had already been implemented, including establishment of production standards and transfer of revenue and receipts audits to the Field Audit Section. He agreed that "refinements in basic principles and organization will have to be made from time to time" and that they would benefit from Westfall's recommendations.[6]

Proposal for a Director of Audits

As Westfall's survey progressed, he became convinced "that the audit responsibilities of the Office cannot be effectively discharged under the present organizational set-up." Noting that the comprehensive audit program was getting under way and that the Korean conflict would necessitate vast defense spending, Westfall argued for "maximum flexibility in the utilization of audit personnel" to ensure the concentration of audit activities on government operations that required immediate attention.

He recommended the appointment of a director of audits, responsible for planning and coordination, with the authority to direct action by the Audit, Corporation Audits, Postal Audit, and Reconciliation and Clearance divisions. The director of audits should be assisted by a small technical staff to help formulate policies and procedures and review division operations and a staff manager to handle recruitment, training, and audit staff assignments. The present division directors would report to the director of audits rather than the comptroller general. Eventually, Westfall proposed, the operating divisions should be organized on an agency basis with complete responsibility for all audit and settlement functions relating to their assigned agencies.

[5]*Westfall Survey Records*, Box 1, Folder: "Audit Survey: Analysis of the Operations and Organization of the Audit Division," September 30, 1950.

[6]Memorandum, Bell to Westfall, April 27, 1951, *Westfall Survey Records*, Box 1, Folder: "Westfall Survey Papers, 1951-1952." Someone, perhaps Westfall, made handwritten notes on this memorandum, questioning whether the changes Bell claimed had already occurred had really been made.

Finally, he recommended reorganizing and strengthening the existing field offices to do all audit work outside Washington.[7]

GAO's division and office chiefs reacted to Westfall's proposal in memorandums to Warren and in a series of meetings. Walter Frese of the Accounting Systems Division agreed completely with Westfall's initiative, saying that the work of his division needed to be completely coordinated with all audit activities. Accounting Systems should be informed of all audit findings showing deficiencies in accounting procedures in order to take corrective action. Also, the division's systems work should be followed by audits to determine the effectiveness of systems operations. Frese added that the present defense effort made implementation of Westfall's recommendations urgent.[8]

The early discussion of Westfall's proposal introduced the notion that the director of audits should be an assistant comptroller general. Westfall explained to Warren why he did not favor this idea. The director of audits, he said, should be concerned with "the day-to-day coordination and direction of the audit activities" and had to be an operator in his own right. It would be quite proper to put an outstanding accountant at the assistant comptroller general level, but this position should be in the policy area, concerned with audit policies and processes as well as accounting systems. Westfall observed that appointment of a new assistant comptroller general would require legislative changes.[9]

Division chiefs who responded to Westfall's proposal for a director of audits generally agreed with it, although some had qualifications. Stephen B. Ives, director of the Corporation Audits Division (CAD), pointed out that increased emphasis on defense audits and the transition to the comprehensive audit suggested the need for overall audit supervision.[10] Gary Campbell, chief of the Postal Audit Division, endorsed Westfall's plan, although he thought that the audit divisions should move to a departmental basis immediately rather than later as Westfall had proposed. He also considered the federal government's structure, laws, and regulations too complex to do field audits on a "pool" basis, as Westfall had suggested.[11]

---

[7]Memorandum, Westfall to the comptroller general, December 29, 1950, *Westfall Survey Records*, ibid.

[8]Memorandum, Frese to the comptroller general, January 4, 1951, ibid.

[9]Memorandum, Westfall to the comptroller general, January 4, 1951, ibid. The Budget and Accounting Act, 1921, provided for one assistant comptroller general.

[10]Memorandum, Ives to the comptroller general, January 5, 1951, ibid.

[11]Memorandum, Campbell to the comptroller general, January 12, 1951, ibid.

E. W. Bell of the Audit Division had reservations about Westfall's plan, especially the conduct of audits in the field. He thought that Westfall's objectives—maximum flexibility in staff use and concentration on defense activities—already were being met for the most part by the existing field audit organization in his division. He argued that Washington division chiefs should have "technical and functional control" of staff under their jurisdiction and that regional office heads should have administrative control of all personnel in their regions, but not responsibility for the technical and functional accomplishment of assigned work.[12]

William L. Ellis, chief of investigations, wrote a thoughtful memorandum to Assistant Comptroller General Frank L. Yates about Westfall's proposal for a director of audits. He began with a minihistory of GAO. GAO was "very much an office of law" 15 or 30 years ago. "Our function began, and too often ended, with a legal decision of a quasi-judicial character upon how much should not have been paid to some one. . . ." Now GAO did not have the "extra-judicial function of decision" on at least 80 percent of government disbursements—that function had been moved to the agencies. "What remains," he concluded, "is sort of an advisory audit, a certain function of checking disbursements but without the omnipotence it once had." GAO, he believed, had "shifted . . . [its] sights from details to operations, from transactions to methods, from end results to organizational approaches." Westfall's proposal was appropriate; GAO needed more coordination and consistency among the four audit divisions. As for a director of audits, "If the right genius be at hand, then let's go ahead with it. If the nominee be one of a little less ducal stature, perhaps a beginning could be found by making the new job a coordinator of policy, methodology, approach, and work distribution, leaving operations where they are."[13]

On April 26, 1951, Warren, Westfall, and the division and office chiefs discussed the proposal for a director of audits. Westfall explained his plan, stating that he thought that the audit divisions should retain technical direction of audits but that the director of audits should have authority both to act in this area if necessary and to decide how field audits should operate. There was a long discussion on whether to have a consolidated audit division or to retain the existing separate divisions under a director of audits. Some officials, such as Frese and General Counsel E. Lyle Fisher, favored one large division. Frese did not think that such an arrangement could be worked out immediately. He again maintained that audit division chiefs should be responsible for the technical performance of the work. Robert F. Keller, an

---

[12]Memorandum, Bell to the comptroller general, January 19, 1951, ibid.

[13]Memorandum, Ellis to the assistant comptroller general, April 24, 1951, ibid.

assistant to the comptroller general, suggested that if GAO could not give the director of audits both the responsibility and the authority for doing the job, the idea be dropped.

At the end of the meeting Assistant Comptroller General Yates summarized the apparent conclusions of the attendees on the powers, the duties, and the responsibilities of the director of audits. He was to coordinate, plan, program, followup on, and review audit work; ensure coverage of all GAO areas of responsibility and be authorized to direct the audit divisions to take action in areas not covered; be responsible for the distribution and the effective use of staff in the audit divisions; and rely on audit division chiefs for detailed performance of audits. The meeting record indicated that no one present objected to Yates's summary.[14]

Comptroller General Warren followed up on this meeting by appointing Ted Westfall as the director of audits. He was to be a staff officer responsible for overall planning, programming, and correlation of audits.[15] The appointment demonstrated Warren's high confidence in Westfall, who had been at GAO for five years and was only 31 years old. Westfall assumed his duties as director of audits and continued to lead the organizational survey assigned to him in 1949.[16]

Survey of Audit Activities in Washington and the Field

Westfall continued the organizational survey with a broad analysis of the full scope of GAO's audit activities, completed in November 1951. He began a report on this analysis by stating that the primary purpose of an audit "should be to determine how well each agency has discharged its financial responsibilities." GAO needed to determine in audits whether an agency was carrying out activities and programs and related spending as authorized by Congress; collecting and properly accounting for revenue; adequately safeguarding, controlling, and using its assets; and issuing reports that "disclose fully the nature and scope of activities conducted and provide the Congress and others with a proper basis for evaluating the agency's operations." Westfall spelled out how GAO should conduct such audits. GAO could use completed audits to assist the appropriations committees and the Bureau of the Budget (BOB) with their examinations of annual budget estimates and

---

[14]Memorandum, unaddressed and unsigned, April 26, 1951, ibid.

[15]Comptroller General's Order No. 1.32, "Establishing the Position of Director of Audits," May 14, 1951, Comptroller General's Orders, 1951 edition, part I, GAO Records. See also GAO, *Annual Report, 1951*, 20.

[16]See pp. 341-57.

"furnish more intelligent comments to the Congress with respect to substantive legislation affecting the operations of the various agencies."

Westfall concluded that the lack of qualified staff was the principal deterrent to completing high-quality audits. He argued that GAO's voucher auditors did not have the necessary training or experience. "Moreover, the high average age (54) of the audit personnel precludes any real success from training or efforts to gain understanding and adopt changed concepts of audit." He also thought that the majority of these auditors, because of their personalities, physical infirmities, and home and family ties, would be unable to accept field employment. He felt that the comprehensive auditors in CAD and the Postal Audit Division were highly competent but that many of them with public accounting backgrounds needed training and reorientation. He expressed particular concern about the limited audit GAO did of military activities. Finally, he proposed establishment of a single field organization to position GAO to make significant progress with the comprehensive audit.[17]

Westfall's survey group visited 19 area field offices (of a total of 28) in the six field zones. The objective was to assess the administrative and technical procedures followed and the overall effectiveness of field audits. The survey disclosed that field offices usually conducted voucher audits and that they emphasized money collections and disclosure of exceptions. "The logical effect of such a philosophy," Westfall's field survey report observed, "is that the entire subject of exceptions is thrown out of its proper perspective in that little attempt is made to eliminate the causes of exceptions and thereby prevent their reoccurrence." The report concluded that the administrators of the field audit unit in the Audit Division provided little direction and that conditions in the field reflected that fact.[18]

A supplement to the report summarized visits to individual area offices. These visits led to a critical conclusion: "Except where otherwise indicated, surveys, programs, working papers and the coordination of audit scope and detail with that of agency audit staffs, have been inadequate, with few individual exceptions, to constitute effective auditing and reasonable efficiency of audit operations." The Washington area office, the largest one, was "poorly administered" and lacked "sufficient qualified personnel" and "intelligent planning." The Oak Ridge area office received credit for moving toward a comprehensive audit of Atomic Energy Commission matters, but "the com-

---

[17]*Westfall Survey Records*, Box 1, Folder: "Audit Survey: An Analysis of the Audit Activities of the General Accounting Office," from the office of the director of audits, November 1951.

[18]*Westfall Survey Records*, Box 1, Folder: "Audit Survey—Report on Survey of Field and Audit Section, Audit Division," undated but internal evidence shows that it was written in 1951.

prehensive phase of the audit was largely ineffective." At San Francisco, "technical supervision is weak" and the auditors "receive little direction." The Detroit area office received criticism for imperfections in the technical aspects of its work but commendations for a broader audit approach, "due principally to the influence and personality of the zone chief." In his area's audits, the zone chief, Kurt W. Krause, encouraged "a keen sense of alertness, inquisitiveness, and some skepticism."[19]

Edward W. Bell, Chief, Audit Division (seated, second from right) and field audit zone chiefs, November 1950. Kurt W. Krause, seated far right; Charles M. Bailey, standing, second from left, and Richard J. Madison, standing, third from left.

The Atlanta office, concerned chiefly with Veterans Administration (VA) tuition and subsistence payments and payrolls, had five suboffices. Westfall's team could not review Atlanta's VA work because audit files for educational institutions were not assembled and could not be examined. "In general," the team concluded, "it did not appear that much had been accomplished recently in the way of completed work." The report noted that the area office supervisor and the zone chief did little personal inspection of the suboffices.

---

[19]See memorandum, Warren to chiefs of divisions and offices and agency heads (for information), January 18, 1952, B-107471, indicating Krause's position as zone chief of the Great Lakes Zone.

The Atlanta zone chief, Richard J. Madison, recorded his impressions of two visits to Atlanta by the survey group, apparently to inform other field office officials of what they might expect.

> Each visit lasted several weeks during which time exhaustive examinations were made of all written programs, instructions and operations. Personnel, both audit and supervisory, were questioned at great length. . . . Maintenance of files, audit programs and the reports of audit were examined in detail. Searching questions . . . were asked. Copies of programs and reports had to be furnished as well as statistics of every nature. The more advance preparation that is made in expectation of such visits the easier it will be when the surveyors arrive and you can be assured that they will stay until they obtain the answers to all of their questions or an unfavorable report . . . will issue showing failure to cooperate.

"You may be assured," he wrote, "that these men call their shots as they see them and all of them that the undersigned has knowledge of are high calibre specialists in this sort of work."[20]

Area Chief Harold L. Ryder of the Santa Monica, California, office re-acted adversely to the report on the survey team's visit to his office in May and June 1951. "The report," Ryder wrote, "is made up of a series of unsupported criticisms apparently aimed at the Area Chief rather than the audit performance of the station as a whole." He complained that the report did not mention the area's "outstanding accomplishments," the volume of work completed by a small staff, and his efforts to institute an audit consistent with principles included in the Budget and Accounting Procedures Act.[21]

In November 1951, Westfall proposed to Warren establishment of a single organization to do all field audits except for those done in the military subdivisions. He recommended that the heads of field offices report to him, with technical instructions issued by the division chiefs responsible for audits of particular agencies. The field organization was "urgently needed" to facilitate training of field staff and establishing site and comprehensive audits in the field and a nationwide program to review military procurement. A single organization would simplify the administrative task and avoid the "empire building" that could happen in separate offices.

---

[20]*Westfall Survey Records*, Box 1, Folder: "Westfall Survey Papers, 1951-1952."

[21]Memorandum, Ryder to Charles M. Bailey, September 14, 1951, *Westfall Survey Records*, Box 1, Folder: "Audit Survey—Loose Correspondence."

Westfall told Warren that he understood that the chiefs of the Postal Audit and Corporation Audits divisions felt that they could not assume responsibility for audits of agencies assigned to them unless they had administrative control of field staff working on audits of those agencies. Westfall said that the solution was to hold division heads responsible only for work done under their administrative control and to assign responsibility for audits done in the field to the director of audits. "To be perfectly plain about it," Westfall told Warren, "I am considerably more concerned with the audit work as a whole for which the Comptroller General must assume final responsibility than I am about the responsibilities of the individual division chiefs."[22]

In a subsequent memorandum, apparently after further thinking, Westfall said that he did not think that it made much difference whether the field offices were in a field operations division with a chief in Washington or reported to him as director of audits through a member of his staff responsible for field operations. This was somewhat of a change from his earlier proposal. The division chief would be responsible for administrative supervision of the field offices, and the auditing divisions would be responsible for providing technical instructions for work on agencies they were assigned to audit. The local heads of field offices would have technical and administrative control over work performed in their offices. While the field organization was building up, Washington divisions would need to send staff to perform work in the field.[23]

Development of a new field system was very important to Westfall and was one of the most prominent recommendations emanating from both his survey of GAO's organization and his initial experience in 1951 as director of audits. Warren took action on Westfall's field operations proposal in 1952 when he established a new regional office system.[24]

Survey of the Corporation Audits Division

Westfall's group issued several other survey reports, including one on the CAD. Westfall did not shy away from criticism in this report, even though he had come to GAO originally to join CAD and had become prominent through participation in audits of the Reconstruction Finance Corporation and the Maritime Commission between 1946 and 1949. The CAD survey

---

[22]Memorandum, Westfall to Warren, November 9, 1951, *Westfall Survey Records*, Box 1, Folder: "Audit Survey: An Analysis of the Audit Activities of the General Accounting Office," November 1951.

[23]Memorandum, Westfall to the comptroller general, December 4, 1951, *Westfall Survey Records*, Box 1, Folder: "Audit Survey—Loose Correspondence."

[24]See pp. 360-62, for information on the 1952 reorganization of field operations.

document criticized the lateness of the division's reports. The Government Corporation Control Act specified that annual audit reports on each corporation were to be issued no later than January 15 following the close of the fiscal year, but the division had failed to meet this deadline. Westfall enumerated the performance defects of CAD assistant directors—assigning audits with little initial instruction; failing to maintain contact with supervisory accountants; and submitting poorly written reports on controversial questions.

The survey report recommended that to alleviate the problems of lateness and quality, the CAD director, deputy director, and assistant directors develop closer coordination on audit scope, progress, and report content. Assistant directors and supervisory accountants should settle any controversial questions, and assistant directors should consult frequently with supervisory accountants and audit staff while reports were being written.

Another criticism was that training in CAD was "hardly more than thinly disguised free CPA [certified public accountant] coaching courses, and as pure theory contribute[d] little to the Division." The report recommended discontinuing the courses and requiring supervisory staff to devote more time to on-the-job training and entering into agreements with other divisions and government agencies to transfer qualified personnel to CAD.

Westfall's group scolded CAD for failing to begin surveys of property accounting systems of agencies, though authorized to do so by the comptroller general early in 1950 on the basis of the Federal Property and Administrative Services Act of 1949. The report recommended that CAD promptly make proposals for carrying out this function.[25]

Survey of the Office of Investigations

The Office of Investigations (OI) came under serious criticism by the Westfall survey team. The OI survey report included several principal findings: (1) the assistant chiefs' responsibilities were not at a level commensurate with their rank; (2) administrative control over assignments was ineffective; (3) assignments took too much time, both in the field and in Washington; (4) the office's procedures manual failed to provide proper guidance for the field in conducting assignments or report writing, and many reports received from the field had been poorly prepared, were too long, and were

---

[25]*Westfall Survey Records*, Box 1, Folder: "Audit Survey—Survey Corporation Audits Division, Section I, Narrative Report," undated.

"burdened with verbose descriptions, citations of references and legalistic rhetoric;" (5) the OI management considered some staff incompetent—"We were informed that upwards of 10 of a total of 37 staff investigators [in Washington] are deemed incapable of productive service in the regular functions of the Office; and that certain others are not sufficiently competent to permit reasonable reliance on their work"—and similar conditions existed in the field; (6) investigators in charge of field offices did not provide enough on-the-job supervision; (7) levels of supervision at Washington were too elaborate, leading to duplication of effort and slow work; and (8) the Washington staff was too large.

The report proposed a long list of changes to solve these problems. They included broadening the duties of assistant chiefs, planning and scheduling assignments well ahead of time when possible, abolishing the position of section head and putting the assignment of investigators in the hands of assistant chiefs, and requiring the assistant chiefs to review reports from the field to get a general understanding of their contents. Other recommendations were to institute a time control system in both Washington and the field, prepare a practical work manual for investigators, require the field to provide complete and finished reports on assignments, and require investigators in charge of field offices to provide on-the-job supervision. To improve the staff, "positive administrative action should be taken to reduce the high percentage of incompetent personnel particularly at Washington and to establish requisites for employment which will facilitate the recruitment of investigators properly qualified for the present character of the work of the Office."[26]

In a separate memorandum to Warren, Westfall mentioned that the report had been discussed extensively with William L. Ellis, the chief of investigations, and that he had generally agreed with the findings and recommendations. Westfall noted that Ellis was aware of the problem of incompetent personnel and was trying to deal with it, although much remained to be done. He suggested to Warren that he give Ellis strong backing in this area and added, "Perhaps some needling on your part would help too."[27]

---

[26] *Westfall Survey Records*, Box 1, Folder: "Report on Survey, Office of Investigations," undated but probably November 1951.

[27] Memorandum, Westfall to the comptroller general, November 30, 1951, ibid. When the author interviewed Ellis in 1990, shortly before his death, he could not recall actually having seen the Westfall survey report on the Office of Investigations, although he remembered discussing it with Westfall many times. See GAO, *William L. Ellis, GAO, 1935-1955*, GAO History Program, Oral History Series, GAO/OP-21-OH (Washington: 1991), 22. See chapter 17, pp. 411-15, 419-20, for further discussion about O.I.

Survey of the Claims Division

Another of Westfall's reports covered the work of the Claims Division. Although a copy of the full survey report is not available, a memorandum prepared by GAO's Office of Administrative Planning reacting to the report sheds some light on its contents. The report recommended reorganizing the Claims Division on a functional basis, instituting a recruitment program to hire competent staff, and appointing an administrator from outside the division. There were also proposals to establish production standards and revise procedures. In commenting on the Claims report, the acting chief of the Office of Administrative Planning wrote: "Claims Division officials should be mindful at all times of the progress of the Office [GAO], and in keeping therewith, should seriously consider the propriety and desirability of discontinuing procedures and instructions of long standing that no longer serve a useful purpose. . . ."[28]

A part of the Claims survey report covered the operations of the Indian Tribal Section of the Claims Division. This section dated back to the 1920s and 1930s, when it handled GAO's earlier work on tribal claims.[29] The section expanded after a new Indian Claims Commission began to operate in August 1946; the Commission was to exist until April 1957, according to the law that created it. By August 1951, the Commission had received 420 petitions from Indian tribes covering 852 separate claims. The principal job of the Indian Tribal Section in the late 1940s was to prepare accounting reports on treaty and trust fund receipts and disbursements for the use of the Indian Claims Commission and the Department of Justice in settling claims.

The problem, as Westfall reported to Warren, was that between 1947 and the end of 1951, the Indian Tribal Commission had disposed of only 56 of the 852 claims. The Commission placed part of the blame for its lack on progress on GAO's slow preparation of the background reports. The chief of the Indian Tribal Section informed Westfall that his section, with 89 staff, would not complete all the accounting reports requested by the Department of Justice until early 1959—about two years after the scheduled statutory end of the Indian Claims Commission. To solve the problem, Westfall made recommendations to reduce and accelerate the work of the Indian Tribal Section.[30]

---

[28]Memorandum, Ellis S. Stone to the comptroller general, June 6, 1952, *Westfall Survey Records*, Box 2, Folder: "Claims Survey—Loose Papers."

[29]See chapter 8, pp. 191-93.

[30]*Westfall Survey Records*, Box 2, Folder: "Claims Survey—An Analysis of the Operations and Organization of the Claims Division Indian Tribal Section, April 1952." The first eight pages of this document are the text of memorandum, Westfall to the comptroller general, April 25, 1952, in which he summarizes the problems of the Indian Tribal Section and makes recommendations.

Survey of General Management Activities

The Westfall survey report on GAO's general management activities, mainly on the work of the Office of Administrative Planning and the executive officer, was hard-hitting and played an important role in Warren's later reorganization actions. The Office of Administrative Planning conducted organizational studies and surveys, developed the annual budget estimates, prepared the comptroller general's annual report, acted as the office's records officer, and performed other duties. The executive officer developed and implemented broad management plans, presided at meetings of the comptroller general's staff to ensure coordination and implementation of the work of the operating divisions, advised the comptroller general on new projects, prepared appropriation estimates for submission to the Bureau of the Budget, and allocated the budget to GAO divisions and offices.

Westfall concluded that the functions of the Office of Administrative Planning and the executive officer "have been poorly performed. The primary reason . . . is the inadequacy of the personnel involved." The executive officer concerned himself mainly with general housekeeping activities, and even they were "ineffectively handled." The Office of Administrative Planning had been effective, Westfall claimed, only in areas involving clerical activities. One example he cited was the office's concern with the design and the processing of a particular form "without realizing that the form itself is not necessary and . . . the operation in which it is used serves no worthwhile purpose."

Westfall recommended that the two offices be abolished. The Office of Administrative Planning should be replaced by a Division of Administrative Services to handle housekeeping activities and the duties of the executive officer, except for the budget, as well as the functions of the Indian Tribal Section, the Records Service Branch of the Division of Audits, and payroll work. Westfall estimated that this division would need 845 staff, the number then handling the functions proposed for it.

Westfall proposed the creation of the position of assistant to the comptroller general for general management. This official's job would be to conduct a continuous management review of GAO operations and assume the budget function. Westfall described this position as "one of the half-dozen most important in the Office and accordingly should be filled with one of the Office's top men." The person should "possess a keen analytical mind," "be impartial and hold himself above petty office politics," and "be tough minded and relentless in the performance of his functions."[31]

John F. Feeney, then the executive officer, understandably reacted adversely to the substance and the conclusions of the general management survey. He argued that Westfall's recommendations were not based on an official survey of or discussions with his office, but rather on general conclusions Westfall had made as a result of his total survey and his work as director of audits. Feeney defended his own performance and listed what he considered the accomplishments of his office. He urged retention of the Office of Administrative Planning and his own office, but suggested that the comptroller general appoint an assistant who would conduct continuous surveys and review the work of all operating divisions and offices.[32]

The general management activities survey report precipitated an extended internal discussion, including a meeting in March 1953 presided over by Assistant Comptroller General Yates and including Frank Weitzel, E. L. Fisher, Robert Keller, and Feeney. This meeting took place almost a year after Westfall left GAO; he was not involved in the debate that followed circulation of his report. Yates reported to Warren after the meeting that no one agreed with all the findings and recommendations in the report. The group favored creation of a Planning Office to replace the Office of Administrative Planning, responsible for audit and review of internal operations, advance planning, the annual report, and orders of the comptroller general. To replace the executive officer there would be an Administrative Office with two functions—(1) budget and finance and (2) administrative services, including records administration, procurement, building management, publications, and internal forms.[33]

Survey of the Office of the General Counsel

That the Westfall group also surveyed the Office of the General Counsel (OGC) is evident, but Westfall did not issue a report on this survey before he left GAO in the spring of 1952. In April 1954, Robert F. Brandt, head of a new Planning Staff established in 1953, forwarded to Warren, a few days before he retired as comptroller general, a comprehensive report on OGC. This report could have been the result of Westfall's earlier work on OGC, although there is no direct evidence of this. In any case, Brandt's report

[31]*Westfall Survey Records*, Box 1, Folder: "General Management Activities—Report on the General Management Activities of the General Accounting Office," undated but internal evidence indicates release of the report in 1952.

[32]Memorandum, Feeney to the comptroller general, November 28, 1952, ibid.

[33]Memorandum, Yates to the comptroller general, March 30, 1953, ibid.

announced completion of the OGC review. There were two major deficiencies in OGC: "First, the number of cases, a great many of which deal with insignificant issues, does not warrant the number of employees presently constituting the Office. Secondly, in considering material issues the Counsel's Office consistently shows a strong tendency to side with the [subject] agency's position."

The report offered nine recommendations for changing OGC:

1. "Establish a closer working relationship between the Counsel's staff and the operating divisions."

2. "Transfer the authority to handle certain claims matters to the Claims Division."

3. "Effect a reduction in force of fifteen . . . attorneys."

4. "Review the grade structure of the attorneys . . . with the objective of raising the grade level."

5. "Institute an on-duty training course for the entire staff of attorneys."

6. "Require written memorandums to be prepared on the results of oral conferences between members of the staff of Counsel's Office and officials from other departments and agencies."

7. "Prepare acknowledgments to inquiries and other transmittals under a simplified routine."

8. "Place the responsibility for ascertaining that internal management procedures of the Counsel's Office are followed with the Special Assistant to the General Counsel."

9. "Delegate authority to the General Counsel for final disposition of Comptroller General's decisions involving, in general, military pay and allowance, exceptions against certifying and disbursing officers, and other matters of a less significant nature."[34]

In his response to the report, General Counsel Fisher complained that he had had no chance to comment on the report before it went to the comptrol-

---

[34]Memorandum, Brandt to the comptroller general, April 28, 1954, filed in *Westfall Survey Records*, Box 2, Folder: "General Counsel Survey."

E. Lyle Fisher, General Counsel, 1947-1958.

ler general. He also censured the reports (presumably referring to the previous Westfall survey reports as well as the one for OGC) for presenting only criticism and not giving any credit for accomplishments. "I am sure you feel," he told Acting Comptroller General Weitzel, "that by and large the General Accounting Office is doing a good job, but if one confined himself to reading these survey reports he could hardly get that impression." Other than agreeing with the proposal to review and raise the grade structure of OGC attorneys, Fisher found problems with most of the recommendations in the OGC report.[35]

While there was continued internal discussion about the Brandt recommendations on OGC, there was no substantial reorganization at this time of the legal office. Perhaps Weitzel, as acting comptroller general, was reluctant to take major steps along these lines.

Clearly the Westfall survey operation between 1949 and 1952 was comprehensive, incisive, and hard-hitting. Westfall did not hesitate to criticize individual division and office heads, and he recommended strong action by the comptroller general to improve GAO's organization along the lines he laid out. Throughout his reports, Westfall's interest in seeing GAO modernize comes through strongly—dead wood had to be cleaned out, new methods should be adopted, and the objectives of the Joint Accounting Improvement Program and the comprehensive audit had to be integrated with GAO's total program. Westfall's survey reports had a decided impact on GAO and certainly shook up the established order. Warren made clear his confidence in Westfall by appointing him director of audits in 1951 and head of the large consolidated audit division early in 1952. One can speculate, however, that when Westfall left GAO a few months later, not all the division and office heads were sorry to see him go.[36]

---

[35]Memorandum, Fisher to the acting comptroller general, May 21, 1954, ibid.

[36]See GAO, *Ted B. Westfall, 1946-1952*, GAO History Program, Oral History Series, GAO/OP-2-OH (Washington: GAO, 1988), 56-57. Westfall explained his departure from GAO: "Money and family responsibilities. Pure and simple." He added: "I was living in a rented apartment; I had just had my fourth child. I did not even see the possibility of being able to buy a house in a reasonable period of time."

Warren's Reorganization

Warren substantially reorganized GAO. Many of the reorganization steps reflected the recommendations of Westfall and the reports of his survey group. Although Congress was interested in the reorganization, for the most part the initiative came from Warren himself. Congress did carefully consider GAO's annual appropriation requests and kept fairly close track of staff size. The House Committee on Expenditures in the Executive Departments, in a 1949 study of GAO functions and operations, wrote this about the Office: "It is not hide-bound and wedded to antiquated methods but it is in a fluid state, alert and alive to modern procedures."[37] The study reflected general congressional approval of GAO and a recognition that changes were already taking place under Warren's leadership.

Early Organizational Changes

In January 1948, in his first major organizational change, Warren created the Accounting Systems Division to provide a home and leadership for JAIP.[38] In October 1950, Warren announced a minor reorganization of the Office of Investigations, by then under the direction of William L. Ellis, previously an assistant to Warren. Ellis succeeded Stuart B. Tulloss, one of the division chiefs who opposed the Frese plan in 1949.[39] At this time, OI operated out of Washington headquarters and 20 investigations field offices.[40] In January 1951, because of the rapid increase in defense spending caused by the outbreak of the Korean conflict, Warren ordered OI to develop investigative and survey programs to guard against wasteful practices and operations in the defense area.[41]

In November 1950, concurrently with the transfer of the Postal Accounts Division to the Post Office Department, Warren created the Postal Audit Division to audit the Post Office Department.[42] In a move effective on December 31, 1950, Warren abolished the Accounting and Bookkeeping Division. Most of its work had been discontinued with adoption of the Frese proposals in late 1949. Its director, J. Darlington Denit, had bitterly opposed the Frese

---

[37]*The General Accounting Office: A Study of Its Functions and Operations*, House Committee on Expenditures in the Executive Departments, H. Rept. 1441, 81st Cong., 1st Sess. (Washington: GPO, 1949), 25.

[38]See chapter 13, pp. 314-15.

[39]See ibid., p. 317.

[40]For information on the 1950 reorganization, see Office Order No. 91, "Functions of the Office of Investigations," October 9, 1950, GAO Records.

[41]*Comptroller General of the United States: Annual Report for the Fiscal Year Ended June 30, 1953* (Washington: GPO, n.d.), 49.

[42]See chapter 13, pp. 334-35.

plan. Elimination of the division required transfer of about 60 of its staff of 325 to other divisions and departure of the rest by a reduction-in-force (RIF) effective in January 1951. In discussing this action before a congressional committee, Assistant Comptroller General Yates remarked that it helped to move unproductive staff out of GAO. He described abolishing the Accounting and Bookkeeping Division and the RIF as "our big opportunities. It is awfully difficult to get rid of anybody in the Government service."[43]

The New Division of Audits

In January 1952, eight months after he created the position of director of audits, Warren established under Westfall a new Division of Audits, consolidating four existing organizations—the Audit, Corporation Audits, Postal Audit, and Reconciliation and Clearance divisions. The idea of a consolidated audit division had come up occasionally during earlier discussion of the Westfall survey reports on audit activities.

In his order establishing the division, Warren spelled out its duties: "to audit the accounts of accountable officers either on a comprehensive, site, or centralized basis, settle such accounts, and examine the fiscal operations of all Government agencies; audit the accounts and books and examine the financial transactions of all Government corporations; prepare reports necessary in connection with the foregoing; reconcile depositary accounts of disbursing officers; and maintain, preserve, and service the files of records in the custody of the General Accounting Office pertaining to settled claims and fiscal officers' accounts." The division was to include the existing Air Force, Army, and Navy Audit branches as well as Civil, Depositary Accounts, Examination and Settlement, and Records Service branches.[44]

In a separate memorandum, Warren appointed the top officials of the Division of Audit: Westfall as director; F. W. Bell, Stephen B. Ives, Gary Campbell, and Irwin S. Decker, the former directors of the divisions subsumed by the Division of Audits, as associate directors of audits; and Ellsworth H. Morse, Jr., and Harry J. Trainor as assistants to the director of audits.[45]

---

[43]Yates testimony, March 13, 1951, *Independent Offices Appropriations for 1952*, Hearings before a Subcommittee of the House Committee on Appropriations, 82d Cong., 1st Sess, pt. 1 (Washington: GPO, 1951), 1477, 1486 (source of quote); and memorandum, T. A. Flynn, GAO director of personnel, unaddressed, October 26, 1950, Warren Papers, Scrapbooks, vol. 14. This memorandum explains the impact of abolishing of the Accounting and Bookkeeping Division on its staff and is an official RIF notice. Denit left GAO to join another government agency.

[44]Comptroller General's Order No. 2.20, "Organization and Functions of the Division of Audits," January 18, 1952, GAO Records.

[45]Memorandum, Warren to chiefs of divisions and agency offices and heads (for information), January 18, 1952, B-107471. See also *Comptroller General of the United States: Annual Report for the Fiscal Year Ended June 30, 1952* (Washington: GPO, n.d.), 2.

Westfall immediately specified his own duties and those of his top managers. He as director of audits would assign site and comprehensive audits to the four associate directors, "who will have top responsibility for the conduct of all phases of the jobs." The associate directors were to assign assistant directors and audit staff to individual jobs. Westfall assigned to each of the associate directors responsibility for specified agencies and other units of the federal government.[46]

Warren reported to Congress shortly after organizing the Divisions of Audits that it had 3,400 personnel—of a total GAO staff of a little over 6,000. He summarized the advantages of the new division: "The consolidation will achieve real economies in that it will cut out duplication of administration and enable a far better and more productive utilization of our auditing personnel. It will make for a better auditing job all around." Westfall estimated that GAO would save annually about $100,000 in the cost of administrative personnel. The principal benefit of the change, Westfall added, was "the extension of our site and comprehensive audits in the field." He indicated that a reorganization of GAO's field activities was forthcoming.[47] Accompanying start-up of operations of the Division of Audits was a RIF of about 400 staff. The *Washington Post* reported at the time that this had lowered employee production and morale. According to the Post, "scores of old-line employees with 20 and 25 years of service are being downgraded several grades and are being fired. That has made the employees believe anything can happen at GAO."[48]

Creation of the New Regional Offices System

On April 1, 1952, Warren established a new regional office system in the Division of Audits. Westfall earlier had strongly recommended a single field organization to replace the existing system of six zones, dating back to the World War II period, and many separate field offices for different divisions and offices scattered all over the country.

In fiscal year 1950, for example, GAO had 2,788 staff in the field—177 from the Office of Investigations, 1,300 from the Audit Division, 406 from the Reconciliation and Clearance Division, 890 from the Postal Accounts

---

[46]Westfall, Division of Audits, Assignment No. 1, January 18, 1952, Legislative Digest Unit Files, Box 48, GAO History Program Archives.

[47]Warren and Westfall testimony, January 23, 1952, *Independent Offices Appropriations for 1953*, Hearings before a Subcommittee of the House Committee on Appropriations, 82d Cong., 2d the Sess., pt. 1 (Washington: GAO, 1952), 485-86, 515 (source of the quote).

[48]Clipping, *Government Employees Exchange*, February 13, 1952, clippings files, GAO History Program Archives; and clipping, *Washington Post*, February 25, 1952, Morse Collection, newspaper clippings folder for 3/1/51-3/1/52, GAO History Program Archives.

Division, and 15 from the Personnel Division. These staff had offices in 63 different locations in the United States. The largest concentrations of field staff were in major cities, including Los Angeles (45), San Francisco (43), Atlanta (34), Chicago (68), Detroit (50), Saint Louis (686, including the Army Audit Branch), New York (108), Cleveland (351, including the Navy Audit Branch), and Philadelphia (35).[49] In January 1952, GAO had 24 field offices

First Regional Managers' meeting, October 1952.

of the Office of Investigations; 3 audit branches at Denver (Air Force), Cleveland (Navy), and Saint Louis (Army); and 4 field offices of the Corporation Audits Division.[50]

Warren's order established regional audit offices under the Division of Audits in 23 cities: Boston; New York; Philadelphia; Richmond; Atlanta; Detroit; Cleveland; Dayton; Chicago; Saint Louis; New Orleans; Saint Paul; Kansas City; Dallas; Billings; Denver; Albuquerque; Salt Lake City; Seattle; Portland, OR; San Francisco; Los Angeles; and Juneau, Alaska. GAO previously had field offices operating out of almost all of these cities. The order abolished the six existing zones and assigned to the director of audits the

[49]Testimony of Warren and others, January 27, 1950, *Independent Offices Appropriations for 1951*, Hearings before a Subcommittee of the House Committee on Appropriations, 81st Cong., 2d Sess., pt. 1 (Washington: GPO, 1950), 865, 866-67 (table with number of personnel in field offices, fiscal year 1950).

[50]Testimony by Feeney (executive officer), January 23, 1952, *Independent Offices Appropriations for 1953*, pt. 1, 497.

determination of geographical jurisdiction for each regional office and the designation of suboffices. Warren's order consolidated all the field offices earlier operated by various GAO units into one office in each location, except that OI continued to maintain separate offices in some locations.[51]

The formation of the regional office system put into effect one of the major recommendations of the Westfall survey. The new regional organization came under Westfall's direction as director of audits. But he left GAO within a month to take a position in private industry. His successor as director of the Division of Audits, E. W. Bell, then became the head of the regional office system.[52]

Establishment of the European Branch

At the same time Warren set up the regional organization, he considered establishing overseas offices in Europe and Asia. The post-World War II U.S. occupation of Japan and part of Germany, development of the Cold War in the late 1940s, and the outbreak of the conflict in Korea in 1950 had forced creation of a far-flung network of U.S. bases and military forces overseas, especially in Europe and eastern Asia, including Japan and Korea. GAO did not have a program before 1952 to perform field audits of these operations, which included not only military and naval installations but also State Department activities and the work of other agencies involved in administering foreign military and economic aid.

After Rep. Albert Thomas (D—Texas), the chairman of the Independent Offices Subcommittee of the House Committee on Appropriations, returned from an inspection trip to Europe, he nudged Warren toward action on a European office. "It is my judgment and hope," Thomas wrote to Warren in January 1952, "that your office should immediately set up a branch in Europe and carefully investigate and check ECA [Economic Cooperation Administration] expenditures in England, France, the BENELUX countries and perhaps others. . . ." Thomas complained about waste in the European rearmament program and about a costly housing project near Bonn, Germany, for U.S. civilian government employees.[53] The contents of Thomas's letter appeared in the newspapers, putting further pressure on Warren.[54]

---

[51]Comptroller General's Order No. 2.26, April 1, 1952, GAO Records; and memorandum, Westfall to regional managers, zone chiefs, and area auditors in charge, April 23, 1952, ibid.

[52]In 1956, the Field Operations Division was established as part of another reorganization under Joseph Campbell, Warren's successor. See chapter 18, pp. 451-61.

[53]Letter, Thomas to Warren, January 8, 1952, B-107366, #1. ECA managed Marshall Plan aid.

[54]See clipping, *Washington Evening Star*, January 11, 1952, clippings files, GAO History Program Archives; and clipping, *Rocky Mountain News*, January 13, 1952, Morse Collection, newspaper clippings folder for 3/1/51-3/1/52, GAO History Program Archives.

Warren responded to Thomas by saying that he was concerned by the magnitude of U.S. government spending abroad. He reported that GAO was developing preliminary plans for an overseas office. In testimony two weeks later, Warren said that GAO was considering offices in both Europe and Japan.[55] In late February 1952, he informed Secretary of Defense Robert A. Lovett that GAO planned to establish offices in Europe and Japan in July or August 1952. He told Lovett that he would send a team to Europe in mid-March 1952 to survey U.S. activities before establishing the office there.[56] Warren provided the same information to the director of the Mutual Security Agency and the secretary of state.[57]

Henry R. Domers (third from right) and members of a GAO survey team that studied the feasibility of establishing an office in Europe, 1952.

Following the return of the survey team from Europe, Warren decided to open, on August 1, 1952, a European Branch with headquarters in Paris.

---

[55]Letter, Warren to Thomas, January 10, 1952, B-107366, #1; and Warren testimony, January 23, 1952, *Independent Offices Appropriations for 1953*, 484.

[56]Letter, Warren to the secretary of defense, February 26, 1952, B-107366, #1.

[57]Letters, Warren to W. Averell Harriman, director, Mutual Security Agency, and to the secretary of state, March 5, 1952, ibid. The members of the European survey team were William L. Morrow, associate general counsel; George H. Staples, Henry R. Domers, and Edwin H. Morse, accountants; and Lee G. Seymour and Richard G. Sinclair, investigators.

Henry R. Domers became the first director of the branch.[58] A suboffice of the European Branch opened immediately in London, and later additional suboffices began operations in Rome (December 1952), Frankfurt (January 1953), and Madrid (1954). The European Branch was responsible for GAO work in Europe, North Africa, and the Near East.[59] The staff of the European Branch was small at first, but the Paris headquarters group grew to 27 by March 1953. At that time, GAO reported to Congress that it expected to have 58 staff at the European Branch headquarters and suboffices by 1954.[60]

Although Warren had indicated that GAO was considering creation of a branch in Japan and a survey team did travel to Japan in 1952, he did not follow through with the plan at the time. In 1956, a Far East Branch opened in Tokyo.[61]

Reorganization of the Claims Division

In September 1953, Warren reorganized the Claims Division on a functional basis. The new divisional organization plan included several branches and sections, with the objective of simplifying the handling of claims. Economy clearly was one of Warren's motives. He explained that Claims was running more than $300,000 over its budget for fiscal year 1954. The reorganization plan included reclassification of positions in the division, reduction in grade of some staff, and a RIF of about 100 technical and clerical staff. Warren expressed regret at the RIF, but said that he wanted a "hard hitting, efficient organization."[62]

Administrative Services and the Planning Staff

In March 1941, early in his term, Warren established a Committee on Organization and Planning, composed of experienced officials in GAO, to consider the Office's organization, procedures, and practices and to present recommendations that would bring greater economy and more-effective per-

---

[58]Letter, Acting Comptroller General Yates to the secretary of defense, July 17, 1952, ibid.; and Comptroller General's Order No. 2.28, "Organization and Functions of the United States General Accounting Office—European Branch," July 22, 1952, GAO Records.

[59]*Report on History, Organization, and Operations of the European Branch, United States General Accounting Office, May 31, 1957* (Washington: GAO, 1957), 1.

[60]Testimony of Warren, Yates et al., March 5, 1953, *Independent Offices Appropriations for 1954*, Hearings before a Subcommittee of the House Committee on Appropriations, 83d Cong., 1st Sess., pt. 3 (Washington: GPO, 1953), 742-43.

[61]*Comptroller General of the United States: Annual Report for the Fiscal Year Ended June 30, 1952* (Washington: GPO, n.d.), 24. See also chapter 19, pp. 491-94.

[62]Comptroller General Order No. 2.4, "Organization of the Claims Division," September 1, 1953, GAO Records; and memorandum, Warren to employees of the Claims Division, September 3, 1953, GAO Records.

formance.[63] In 1945, Warren adopted a more formal structure by setting up the Office of Administrative Planning. The Office's duties included conducting studies of GAO's work and its relationships to other government agencies and Congress and developing management and operating techniques for doing the work. The office was also to assist in budgetary planning and prepare the comptroller general's annual report.[64]

In September 1953, in his last reorganization action, Warren responded to the Westfall report on general management, which severely criticized the offices of Administrative Planning and the executive officer. He abolished these offices and formed an Office of Administrative Services to be responsible for internal budget and finance, records management, and various internal services. He also established a small Planning Staff to undertake a continuous review of GAO's internal operations.

The Significance of Warren's Reorganization

By the end of his term in 1954, Warren had substantially changed the organizational structure of GAO, highlighted by the consolidation of the audit divisions and the formation of an integrated regional office system. His central objectives were to promote economy and efficiency in operations and to make the results of GAO's audits and other activities more useful to Congress and the executive branch. To a significant degree, Warren cleared out the old systems and much of the veteran staff devoted to them, and replaced them with new systems, organization, staff, and leadership, personified by staff such as Walter Frese and Ted Westfall.

The influence of Frese and Westfall cannot be overestimated. Both were outsiders, who were not wedded to GAO's time-honored work agenda or to its approaches to doing that work. Frese, an expert accountant, came out of the Treasury Department with ideas on GAO gained from the perspective of the executive branch. Both Frese and Westfall, when asked by the comptroller general to make recommendations for improving GAO's organization and work, were willing to speak clearly and frankly, even if they found it necessary to place the blame for outmoded or irrelevant practices and procedures directly on division and staff office heads.

Warren's organizational moves were also clearly related to the program changes he had decided upon by 1949—the comprehensive audit and the

---

[63]Office Order No. 1, March 15, 1941, 235 MS 930a; and *Annual Report of the Comptroller General of the United States for the Fiscal Year Ended June 30, 1941* (Washington: GPO, 1942), iv.

[64]Office Order No. 5—Revised, October 26, 1945, 290 MS 2018a.

Joint Accounting Improvement Program—and their endorsement by Congress in the Budget and Accounting Procedures Act of 1950. A common objective of these two programs was to work cooperatively with agencies to improve accounting and controls in the executive branch and make it easier for GAO to conduct its audits. The old adversarial approach that had been common in GAO in the days of Comptroller General J. R. McCarl was to be discarded in favor of cooperation. Warren believed that his reorganization efforts had been successful. In 1953, he stated in his annual report, "I have come up with what I consider a well-rounded, hard-hitting, and efficient organization." In this report, Warren exhibited considerable pride in his reorganization accomplishments.[65]

It is significant that a few months after Warren retired in April 1954, the Planning Staff that he had set up in 1953, headed by Robert F. Brandt, issued a critical report on GAO organization. Given the extent of Warren's reorganization and the planning behind it, the report's criticisms were startling. It described the existing organizational structure as "archaic." Brandt listed what he considered the shortcomings of GAO: reports were not timely; there was inadequate auditing of major expenditure areas; report content was not always useful to Congress; activities overlapped among the Division of Audits, the Office of Investigations, and the Accounting Systems Division; the work of the Office of the General Counsel was not coordinated with other divisions; the field organization was "cumbersome and uneconomical;" the administrative service setup was costly; and a separate planning and budgeting section was unnecessary.

Brandt proposed putting line audit functions on a departmental basis— for Defense, Interior, State, and the other cabinet agencies. He explained, "The welding together of the efforts of the auditors, accountants, investigators, and attorneys in each departmental unit would permit more effective overall evaluation of an agency's performance." He also recommended establishing one regional office in each of 17 geographical areas, instead of the existing separate Division of Audits regional offices and Office of Investigations field offices. He proposed, among other things, setting up an Office of Management Surveys "to advise the Congress and top management of the departments and agencies on specific management problems."

Brandt closed his report with this statement: "Speaking frankly, the proposed reorganization will not in itself cure all the deficiencies which now hamper our efforts. Many individuals in the Office have been schooled in

---

[65]GAO, *Annual Report, 1953*, 1-2, 15-16.

the ways of the old General Accounting Office and steeped in its early traditions. The new and broader objectives on which the Office set its sights,
starting about ten years ago, are not fully understood or accepted."[66]

Brandt's proposals demonstrate that not everyone in GAO felt that Warren's
reorganization had made the changes necessary to enable GAO to operate
and do its work effectively. Whether these proposals represented Brandt's
own personal views or reflected wider opinion in GAO is not clear. In any
case, Acting Comptroller General Weitzel took no immediate action on them.
Just three months later, in December 1954, a new comptroller general, Joseph Campbell, arrived at GAO. He moved soon to reorganize GAO again,
but there is no direct evidence that he was influenced by the Brandt report.[67]

---

[66]The summary of the Brandt proposals is based on *Westfall Survey Records*, Box 2, Folder: "A Plan for
Reorganization of the General Accounting Office," September 1954.

[67]See chapter 17, pp. 416-20, for information on Campbell's reorganization.

CHAPTER 15

Audits and Other Activities, 1945-1954

The pace and the substance of activities of the General Accounting Office (GAO) increased greatly during Lindsay C. Warren's term as comptroller general between 1940 and 1954. The defense and war effort between 1940 and 1945, the assumption of responsibility for annual audits of government corporations, the new emphasis on financial management, and the adoption of a more comprehensive approach to audits brought about major changes in GAO's agenda. The Cold War and the creation of a vast U.S. military establishment led GAO into more emphasis on defense audits. The outbreak of a hot war in Korea in 1950 also affected the size of GAO's audit load.

The several audit divisions existing in GAO before 1952 and thereafter the consolidated Division of Audits were responsible for many audit reports issued by the Office. The Office of Investigations (OI) also issued a substantial number of reports. Other divisions, such as Claims and Accounting Systems, carried heavy workloads during the period.

Work of the Audit Division and the Division of Audits

Before 1952, the old Audit Division, formed in 1926, was responsible for the general audit work of GAO. The Corporation Audits and Accounting Systems divisions handled specialized audits of government corporations and accounting systems work. In 1952, these three divisions and the Reconciliation and Clearance Division merged into the Division of Audits under the director of audits. At this point, GAO's audit work was in a transition from the traditional voucher checking and settlement of disbursing officers' accounts to site and comprehensive audits.

What GAO referred to by 1952 as site audits were conducted at agency offices, installations, or project locations around the country, including Washington, D.C., rather than in GAO offices. During fiscal year 1951, GAO conducted site audits at 944 locations, an increase of 354 field audit locations over the previous year. "Site audit programs," Comptroller General Warren explained, "recognize the accounting and internal control of each agency as the basic starting point for effective control of the Government's financial operations." Objectives of site audits included evaluating internal controls, detecting deficiencies, establishing or improving controls, and formulating auditing programs based on sound auditing principles.[1]

During this period, Warren spoke of both site audits and comprehensive audits. Comprehensive audits often took place at field sites, but their nature and scope differed from those of site audits. What Warren labeled site audits were essentially GAO's traditional audits—emphasizing account accuracy, procedural correctness, and legal legitimacy.

The two principal kinds of site audits conducted in the early and mid-1950s were payroll audits covering federal civilian employees' pay and audits of payments under cost-type government contracts.[2] During fiscal year 1953, GAO conducted civilian payroll account audits at about 1,200 sites. These audits emphasized improving agency payroll operations. Division of Audit staff advised agency management on specific payroll issues, such as the lack of internal controls on overtime and leave. They also undertook overall reviews of payroll operations to provide recommendations to agency management for improvements.[3]

At the end of fiscal year 1953, GAO had under audit about 12,000 cost-type contracts awarded to 3,000 contractors. For the most part, these were military contracts. An important objective of these audits was evaluating the internal audits of military department auditors, to help them improve the reliability and the quality of their work. GAO also had increased the scope of its audits of contracts and contractors' records—leading to recovery of improper payments to contractors and disclosure of other problems. In one instance, for example, GAO auditors called to the attention of a military contracting officer certain factors that would affect the remaining cost of the contract he was renegotiating. With this information, the contracting officer negotiated a new price, saving $2,811,041. In another case, GAO discovered that a contractor was using separate purchase orders for several items bought from a supplier. The military department auditors had previously noted this problem, but it had not been corrected. As a result of GAO's advice, the contracting officer began to use multiple-item purchase or-

---

[1]*Comptroller General of the United States: Annual Report for the Fiscal Year Ended June 30, 1951* (Washington: GPO, n.d.), 28-29.

[2]*Comptroller General of the United States: Annual Report for the Fiscal Year Ended June 30, 1953* (Washington: GPO, n.d.), 29.

[3]Testimony of Warren et al., January 13, 1954, *Independent Offices Appropriations for 1955*, Hearings before a Subcommittee of the House Committee on Appropriations, 83d Cong., 2d Sess., pt. 1 (Washington: GPO, 1954), 369.

ders, reducing the amount of paperwork on procurement and saving over $50,000 on the contract.[4]

In other testimony, GAO provided details of additional accomplishments re sulting from audits. In March 1952, the Board of Directors of the Panama Canal Company adopted GAO's recommendations to reduce the staff in its Washington office from 129 to 7 and to increase the procurement staff in the New York office by 19, resulting in an annual savings of $500,000. Also on the basis of a GAO recommendation, the company cut the cost of a long-range housing construction program from an estimated $80 million to $40 million, resulting in an annual oper- ating expense reduction of about $1.5 million. During an audit of the Bureau of Land Management, GAO discovered that the bureau was misinterpreting a law on distribution of proceeds from timber sales to certain counties in Oregon. As a result, the bureau reduced the amount to be distributed by $719,000.[5]

During this period, GAO's objective was to shift from the old voucher audits and limited site audits to the comprehensive audit. In January 1954 testimony, Warren used the term comprehensive audit "to designate those audit assignments which have as their objective the discharge of all statutory audit responsibilities of . . . [GAO] relating to the receipt, disbursement, and application of public funds. It includes the detailed examination of financial transactions and accounts neces- sary to verify the accuracy and reliability of the agency's financial statements and reports." He added that GAO classified audits of government corporations as comprehensive audits. During fiscal year 1953, Warren stated, GAO converted several additional audits from centralized voucher audits to comprehensive or site audits. During the year, in addition to corporation audits, 57 other comprehensive audit assignments were in process. He explained that further conversions from centralized audits to site audits "will depend primarily on the availability of person- nel capable of doing this type of audit."[6]

The Civil Audit Branch of the Division of Audits, located in Washington, au- dited accounts of federal civil agencies not assigned to site audits. The branch performed these audits on a selective basis by agency or bureau rather than by class of voucher, the previous procedure. There were advantages to this ap- proach. Staff doing auditing on an agency basis could become well-acquainted with the laws applicable to the specific agency and with its regulations and prac- tices. Also, the use of selective audit techniques on the basis of extensive expe-

[4]Ibid., 368-69.

[5]Testimony of Warren et al., *Independent Offices Appropriations for 1954*, Hearings before a Subcom- mittee of the House Committee on Appropriations, 83d Cong., 1st Sess., pt. 3 (Washington: GPO, 1953), 751-52.

[6]Warren testimony, January 13, 1954, *Independent Offices Appropriations for 1955*, pt. 1, 365.

rience with an agency lowered the cost of the audit without a significant loss of effectiveness.[7]

Although GAO deemphasized the voucher audit, it continued to do a significant number in the late years of Warren's term. During fiscal year 1953, for example, the Civil Audit Branch audited nearly 19 million vouchers and 900,000 contracts and related documents on a selected basis in its centralized audit. Other units of the Division of Audits, including the Examination and Settlement Branch, audited additional vouchers.[8]

Audit Reports

Increased Number of Reports

The number of reports issued between 1945 and 1954 by GAO to Congress and its committees grew gradually and their subject matter broadened. In its fiscal year 1945 *Annual Report*, GAO began to print lists of reports sent to Congress and indicated the number of replies GAO had made to miscellaneous inquiries from members of Congress. Between fiscal years 1945 and 1951, GAO provided 2,716 reports to Congress, the total varying from 139 in fiscal year 1945 to 686 in 1951. The number of inquiries handled ranged from 3,300 in 1945 to 6,605 in 1947. Beginning in the 1952 report, GAO listed totals for reports and inquiries without breaking them down into categories. For 1952-1954, there were 11,490 reports and inquiries. If the breakdown for the earlier years held true for 1952-1954, which is likely, about 90 percent of the total over the 1945-1954 period were answers to miscellaneous inquiries and about 10 percent written reports.[9] In addition, each year GAO sent a few reports, either requested or required by law, to the president and a larger number to the director of the Bureau of the Budget (BOB) on pending legislation and enrolled enactments.[10]

Three Forms for Audit Reports

During the Warren period, GAO began to bind many of its reports in blue covers, establishing a practice that remains in use in the mid-1990s. Some early reports of the Corporation Audits Division had blue covers, as did other reports issued by the audits divisions in the late 1940s. The first *Report Manual* of the Division of Audits, published in 1954, formalized the practice. This manual speci-

---

[7]Ibid., 369-70.

[8]Ibid., 370.

[9]See appendix VII. Data for 1945-1954 come from GAO's *Annual Reports* for these years.

[10]See *Annual Reports*, fiscal years 1945-1954. The annual reports indicate how many reports went to the president each year but do not provide the subject matter or titles of these reports.

fied three forms for audit reports: bound reports with blue covers, unbound reports with white fly-sheet covers, and letters. The manual specified that "audit reports transmitted to the Congress or its committees will normally be in bound form"; thus their covers would be blue.[11] For a time in the years after Warren's retirement, reports issued to agency officials rather than Congress had gray covers.[12]

Variety of Subjects Covered

The subjects of GAO's reports to Congress during these years varied from the routine—"Examination of Fiscal Offices of the Canal Zone for the Last Half of Fiscal Year 1944 by the General Accounting Office"—to the unique—"Economic Cooperation Administration: Propriety of Contracts under China Program." Reports on defense and foreign policy issues were frequent, for example, reports on U.S. participation in a proposed Inter-American military cooperation program, a Navy housing program on Guam, use of U.S.-flag vessels to transport commodities under foreign aid programs, extension of federal benefits to military personnel serving in Korea, establishment of Daylight Savings Time for national security purposes, a sports-car-racing program for the Strategic Air Command, contract and procurement activities of the European command, joint administration of the stockpiling program by the General Services Administration (GSA) and the Defense Materials Procurement Agency, Air Force production contracts, misuse of public funds at an Air Force base, and alleged Corps of Engineers contract irregularities on construction work in Iceland.

GAO issued numerous reports during this period on the problems and the status of American Indians, for example, a 1946 report on authorization for western bands of the Shoshone Nation to sue in the Court of Claims. Other reports covered a proposal to confer unqualified citizenship on American Indians in the territory of Alaska and the United States, the amounts in tribal funds, and compensation for injuries and deaths occurring in the massacre of the Sioux at Wounded Knee in the late 19th century.

Other reports considered a panoply of subjects: the government of Puerto Rico; slum areas in Washington, D.C.; funds for the Pan American Highway; the aircraft industry; local public health services; multiple sclerosis; the government loyalty program; small business; presidential impounding of funds; timber sales; the Export-Import Bank; and even the sale of the Bluebeard's Castle Hotel in the Virgin Islands.

---

[11]GAO, Division of Audits, *Report Manual* (Washington: GAO, 1954), 4-1, 4-2.

[12]Memorandum, Ellsworth H. Morse, Jr., to the administrative officer, November 9, 1956, GAO Records.

Bill Comments

Committees and members of Congress frequently asked GAO to comment on proposed or pending legislation. GAO's comments usually were in letter form. In 1946 and 1947, GAO commented on a bill to establish a National Science Foundation (NSF). On both occasions, the Office objected to provisions in the bill that set no limits on travel expenses and authorized NSF to enter into contracts without following normal legal requirements. Both Assistant Comptroller General Frank L. Yates and Warren said that established legal doctrine should not be ignored in the bill and warned that doing so could lead to abuse.[13]

In 1948, GAO analyzed a bill that proposed a Department of Transportation, to include the Interstate Commerce Commission, the Maritime Commission, the Civil Aeronautics Authority, the Civil Aeronautics Administration, the Weather Bureau, the Inland Waterways Commission, and the Office of Defense Transportation. Writing for GAO, Yates noted previous GAO recommendations to centralize responsibility for federal transportation activities and said that the bill would serve a useful general purpose. He observed that not all transportation units in the government would be transferred to the new department, thus risking duplication of effort. Yates suggested that this important bill be considered carefully and reminded the House committee handling the bill that the Hoover Commission on the Organization of the Executive Branch was studying transportation and might provide useful information to the committee.[14]

Warren, at BOB's request in 1948, commented on a bill providing for the administration of the Central Intelligence Agency (CIA), established by the National Security Act of 1947. He noted that while some provisions of the bill—those on procurement of supplies, transfer and use of funds, and other matters—granted more authority to the CIA than was normal, the CIA was so important that such extraordinary authority was justified. "In an atomic age," Warren wrote, "where the act of an unfriendly power might, in a few short hours, destroy, or seriously damage the security, if not the existence of the nation itself, it becomes of vital importance to secure in every practical way, intelligence affecting its security."[15]

---

[13]Letter, Yates to Rep. Clarence F. Lea, chairman, House Committee on Interstate and Foreign Commerce, March 7, 1947, 307 MS 554. Congress passed a National Science Foundation bill in 1947, but President Harry S. Truman vetoed it because it did not provide for a presidentially appointed director and advisory board. On May 10, 1950, Truman signed a bill creating NSF, with a director and a board appointed by the president. See George T. Mazuzan, *The National Science Foundation: A Brief History* (Washington: NSF, 1988), 1-6.

[14]Letter, Yates to Rep. Clare E. Hoffman, chairman, House Committee on Expenditures in the Executive Departments, January 21, 1948, 317 MS 1966. Warren expressed the same points regarding a similar Senate bill in a letter to Sen. Edwin C. Johnson, chairman, Senate Committee on Interstate and Foreign Commerce, January 17, 1949, 332 MS 609.

[15]Letter, Warren to the director of BOB, March 12, 1948, 319 MS 1424.

Assistant Comptroller General Frank L. Yates.

Another matter that Congress considered during these years was the presidential impoundment of appropriated funds. In 1949, Warren commented on a Senate bill proposing to grant to the president the power to transfer to the Treasury funds provided for any item that he determined was not in the national interest. The amount then would not be available for expenditure unless Congress reappropriated it. Warren expressed general agreement with the concept of impoundment but felt that the power should apply only to executive branch spending. He also thought that impounded funds should go into the surplus fund rather than to miscellaneous receipts, an account established to receive income and collections. Warren recommended appropriate safeguards to ensure that Congress did not abdicate its control over public funds.[16]

In 1951, a line-item veto bill came up, proposing to allow the president to veto separate and distinct items in appropriations bills. Yates commented, indicating that GAO was "a strong advocate of any legislation that would promote more efficient and economical management of appropriations." As Warren did on im-

---

[16]Letter, Warren to Sen. John L. McClellan, chairman, Senate Committee on Expenditures in the Executive Departments, August 3, 1949, 336 MS 224.

poundment, Yates suggested that the line-item veto power of the president, consistent with the principle of separation of powers, be restricted to executive branch appropriations.[17]

A final example of bill comments was Warren's reaction to a 1950 bill prohibiting both a husband and wife from working for the federal government if their combined annual income exceeded $7,500 or if one spouse received over $5,000. The bill excluded married couples from its terms if both were elected officials or were appointed by the president with Senate consent or if they were warrant officers or enlisted military personnel. Warren thought that this plan would result in greater distribution of federal employment among families but stated that current conditions did not warrant such a measure. He opposed the legislation, stating that it would result in the separation from federal service of trained and experienced personnel who had earned their grades by merit and would disrupt orderly programs of staff reduction already under way in many agencies.[18]

Impact of the Korean War: Defense Audits

The outbreak of the Korean conflict in June 1950 and the subsequent three years of combat directly affected GAO programs. Warren did not want GAO to hinder the Defense Department's efforts to expand, equip, and train U.S. military forces, but at the same time, he hoped to avoid the spending problems that had accompanied the military effort during World War II.[19] He laid out GAO's defense audit program in January 1951: "With the national debt standing at over a quarter of a trillion dollars, it is essential to our economic survival not only that the national defense be strengthened but that this be done as effectively and as economically as possible in terms of expenditures. The nation cannot afford to repeat the mistakes and extravagance which were permitted in World War II under the guise of necessity to the war effort."

GAO's concentration on defense spending had two objectives: to "seek out excesses, waste and extravagances including those in procurement and contracting" and to "actively cooperate with and assist the defense fiscal staffs to meet

[17]Letter, Yates to Rep. William L. Dawson, chairman, House Committee on Expenditures in the Executive Departments, March 23, 1951, 355 MS 1548. The line-item veto issue persisted for many years, and GAO dealt with it from time to time in later years. For example, see *Line Item Veto: Estimating Potential Savings* (GAO/AFMD-92-7, January 22, 1992).

[18]Letter, Warren to Rep. Thomas Murray, chairman, House Committee on Post Office and Civil Service, April 14, 1950, 344 MS 918.

[19]See chapter 11, pp. 249-78.

their monumental problems of organization, method and control." Warren indicated that he did not anticipate any significant expansion of staff, but he wanted defense operations to be given priority.[20]

Specifically, Warren directed the replanning and the coordinating of all defense audit work, with special consideration to extending site audits and retaining documents in the field, comprehensive audits for agencies involved in the defense effort, active efforts to uncover wasteful practices and operations, and increased use of selective audit techniques when appropriate. He detailed particular objectives for various GAO offices and divisions. The Accounting Systems Division was to help defense agencies establish effective accounting and internal control systems; the Office of Investigations was to develop programs to assist the defense effort and uncover waste; the Office of the General Counsel was to give priority to comptroller general decisions and other work related to the defense effort; the Claims Division was to give priority to defense claims and to "the collecting of all moneys due the Government;" and the Transportation Division was to work to ensure that both military and civilian transportation payments and carrier claims for refunds were handled promptly.[21]

A letter Warren wrote to Secretary of Defense George C. Marshall provides further evidence of Warren's determination to avoid waste during the Korean conflict. Noting that Congress had passed legislation to amend and extend the First War Powers Act of 1941, Warren urged vigilance on the part of the Department of Defense. The amended legislation, Warren wrote, "will result in extraordinary power being given to the Department of Defense, particularly with respect to the making, performance, amendment and modification of contracts." He urged that the Department of Defense (DOD) exercise these broad powers judiciously and see that "the abuses of similar authority which occurred during World War II are reduced to a minimum or entirely eliminated." Warren particularly urged that exercise of authority to make advance payments and contract amendments be kept at a high level in DOD "and not delegated indiscriminately to all contracting officers."[22]

In April 1951, Warren informed Secretary Marshall of GAO's intention to extend the comprehensive audit to DOD and to provide more assistance to DOD

[20]Memorandum, Warren to chiefs of divisions and offices, January 12, 1951, B-100711.

[21]Ibid. See also testimony of Yates, Weitzel, et al., March 13, 1951, *Independent Offices Appropriations for 1952*, Hearings before a Subcommittee of the House Committee on Appropriations, 82d Cong., 1st Sess. pt. 1 (Washington: GPO, 1951), 1480-83, for further information about Warren's January 12, 1951, memorandum and GAO's defense program.

[22]Letter, Warren to Marshall, undated, the Papers of Lindsay C. Warren, Southern Historical Collection, Wilson Library, University of North Carolina at Chapel Hill, Folder 614 (hereafter referred to as Warren papers). Marshall became secretary of defense in September 1950, three months after the Korean conflict began, and served until September 1951. This letter appears to have been written to Marshall during the early months of his tenure as secretary of defense.

on accounting problems and systems. GAO's staff was already examining existing accounting and internal control systems under the DOD comptroller and would do so in field offices and installations as soon as practical. GAO, Warren wrote, would do everything it could to coordinate the comprehensive audit program with development of approved accounting procedures in DOD. Warren noted that the DOD comptroller and the comptrollers of the military departments were in accord with GAO's approach.[23]

GAO had mixed success in gaining cooperation from the military establishment during the war period. In January 1952, Chief of Investigations William L. Ellis testified that in some instances when his staff examined military installations, considering among other things fiscal and accounting methods and business practices, local commanders responded to their suggestions by making immediate changes. But in other situations, Ellis reported, GAO and the military did not get along well. He referred especially to unofficial funds and welfare activities, which the military authorities did not consider within GAO jurisdiction. "We have been physically excluded from some places," Ellis testified, "including one Navy location where they put us in the brig for trying. In this one field we did not get along, because we think they are public funds, public records, and we should look at them. But the military for 25 years have thought otherwise." Ellis explained that when GAO had complained at specific installations about appropriations spent for unofficial welfare and recreational activities, the local commanders had maintained that such spending was a command prerogative.[24]

Except for access to records, relationships between DOD and GAO at the higher levels, both in the Office of the Secretary of Defense and the military departments, were very good. A letter from Secretary of Defense Charles E. Wilson to Warren in June 1953 illustrates this point. Warren had given Wilson copies of a GAO report of findings and recommendations after a GAO-BOB-DOD survey of financial practices and obligation of funds under the Mutual Security Program. Wilson described GAO's recommendations for improvement of DOD financial and accounting practices as "constructive contributions toward improving and developing our accounting to permit comprehensive auditing."[25]

Frank Pace, Jr., secretary of the Army, also expressed his appreciation for GAO's efforts, including cooperation in developing an accounting system for the Corps of Engineers and surveying procurement policies and practices in the Ord-

[23]Letter, Warren to the secretary of defense, April 10, 1951, 356 MS 614.

[24]Ellis testimony, January 23, 1952, *Independent Offices Appropriations for 1953*, Hearings before a Subcommittee of the House Committee on Appropriations, 82d Cong., 2d Sess., pt. 1 (Washington: GPO, 1952), 536-37.

[25]Letter, Wilson to Warren, June 8, 1953, Warren Papers, Folder 459.

nance Corps. Pace estimated that the savings resulting from GAO work totaled millions of dollars.[26] In a later letter, Pace again thanked Warren for his cooperation: "I would like to dwell for a moment on the increasingly worthwhile relationship established between the Army and the General Accounting Office to the real benefit of the taxpayer. The concept of having the GAO correcting fundamental ills as opposed to merely pointing them out after they occur is of inestimable value to our nation. This close working relationship has resulted in many gains that could not have been accomplished had it not been for your broad constructive point of view."[27]

Wilfred J. McNeil, assistant secretary of defense (comptroller), with whom GAO representatives had considerable contact during the Korean War, also supported the Office's defense work and tried to promote understanding of GAO's objectives and programs in other areas of DOD. In a memorandum to the service secretaries and other DOD officials, McNeil observed that the comptroller general had "adopted a progressively greater cooperative and constructive approach to the carrying out of his audit responsibilities. The result . . . has been correction of the deficiencies through cooperation with the agency staffs rather than mere reporting thereof to the Congress." He advised his colleagues to give full cooperation to GAO staff and to pay adequate and prompt attention to GAO reports.[28]

GAO had a serious problem with the DOD during the Korean War period on access to records. This issue became more pressing with the opening in August 1952 of the European Branch. In May 1952, in anticipation of the opening of this office, Secretary of Defense Robert A. Lovett proposed to Warren a plan for GAO access to classified DOD materials. Lovett recognized GAO's need for access but qualified his recognition by stating that "the military departments and other [Defense] agencies . . . must exercise strict control over the dissemination of many categories of important military information. The command concept of security and the authority and responsibility of those charged with the protection of military secrets must remain inviolate." He said that he doubted that GAO would have frequent need for information about the number and the disposition of military units, their armaments, and numbers of personnel.

Lovett spelled out proposed procedures for GAO access to DOD activities, classified or unclassified. He proposed that the comptroller general notify the appropriate DOD official by letter of GAO's intention to visit an installation, pro-

---

[26]Letter, Pace to Warren, October 31, 1952, reprinted in *Independent Offices Appropriations for 1954*, pt. 3, 754.

[27]Letter, Pace to Warren, January 15, 1953, Warren Papers, Folder 453.

[28]Memorandum, McNeil to the secretaries of the Army, the Navy, and the Air Force and the chairmen of the Munitions Board and the Research and Development Board, April 3, 1952, B-107366, #1.

viding the date, the purpose, and the scope of the visit and names and clearance levels of persons designated to make the visit. The comptroller general would also be responsible for the proper safeguarding of classified matter and would not disseminate information from such materials before obtaining approval from the originating military agency.[29]

Warren objected to the proposed notification of visit procedures. GAO, he wrote, had for years been operating on the basis of no advance notification: "I am sure you will agree that the element of surprise is absolutely essential to certain audit and investigative work." Warren said that the question of access to classified materials had become important because of GAO's extensive reviews of procurement practices. He concluded that he agreed with Lovett's proposal except for the advance notification procedure and the need to get prior approval before disseminating classified information outside GAO. He expressed confidence that these differences could be worked out.[30]

In January 1953, Secretary of Defense Wilson, Lovett's successor, sent Warren a revised draft of the access plan, following discussions between DOD and GAO representatives. The new plan focused on a "need to know" requirement for access to classified information. "It is considered that in a majority of instances where General Accounting Office personnel will be performing audits, surveys, examinations and investigations they ordinarily will not have need for access to classified security information," Wilson wrote. When its staff needed access, GAO was to make arrangements with the head of the military department or defense agency involved. This draft directive made no mention of the earlier advance notification requirement.[31]

Thomas A. Flynn, GAO director of personnel, whom Warren made responsible for discussions with DOD on the matter, recommended that the DOD draft directive be accepted. He made this recommendation even though Henry Domers, the director of the European Branch, had informed him that Army and Air Force officials were denying GAO auditors and investigators access to classified information. Domers also felt that the section of the proposed directive stating that GAO normally would not need access to classified information should not apply to the European Branch because almost all the information GAO required in Europe was classified. Flynn said that he thought that the draft directive should be approved "because I am fearful that any meeting between members of this Office and the Office of the Secretary of Defense concerning a component of the pro-

---

[29]Letter, Lovett to the comptroller general, May 15, 1952, ibid.

[30]Letter, Warren to the secretary of defense, August 14, 1952, ibid.

[31]Letter, Wilson to the comptroller general, January 30, 1953, ibid.

gram will tend to delay the effecting of the whole program which is now within our grasp and which we have been working on for a period of time in excess of a year." Robert F. Keller, Warren's special assistant, noted on Flynn's memorandum that the problems Domers had been having in Europe had been resolved. In a separate memorandum to Ellis, Keller said that he thought that the proposed DOD directive was the best GAO could get at the moment.[32]

Soon thereafter, Frank Yates, acting comptroller general, wrote to the secretary of defense approving the draft directive. He stipulated that if conditions changed and the arrangement became unworkable, GAO would request its revision.[33] In this case, GAO acquiesced in an agreement that was not totally satisfactory but appeared to be all that DOD was willing to grant at the time. In subsequent years, access to records remained a problem for GAO.

Work of the Office of Investigations

OI remained through the end of Warren's term an active and important component of GAO operations, even though Westfall's report on OI was very critical.[34] Warren continued to support the office.[35] In 1949, before Westfall's survey, Warren had appointed William Ellis, one of his closest associates, as chief of investigations. Probably the fact that Ellis headed OI strengthened Warren's support for the office. Ellis spoke highly of his staff in 1951: "They know more about the fiscal workings of our Government than . . . any other one group of people . . . ."[36]

OI had four basic functions—inspections, investigations, investigative surveys, and special audits. *Inspections* involved periodic examination of government installations where financial operations were carried out and where accountable property was located. An inspection could be a full examination or a test check of all matters related to the functions of an installation. Not only could irregularities in financial and property matters be pinpointed, but also the periodic, unannounced inspections had a deterrent effect, encouraging financial responsibility.

---

[32]Memorandum, Flynn to Keller, February 9, 1953, ibid. Attached is a handwritten memorandum from Keller to Ellis.

[33]Letter, Yates to the secretary of defense, February 19, 1953, B-107366, #1.

[34]See chapter 14, pp. 351-52.

[35]In testimony on January 13, 1954, *Independent Offices Appropriations for 1955*, pt. 1, 346, Warren said that OI had done an outstanding job and requested authorization of a grade 18, the highest civil service rank, for Chief of Investigations Ellis.

[36]"Statement of W. L. Ellis . . . before the Senate Committee on Expenditures in the Executive Departments," June 19, 1951, LDU Subject Files, Box 88, Folder: Legislative Reorganization, GAO History Program Archives.

Investigations supplemented audit and settlement procedures in an effort to disclose problems that were often not caught in regular audits. Such an investigation was "geared to detecting fraud or irregularity in accounts and determining in general the propriety and effectiveness of the use of public funds and property, and the adequacy of the accounting for such use." Investigative reports could be the basis for several steps—criminal prosecution by the Department of Justice, civil suits to collect money due the government, accounting systems changes to prescribe or develop corrective procedures, reports to Congress, reports to federal staff agencies (especially BOB), and reports recommending corrective action to the involved agency. *Investigative surveys* covered, like inspections and investigations, matters relating to the receipt, the disbursement, and the application of public funds. The objective was to discover the facts of a fiscal problem; analyze an entire agency's or program's fiscal structure; broadly evaluate the practices and the policies; and report problems to Congress, the agency concerned, and others as necessary. OI conducted *special audits* when directed by the comptroller general "in matters of particular difficulty, distinctiveness, and delicacy" of agencies or activities, including the periodic audit of some congressional offices in the Capitol.[37]

In 1952, the Office of Investigations had 231 staff, 70 in Washington and 161 in 24 field offices located in major cities.[38] OI's reports covered various subjects. Warren's prepared statement for appropriation hearings in March 1953, for example, described representative OI jobs. One was an examination of the Commodity Credit Corporation (CCC), done at the request of the Senate Agriculture Committee. OI looked into cases of losses and spoilage of government-stored grain, discovering large monetary losses that were due to poor administration and controls by CCC's Production and Marketing Administration. The Senate Agriculture Committee considered GAO's report, and CCC moved to correct some conditions and make substantial personnel changes.[39]

Another example was OI's examination of military housing construction contracts administered by U.S. Army engineers at Elmendorf Air Force Base in Alaska. GAO found serious deficiencies and deviations, caused by disregard for specifications and standards. OI investigators went to Alaska with a subcommittee of the House Committee on Expenditures in the Executive Departments for hearings, which confirmed what GAO had reported. GAO expected as a result of

---

[37]Testimony of Warren et al., January 13, 1954, *Independent Offices Appropriations for 1955*, pt. 1, 351-52; and *Comptroller General of the United States: Annual Report for the Fiscal Year Ended June 30, 1952* (Washington, GPO, n.d.), 34.

[38]Ellis testimony, January 23, 1952, *Independent Offices Appropriations for 1953*, pt. 1, 498, 531-32.

[39]Warren's written statement, hearing of March 5, 1953, *Independent Offices Appropriations for 1954*, pt. 3, 746-47.

its work that future management of the $200 million housing construction project in Alaska would be significantly improved.[40]

During these years, OI undertook numerous investigations of questionable practices by educational institutions that had acquired surplus government property on the basis of legislation passed in the late 1940s. In 1951, OI did a broad investigation at the state level of the acquisition of federal surplus property by state and local government educational institutions. OI learned that in 1949 and 1950, the Defense Department, the General Services Administration (GSA), and other federal agencies had donated to such institutions property valued at over $91 million. While the law said that surplus property was to be acquired on the basis of necessity, much of it was provided merely because it was available. Also, some of the property, instead of being used, was being stockpiled in local warehouses. State accounting records were fragmentary. Much of the property had been resold, with the proceeds retained by local agencies and in some cases by private individuals. GAO provided OI's report on this matter to the House committee, GSA, and the Federal Security Agency.[41]

OI also investigated in 1952 the construction of a golf course costing more than $66,000 at a West Coast Air Force base. The project was contrary to Air Force regulations, and the local command had received authorization for the expenditure by misleading Department of the Air Force officials. When OI disclosed this matter, construction of the golf course stopped. OI also discovered that over $24,000 of appropriated funds and $16,000 of nonappropriated funds had been illegally spent or obligated to remodel a civilian employees' club at the same base.[42]

Another instance of waste reported by OI was the purchase in June 1951 by the Air Force Air Materiel Command of 748,368 linear feet (142 miles) of chain link fence at a cost of $1.5 million. The Air Materiel Command shipped the fencing to 27 Air Force installations. OI's investigation at 19 of the 27 installations disclosed than more than 70 percent of the fencing shipped to these places remained unused a year and a half after the Air Force had bought it. OI found also that the Air Force had purchased the fencing under emergency procedures at the end of the fiscal year.[43]

---

[40]Ibid., 747.

[41]Ibid., 748.

[42]Ibid.

[43]Warren's written statement, January 13, 1954, *Independent Offices Appropriations for 1955*, pt. 1, 352-53.

A final example, which GAO described as "a small item of waste and extravagance, . . . but typical of the myriad of such matters arising in inspections," was the construction, on orders from the commanding general, of a fence, a dog run, and a kennel at an Army installation. The work request stated that the project was "in the best interest of the Government for security purposes." The items constructed, costing $1,200, included a kennel to house several dogs owned by the general and a 90-by-60-foot fenced dog run. "A wooden floor was installed in the kennel so the dogs would not lie on the bare earth." The general involved served only five months at this post, and after he left, the fence was removed at additional cost to the government.[44]

While the OI had serious organizational and personnel problems, at least according to the Westfall survey report, its extensive work continued under Warren. As these examples demonstrate, OI's work resulted in disclosure of serious problems and corrective action in many cases. Rep. John Phillips (R—California) made this point during GAO's appropriations hearings in January 1954. He suggested that publicly disclosing the names of individuals responsible for waste in the government might be the best way to prevent improper spending. He asked GAO to provide the names of persons involved in specific OI investigations. Phillips suggested that "a little adverse publicity" might have the desired effect.[45]

Accounting Systems Work

The main mission of the Accounting Systems Division was to implement, in cooperation with BOB and the Treasury Department, the Joint Accounting Improvement Program. Walter Frese, the division's director, defined the program in 1949 testimony: "This is being handled on the basis that all phases of accounting should be developed in proper relation to each other, that is in terms of a consistent and tied-in accounting system for the Government as a whole, with an operating center in the Treasury Department in the light of that Department's financial reporting responsibilities; it envisions adequate systems in each agency that will meet the needs of agency management and also conform to certain standards and principles considered important for the Government as a whole."

Frank Weitzel added that an ultimate objective was to eliminate duplication of effort in the accounting area. This would result eventually in economies in gov-

---

[44]Ibid., 354.

[45]Hearing, January 13, 1954, *Independent Offices Appropriations for 1955*, pt. 1, 359-63. See chapter 17, pp. 411-14, 419-20, for later activities of the Office of Investigations and its abolition by Comptroller General Joseph Campbell in 1956. See chapters 19 and 20 for further discussion of the question of naming responsible officials in GAO reports.

a large number of Indian claims, greatly increased the Claims Division's workload and slowed down the decline in staff.[52]

The volume of claims received and settled in the first postwar decade fluctuated from year to year but remained large, as shown in table 15.1.[53]

As a result of its claims work, each year GAO collected and returned to the Treasury substantial amounts of money. For example, GAO reported that debt collections resulting from the work of the Claims Division during fiscal year 1953 were $7,363,035.[54]

Occasionally GAO had to deal with some very old claims as well as current ones. An example was the case of a Navy man who had twice enlisted in the Navy and had deserted both times. The first enlistment period was from October 10, 1898, to desertion on October 24, 1900; the second was from March 8, 1909, to desertion on April 30, 1909. The seaman apparently was not apprehended until August 1939, when he surrendered at a Navy Recruiting Station in Detroit, after which he received undesirable discharges for both enlistments. He based his specific claim, for $380 left in the ship's bank aboard the U.S.S. *Albatross* when he deserted in 1900, on the argument that he had neither been court-martialed nor received a dishonorable discharge. GAO denied the claim, stating that it had long been established that for purposes of forfeiture of all money due, including deposits, desertion was a fact and did not need to be established by court-martial findings.[55]

Conclusions

In his annual report for fiscal year 1949, Warren observed that "the General Accounting Office as it stands today is not the same as it was a few years ago. . . . Many new duties have been added and, more important, new approaches have been taken in performing the work. It is not hide-bound and wedded to antiquated methods but it is in a fluid state, alert and alive to modern procedures."[56] Two years later, he proclaimed that "the General

---

[52]Testimony of Warren et al., February 9, 1949, *Independent Offices Appropriation Bill for 1950*, vol. I, 977.

[53]Statistics for 1946-1951 were printed with testimony of Warren et al., January 23, 1952, *Independent Offices Appropriations for 1953*, 501; 1952-1954 statistics are taken from GAO, *Annual Report, 1952*, 95; GAO, *Annual Report, 1953*, 121; and *Comptroller General of the United States: Annual Report for the Fiscal Year Ended June 30, 1954* (Washington: GPO, n.d.), 137.

[54]Testimony of Warren et al., January 13, 1954, *Independent Offices Appropriations for 1955*, pt. 1, 380.

[55]Letter, Yates to Maurice Clifford, May 27, 1949, 333 MS 2702.

[56]*Comptroller General of the United States: Annual Report for the Fiscal Year Ended June 30, 1949* (Washington: GPO, n.d.), iv.

Accounting Office today is far different from the General Accounting Office of 1940. It would take pages to detail the changes which have taken place during these years under the new legislation enacted by Congress and the new approaches employed to enable us to perform better our primary functions." He mentioned site and comprehensive audits, audits of government corporations, audits of property accounts and transactions, and improved handling of claims. "The investigative work has shown added enthusiasm and vigor resulting in searching and enlightening reports." Other important improvements included accounting systems work and the Joint Accounting Improvement Program.[57]

GAO's efforts, Warren reported in 1951, were based on six central operating policies:

• Recognition of the mission of the Office as an agency of the Congress to check on Federal financial transactions;

• cooperation with both the Congress and the executive branch toward informed and improved governmental administration;

• appropriate decentralization of operations;

• regard for generally accepted principles of auditing, including consideration of the effectiveness of agency accounting organizations and systems, internal audit and control, and related administrative practices;

• elimination of unnecessary, duplicative, or overlapping functions, records, and procedures; and

• concentration on defense spending and assistance to the defense fiscal staffs.[58]

Clearly Warren thought that GAO operations under his leadership, particularly considering the changes in organization and approach that had taken place since World War II, had vastly improved. He asserted in 1952 that "the need for . . . [GAO] as a nonpartisan and nonpolitical agency of the Congress has never been greater." The existence of GAO, to watch over and control expenditures for domestic programs, foreign aid expenditures, and "a defense program almost unparalleled in history," was of high importance.[59]

[57]GAO, *Annual Report, 1951*, 3.
[58]Ibid., 3-4.
[59]GAO, *Annual Report, 1952*, v-vi.

Comptroller General Warren and top GAO officials, 1954.

The results of the work of the audit divisions, the Accounting Systems Division, the Office of Investigations, and the Claims Division, along with the products of other GAO units, led to significant accomplishments that Warren emphasized in his efforts to demonstrate GAO's importance and effectiveness. Both actual collection of funds and savings resulting from findings and recommendations that improved the operating efficiency of government agencies, reduced expenditures, and prevented illegal and improper use of public funds were important, Warren thought. At the time of his retirement, he estimated that GAO had collected $915,000,000 between 1941 and 1954.[60] This amount was more than twice what Congress had appropriated for GAO operations during the period.[61]

The personal satisfaction Warren achieved from the changes he made at GAO between 1940 and 1954 seems entirely justified. GAO *was* a very different and more-cooperative organization in 1954 than it had been in 1940. Warren showed no hesitation in casting off outmoded methods and approaches, unnecessary duties, and even aspects of GAO's traditional culture. External events, both domestic and international, conditioned GAO's transformation during the Warren years. World War II, the international problems that followed it, changes in the domestic and international economic structures, and

---

[60]Warren, letter to members of Congress, March 31, 1954, reprinted in *GAO Review* (summer 1981): 7-8.

[61]See appendix VI.

many other factors would have forced change in GAO no matter who happened to be leading the Office at the time. But Warren deserves much credit for the progress GAO made during his tenure. His successor, Joseph Campbell, headed a much more vital organization when he entered office in 1954 than Warren had found in 1940.

CHAPTER 16

Financial Management Work Under Campbell

Joseph Campbell entered office as comptroller general of the United States on an interim appointment by President Dwight D. Eisenhower on December 14, 1954.[1] His predecessor, Lindsay C. Warren, had placed great emphasis on the work of the General Accounting Office (GAO) in the area of financial management. He had taken leadership in establishing the Joint Accounting Improvement Program (JAIP) in cooperation with the Treasury Department and the Bureau of the Budget (BOB). The Budget and Accounting Procedures Act of 1950 sanctioned the joint program and reaffirmed GAO's long-standing role in development and installation of accounting systems in federal agencies. Warren in 1948 had established the Accounting Systems Division to handle GAO's financial management work.

Given his own background as an accountant, it was reasonable to expect that Comptroller General Campbell would continue the emphasis on this aspect of GAO's work. Under his leadership, however, GAO concentrated more attention on other duties. This is not to say that GAO ignored its accounting systems work and the general improvement of financial management in the federal government. Almost all the new professional staff who joined GAO during Campbell's tenure were, in fact, professional accountants. But compared with audit activities in the Warren period, the major audit activities during Campbell's term overshadowed financial management work, including accounting systems and JAIP operations.

Accounting Systems Work Early in the Campbell Period

When Campbell entered office, accounting systems work was the responsibility of the Accounting Systems Division under Walter F. Frese. In testimony in February 1955, two months after Campbell joined GAO, he stressed the current importance of the division's activities: "The momentum of agency efforts has stepped up materially with every succeeding year until the present, when it has reached an alltime high. The result is that today there is more and more activity

---

[1]See chapter 5, pp. 101-08, for information on Campbell's background and appointment.

which the Accounting Systems Division . . . needs to participate in if all these developments are to be kept moving in the right direction."[2]

Although Campbell announced his preliminary reorganization plans in November 1955, there was no indication then that accounting systems and financial management work would be deemphasized.[3] When Campbell, Frese, and others testified on GAO's budget in February 1956, they put considerable emphasis on accounting systems work and the progress in that area.[4]

In his November 1955 outline of anticipated changes in GAO organization, Campbell stated that the Office's operation "can be further strengthened by improved coordination in our accounting and auditing relationships with the executive agencies and by more emphasis on the development of accounting and auditing policy and the consistent application thereof in our daily work." He said that "cooperative accounting systems work with the agencies will be vigorously continued, with added emphasis on the constructive review and evaluation of existing systems." Campbell proposed to set up an accounting policy and procedures group, whose duties would include developing accounting principles and standards and responsibility for governmentwide accounting and fiscal procedures. He indicated that Frese would head this group. He also anticipated establishing a separate group to handle auditing policy and practices. "Particular emphasis," Campbell wrote, "will be devoted to the coordination of audit and systems work on an agency basis."[5]

One of the reorganization orders Campbell released on March 22, 1956, established the Accounting and Auditing Policy Staff (AAPS), which was a combination of the two groups for accounting policy and procedures and auditing policy and practices he anticipated in November 1955. The new office was to formulate accounting policy and prescribe accounting principles and standards for guidance of executive agencies and develop auditing policy, standards, and practices for guidance of the new Civil Accounting and Auditing Division (CAAD) and Defense Accounting and Auditing Division (DAAD). The order spelled out the accounting systems and financial management duties of AAPS. They included

---

[2]Statement on Accounting Systems Division, printed with testimony for February 22, 1955, *Independent_Offices Appropriations for 1956*, Hearings before a Subcommittee of the House Committee on Appropriations, 84th Cong., 1st Sess., pt. 1 (Washington: GPO, 1955), 763-64.

[3]See chapter 17, pp. 416-20, for details of the 1956 reorganization.

[4]GAO budget justification statement, printed with testimony of February 10, 1956, *Independent Offices Appropriations for 1957*, Hearings before a Subcommittee of the House Committee on Appropriations, 84th Cong., 2d Sess., pt. 2 (Washington: GPO, 1956), 1366, 1369.

[5]Campbell, "Outline of Planned Changes in Organization and Operations," November 30, 1955, ibid., 1342-45; also in A-16251, #1.

maintaining effective working relationships with Treasury and BOB in JAIP.[6]
With the establishment of AAPS, initially headed by Frese, the Accounting
Systems Division ceased to exist. Central to Campbell's reorganization was
the idea that the audit divisions should integrate accounting systems and
auditing work in their everyday activities. The establishment of AAPS, to be
concerned with policy for both accounting systems and audits, reflected this
central concept.

The Second Hoover Commission and the Lipscomb Report

Besides Campbell's ideas on integration of accounting systems work and
audits, two concurrent reports influenced his reorganization plan and especially his decision to abolish the Accounting Systems Division—the Hoover
Commission report on accounting and auditing (1955) and the report (1956)
of a subcommittee of the House Committee on Government Operations,
headed by Rep. Glenard P. Lipscomb (R—California).

President Eisenhower established the second Hoover Commission on
Organization of the Executive Branch of the Government in 1953 to study
public policy, organization, and management and to recommend improvements. One of the commission's task forces looked at budgeting and accounting and made numerous proposals that for the most part the full commission eventually adopted.[7]

Ironically, given GAO's adverse reaction to the budget and accounting proposals of the first Hoover Commission in 1949, the second Hoover Commission
had its main offices in the GAO Building. Hoover told reporters that space in the
building was available because GAO had decreased its staff on the basis of economy
recommendations made by the first Hoover Commission. This remark infuriated
Comptroller General Warren, still in office in 1953 when the Hoover Commission
began its work. He referred to Hoover's remark as "a lie of the whole cloth.
Neither Herbert Hoover nor the Hoover Commission had anything whatever to do
with the reforms I have made in the General Accounting Office. . . . All that has

---

[6]Comptroller General's Order No. 2.30, March 22, 1956, A-16251, #1.

[7]For background, see Frederick C. Mosher, *The GAO: The Quest for Accountability in American
Government* (Boulder, CO: Westview Press, 1979), 138-39 (hereafter cited as Mosher, *GAO*). For
official reports of the Hoover Commission, see *Report on Budget and Accounting in the United States
Government*, prepared by the Commission Task Force on Budget and Accounting, June 1955 (hereafter
cited as Hoover Commission Task Force, *Report on Budget and Accounting in the United States Govern-
ment)*, and *Budget and Accounting*, a Report to the Congress by the Commission on Organization of the
Executive Branch of the Government, June 1955, both in LDU Subject Files, Box 82, Folder #2, GAO
History Program Archives.

been accomplished in . . . [GAO] has been in spite of the feelings and desires of Mr. Hoover. . . . He failed both as President and as head of the Hoover Commission to abolish the Office which he so cordially hates."[8]

The second Hoover Commission did not make any radical or far-reaching proposals affecting GAO, in contrast to the first Hoover Commission. The task force on budget and accounting noted the accomplishments of JAIP, but described it as "a piecemeal effort" and argued that "the motivating and stimulating force required for such improvement must be supplied by the executive branch." The solution should be establishing an Office of Accounting in BOB to develop an accounting plan "consistent with broad policies and standards prescribed by the Comptroller General." Also, comptrollers should be appointed in all federal agencies.[9]

Comptroller General Campbell expressed general agreement with the Hoover Commission recommendations on budgeting and accounting in a written commentary prepared in response to a request from Rep. William L. Dawson, chairman of the House Committee on Government Operations. Regarding some recommendations, Campbell merely said that the matter was up to Congress to decide. Regarding others he expressed complete agreement.

Campbell approved a recommendation that the executive budget and congressional appropriations be in terms of estimated annual accrued expenditures,[10] but he thought that such a change should be approached on the basis of individual agency programs rather than across the board. Campbell had no problem with the recommendation to create an accounting office in BOB but observed that JAIP and individual executive agencies had "a part to play in the total operation and that the desired elements can only be achieved through joint efforts carried out with mutual respect for the responsibilities of each." Campbell endorsed the Commission's recommendations that government accounts be kept on an accrual basis to show resources, liabilities, and operations costs. He said that experience under JAIP showed the advantage of the accrual basis—"a major factor in providing better control over

---

[8]See clipping, "Washington Scrapbook," *Washington Times-Herald*, October 3, 1953, with attached Warren memorandum, the Papers of Lindsay C. Warren, Southern Historical Collection, Wilson Library, University of North Carolina at Chapel Hill, Scrapbooks, vol. 17.

[9]Hoover Commission Task Force, *Report on Budget and Accounting in the United States Government*, 56-61.

[10]Mosher defines "accrued expenditures" as "charges incurred during a given period requiring the provision of funds" for goods and tangible property received; services by employees, contractors, and others; and amounts owed under programs requiring no performance or current service, such as annuities and other benefit payments. See Mosher, *GAO*, 162.

resources and liabilities and . . . an essential element in obtaining adequate cost data."

The Commission also recommended that GAO and BOB undertake an intensive study to determine the "adequacy of internal accounting in Government agencies and what steps should be taken to improve it." Campbell responded that GAO, through the comprehensive audit and accounting systems work, continuously studied these matters but that GAO would be glad to cooperate in any special effort to improve internal accounting.[11]

Subsequently, in 1956, BOB established a new staff Office of Accounting under an assistant director, but it apparently had little impact and did not affect GAO's work.[12] In August 1956, the president signed a law implementing some of the Hoover Commission proposals on budgeting and accounting. The law required agencies to develop requests for appropriations, to the extent desired by the president, from cost-based budgets. A cost-based budget, according to a 1961 congressional report on financial management, "identifies, in terms of the goods and services consumed by each activity, the costs of the program planned by the agency. . . . A cost-type budget shows the obligating authority required to place orders for additional goods and services needed to accomplish the planned program and maintain the resources at hand at a level appropriate to the agency's reporting requirements." In the following years, the number of cost-based budgets increased; by 1961 such budgets covered more than 50 percent of all appropriation items.[13]

The effects of the Hoover Commission recommendations on GAO's work were limited and at best subtle. Frese in a later interview observed that the Hoover Commission report had urged BOB to be more active in promoting accounting systems improvement in the executive branch. "This, of course, would indicate for the GAO that it should work more on the auditing side.

---

[11]Letter, Campbell to Dawson, October 26, 1955, with attachment, "Statement Setting Forth the Views of the Comptroller General on the Budget and Accounting Report of the Hoover Commission," 15 pages, B-125294; also in LDU Subject Files, Box 82, Hoover Commission, Folder 2, Budget and Accounting, GAO History Program Archives.

[12]See White House Press Release, April 29, 1956, LDU Subject Files, Box 82, Hoover Commission, Folder 2, Budget and Accounting, GAO History Program Archives. See also Frederick C. Mosher, *A Tale of Two Agencies: A Comparative Analysis of the General Accounting Office and the Office of Management and Budget* (Baton Rouge, LA, and London: Louisiana State University Press, 1984), 108. Mosher mentions the establishment of the office but says nothing further about it.

[13]Public Law 84-863, 70 Stat. 782, approved August 1, 1956; and Staff of the Senate Committee on Government Operations, *Financial Management in the Federal Government*, 87th Cong., 1st Sess., S. Doc. 11 (Washington: GPO, 1961), 92, 95-96 (hereafter cited as *Financial Management*, 1961).

The Accounting and Auditing Policy Staff . . . was set up in GAO to provide policies for the appropriate coordination of those functions."[14]

The House Committee on Government Operations in February 1955 established a special subcommittee, headed by Representative Lipscomb, to study GAO organization and administration. Lipscomb, before his House service began in 1953, had been a senior partner in a California public accounting firm and thus had a special interest in GAO's work. Chairman Dawson of the Government Operations Committee also was a member of the subcommittee, but Lipscomb was the major influence on its work and the report issued in June 1956.[15]

Lipscomb's report surveyed the major GAO units, including the Audit, Accounting Systems, Claims, and Transportation Divisions; the Office of the General Counsel; and the Office of Investigations.[16] Lipscomb stated in the report that after reviewing the work of the Accounting Systems Division, he thought that the executive agencies should assume primary responsibility for accounting systems. "Cooperative systems work with the agencies," the report concluded, "should be designed primarily to assist in the development of practical solutions to new or unique problems and not as a substitute for agency initiative. This approach would leave the General Accounting Office in a better position to make objective appraisals of agency systems and minimize the possible embarrassment of having to make adverse reports on systems designed by the General Accounting Office." The report recommended that GAO and executive agencies give major attention to accounting systems improvements to enable the systems to produce "unqualified certification of financial statements of such agencies in the opinions of the General Accounting Office auditors as expressed in the Office's audit reports."

Lipscomb recommended also abolishing the Accounting Systems Division and reconstituting its functions in other GAO offices: development of principles, standards, and related accounting requirements in one group and integration of the cooperative accounting systems work in the agencies with GAO's audit work. Audit reports should include the results of accounting

---

[14]Walter F. Frese, *Early History of the Joint Financial Management Improvement Program*, as interviewed by Ellsworth H. Morse, Jr., and Donald C. Kull (typescript, Joint Financial Management Improvement Program (JFMIP), April 1980), 246 (hereafter cited as Frese, *Early History of JFMIP*).

[15]Mosher, *GAO*, 149.

[16]*The General Accounting Office: A Study of Its Organization and Administration with Recommendations for Increasing Its Effectiveness*, Seventeenth Intermediate Report of the Committee on Government Operations, 84th Cong., 2d Sess., H. Rept. 2264 (Washington: GPO, 1956) (hereafter cited as *Lipscomb Report*). For information on Representative Lipscomb's comments on the Office of Investigations see chapter 17, p. 415.

systems reviews and evaluation along with other findings and recommendations for corrective action. Lipscomb also proposed that GAO include an objective appraisal of accounting systems drawn from its audit reports in JAIP's annual progress report.[17]

The Lipscomb Report was neither a shock nor a major problem for GAO. By the time the House Government Operations Committee issued the report, Campbell had announced the major elements of his 1956 reorganization plan, including abolition of the Accounting Systems Division, establishment of a group to develop accounting principles and standards (the Accounting and Auditing Policy Staff), and integration of systems and regular audit work in CAAD and DAAD. Ellsworth H. Morse, Jr., who succeeded Frese as director of AAPS in August 1956, stated in a meeting of his staff shortly after issuance of the Lipscomb Report that "reorganization changes in the General Accounting Office have been made as a result of official consideration and decision by the Comptroller General and not because of recommendations made in the report."[18]

There was great similarity, however, between Lipscomb's recommendations and Campbell's organizational changes in the accounting systems area. It is hard to believe that Campbell was not influenced by them to some degree. Perhaps conversely the organizational changes Campbell had made influenced Lipscomb because they occurred before official release of his report. It is clear from the Lipscomb Report that there was extensive communication between the GAO and Lipscomb staffs, and perhaps contact between Campbell and Lipscomb, although no direct evidence of this has been found.

Campbell responded formally to the Lipscomb Report on November 1, 1956. He had only a few disagreements with Lipscomb and accepted most of what the report contained, with respect to not only accounting systems but other aspects of GAO operations. He stated that he thought that the report's concentration on problem areas and need for urgent action did "not present the complete picture of the operations and activities of . . . [GAO] and its accomplishments in recent years" and added that the recommendations dealt

---

[17]*Lipscomb Report*, 6-7.

[18]Morse, *Daily Notes*, 1956, as reported in a memorandum for the files, subject: Director's meeting, August 8, 1956, by Walter C. Shupe, August 9, 1956.

with programs on which GAO had been working for some time or for which foundations had already been established.[19]

Campbell pointed out that GAO had already implemented two of the three specific recommendations on the Accounting Systems Division: The division had been abolished and its work had been integrated with audit work in the new CAAD and DAAD. As for Lipscomb's third recommendation, that JAIP's annual progress report include an appraisal by GAO of agency systems based on GAO audit findings, Campbell demurred in part. He pointed out that the JAIP report was not a GAO document but rather a joint publication agreed to by the three cooperating agencies. Campbell thought that it was "inappropriate to use it as a vehicle for a unilateral appraisal by one of the agencies involved in the joint program." He added that the call for materials for the 1956 progress report included a request for agency plans for improvements, as well as accomplishments in the past year.[20]

Accounting Systems Work After 1956

The Accounting Systems Division had 107 staff early in 1956, just before Campbell abolished it and integrated its work into the Civil and Defense Accounting and Auditing Divisions. At this time, two-thirds of the Accounting Systems Division staff worked directly in agency offices to perform their duties, including, for example, 13 in the Defense Department, 6 in Treasury, 4 in Agriculture, and 3 each in Interior and the Veterans Administration.[21] A year later, Campbell testified that GAO auditors were doing both accounting systems work and their regular audit work and that GAO was emphasizing review and evaluation of agency systems. Campbell spoke especially about the importance of electronic data processing (EDP) and noted that some agencies, such as the Social Security Administration, the Federal Bureau of Investigation, the Post Office Department, and the Defense Department, had started "progressive studies and adaptations" of EDP in their operations. He indicated that GAO had begun a governmentwide survey on present and planned use of EDP to determine progress in the field and EDP's effects on federal financial management processes.[22]

---

[19]Transmittal letter, Campbell to Dawson, November 1, 1956, in *Comments of the Comptroller General of the United States on Report of the Committee on Government Operations, House of Representatives, Entitled "The General Accounting Office - A Study of Its Organization and Administration with Recommendations for Increasing Its Effectiveness (House Report No. 2264, 84th Congress, 2nd Session, November 1, 1956,* copy in GAO History Program Archives. This document contains 69 pages.

[20]Ibid., 51-56.

[21]Testimony of Campbell et al., February 10, 1956, *Independent Offices Appropriations for 1957,* 1366, 1370.

[22]Campbell testimony, February 26, 1957, *Independent Offices Appropriations for 1958,* Hearings before a Subcommittee of the House Committee on Appropriations, 85th Cong., 1st Sess., pt. 2 (Washington: GPO, 1957), 1927-28.

In fact, after 1956, while GAO still officially included accounting systems work in its audit programs, activity in the area languished somewhat. Morse, the director of AAPS, maintained interest in it and discussed it from time to time in his staff meetings. He queried the audit divisions on occasion about the status of their accounting systems work and delays in approving accounting systems.[23] Campbell reported in 1959 that GAO had issued guidelines to agencies for submitting formal requests for approval of accounting systems and that he approved eight systems during fiscal year 1959.[24] Morse recorded in his daily notes in April 1960, after a discussion with Campbell about accounting systems, the comptroller general's view that GAO's "audit function and related reports, critical though they were, were more effective in stimulating systems improvements than other types of operations."[25]

Walter Frese, at the time a professor at Harvard University, criticized GAO's lack of attention to systems work at a public meeting in Chicago in 1961. Morse, who attended the meeting, complained that Frese had commented adversely on GAO's current emphasis on audit evaluations and that he "was not reluctant to tell anybody that he thinks more cooperative [systems] work should be done." Morse did not think that GAO should return to the level of emphasis on systems work that had existed in the early and mid-1950s, but he wrote: "By promoting a better integration of our accounting and auditing work, we can restore this balance by concentrating in each assignment on not only developing our findings but consciously considering how if at all involved the function of accounting can contribute to the improvement of the situation or otherwise to effective or better management."[26]

The Decline of the Joint Accounting Improvement Program

GAO's work on accounting systems and other aspects of financial management in the federal government obviously declined during Campbell's term. Morse, who was a very close adviser to Campbell, kept the subject alive but could not push the work in the face of Campbell's lack of interest and his concentration on audit activities, especially in the defense area. The history of JAIP during Campbell's tenure illustrates the problem well.

---

[23]See entry for meeting of May 21, 1957, Notes of Meetings of the Accounting and Auditing Division Heads, September 1956 through June 1957, Morse Papers, GAO History Program Archives; entry for July 10, 1958, Morse, *Daily Notes*, 1957-1958; and entry for April 29, 1959, Morse, *Daily Notes*, 1959-1960.

[24]*Annual Report of the Comptroller General of the United States for the Fiscal Year Ending June 30, 1959* (Washington: GPO, 1959), 45-46.

[25]Entry for April 19, 1960, Morse, *Daily Notes*, 1959-1960.

[26]Entry for October 31, 1961, Morse, *Daily Notes*, 1961-1962.

Frese said years later that he had accepted Campbell's 1956 reorganization plan that consolidated accounting systems work with the audits of the two new auditing divisions. "I felt," he said, "that this work ought to be synchronized with audits that would review not only the constructive things that had been done, but also some of the areas that needed further improvement and development, and that closer coordination was probably needed between this review and evaluation process and the constructive process of working with the agencies." Frese hoped that after the reorganization, there would be more coordination of the audit and systems functions; the auditors, he hoped, would take a constructive approach in their reviews, stressing areas where improvements could be made and making appropriate recommendations to the agencies.

Frese also noted that Lipscomb seemed greatly concerned about GAO's independence and thought, as Frese put it, "that our cooperative work with the agencies may well be jeopardizing the independence of the GAO." He made clear that he did not agree with Lipscomb on this point. Nevertheless, Frese observed, "the cooperative part of the work sort of died on the vine for a while."[27] Frederick Mosher concluded in his study of GAO that the abolition of the Accounting Systems Division "was a setback to the cooperative work with executive agencies toward improving accounting practices, and the joint program thereafter had declining momentum for many years."[28]

There is ample evidence that Campbell did not have a high regard for JAIP and was unwilling to participate in its activities to any significant degree. His successor as comptroller general, Elmer B. Staats, remarked in a much later interview about Campbell's "overconcern about allowing GAO people to get involved in anything other than strictly internal." Staats, who as a BOB official in the late 1940s had been involved in JAIP's establishment, thought that Campbell had been wrong in deemphasizing the cooperative work.[29]

Arthur Schoenhaut, a CAAD official who knew Campbell well, observed that Campbell did not think that accounting systems and financial management work was a "high priority area." He also noted that "certain staff members in GAO viewed working on systems like being assigned to Siberia. If you got assigned to accounting systems work, you thought you were on your way out. . . . I think it all stemmed from Joe Campbell. He didn't believe it

---

[27]Frese, *Early History of JFMIP*, 244-46, 278.

[28]Mosher, *GAO*, 151.

[29]GAO, *Elmer B. Staats*, GAO History Program, Oral History Series, GAO/OP-1-OH (Washington: 1987), 7-8.

was important. He thought that it was important to do audits and to be independent and that you should not have to help the agencies with anything."[30]

After Ellsworth Morse became director of AAPS in 1956, Campbell assigned him to represent GAO in the joint program and Joseph Sullivan, a member of Morse's staff, served on the JAIP Operations Steering Committee, an advisory-liaison group, along with representatives from Treasury and BOB.[31] Campbell met with the secretary of the treasury and the BOB director in regular annual meetings of the joint program principals through January 1959 but not thereafter; the principals did not meet again until after Campbell left office.[32]

On a number of issues during these years, the agencies in the joint program had disagreements that impeded progress. GAO—with Morse and Campbell involved—objected to an article published by Percival Brundage, the director of BOB, in the February 1958 issue of the *Journal of Accountancy*, ascribing leadership of the joint program to Percy Rappaport, BOB's top staff representative to the program.[33] There was also dissension over a proposal that JAIP undertake a study of the need for detailed central accounting in the Treasury Department. When the subject first arose in February 1958, the Treasury representative objected vigorously, saying that Treasury would not participate in a study that might result in curtailing Treasury accounting. Morse observed that the Treasury representative apparently "wants to be in a position to object strenuously to any study group's conclusion that Treasury reporting be based on agencies' reports to the Treasury." Morse added that GAO's position was that it would not agree to studies in which Treasury did not participate.[34]

By the late 1950s, it was clear that Campbell's interest in JAIP was waning. He declined an invitation to a meeting of President Eisenhower's cabinet in July 1959, at which Maurice Stans of BOB planned to report on JAIP's functions and accomplishments. Morse noted that "Mr. Campbell rejected the invitation flatly on the theory that it was inappropriate for him to attend such meetings."[35] When Campbell learned that the director of BOB had questioned the need for a meeting of the joint program principals scheduled

---

[30] GAO, *Arthur Schoenhaut*, GAO History Program, Oral History Series, GAO/OP-4-OH; (Washington: 1988), 31-32.

[31] Entry for August 9, 1956, Morse, *Daily Notes*, 1956; and record of meeting of September 13, 1956, Notes of Meetings of the Accounting and Auditing Division Heads, September 1956 through June 1957, Morse Papers.

[32] Entry of January 30, 1957, Morse, *Daily Notes*, 1957-1958 (reporting meeting of principals on this date), entry of January 3, 1958, ibid. (reporting meeting of principals); and entry of January 9, 1959, Morse, *Daily Notes*, 1959-1960 (reporting meeting of principals).

[33] See entries for February 10, 21, 27 and March 4, 1958, Morse, *Daily Notes*, 1957-1958.

[34] Entry for February 10, 1958, ibid.

[35] Entry for June 30, 1959, Morse, *Daily Notes*, 1959-1960.

Joint Financial Management Improvement Program principals Joseph Campbell,
Robert Anderson, and Maurice Stans examining the Tenth Annual Progress Report,
January 1959.

for December 6, 1960, he, according to Morse, "stated that he didn't really care." When a proposal came up soon thereafter to have a meeting involving Campbell, the secretary of the Treasury, and the director of BOB in the new administration of John F. Kennedy, Campbell showed no enthusiasm but said that he would attend if the meeting took place.[36] A meeting of the JAIP principals scheduled for December 19, 1961, was canceled at the last minute because the BOB director had other commitments. When Morse discussed plans for this meeting with Campbell before its cancellation, "Mr. Campbell stated that a meeting of this kind for as much as a half-hour is plenty long. He apparently does not expect much to come out of it."[37]

When BOB tried to arrange a gathering of the principals in January 1962, Campbell pointed to cancellation of the previous month's meeting as an indication that there was no real need for it and did not agree to the current BOB proposal.[38] Early in 1964, Elmer Staats, deputy director of BOB, pro-

[36]Entry for November 18, 1960, ibid.; and entry for January 25, 1961, Morse, *Daily Notes*, 1961-1962. The meeting was not held.

[37]Entries for December 5, 18 (source of the quote), and 19, 1961, ibid.

[38]Entry for January 11, 1962, ibid.

posed that in recognition of the joint program's 15th anniversary, there be some fanfare with issuance of the program's 15th progress report as well as a meeting of the principals. Campbell thought that the report ought to be released but exhibited no enthusiasm for the proposed meeting, which did not take place.[39]

Notwithstanding the lack of enthusiasm during the Campbell period, the joint program continued to exist and carried on some aspects of its work. Besides the Operations Steering Committee established by the program in 1956, another standing committee, set up to handle joint matters of financial management and improvement in the Department of Defense, began work at the same time.[40] In 1959, recognizing that JAIP's work had broadened from its initial emphasis on improving accounting operations to using accounting information for program decisions, budgeting, reporting, and control, the participating agencies changed its name to Joint Financial Management Improvement Program (JFMIP).[41]

In 1961, the Senate Committee on Government Operations recognized JFMIP's work. According to the committee, "Many improvements in budgeting, accounting, and reporting have resulted from the work done under the joint program and the committee is vitally interested in its continued progress."[42] In reporting on "15 years of progress" in 1963, JFMIP provided specific examples from government agencies, including legislation, federal budgeting, central financial operations, agency reporting practices and internal audit operations, and others. In the same report, JFMIP specified two areas of inadequate progress—accrual accounting systems tailored to agency needs and effective use of cost information for purposes of agency internal management.[43]

Financial Management Work under Campbell: An Assessment

Comptroller General Warren, by leading in establishment of JAIP and creation of the Accounting Systems Division, had elevated financial management issues, especially accounting systems, to a high priority in GAO. His successor, Joseph Campbell, continued that work at the same pace during his first year or so. But then, perhaps influenced by the work of the

---

[39]Entry for February 13, 1964, Morse, *Daily Notes*, 1963-1964.

[40]Frederic H. Smith, "The Joint Financial Management Improvement Program is 20 Years Old," *GAO Review* (winter 1969): 86.

[41]JFMIP, *Improvement of Financial Management in the United States Government: Progress 1948-1963* (Washington: GPO, 1963), 1 (hereafter cited as JFMIP, *Progress 1948-1963*).

[42]Senate Committee on Government Operations, *Financial Management*, 1961, 4.

[43]JFMIP, *Progress 1948-1963*, 3, 5-102.

second Hoover Commission and the Lipscomb committee, Campbell made substantial changes in GAO's organization and leadership in the financial management area. He abolished the Accounting Systems Division, Frese left, and systems work moved to two large auditing divisions.

While there were still high-level officials in GAO, like Morse and Assistant Comptroller General Frank Weitzel, committed to the joint program's objectives and work as well as the agenda of the former Accounting Systems Division, there was little they could do to prevent backsliding in the face of Campbell's lack of commitment to such work. Campbell froze Weitzel out of most important issues, and Morse, although very close to Campbell, chose not to push for something that the comptroller general did not favor. The very fact that accounting systems work became one element of the duties of two divisions that had other priorities contributed to its downgrading. Morse kept GAO's official participation in the joint program alive, but as an organization, JFMIP was weak and divided when Campbell's term ended in 1965. Without support from the comptroller general, who declined after 1959 to meet with the other principals, JFMIP just limped along.

This interpretation is affirmed by Gerald Murphy, who began at the Treasury Department in 1959, was involved in JFMIP leadership for a long time, and eventually rose to the position of fiscal assistant secretary of the Treasury. According to Murphy, the Joint Accounting Improvement Program was very energized in its early years, 1950-1955 in particular. During this period, the central agencies put staff resources into the program and there was a feeling that massive change was possible. According to Murphy, things slowed down considerably under Campbell, especially after 1959. In the participating agencies other than GAO, there was great concern about Campbell's negative impact on JFMIP, particularly his stand on the independence of auditing. At the same time, according to Murphy, BOB did not allocate resources to JFMIP projects and staff resources generally were low. The willingness of the central agencies to provide staff to get important jobs done determined the degree of success. Without GAO's exerting its authority to make things happen, the joint program, according to Murphy, could not operate effectively.[44]

---

[44]Telephone interview, Roger R. Trask with Gerald Murphy, Washington, DC, March 10, 1989.

The future of JFMIP by 1966 depended on the interest of Elmer Staats, Campbell's successor, in the program. Before Staats arrived at GAO in March 1966, Acting Comptroller General Weitzel began renewed emphasis on the program, and Staats, long interested in JFMIP during his many years in BOB, moved rapidly to reinvigorate it.[45]

.

---

[45]This period in JFMIP history is beyond the scope of this book. For summary information see Roger R. Trask, "The Joint Financial Management Improvement Program: An Overview, 1948-1981," typescript, GAO History Program Archives.

CHAPTER 17

Audits and Operations in the Campbell Era, I

The emphasis in the General Accounting Office (GAO) during the term of Comptroller General Joseph Campbell was predominantly on audits of government agencies and programs and less on accounting systems and financial management. Campbell particularly thought GAO's work in the defense area ought to be expanded, leading to a proliferation of reports on defense contracts. He devoted much attention early in his term to how GAO ought to be organized. He was concerned about the quality of the staff, which he believed should be upgraded and professionalized. During his first year the "cheese squeeze," the "zinc stink," and the Lipscomb Report increased in his mind the need for reorganizing and for a professional upgrading of the audit staff. Campbell also felt that more work should be done in the field, hence his interest in the activities of the regional offices and overseas branches. The era of change that Comptroller General Lindsay C. Warren initiated in GAO after World War II continued under Campbell, although he deemphasized some areas that had been priorities for Warren.

The Cheese Squeeze, the Zinc Stink, and the Lipscomb Report: Preliminaries to Reorganization

The Cheese Squeeze

The cheese squeeze, as it came to be called in GAO, involved the purchase and the resale of cheese by the Department of Agriculture's Commodity Credit Corporation (CCC). On the basis of the Agricultural Act of 1949, the Department of Agriculture supported farmers between April 1, 1953, and March 31, 1954, at 90 percent of parity[1] by buying dairy products—cheese,

---

[1]*Webster's New Collegiate Dictionary* (1980) defines "parity" as "an equivalence between farmers' current purchasing power and their purchasing power at a selected base period maintained by government support of agricultural commodity prices." The base period was 1909-1914, when farm profits were very good and agricultural prices were "balanced" with other prices. The goal of federal farm subsidies in later years was to achieve this balance again. Government purchases of farm products gave farmers a secure market when otherwise they could not sell all their products on the open market at sufficient profit. Often the government stored such products until the supply declined, then sold them on the open market at more than it had paid the farmers.

butter, and dried milk—from dairy product processors. In the case of cheese, Agriculture bought cheddar cheese until March 31, 1954, at 37 cents a pound and sold it through the CCC at 39 cents a pound. In February 1954, the Department of Agriculture announced that the price of cheese purchases would be reduced to 75 percent of parity, and that beginning on April 1, 1954, it would pay 32-1/4 cents per pound. In March 1954, Agriculture announced that it would sell this cheese for 34-1/4 cents per pound—2 cents more than the purchase price, as in previous practice.[2]

The problem developed when Agriculture allowed the cheese processors, beginning on April 1, 1954, to buy for 34-1/4 cents per pound the cheese they had previously sold to the government for 37 cents a pound. This gave the processors an extra profit of 2-3/4 cents per pound and cost the government the same amount. The processors stored the cheese bought and sold by the government; it never came physically into Agriculture's hands. The processors that had entered into contracts with CCC received checks for the price differential.[3] These transactions led to the resale of more than 86 million pounds of cheese to processors at a cost more than $2 million less than the government had originally paid for the cheese. Some of the major companies involved were Kraft Foods, Chicago; Lakeshire Marty Company, Plymouth, Wisconsin; National Biscuit Company, New York; Tillamook County Creamery Association, Tillamook, Oregon; and C. J. Berst and Company, Portage, Wisconsin.[4]

The Department of Agriculture openly published details of the cheese repurchase program and justified it by saying that it had "averted the temporary shortage of cheese which would otherwise have developed in retail trade channels because obviously no processor would have retained cheese in inventory at the close of business March 31 [1954] knowing that the support purchase price would drop nearly 5 cents per pound overnight. Had there been no cheese in commercial channels for a period of several days, consumption would have suffered and the government would have been forced to make even larger subsequent purchases of cheese and other dairy prod-

---

[2]Memorandum, Carlile Bolton-Smith, American Law Division, Legislative Reference Service, Library of Congress, to Rep. Lawrence H. Fountain, chairman, Intergovernmental Relations Subcommittee, House Committee on Government Operations, July 6, 1955, 1-8. This 20-page memorandum explains in detail Agriculture's cheese purchase program and the sequence of events constituting the cheese squeeze.

[3]Memorandum, Bolton-Smith to Fountain, July 6, 1955, 8-12; letter, Secretary of Agriculture Ezra Taft Benson to Berry H. Akers, editor-in-chief, *Saint Paul* (MN) *Farmer*, undated, attached to Office of the Secretary of Agriculture, note to correspondents, July 20, 1955, in B-124910, #1.

[4]"Cheese purchased by CCC in March 1954 and immediately contracted for sale back to the sellers in April 1954 under LD-112," undated and unsigned, ibid. This seven-page document, probably from the Department of Agriculture, lists 108 companies and the amounts of their purchases, totaling 86,639,277 pounds of cheese.

ucts." Agriculture argued that the cheese processors had not gotten a $2 million windfall; "They had paid farmers for milk used in the production of cheese under a program reflecting a higher price support. This same cheese moved into consumption after price supports were reduced. It was sold at a lower price with consumers obtaining price reductions."[5]

Publicity about the cheese transactions and accusations that they were not legal led to an investigation and hearings by the Intergovernmental Relations Subcommittee of the House Government Operations Committee chaired by Rep. Lawrence H. Fountain (D—North Carolina). In July 1955, Fountain asked Comptroller General Campbell to give his opinion on whether the 1954 cheese purchase and resale program was legal under the Agricultural Act of 1949 or any other legislation. In his decision, provided to Fountain in August 1955, Campbell concluded that the transactions were "unauthorized and improper" under the Agricultural Act of 1949. He added that he was not inferring any intentional wrongdoing by any official involved.[6]

The Department of Agriculture disagreed with Campbell's opinion and eventually referred the matter to the attorney general for his determination on whether legal action was necessary. Fountain responded by writing to Secretary of Agriculture Ezra T. Benson, "I am sure you recognize . . . that an opinion of the Comptroller General is binding upon the Department of Agriculture whether the Department agrees with it or not."[7] In the meantime, Fountain disclosed that in 1954, Agriculture paid butter dealers about $280,000 in purchase-resale transactions similar to the cheese transactions, and stated that Campbell's opinion applied to the butter deals as well.[8]

For several months, the Department of Agriculture delayed responding definitively to Fountain, claiming that it was waiting for an opinion from the attorney general on the cheese matter. Fountain reiterated to Agriculture his view that the transactions were illegal, urged the department to secure voluntary repayments from the cheese processors, and said that legal action should be taken if voluntary refunds could not be obtained.[9] By mid-April 1956,

---

[5]Letter, Benson to Akers, undated, ibid. See also Department of Agriculture, Commodity Stabilization Service, "Dairy Price Support Operations," May 27, 1955, ibid.

[6]Letter, Fountain to Campbell, July 29, 1955, ibid; and letter, Campbell to Fountain, August 15, 1944, ibid.

[7]Letter, Earl L. Butz, acting secretary of Agriculture, September 2, 1955, to Fountain, attached to letter, James R. Naughton, counsel, Intergovernmental Relations Subcommittee, to Campbell, September 8, 1955, ibid; and letter, Fountain to Benson, September 16, 1955, ibid. See also Fountain, press release, September 17, 1955, ibid.

[8]Fountain, press release, October 15, 1955, ibid.

[9]Letter, Fountain to Benson, November 30, 1955, ibid.; and letter, Fountain to Attorney General Herbert Brownell, Jr., February 13, 1956, ibid.

Fountain had lost patience with both the Department of Agriculture and the attorney general for dragging their feet on the cheese case. All his letters to Secretary Benson had been answered by subordinates in Agriculture, Fountain complained, and the department had failed to do its duty. He asked Benson to appear before his subcommittee within two weeks.[10]

Despite Fountain's complaints, the under secretary of agriculture rather than Benson answered this letter and said that he and other department representatives would be happy to meet with Fountain's subcommittee. Fountain wrote back to Benson, expressing indignation over the under secretary's letter and stating again that it was the secretary of agriculture's duty to recover the improper cheese payments.[11] Fountain then met with the attorney general, who said that the Justice Department agreed with Campbell's opinion and would demand that the cheese processors repay the unauthorized amounts. If voluntary payments were not forthcoming, Justice would take legal action. Subsequently, in May and June 1956, Justice filed suit against some major companies involved—National Biscuit Company, A and P stores, Swift and Company, Kraft Foods Company, and H. J. Heinz Company. Fountain, in summarizing these developments, severely criticized Agriculture and CCC for continuing to uphold the opinion that the cheese transactions were legal while the Justice Department was engaged in litigation to recover funds from the processors. He also suggested that Agriculture submit questionable transactions to GAO for an opinion before committing funds.[12]

Eventually, the Justice Department brought suit on test cases in Baltimore; Minneapolis; and Madison, Wisconsin, as well as in 120 other cases in various locations. The courts decided for the government in all these cases, and by November 1959, the government had recovered $2,227,983 in principal and interest from the processing companies and expected to recover more than $216,000 in addition from concerns against which actions were still pending.[13]

The cheese squeeze demonstrated to GAO the importance of work on government procurement and contracts. In this case, the courts affirmed Campbell's August 1955 opinion on the cheese purchase-resale episode and

---

[10]Letter, Fountain to Benson, April 13, 1956, attached to Fountain, press release, April 15, 1956, ibid.

[11]Letter, True D. Morse, under secretary of Agriculture, to Fountain, April 20, 1956, ibid.; and letter, Fountain to Benson, April 25, 1956, ibid.

[12]"Committee on Governmental Operations, Intergovernmental Relations Subcommittee, Report on 'Purchase-Resale' Transactions of the Commodity Credit Corporation," unsigned typescript, 25 pages, for release on July 27, 1956, ibid.

[13]Court decisions, United States District Court for the District of Maryland, filed July 3, 1947, mimeographed copy, in ibid.; and letter, George C. Doub, assistant attorney general, Civil Division, Department of Justice, to the GAO general counsel, November 18, 1959, ibid.

GAO benefited from the favorable publicity gained in the process.[14] Also, the fact that Campbell took a stand against the actions of a cabinet-level department in the Eisenhower administration during his first year in office helped to dispel the concern expressed during his confirmation hearings that he would be subservient to the administration's views as comptroller general.[15]

The Zinc Stink

The zinc stink occurred during the same period as the cheese squeeze. GAO's Office of Investigations (OI) in June 1955 issued *Report of Investigations of the Program for Development and Expansion of Strategic and Critical Materials in the Interest of National Defense.* The report discussed contracts issued by the Defense Materials Procurement Agency (DMPA) to three firms—Mid-Continent Mining Corporation; MacArthur Mining Company, Inc.; and W. M. & W. Mining Company, Inc., for the production of zinc. DMPA, headed by the administrator of General Services, had authority under the Defense Production Act of 1950 to expand facilities to produce strategic and critical materials needed for defense production, a national stockpile, and civilian purposes. DMPA had authority to use purchase contracts, loans, subsidies, and accelerated tax amortization to meet its objectives. Between September 1951 and May 1953, the deputy administrator of DMPA, who ran the strategic materials program, was Howard I. Young, president of both the American Zinc, Lead & Smelting Company and the American Mining Congress. Young served the government as a dollar-a-year man.[16]

After receiving information about DMPA's zinc program in 1953, investigators in the GAO Office of Investigations (OI) field office in Kansas City began looking into the matter; subsequently the Washington Headquarters of OI, under Chief of Investigations William L. Ellis, took over the job. In June 1955, Ellis sent OI's report to Comptroller General Campbell, who forwarded it to the Joint Committee on Defense Production and other congressional committees.

In summarizing the three cases considered in the report, the OI said that they had certain common elements: "The Government provided financial

---

[14]See, for example, clipping, "House Unit Acts on Cheese Deal," *New York Times*, September 18, 1955, ibid; and clipping, "Fantasy in Cheese," *Washington Daily News*, August 19, 1955, ibid.

[15]See chapter 5, pp. 105-08. See also the account of the cheese squeeze in Frederick C. Mosher, *The GAO: The Quest for Accountability in American Government* (Boulder, CO: Westview Press, 1979), 146-47.

[16]*Defense Production Act*, Hearings before the Joint Committee on Defense Production, 84th Cong., 1st Sess., to hear witnesses on Defense Production Act Contracts entered into by the Defense Materials Procurement Agency (Washington: GPO, 1955), 181-84 (hereafter cited as *Defense Production Act*, Hearings, 1955.)

assistance to three marginal producers of zinc ore; the zinc situation was not so critical as to require the assistance given these companies; Government funds of nearly $400,000 were risked and lost to develop or continue these ventures; and the American Zinc, Lead & Smelting Co., of which Howard I. Young, Deputy DMPA Administrator, was president, or its subsidiaries, made contracts to smelt or buy concentrates produced by these companies and by which it could sell zinc in an assured market."

GAO's report explained these charges in detail, including the fact that the three companies assisted financially by DPMA had failed to reach production. The report, among other things, clearly raised the question of conflict of interest by Young.[17] Young wore three hats during these events, GAO reported; he was a government official, a company executive, and a mining industry spokesman.

> As Deputy Administrator of DPMA and as its key operative official, it was his duty to insure needed defense materials at the least cost to the Government. As a member of key Government committees it was his duty to help formulate national defense policy in the fields of stockpiling, allocation, industry expansion, ceiling prices, etc. As president of American Zinc he obtained added sources of zinc concentrates to feed the smelters of his company. As president of the American Mining Congress he sought to help domestic industry. His varied activities, which cannot always be completely revealed, stem from the fact that he was serving in this triple capacity; service to three masters, with equal loyalty to each, became plainly incompatible.[18]

After receiving GAO's zinc report, the Joint Committee on Defense Production held hearings in July 1955. On July 6, Ellis, Robert F. Keller (assistant to the comptroller general), and five investigators from OI represented GAO. On July 14, Ellis and the five investigators testified; Howard Young was there also, along with legal counsel John Lane, as was Jess Larson, who as GSA administrator appointed Young to his DPMA position in 1951. Comptroller General Campbell; Assistant Comptroller General Frank H. Weitzel; Ellis; and Charles E. Eckert and David M. B. Lambert, legislative attorneys, testified for GAO on July 27, the third and final hearing day.[19]

---

[17]See *Defense Production Act*, Hearings, 1955, 181-309, for the text of the report and related material.
[18]Ibid., 187 (from text of the GAO report).
[19]Ibid., 1, 19, 125.

The first day's hearing lasted less than an hour and consisted mainly of Ellis's presentation of the details of GAO's zinc reports. At its conclusion, the committee decided to invite Howard Young to appear at the next hearing session.[20] The hearing on July 14 lasted more than six hours. Young denied that he was guilty of conflict of interest—GAO had not directly so charged him but had certainly implied it—and contested with Ellis both the broad conclusions and some specific details in the GAO report. At the end of the hearing, Sen. Homer E. Capehart (R—Indiana) suggested that Young meet with GAO officials to resolve their differences over report details that Young had charged were erroneous.[21]

The third day's hearing became quite contentious. Although Young and GAO officials met several times between the second and third sessions, they did not settle all their differences. John Lane, Young's counsel, raised what he termed "extremely important policy considerations" for the committee, Congress, and the comptroller general: "Does the Congress intend its own agency, the GAO, to provide it with reliable, accurate and supportable reports, as a basis for its determination of important legislative policy?" He went on: "Does the Congress intend that the appropriations it provides for the General Accounting Office shall be utilized to the extent here evidenced to hound and harass a citizen, to defame his character, to have his name dragged in the mud of sensational newspaper publicity, to attack his character, to adversely affect his relations within his industry and with his Government, when his only offense is that he is an honest businessman doing a notoriously successful job for his Government?" He continued: "To what extent does the Congress . . . want its administrative arm, the General Accounting Office, to be unbiased, to be impartial in its report of finding of fact. . . ?"   Finally, he asked: "Does the Congress wish it to be known throughout the land that no honest businessman can come into Government and do a job for his country without running the risk of personal persecution and character assassination from the General Accounting Office?" Lane suggested that the committee request the comptroller general to publicly apologize to Young.[22]

Campbell admitted in testimony that GAO had made a mistake in its report on an issue that Young had argued during the second day's hearing. DMPA under Young had made a loan of $325,000 to the Mid-Continent Mining Corporation; Mid-Continent Mining spent $60,000 of this money to buy mining equipment. GAO stated in its report that this equipment had

---

[20]Ibid., 1-17.
[21]Ibid., 19-123; Capehart's suggestion is on 97-98.
[22]Ibid., 139-40.

been purchased from Young's firm, American Zinc, Lead, & Smelting Company, on the recommendation of representatives from that company. Campbell conceded that GAO was wrong on this point and that the equipment had been bought from Western Machinery Company. He maintained, however, that use of the equipment had benefited American Zinc "since it held an interest in the process patent for the process used by the machine, rather than the title to the machine itself."[23]

This admission of error in effect cast doubt on the general substance of GAO's zinc report, although Weitzel argued that Young had made errors in his testimony as well.[24] Both Senators Capehart and John W. Bricker (R—Ohio) severely criticized GAO after Campbell admitted the error. Bricker argued that GAO could have discovered the facts and avoided submitting an erroneous report to the committee. Senator Capehart's comment was more scorching: "Now the thing I objected to, and still object to, is that you fellows come in here as prosecuting attorneys . . . when your job, as I understand it, is to be factual and is to advise us and be just as much interested in defending one side as you are condemning another. Now, maybe I am wrong about it. However, my observation of your attitude all the way through has been one of fighting this thing, of condemning this man and I do not think that is your job. Frankly, I sort of resented it, and I still resent it."[25]

During this hearing, Chairman Paul Brown (D—Georgia) was abrupt with GAO representatives, including Weitzel, and by interrupting prevented them from presenting all that they had to say. There was little discussion of mistakes GAO contended Young had made, and the emphasis was on GAO's error. While GAO stood its ground on the substance of the zinc reports, Campbell's admission of error substantially weakened the strength of its conclusions. Ellis stated many years later that he had read the draft zinc report before GAO issued it, but he had not read the full file. "And it was a bum report," he said. Campbell was "just livid" about it and Ellis, according to his own recollection, offered to resign. Campbell initially declined his offer but later accepted, ending Ellis's 20-year career at GAO and dismissing a man who had been one of Comptroller General Warren's most trusted officials.[26] Campbell's 1956 disbanding of the Office of Investigations certainly stemmed in part from the zinc stink.[27]

---

[23]Ibid., 152-53.

[24]Ibid., 171.

[25]Ibid., 172.

[26]GAO, *William L. Ellis, GAO, 1935-1955*, GAO History Program, Oral History Series, GAO/OP-21-OH (Washington: 1991), 2-3.

[27]See below, pp. 419-20.

The Lipscomb Report

The report on GAO issued in 1956 by the House Government Operations Committee, familiarly known as the Lipscomb Report, had much to say about the Office of Investigations.[28] After reviewing OI's work, Rep. Glenard P. Lipscomb concluded that the office "dealt with specific instances of waste or irregularity rather than general significant deficiencies in financial administration." He also noted "inadequate foundation and documentation for some allegations" in OI's reports and insufficient coordination with the Division of Audits and the Accounting Systems Division in its investigations. Lipscomb commented on OI's slowness in sending reports to Congress and asserted that it sometimes revised draft reports too extensively in response to agency or individual comments. Lipscomb concluded that OI's reports "have not, for the most part, been of value to the Congress and the agencies in revealing significant areas of weakness in financial administration."

Lipscomb specifically recommended that the comptroller general review OI to determine whether it should continue as a separate organization. Whether it continued or not, investigative work should be confined to specific cases that did not fit into regular audits or required techniques beyond the scope of such audits. Lipscomb recommended also that investigative staff be highly qualified, that investigative activity be closely coordinated with the work of GAO's audit and other divisions, and that documentation of investigative cases be improved. Finally, he proposed that GAO continue to detail qualified investigators when Congress and its committees requested them.[29]

In his response to Lipscomb in November 1956, Campbell disagreed that OI's reports had been of little value to Congress but accepted the other recommendations. This happened five months after Lipscomb issued his report, and by that time, Campbell had made substantial changes in the organization of GAO investigative work.[30]

---

[28]See chapter 16, pp. 396-98, for background on the committee and its recommendations on GAO's accounting systems work.

[29]*The General Accounting Office: A Study of Its Organization and Administration with Recommendations for Increasing Its Effectiveness*, Seventeenth Intermediate Report of the Committee on Government Operations, 84th Cong., 2d Sess., H. Rept. 2264 (Washington: GPO, 1956) (hereafter cited as *Lipscomb Report*), 7-8, 33-37.

[30]*Comments of the Comptroller General of the United States on Report of the Committee on Government Operations, House of Representatives, entitled "The General Accounting Office - A Study of Its Organization and Administration with Recommendations for Increasing Its Effectiveness (House Report No. 2264, 84th Congress, 2d Session, November 1, 1956)*, 57-62 (hereafter cited as Campbell, *Comments on Lipscomb Report*).

The Reorganization of 1956

On November 30, 1955, Campbell issued a document entitled "Outline of Planned Changes in Organization and Operations."[31] By this time, GAO had experienced the cheese squeeze and the zinc stink and had advance knowledge of what Lipscomb would recommend in his report a few months later. Also, Campbell had been in office nearly a year and had had time to observe GAO operations. His outline disclosed in general the actions he expected to take and made preliminary designations of officials to head a new structure of divisions and offices. Campbell's outline dealt with GAO organization in four areas—the comptroller general's office; legal work; legislative liaison, general administration, and specialized functions; and accounting and auditing. He anticipated organizing activities in the accounting and auditing area around six functions: accounting and auditing procedures, accounting and auditing policy and practices, defense audits, civil audits, staff management for accounting and auditing, and field operations. Campbell indicated that specific orders establishing the new functional groups would be forthcoming.[32]

On March 22, 1956, Campbell issued five orders to implement his reorganization plan. Order No. 2.30 established the Accounting and Auditing Policy Staff (AAPS) to develop accounting and auditing policy, standards, and practices and to cooperate with the Treasury Department and the Bureau of the Budget (BOB) in reviewing and developing central accounting processes and financial reporting. AAPS was also to review audit division programs "for consistency with policy and adherence to broad program objectives" and to review draft reports. AAPS received a special assignment to conduct research in methods and procedures of electronic data systems to stimulate the development and the effective use of such equipment in auditing and accounting. All in all, Campbell gave AAPS a broad mandate, and as the unit developed in subsequent years under its director, Ellsworth H. Morse, Jr., it played a very important role in GAO's ongoing work.[33]

In the audit area, Campbell divided the Division of Audits, created in 1952, into two divisions—Defense Accounting and Auditing (DAAD) and Civil Accounting and Auditing (CAAD). DAAD was to carry out accounting and auditing functions in the Department of Defense (DOD) and the military departments. DAAD's Washington staff; GAO's Navy, Army, Air Force, and

---

[31]In A-16251, #1.

[32]Ibid.

[33]Comptroller General's Order No. 2.30, March 22, 1956, ibid. The changes Campbell made in the accounting area, including abolition of the Accounting Systems Division, are discussed in detail in chapter 16, pp. 391-405. See below for a further discussion of AAPS's work during the Campbell period.

Ellsworth H. Morse, Jr., who directed GAO's policy office from 1956 to 1977.

Marine Corps Audit Branches located in Cleveland, Indianapolis, Denver, and Washington; and the regional offices, "in accordance with work plans and programs provided by the Washington staff," would handle the division's work.[34] CAAD was responsible for accounting and auditing work in all agencies except those assigned to DAAD. The work of the division was the responsibility of its Washington staff, its two branches—Civil Audit and Depository Accounts—and regional offices. DAAD and CAAD were to cooperate with two other new organizations, the Office of Staff Management (OSM) and the Field Operations Division (FOD), "in the development and execution of a professional career program designed to increase the overall effectiveness of the accounting and auditing staff."[35] An important feature of Campbell's plan was the consolidation within these two divisions of both the accounting systems work done previously by the Accounting Systems Division and the audit work of the Division of Audits. One result of this consolidation was the death of the Accounting Systems Division that Comptroller General Warren had valued so highly.

Campbell also announced in March 1956 the establishment of FOD under a director responsible to the comptroller general. The division was to have a small central office in Washington. The director was to review work programs involving the regional offices and was responsible for their administrative direction through regional managers reporting to him. He was also responsible for scheduling, in cooperation with the directors of CAAD and DAAD, all work programs coming out of Washington. He was to cooperate with the Office of Staff Management on recruiting, appointing, and training regional office staff. The regional managers were responsible to the CAAD and DAAD directors "for the accomplishment and technical adequacy of all phases of accounting and auditing assignments made by them" and to the director of FOD "for the overall quality of performance."[36] Campbell's purpose in setting up FOD was to establish central direction in Washington of regional operations and to integrate the work of the regional offices and the Washington audit divisions.

Campbell's fifth order in March 1956 created the Office of Staff Management. Its functions included establishing a recruiting program "designed to obtain a high quality professional staff of accountants and auditors from colleges, universities, professional fields and industry" and setting up a training and career program "designed to increase the abilities of the accounting and auditing staff to maximum usefulness." The office also was to exercise

---

[34]Comptroller General's Order No. 2.31, March 22, 1956, A-16251, #1.

[35]Comptroller General's Order No. 2.32, March 22, 1956, ibid.

[36]Comptroller General's Order No. 2.33, March 22, 1956, ibid.

general control over staff placement in cooperation with the accounting and auditing divisions and to develop a program to gain recognition of the staff's accounting and auditing work as qualifying experience for the certified public accountant (CPA) examination. The creation of OSM signaled Campbell's determination to upgrade the staff through both recruiting and training and to enable GAO to prepare higher-quality reports for Congress and the agencies under audit.

Campbell made two other organizational changes after issuing his March 1956 orders, both effective on July 1, 1956. He established the Office of Legislative Liaison (OLL) to improve GAO's congressional contacts and relationships. OLL initially was in the Office of the Comptroller General, under the direction of Robert F. Keller, one of Campbell's assistants and later general counsel.[37]

The other change was abolition of the Office of Investigations. By this time, Campbell knew of the Lipscomb Report's criticisms of OI and he had gone through the difficult congressional hearings over the zinc cases in the summer of 1955.[38] Some portent of things to come occurred in November 1955 when Campbell transferred OI's director and deputy director, William L. Ellis and Ralph Ramsey, to the Office of the General Counsel and brought in Kirt W. Johnson from the New York Regional Office as acting chief of investigations. The press reported at the time a GAO spokesman's statement that Ellis and Ramsey wanted to be transferred but gave prominent mention to the zinc stink as a probable cause for the change.[39] A few months later, Ellis was in effect fired when Campbell accepted his resignation.[40]

Campbell announced changes in the organization of investigative work in June 1956. He emphasized the importance of the investigative function but said that it should be integrated with accounting and auditing work to "bring about an improved performance of the work of the General Accounting Office as a whole." Campbell transferred OI's duties, work in process, and staff to CAAD and DAAD; in each of these divisions, an assistant director would serve as chief of investigations responsible to the division's director. OI's regional offices were consolidated with the 19 regional audit offices. In each regional office, an investigator-in-charge would report to the

---

[37]See chapter 5, p. 120.

[38]Ted B. Westfall issued a very critical report on OI in late 1951. Campbell apparently was not familiar with it when he made changes involving OI in 1955 and 1956. Morse gave Campbell a copy of Westfall's report in 1958 when Campbell said that he had never seen it. See entry for December 19, 1958, Morse, *Daily Notes*, 1957-1958, GAO History Program Archives. See also chapter 14, pp. 351-52.

[39]Clipping, *Washington Post*, "Probe Unit for GAO Shaken Up," November 3, 1955, in clippings CG, 1954-1962, GAO History Program Archives.

[40]See above, p. 414.

regional manager. The heads of the accounting and auditing divisions and regional offices received authorization "to utilize the investigative, auditing, and accounting personnel under their jurisdiction in such manner as will best meet the requirements of the work to be performed, consistent with position classification."[41]

By July 1, 1956, Campbell had his new organization in place. Its centralizing principle was the integration of accounting systems and audit work in the two main audit divisions—CAAD and DAAD—supported by other offices, especially Staff Management, the Accounting and Auditing Policy Staff, and the Field Operations Division. Upgrading GAO's staff—its professionalization—was another key motive of Campbell. OSM, which had no comparable predecessor in GAO, was a very important Campbell innovation. He also wanted more centralized and direct attention given to accounting and auditing policy and procedures, hence the establishment of AAPS. Also, clearly Campbell desired to increase GAO's audit work in the defense area, including defense procurement contracts. Henry Eschwege and Victor L. Lowe, auditors in CAAD when it began operations in 1956, both observed later that one of Campbell's main reasons for separating the Division of Audits into civil and defense divisions was to put more emphasis on defense audits.[42]

Obviously, Campbell had devoted considerable thought to the reorganization, which he planned without much input from division and office heads. When Chairman Albert Thomas (D—Texas) of the Subcommittee of the House Appropriations Committee asked him if the reorganization had worked out as he had anticipated, Campbell replied: "I am convinced that we have done the right thing, and that it has worked out very, very well."[43]

The Accounting and Auditing Policy Staff

Campbell initially anticipated setting up a group for accounting policy and procedures, to be headed by Walter F. Frese, and a second group for audit policy and practices, directed by Ellsworth H. Morse, Jr. Later he decided to combine the two groups into the Accounting and Auditing Policy Staff and appointed Frese as its first director. He selected Morse to be the

---

[41]Campbell, "Proposed Changes in the Office of Investigations," June 6, 1956, *GAO Inter-Office Memorandums*, vol. 2, 1954-1968, GAO Law Library.

[42]GAO, *The Civil Division, 1956-1972: Interview with Gregory J. Ahart, Henry Eschwege, and Victor L. Lowe*, GAO History Program, Oral History Series, GAO/OP-22-OH (Washington: 1992), 14.

[43]Campbell testimony, March 3, 1958, *Independent Offices Appropriations for 1959*, Hearings before a Subcommittee of the House Committee on Appropriations, 85th Cong., 2d Sess., pt. 2 (Washington: GPO, 1958), 1247.

director of the new Civil Accounting and Auditing Division.[44] After Frese left GAO a few months later to take a professorship at Harvard University, Campbell moved Morse to AAPS and appointed Adolph T. Samuelson as director of CAAD. When Morse agreed to take the AAPS job in August 1956, Campbell told him that he regarded the position "as the top accounting and auditing job in the office." Morse's duties included directing the policy staff; coordinating the activities of the five accounting, auditing, and investigative groups (AAPS, CAAD, DAAD, FOD, and OSM); and representing the comptroller general in the Joint Accounting Improvement Program.[45]

When Morse took over AAPS in August 1956, it had 42 staff, which Campbell thought was too many.[46] Gradually AAPS's staff size declined— to 34 in 1960, 28 in 1962, and 27 in 1964—consistent with the overall decrease in GAO's staff during the period.[47]

As director of AAPS, Morse, known to his friends and associates as Mose, became a very influential official in GAO. He was probably closer to Campbell than any other office head or division director; his *Daily Notes*, which he recorded between 1956 and 1968, reveal almost daily contact with the comptroller general on a wide variety of subjects—AAPS matters as well as broader questions related to GAO's work and operations. Campbell indeed did consider Morse the top accounting and auditing official in GAO and usually took his advice, even on issues where there were differences of opinion between Morse and another division or office head. Although Morse was modest and reserved, a reading of his daily notes demonstrates the range of his interests and the influence he had with Campbell.

In 1963, at the annual appropriations hearings when Rep. Albert Thomas asked Campbell if the policy staff was the "blue-ribbon crowd" in GAO, Campbell answered yes. Annually at these hearings, he summarized

[44]Campbell testimony, February 10, 1956, *Independent Offices Appropriations for 1956*, Hearings before a Subcommittee of the House Committee on Appropriations, 84th Cong., 1st Sess., pt. 2 (Washington: GPO, 1955), 1345.

[45]Entries for August 6 and 9, 1956, Morse, *Daily Notes*, 1956.

[46]Entry for August 10, 1956, ibid.; and *Annual Report of the Comptroller General of the United States for the Fiscal Year Ending June 30, 1956* (Washington: GPO, 1956), 42.

[47]Table, hearing of March 3, 1958, *Independent Offices Appropriations for 1959*, pt. 2, 1281; table, hearing of March 7, 1960, *Independent Offices Appropriations for 1961*, Hearings before a Subcommittee of the House Committee on Appropriations, 86th Cong., 2d Sess., pt. 2 (Washington: GPO, 1960), 766; table, hearing of February 9, 1962, *Independent Offices Appropriations for 1963*, Hearings before a Subcommittee of the House Committee on Appropriations, 87th Cong., 2d Sess., pt. 2 (Washington, GPO, 1962), 72; and table, hearing of February 25, 1963, *Independent Offices Appropriations for 1964*, Hearings before a Subcommittee of the House Committee on Appropriations, 88th Cong., 1st Sess., pt. 2 (Washington: GPO, 1963), 196.

AAPS's official duties—generally, to develop and coordinate within GAO "the studies and data from which policies and procedures are evolved." Specifically, Campbell listed the policy staff's principal work: (1) to develop accounting principles, standards, and policies; (2) to develop and review "auditing and investigative policy, principles, standards, guidelines, and related requirements" for CAAD, DAAD, and FOD; (3) to participate in the review of and consultation on agency automatic data processing (ADP) systems; (4) to develop and review fiscal procedures, including coordination and development with Treasury and the Bureau of the Budget of the federal government's central accounting and financial reporting; and (5) to participate with Treasury and BOB under the Joint Financial Management Improvement Program in development and review of joint projects and programs to improve financial management in separate agencies and in the federal government as a whole.[48]

A large part of GAO's work was preparation and issuance of reports. Thus the development of report policy was a central task of AAPS. To some degree, congressional interest in GAO reports influenced report policy development. For example, in January 1957, Sen. Allen J. Ellender (D—Louisiana), chairman of the Subcommittee on Public Works, Senate Committee on Appropriations, wrote to Campbell about a GAO report on local participation in Army Corps of Engineers flood control and navigation projects. GAO had made legislative recommendations in the report, including one to govern the extent of local participation in such projects. Ellender pointed out that Congress, which received survey reports from the Corps of Engineers, held hearings on such matters. "It appears to me," he wrote, "that in recent years there has been a decided increase in the number of unsolicited reports on various aspects of Federal Programs authorized by Congress suggesting that the Congress may wish to write a new policy on the particular program under discussion." "To my knowledge," he continued, "the committees of Congress have not enacted legislation as a result of the reports submitted." He added that it would be better for GAO to spend its time preparing information specifically requested by a committee or member of Congress.[49]

After receiving this letter, Morse and several other GAO officials met with two staff members of the Senate Appropriations Committee to discuss it. Kenneth Bousquet, one of the subcommittee staff, stated that the reports the subcommittee had received from GAO were of no value and said "he had not been able to find out who would get anything out of them." Bousquet talked at length about reports on the Corps of Engineers and suggested that

---

[48]Campbell testimony, February 25, 1963, ibid.
[49]Letter, Ellender to Campbell, January 9, 1957, bound in Morse, *Daily Notes*, 1957-1958.

GAO did not have complete information on congressional consideration of these matters. Both Bousquet and William Woodruff, the other committee staffer, complained that GAO never said anything good about an agency in its reports. Morse wrote that the GAO and committee representatives "finally agreed that working relationships could be developed whereby when we were planning work for a new year informal discussions would be held with committee staff members to ascertain whether they wished to make suggestions as to specific areas of coverage in our work."[50]

A few weeks later, Campbell wrote to Ellender, stating that arrangements had been made for periodic contact between GAO representatives and the committee staff. This "should provide a better method of enabling us to ascertain problem areas of interest to the Congress," Campbell wrote. He also said that as a result of the recent discussions, he believed that GAO would be able to make its audit reports more useful and generally "to render improved service to Congress."[51]

Shortly after this episode, but apparently not in relation to it, Morse, Campbell, and others from GAO attended an executive session of the Subcommittee on International Operations, House Committee on Government Operations, chaired by Rep. Porter Hardy, Jr. (D—Virginia). The subject of the session was a recommendation of the subcommittee in a report on Iran (H. Rept. 10, 85th Cong., 1st Sess.) about GAO's relationships with the International Cooperation Administration (ICA). The subcommittee recommended that GAO establish, and require ICA to use, an accounting system ensuring accurate end-use accounting for expenditures of foreign aid funds. The subcommittee also recommended that GAO "expand and strengthen its audits of economic aid expenditures to assure timely, accurate, and fully detailed reports to the Congress." Hardy commented that GAO recommendations were of little use unless there was follow-up to make sure that actual improvements were under way. Rep. Glenard Lipscomb added that GAO did not go into enough detail in its reports.[52]

Another example of congressional concern about GAO reporting policy occurred in 1958. Campbell received a telephone call from Sen. John L. McClellan (D—Arkansas) about proposed GAO comments in a report re-

---

[50]Morse, "Meeting with Staff of Senate Appropriations Committee," January 23, 1957, in Morse, *Daily Notes*, 1957-1958. See also Edward T. Johnson, GAO legislative attorney, "Memorandum for the Legislative Contact File," February 12, 1957, ibid.; these are Johnson's minutes of the January 23, 1957 meeting.

[51]Letter, Campbell to Ellender, February 13, 1957, ibid.

[52]Entry for February 19, 1957, ibid., with attachment: summary of the meeting by George Staples of GAO.

viewing the economic benefits of the Arkansas River and Tributaries Project. In a subsequent meeting involving McClellan and Campbell, McClellan questioned GAO's authority to inquire into some matters covered in the draft report. GAO agreed to reconsider the report. Morse, not present at this meeting, noted that the incident had raised the issue of whether GAO should question congressional decisions in cases when Congress had already made appropriations. "One outcome we would hope to avoid," Morse wrote, "would be the admonition to confine our work to accounts and vouchers and not undertake to review and evaluate agency operations."[53] When Morse discussed this matter with him, Campbell said that he did not entirely agree that GAO should avoid work that resulted in findings questioning decisions of Congress.[54]

Eventually Morse; Keller; Samuelson; and Elmer W. Muhonen, the assistant director responsible for the project, agreed to recommend to Campbell deletion of the summary finding point to which McClellan had objected and to concentrate in the report on the historical and factual aspects of the matter. Morse and Keller agreed that GAO should not challenge Congress's legislative decisions unless the agency concerned, in this case the Corps of Engineers, had misrepresented the situation.[55] Campbell concurred in this recommendation, suggesting that if anyone questioned the deletions, GAO should say that it was not sure it should criticize or make recommendations on a matter approved by Congress.[56]

There were other instances of the same kind of concern from congressional committees and individual congressmen during the Campbell period. GAO, without sacrificing the integrity of its reports, tried to respond as positively as it could. In December 1964, late in Campbell's term, the chief counsel of the House Government Operations Committee remarked to a group of GAO trainees that some of the Office's reports were not particularly significant. Morse, who was displeased by the remark, suggested to Campbell, who agreed, that GAO include in report transmittal letters "some kind of a highlight comment as to why the matter reported was considered by us to be of sufficient significance to report to the Congress."[57]

---

[53]Entry for May 22, 1958, ibid.
[54]Entry for May 27, 1958, ibid.
[55]Entry for June 4, 1958, ibid.
[56]Entry for June 5, 1958, ibid.
[57]Entry for December 1, 1964, Morse, *Daily Notes*, 1963-1964.

In 1962, Campbell issued an important instruction on GAO's audit effort and reporting policies. He stated that GAO could be proud of its accomplishments, but "we cannot conclude that all our efforts in reviewing Federal agency operations are as productive as they should be." He discussed three points extensively: (1) Resources should be used to review agency operations "that are most likely to be productive of significant findings as to the manner in which public funds are applied and reporting our findings to the Congress. . . ." (2) GAO needed to obtain greater benefits from its findings. "To help obtain greater benefits . . . , our recommendations should provide for corrective action of a nature broader than curing the specific weaknesses on which we base our findings." (3) GAO should relate deficiencies it discovered to the organization and persons responsible for them. "By this, I refer not only to department, agency, or bureau heads who are responsible for all operations, but to the lower levels of performance or decision-making more directly involved in the operations we review." Campbell stated that GAO would include such identification in reports only "when we consider the inclusion of such information necessary to obtain proper consideration and corrective action on our findings and recommendations." GAO audit units should try to get such information for all reports and be prepared to supply it if necessary to congressional committees and concerned government officials.[58]

In a meeting with accounting and auditing division heads, Morse indicated how AAPS would implement the three instructions. Direction of effort would be considered in AAPS work on authorization of specific assignments; broadening of recommendations to obtain greater benefits would be considered in the reports review process; and on the matter of naming names, AAPS would see that the procedure was used if necessary to get corrective action on problems GAO identified.[59]

Campbell's November 1962 instruction probably reflected congressional concern about GAO as well as his own increasing emphasis on reporting accomplishments, monetary and otherwise. The instruction was fateful to the extent that it adopted an official policy of naming persons allegedly responsible for problems identified in GAO reports. The Defense Accounting and Auditing Division in particular used this technique heavily in its growing number of reports on defense contracts. The ultimate result was extensive hearings in 1965 chaired by Rep. Chet Holifield (D—California) on

---

[58]Memorandum, Campbell to directors of AAPS, CAAD, and FOD, Subject: Direction of audit effort and related reporting policies, November 30, 1962, in *GAO Intra-Office Memorandums*, vol. 2, 1954-1968, GAO Law Library.

[59]Notes of meeting of December 18, 1962, Morse, Notes of Meetings of the Accounting and Auditing Division Heads, July 1960 through July 1964.

GAO's defense contract reports, leading to serious criticism of GAO and significant changes in reporting policy.[60]

"Reports review" was an important function assigned to AAPS at the time of its founding in 1956. Campbell charged the office with reviewing draft CAAD and DAAD reports "from the standpoint of policy, existing standards, and reporting objectives."[61] In the background of this assignment was the occasional inadequate review of reports. A prime example was the 1955 zinc report, which included an error Campbell had to admit publicly in congressional testimony. In April 1956, when Morse was still director of CAAD, he met with Karney Brasfield, one of Campbell's assistants, and other officials, including Walter Frese, the first director of AAPS, to discuss problems in the process for reviewing draft reports. Brasfield explained that representatives of the Office of the General Counsel (OGC) and the Office of the Comptroller General (OCG) sometimes did not have sufficient opportunity to review reports that went to agency heads. Brasfield suggested that the AAPS staff review all reports addressed to both agency heads and Congress before issuance. This would ease the pressure on OGC and OCG, which could at least review report summaries. Another suggestion was that the policy staff and the operating division that had prepared a report be in agreement before it went to OGC and OCG for review.[62]

AAPS gradually acquired a reputation for being very tough in the review of draft reports. Allen R. Voss, an auditor who moved from CAAD to AAPS as a report reviewer in 1963, remarked years later that people in the operating divisions feared the policy staff; report reviewers "were always in a confrontational stage with the operating people over report reviews." "The CG [comptroller general]," Voss added, "would not want any report to come up to his desk for signature without being reviewed by the . . . [AAPS] staff. Report review was a big function in AAPS." Voss's immediate superior in AAPS, Robert L. Rasor, was the consummate reviewer; Voss had to thoroughly review each report Rasor gave him, "because I knew it was going to get a complete, detailed review by him and that there was no exception."[63]

Donald J. Horan, an auditor who transferred from a regional suboffice to AAPS in 1965, noted the thoroughness of reports review. "I remember reports on which we would have maybe 100 comments. Some of those early

[60]See chapter 20, pp. 505-12.

[61]Comptroller General's Order No. 2.30, March 22, 1956, A-16251, #1.

[62]Entry for April 30, 1956, Morse, *Daily Notes*, 1956.

[63]GAO, *Policy Guidance, 1963-1986: Interview with Donald J. Horan, Eugene L. Pahl, and Allen R. Voss*, GAO History Program, Oral History Series, GAO/OP-23-OH (Washington: 1992), 3, 6, 29.

ADP reports . . had over 100 comments. Many of them were very substantive things about the evidence to support positions, and a lot of them were not very substantive but involved such things as problems with the presentation of findings," Horan recalled.[64] Gregory Ahart, a CAAD auditor who eventually became deputy director of the division, felt, as one whose reports were reviewed by AAPS, that the process worked fairly well, even though there were some ruffled feathers at times. "But on the whole," Ahart said, ". . . report review was very useful in helping upgrade the quality of the product and upgrade the quality of the writing that went into the product. It wasn't always a most comfortable relationship probably on either side."[65]

An example of report review, perhaps more extreme than most but not unique, was one AAPS performed for the Defense Accounting and Auditing Division in April 1960. The AAPS comments covered a DAAD review of an ADP system at the Army Transportation Materiel Command. Frederic H. Smith, deputy director of AAPS, informed DAAD that AAPS had partially reviewed the draft report but had so many comments that AAPS was returning it for further work before proceeding. "Please submit it again," Smith wrote, "when it is, in your opinion, ready for final review." The five-page, single-spaced AAPS review began with the observation that the DAAD report "leaves the impression that it has not been reviewed since assembly in its present form. . . . Reports submitted to AAPS should represent the best effort of the originating division." Other AAPS comments:

• "This draft is embarrassingly stale. If it could have been issued eighteen months ago it would have been useful and of real interest."

• "Too many military abbreviations are encountered by the reader."

• "Your tale . . . about the depot refusals may be very interesting, but you should explain it for a reader."

The AAPS comments detailed numerous errors and incomplete or misleading information in the DAAD report.[66]

---

[64]Ibid., 31.

[65]GAO, *The Civil Division, 1956-1972: Interview with Gregory J. Ahart, Henry Eschwege, and Victor L. Lowe,* GAO History Program, Oral History Series, GAO/OP-22-OH (Washington: 1992), 37.

[66]Memorandum, Smith to Defense Accounting and Auditing Division, April 27, 1960, with attached "AAPS Review Comments, Report on Review of ADP System at Transportation Materiel Command," in Morse Papers, Box 31, Folder: Federal Government, Executive Branch—Defense, Department of—Army [December 1956-April 1960], GAO History Program Archives.

There were differences in AAPS relationships with CAAD and DAAD. Samuelson, the director of CAAD, got along better with Morse and was more willing to resolve disputed issues in report reviews. Furthermore, his division seemed to review draft reports more thoroughly than DAAD before they sent them to AAPS.[67] Voss explained how AAPS and the divisions resolved differences. The normal process was for division assistant or associate directors to confer with AAPS reviewers, including the reviewer who had gone over the report at issue. Usually the matter was settled amicably at this stage. When this process did not work, Robert Rasor took up the case with division representatives. Usually, Voss commented, Rasor convinced the division staff to accept AAPS's point of view, resulting in changes in the draft report. If settlement did not come at this level, Morse and the division director discussed the draft report, and for most cases that got this far, settlement came at this stage. The next step was to take the case to Comptroller General Campbell; everybody concerned was reluctant to do that.[68]

Morse and Samuelson occasionally had differences about report review. For example, in 1957, Samuelson complained to Morse about the extent of AAPS's detailed reviews, saying that he thought that they were to be restricted to policy matters. Morse summarized this discussion by saying that it "ended on the note that there really was not too much difference in our viewpoints and that the process would shake itself out satisfactorily in due course."[69] On another occasion, Morse discussed with Samuelson the AAPS preference to receive report drafts only after incorporation of comments from the agency reviewed. Samuelson felt that this would take more processing time, but he finally agreed to it after Morse said that AAPS would try to expedite the return of drafts to the division.[70]

In 1960, Morse drew up proposals requesting DAAD and CAAD to strengthen the division review process so that AAPS could cut the detailed review somewhat and concentrate more on policy questions. When Morse discussed the proposals with Campbell, the comptroller general thought that they were appropriate and said that AAPS ought to insist on receiving reports in good shape and should not have to be concerned with grammar and format.[71]

---

[67]Comment of Henry Eschwege in GAO, *The Civil Division, 1956-1972*, 37; and comment of Donald Horan in GAO, *Policy Guidance, 1963-1986*, 32.

[68]Voss comments, ibid., 30.

[69]Entry for May 3, 1957, Morse, *Daily Notes*, 1957-1958.

[70]Entry for August 7, 1958, ibid.

[71]Entry for November 18, 1960, Morse, *Daily Notes*, 1959-1960.

On occasion, Campbell was disappointed with the AAPS review of reports. In 1962, he raised questions about a proposed report on the San Francisco and New York offices of the Public Housing Administration. The report had extensive information on San Francisco and little on New York. Campbell thought that there should be separate reports on each office, with much more information on New York, which Campbell pointed out had a large low-rent housing program. As Morse recorded the matter, "Mr. Campbell expressed his difficulties first to Mr. [John] Abbadessa, Deputy Director, CAAD, and later to me. His inquiry to me added up essentially to why in the Policy Staff review we did not question the report treatment. Mr. Campbell suggested that I familiarize myself with the report and our review and discuss it with him later."

After his subsequent discussion with Campbell, Morse concluded that "the conversation added up to a greater recognition of the need in AAPS to review reports with an overall viewpoint and to watch for outside reader reaction as well as to make sure as best we can that the perspective of our findings is properly set forth."[72] About the same time, Campbell asked Morse if the report review process was "tight enough to prevent the possibility of improper reports getting out. He emphasized that he did not have the time to go into very many of the reports in much detail." Morse assured Campbell that AAPS did not think that any seriously defective reports could go forward.[73]

Campbell was interested in the procedures used by AAPS and the operating divisions to begin work on specific jobs. When Campbell brought this matter up in 1962, he asked Morse to what extent AAPS was involved in decisions to do jobs. Morse explained that he made suggestions on jobs but did not directly participate in decisions to begin them. Campbell suggested that Morse study the job approval system centered in the divisions; he thought that there should be provision for signed approval of all jobs before they started, to make sure that, among other things, they were worth doing. As Morse recorded it, "He mentioned that we seemed to be well versed in the Federal Prison Industries, as an example, but have done very little work in NASA [National Aeronautics and Space Administration] so far."[74]

In a subsequent meeting, Campbell said that some work that he personally had requested had not been done. He mentioned specifically requests he had made to the director of DAAD to look into cost overruns in missile

---

[72]Entries for March 7 and March 8, 1962, Morse, *Daily Notes*, 1961-1962.
[73]Entry for March 21, 1962, ibid.
[74]Entry for February 16, 1962, ibid.

base work and to CAAD for information about supergrade and equivalent job levels in the federal government. Campbell made clear that he wanted the AAPS staff to do more to make sure that GAO staff were working where they would do the most good. "There was some feeling of lack of confidence in our present system and particularly the abilities of the operations division directors to provide suitable long-range thinking and follow-up in view of their multitudinous daily responsibilities."[75]

Morse worked on these questions immediately and announced improvements in the planning, information, and control system in mid-March 1962. A new system of advance approval for each accounting and auditing job assignment, including an authorization form, would go into effect on July 1, 1962. There was also to be an inventory of jobs in progress and a monthly reporting system for each job in progress, showing the current month's staff time charges and total time on each job. Also, the "Blue Book," a semiannual report of estimated staff requirements used up to this time mainly in the Field Operations Division, would be extended to the headquarters divisions and eventually to the overseas branches. Finally, Morse said that a special system for following up on special work commitments, such as those made during appropriations hearings and those made as a result of suggestions by the comptroller general, would be established.[76]

When Campbell established AAPS in 1956, he included among its functions the development and the direction of a coordinated program to ensure effective application of modern electronic systems and other advanced scientific management methods and techniques to the accounting, the auditing, and the other financial operations of the federal government.[77] In the next few years, GAO issued a series of reports about the governmentwide use of automated data processing equipment; the work on these reports centered in AAPS. In June 1958, GAO issued a report criticizing the government's management of ADP, especially the agency-by-agency approach and the lack in the federal government of a single agency charged with directing and coordinating ADP developments. Edward Mahoney, an ADP expert on Morse's staff, was the principal author of this report, which proposed a joint program for coordination of ADP matters in the government.[78]

---

[75]Entry for March 5, 1962, ibid.

[76]Notes of meeting of March 13, 1962, Morse, Notes of Meetings of the Accounting and Auditing Division Heads, July 1960 through July 1964.

[77]Comptroller General's Order No. 2.30, March 22, 1956, A-16251, #1.

[78]Entry for May 5, 1958, Morse, *Daily Notes*, 1957-1958; Senate Committee on Government Operations, *Financial Management in the Federal Government*, vol. II, 92d Cong., 1st Sess., S. Doc. 92-50 (Washington: GPO, 1971), 75 (hereafter cited as *Financial Management*, 1971). This publication, prepared by GAO for the Senate committee, was a followup to the volume with the same title published in 1961.

On December 30, 1960, GAO issued a second report again emphasizing the need for governmentwide ADP coordination. The report noted that BOB had made progress in calling attention to the need for leadership in the executive branch on ADP, but it stressed the need for more long-range planning, especially on such things as integration of systems between agencies and with industry.[79] Another report, issued on March 6, 1963, argued that the federal government could save $100 million over a five-year period if it bought rather than leased ADP equipment. The report recommended that the president establish an office to provide central management of procurement and use of ADP equipment.[80]

In April 1964, GAO issued another report stating that optimum efficiency and effectiveness in the ADP field depended on adopting a governmentwide program.[81] In October 1965, Congress passed an act providing for coordination of federal ADP programs. BOB would be responsible for exercising control over fiscal and policy matters on ADP equipment used by government agencies, and the General Services Administration (GSA) would operate a revolving fund for equipment acquisition. GSA was to buy ADP equipment and rent it to agencies; the rental proceeds were to go into the revolving fund. The agencies themselves were to select their own equipment consistent with their requirements.[82] This law was a direct result of GAO's recommendations on ADP.

To provide a basis for its work and leadership in the ADP area, GAO developed a training course for selected staff under the auspices of the Office of Staff Management; AAPS staff provided substantial input. The first session of the course took place in August 1957; at least one person from each regional office was in the class.[83]

The Office of Staff Management—Recruiting and Training

Campbell placed much emphasis on staff professionalization, which he felt was necessary to improve the quality of the Office's work. Recruiting

---

[79]Entry for November 9, 1960, Morse, *Daily Notes*, 1959-1960 (summarizes a discussion among Morse; Mahoney; and Thomas D. Morris, assistant director of management and organization at BOB, about the forthcoming report); and Senate Committee on Government Operations, *Financial Management*, 1971, 75.

[80]Entry for February 1, 1963, Morse, *Daily Notes*, 1963-1964; Senate Committee on Government Operations, *Financial Management*, 1971, 75; and *Annual Report of the Comptroller General of the United States for the Fiscal Year Ended June 30, 1963* (Washington: GPO, 1963), 52.

[81]Senate Committee on Government Operations, *Financial Management*, 1971, 75.

[82]Ibid., 75-76.

[83]Entries for January 8, 28, and 29, 1957, Morse, *Daily Notes*, 1957-1958; and Leo Herbert, "Memorandum Regarding Electronic Data Processing Course," January 25, 1957, attached to entry for January 28, 1957, ibid.

new staff and training both current and new staff were the primary approaches Campbell chose to achieve these objectives. To manage this process, he created OSM and recruited Leo Herbert to head it. Herbert, who earned an M.B.A. degree in 1941 and a Ph.D. in 1944 at Louisiana State University, was also a certified public accountant. In addition to having held several teaching positions, he had been assistant state auditor of Louisiana from 1952 to 1956. When he moved to GAO in April 1956, he was a professor of accounting and head of the Department of Business Administration at the Louisiana Polytechnic Institute.[84]   Herbert later stated, "Mr. Campbell had an idea that what he wanted here was a very highly professional staff of accountants instead of high-class bookkeepers, or what they used to call voucher auditors." Herbert at first assumed that he would be at GAO a relatively short time, but he stayed 19 years until his retirement in 1974.[85]

Herbert's job was to develop and manage recruiting and training programs. One of the first things he did was to analyze the GAO staff in the accounting series (Civil Service classification 510). Herbert found that of the 1,226 staff in this series (total GAO staff numbered about 5,000), only 226 were what he considered professional accountants. The rest—1,000— were still working as voucher-, cost-, or clerical-type auditors.[86] Since Campbell wanted professional accountants, this gave Herbert a quick indication of what his recruiting task was.

One of Herbert's recruiting problems was the existing ratings and salary levels for accountants established by the U.S. Civil Service Commission. New college graduate accountants had to be hired at the GS-5 level, a comparatively low level on the civil service scale. As Herbert put it, "Trying to get the Commission to understand what GAO was so we could get the salaries up, comparable to what the public accounting firms were paying people, was one of the major issues I ran into. . . . Also I had to acquaint the rest of the government with GAO." Within two years of Herbert's start at GAO, the Civil Service Commission authorized the Office to maintain its own civil service register, a list of job candidates, enabling the Office to inform applicants quickly whether they would be offered appointments. Also, the Commission agreed that candidates who had master's degrees or who had graduated in the upper 25 percent of their classes could begin their service at the GS-7 level.[87] Although there was an effort to bring in experienced accountants at higher grades, and a few came to GAO in that way, Herbert's recruit-

---

[84]See GAO, *Leo Herbert, GAO, 1956-1974*, GAO History Program, Oral History Series, GAO/OP-7-OH (Washington: 1988), v, 1-2.

[85]Ibid., 1, 2-3.

[86]Ibid., 3.

[87]Ibid., 6-8.

ment program concentrated on the hiring of high-quality new college graduates. Herbert thought that these accountants could rise to a professional working level in two to three years, and five years at a maximum. According to Herbert, "It was quicker than if we got these people out of public accounting, because you had to knock things out of their [public accountants] heads and put new stuff into their heads."[88]

Herbert's recruitment program began to show almost immediate results. Campbell spelled out the results in his 1956 annual report: In June 1956, GAO made auditor appointment offers to graduates of 104 colleges and universities in 42 states; 126 candidates accepted and came to the Office as junior auditors. "In our recruiting," Campbell reported, "quality of personnel is being stressed." Also, in the summer of 1956 GAO began an internship program for college-level juniors, a college faculty residency program, a program to recruit upper-level accountants, and an attorney recruitment and training program.[89]

Recruiting of accountants went on at a rapid pace in the remaining nine years of Campbell's term. In 1957, Herbert's second recruiting year, GAO hired 290 accounting majors from 133 educational institutions in 40 states, including some accountants hired directly by individual regional offices for placement in those locations. New hires in subsequent fiscal years included 126 in 1958, 135 in 1959, 246 in 1960, 342 in 1961, 262 in 1962, 311 in 1963, 268 in 1964, and 330 in 1965. In addition, in the early years of this period, GAO reappointed numerous previously employed college graduate accountants returning from military service, for example, 36 in 1958 and 21 in 1960.[90]

While substantial numbers of new accountants agreed to come to GAO, there were problems along the way, including recruiting competition in some areas of the country with commercial interests. Herbert pointed this out in 1956 with reference to Detroit, where GAO had a regional office. Starting salaries for accounting graduates in commercial firms in Detroit at the time were $375 per month and were expected to increase in the spring of 1957 to $425. At the same time, GAO received authorization to offer new graduates no more than $306 per month at the GS-5 level.[91] GAO lost some of the newly appointed accountants early in their tenure. Campbell raised ques-

---

[88]Ibid., 9.

[89]GAO, *Annual Report, 1956*, 4-6. See below, pp. 31-33.

[90]Recruitment figures from GAO, *Annual Report*, as follows: 1957, p. 3; 1958, p. 227; 1959, p. 243; 1960, p. 257; 1961, p. 244; 1962, p. 230; 1963, p. 264; 1964, p. 306; and 1965, p. 202.

[91]Herbert statement in meeting of September 17, 1956, Morse, Notes of Meetings of the Accounting and Auditing Division Heads, September 1956 through June 1957.

tions about the recruiting effort in September 1957, noting that only half of the GS-5s who came to GAO in June 1956 were still there.[92]

Retaining new hires in the competition for accountants with other government agencies and private industry was a continuing problem. Herbert stated in mid-1957 that 40 percent of the staff leaving GAO transferred to other agencies, most of them getting promotions in the process. Adolph Samuelson of CAAD suggested that departing staff knew that GAO would rehire them if the new positions proved unsatisfactory. Samuelson thought that removing this assurance would cut the number of transfers.[93] Campbell testified in 1961 that GAO was making progress in its college recruiting but faced stiff competition. Auditors, according to Campbell, were "now No. 2 on the critical professional shortage list." In response to a question on how GAO persuaded young recruits to come to the Office given a starting salary that was less than what prevailed in private industry, Campbell said that GAO recruited in person at colleges and universities and promised potential job applicants "that the training they will receive from us will benefit them and that we think our work is the most interesting work that a young accountant can possibly become engaged upon."[94]

In 1964, Campbell testified that the colleges were not turning out enough accounting majors to meet the demand and that competition was keen. Government starting salaries were about $1,000 per year less than salaries in private industry. He said that GAO might hire 300 new accountants in a given year but lose 100 of them to agencies promising promotions. Campbell also noted that GAO lost significant numbers of newly hired accountants to the private sector and by draft to the military services.[95]

GAO continued to try to hire upper-level accountants throughout the Campbell period, even though the bulk of recruiting was aimed at entry-level hires. GAO division directors felt that upper-level hiring should continue. They wanted some experienced staff who could move ahead quickly with their work and who could supervise other staff. Recruiting done by regional office managers often did not concentrate much on upper-level hires because such staff usually were not used in those offices. But on occasion, there was need for upper-level staff in regional offices because many of the

---

[92]Entry for September 10, 1957, Morse, *Daily Notes, 1957-1958.*

[93]Notes of special meeting, July 1, 1957, Morse, Notes of Meeting of Accounting and Auditing Division Heads, July 1957 through June 1958.

[94]Campbell testimony, March 15, 1961, *Independent Offices Appropriations for 1961*, pt. 1, 316, 331.

[95]Campbell testimony, February 6, 1964, *Legislative Branch Appropriations for 1965*, Hearings before a Subcommittee of the House Committee on Appropriations, 88th Cong., 2d Sess. (Washington: GPO, 1964), 31-32.

new entry-level accountants were assigned to them.[96]   Samuelson suggested on one occasion an effort to recruit former employees of public accounting firms who had been let go when they had not risen to the position of audit manager within the normal five-year period. Morse thought that this was a good idea, and the division directors discussed the possibility of asking accounting firms to advise GAO of accountants they planned to release.[97]

Campbell had some reservations about upper-level hiring. In a 1958 conversation with Morse, "he observed that in his opinion there is no comparison between the character of the experience a college man obtains with us during his first five or six years and that obtained in small time public accounting where we are trying to attract upper level staff members. He repeated his idea . . . that our real hope for expansion lies in the college recruits with intensive training and experience." In a later meeting, Campbell suggested to Morse that GAO discontinue upper-level recruiting.[98] Although in fact such hiring was not ruled out, few candidates acceptable to GAO at the upper levels were available.[99]

Campbell was not interested in recruiting persons who were specialists in disciplines other than accounting. In a 1964 hearing, Rep. Thomas J. Steed (D—Oklahoma) asked Campbell if GAO was interested in having specialists in the space and nuclear energy fields. Campbell said no and added, "It is obvious that we could not possibly set ourselves up with engineering and scientific know-how. I do not think it is necessary. I think you do not have to be . . . a hen to know a rotten egg." He went on to say, "I think our people can go in and ask questions. They may not get the whole answer, but they get a pretty good picture of what is right and what is wrong."[100]

While the total size of GAO's staff declined considerably during Campbell's term, from 5,913 on June 30, 1954, to 4,278 on June 30, 1965, there was a clear shift in the proportion of the total staff made up of professionals. During fiscal year 1954, there were 1,340 accountants, auditors, and investigators of a total staff of 5,913; the number in this category climbed steadily thereafter, reflecting in part the success of Herbert's recruiting pro-

---

[96]Notes of meetings of November 20 and December 17, 1956, and January 7, 1957, Morse, Notes of Meetings of the Accounting and Auditing Division Heads, September 1956 through June 1957.

[97]Notes of meeting of June 11, 1956, ibid.

[98]Notes of meetings of March 5 and June 25, 1958, Morse, Notes of Meetings of the Accounting and Auditing Division Heads, July 1957 through June 1958.

[99]Notes of meeting of April 27, 1962, Morse, Notes of Meetings of the Accounting and Auditing Division Heads, July 1960 through July 1964.

[100]Campbell testimony, February 6, 1964, *Legislative Branch Appropriations for 1965*, 41-42. Later, under Elmer B. Staats, Campbell's successor as comptroller general, GAO began to bring in specialists in various fields.

gram. At the end of fiscal year 1960, there were 1,850 accountants, auditors, and investigators in a total staff of 5,203 and at the close of fiscal year 1963, 2,156 in a total staff of 4,659. The percentage of staff composed of accountants, auditors, and investigators increased from 22.6 in 1954 to 46.2 in 1963.[101] Campbell was pleased with these trends but still had some doubts about the professional staff. In a conversation with Morse just six months before he retired, Campbell "expressed concern about the continuing problem of deadwood in our organization and indicated that we were still going to try to work out some effective procedures to eliminate it. He estimated that about 10% of our professional staff could be classified in this category."[102]

What Campbell described as "deadwood" included, at least for earlier years in his term, some of the Office of Investigations staff that GAO distributed among the accounting and auditing divisions after OI's abolition in 1956. At first, the investigators in each regional office continued to work for the most part on investigative duties if such activity was necessary, but the GAO criteria and guidelines for investigative work were hazy. The initial plan was to control such work from Washington headquarters.[103] Campbell felt that specialized investigative work was still necessary but worried about the program. Morse recorded after a January 1957 meeting that Campbell "stated that he was far from satisfied with the present investigative supervisors, [and] indicated lack of confidence in the investigators generally. . . ."[104]

Campbell met with Morse, Herbert, Samuelson, and other officials in January 1957 to discuss the investigative function. One prominent topic in the meeting was whether investigators should confine their work to fact-finding or go on to evaluating the information gathered. Campbell believed that the investigators should be fact-finders and that evaluation should be left for the accounting and auditing staff who were trained to evaluate information. Campbell proposed procedures for the operating divisions to better integrate investigative work:

• Herbert should develop a special training program for present investigators and selected accountants and auditors.

• investigators who were also accountants should be considered for transfer to the audit groups.

---

[101]Campbell testimony, February 6, 1964, *Legislative Branch Appropriations for 1965*, 10.
[102]Entry for January 6, 1965, Morse, *Daily Notes*, 1965-1966.
[103]Meetings of September 13 and November 13, 1956, Morse, Notes of Meetings of the Accounting and Auditing Division Heads, September 1956 through June 1957.
[104]Entry for January 24, 1957, Morse, *Daily Notes*, 1957-1958.

- investigators who were lawyers should remain as investigators and used to the extent possible in existing work assignments.

- the rest of the investigative group "who represent a considerable problem in ability, character, personality, and similar factors, are to be considered as individual problems to be assigned, utilized, or disposed of as best we can."[105]

After this meeting, Morse, Herbert, and the accounting and auditing division heads had lengthy discussions about procedures for converting investigators to the audit series. Eventually, Campbell decided that the directors of CAAD, DAAD, and the Field Operations Division should recommend specific staff for conversion. Investigators would not be converted without their concurrence, and investigators who were attorneys would be considered for transfer to the Office of the General Counsel. The investigator series would be retained for staff not converted to the auditor or the attorney series.[106]

Actually integrating the investigators into the accounting and auditing divisions proved difficult in some cases. Henry Eschwege, working in 1956 with the GAO audit group at the Department of Agriculture, spoke of one investigator placed with his group: ". . . we really did not know how to utilize that person. He was a fine gentleman, but he was completely lost." Eschwege added that later he found some investigators who were very useful in doing work relating to audits and program evaluation.[107]

As adjuncts to the recruiting program, GAO, under Leo Herbert's guidance, established several programs designed to enhance the college recruiting effort. These programs involved both students and faculty. The summer faculty-resident program got under way soon after Herbert became head of the Office of Staff Management. During the summer of 1957, GAO brought in 15 faculty-residents and assigned them to various offices and divisions,

---

[105]"Discussion of Investigations Function with the Comptroller General," January 25, 1957, ibid. The quotation is from Morse's notes rather than a direct record of Campbell's words. The first investigative training class was held in the fall of 1957. See notes of meeting of November 12, 1957, Morse, Notes of Meetings of the Accounting and Auditing Division Heads, July 1957 through June 1958.

[106]Notes on meeting attended by Campbell on June 18, 1957, Morse, Notes of Meetings of the Accounting and Auditing Division Heads, September 1956 through June 1957.

[107]GAO, *The Civil Division, 1956-1972*, 9. For an interesting summary of the career of a GAO investigator see GAO, *Charles E. Wolfe, 1935-1988*, GAO History Program, Oral History Series, GAO/OP-8-OH (Washington: 1988). Wolfe began work at GAO in 1935 as a junior typist, and became a field investigator in 1937, working mainly in the New York area. After abolition of the Office of Investigations in 1956, he worked on comprehensive audits in the New York Regional Office. Later he served on detail as a staff member of two Senate committees and ended his GAO career in 1988, after 53 years of continuous service, as chief referencer of the Washington Regional Office.

including AAPS, CAAD, DAAD, OSM, and the Saint Paul Regional Office. The primary benefit GAO expected was "missionary work" by the faculty after they returned to their home institutions. As recorded after a discussion of the matter by the accounting and auditing division heads, "It is expected that these men will play some part in influencing top accounting students to join GAO in the future years." An initial secondary goal was to gain from the professors an evaluation of GAO audit standards, programs, procedures, and reports, with the hope that this would help the Office in its efforts to get GAO experience counted toward earning the CPA certificate.[108]

Campbell had reservations about the effectiveness of the faculty-resi- dent program right from the beginning. He told Morse early in 1958 that "he didn't want a repetition of last summer's experience and that he wanted to avoid any possible criticism which might result if we repeated last year's plan." He was concerned with the costs of the program, and he doubted that it had resulted in the recruitment of many new accountants. Campbell told Morse that he thought that faculty should be brought in only if requested by the policy staff or DAAD and CAAD for direct use in their work. Morse concluded that Campbell had abandoned the original plan to use college faculty as missionaries for GAO.[109] GAO used a few faculty consultants in the later Campbell years in selected regional offices, but the larger program Herbert started in 1956 did not last long.[110]

Another group that helped GAO on recruiting and other more general areas was the Educator-Consultants Panel. Campbell established the group in 1955 on the recommendation of his assistant, Karney Brasfield, and Walter Frese of the Accounting Systems Division. Herbert had responsibility for the panel later. GAO used the group, which had a membership of six to eight educators from leading schools of business administration, to advise on, and assist in the establishment of, the long-range recruiting and training pro- gram.[111] Campbell generally appreciated their contributions and usually at- tended their meetings. He did show some annoyance when he learned that the group members at one meeting had discussed issues beyond the scope of their mandate, for example, whether Campbell should attend the meetings of

---

[108]Memorandum for the files, April 30, 1956, Morse, *Daily Notes*, 1956; notes of meeting of April 16, 1957, Morse, Notes of Meetings of the Accounting and Auditing Division Heads, September 1956 through June 1957; and GAO, *Leo Herbert*, 11.

[109]Entries for April 29, 1957, and March 5, 1958, Morse, *Daily Notes*, 1957-1958.

[110]Campbell's printed statement, February 9, 1962, *Independent Offices Appropriations for 1963*, pt. 1, 75.

[111]Entry for April 12, 1957, Morse, *Daily Notes*, 1957-1958; and *Annual Report of the Comptroller General of the United States for the Fiscal Year Ended June 30, 1961* (Washington: GPO, 1961), 243.

division heads. Campbell told Morse that "the work with these consultants would have to be watched closely from here on out."[112]

Campbell met with the panel in Ann Arbor, Michigan in December 1957. He said that his purposes in traveling to Ann Arbor had been to find out how familiar the educator-consultants were with GAO's work and how they felt about urging state governments to recognize GAO experience as qualifying for CPA certification.[113] At its November 1958 meeting, the panel discussed the possible participation of GAO staff in external management training programs. Campbell attended this meeting and expressed his view that GAO's top officials needed this kind of broadening experience. Their association with business executives and others in such training programs would broaden their perspectives and help by "providing the group of key people in many industries with an opportunity to learn something about the GAO and the calibre of its officials."[114] Morse noted the views expressed at this meeting by Professor William A. Paton of the University of Michigan. "Professor Paton . . . stated at one point that while he had always been identified as more or less anti-Government, he was coming around to recognizing that we have big Government and that there is need for a suitable mechanism to help police its operations and that to the extent GAO helped fill this need, he counted himself as a strong supporter of GAO. (This is a notable statement from this man and once he starts talking more widely in this direction, our cause should be helped immeasurably)."[115]

GAO established a student summer intern program shortly after Herbert arrived. The goal was to introduce undergraduate students between their junior and senior years to the type of accounting and auditing work done by GAO. The program's objectives were eventually to recruit these students as GAO staff and to get favorable publicity from the word spread by the students at their colleges and universities.[116]

Staff training was the other side of OSM's responsibilities. Both the new college graduate accountants brought in by the recruiting program and more-experienced GAO staff required training. Herbert tried to teach a conceptual framework of "planning, doing, reviewing" during training, but it was not always fully understood by the GAO staff. Herbert linked this framework to

---

[112]Entry for April 12, 1957, Morse, *Daily Notes*, 1957-1958.

[113]Entry for December 2, 1957, Morse, ibid.

[114]Morse, "Educator-Consultants Meeting, November 17 and 18, 1958, Miscellaneous Notes," ibid. The quotation is Morse's paraphrasing of Campbell's statement.

[115]Ibid.

[116]"Memorandum for the Files, Subject: Directors Meeting," April 26, 1956, Morse, *Daily Notes*, 1956; and GAO, *Leo Herbert*, 14.

"criteria, cause, and effect." He thought that auditors needed to understand the criteria, or standards, that an auditor would use to evaluate the operations of a particular federal program. Through analyzing the condition of a program at a given time and comparing it with the crtiteria, the auditor could determine how the program should be operating and how it was actually operating. By using accepted audit techniques, the auditor could identify both the causes and the effects of program operations.[117]

The first new training program developed during the Campbell period was for GS-5s, the new college graduates brought in to join the accounting and auditing staffs. When GAO received permission to bring in new recruits at the GS-7 level, they also participated in this program. GAO decided to offer the GS-5 course just before Herbert's arrival in the spring of 1956. Edward Breen, a University of Illinois accounting professor initially hired as a consultant and later deputy director of OSM, planned the course.[118] The first two three-week sessions of the GS-5 program met in June and July 1957, under Breen's direction. In the early years, all new recruits, including those from the regional offices, attended these classes in Washington. The course outlined GAO's duties, responsibilities, and objectives and included case studies work to support the material presented in lectures. After these classes, the trainees moved to audit sites, either in Washington or the regions, for on-the-job experience.[119]

Subsequently, Herbert's office held several sessions of the training course for GS-5s and GS-7s each year. Besides participating in the core course, the new hires later periodically attended seminars on specialized subjects and rotated to GAO audits in various government agencies and activities.[120] In the later years of Campbell's term, some of the introductory courses were taught in regional offices. In fiscal year 1961, 210 staff received the training, consisting then of 4 weeks of intensive classroom work and 11 months of on-the-job experience.[121] Most of the rotation of new accountants was intradivisional, although the policy called for rotation between divisions as well. The latter practice did not work well for various reasons, including the fact that DAAD was not interested in transferring highly competent members of its staff to CAAD.

---

[117]GAO, *Leo Herbert*, 25; and Roger L. Sperry, Timothy D. Desmond, Kathi F. McGraw, and Barbara Schmitt, *GAO 1966-1981: An Administrative History* (Washington: GAO, 1981), 175.

[118]Entry for March 8, 1956, Morse, *Daily Notes*, 1956; and memorandum for the files on director's meeting, April 26, 1956, ibid.

[119]Memorandum for the file on director's meeting, April 26, 1956, ibid.; and GAO, *Leo Herbert*, 1956, 5.

[120]*Annual Report of the Comptroller General of the United States for the Fiscal Year Ending June 30, 1960* (Washington: GPO, 1960), 258.

[121]Campbell's printed statement, February 9, 1962, *Independent Offices Appropriations for 1963*, pt. 2, 74-75.

THE SECOND GS-7 TRAINING PROGRAM FOR THE YEAR 1962 GIVEN BY THE OFFICE OF STAFF MANAGEMENT was conducted in Washington, D. C., July 9 through 20.   Reading from left, ROW 1: John F. Elliott, Philadelphia Regional Office, Counselor; David Rettiger, Kansas City Regional Office, Counselor; Leo Herbert, Director, Office of Staff Management; Joseph Campbell, Comptroller General of the United States; Edward Breen, Assistant Director, Office of Staff Management; Cornelius Tierney, Boston Regional Office, Counselor; James Kelly, Civil Accounting and Auditing Division, Counselor.   ROW 2:   Joann H. Olson, Speight W. Burrus, Jack H. Vital, Judith A. Howe.   ROW 3:   David S. Shupe, L. Thomas Snyder, Richard L. Maynard, Archie Granda, William Hill, Robert Procaccini, Robert W. Jones, James S. Whitt, Jr., Joseph T. Valonis, Fred C. Conant, Robert R. Lindemuth, Charles H. Wehring.   ROW 4:   Ken Earnest, Jerry Lininger, John Navarre, Jerry Brenner, Larry Kortick, William C. Lynch, Charles V. Carroll, William B. Diepenbrock, Donald C. Hahn, Joel R. Berman, Robert E. Pavlik, Robert A. Indresano.   ROW 5:   James M. Mathews, Francis K. Boland, Larry J. Simon, Victor L. Wells, Jr., Arthur L. Hale, Ramon A. Looney, John A. Remke, Ben F. Gardner, Robert Clark, Vern F. Amick, Matthew R. Solomon, Joe E. Totten.   ROW 6:   J. F. Sparks, J. L. Magnes, L. R. Drewett, F. E. Harzer, J. K. Seidlinger, R. D. Robertson, S. Krywucki, J. P. Kelly, S. Correira, Jr., G. R. Demers, R. D. Gerring, J. R. Tipton.   ROW 7:   Robert Farabaugh, Leonard Burns, Earl Ellison, Brian Crowley, Orian A. Archambault, Donald H. Leppla, Larry C. Hanna, Gene W. Mindling, A. Herman Meyer, Jr., Billy R. Gilliland, Joseph S. Azzarano, Walter Smith.   ROW 8:   Ralph E. Anderson, James B. Perkins, Michael D. Pecovish, Harold D. Edwards, Kermit S. Mohn, Leo Ganster, Thomas J. Kingfield, David E. Overman, Jr., Donald E. Whitteaker, Gerald H. Springbom, Enil C. Cracker, Cecil B. Carter.

GAO's GS-7 training class for 1962.   Seated, front center; Leo Herbert; Comptroller General Campbell; Edward Breen.

In 1957, Herbert proposed a training program for GS-7 and GS-9 accountants. Morse opposed the plan, arguing that it was unnecessary and would divert resources and attention from more important training programs. Campbell accepted Morse's arguments. Herbert was reluctant to give up the idea but had to accept Campbell's decision.[122] Later, in 1960, OSM developed an intermediate training program for GS-9 to GS-11 staff. The revised *Comprehensive Audit Manual* (released in 1958) was the basis of the course, and the classes used case studies extensively. In 1961, 293 staff took this course, and 250 took it in 1962, from both Washington and the regional offices.[123]

In 1959, GAO began a report training course for accountants, auditors, and investigators. Herbert developed tentative plans and an outline for the course, and Morse strongly supported it, even though Samuelson questioned the need for it and said that on-the-job training was the only effective approach. Morse thought that such a course was necessary because of failures to provide satisfactory on-the-job supervision and the need to emphasize reporting policy, cut the time and the effort in report preparation, and acquaint GAO staff with the revised *Comprehensive Audit Manual*. Campbell agreed on the need for the course; the first one-week session was held in January 1959.[124] More than 1,100 accountants, auditors, and investigators took the course during fiscal year 1960.[125]

Campbell, as noted earlier, was determined to increase the number of GAO staff who were CPAs. He worked hard to expand the number of states recognizing GAO experience in granting CPA certification. As part of the Office's training program, a CPA coaching course began in 1957; classes were held both at headquarters and in some regional offices.[126]

Finally, GAO began a program under Campbell to send upper-level officials to professional management training programs at leading universities, including Harvard, Michigan, and Stanford. This effort resulted partly from a 1958 suggestion by James Lanigan, associate counsel of the House Government Operations Committee, that GAO set up a unit of trained and experienced management experts who could help the committee determine the

---

[122]Entries for September 25, 1957, and February 4, 19, and 21, 1958, Morse, *Daily Notes*, 1957-1958.

[123]Entry for August 12, 1960, Morse, *Daily Notes*, 1959-1960; Campbell's printed statement, February 9, 1962, *Independent Offices Appropriations for 1963*, pt. 2, 75; and Campbell's printed statement, February 25, 1963, *Independent Offices Appropriations for 1964*, pt. 2, 199.

[124]Entries for July 25 and 30, and August 1, 1958, Morse, *Daily Notes*, 1957-1958; and notes of meeting of January 13, 1959, Morse, Notes of Meetings of the Accounting and Auditing Division Heads, July 1958 through June 1960.

[125]GAO, *Annual Report, 1960*, 258.

[126]See chapter 5, p. 113; and GAO, *Leo Herbert*, 26.

New certified public accountants at the General Accounting Office, 1956.

Seated left to right: Sidney F. Hecker, John F. Utley, Gail Yingling, Roger M. Melanson, John R. Moore, Jr., and George E. Wentworth. Standing left to right: Ira G. Sherman, Edward C. Messinger, Samuel Willner, John D. Carrico, William L. Martino, Edwin J. Kolakowski, Raymond F. Masino, Dennis J. Huggins, Raymond A. Beaudet, Gerald W. Hicks, Francis C. Chlan, Wayland B. Coe and Harlan B. Epley. Kent H. Crowther was not present when picture was taken.

overall management efficiency of government agencies. Morse, the division heads, and Campbell all rejected Lanigan's proposal.[127] In the context of this discussion, Campbell brought up the idea of sending selected GAO staff to management training courses at Harvard University, programs that Campbell described as the best in the nation.[128] By 1960, Campbell had decided to send staff to Harvard.[129] Selected GAO middle managers attended the Program for Management Development (PMD), while higher-level managers participated in the Advanced Management Program (AMP).

Victor L. Lowe of CAAD was one of the first officials chosen to attend a program; others who went during this period were Gregory Ahart and Henry Eschwege of CAAD and Morse himself in 1963.[130] Campbell reported that

---

[127]Notes of meeting of October 28, 1958, Morse, Notes of Meetings of the Accounting and Auditing Division Heads, July 1958 through June 1960; and entries for October 29 and 31 and November 6 and 7, 1958, Morse, *Daily Notes, 1957-1958.*

[128]Entry for October 29, 1958, ibid.; and entries for March 3, May 3 and 9, 1960, Morse, *Daily Notes,* 1959-1960.

[129]Entry for May 3, 1960, ibid.

[130]GAO, *The Civil Division, 1956-1972,* v-vi, and 49-51; and note between entries for February 13 and May 21, 1963, Morse, *Daily Notes,* 1963-1964. See also GAO, *Leo Herbert,* 35-38.

during fiscal year 1961, twelve managers attended courses at Harvard, Stanford, and the University of Michigan.[131]

Recruiting and training were extremely important aspects of Campbell's program to professionalize the GAO staff and upgrade the quality and the usefulness of GAO reports and other work. The impact of the recruiting and training programs run by Leo Herbert and the Office of Staff Management was widespread and profound, both on the two main auditing divisions and the rest of GAO's units.

---

[131]GAO, *Annual Report, 1961,* 249.

CHAPTER 18

Audits and Operations
in the Campbell Era, II

The Comprehensive Audit

When Joseph Campbell became comptroller general, the General Accounting Office (GAO), was emphasizing the comprehensive audit. The program to expand its use, inherited from the Warren period, continued in force. There was still some lack of understanding among GAO staff of the meaning and the purposes of the comprehensive audit. In 1958, Charles W. Moore, the regional manager in Detroit, said that the problem was "the lack of a sufficient understanding of the basic philosophy, principles, and objectives of the comprehensive audit program. Without a keen insight into the real purpose of our audit, and generally how it is to be accomplished, a certain amount of inefficiency and floundering will result, which will be reflected in the reporting efforts."[1] Henry Eschwege, in recounting his experience in the 1950s auditing the Commodity Credit Corporation (CCC), said that he and his colleagues had "looked at the management" rather than at balances on financial statements. Comprehensive audits, Eschwege observed, were really "management-type audits."[2] A second group verified balances on the financial statements.

Apparently there was some problem in getting staff to read the *Comprehensive Audit Manual*, which GAO had issued originally in 1952. Kenneth A. Pollock, an auditor who joined the San Francisco Regional Office in November 1955, remarked later about the manual's large size and the difficulty of reading it: "It was hard. It was really tough reading. When I came on board . . . , the entire training program consisted of 'Here's the *Comprehensive Audit Manual*. Read

---

[1]Memorandum, Moore to Ellsworth H. Morse, September 15, 1958, Morse Papers, Subject Files, Box 53, Folder: Field Operations Division—1956 through April 1962, GAO History Program Archives.

[2]GAO, *The Civil Division, 1956-1972: Interview with Gregory J. Ahart, Henry Eschwege, and Victor L. Lowe*, GAO History Program, Oral History Series, GAO/OP-22-OH (Washington: 1992), 12.

sive Audit Manual. Read it.'" Pollock said that he was appalled when he got the manual and that he "went crazy" trying to read it.[3]

When the Accounting and Auditing Policy Staff (AAPS) staff began a revision of the manual in 1957, they decided that it should be issued in smaller physical form, brought up-to-date, and cleared of errors. Ellsworth H. Morse, the director of AAPS, and his staff agreed that "no amount of rewriting will assure that staff members in the office will read it. This compulsion must come from other ways, such as through training programs, supervision, research, and personal interest." Somewhat later, while the manual revision was still under way, Morse recommended to Campbell that the word "comprehensive" in the description of GAO audits be dropped but

pointed out that the directors of the Civil Accounting and Auditing Division (CAAD) and the Defense Accounting and Auditing Division (DAAD) disagreed on this point. Campbell did not respond to this suggestion at the time, but GAO did gradually stop using the term "comprehensive audit" in the late 1950s, although it remained in the title of the audit manual.[4]

The Civil Accounting and Auditing Division

Morse headed CAAD during its early months of operation in 1956; when he became head of AAPS, Campbell appointed Adolph T. Samuelson to head CAAD. A World War II Navy veteran and certified pub-

Adolph T. Samuelson, Director, Civil Accounting and Auditing Division (later Civil Division), 1956-1972.

---

[3]GAO, *The San Francisco Regional Office, 1954-1987: Interview with Harold J. D'Ambrosia, Kenneth A. Pollock, Richard A. Sheldon, and Charles F. Vincent*, GAO History Program, Oral History Series, GAO/OP-20-OH (Washington: 1991), 9. See also John C. Fenton, "The Corporation Audits Division—Its Legacy to the Seventies," *GAO Review* (summer 1971): 95. The Corporation Audits Division did the first work on the *Comprehensive Audit Manual* in 1950.

[4]Entry for April 18, 1957, Morse, *Daily Notes*, 1957-1958; and entry for September 24, 1959, Morse, *Daily Notes*, 1958-1960. For a favorable congressional assessment of GAO audits, including comprehensive audits, issued in February 1956, just before Campbell's reorganization, see *Review of Audit Reports of the Comptroller General*, Report of the Senate Committee on Government Operations, 84th Cong., 2d Sess., S. Rept. 1572 (Washington: GPO, 1956).

joined GAO's Corporation Audits Division in 1946 and later worked on civil audits. Known as "Sammy" or "Sam" to his staff, Samuelson headed CAAD until a 1972 reorganization split it into several specialized audit units.[5] On July 1, 1956, CAAD had 1,045 staff—490 auditors, investigators, and systems accountants in the central division; 189 in the Civil Audit Branch; and 366 in the Depository Accounts Branch.[6] Gradually between 1956 and 1965, the division staff declined to between 700 and 800, reflecting the shrinking of GAO's total staff from 5,552 to 4,278 during that period.[7]

Broad Range of Activities

Transportation audits excepted, CAAD at its inception in 1956 had responsibility for auditing, investigations, and accounting systems work for all non-defense agencies. The Transportation Divison handled transportation audits. CAAD covered nine cabinet-level departments—Agriculture; Commerce; Health, Education, and Welfare; Interior; Justice; Labor; Post Office; Treasury; and State—as well as about 115 independent executive branch corporations, boards, commissions, and agencies and various offices in the legislative and judicial branches. Much of this audit work took place at sites of agency operations in Washington and elsewhere. The regional offices supported the work of the divisions as required.

CAAD's Civil Audit Branch audited the accounts of those agency accountable officers required to transmit them to GAO. The branch also issued certificates of settlement of accounts of disbursing officers. The Depository Accounts Branch handled the audit, the reconciliation, and the adjustment of disbursing officers' depository accounts.[8] When GAO transferred the function of reconciliation and adjustment of these accounts to the Treasury Department in 1959, the staff of the Depository Accounts Branch began to perform other duties in the division.[9]

---

[5]GAO Press Release, October 30, 1956, in Morse, *Daily Notes*, 1956. See also GAO, *Adolph T. Samuelson, 1946-1975*, GAO History Program, Oral History Series, GAO/OP-11-OH (Washington: 1989). This publication contains excerpts from two interviews with Samuelson that took place in 1979 and 1980.

[6]Campbell's printed statement, testimony of February 26, 1957, *Independent Offices Appropriations for 1958*, Hearings before a Subcommittee of the House Committee on Appropriations, 85th Cong., 1st Sess., pt. 2 (Washington: GPO, 1957), 1960.

[7]See Appendix V.

[8]Campbell's printed statement, testimony of February 26, 1957, *Independent Offices Appropriations for 1958*, 1960.

[9]Testimony of Campbell et al., March 7, 1960, *Independent Offices Appropriations for 1961*, Hearings before a Subcommittee of the House Committee on Appropriations, 86th Cong., 2d Sess., pt. 2 (Washington: GPO, 1960), 774-75.

The broad range of CAAD's audit activities prevented the division from performing a yearly audit of each agency under its jurisdiction. The division programmed for periodic reviews of activities, as time and staff resources permitted. Typically, CAAD issued reports to both Congress and agency officials. For fiscal year 1958, for example, CAAD issued 131 reports to Congress and 118 to agency officials. For fiscal year 1962, the numbers were larger—130 to Congress and 294 to agency officials.[10] GAO's *Annual Report* for each fiscal year during the Campbell period listed the titles and the subject matter of all these reports, and in the Office's annual appropriations testimony, Campbell and other top officials discussed examples of the nature of CAAD's work and the substance of its findings.

For example, during fiscal year 1959, CAAD conducted audits of the Department of Agriculture in the central offices of 10 agencies in Washington and in 115 field offices and issued 18 reports to Congress and seven to agency officials. These reports detailed various problems in Agriculture units. The audit of the central office and five field offices of the Meat Inspection Division, Agricultural Research Service, disclosed unsanitary conditions at some locations because resident inspectors and supervisors had not required conformance with laws and regulations on sanitation standards. GAO also commented on deficiencies in meat inspectors' training.

During fiscal year 1959, GAO issued a report to Congress on the Commodity Credit Corporation, disclosing that during the marketing year 1958-1959, CCC had maintained prices for cotton available for export "at levels in excess of competitive world prices," contrary to the requirements of the Agricultural Act of 1956. The report recommended that the secretary of agriculture periodically adjust cotton export prices and annually determine the volume of cotton exports necessary to maintain a fair historical share of the world market for the United States. In another report, GAO disclosed that CCC had packaged nonfat dry milk and processed cheese for donation abroad in tin cans instead of plastic bags in cartons, costing the government an additional $7 million.

A 1959 report on Agriculture's Foreign Agricultural Service (FAS) noted that FAS had used U.S. dollars rather than foreign currency to pay foreign travel and other expenses even though FAS could have secured foreign currency on hand in the Treasury. Foreign currencies to pay for $16,000 (17 percent) of $93,000 in payments over a six-month period were available. In response to

---

[10]Testimony of Campbell et al., April 15, 1959, *Independent Offices Appropriations for 1959*, Hearings before a Subcommittee of the House Committee on Appropriations, 85th Cong., 2d Sess. pt. 2 (Washington: GPO, 1958), 1038; and testimony of Campbell et al., February 25, 1963, *Independent Offices Appropriations for 1964*, Hearings before a Subcommittee of the House Committee on Appropriations, 88th Cong., 1st Sess., pt. 2 (Washington: GPO, 1963), 203.

GAO's recommendations, FAS said that in the future, it would use foreign currencies for these expenses to the extent possible.[11]

During fiscal year 1961, CAAD issued three reports on the federal-aid highway program administered by the Bureau of Public Roads, Department of Commerce, based on reviews at the Bureau's Washington office and six regional and seven division offices. A report on the program in Arkansas, Louisiana, and Oklahoma revealed problems in highway rights-of-way acquisition and the need for stronger contracting and preaward procedures. In a report on the program in Montana and Oregon, GAO pointed out weaknesses in state contracting and preaward procedures, an inadequate study in Montana of a proposed interstate highway route, and lack of control over rights-of-way acquisition. A report on the program in Wyoming and New Mexico revealed some of the same problems, as well as the fact that the basis for payment of fees to consulting engineer firms in New Mexico was usually a percentage of the engineers' estimate of construction costs. GAO felt that this was undesirable and recommended a basis related to other factors, including required technical competence and project engineering character. On this recommendation as well as others, GAO reported, the Bureau of Public Roads indicated general agreement and took action to implement them.[12]

Also during fiscal year 1961, GAO issued a report on the federal grants program for school construction administered by the Office of Education, Department of Health, Education, and Welfare. According to the then-current law, school districts eligible for federal construction grants had to demonstrate increased school enrollment resulting directly from the activities of the U.S. government. GAO's report showed that the Office of Education's policies, procedures, and practices had allowed grants on inadequate evidence of school district eligibility for the aid. GAO recommended to the commissioner of education that aid applications be approved only on the basis of adequate documentation of eligibility and that proper criteria, procedures, and instructions be issued to require clear proof that increases in school enrollment actually resulted from federal activities.[13]

A 1961 report on Interior's Bureau of Indian Affairs (BIA) discussed the program for terminating federal supervision over Indian affairs. GAO criticized Interior for not proposing legislation for terminating supervision over

---

[11]Reports on Department of Agriculture audits, summarized in testimony of Campbell et al., March 7, 1960, *Independent Offices Appropriations for 1961*, pt. 2, 775-76.

[12]Testimony of Campbell et al., February 9, 1962, *Independent Offices Appropriations for 1963*, Hearings before a Subcommittee of the House Committee on Appropriations, 87th Cong., 2d Sess., pt. 2 (Washington: GPO, 1962), 81.

[13]Ibid., 82.

certain tribes or groups even though BIA's surveys showed that they were ready for termination. GAO also reported that Interior had not required BIA to develop long-range federal supervision termination plans over all Indian groups and instead relied on the Indians to do most of the termination planning. GAO recommended that Congress pass legislation requiring the secretary of the Interior to prepare a long-range termination plan for each tribe or group, report annually to Congress on progress of the program, and submit draft legislation for termination of supervision over tribes considered ready for such action. Interior did not agree with the recommendation on changing its supervision termination policies.[14]

These examples illustrate the broad range and specific subjects of the hundreds of reports issued by CAAD each year. The reports dealt not only with the financial aspects of government program administration but also with the efficiency and the effectiveness of program implementation. Even though accounting systems work was to be a part of CAAD's responsibilities after the 1956 reorganization, it declined in importance as Campbell's tenure progressed. For the early years of CAAD, the systems staff operated somewhat separately from the auditors, although they worked out of the same audit sites. Gradually they were more fully integrated into the division. Victor Lowe observed that the status of the systems people was lower than that of the auditors: "It didn't take long to figure out that if you put a lot of time, effort, and energy into accounting systems, you would be a very unhappy guy and probably nobody would know your name and you'd never get promoted. If you put a lot of time into developing good findings and putting out reports, you got rewards. It didn't take long for accounting systems to sort of slide into the background."[15]

CAAD Organization

Gradually CAAD's organization evolved under Adolph Samuelson's leadership. The division's organization chart in 1964 showed Arthur Schoenhaut as deputy director and three associate and 19 assistant directors, each responsible for one or more civil agencies. For example, Assistant Director Clerio P. Pin was responsible for audits in the Department of Commerce, the Federal Trade Commission, the Interstate Commerce Commission, the Panama Canal Company and the Canal Zone Government, and the Saint Lawrence Seaway Development Corporation. Associate Director L. A. Nelson's realm included the Departments of Health, Education, and Welfare; Justice; and Labor, as well as the Civil Service Commission, the Railroad Retirement Board, and the judicial branch. The responsibility of Assistant Director L. H. (Mike) Drennan, Jr., encom-

[14]Ibid.
[15]GAO, *The Civil Division, 1956-1972*, 16.

passed only the District of Columbia government. Four assistant directors were responsible for program review and special projects.[16]

Differences between CAAD and DAAD

The Civil Accounting and Auditing Division had a different character, and its operating methods differed somewhat from those of its counterpart in the defense area. The Defense Accounting and Auditing Division dealt mainly, but not exclusively, with the Defense Department, and its Washington staff tended to operate from the GAO Building rather than at audit sites, as CAAD did. A major explanation for problems between the two divisions, and indeed their sometimes intense competition, was that their heads had contrasting temperaments. According to Henry Eschwege, "there was some discomfort on the part of the two heads of the Divisions to even discuss things," especially after William A. Newman became head of DAAD in 1959. Victor Lowe observed that "Bill Newman and A. T. Samuelson could not have been further apart. Samuelson was sort of an introvert, quiet. Bill Newman was, if anything, the exact opposite of that." When Charles M. Bailey succeeded Newman in 1968, Samuelson's relations with him were a little better than with Newman, but still were strained. Gregory Ahart, Samuelson's deputy between 1967 and 1972, said that he had gotten along with Richard Gutmann, Bailey's deputy, and that when Samuelson and Bailey had a problem, he and Gutmann had handled it.[17]

One thing that distinguished the two divisions, according to some observers, was CAAD's emphasis on training, which Samuelson pushed vigorously. According to Eschwege, this reflected Samuelson's people orientation; the training "changed the quality of the people that wound up in the Civil Division as opposed to the ones that got into the Defense Division." Ahart said, "I don't think . . . [DAAD] ever put that great an emphasis on the career development and the growth of the individuals within the organization."[18]

The Field Operations Division and the Regional Offices

Campbell established the Field Operations Division (FOD) in March 1956 to provide central direction for the regional offices and to promote the inte-

---

[16]CAAD organization chart, *Annual Report of the Comptroller General of the United States for the Fiscal Year Ended June 30, 1964* (Washington: GPO, 1964), 322. Other associate directors were Philip Charam and L. K. Gerhardt; other assistant directors were John C. Fenton; Henry Eschwege; I. M. Crawford; J. E. Milgate; Max Neuwirth; J. T. Hall, Jr.; Max Hirschorn; L. G. Smith; F. H. (Doc) Studt; Louis W. Hunter; E. W. Stepnick; W. Parker; J. F. Utley; R. S. Lindgren; O. D. McDowell; F. K. Rabel; and J. A. Vignali.

[17]GAO, *The Civil Division, 1956-1972*, 18, 20, 31-32.

[18]Ibid., 18-19.

gration of the work of the two main Washington audit divisions—CAAD and DAAD—and the regional offices.[19] When Campbell announced his preliminary reorganization plan in November 1955, he indicated that John E. Thornton would become the director of FOD. Thornton, a CPA, a joined GAO in 1935. Between 1936 and 1954, he worked chiefly in the field, primarily in California. When Comptroller General Lindsay C. Warren created the new regional office system in 1952, Thornton was chief of the Western Zone of field operations. Between 1952 and 1954, he was manager of the San Francisco Regional Office. When he returned in 1954 to headquarters, he became assistant director for field operations in the Division of Audits. With the creation of FOD in 1956, Thornton assumed the position of division director, which he held until his retirement in 1976.[20]

In 1956, there were 19 regional offices. Four of the offices established in 1952—Juneau, Albuquerque, Billings, and Salt Lake City—had been closed by this time. Some regional offices had suboffices—for example, Fort Worth under Dallas, Sacramento under San Francisco, and Phoenix under Los Angeles. With the abolition of the Office of Investigations (OI) in 1956, the regional offices took over the work and the staff of the separate OI field offices, which closed. Campbell summarized the functions of the regional offices in 1957 testimony: to cooperate with government agencies in developing accounting systems; to review and evaluate accounting systems; to audit the activities, the financial transactions, and the accounts of agencies and their contractors; to investigate agencies concerning the receipt, the disbursement, and the application of public funds; and to participate in property accounting surveys.[21]

The FOD central office in Washington provided administrative direction to the regional offices as well as certain services to the accounting and auditing units in Washington, including typing and stenographic work on reports; maintaining allotment records, cost data, and other fiscal and accounting information; preparing travel orders; maintaining general records and central files; and handling

---

[19]Comptroller General's Order No. 2.33, March 22, 1956, A-16251, #1. See chapter 17, p. 418 for information on the establishment of FOD. For brief general histories of FOD, see C. E. Merrill, "History of the Field Operations Division," *GAO Review* (summer 1971): 128-35, and Elizabeth M. Williams and Alvin S. Finegold, "Remembering GAO's Field Operations Division," *GAO Review* (spring 1984): 21-25, 39-40.

[20]Comptroller General of the United States, "Outline of Planned Changes in Organization and Operations," November 30, 1955, A-16251, #1. See also GAO, *John E. Thornton, 1935-1976*, GAO History Program, Oral History Series, GAO/OP-3-OH (Washington: GAO, 1988), v, 1-4.

[21]Campbell's printed statement, testimony of February 26, 1957, *Independent Office Appropriations for 1958*, pt. 2, 1943.

mail.[22] Eventually these housekeeping functions devolved to the separate divisions and other GAO units, freeing FOD to concentrate on field operations.[23]

On July 1, 1956, FOD had 98 staff in Washington and 967 in the regional offices. A year later, the central office staff was down to 20, reflecting the transfer of the housekeeping functions, and the staff in regional offices had increased to 1,150.[24] The largest regional offices at the end of calendar year 1957 were New York (112 staff), Philadelphia (92), Atlanta (78), Denver (74), San Francisco (72), and Dallas (70).[25] FOD's staff size varied in subsequent years—1,216 in 1961, 1,326 in 1962, and 1,688 in 1963.[26]

Over time there were changes in the locations of regional offices and a further decline in the total number. A new regional office opened in Cincinnati in January 1958, replacing the Dayton office. That office devoted most of its resources to work on the activities of the Air Materiel Command, which had headquarters in Dayton. Morse and the heads of the accounting and auditing organizations recommended to Campbell in the fall of 1957 that the staff at Dayton who concentrated on Air Force work remain there but be responsible to DAAD's Air Force group in Washington and that a new regional office be opened at Cincinnati to do the rest of GAO's work in the region.[27]

From time to time, Campbell suggested creating additional regional offices—in places such as Jacksonville, upstate New York (Syracuse or Rochester), and Long Island. The accounting and auditing divisions heads discussed these suggestions but did not recommend opening any new full re-

---

[22]Ibid.

[23]Memorandum, Morse to directors of the Office of Staff Management, the Civil Accounting and Auditing Division, the Defense Accounting and Auditing Division, and the Field Operations Division, April 24, 1957, Morse Papers, Subject Files, GAO Offices and Divisions, Box 53, Folder: FOD, 1956 - April 1962, GAO History Program Archives; and Campbell's printed statement, testimony of March 3, 1958, *Independent Offices Appropriations for 1959*, pt. 2, 1288.

[24]Campbell's printed statement, testimony of February 26, 1957, *Independent Offices Appropriations for 1958*, pt. 2, 1944; and Campbell's printed statement, testimony of March 3, 1958, *Independent Offices Appropriations for 1959*, pt. 2, 1288.

[25]Printed table, Campbell testimony of March 3, 1958, ibid., 1267.

[26]Campbell testimony, March 15, 1961, *Independent Offices Appropriations for 1962*, Hearings before a Subcommittee of the House Committee on Appropriations, 87th Cong., 1st Sess., pt. 1 (Washington: GPO, 1961), 354; Campbell testimony, February 9, 1962, *Independent Offices Appropriations for 1963*, pt. 2, 44; and Campbell testimony, February 25, 1963, *Independent Offices Appropriations for 1964*, pt. 2, 204.

[27]Memorandum for the file, meeting of May 14, 1957, in Morse, Notes of Meetings of the Accounting and Auditing Division Heads, September 1956 through June 1957; memorandum, Leo Herbert, Morse, Thornton, Lawrence J. Powers, and Samuelson to the comptroller general, September 17, 1957, in Morse Papers, Subject Files, GAO Offices and Divisions, Box 53, Folder: FOD, 1956-April 1962, GAO History Program Archives; and memorandum, Thornton to heads of divisions and offices and regional managers, December 18, 1957, ibid.

gional offices. Occasionally new suboffices were opened—for example, those at Syracuse in 1960 and Mitchell Field on Long Island in 1964.[28]

In September 1957, the headquarters of the Richmond Regional Office transferred to Norfolk and GAO staff remaining in Richmond became a suboffice of the Norfolk region.[29] In 1960, there was a major realignment of several regions, resulting in the closing of four regional offices. The Cleveland office closed in April 1960, with its territory divided among the Cincinnati, Detroit, New York, and Philadelphia offices. The staff at Cleveland became a suboffice of the Detroit region and the staff at Pittsburgh, formerly under Cleveland, became a suboffice of the Philadelphia region.[30] In May 1960, three other regional offices closed: Portland, to become a suboffice of Seattle; St. Louis, to become a suboffice of Kansas City; and St. Paul, to become a suboffice of Chicago.[31] These changes resulted primarily from the need to better use regional office staff where work existed. The number of regional offices declined from 19 in 1956 to 15 in 1960.

Late in his term, Campbell decided to establish a new regional office in the Washington, DC, area. Opening the office was Campbell's personal idea; he thought that it would help to cut CAAD's heavy workload and make possible better coverage of contractor activities in the Washington area.[32] Thornton believed that Campbell wanted a regional office in Washington because he "felt that there was quite a bit of work around that was not being done that probably should have been done. . . . He set up the group to audit these field-type installations."[33] The directors of CAAD and DAAD, Samuelson and Newman, initially disagreed on the need for the Washington office. Newman welcomed the sug-

---

[28]Entries for August 1 and September 17, 1957, Morse, *Daily Notes*, 1957-1958; notes of meeting on September 17, 1957, Morse, Notes of Meetings of the Accounting and Auditing Division Heads, July 1957 through June 1958; entry for December 10, 1957, Morse, *Daily Notes*, 1957-1958; entry for December 1, 1959, Morse, *Daily Notes*, 1959-1960; and memorandum, Thornton to the comptroller general, August 20, 1964, Morse Papers, Subject Files, GAO Offices and Divisions, Box 53, Folder: May 1962 - December 1965.

[29]Notes of meeting of September 13, 1956, Morse, Notes of Meetings of Accounting and Auditing Division Heads, September 1956 through June 1957; and memorandum, Thornton to heads of divisions and offices, August 27, 1957, Morse Papers, Subject Files, GAO Offices and Divisions, Box 53, Folder: FOD, 1956 - April 1962.

[30]Thornton, "Notice of Change in Regional Boundaries," March 7, 1960, ibid.; and notes of meeting of March 8, 1960, in Morse, Notes of Meetings of the Accounting and Auditing Division Heads, July 1958 through June 1960.

[31]Thornton, "Notice of Changes in Regional Boundaries," April 11, 1960, Morse Papers, Subject Files, GAO Offices and Divisions, Box 53, Folder: FOD, 1956 - April 1962; and notes of meeting of April 29, 1960, Morse, Notes of Meetings of Accounting and Auditing Division Heads, July 1958 through June 1960.

[32]Entry for June 4, 1963, Morse, *Daily Notes*, 1963-1964; and GAO, *Regional Offices and the Field Operations Division: Interview with Francis X. Fee, Walter H. Henson, and Hyman L. Krieger*, GAO History Program, Oral History Series, GAO/OP-15-OH (Washington: 1990), 4.

[33]GAO, *John E. Thornton*, 67.

gestion, feeling that it would result in better coverage of defense contract and military installation work in the area. Samuelson saw few advantages for his division. According to Morse, Samuelson was "not prepared to endorse turning over the performance of work in national agency headquarters to such an office without a much more penetrating study and realignment of the way things are handled in our office."[34]

Despite these differences, Campbell decided to go ahead with establishment of the office. He thought that its headquarters should not be in the GAO Building but in the immediate metropolitan area. Eventually he accepted the recommendation of Morse and the division directors that it be housed in the Rosslyn area of Arlington, Virginia, just across the Key Bridge from the District of Columbia. The Washington Regional Office opened in mid-1964. Many of its staff came from existing regional offices and others from the accounting and auditing divisions in Washington. Donald L. Scantlebury was the first manager of the office. With its creation, the number of regional offices rose to 16.[35]

CAAD and DAAD developed most of the work assignments of the regional offices, with coordination through Thornton and the Field Operations Division. When FOD began to operate in 1956, one of its guidelines was that the Washington staff were to explain clearly to regional managers the reasons for requested work. The headquarters divisions were to coordinate field trips of Washington staff with the FOD director, and such visitors were to communicate with regional managers when visiting regional office cities.[36]

The usual procedure during Campbell's term was for the regional offices to do jobs assigned to them by one of the operating divisions. The information and the evidence they gathered along with tentative findings went to the appropriate Washington divisions for incorporation into formal reports on the jobs. Sometimes the involved regional offices drafted reports on assignments. By the late 1950s, the "lead region" approach began to be used. One regional office was designated to take the lead on an assignment involving work in the territory of two or more regions. The secondary regions involved in such an assignment did "assist work" in their own areas as requested by the lead region. The benefits of this system were intended to be easing the workload of Washington headquarters supervisory staff, more effective use of regional staff, faster report preparation, and assignment of greater responsibility to the regions. Some regional offices, such as San

---

[34]Entries for June 6 and 11, 1963, Morse, *Daily Notes*, 1963-1964.

[35]Entries for October 30 and November 18, 1963, Morse, *Daily Notes*, 1963-1964; notes of meeting of July 8, 1964, Morse, Notes of Meetings of the Accounting and Auditing Division Heads, July 1960 through July 1964; and entry for September 23, 1964, Morse, *Daily Notes*, 1963-1964.

[36]Memo for the files on director's meeting, August 8, 1956, Morse, *Daily Notes*, 1956.

Francisco and Seattle, were eager to have lead assignments and on occasion took the initiative in developing assignments for which they could take the lead.[37]

Although GAO used the lead region approach on some jobs, it was not the general rule during the Campbell period. Its usage depended on the capabilities of individual regional office staffs and managers and their interest in such a role and on the willingness of headquarters divisions to allow regional offices to play a larger part in project management. Campbell was very much interested in the regional office system and devoted considerable

Comptroller General Campbell with regional managers, Denver, 1957.

personal attention to its development. He visited regional offices when he could; for example, in the fall of 1957, he visited Chicago, Denver, Seattle, Portland, San Francisco, Los Angeles, and Dallas.[38] During Campbell's term, there were annual meetings of the regional managers, usually in Washington but on occasion elsewhere, such as Denver in 1957. Campbell attended some of these meetings, along with other top headquarters officials, including Assistant Comptroller General Frank H. Weitzel; Morse; Thornton; Samuelson; Leo Herbert, head of the Office of Staff Management; General Counsel Robert F. Keller; and the DAAD directors, Lawrence Powers through 1959 and William A. Newman thereafter.[39]

Campbell considered the regional managers his personal representatives in the field, and he maintained direct relationships with them. When a re-

---

[37]GAO, *Regional Offices and the Field Operations Division*, 24-26; GAO, *The San Francisco Regional Office, 1954-1987*, 50; and GAO, *John E. Thornton*, 62-66. See also Williams and Finegold, "Remembering GAO's Field Operations Division," 23.

[38]Entry for October 21, 1957, Morse, *Daily Notes*, 1957-1958.

[39]See binder entitled *"Regional Managers Conferences 1956-1963"*, GAO Law Library. This contains the minutes of the annual regional managers' meetings.

gional manager visited Washington, a call on Campbell was obligatory. According to Walter H. Henson, a staff member in the Seattle Regional Office between 1957 and 1964 and thereafter regional manager in New Orleans and Norfolk, "Mr. Campbell had a very, very detailed and acute knowledge of the field people. . . . He knew our people as well as we did, and he would discuss them in detail—and we had better know our people."[40]

Hyman L. Krieger, who served under Campbell as regional manager in Chicago and New York and as deputy director of FOD, noted Campbell's interest in the regions and the importance of his support for regional managers. He recounted one episode while he was in New York. Thomas Watson, the president of International Business Machines, asked to meet with Krieger. Krieger knew that Campbell and Watson were acquainted, and he asked Campbell if he would like to come to New York to attend the meeting. Campbell's response was, "Who is my Regional Manager in New York?" Krieger said he "got the message very loudly and clearly." Campbell's approach, Krieger explained, "was that you were in the field and you were his representative; you'd better do the best job you were capable of doing. He could be quite concerned if you didn't live up to his expectations."[41]

Campbell appointed Krieger to an experimental position in January 1962 as part of his effort to strengthen the regional office system. He created the Northeast District of FOD, covering the territories of the Boston and New York Regional Offices, and appointed Krieger as the district manager with his office in New York. There was no change in the organization and the responsibilities of the two regional offices, but the two managers were responsible to Krieger for work performed in their areas.[42] A few months before he created the district manager position, Campbell told Morse that he thought that the field offices should be strengthened and be more autonomous. Campbell "expressed concern about the extent of Washington control of field office operations."[43] Campbell explained to Morse that Krieger's assignment "involved among other things the study of whether our field staffs were being properly utilized." A little later, Campbell asked Morse about the extent to which regional office draft reports "were torn apart and overhauled by the Washington staff." He told Morse that he wanted serious consideration to giving the regional offices greater autonomy in performing their work and preparing reports.[44]

---

[40]GAO, *Regional Offices and the Field Operations Division*, 15-16.

[41]Ibid., 13-14.

[42]Memorandum, Campbell to heads of divisions and offices, January 11, 1962, Morse Papers, Subject Files, GAO Offices and Divisions, Box 53, Folder: 1956 - April 1962.

[43]Entry for June 20, 1961, Morse, *Daily Notes*, 1961-1962.

[44]Entries for February 16 and March 8, 1962, ibid. Washington-regional relationships became a serious issue in the 1970s and 1980s. The problem Campbell identified in the 1960s was not solved at the time.

Krieger's assignment as a district manager lasted only three months. In late March 1962, Campbell dropped the district manager concept and brought Krieger to Washington as deputy director of FOD under Thornton. By this time, Campbell had decided that the regional system could be improved by strengthening the central office of FOD and giving greater responsibility to its director. Assigning Krieger as Thornton's deputy was part of this process.[45] Krieger later explained that after a few months as district manager, he had concluded that the approach had little merit; when he reported this to Campbell, the comptroller general dropped the plan and appointed Krieger to his new FOD post.[46]

Campbell's decision to strengthen the regional system generated discussions on what changes should be made to accomplish his objectives. Krieger was to be responsible mainly for the technical operations and the performance of the regional offices, with the goals of strengthening their performance and assigning greater responsibility to the field staff. At a meeting in mid-April 1962, Newman, the DAAD director, suggested that Krieger attend the kickoff conferences on audit assignments involving field staff under the direction of Washington divisions to thoroughly acquaint FOD with the nature of the jobs. He also suggested that the field offices gradually be given the authority and the responsibility to plan, program, and complete certain jobs, such as contract reviews. The regional offices would submit draft reports to the appropriate Washington operating division for review.

At this meeting, Thornton and Krieger listed some matters requiring consideration in increasing regional office responsibilities: (1) faster movement of regional office staff between jobs, (2) the need to make field staff more aware of their responsibilities, (3) the need for the Washington divisions to respond more quickly to the regional offices on acceptability of their work, (4) and an end to the idea in the regions that Washington staff would correct errors that their draft reports might contain. Thornton and Krieger also stressed the importance of developing effective report review machinery in the regional offices and expanding the practice of bringing in field supervisors to work with the Washington staff in completing reports.[47]

In 1963, Morse and Campbell discussed the idea of assigning some jobs exclusively to regional offices—for example, audits of the Tennessee Valley Authority, the Railroad Retirement Board, the International Boundary and Wa-

---

[45]Entries for March 28 and 30, 1962, ibid.

[46]GAO, *Regional Offices and the Field Operations Division*, 3-4.

[47]Notes of meeting of April 11, 1962, Morse, Notes of Meetings of Accounting and Auditing Division Heads, July 1960 through July 1964.

ter Commission, and the Saint Lawrence Seaway Development Corporation.[48]
A few months later, Morse proposed to Campbell, as part of an effort to
advance the autonomy of the regional offices, that certain contractors be
assigned for audit to specific regions. Campbell suggested that the Philadelphia, San Francisco, and Atlanta offices be selected for this project, presumably because of the volume of defense contract work in those regions.[49]
Shortly thereafter, Campbell signed an order putting this plan into effect by
assigning specific contractors to designated regional offices and giving the
regions full authority for auditing, reporting, and follow-up activities.
Newman, even though earlier receptive to the idea, opposed this, arguing
that defense contractor reports should go through his division for review and
transmission to the Department of Defense. He was unwilling to cede full
authority throughout the whole process to regional offices. Morse and
Campbell did not back down; Campbell asked Morse to continue his efforts to get
Newman to support the new system.[50]

Newman then gave Morse a memo making counterproposals that "would all
have the effect of retaining DAAD control of reports and liaison as is now done."
Morse informed Newman that Campbell wanted to go ahead as planned, but "Mr.
Newman informed me flatly that he refused to go along with any such arrangement and stated that he and I both should discuss the matter with Mr. Campbell."
Morse and Newman did meet with Campbell. Newman explained his objections
and said that he did not understand how regional officials could develop suitable
working arrangements with the Department of Defense. Newman also asserted
that the FOD director, in Morse's paraphrase, "did not have the background and
experience necessary to deal with them either." Campbell made clear that he
wanted to proceed with the plan to see whether the regional managers could do
the job. He did not think that regional managers were working up to a level
consistent with their rank. He wanted to increase their responsibilities and give
them greater freedom from the Washington operating divisions. "Whether Mr.
Newman fully understands this feeling was not entirely clear," Morse observed.[51]

Despite Campbell's efforts to increase the responsibilities and the autonomy of the regional offices, there is not much evidence of significant
progress during the remainder of his term. The 1964 comments of William
N. Conrardy, the Seattle regional manager, illustrate this point. Conrardy
had issued a memorandum to his staff on reporting objectives for preliminary survey and review and detailed examination assignments. When Morse

---

[48]Entry for June 4, 1963, Morse, *Daily Notes*, 1963-1964.

[49]Entry for October 23, 1963, ibid.

[50]Entry for November 13, 1963, ibid.

[51]Entry for November 15, 1963, ibid. Newman's statements and opinions are paraphrased by Morse
rather than directly quoted.

asked him for information on these instructions, Conrardy argued that there was a need for increased emphasis by the regional offices on planning and programming. He stated that during the recent past, the number of assignments from the Washington divisions for execution in the field had decreased significantly. Conrardy wrote: "This has created an urgent need for this Region to increase its programing and planning efforts . . . to achieve effective utilization of available resources and to assure that available resources will be productively directed toward meeting the reporting responsibilities of the General Accounting Office."

Conrardy supported his position by citing statistics: As of April 24, 1964, 12 Seattle staff were working on assignments from Washington or doing assist work for other regional offices and 72 staff members, or 85 percent of the Seattle personnel, were working on assignments initiated within the region. "Without the increased emphasis on planning and programing [sic], which resulted in these locally initiated assignments, much of the Region's resources would not have been productively employed at April 24," Conrardy reported to Morse.[52]

Another example was the complaint of Forrest Browne, the Kansas City regional manager, to Morse in 1965 about the extent to which some groups in CAAD rewrote draft reports prepared by his office before they went for comment to the agency concerned. Browne considered this practice inefficient and undesirable and suggested that the Washington groups return draft reports to the regional office if they were dissatisfied, with suggestions on how to revise them. Browne thought that his staff who did the audits were in the best position to rework the reports "and this pattern of operation is more closely in line with the trend to expect more complete and final work by regional office personnel." Morse agreed with Browne and observed that he thought the pattern Browne favored "would become standard in years to come."[53]

Clearly Campbell had followed the tradition of his predecessor, Lindsay Warren, in his deep interest in the regional offices and had taken steps to increase their prerogatives and the scope and the importance of their work. He achieved some degree of success, but much remained to be done. There still existed in the minds of some Washington officials and staff the conviction that the regional offices were second-class organizations that ought to assist the headquarters divisions but not operate autonomously or with increased authority.

---

[52]Memorandum, Conrardy to Morse, April 27, 1964, Morse Papers, Subject Files, GAO Offices and Divisions, Box 53, Folder: May 1962 - December 1965, GAO History Program Archives.

[53]Entry for May 18, 1965, Morse, *Daily Notes*, 1965-1966.

The regional offices varied a great deal, of course, and their importance was to a degree determined by the significance of the assignments they received from Washington or generated locally. It also made a difference who the regional manager was—how well he organized and motivated his staff, what the nature of his relations with the Washington divisions was, and what steps he took to generate work for his office. Alfred M. Clavelli, the long-time regional manager at San Francisco, for instance, a very strong office head, was a master at planning jobs and marketing them at GAO headquarters—getting a division or a group there interested in the proposal and authorizing him to go ahead with it.[54] There were others, such as Charles W. Moore in Detroit, who operated in a similar fashion.

The Office of Administrative Services

The Office of Administrative Services (OAS), established in 1953, continued to operate during Campbell's term. During fiscal year 1956, it had 307 personnel; its staff size increased somewhat in the next few years but never, during Campbell's term, exceeded 365, its total during fiscal year 1963.[55] OAS, headed by John F. Feeney, had a small administrative office and two branches, Budget and Finance and Records Management and Services.

The Budget and Finance Branch prepared and administered GAO's budget and maintained the Office's accounting system, as well as various internal financial records, including travel records for the accounting, auditing, and investigative activities. It was also responsible for the preparation of the GAO payroll, the maintenance and the audit of leave and retirement records, and the accounting control and the deposit of GAO money collections received in Washington. Finally, the branch was responsible for electrical accounting machine operations involved in preparation of statistical and reporting data for all GAO divisions and offices.[56]

The Records Management and Services Branch was charged with the preservation, the disposal, and the security of GAO records and for certain functions related to the records of executive agencies, including decisions on requests for authority to dispose of financial records and for transfer of

---

[54]GAO, *Regional Offices and the Field Operations Division*, 26.

[55]Campbell testimony, February 10, 1956, *Independent Offices Appropriations for 1957*, Hearings before a Subcommittee of the House Committee on Appropriations, 84th Cong., 2d Sess., pt. 2 (Washington: GPO, 1956), 1371; and Campbell testimony, February 25, 1963, *Independent Offices Appropriations for 1964*, 185.

[56]Printed statement, testimony of Campbell et al., April 15, 1959, *Independent Offices Appropriations for 1960*, Hearings before a Subcommittee of the House Committee on Appropriations, 86th Cong., 1st Sess., pt. 2 (Washington: GPO, 1959), 1063.

fiscal records to federal records centers. The branch also secured and distributed supplies, utilities, and equipment for GAO; reproduced and distributed Office publications; handled incoming and outgoing mail; and furnished transportation and various building management services.[57]

The scope of the records management function is demonstrated by activities covering GAO records during fiscal year 1962: disposal of 227,342 cubic feet of fiscal records and the transfer to federal records centers of 248,462 cubic feet of records. The branch also approved 129 schedules for disposal of fiscal records. At the end of this fiscal year, there were 520,197 cubic feet of GAO records in federal records centers and 630,943 cubic feet in GAO offices in Washington, at audit sites, at regional offices, and at a records storage facility at Cameron Station in Alexandria, Virginia.[58]

OAS was a housekeeping operation, providing essential services to all GAO divisions and offices. A large proportion of its staff worked in the Records Management and Services Branch. Between 1960 and 1964, OAS also included the Indian Tribal Claims Branch, which earlier had been part of the Claims Division. In 1964, the section moved to the Civil Accounting and Auditing Division.[59]

The Office of the General Counsel

The Office of the General Counsel (OGC) continued to play a very important role during Campbell's term. The general counsel until 1958 was E. L. Fisher, who had held the position since 1947. In 1958, Campbell appointed Robert F. Keller to head OGC. Keller began work at GAO in 1935; served in the U.S. Navy during World War II; worked as a GAO legislative attorney between 1945 and 1950; and then became an assistant to the comptroller general, under Warren until 1954 and then under Campbell.[60] As an assistant to Campbell, Keller directed the activities of the Office of Legislative Liaison, established by the comptroller general during the reorganization of 1956.[61]

The OGC staff when Campbell became comptroller general included about 100 lawyers, and that number increased only slightly during his term. Except for two lawyers assigned overseas, one to the European Branch and

[57]Ibid.

[58]Printed statement, testimony of Campbell et al., February 25, 1963, *Independent Offices Appropriations for 1964*, pt. 2, 186-87.

[59]See below, pp. 467-68, for information on Indian tribal claims work.

[60]Keller headed OGC until 1969. Then he served under Comptroller General Elmer B. Staats as assistant comptroller general (1969-1971) and as the first deputy comptroller general (1971-1980).

[61]See chapter 17, p. 419.

one to the Far East Branch, all these lawyers worked at GAO headquarters. OGC's support staff during the same period stabilized at about 80 persons.[62]

The functions of OGC, as defined in a comptroller general's order, were as follows:

Robert F. Keller, General Counsel, 1958-1969.

- to prepare decisions of the comptroller general as required by law;

- to prepare intraoffice decisions and instructions on legal questions arising in GAO work;

- to advise and assist division and office heads on legal aspects of matters under their jurisdiction;

- to issue letters on legal matters to agencies, claimants, debtors, and others;

- to consult with and assist the Justice Department on debt collection matters and collaborate with Justice when requested in the development and the trial of suits involving GAO interests;

- to conduct conferences with government officials and private citizens on matters affecting their interests;

- to maintain continuous contact with Congress and its committees and members to carry out legislative liaison responsibilities;

- to prepare reports and recommendations to Congress and the Bureau of the Budget on pending or proposed legislation;

- to analyze and digest decisions, memorandums, and other materials for publication or inclusion in various reference records and disseminate information on decisions;

---

[62]Testimony of Campbell et al., February 10, 1956, *Independent Offices Appropriations for 1957*, pt. 2, 1395; testimony of Campbell et al., March 7, 1960, *Independent Offices Appropriations for 1961*, pt. 2, 762; and testimony of Campbell et al., February 25, 1963, *Independent Offices Appropriations for 1964*, pt. 2, 189.

- to maintain files of decisions and other case materials;

- to maintain a law library; and

- to maintain legislative files for use by GAO divisions and offices and to distribute legislative materials to these offices.[63]

To accomplish these functions, OGC included, besides its complement of attorneys, a law library; an index and files section; a digest section; and beginning in fiscal year 1959, the Office of Legislative Liaison and a legislative digest unit.

The lawyers in OGC spent most of their time on decision work. The Budget and Accounting Act, 1921, authorized agency heads and disbursing and certifying officers to request decisions from the comptroller general on any questions involving payments to be made or presented to them for certification. The comptroller general also made decisions related to GAO's day-to-day work in the form of instructions to division and office heads; many of these decisions involved interpretations of law in the light of GAO's statutory responsibilities. The comptroller general also rendered decisions to claimants who requested review or reconsideration of claims previously disallowed.

Classified according to subject matter, these three groups of decisions covered (1) federal civilian personnel matters, including pay; (2) contract matters—procurement of services and supplies, construction projects, federal leases, and sale and disposition of government property; (3) military matters, such as pay and allowances, retirement benefits, and travel; (4) transportation, covering all legal matters relating to government shipments and relationships of the United States with common carriers; (5) appropriations and miscellaneous matters, such as appropriations availability and obligation and application of appropriations limitations; (6) legislation; and (7) miscellaneous private inquiries.[64]

Of these seven categories, OGC's heaviest workload was in civilian pay, appropriations, contracts, military pay and allowances, and transportation.[65] The volume of decisions rendered by the comptroller general based on the legal work of the OGC lawyers was large. For example, during fiscal year 1959, in these five areas, the comptroller general issued 5,876 decisions; the largest volume, 1,920, concerned contracts; military pay and allowances

---

[63]Comptroller General's Order No. 2.1, "Office of the General Counsel," October 15, 1959, in *Comptroller General's Orders*, 1959 edition, GAO Records. This version of the order was in effect from 1959 to 1969.

[64]Printed statement, testimony of Campbell et al., March 7, 1960, *Independent Offices Appropriations for 1961*, pt. 2, 761.

[65]Keller testimony, March 7, 1960, ibid., 762.

(1,178) and transportation (1,100) followed.[66] Campbell reported, illustrating the diversity of legal matters subject to decisions, that in fiscal year 1961, OGC prepared 11 decisions at the request of the Department of Agriculture. They dealt with such questions as whether Agriculture could pay members of a state National Guard for fighting a fire in a national forest; whether the secretary of agriculture under the Soil Bank program could relieve unforeseen hardships of producers; and whether the Commodity Credit Corporation, with respect to grain mortgaged to CCC by a producer and stored by the producer under a price support loan, could take delivery of the grain at the farm where it was stored in satisfaction of the loan.[67]

Bid protests on contracts let by the federal government constituted a large part of decision work. Keller testified that OGC handled about 1,500 bid protest cases in fiscal year 1962. When a bidder filed a protest with GAO concerning a contract awarded by a federal agency to another bidder, GAO's first step was to request a report on the matter from the agency. Sometimes OGC met with the bid protester's attorney, and the bidder could file legal briefs. On occasion, OGC asked one of the accounting and auditing divisions to investigate the matter. OGC also used court precedents and previous comptroller general decisions when appropriate. Pending OGC's final recommendation to the comptroller general on the protest, the contracting agency usually held up implementation of the contract. The comptroller general's decision on the legality of the contract award answered the question of whether it met all the requirements of law and federal procurement regulations. Keller reported that OGC decided in favor of the bid protesters in 7 to 10 percent of the 1,500 bid protests received during fiscal year 1962.[68]

Related to decision work, OGC made reports and recommendations to the U.S. attorney general, on his request, on suits filed in the Court of Claims or U.S. district courts concerning the collection of money owed to the government by disbursing and certifying officers or by other persons and companies.[69]

While OGC during Campbell's term continued to be influential, the influx of trained and experienced staff in the accounting and auditing divisions, many being CPAs, greatly expanded the number of professionals in GAO. Until the end of World War II, the lawyers were the only large professional group in GAO. While the number of lawyers did not decrease, the

---

[66]*Annual Report of the Comptroller General of the United States for the Fiscal Year Ending June 30, 1959* (Washington: GPO, 1959), 277.

[67]Campbell's printed statement, testimony of February 9, 1962, *Independent Offices Appropriations for 1963*, pt. 2, 61.

[68]Keller testimony, February 25, 1963, *Independent Offices Appropriations for 1964*, pt. 2, 190-91.

[69]Campbell's printed statement, testimony of February 9, 1962, *Independent Offices Appropriations for 1963*, pt. 2, 66.

accountants brought in, first by Comptroller General Warren for the Corporation Audits Division and later by Campbell in much larger numbers, tended to mute somewhat the influence of OGC in GAO as a whole. As Campbell put more and more emphasis on the reporting activities of the accounting and auditing divisions, especially CAAD and DAAD, the lawyers became a less dominant group, although their work did not diminish in importance.

Claims Work

Claims work, one of GAO's original functions, continued during the Campbell period. Before Campbell's term, GAO typically received thousands of claims cases each year, including claims against the government (payment claims) and claims by the government (debt claims). The Claims Division did the bulk of its work in headquarters; its only field operations were in Indianapolis, where GAO staff handled debt claims involving military personnel.[70] A reorganization of the Claims Division during fiscal year 1955 along functional lines to distinguish among three basic types of claims activity—claims against the government by members or former members of the armed forces, other claims against the United States, and claims on behalf of the United States—facilitated handling of claims and made possible some reduction in staff. At the same time, GAO began to cooperate with government agencies to improve their internal handling of claims to make more efficient the total claims-processing task and lighten GAO's claims load.[71]

Also helpful was the passage of a law in July 1956, strongly supported by GAO, authorizing agencies to make payment on claims from lapsed appropriations without referral of the cases to GAO if no questions of fact or law were involved.[72] As GAO expected, the law resulted in a reduction in the number of claims received for settlement. In the fiscal year before passage of the law, GAO received 96,853 claims; in the next fiscal year, the number was 48,897.[73]

The number of staff in the Claims Division before passage of the 1956 law was slightly over 700. After 1956, the staff size declined gradually, to

---

[70]Testimony of A. Banks Thomas, director of the Claims Division, February 10, 1956, *Independent Offices Appropriations for 1957*, pt. 2, 1377.

[71]Testimony of Campbell et al., February 22, 1955, *Independent Offices Appropriations for 1956*, Hearings before a Subcommittee of the House Committee on Appropriations, 84th Cong., 1st Sess., pt. 1 (Washington: GPO, 1955), 745-46.

[72]Public Law 84-798, 70 Stat. 647, approved July 25, 1956. See also *Annual Report of the Comptroller General of the United States for the Fiscal Year Ending June 30, 1956* (Washington: GPO, 1956), 7.

[73]*Annual Report of the Comptroller General of the United States for the Fiscal Year Ending June 30, 1957* (Washington: GPO, 1957), 5.

346 in 1962.[74] Typically in the years before 1956, the Claims Division had a large backlog of unsettled claims. With the efficiencies gained by the division's reorganization and especially the decline in number of claims received, the division eventually eliminated the backlog. Early in 1962, Campbell testified that the backlog had been reduced to the point where newly received claims could be processed expeditiously. At the same time, the director of the division noted the 50-percent decrease during the past few years in both the workload and the staff of the division. He estimated that the division was receiving about 1,400 payment cases and 5,000 debt cases per month. More than 50 percent of the debt cases came from the military.[75]

GAO's annual collections on debts owed to the government between 1956 and the end of Campbell's term ranged from around $5 million (calendar year 1961) to almost $11 million (calendar year 1957). Amounts that GAO certified to be paid out by the government in settlement of claims also varied—for example, about $31 million in fiscal year 1961 compared with $11 million in 1962.[76]

A special activity of the Claims Division, as in the past, was the work on American Indian claims against the U.S. government. The Indian Tribal Claims Section was responsible for preparing detailed reports for the attorney general on Indian claims filed with the Indian Claims Commission and the U.S. Court of Claims. In preparing the reports, which included information on Indian treaty obligations of the government, an accounting of Indian trust and investment funds, and other matters, the section did extensive research in records dating back to the late 18th century. The volume of Indian claims work was heavy; in mid-1958, for example, the section had 196 reports pending.[77]

In November 1959, GAO transferred the Indian Tribal Claims Section to the Office of Administrative Services, where it became the Indian Tribal Branch, with 82 staff. The group was moved because its work was reporting and accounting rather than adjudicating and settling claims.[78] By this time,

---

[74]Testimony of Campbell et al., February 10, 1956, *Independent Offices Appropriations for 1957*, pt. 2, 1374; and testimony of Campbell et al., February 9, 1962, *Independent Offices Appropriations for 1963*, pt. 2, 52.

[75]Testimony of Campbell et al, February 9, 1962, ibid., 52-54.

[76]Testimony of Campbell et al., March 3, 1958, *Independent Offices Appropriations for 1959*, pt. 2, 1245; testimony of Campbell et al., February 9, 1962, *Independent Offices Appropriations for 1963*, pt. 2, 53; and testimony of Campbell et al., February 25, 1963, *Independent Offices Appropriations for 1964*, pt. 2, 164.

[77]Testimony of Campbell et al., April 15, 1959, *Independent Offices Appropriations for 1960*, pt. 2, 1064-65.

[78]Testimony of Campbell et al., March 7, 1960, *Independent Offices Appropriations for 1961*, pt. 2, 731.

Comptroller General Campbell was concerned about the number of staff involved in this activity and began to consider transferring the function to another agency.   Morse thought that to move the tribal claims work to the Department of Justice would be logical because it was the defendant in cases of tribal claims brought against the United States.   Campbell responded that both the Justice Department and the Indian Tribal Claims Commission depended on GAO to prepare objective reports on tribal claims and that if either organization prepared the reports, there inevitably would be disputes over their accuracy.   Campbell recommended that Morse assign someone in the Accounting and Auditing Policy Staff to study the matter.[79]

The AAPS study, completed in the fall of 1960, concluded that while the Indian claims function did not fit in well in GAO, there was no other logical place in the government for it and GAO should be prepared to keep it.[80]   Campbell continued to hope that Indian claims could be moved from GAO.   When asked to comment on the Indian Tribal Branch at a hearing in 1964, Campbell said that he did not think that GAO ought to be doing Indian claims work but admitted that the Departments of Justice and the Interior as well as the Indian Tribal Claims Commission all valued GAO's reports on the claims.   Campbell said that he was trying to persuade the Interior Department to take the job. General Counsel Keller remarked, "It is one of those things started many years ago, and we have never been able to get rid of it."[81]

In July 1964, GAO moved the Indian Tribal Branch from the Office of Administrative Services, where it did not really fit, to the Civil Accounting and Auditing Division.   During 1965, GAO transferred the function to the National Archives and Records Service, an agency of the General Services Administration, on the basis of on an agreement between GAO and GSA.[82]

The Transportation Division

The Transportation Division had responsibility for auditing government transportation payments to common carriers, a function dating back to the early years of GAO.   When Campbell entered office, the division was one of GAO's

[79]Entries for February 26 and March 1, 1960, Morse, *Daily Notes*, 1959-1960; and testimony of Campbell et al., March 7, 1960, *Independent Offices Appropriations for 1961*, pt. 2, 753-54.

[80]Entry for September 30, 1960, Morse, *Daily Notes*, 1959-1960.

[81]Testimony of Campbell and Keller, February 6, 1964, *Legislative Branch Appropriations for 1965*, Hearings before a Subcommittee of the House Committee on Appropriations, 88th Cong., 2d Sess. (Washington: GPO, 1964), 48.

[82]Entry for June 26, 1964, Morse, *Daily Notes*, 1963-1964; and *Annual Report of the Comptroller General of the United States for the Fiscal Year Ended June 30, 1965* (Washington: 1965), 158.

largest units, with 1,452 staff during fiscal year 1955. Campbell described in 1956 testimony the "staggering volume of activity" of the division during fiscal year 1955:

> During the fiscal year 1955, the Transportation Division examined 3,993,128 bills of lading and 3,209,821 transportation requests; furnished other Government agencies information as to 87,124 rate situations; reaudited 5,730,558 bills of lading and 3,000,716 transportation requests; adjudicated or settled 40,674 freight and 4,689 passenger transportation claims; settled 9,980 claims by the United States against carriers in connection with free billing, administratively reported debts and export traffic; disposed of 40,607 appeals and protests in connection with actions taken; reported debts totaling $1,651,789 to the Department of Justice for collection involving 7,095 bills of lading and transportation requests and considered and furnished reports to the Attorney General as to 17,989 bills of lading and transportation requests, each of which was the subject of legal action against the United States. In the performance of this work there were issued to carriers of all types 118,157 freight and 53,550 passenger notices of overpayment in the aggregate sums of $41,772,949 and $9,481,409, respectively. In addition to direct collections and deposit of $38,512,444 the Transportation Division collected and forwarded to administrative agencies refunds from carriers aggregating $334,405, and there were issued—in connection with Reconstruction Finance Corporation liquidation—notices of overpayments to carriers of over $800,000 due to audits and formulas furnished by the freight subdivision respecting vouchers RFC had submitted to the Division for examination.[83]

The backlog of transportation audits was large in the early years of Campbell's term. A major reason for this condition was the ongoing reaudit that began in 1948 of World War II transportation charges.[84] GAO did not finish the reaudit until December 1961. Campbell reported to Congress that total overcharges identified by the reaudit amounted to $250 million.[85] The reaudit burden made it difficult for the Transportation Division to keep up with the audit of current charges, contributing to the backlog. In February

---

[83]Testimony of Campbell et al., February 22, 1955, *Independent Offices Appropriations for 1956*, pt. 1, 748 (staff size); and testimony of Campbell et al., February 10, 1956, *Independent Offices Appropriations for 1957*, pt. 2, 1341, 1378.

[84]See chapter 11, pp. 266-73.

[85]Campbell testimony, February 9, 1962, *Independent Offices Appropriations for 1963*, pt. 2, 14-15.

1957, the division was 28 months behind in auditing freight transportation charges; the lag was about 12 months for both freight and passenger payments in April 1959, 6 months in February 1962, and down to 4 months in February 1964.[86]

GAO was able to complete the reaudit work and bring ongoing transportation audits near current despite a declining workforce during the Campbell years. Transportation's staff decline was due to both the gradual cut in personnel under Campbell and the comptroller general's special concerns about the Transportation Division. He remarked to Morse in 1957 that the division accounted for 25 percent of GAO's current budget. He also noted that the transportation audit was way behind "and presumably not catching up very fast."[87] Campbell had questions about the quality of work in the division.

Thomas E. Sullivan, who became associate director of the division in 1960 and director in 1962, observed that the Transportation staff was "a nonprofessional group of people looked upon, probably, as more clerical and technical, and yet . . . were performing a lot of technical work. We were the stepchild of GAO." Working conditions in the division, especially before 1959, were dismal, according to Sullivan. He suggested that the fact that Transportation was the "predominantly . . . black organization" in GAO helped explain the division's situation.[88]

Campbell, according to Sullivan, wanted to curtail Transportation's activities and cut the payroll.[89] There is no evidence that Campbell related these objectives to the fact that much of the division's staff was black. From 1,452 in fiscal year 1955, the staff declined gradually to 1,116 in 1962 and 817 in 1965, Campbell's last year in office.[90]

Early in 1959, Campbell appointed John P. Abbadessa from CAAD as the director of the Transportation Division and asked him to do a study and

---

[86]Testimony of Campbell et al., February 26, 1957, *Independent Offices Appropriations for 1958*, pt. 2, 1957; testimony of Campbell et al., April 15, 1959, *Independent Offices Appropriations for 1960*, pt. 2, 1043; testimony of Campbell et al., February 9, 1962, *Independent Offices Appropriations for 1963*, pt. 2, 57; and testimony of Campbell et al., February 6, 1964, *Legislative Branch Appropriations for 1965*, 11.

[87]Entry for March 13, 1957, Morse, *Daily Notes*, 1957-1958.

[88] GAO, *Transportation Activities, 1946-1975: Interview with Joseph P. Normile, Fred J. Shafer, and Thomas E. Sullivan*, GAO History Program, Oral History Series, GAO/OP-24-OH (Washington: 1992), 20. In the late 1960s and the 1970s, the question of race relations and equal employment opportunity became a contested issue, leading eventually to court cases. For a discussion of these matters, see ibid., 41-49, and Roger L. Sperry, Timothy D. Desmond, Kathi F. McGraw, and Barbara Schmitt, *GAO 1966-1981: An Administrative History* (Washington: 1981), 194-207.

[89]GAO, *Transportation Activities, 1946-1975*, 21.

[90]Testimony of Campbell et al., February 9, 1962, *Independent Offices Appropriations for 1963*, pt. 2, 56; and GAO, *Annual Report, 1965*, 385.

make recommendations on the future of the division. Abbadessa recalled later that Campbell had questioned whether the division "fitted in because it was kind of the last vestige of the old voucher audits" and that he was also concerned about the budget.[91] Abbadessa reorganized the division, installed controls and production reporting, and shifted some staff from rail to motor and airline audits. He also improved working conditions in the division offices.[92]

During Abbadessa's short term in the Transportation Division, a new law and two Supreme Court decisions significantly affected the transportation audit. The law imposed a three-year time limit on the government's right to recover money for overcharges and other reasons due from carriers. This necessitated an effort in the Transportation Division to get more up-to-date on the examination of transportation payments and to collect from carriers before the three-year limit on each case. To do this, Abbadessa moved about 80 staff from the reaudit to current work.[93]

One of the Supreme Court decisions held that the government could not recover unreasonable charges by motor carriers when no specific statutory provision allowed such recovery.[94] An unreasonable charge could be legal, while an overcharge represented a violation of established rates and was recoverable. Between May 1959, when the Court reached this decision, and June 30, 1960, GAO found unreasonable charges of about $900,000 that were not recoverable under the decision.[95]

In the second case, the Supreme Court held that under admiralty law, deductions from payments due a carrier on other maritime transactions could not be made by the government to satisfy a claim. The Court ruled also that under maritime law, suits to recover maritime claims would be barred unless they were presented in court within one year of the causes of the actions. During fiscal year 1959, before the decision in this case, GAO collected over $70,000 in maritime claims by deduction from other amounts due carriers.[96]

---

[91]GAO, *John P. Abbadessa, 1947-1962*, GAO History Program, Oral History Series, GAO/OP-18-OH (Washington: 1990), 4; and press release, January 5, 1959, announcing Abbadessa's appointment, Morse, *Daily Notes*, 1959-1960.

[92]GAO, *John P. Abbadessa*, 4-6; and GAO, *Transportation Activities, 1946-1975*, 21.

[93]Public Law 85-762, 72 Stat. 859, approved August 26, 1958; Abbadessa testimony, April 15, 1959, *Independent Offices Appropriations for 1960*, pt. 2, 1070; and testimony of Campbell et al., March 7, 1960, *Independent Offices Appropriations for 1961*, pt. 2, 755.

[94]*Time Inc. v. United States; Davidson Transfer and Storage Co., Inc. v. United States*, 359 U.S. 464.

[95]Comment of Fred J. Shafer in GAO, *Transportation Activities, 1946-1975*, 31; and testimony of Campbell et al., March 15, 1961, *Independent Offices Appropriations for 1962*, pt. 1, 342.

[96]*The United States v. Isthmian Steamship Co.*, 359 U.S. 314; testimony of Campbell et al., March 7, 1960, *Independent Offices Appropriations for 1961*, pt. 2, 755-756; and testimony of Campbell et al., March 15, 1961, *Independent Offices Appropriations for 1962*, pt. 1, 342-43.

GAO drafted bills that were introduced in Congress to supersede these decisions, but Congress did not pass them.

GAO's collections as a result of transportation audit work were considerable during the Campbell period. Some of the total represented collections resulting from the World War II reaudit. For example, during fiscal year 1958, the Transportation Division collected $40,162,000, including $22,016,000 from the reaudit.[97] During fiscal year 1956, total transportation collections were $52,097,027; during fiscal year 1961, $24,070,443.[98]

Although there were still problems in the Transportation Division at the end of Campbell's term in 1965, Abbadessa and his successors as directors of the division had made improvements in organization and staffing during their terms and given the amount of annual collections from carriers, could certainly show some significant accomplishments.[99]

---

[97]Testimony of Campbell et al., April 15, 1959, *Independent Offices Appropriations for 1960*, pt. 2, 1043.

[98]Testimony of Campbell et al., February 26, 1957, *Independent Offices Appropriations for 1958*, pt. 2, 1933; and testimony of Campbell et al., February 9, 1962, *Independent Offices Appropriations for 1963*, pt. 2, 56.

[99]In 1975, under Comptroller General Elmer B. Staats, GAO transferred the transportation audit work to the General Services Administration, as authorized by the GAO Act of 1974 (Public Law 93-604, 88 Stat. 1959, approved January 2, 1975). See GAO, *Transportation Activities, 1946-1975*, 49-52, for a discussion of the transfer.

CHAPTER 19

Defense and International Work Under Campbell

When Comptroller General Joseph Campbell reorganized the accounting and auditing organizations of GAO in 1956, one of his central objectives was to improve the Office's ability to handle defense audits. The Cold War, the conflict in Korea, the involvement of the United States in the North Atlantic Treaty Organization and other regional security groups, programs of economic and military assistance, the stationing of large contingents of the U.S. armed forces overseas, and the development of new strategic and conventional weapon systems all contributed to the increasing volume and importance of GAO's defense and international work.

GAO officials Harold Rubin and William Conrardy inspecting a nuclear power facility at Fort Greeley, Alaska, 1960.

In his fiscal year 1956 annual report, Campbell noted the "tremendous importance" of GAO's defense work—in procurement and contracting, industrial and commercial-type activities, pay and allowances, operations at military installations, transportation, and various aspects of financial management. "Plans and programs," he wrote, "are now in effect, and others are being formulated, whereby all facets of our systems, audit, and investigative work will be strengthened and our coverage of defense operations substantially extended. . . . Increased emphasis will be given to the review and evaluation of certain financial management aspects of the defense organizations."[1]

The Defense Accounting and Auditing Division (DAAD), created in 1956, was the central organization for defense work. The overseas branches in Europe and the Far East were important adjuncts of DAAD. An increasingly important aspect of DAAD's audit work in the United States, as Campbell intended, was procurement and contracting. As this activity increased, especially in the 1960s, it became controversial, significantly affecting GAO's relationships with both the Department of Defense (DOD) and defense contractors. Hearings in 1965, chaired by Rep. Chester (Chet) E. Holifield (D—California), brought considerable criticism to both GAO and DOD and constituted the last major event of Campbell's term as comptroller general.[2] The controversy over defense contract audits and the overall effects of the hearings on GAO's organization and program ushered in a new era in the Office's history, under a new comptroller general.

The Defense Accounting and Auditing Division

DAAD, created on March 22, 1956, was staffed by personnel involved in defense accounting and auditing work formerly done by the Division of Audits.[3] The division's first director was Lawrence J. Powers; his deputy and successor in 1959 was William A. Newman.[4] DAAD's organization included defined groups for the Army, the Navy, the Air Force, and other areas, including DOD in general and military assistance. Initially, there was also a group assigned to contract audit work. Later DAAD discontinued this group and assigned defense contract work directly to the Army, Navy, and Air

---

[1]*Annual Report of the Comptroller General of the United States for the Fiscal Year Ending June 30, 1956* (Washington: GPO, 1956), 21.

[2]See chapter 20.

[3]Comptroller General's Order No. 2.31, March 22, 1956, A-16251, #1.

[4] GAO, *Defense Related Audits, 1937-1975: Interview with Hassell B. Bell, J. Kenneth Fasick, and James H. Hammond*, GAO History Program, Oral History Series, GAO/OP-9-OH (Washington: GAO, 1989), 6-7; and press release, December 17, 1959, Morse, *Daily Notes*, 1959-1960 (on appointment of Powers as assistant to the comptroller general, effective December 24, 1959); and press release, December 24, 1959, Morse, *Daily Notes*, 1959-1960 (on Newman's appointment as director of DAAD, effective December 27, 1959.

Force groups.[5] The division included, until 1963, the Far East Branch at Tokyo, created in 1956;[6] the accounting and auditing staff in Dayton, Ohio; the Army Audit Branch in Indianapolis; the Navy Audit Branch in Cleveland; the Air Force Audit Branch in Denver; and the Marine Corps Audit Branch in Washington, DC. The service audit branches were responsible chiefly for the centralized audit and settlement of accounts of accountable offices of the military departments. They were distinct from the Army, Navy, and Air Force groups that were part of DAAD's headquarters staff in Washington. In 1962, GAO transferred the staff servicing military records in Indianapolis, Cleveland, and Denver to the respective military departments and changed the offices themselves to audit sites under the Cincinnati, Detroit, and Denver regional offices. GAO discontinued the Marine Corps audit group in 1964.[7]

DAAD's staff included 754 persons when the division began operations on July 1, 1956—167 in Washington and 587 distributed among the military audit branches, with the largest number, 252, in the Army branch in Indianapolis. The division staff increased to slightly over 800 during DAAD's first year of operations, and it approximated that number until 1962. In that year, the staff in the military audit branches transferred to the Field Operations Division, and in 1963, additional staff, including those in the Far East Branch, moved to the new International Operations Division. On June 30, 1964, as a result of these changes, DAAD had 303 staff.[8]

In 1957 testimony, Campbell summarized the duties of DAAD. The office of the director was responsible for supervision and direction of the division, including coordinating the work of the accounting, auditing, and investigative groups; processing of reports; and developing policy and procedures. The

---

[5]Ibid., 6, 10, 11, 14. DAAD's leadership in the last year of Campbell's term included Newman as director and Charles M. Bailey as deputy director. Richard W. Gutmann, an associate director, headed the Army group, with Assistant Directors W. F. Coogan, J. F. Flynn, and S. S. Warren. Associate Director J. H. Hammond ran the Air Force group, aided by assistant directors M. Gradet, P. C. Newell, and Robert G. Rothwell. In the Navy group, J. Kenneth Fasick was associate director, with James L. DiGuiseppi, Donald L. Scantlebury, and J. M. Sullivan. The DOD group included Associate Director H. H. Reuben and Assistant Directors R. B. Hall, Jr.; W. J. Wilson; and Irving Zuckerman. The Program Review and Special Projects group included Hassell B. Bell and S. B. Savage. See DAAD organization chart in *Annual Report of the Comptroller General of the United States for the Fiscal Year Ended June 30, 1964* (Washington: GPO, 1964), 323.

[6]See below, pp. 491-94.

[7]Table, Number of Employees, June 30, 1954 through June 30, 1965, *Annual Report of the Comptroller General of the United States for the Fiscal Year Ended June 30, 1965* (Washington: GPO, 1965), 356.

[8]Testimony of Campbell et al., February 26, 1957, *Independent Offices Appropriations for 1958*, Hearings before a Subcommittee of the House Committee on Appropriations, 85th Cong., 1st Sess., pt. 2 (Washington: GPO, 1957), 1958-59; testimony of Campbell et al., February 9, 1962, *Independent Offices Appropriations for 1963*, Hearings before a Subcommittee of the House Committee on Appropriations, 87th Cong., 2d Sess., pt. 2 (Washington: GPO, 1962), 76-77; testimony of Campbell et al., February 25, 1963, *Independent Offices Appropriations for 1964*, Hearings before a Subcommittee of the House Committee on Appropriations, 88th Cong., 1st Sess., pt. 2 (Washington: GPO, 1963), 201; and table, Number of Employees, June 30, 1954 through June 30, 1965, GAO, *Annual Report, 1965*, 356.

Washington groups were to carry out cooperative accounting systems development and auditing and investigative functions in DOD, including the military departments. They were also to plan and supervise work programs related to defense activities carried out by regional offices. Campbell stated that the wide scope and the volume of DOD operations and the size of the defense budget "makes our task in this area one of tremendous importance." He pointed out that defense appropriations for fiscal year 1957 were over $36 billion and that actual spending during fiscal year 1956 amounted to $35.6 billion. He added that GAO intended to expand its coverage of defense operations as fast as it could recruit and train qualified personnel.[9]

Campbell pointed out some specific aspects of DAAD's defense work. The division was reviewing and evaluating the military assistance program, procurement, supply management functions and operations; defense contract negotiations; and administration and contractor operations. GAO also was developing selective comprehensive audits of military installations to determine whether authorized programs were being carried out as planned and whether resources were being used efficiently and effectively. "This review will complement the findings in related logistical, operational, and financial management areas, so as to provide a basis for department wide evaluation of specific programs."[10]

The total number of reports produced by DAAD and submitted to Congress and agency officials was substantial. For example, in fiscal year 1961, the division issued 78 to Congress and 321 to agency officials, and in fiscal year 1962, 138 to Congress and 254 to agency officials.[11]

Campbell's testimony in March 1960 demonstrated GAO's increasing emphasis on contract audits. He indicated that DAAD would concentrate on selected programs to ensure coverage of major procurement activities of each military service. He mentioned specifically several weapon systems contracts: the B-58 strategic bomber, General Dynamics Corporation; the KC-135 jet tanker, the B-52 bomber, and the BOMARC missile, Boeing Airplane Company; the Redstone Jupiter missile and the M-48 medium tank, Chrysler Corporation; the

---

[9]Campbell's printed statement, testimony of February 26, 1957, *Independent Offices Appropriations for 1958*, 1958-59. For a table showing total obligational authority for DOD covering the fiscal years 1947 through 1985, see Roger R. Trask, *The Secretaries of Defense: A Brief History, 1947-1985* (Washington: Historical Office, Office of the Secretary of Defense, 1985), 63. DOD's total obligational authority in current dollars rose from $33.79 billion in fiscal year 1955 to $49.561 billion in fiscal year 1965, the years of Campbell's term.

[10]Testimony of Campbell et al., February 26, 1957, *Independent Offices Appropriations for 1958*, pt. 2, 1925.

[11]Testimony of Campbell et al., February 9, 1962, *Independent Offices Appropriations for 1963*, pt. 2, 76; and testimony of Campbell et al., February 25, 1963, *Independent Offices Appropriations for 1964*, 200.

Polaris missile, Lockheed Aircraft Corporation; and the Navy F-3H fighter bomber, McDonnell Aircraft Corporation.[12]

DAAD's reports demonstrated the wide variety of subjects covered. The division placed considerable emphasis on accomplishments—number of reports issued, cash collections, and estimated savings other than cash collections. During fiscal year 1960, DAAD reported cash collections of $12.1 million and nearly $75 million in estimated savings due to several actions: reductions in prices of negotiated contracts, $3.5 million; cancellation of proposed purchases, $4.5 million; cancellation of requisitions for materials and supplies not required, $46.5 million; transfer of materials from one military department to another, $16.5 million; termination or consolidation of facilities, $2.8 million; more effective interagency use of repair facilities, $200,000; and cancellation of unnecessary movement of materials, $500,000.[13]

DAAD's review of an airfield being used mainly for pilot proficiency training and accommodation of aircraft flying from one airfield to another was an example of work resulting in significant savings. GAO discovered that other airfields in the vicinity could handle the bulk of the operations at this location and that transfer of operations would not increase costs significantly. GAO urged the military department responsible for this airfield to reappraise its use and that it do so expeditiously because of a pending proposal to improve the field at a cost of about $2 million. On the basis of GAO's review, the department reduced the airfield to auxiliary status, eliminating the improvement cost and making possible an annual savings of about $600,000.[14]

Another example was a 1963 report on reenlistment of undesirable military personnel. GAO claimed that the military services reenlisted men who were undesirable, according to their personnel records, at a cost to the government of about $15 million per year. Later, before these men completed their reenlistment periods, they were discharged on the basis of unsatisfactory performance. The involved service then had to collect the part of the reenlistment bonuses covering the period of uncompleted service. Much of this bonus money, amounting to about $900,000 per year, proved uncollectible. GAO

---

[12]Campbell's printed statement, testimony of March 7, 1960, *Independent Offices Appropriations for 1961*, Hearings before a Subcommittee of the House Committee on Appropriations, 86th Cong., 2d Sess., pt. 2 (Washington: GPO, 1960), 770.

[13]Campbell's printed statement, testimony of March 15, 1961, *Independent Offices Appropriations for 1962*, Hearings before a Subcommittee of the House Committee on Appropriations, 87th Cong., 1st Sess., pt. 1 (Washington: GPO, 1961), 348.

[14]Ibid., 349.

reported that DOD agreed that it had serious problems in reenlistment procedures and was taking corrective action.[15]

The Access-to-Records Issue

In April 1959, at a hearing before a subcommittee of the House Appropriations Committee, Chairman Albert Thomas (D—Texas) asked Campbell if GAO had any serious problems. Campbell responded, "I think that really the most serious problem we have . . . [which] could be almost fatal to our office is the matter of access to records."[16] Access to records, guaranteed to GAO in the Budget and Accounting Act, 1921, was especially critical for work in DOD, which had a high incidence of classified materials.

A difficult problem over access to Army records developed for GAO in 1956. In October 1956, Campbell wrote to Secretary of the Army Wilbur M. Brucker, indicating that GAO would extend its comprehensive audit program to the Department of the Army and that it would begin an audit of the Ordnance Tank-Automotive Command in January 1957. He asked Brucker for the Army's cooperation in arranging for this audit and in providing official documents, records, and reports.[17] Brucker's response precipitated a serious controversy. He explained that the "Army should not be asked to make available internal audit reports or any related workpapers" until completion of internal processes. He added that when the Army did an internal audit, it allowed time for careful review of the report by Army officials and development of plans for corrective action. He also asked that GAO send requests for reports and workpapers to his office rather than to field installations or other Army staff elements. He requested that GAO submit separate copies of draft reports to installation or activity commanders, the supervising command, and Army management echelons, including the deputy chief of staff for logistics, the comptroller, and his own office. Brucker concluded that, subject to these conditions, "all official documents, records and reports not otherwise prohibited for release are made available as necessary in the conduct of the audit after clearance by my office."[18]

Campbell responded that the Army rules so limited the availability of documents "that the effective performance of the statutory responsibilities of

---

[15]Testimony of Campbell et al., February 25, 1963, *Independent Offices Appropriations for 1964*, pt. 2, 155-59.

[16]Campbell testimony, April 15, 1959, *Independent Offices Appropriations for 1960*, Hearings before a Subcommittee of the House Committee on Appropriations, 86th Cong., 1st Sess., pt. 2 (Washington: GPO, 1959), 1044-45.

[17]Letter, Campbell to the secretary of the army, October 9, 1956, Morse Papers, Subject Files, Box 1, Folder: Access to Records, #1.

[18]Letter, Brucker to the comptroller general, December 19, 1956, ibid.

. . . [GAO] would be seriously impaired." He invoked the Budget and Accounting Act, 1921, arguing that the Army procedures were inconsistent with that law. Campbell added that he would provide a copy of his letter to the secretary of defense because of the importance of the access question and the need for a more clearly defined policy in DOD.[19]

In May 1957, Campbell informed the secretary of defense that the Army rules had seriously impaired GAO operations and noted that discussion between GAO and Army representatives had failed to resolve the problem. "We believe," Campbell wrote, "that you will appreciate the seriousness of this matter and that our statutory responsibility will not permit us to accept the continued existence of the . . . restrictions. We must insist, therefore, that remedial action be taken without further delay and our Office be so notified."[20]

After Sen. John L. McClellan (D—Arkansas), chairman of the Senate Committee on Government Operations, wrote to Secretary of Defense Charles E. Wilson about the GAO access problem, mentioned the possibility of holding hearings on the matter, and asked for an immediate report, the Army responded.[21] Brucker, in a memorandum to the Army chief of staff, explained the GAO comprehensive audit program in detail and stated that all Army levels should cooperate with GAO auditors, providing proper working space and timely assistance in making information and records available. Brucker told the chief of staff, "I have agreed that requests for the release of internal audit reports and working papers at the field level will be honored and such release effected at that level. In addition, I have agreed that internal audit reports may be released prior to the formulation of an Army position and the establishment of a program for corrective action as I had previously requested."[22]

This solved the immediate problem with the Army, but not the broader question with the Department of Defense. On July 8, 1957, DOD released Directive 5200.1, a revised directive on access to DOD records, replacing one issued in 1953. William A. Newman, deputy director of DAAD, thought that the new directive's key provisions, which were very similar to the 1953 version, "have the effect of restricting the ready availability of information which is vital to the con-

---

[19]Letter, Campbell to the secretary of the army, February 7, 1957, ibid.

[20]Letter, Campbell to the secretary of defense, May 2, 1957, ibid.

[21]Letter, McClellan to Wilson, August 15, 1957, ibid.; and notes of meeting, August 20, 1957, Morse, Notes of Meetings of the Accounting and Auditing Division Heads, 1957-1958.

[22]Brucker, memorandum to the chief of staff, Subject: General Accounting Office Expanded Audit Program, August 20, 1957, with attachment, "Guidelines Relative to General Accounting Office Comprehensive Audits," Morse Papers, Subject Files, Box 1, Subject: Access to Records, #1.

duct of our audits. . . . Requirements that clearances be obtained from the Secretary level prior to release of information are extremely time-consuming, and also result in awkward working relationships."[23] Robert Keller, assistant to the comptroller general, and Lawrence Powers, director of DAAD, in a meeting with congressional staff, explained that when DOD issued the 1953 directive, the provisions on access to classified information did not constitute a problem for GAO. But in later years, expansion of defense auditing had altered the situation; in 1957, 80 percent of DAAD's defense work was in sensitive areas of classified security information. DOD had not discussed the new directive with GAO before issuing it. Keller and Powers explained that GAO did not have serious problems with DOD at the time with access to classified matter. Nevertheless, the committee staffers concluded that the new DOD directive ought to be revised.[24]

William A. Newman, Jr., Director, Defense Accounting and Auditing Division (later the Defense Division), 1959-1968.

Subsequently Comptroller General Campbell wrote to the secretary of defense explaining the expanded volume of GAO defense auditing and requested that DOD amend Directive 5200.1 to provide GAO staff with "generally unrestricted access" to classified information. After receiving a copy of Campbell's letter, Rep. John A. Moss, chairman of the Government Information Subcommittee, wrote to Secretary of Defense Neil H. McElroy asking him to remove the access restrictions. Moss stated publicly that "when classified information is denied to GAO to the point where it cannot fulfill its statutory responsibility our tax dollars are being spent without one of the most effective checks Congress has on potential inefficiency and irresponsibility."[25] Defense's response noted that GAO had agreed to the wording of the 1953 access restrictions and that DOD had had

---

[23]Memorandum, Newman to Owen A. Kane, legislative attorney, October 1957, B-107366, #1.

[24]Keller, memorandum for congressional contact file, October 10, 1957, ibid.

[25]Letter, Campbell to the secretary of defense, November 20, 1957, B-134192; letter, Campbell to Moss, November 20, 1957, ibid.; clipping, *Washington Evening Star*, December 12, 1957, Morse Papers, Subject Files, Box 1, Subject: Access to Records, #1.

no formal request for reconsideration of the 1957 directive until Campbell's November 1957 letter. DOD was now studying Campbell's request.[26]

In the meantime, Rep. William L. Dawson (D—Illinois), head of the House Government Operations Committee, informed the chairs of all House committees and subcommittees about GAO's problem of access to classified DOD documents.[27] After further prodding by Campbell, the Defense Department in March 1958 developed two documents—a draft directive on access to unclassified information and a revision to Directive 5200.1 on access to classified information. After making minor suggestions for revision, Campbell stated that the draft documents were satisfactory but added that if the procedures proved unworkable, GAO would insist that they be reconsidered.[28]

Although Campbell appeared willing at this point to accept the DOD directive, congressional sources, including Moss and Rep. F. Edward Hebert (D—Louisiana), chairman of the Subcommittee for Special Investigations of the House Armed Services Committee, were not. Moss emphasized that GAO was an arm of Congress, independent of the executive branch, and that the executive branch had no authority to restrict GAO's functions and activities.[29] In the meantime, GAO experienced some problems in getting access to classified information. In March 1958, GAO's European Branch requested access to a logistics section of a USAREUR (U.S. Army, Europe) plan and a USAREUR supply operations report prepared by the Operations Research Office of the Johns Hopkins University. The Army declined access to these documents, stating that the top secret logistics report did not fall into the Army's definition of "need to know" and that the Johns Hopkins report was an internal study that did not establish USAREUR policy. After Assistant Comptroller General Weitzel wrote to the secretary of the army requesting access to these documents, the Army agreed to provide them to the European Branch.[30]

---

[26]Letter, Deputy Assistant Secretary of Defense (Manpower, Personnel, and Reserves) Stephen S. Jackson to Moss, January 8, 1958, ibid.

[27]Letter, Dawson to colleagues, January 14, 1958, and Kane, memorandum for the congressional contact file, February 5, 1958, both in ibid.

[28]Letter, Campbell to the secretary of defense, March 3, 1958, ibid.; and letter, Wilfred J. McNeil (assistant secretary of defense (controller) to Campbell, March 14, 1958, and letter, Campbell to McNeil, March 21, 1958, both in B-107366, #1.

[29]Letter, Hebert to Campbell, March 28, 1958, and letter, Moss to Campbell, March 31, 1958, both in ibid.

[30]Letter, Weitzel to the secretary of the army, April 8, 1958, and letter, Robert Dechert (general counsel, DOD) to the comptroller general, April 11, 1958, both in ibid. See also letter, Campbell to Moss, April 18, 1958, Morse Papers, Subject Files, Box 1, Subject: Access to Records, #1. This six-page letter summarizes instances of GAO access-to-records problems from 1956 to 1958.

After two congressional hearings and a long round of meetings between April and July 1958 involving representatives from GAO, DOD, and the Moss and Hebert subcommittees,[31] DOD issued Directive 7650.1 and a change to Directive 5200.1 on July 9, 1958. The change to 5200.1 was minor and was not a subject of contention. But 7650.1, pertaining to GAO comprehensive audits in DOD, was unsatisfactory to GAO. Campbell informed Hebert that the problem was two paragraphs in the directive that "in substance provide that the reports of the Inspector General and any information on which a question exists as to being furnished to a member or committee of Congress shall not be furnished except upon the approval of the appropriate departmental secretary." Campbell told Hebert that "these restrictions could seriously hamper the General Accounting Office in performing its statutory responsibilities and will impede the performance of our work." Campbell indicated that GAO would report any future problems of access to records to the House Armed Services Committee and other appropriate committees.[32]

In subsequent years, GAO continued to have problems with DOD regarding access. Keller, testifying before a Senate subcommittee in March 1959, listed three particular problem areas: (1) information on procurement and other internal files containing materials used in making decisions; (2) information in internal reviews, such as staff studies, providing a basis for supply, logistics, and financial management determinations; and (3) information about operations and program execution in departmental inspections, surveys, and examinations. Keller concluded that withholding information "permits concealment of adverse conditions by those basically responsible. It also permits delay and laxity in accomplishing improvements. . . . At the very least these practices . . . result in greatly increased costs of external reviews representing an unjustifiable waste of the taxpayer's money."[33] Testifying the next month, Campbell said that GAO's access-to-records problems principally were with the armed services and the International Cooperation Administration (ICA), which denied access to evaluation reports on assistance programs to several foreign countries, including Taiwan, Laos, Pakistan, India, Bolivia, Brazil, and Guatemala.[34]

---

[31]Documents supporting this statement are in B-107366, #1.

[32]Letter, Campbell to Hebert, July 25, 1958; and letter, McNeil to the comptroller general, July 22, 1958, (transmitting copies of DOD Directive 7650.1 and change 3 to DOD Directive 5200.1, July 9, 1958), both in ibid.

[33]Keller testimony before the Subcommittee on Constitutional Rights, Senate Judiciary Committee, March 13, 1959, Morse Papers, Subject Files, Box 1, Subject: Access to Records, #4.

[34]Testimony of Campbell et al., April 15, 1959, *Independent Offices Appropriations for 1960*, pt. 2, 1045-53.

Congress reflected its concern about access in the terms of two laws—the Mutual Security Act of 1959 and the Mutual Security Appropriations Act of 1960—that required that information on foreign aid programs be made available to GAO and congressional committees. In commenting on these laws, Campbell observed that they did not solve completely GAO's access-to-records problem but that they showed "a clear intention on the part of the Congress toward achieving the full exercise of its constitutional control of the public monies."[35]

During this period, President Dwight D. Eisenhower came under press criticism for his apparent support of DOD's and ICA's withholding of records from GAO. Eisenhower was visibly annoyed when asked at a press conference in July 1959 about the use of executive privilege by government agencies to deny access to information to GAO. Sen. Michael J. Mansfield (D—Montana) entered into the *Congressional Record* a *Wall Street Journal* editorial on the matter; the *Journal* suggested that if Eisenhower looked into the extent of secrecy in the executive branch, "we have an idea the President would be far more angered at some of his own bureaucrats than at the reporter who brought the secrecy to his attention."[36]

While GAO debated access problems with the Office of the Secretary of Defense, it experienced concurrent difficulties with the Air Force. In June 1958, GAO requested a copy of the Air Force inspector general's (IG) report entitled *Survey of Management of the Ballistic Missiles Program*. Secretary of the Air Force James H. Douglas denied the request, stating that IG reports were exclusively for the use of Air Force officials and that release of the report would have an adverse impact on effective administration of the department. Campbell reported the matter to Representative Hebert and sent copies of his letter to several other House and Senate committee chairs, arguing that the Air Force position violated the Budget and Accounting Act, 1921, and, by preventing review of Air Force actions, delayed improvements and made possible the waste of taxpayers' money.[37] Chairman Moss of the House Government Information Subcommittee told Campbell that his committee would fully support his position.[38]

In the meantime, Secretary Douglas gave Campbell a statement of facts from the Air Force IG's report on management of the ballistic missiles program but

---

[35]*Annual Report of the Comptroller General of the United States for the Fiscal Year Ending June 30, 1959* (Washington: GPO, 1959), 12-13.

[36]Clipping from *Congressional Record*, July 17, 1959, A6904, extension of Mansfield remarks, including editorial in *Wall Street Journal*, July 17, 1959, GAO History Program Archives.

[37]Letter, Secretary of the Air Force James H. Douglas to the comptroller general, July 30, 1958, Morse Papers, Subject Files, Box 1, Subject: Access to Records, #2; and letter, Campbell to Hebert, September 10, 1958, B-107366, #1. In this letter, Campbell refers to his letter to Douglas of June 13, 1958, and Douglas's reply of July 30, 1958.

[38]Letters, Moss to Campbell, September 23 and October 20, 1958, ibid.

omitted sections on opinions, conclusions, and recommendations for the same reasons given in his initial refusal to release the report. Campbell declared this response unsatisfactory and repeated his request for the entire report.[39]

When Campbell testified before the House Government Information Subcommittee in November 1958, he summarized the broad problem of access with DOD dating back to 1956, as well as the current problem with the Air Force. He again contended that the Air Force action violated the Budget and Accounting Act, preventing GAO from "a proper discharge of our statutory responsibilities."[40] President Eisenhower publicly backed the position presented by the Air Force in the hearings. He wrote to a member of Congress, as reported in the press, that "the public interest is not necessarily served by divulging the advice, suggestions, or recommendations which subordinate employees periodically make to their superiors." The *Washington Post* concluded that the controversy involved the separation of powers between the executive and legislative branches.[41] The two sides in this dispute were at an impasse, and the problem was not settled at the time.

GAO's problems of access to records of DOD and other agencies, including the Department of State, were not resolved during the Campbell period. In 1965, before Campbell left office, GAO issued instructions to its divisions that information on serious access problems should be mentioned in reports to Congress and agencies.[42]

Besides experiencing access problems with the armed services, GAO had some with private corporations doing defense contract work. An example was the refusal of the General Motors Corporation, Cadillac Cleveland Ordnance Plant, to grant access to records on uncompleted contracts and subcontracts. The firm contended that GAO had the right of access only to completed contracts, citing as its source Public Law 82-245 (approved October 31, 1951). Campbell argued that the law authorized GAO access to contractor records from the time of contract negotiation until three years after completion.[43] In view of Campbell's demand for access to these records and pressure exerted by Representative Hebert, General Motors conceded the issue. While standing by its arguments against

---

[39]Letter, Douglas to the comptroller general, October 30, 1958, and letter, Campbell to the secretary of the Air Force, November 7, 1958, both in ibid.

[40]Campbell's printed statement, testimony of November 12, 1958, ibid. See also clipping, *Washington Post*, November 13, 1958, Morse Papers, Subject Files, Box 1, Subject: Access to Records, #2.

[41]Clipping, *Washington Post*, November 14, 1958, ibid. A summary of the Air Force testimony is in M. J. Nevins, GAO assistant general counsel, memorandum for congressional contact file, November 14, 1958, B-107366, #1.

[42]Entry for May 12, 1965, Morse, *Daily Notes*, 1965-1966.

[43]Letter, Campbell to Harlow H. Curtice, president, General Motors Corporation, April 26, 1957, Morse Papers, Subject Files, Box 1, Subject: Access to Records, #1.

access, the company agreed to grant GAO auditors access to the records at the Cadillac Cleveland Ordnance Plant.[44]

Another case involved the refusal of the Hewlett-Packard Company to grant access to cost records on several Air Force contracts to representatives of the San Francisco Regional Office. Hewlett-Packard contended that cost data were not pertinent because costs had not been a factor in contract negotiation and that only price analysis was necessary in contract audits.[45] Rep. Charles S. Gubser (R—California), defending the position of Hewlett-Packard, located in his district, brought the matter to the attention of the Special Investigations Subcommittee, House Armed Services Committee.[46]

The Hewlett-Packard access matter eventually went to the courts. After Campbell retired, a U.S. district court ruled in March 1966 in favor of GAO, stating that the law governing access to contractor records allowed examination of production cost records, even though such costs had not been considered in contract negotiation. A U.S. Court of Appeals upheld this decision in 1967, and early in 1968, the Supreme Court denied certiorari, thus affirming the lower court ruling.[47]

The European Branch

Most of the work of GAO's overseas branches involved defense and foreign relations issues. The European Branch (EB), set up in Paris in August 1952 with later-established suboffices in London, Rome, Frankfurt, and Madrid, was the first permanent GAO force stationed overseas. Its original jurisdiction included all of Europe, the Near East, and North Africa; later its area extended to all of Africa plus India and Pakistan.[48] Between 1955 and 1963, the European Branch reported to Assistant Comptroller General Frank Weitzel. The European Branch

[44]Press Release, Hebert, July 29, 1957, and letter, Henry H. Hogan, general counsel, General Motors Corporation, to Campbell, July 25, 1957, both in ibid.

[45]Letter, W. F. Cavier, vice president-finance, Hewlett-Packard Company, Palo Alto, CA, to Alfred M. Clavelli, GAO regional manager, San Francisco, November 21, 1962, and memo, Clavelli to Hassell B. Bell, associate director, DAAD, December 3, 1962, both in Morse Papers, Subject Files, Box 1, Subject: Access to Records, #7. See also letter, Campbell to the chairman, Subcommittee for Special Investigations, House Armed Services Committee, January 16, 1963, ibid. In response to the subcommittee's inquiry, Campbell provided a detailed explanation of both the Hewlett-Packard and GAO arguments regarding the matter.

[46]Bell, memorandum for the congressional contact file, January 17, 1963, reporting on a meeting involving himself, Campbell, and Keller with Representative Gubser, ibid.

[47]*Hewlett-Packard Company v. the United States*, 385 F.2d 1013 (1967).

[48]See Charles E. Hughes, "The Overseas Offices of the General Accounting Office," *GAO Review* (summer 1971): 136-143; Charles D. Hylander, "Overseas Activities of the General Accounting Office,", *GAO Review* (fall 1966): 15-20; and "The European Branch: GAO in the Center of the Old World," *GAO Review* (fall 1982): 33-40. See also chapter 14, pp. 362-64.

had 50 staff on June 30, 1955; 49 on June 30, 1959; 61 on June 30, 1963; and 37 on June 30, 1965.[49]

During the early years of operations, the branch gave special attention to offshore procurement under the mutual defense assistance program and to military supply activities. For example, GAO, in 1957 testimony, summarized its findings and accomplishments in two European procurement cases. In one case, the Army changed a contract for ammunition to be delivered in metal boxes to allow delivery in wooden containers. In negotiations with the contractor, Army officials stated that a $50,000 reduction in the contract price would be acceptable, but GAO recommended not settling until an audit of the contractor's records determined the actual savings to the firm because of the packaging change. After an audit by the Army Audit Agency, a contract amendment reduced the Army's cost by $100,000. The second case involved an Air Force contract in Germany for document reproduction services that had been renewed for several years at prices based on the contractor's original offer. GAO recommended that new bids be solicited; the result was awarding of a contract at a lower price to the services, saving an estimated $52,500 in the first year.[50]

As early as 1955, there were indications of concern within the House Government Operations Committee about the quality of work at the European Branch.[51] In 1957, a subcommittee of the House committee conducted a study of European Branch operations. One reason the subcommittee undertook the study was that GAO had not issued any EB reports to Congress from the time the branch opened in August 1952 until the subcommittee began its study in 1957.[52] The subcommittee published its report, House Report No. 1281, in January 1958.

The report listed several objectives: (1) to review GAO activities in Europe, Africa, and the Near East "to ascertain the adequacy of its coverage of the multibillion dollar expenditure of the United States in that area"; (2) to review GAO methods and procedures in Europe; (3) to review all reports issued by EB to

---

[49]Table, Number of Employees, June 30, 1954 through June 30, 1965, GAO, *Annual Report, 1965*, 356. These statistics are in most cases lower than what GAO had reported in annual appropriations hearings. For example, while the table lists 49 staff in Europe on June 30, 1960, GAO officials testified in March 1960 that there were 58 staff in the branch. See testimony of Campbell et al., March 7, 1960, *Independent Offices Appropriations for 1961, pt. 2, 777.*

[50]Testimony of Campbell et al., February 26, 1957, *Independent Offices Appropriations for 1958*, pt. 2, 1949.

[51]Testimony of Campbell et al., February 22, 1955, *Independent Offices Appropriations for 1956*, Hearings before a Subcommittee of the House Committee on Appropriations, 84th Cong., 1st Sess., pt.1 (Washington: GPO, 1955), 794.

[52]Milton J. Socolar, who served as an auditor and later as a lawyer in the European Branch in the 1950s and again in the 1960s, noted that much of what the branch produced actually came out as reports from DAAD or CAAD. See Socolar interview, April 22, 1994 (draft of February 1995), GAO History Program Archives.

determine comprehensiveness of coverage and the accuracy and the significance of report findings; (4) to review selected programs on which the branch was conducting reviews or had issued reports; and (5) to review selected agencies to determine, independently of GAO work on them, the efficiency and the economy of their operations. To carry out these objectives, subcommittee staff and members reviewed reports and workpapers at the Paris office and GAO operations in U.S. programs in England, Germany, Italy, Turkey, Greece, Pakistan, Spain, the Netherlands, and Belgium. In addition, the group held hearings in Paris, Bonn, London, Heidelberg, Wiesbaden, and Rome and an open briefing in Madrid.[53]

In its survey in Europe, the subcommittee looked at organization of the branch, its use of the comprehensive audit, the number and the disposition of reports, access to records, and security classification of reports. The subcommittee also studied several program areas—military assistance, procurement, construction, and military supply operations. House Report 1281 stated that the European Branch had functioned well and had an impressive record of accomplishments.[54] But it questioned whether the branch's staff, then numbering 52, was enough to provide timely coverage of U.S. programs in Europe. It noted the frequent considerable lapse of time between assignment starts and report or action completion.[55] The report questioned the comprehensiveness of the comprehensive audit in Europe; the branch, the subcommittee reported, reviewed specific phases of agency operations rather than undertaking a total agency review. The report also recommended that the comptroller general study the question of expanding the comprehensive audit.[56]

The House report concluded that "less than one-fourth of the reports [of EB] ... are of such significance that the findings and recommendations are brought to the attention of the department concerned or of the Congress." It stated that perhaps there was a proliferation of reports and again recommended that the comptroller general review the matter.[57] Working relationships between EB and U.S. agencies operating in its area were excellent, the report noted. EB had good access to records, with some significant exceptions. The subcommittee recommended that agencies restricting GAO access rescind orders or directives restricting access. The subcommittee described the Defense Department's prac-

---

[53]*Report on Review of General Accounting Office Operations in Europe and the Major Programs Covered by the General Accounting Office in the European Area*, Seventeenth Report by the Committee on Government Operations, H. Rept. 1281, 85th Cong., 2d Sess., January 16, 1958 (Washington: GPO, 1958), 1-2 (hereafter cited as *Review of GAO Operations in Europe*, H. Rept. 1281.

[54]Ibid., 3-13.

[55]Ibid., 3-4.

[56]Ibid., 4.

[57]Ibid., 4-6.

tice of classifying almost all EB reports as secret or top secret as "anomalous and indefensible" and said that it should be ended.[58]

Regarding specific EB program areas, the report summarized GAO's findings and made recommendations to the Departments of Defense and State relative to these findings. GAO had concluded that the amount of U.S. military assistance exceeded in some cases the recipient nations' capacity to use the funds effectively and that sometimes political and economic considerations influenced the types and the levels of aid. The subcommittee recommended that DOD review the military assistance program.[59] The offshore procurement program had been successful in providing a production base and improving economic conditions in European countries, but millions of dollars had been wasted in excess costs, poor contract administration, and laxity in protecting U.S. interests. House Report 1281 included several recommendations to DOD and the State Department on offshore procurement.[60]

The subcommittee's views on construction of bases and other installations in Europe with U.S. funds were quite critical. It noted that in England, where many such installations had been returned or were being returned to the British government, there had been no negotiations on an agreement for compensation to the United States for facilities and equipment being left behind.[61] The subcommittee also studied EB's work on Spanish base construction, one of the branch's early big jobs. GAO had raised serious questions about the decision to locate the Torrejon Air Base near Madrid. Another base, at Moron, had originally been slated to be an Air Force supply depot. The Air Force had changed its plans after the project began, deciding to use the base for a hospital and a pipeline control station for petroleum and lubricants. EB concluded that these facilities could have been located at nearby installations, thus saving the United States millions of dollars.[62]

The subcommittee found "that the deplorable conditions previously reported . . . still exist" in military supply operations in Europe. The Air Force and Army planned to cut supply depot operations in Europe by supplying units in the field directly from depots in the United States. Without proper safeguards, the subcommittee concluded, "these base stocks may well assume the proportions of small depots and thereby compound the problems sought to be eliminated."[63]

---

[58]Ibid., 5-6.
[59]Ibid., 7-10.
[60]Ibid., 10-12.
[61]Ibid., 12.
[62]Ibid., 44-46.
[63]Ibid., 13.

Campbell responded to the subcommittee's report in mid-April 1958. He concluded that the present staff of 54 was satisfactory. He stated that the branch's future workload might decline because of ongoing reductions in offshore procurement and progress already made in GAO reviews of the military assistance program.[64] He concluded also that EB's approach to the comprehensive audit was consistent with its use in other GAO audit areas.[65] As for the limited flow of reports, Campbell explained that decisions on sending reports to Congress depended on significance of findings. He also pointed out that many of the 462 EB reports the subcommittee mentioned were not really reports—some were information documents used internally by GAO. Campbell added that GAO would begin to provide to Congress a monthly list of EB reports after April 30, 1958.[66] On the access issue, Campbell said that GAO had been working with DOD on the matter and that directives had been drafted.[67]

House Report 1281 was not a long-range problem for GAO, but it generated considerable internal discussion of the branch's operations, reporting policy, and number and disposition of reports. The report language was not overly critical and in fact provided a broad rationale for EB's continuation. Campbell obviously gave much thought to the branch's organization and activities in future years. Morse reported in 1959 that Campbell "generally thinks the Branch has been ballooned way out of its importance." He raised questions about the suboffices in Rome and Madrid, which by this time were being phased out, and thought that having even three staff in London was questionable. Campbell thought that maintaining two offices in Europe, in Paris and Frankfurt, each eventually with its own manager, might be a suitable arrangement.[68]

In late 1960, the State Department suggested that GAO move its European headquarters from Paris to Frankfurt. State said that it was concerned about "the inimical effects on Franco-American relations of the unduly large American official colony in Paris and has recognized the pressing need to limit United States Government representation there to the minimum necessary for the official conduct of our bilateral responsibilities."[69] The increasing difficulties between the United States and France after Charles de Gaulle's

---

[64]Memorandum, Campbell to William L. Dawson, chairman, House Government Operations Committee, April 14, 1958, 1-3, B-125299. This document includes a one-page transmittal letter and a 14-page report providing the comptroller general's comments on House Report 1281. The page numbers refer to the 14-page report.

[65]Ibid., 4-5.

[66]Ibid., 6-8.

[67]*Review of GAO Operations in Europe*, 9-14, H. Rept. 1281.

[68]Entry for January 26, 1959, Morse, *Daily Notes*, 1959-1960.

[69]Letter, Lane Dwinell, assistant secretary of state, to Campbell, December 22, 1960, B-107366, #2.

return to the French presidency in 1958 probably conditioned the department's views, although the department did not mention this.

Campbell informed the department that GAO preferred to retain EB in Paris, still the center of much of its work.[70] In July 1964, the European Branch did move to Frankfurt and GAO closed the Paris office. The difficulty of maintaining suitable office space in Paris and continued problems between the United States and de Gaulle's government explain this move.[71]

Throughout the Campbell period, most EB work concentrated on military spending; in February 1962, GAO estimated that 90 percent of the branch's workload concerned reviews of the activities of DOD and the separate military departments. GAO testified that the European Branch "continued to find millions of dollars of equipment programed and delivered under the military assistance program where no valid requirements existed. This deficiency stems primarily from a failure by responsible [U.S.] military officials to adequately monitor the program."

In Turkey, there were serious spare parts deficiencies in the Turkish Army and Air Force, long delays in disposal of excess property, inadequate controls over budgetary support funds supplied by the aid program, and delay in completion of an aircraft control and warning system. The problems in Greece were similar: unnecessary deliveries of supplies, failure to redistribute excess materials to other military assistance program countries where they were needed, excessive ordering of materials by the Greek armed forces, delivery of equipment without related materials needed for operational capability, and inadequate control by U.S. agencies over military budget support funds contributed to Greece.[72]

During fiscal year 1962, GAO sent six reports to Congress resulting from European Branch reviews. They covered the military assistance programs for Greece and Turkey; use of local currencies in Spain for U.S. administrative and contracting purposes; housing allowances for U.S. military personnel in France; requisition actions by the Ordnance Supply Management Agency, USAREUR; and signal supply operations, USAREUR.[73] An example of nonmilitary work was a review of the adequacy of fiscal controls and administrative practices at U.S. embassies and consulates in Germany, Italy, and the United

---

[70]Letter, Campbell to the secretary of state, May 17, 1961, ibid.

[71]"The European Branch: GAO in the Center of the Old World," 33; and Hughes, "The Overseas Offices of the General Accounting Office," 139-40.

[72]Campbell's printed statement, testimony of February 9, 1962, *Independent Offices Appropriations for 1963*, pt. 2, 46-47.

[73]Testimony of Campbell et al., February 25, 1963, *Independent Offices Appropriations for 1964*, pt. 2, 205.

Kingdom. GAO found that local currency balances maintained by the embassies in Bonn, Rome, and London were not earning maximum interest rates. As a result of GAO's review, the London embassy moved $16.5 million sterling from non-interest-bearing accounts with the Bank of England to interest-bearing accounts with U.S. banks in London. Within six months of this transfer, the funds earned more than $166,000 in interest.[74]

Until 1963, EB reported to Assistant Comptroller General Weitzel, while the Far East Branch, established in 1956,[75] was under DAAD's jurisdiction. Campbell explained in a 1960 hearing that practically all the Far East work was defense-related, while the European office also covered State Department and other civil programs. He added that when EB began operations in 1952, it was an innovation and required high-level supervision from Washington headquarters.[76]

William Newman, DAAD's director, was uncomfortable with his lack of control over the European Branch. He complained in 1961 about the quality and the usefulness of some EB reports and about the fact that he did not control its work assignments. Subsequently, on Ellsworth Morse's suggestion, Newman met with Weitzel to plan for more rigid Washington control over EB's work program and plans. Weitzel agreed to the changes, but he retained responsibility for the branch's operations. A few months later, when Campbell appointed a new director of the European Branch, Newman was unhappy because that person had not come from DAAD.[77]

The Far East Branch

GAO had considered establishing branches in both Europe and the Far East in 1952. A GAO team consisting of Donald Bacon and E. P. Schaffer, Division of Audits; J. E. Welch, Office of General the Counsel; and Irving Zuckerman, Accounting Systems Division, conducted a survey beginning in May 1952 to determine the extent of U.S. government fiscal activities in the Far East and the need for a GAO office in the region. One or more members of the survey team visited Japan, Korea, Okinawa, Formosa, the Philippines, Guam, Hong Kong, Indochina, Thailand, Burma, India, and Pakistan. In their report to Comptroller General Warren on the Far East survey, Zuckerman and Welch recommended creating a Far East branch in Tokyo or Yokohama, with a suboffice in Manila and perhaps another suboffice in Bangkok, Thailand, or New Delhi, India. Bacon and Schaffer sepa-

---

[74]Campbell's printed statement, March 15, 1961, *Independent Office Appropriations for 1962*, pt. 1, 356.

[75]See below, pp. 491-94.

[76]Campbell testimony, March 7, 1960, *Independent Offices Appropriations for 1961*, pt. 2, 748-49.

[77]Entries for April 7 and 21 and September 18, 1961, Morse, *Daily Notes*, 1961-1962.

rately recommended that GAO operate in the Far East, but for the time being on an itinerant basis.[78] Warren chose to follow the latter recommendation in 1952, about the same time he decided to create the European Branch.

The need for a Far East office became increasingly clear in the next few years, and as in the case of Europe in 1952, there was congressional pressure to establish a presence there. In January 1954, Rep. Charles B. Brownson (R—Indiana), chairman of the International Operations Subcommittee of the House Government Operations Committee, wrote to Comptroller General Warren about recent subcommittee investigations on embassy housing construction costs in Tokyo, "where there is a real question as to whether or not the United States obtained value received for dollars spent." Brownson said that he was acquainted with EB's work and was surprised to learn that GAO had no auditors in place in the Far East. Warren responded that there were certain matters GAO wanted to look into in the Far East and that he would send four investigators there for six to eight months; they would examine the matter Brownson had written about if time permitted, he said.[79]

Warren left office shortly after this exchange, but the team did go to the Far East as promised. At a hearing in February 1956, Rep. Albert Thomas asked Campbell about the prospects of GAO's opening a Far East office, given the fact that the United States annually spent at least $3 billion in the Pacific area. Campbell explained that GAO, before he entered office, had decided that the best approach was to send teams to the Far East rather than to establish a formal office, but he was inclined to favor a permanent staff, preferably in Tokyo.[80] After considerable internal discussion, Campbell decided in June 1956 to create a Far East Branch (FEB) in Tokyo as part of DAAD.[81] The branch's work area included Japan, Formosa, the Philippines, the Mariana Islands, Cambodia, Laos, Vietnam, Thailand, and Pakistan.[82] Robert F. Brandt was the first director of the Far East Branch.

---

[78]Irving Zuckerman and J. E. Welch to the comptroller general, "Report on Far East Survey," undated but clearly late summer or fall 1952, GAO Records.

[79]Letter, Brownson to Warren, January 25, 1954, and letter, Warren to Brownson, February 5, 1954, both in B-118460.

[80]Campbell testimony, February 10, 1956, *Independent Offices Appropriations for 1957*, Hearing before a Subcommittee of the House Committee on Appropriations, 84th Cong., 2d Sess., pt.2 (Washington: GPO, 1956), 1356-57.

[81]Comptroller General's Order 2.35, June 14, 1956, GAO Records; entries for April 16 and 19, May 15 and 28, and August 23, 1956, Morse, *Daily Notes*, 1956. See also memo, J. M. Sullivan to Karney Brasfield, February 17, 1956, "GAO Audit of Far East Activities," and memo, Lawrence J. Powers (DAAD director) to the comptroller general, May 25, 1956, both in GAO Records. Both these documents recommended creating a Far East branch.

[82]GAO, *Annual Report, 1956*, 4.

The branch was slow in starting substantive operations because of the need to recruit qualified staff from elsewhere in GAO. On December 31, 1956, the branch had 10 staff—the director, six accountants, two investigators, and an attorney-advisor. A year later, the branch had 13 staff.[83] In February 1957, Campbell explained that FEB's work would focus mainly on the military area, specifically review and examination of the military assistance program, procurement by the military services in Japan, inventory and supply management, and obligating practices of the military departments. In his brief history of FEB written in 1959, Brandt confirmed that the branch's two most significant work areas between 1956 and 1959 were review of Army and Air Force supply management practices and procedures in Japan, Korea, Okinawa, Guam, and the Philippines and a comprehensive examination of the military assistance program in Japan, Korea, Taiwan, Vietnam, Cambodia, and Laos.[84]

Although DAAD looked into the possibility of creating a suboffice of FEB in Honolulu in 1957, that was not done, and for the time being, GAO work out of Honolulu was the responsibility of the San Francisco Regional Office, which maintained a small staff there and sent others on a temporary duty basis.[85] The staff of FEB during Campbell's term reached a high of 35 on June 30, 1963, and then declined, reflecting general cuts in the GAO staff, to 19 two years later.[86] Given the enormous geographical area covered by the branch, the staff traveled widely by air, by Campbell's count about 50 percent of the time. Although they received the same pay as their colleagues in the United States, they did get quarters or allowances to live on military posts.[87]

In his branch history, Brandt listed 36 draft reports prepared by FEB by June 30, 1959, most of them concerned with supply management and military assistance.[88] During fiscal year 1962, GAO provided six reports to Congress resulting from reviews made by FEB. They covered Army equipment maintenance and supply support furnished under the military assistance program to Far East nations; stock and related consumer funds to purchase repair parts and other mate-

---

[83]Robert F. Brandt, "A Brief History of the Far East Branch, United States General Accounting Office, for the three years ended June 30, 1959," 2, GAO Records; and table, Number of Employees, June 30, 1954 through June 30, 1965, in GAO, *Annual Report, 1965*, 356.

[84]Testimony of Campbell et al., February 26, 1957, *Independent Offices Appropriations for 1958*, pt. 2, 1929-30; and Brandt, "A Brief History of the Far East Branch," 2-3.

[85]Notes of meeting of April 16, 1957, Morse, Notes of Meeting of the Accounting and Auditing Division Heads, September 1956 through June 1957; and GAO, *The San Francisco Regional Office, 1954-1987: Interview with Harold J. D'Ambrogia, Kenneth A. Pollock, Richard A. Sheldon, and Charles F. Vincent*, GAO History Program, Oral History Series, GAO/OP-20-OH (Washington: 1991), 24-27.

[86]Table, Number of Employees, June 30, 1954 through June 30, 1965, GAO, *Annual Report, 1965*, 356.

[87]Campbell testimony, February 9, 1962, *Independent Offices Appropriations for 1963*, pt. 2, 48.

[88]Brandt, "A Brief History of the Far East Branch," appendix.

rials from the stock fund inventories in the 8th U.S. Army, Korea; central rebuilding of World War II vehicles and assemblies under the military assistance program in the Pacific Area Command; management of spare parts for Army equipment provided to Far East countries; repair parts supply for ordnance tank-automobile vehicles, 8th U.S. Army, Korea; and examination of the economic and technical assistance program for Korea.[89]

Given the expanding activities of the United States in South Vietnam during these years, the volume of FEB work there expanded greatly. An example was the extensive work on the U.S. foreign aid program in Vietnam done by the branch between 1962 and 1964.[90]

Establishment of the International Operations Division

Reflecting the importance of GAO's overseas work, especially its emphasis on defense and foreign assistance activities, Campbell established the International Operations Division (IOD), effective August 19, 1963, and appointed Oye V. Stovall as its first director. The new organization grew out of discussions Campbell initiated in 1962 about the possibility of placing responsibility for reviews of foreign assistance programs in one GAO group.[91] There also is evidence that differences between CAAD and DAAD about overseas audit jurisdictions influenced Campbell. CAAD thought that it should be responsible for economic aid, a civil activity, whereas DAAD thought that it should do country reviews covering both economic and military programs. These differences of opinion came to Campbell's attention. He settled the problem by creating the new division to handle all international activities. Newman, DAAD's director, reportedly was very disappointed because his division lost jurisdiction over FEB and overseas defense work as well as the military assistance program.[92]

IOD was to carry out GAO's accounting, auditing, and investigative functions related to U.S. government programs and activities in foreign nations, in both the military and civil areas. The division's mandate extended to the programs of the Department of State, including the Agency for International Development; the Peace Corps; the Department of Defense; the Export-Im-

---

[89]Campbell's printed statement, testimony of February 25, 1963, *Independent Offices Appropriations for 1964*, pt. 2, 208.

[90]Entry for July 8, 1964, Morse, *Daily Notes*, 1963-1964. After Campbell left office, GAO created an office under FEB in Saigon, Vietnam, in 1966. See Roger R. Trask, *GAO History, 1921-1961* (Washington: GAO, 1991), 84.

[91]Entries for March 22 and 28, 1962, Morse, *Daily Notes*, 1961-1962.

[92]This explanation of IOD's origins is put forward by James A. Duff and J. Kenneth Fasick in GAO, *International Activities, 1956-1981: Interview with James A. Duff, J. Kenneth Fasick, and Charles D. Hylander*, GAO History Program, Oral History Series, GAO/OP-19-OH (Washington: GAO, 1991), 7. This oral history covers both the origins and the history of IOD, later renamed the International Division.

port Bank; the United States Information Agency; the international programs of the Department of Commerce; the foreign functions of the Department of Agriculture; and the international finance functions of the Treasury Department. Campbell transferred the European and Far East Branches to IOD and directed CAAD and DAAD to provide appropriate staff to the division.[93]

After IOD began its work, there were still jurisdictional differences between it and other divisions. Late in 1963, Adolph Samuelson, the CAAD director, indicated his opposition to both IOD and CAAD working in the agriculture area; he thought that if IOD had overseas work in agriculture, it should be done for IOD by a CAAD group on an assist basis. Eventually, Campbell, Morse, Samuelson, and Stovall agreed that IOD should do overseas agriculture work.[94]

In 1964, DAAD developed plans for a preliminary survey of military pay and allowance matters in Europe. DAAD's Navy Group in Washington would direct the project and would use staff from the military audit groups in regional offices to do the survey and review work in Europe. Campbell gave preliminary approval of the project after Newman had proposed it to him. Morse discussed the proposal with Campbell, noting that it violated the comptroller general's order establishing IOD. Campbell told Morse that he thought that Newman had coordinated the matter with Stovall. Morse noted, "I pointed out that it was my understanding that most of this coordination was a matter of Mr. Newman telling Mr. Stovall what he intended to do." Stovall then

Oye V. Stovall, Director, International Division, 1963-1973.

prepared an instruction to the divisions, signed by Campbell, which repeated

---

[93]Memorandum, Campbell to heads of divisions and offices, July 19,1963, filed in Morse, *Daily Notes*, 1963-1964. See also GAO, *Annual Report*. 1964. 205.

[94]Entry for November 13, 1963, Morse, *Daily Notes*, 1963-1964.

the earlier order assigning work abroad to IOD and indicated how such work would be accomplished.[95]

By the end of Campbell's term in 1965, GAO had broadly extended its overseas activities, centered in the European and Far East Branches. The increasing volume of foreign work, generated by programs of the Defense and State Departments and other agencies with overseas interests, explains the increased activity. The establishment of IOD in 1963 provided for unity and coordination of overseas work. The role that Congress played in the creation of both the European and Far East Branches indicated its great interest in this aspect of GAO's audit programs. The tremendous amounts of money spent by the United States on international programs obviously convinced Congress of the need for GAO review of these programs.

---

[95]Entries for February 17 and 20, 1964, ibid.

CHAPTER 20

Defense Contract Audits and the
Holifield Hearings, 1965

As the term of Comptroller General Joseph Campbell progressed, the General Accounting Office (GAO) concentrated more and more on auditing defense contracts, using both contractor and Department of Defense (DOD) records. A 1951 law had authorized GAO to examine the records of companies awarded negotiated defense contracts.[1] During Comptroller General Lindsay C. Warren's term, given the expanded military effort during the Korean conflict and continued emphasis on defense thereafter, the volume of defense audit work had increased significantly.[2] Campbell's emphasis on the financial benefits of GAO's audit work resulted in expanded attention to the fruitful field of government contracting, especially in the defense area. The Truth in Negotiations Act (1962), based to a significant extent on GAO disclosure of problems, tightened up contracting rules and procedures and gave GAO a clearer basis for scrutinizing and criticizing defense contracts. Most contracts by 1960 were either negotiated agreements determined by calculations of contractor costs plus a fixed fee or negotiated agreements including a fixed price. A third type of contract, based on open advertisement for bids and competitive bidding, had been common until World War II but thereafter was used much less than negotiated contracts, especially in the defense area.[3]

The Truth in Negotiations Act required advertisement of proposed contract projects and competitive bidding, except for certain specified exemptions, and required contractors involved in negotiated contracts to certify that "the cost or pricing data . . . submitted was accurate, current, and complete." The government had authority to recover contractor overcharges resulting from cost data that did not meet these standards.[4] In his 1962

---

[1]Public Law 82-245, 65 Stat. 700, approved October 31, 1951.
[2]See chapter 15, pp. 376-81.
[3]Frederick C. Mosher, *The GAO: The Quest for Accountability in American Government* (Boulder, CO: Westview Press, 1979), 152 (hereafter referred to as Mosher, *GAO.*)
[4]Public Law 87-653, 76 Stat. 528, approved September 10, 1962.

annual report, Campbell spelled out the important features of the law: It required more use of formal competitive bidding in the contracting process, more precise written justification for negotiated contracts, and more competition on negotiated government purchasing.[5]

As defense contract audits increased under Campbell, GAO periodically wrestled with the question of whether to include in contract audit reports the names and the locations of involved contractors and subcontractors and government contracting officials. Gradually, especially after 1960, GAO became more specific about those persons it considered responsible for overcharges, excessive profits, and other problems in defense contracts. Pressure from the press and congressional sources contributed to this trend. In 1959, for example, a representative of the Gannett newspapers suggested to Ellsworth Morse, the director of the Accounting and Auditing Policy Staff (AAPS), that GAO include in its reports the locations of mentioned contractors and subcontractors. The representative stated that it would be useful for his organization to know such locations when deciding which newspapers might be interested in particular reports. When Morse discussed this suggestion with Campbell, they agreed that it was a good idea. Morse then issued instructions to implement it.[6]

Early in 1961, Morse asked Campbell how he felt about including in reports the names of top officials responsible for problems. Campbell, according to Morse, "expressed wonderment" that GAO was not doing this but said that perhaps the exclusion of names was deliberate, enabling the Office to "stay out of personalities." Campbell suggested that he meet with Morse and other officials to discuss the matter.[7] Soon after this exchange, Rep. Charles R. Jonas (R—North Carolina) inquired in a House hearing, after Campbell referred to $46 million in unnecessary defense requisitions, whether GAO had identified the officers in the field responsible for the requisition orders. Campbell questioned whether placing all the blame on the field officers was proper. "I think it is very difficult for me," he said, "to justify pointing to a man way down the line. When we submit our report on the whole problem to the Department [of Defense], we might get what amounts to a whitewash right back from them in the form of a five or six page . . . letter. I have one right here, completely justifying all of the actions of the Department, and as far as it is concerned, we [GAO] are irresponsible. It follows that that is where the problem is—the unresponsiveness, sometimes,

[5]*Annual Report of the Comptroller General of the United States for the Fiscal Year Ended June 30, 1962* (Washington: GPO, 1962), 30.

[6]Memorandum for the file, discussion with Arthur Hermann of Gannett newspapers, May 22, 1959, and entry for May 27, 1959, both in Morse, *Daily Notes*, 1959-1960.

[7]Entry for February 9, 1961, Morse, *Daily Notes*, 1961-1962.

at the top levels." Morse noted that Jonas's remarks were very interesting in view of the fact that GAO was then beginning to put names of top officials responsible for problems in its reports.[8]

Adm. Hyman L. Rickover, the "father of the nuclear navy," played a notable role in GAO's increasingly common practice of naming names in reports. Rickover met with Campbell in August 1962 to discuss a recent GAO report on a Westinghouse Electric Company contract with the Navy for nuclear components. During this meeting, Rickover suggested several ways GAO could increase its effectiveness: broaden its recommendations to cover systems defects leading to problems rather than emphasizing recoveries or overpayments in particular cases, be specific about the persons involved, and concentrate more on important areas. Rickover also suggested that GAO include in its annual report the names of companies that had not agreed to refund overcharges. Campbell was receptive to Rickover's suggestions and directed Morse to work on means to implement them.[9]

Morse drafted a policy statement that Campbell issued in late November 1962. The statement did not require disclosing the names of individuals responsible for deficiencies but instructed GAO units to be able to provide this information when necessary. Campbell had reservations about identifying persons at lower levels who acted on orders from higher officials, but he did not prohibit publication of their names if it would help to correct deficiencies.[10]

At the same time GAO began to name names, the number of reports proliferated and their titles became more strident and provocative. Campbell included in his 1964 annual report an extensive table listing defense reports in which GAO charged "waste and mismanagement." Titles of cited reports included such expressions as "uneconomical use," "overprocurement," "noncompetitive procurement," "unnecessary costs," "illegal use," "excessive cost," "overcharges," "unsatisfactory condition," "overpricing,", "overestimated costs," "uneconomical replacement," "wasteful practices," "improper charges," "illegal award," and others. The table listed some civil agency security-related reports, on the Atomic Energy Commission (AEC) and the

---

[8]Jonas remarks and Campbell response during testimony of Campbell et al., March 15, 1961, *Independent Offices Appropriations for 1962*, Hearings before a Subcommittee of the House Committee on Appropriations, 87th Cong., 1st Sess., pt. 1 (Washington: GPO, 1961), 323-325; and entry for March 15, 1961, Morse, *Daily Notes*, 1961-1962.

[9]Morse memorandum, undated, summarizing the Campbell-Rickover meeting, filed between entries for September 4 and 5, 1962, and entry for September 5, 1962, both in Morse, *Daily Notes*, 1961-1962.

[10]Entries for October 31 and November 14, 21, and 27, 1962, ibid.

Comptroller General Campbell.

National Aeronautics and Space Administration (NASA), using similar terms, but the incidence for defense reports was much higher.[11]

GAO noted that it had submitted to Congress during fiscal year 1964 nine reports on "the effectiveness of the administrative controls exercised by the military departments to assure contractors' compliance with the terms and conditions of defense contracts" and that these reports "revealed weak-

---

[11]*Annual Report of the Comptroller General for the Fiscal Year Ended June 30, 1964*, (Washington: GPO, 1964), 341-55.

nesses which resulted in excessive costs or avoidable losses to the Government." Specific problems identified included interest-free contractor use of government funds through excessive progress payments, inapplicable costs charged to a contract, refunds not credited to a contract, acceptance of defective materials because of poor inspection procedures, use of uneconomical practices in furnishing supplies to contractors, unauthorized use by a contractor of materials acquired from a surplus parts dealer, and awarding of a contract for items the government already owned.[12]

While GAO accelerated the pace and increased the scope of defense contract audit reporting, the press frequently took note of increasing tension between the Office on the one hand and defense contracting officers and contractors on the other. In April 1960, the journal *Armed Forces Management* ran an article entitled "The GAO: What Price A Headline?" If military contracting officers and defense contractors could organize their own combat units, the article stated, the "next limited war would almost certainly break out somewhere in the vicinity of GAO headquarters at 441 G Street, N.W., in the District of Columbia." Contract negotiators did not like GAO and complained that the organization looked at extremes to "twist and puff them into something out of all relation to their original environment." "Such GAO shenanigans," the article concluded, "force thoughtful sideline observers to assume either (1) GAO has an appalling lack of knowledge about how defense contracting is handled—which seriously questions their credentials to do an audit of it; or (2) they are playing to the gallery rather than performing as their job description says they should."[13]

The *Saturday Evening Post* ran an editorial in 1961 generally favorable to GAO but did note that "opinion as to the services of GAO is not universally laudatory." The *Post* explained that defense manufacturers had complained that GAO's "meticulous attention to the precise terms of a contract" adversely affected the nation's defense posture and that the armed services thought that the Office's criticisms of military equipment purchases "take too little account of the emergency conditions under which this kind of material has to be purchased."[14]

---

[12]Ibid., 91.

[13]*Armed Forces Management* (April 1960), in clippings, CG [Campbell] 1954-1962, GAO History Program Archives.

[14]"One Federal Bureau Aims to Curb the Spenders," *Saturday Evening Post*, June 24, 1961, ibid.

Questions from Holifield and GAO's Response

The number of reports on defense contracts submitted to Congress increased rapidly—36 in fiscal year 1963, 48 in 1964, and 57 in 1965.[15] Hundreds of other reports, on contracts and other matters, went directly to DOD or to the military services. By 1964, objections to the volume and the tone of these reports by both DOD and defense contractors had reached a high level. They attracted the attention of Rep. Chet Holifield (D—California), the chairman of the Military Operations Subcommittee of the House Committee on Government Operations.

Holifield's personal motives in becoming involved in this matter are not clear. He represented a congressional district in the Los Angeles area. Although there was not much defense industry in his district, there were in California many defense and aerospace contractors whose concern about GAO audits may have reached him or at least his staff. Given his position as chairman of the Military Operations Subcommittee, Holifield perhaps heard complaints about GAO audits from sources in the Office of the Secretary of Defense or the military departments. Herbert Roback, who was the staff administrator of Holifield's subcommittee and who played a leading role in subsequent hearings, may have influenced Holifield. Perhaps House colleagues who represented districts with defense industries pressed him to take action.

Holifield's biographers, Richard W. Dyke and Francis X. Gannon, acknowledge that Holifield supported both the U.S. role in Vietnam during the 1960s and the Defense Department in general, as did Roback. But they say that Holifield's criticism of GAO defense contract audits can be explained best by his commitment to civil liberties. Holifield thought, his biographers argue, that by publicizing the names of individuals and companies alleged to have done wrong, GAO was endangering their individual rights. Dyke and Gannon state that suggestions, including some from other members of Congress, that he was attacking GAO on behalf of California defense and aerospace interests, angered Holifield a great deal.[16]

On October 5, 1964, Holifield wrote to Campbell about GAO defense contract audits and the role GAO played in contractor overcharge cases and in cases referred to the Department of Justice. This letter began the chain of

---

[15]Campbell reported slightly higher numbers subsequently—41 for 1963 and 52 for 1964. See letter, Campbell to Rep. Chet E. Holifield, March 11, 1965, B-155327, #1.

[16]Richard W. Dyke and Francis X. Gannon, *Chet Holifield: Master Legislator and Nuclear Statesman* (Lanham, MD: University Press of America, 1996), 139-140.

events leading to hearings before Holifield's subcommittee in May 1965. Holifield discussed specifically two Westinghouse cases involving Navy claims against the company for $2,241,000 (by later Navy calculations, $2,930,195) and $1,066,000. These claims grew out of fixed-price contracts for nuclear components under a prime contract awarded in October 1956 and on which GAO had reported. Westinghouse contended, according to Holifield, that improper procedures had led to disallowance of these charges and that GAO and the Justice Department had made "extralegal intrusions upon an administrative process defined in the contract and subscribed to in good faith by the contracting parties." Holifield posed seven questions to Campbell relating to the Westinghouse matters and more generally to GAO procedures.[17]

Campbell took almost two and one-half months to respond to Holifield's inquiry. General Counsel Robert Keller and other officials in GAO helped draft Campbell's letter.[18] The first six pages of Campbell's 16-page reply provided details of GAO's two reports (dated July 23 and December 26, 1962) on the disputed contracts. Campbell pointed out that the Navy, not GAO, had suspended certain costs of the contract but that the Navy based its action on GAO reports. Then Campbell answered the seven questions Holifield had asked in his October 1964 letter.

• Was Westinghouse right in arguing that it had been subject to undue delay in resolving the dispute? Possibly, Campbell responded, but he explained that at the time, the Navy had under consideration several Westinghouse overpricing reports.

• Had Westinghouse been denied due process because the Navy had suspended payments rather than determining cost allowability? Campbell's lengthy response, full of citations to various legal decisions, did not provide a definitive answer.

• Did procedural due process hinge on the amount of time lapsing after suspension of payments? Again Campbell's answer was inconclusive, but he stated that Westinghouse was free to file a suit in the Court of Claims if it felt that it had a case.

• Under what circumstances did GAO refer investigative and audit reports to the Department of Justice? Campbell responded that GAO referred cases

---

[17]Letter, Holifield to Campbell, October 5, 1964, ibid. Additional documents in this file provide details of the Westinghouse cases.

[18]Memorandum, Keller to Campbell, December 14, 1964, ibid.

when it thought that legal remedies might be available to the government. When GAO reviews disclosed "that overpricing may have resulted from overreaching conduct, questionable cost or pricing information, or from the withholding of information pertinent to pricing," the Office referred reports to Justice. "This type of referral," Campbell wrote, "is indicative of possible fraud taint in the case."

• In the Westinghouse case, was GAO authorized to enforce its recovery recommendations by taking exception to payments by Navy disbursing officers, and if so, why had this authority not been used in this case? Campbell said that he thought that Justice should have an opportunity to evaluate the findings "before any efforts were made to effect collection or recovery."

• What were the respective authorities and interrelationships of GAO and Justice in claims settlement? Was Justice authorized to negotiate settlement of disputed matters in government contracts whether or not litigation was involved? Campbell said that GAO's opinion was that when claims were referred to Justice, that department had exclusive jurisdiction over the matter.

• Did GAO have suggestions "for more adequately protecting both the rights of the Government and the contractor in contract disputes of the kind here involved?" Campbell responded that it would be appropriate to provide, in cost-reimbursement-type contracts, a reasonable time during which the contracting agency must allow or disallow payments, if fraud or illegality was absent.[19]

In response, Holifield requested additional information on GAO's role in voluntary or other recovery of funds from contractors. He asked for data covering reports issued by GAO on DOD, the military departments, the National Aeronautics and Space Administration, and the Atomic Energy Commission for the calendar years 1959 through 1964. Holifield wanted, among other things, statistics on the total number of reports GAO had issued each year; the number dealing specifically with contract matters; a list of reports recommending efforts to collect voluntary refunds from contractors and recoveries made or reported to GAO; the number of cases referred to the Department of Justice for possible fraud; and a list of reports in which GAO identified illegal contracts.[20]

---

[19]Letter, Campbell to Holifield, December 15, 1964, ibid.
[20]Letter, Holifield to Campbell, January 7, 1965, ibid.

Campbell responded in March 1965. He indicated that between 1959 and 1964, GAO issued 582 reports on DOD, eight on NASA, and 24 on AEC. Of these totals, 216 dealt with contract matters in DOD, four in NASA, and 19 in AEC. During the period, GAO referred 39 DOD cases and two AEC cases to Justice. In attached lists, Campbell indicated cases reported to Congress disclosing excessive negotiated prices or costs erroneously claimed and paid under government contracts, illegal contract awards, and cases on which GAO had taken formal exception to disbursing officers' accounts with respect to contract payments.[21]

The Holifield Hearings

By this time, given Holifield's extensive requests for information from GAO, it was clear that the Office had a potentially serious problem. Holifield soon announced that the Military Operations Subcommittee would hold hearings on GAO contract audits. The hearings began on May 10, 1965, and continued on ten subsequent days—May 11, 18, 19, 20, 25, 26, and 27; June 1 and 3; and July 8. The hearings resulted in a detailed analysis of GAO defense contract auditing work, with DOD and defense industry representatives quite critical and GAO explaining and justifying its position.[22] Twenty-three principal witnesses testified—eight from DOD (including the military services), ten from industry, two from other government agencies, one former defense contractor, and two from GAO—Comptroller General Campbell and Assistant Comptroller General Frank H. Weitzel.[23] From Holifield's subcommittee staff, the most important participants were Herbert Roback, staff administrator, and Douglas Dahlin, staff attorney.

As the hearings began, a prominent journalist suggested that Holifield was in the clutches of the defense industry. Columnist Drew Pearson wrote that Holifield was "lined up behind big business" and that he was "strangely found on the side of luxurious shuffleboard courts, table tennis facilities, a scenic mall, out-door dining rooms for the Aerospace Corp., all paid for by the taxpayer." Pearson's colleague, Jack Anderson, identified several large defense contractors that were behind Holifield's investigation. "Doubtless the contractors can cite some GAO abuses. But what they really want is to silence the watchdogs altogether. In the great corporate scramble for de-

---

[21]Letter, Campbell to Holifield, March 11, 1965, ibid.

[22]*Comptroller General Reports to Congress on Audits of Defense Contracts*, Hearings before a Subcommittee of the House Committee on Government Operations, 89th Cong., 1st Sess. (Washington: GPO, 1965). In this volume, pp. 1-667 present hearings transcripts and pp. 669-1075 contain appendixes.

[23]Ibid., iii-iv.

fense dollars, the big contractors all too often have turned pull and politics into private profit."[24]

Holifield opened the hearings on May 10, 1965, by explaining that they would deal mainly with contract issues and problems. He noted the great concern of the defense industry and DOD "over the difficult and sometimes awkward situations created by the GAO audit reports." He identified GAO findings of overpricing in government contracts and the extent of GAO's right to examine the books and records of contractors as major problem areas. "Is the GAO," Holifield asked, "as some Government and industry parties believe, enforcing its own standards of procurement on Government and industry without authority of law or without the benefit of the intimate technical and business experience which resides in the parties to the procurement process? Is there developing a basic clash of procurement philosophies between GAO and DOD?" Holifield added that his subcommittee had excellent working relationships with GAO and depended heavily on the Office. "It does not hurt once in a while, however, to examine the operations of the General Accounting Office itself. . . . In this hearing we hope to get a better understanding of how the GAO does its contract audit work and what benefits and burdens result therefrom."[25]

Paul R. Ignatius, assistant secretary of defense (installations and logistics), the principal DOD witness, testified at the first day's hearings. He began by stating that Secretary of Defense Robert S. McNamara took a personal interest in GAO reports on DOD and had directed "prompt, clear, and positive action" on these reports. He noted the substantial increase during the previous three years in the number of draft and final reports pertaining to DOD. He recognized that given the extent and the complexity of defense work, some mistakes were inevitable, but DOD did not, he stated, believe "that the increase in the number of reports is a barometer of the number of deficiencies in procurement." Ignatius concentrated on three areas of disagreement between DOD and GAO—integrity of contracts, pricing policy, and government involvement in contractor operations.[26]

On integrity of government contracts, Ignatius's biggest complaint concerned the GAO practice of urging voluntary refunds from contractors when

[24]Clippings, Drew Pearson, *Washington Post*, May 14, 1965, and Jack Anderson, *Washington Post*, May 18, 1965, both in Legislative Digest Unit Files, Box 38, Folder 18, GAO History Program Archives.

[25]*Comptroller General Reports to Congress on Audits of Defense Contracts*, 2-3. See GAO, *Chet Holifield*, GAO History Program, Oral History Series, GAO/OP-5-OH (Washington: 1988). In this oral history interview Holifield did not disclose many details of the hearings or his own interest and motivations. At the time of the interview, in September 1987, Holifield was 84 years old and was in poor health.

[26]Ibid., 5-6.

it decided that prices included "unnecessary," "excessive," or "unwarranted" costs. DOD did not rule out seeking voluntary refunds, but its policy was that this was an extraordinary remedy to be used when it was clear both that the government had been overcharged in contract pricing or inadequately paid for the use or the purchase of government property and that retention by the contractor of the amount involved "would be contrary to good conscience and equity." Ignatius also had problems with cases where GAO declared contracts illegal after they had been fully performed and recommended withholding payment and with instances where GAO action interfered with established contractual remedies for settling claims and disputes, including usage of the Armed Services Board of Contract Appeals.[27]

Regarding pricing policy, Ignatius explained, the difference between GAO and DOD was primarily in their opinions of the benefits to the government of the cost-type approach to defense contracting versus the benefits of the fixed-price approach. DOD thought that providing strong incentives to defense contractors for sound contract management was important in reducing procurement costs and that this could be achieved best by fixed-price contracts. In cost-type contracts, contractors were paid on the basis of costs actually incurred, but the problem with such contracts, according to Ignatius, was that they offered no incentives to the contractors to reduce costs. He said that such contracts sometimes led to final costs 50 to 100 percent higher than estimated costs and delayed contract deliveries by a year or more. Ignatius claimed significant savings for DOD as a result of the shift, beginning in 1961, to fixed-price contracts. Under these contracts, the contractors could make higher profits by increasing efficiency and lowering costs and DOD's costs for the contracts were less than those under cost-type contracts. Ignatius complained that GAO frequently criticized DOD's use of fixed-price contracts, sometimes arguing that contractors had earned excessive profits because actual costs had been lower than estimates.[28]

DOD's differences with GAO in the area of government involvement in contractor operations was the third major area Ignatius discussed. GAO sometimes argued that it would be cheaper for the government to furnish components and subsystems to prime contractors; unnecessary costs could be incurred in profits and fees paid to contractors on subcontract materials. GAO had recently recommended that DOD adopt as general policy the practice of furnishing components and subsystems except in cases where the prime contractors helped produce the items or provided technical assistance to the subcontractors. Ignatius pointed out that units of DOD often operated as

---

[27]Ibid., 6-9.
[28]Ibid., 9-11.

GAO had recommended; for example, government-furnished equipment constituted about 35 percent of the total purchase price of Navy ships. But often the alternative approach was more cost-effective.

Ignatius identified other problems in this area, including GAO's repeated recommendation that the government buy electronic data processing equipment and provide it to contractors rather than permitting them to lease such equipment. Ignatius argued that an increase in government control and intervention should be avoided in favor of a contracting approach that provided "maximum incentive for efficient and economical contract performance."[29]

In Frederick Mosher's opinion, Ignatius set "the critical tenor of the hearings" with his testimony. "From the onset, GAO was the 'defendant.'"[30] Actually, Ignatius's testimony was both polite and pointed. He acknowledged more than once the value of GAO reports to DOD, but was very clear in his statements on specific areas of disagreement between GAO and DOD. Comptroller General Campbell, accompanied by Robert F. Keller; William A. Newman, director of the Defense Accounting and Auditing Division (DAAD); and several other GAO officials, appeared before the subcommittee on the second hearing day, May 11, 1965. Campbell reviewed GAO's statutory authority for audit work and access to records and explained what GAO was looking for in audits of negotiated contracts. These audits might include reviews of contractors' cost estimates and pricing proposals; comparison of contractor cost estimates with the firms' previous cost experiences; comparison of estimated and actual costs in performance of contracts; and reviews of the contractors' negotiation and administration of subcontracts. "The underlying causes of weak or extravagant procurement practices are sought and recommendations are made for improving contracting practices and administration," Campbell explained. He emphasized that the cases at issue involved negotiated contracts rather than those awarded on sealed bids after formal advertising. For the latter type of contract, the federal government did not have authority to audit contractors' books and records except on change orders over $100,000. Campbell argued that full and free competition did not exist for negotiated contracts and pointed out that GAO had long urged that advertised procurement be used to the extent possible.[31]

On subsequent hearing days, Holifield's subcommittee heard testimony from various representatives of the government and the defense industry:

---

[29]Ibid., 12-14.

[30]Mosher, *GAO*, 155.

[31]Campbell statement, hearing of May 11, 1965, *Comptroller General Reports to Congress on Audits of Defense Contracts*, 40-50.

On May 18, John W. Douglas, assistant attorney general, Civil Division, Department of Justice, discussed procedures for handling cases referred to Justice by GAO or agencies; on May 19, Elmer B. Staats, deputy director, Bureau of the Budget (BOB), testified; on May 20, John P. Abbadessa, controller, AEC, testified on GAO audits of AEC contracts; on May 25, Daniel M. Luevano, assistant secretary of the army (installations and logistics), and other Army representatives discussed GAO audits of Army contracts; on May 26, Graeme C. Bannerman, assistant secretary of the navy (installations and logistics), and other Navy representatives testified on audits of Navy contracts; on May 27, Robert H. Charles, assistant secretary of the air force (installations and logistics), and other Air Force representatives, discussed audits of Air Force contracts; and on June 1 and June 3, representatives of specific companies and industry associations testified.[32]

The general approach of those testifying for the military was to acknowledge positive assistance from GAO but to take issue in reference to specific reports as well as the three areas of disagreement Ignatius had discussed in his testimony. The comment of Robert H. Charles, assistant secretary of the air force, was representative:

> The efforts of the General Accounting Office have been, and I am sure will continue to be, of substantial help to us in identifying shortcomings and in developing better management procedures and controls. With their assistance, we have been able to obtain price reductions and refunds in many cases where the General Accounting Office recommendations were predominately based on demonstrable cost and pricing factors rather than on judgment or interpretation of policy. There is no doubt in my mind that GAO and the Air Force have the same basic objective, namely, the judicious application and utilization of public moneys and the resources of the Government. Where we sometimes differ is in the area of judgment—the judgment of the Air Force in the light of circumstances existing at the time of the negotiation versus the judgment of the General Accounting Office based on reconstruction of the case after the fact and in light of what actually happened.[33]

The statement of Elmer Staats, deputy director of BOB, was quite positive about GAO's work and contributions. Staats called attention to the mes-

---

[32]The testimony listed here is in ibid., 87-571.
[33]Ibid., 364.

sage of President Lyndon B. Johnson to federal agency heads on May 2, 1964, stating that he wanted "prompt and thorough attention" given to reports by GAO and congressional committees. If criticisms in these reports were justified, Johnson said, he wanted "corrective action so that the error is not repeated." Staats pointed out that BOB, in implementing the president's directive, required agency heads to carefully consider GAO reports and promptly initiate corrective actions when appropriate. Agency heads were to disclose to BOB, within 60 days after issuance of reports, their views on the reports' findings and corrective steps taken. Staats added that most of BOB's follow-up action on audit reports came in the examination of budget requests. He cited examples of instances when GAO reports had been helpful to BOB—on lease versus purchase of automated data processing equipment, the timing of federal disbursements, standardized government travel regulations, and failure to use excess foreign currency to the maximum extent possible. Staats concluded by saying that the president and BOB "regard GAO reports as an important source of assistance in working toward our goal of strengthened agency management."[34]

On his second day of testimony, May 19, 1965, Campbell submitted a statement for the record responding to the three areas that Ignatius identified as problems on May 10. In response to questions posed mainly by Herbert Roback, Campbell, Keller, and Newman explained GAO policies and procedures on several matters, including suspensions and disallowances of payments to contractors, voluntary refunds, access to contractor records, and GAO reporting policy. Roback's questions were pointed and exhibited some skepticism about the way GAO operated, but on the whole, the hearing was not exceptionally contentious.[35] As it turned out, this was Campbell's last appearance at the hearings. The subcommittee planned to have him back for another hearing after six additional days of testimony in May and early June 1965 by representatives of the Department of Justice, the military services and the defense industry. But Campbell became ill and decided at the end of June 1965 to retire on disability, effective on July 31, 1965.[36]

On July 8, 1965, when Holifield's subcommittee held its last hearing, Assistant Comptroller General Weitzel, soon to become acting comptroller general, was GAO's principal witness. Keller, Morse, and Charles M. Bailey, deputy director of DAAD, accompanied Weitzel. William Newman, DAAD's director, was traveling in Alaska at the time. In the course of Weitzel's statement, the subcommittee accepted for the record written responses by GAO

---

[34]Staats testimony, May 19, 1965, ibid., 173-76.

[35]Hearing of May 19, 1965, ibid., 131-65 (discussion), 166-73 (Campbell's printed statement).

[36]For details of Campbell's illness and retirement, see chapter 5, pp. 124-26.

Robert F. Keller and Frank H. Weitzel.

to the previous testimony of industry and military representatives as well as statements on several of GAO's reports on defense matters.[37]

Weitzel began his testimony by expressing concern about objections by defense contractors to GAO efforts to fulfill its statutory responsibilities. He reviewed GAO's statutory authority, particularly the Budget and Accounting Act, 1921, to make clear that GAO had full authority to do audits. He said, "We have tried to carry out our responsibilities to the best of our ability in a fair and impartial manner even though the results of our work may reflect unfavorably upon the agency or contractor under audit. We do not see how this result can be avoided if we are to carry out the duties we think Congress intended us to do."[38]

Rep. Howard H. Callaway (R—Georgia) praised GAO extensively during his questioning of Weitzel but recognized the merits of contractor problems. He asked Weitzel to explain the meaning of the term "audit" as understood by GAO and the Office's policy on recommendations for voluntary refunds.[39]

---

[37]Hearing of July 8, 1965, *Comptroller General Reports to Congress on Audits of Defense Contracts*, 581-629.

[38]Ibid., 575-79 (quote on 577).

[39]Ibid., 629-37.

At this hearing, Holifield criticized GAO's practice of naming persons charged with errors or other problems in contract management. He asked Weitzel, "Do you think it is necessary to make this type of a public disclosure on the basis of your judgment?" Weitzel said that it was not absolutely essential for GAO to name names, but pointed out that several congressional committees had asked GAO to do it. Holifield suggested that a better course might be for GAO to provide names to chairs of involved congressional committees rather than publishing them in reports. Weitzel agreed that this might be acceptable and promised to consider it.[40]

Douglas G. Dahlin, a staff attorney with Holifield's subcommittee, questioned Weitzel about GAO's use of attention-getting titles. Weitzel said that GAO wanted its reports to be meaningful and conducive to action. He said, "So we tried to work toward making what we say mean something and give it a description which people can grasp, where people do not have too much time to read, where they can grasp what it is all about . . . . If we just put out a report and said that this is the report on the audit of contract DOD, such and such a number, it would not attract very much attention—no one might read it." Weitzel said that GAO was considering the matter of titles of reports and wanted to be accurate and concise without shading the meaning. Roback observed that "when the Comptroller General resolves in his own mind whether he is trying to hit the headlines, or report to the Congress, that will not be much of a problem any longer. I would take it as an insult if anyone believed I pick these reports to read on the basis of the title or the headlines."[41]

Several other subjects, including suspension or disallowance of payments to contractors, came up during questioning of Weitzel. Again Roback's queries suggested a bias against GAO and in favor of contractors. But on the whole, the hearing did not result in serious damage to GAO. Weitzel and his colleagues upheld the Office's position strongly while exhibiting willingness to reconsider certain policies, such as naming names in reports. Morse concluded in his journal after the July 8 hearing that "there seems to be no evidence that the calibre of our work on defense contractors and the substance of our findings will be successfully challenged."[42]

In fact, before the hearings ended on July 8, 1965, GAO began discussions on possible changes in reporting practices. At the end of June, Weitzel, Keller, and other GAO officials met twice with Holifield and Rep. Frank J. Horton (R—New York), a member of the Military Operations Subcommittee, to discuss reporting practices. Subsequently, GAO decided to cut overem-

---

[40]Ibid., 645-46.
[41]Ibid., 661-63.
[42]Entry for July 8, 1965, Morse, *Daily Notes*, 1965-1966.

phasis on deficiencies in report titles, eliminate recommendations for disciplinary actions, and resume the earlier practice of listing only agency officials at the bureau level and above. GAO pledged to provide balance in reports, state both sides of issues, separate fact and opinion, and stop mentioning referrals to the Department of Justice in published reports. These changes, specified internally in early July 1965, were to be applied selectively to individual reports and not formally promulgated until the Holifield committee issued a report on the hearings.[43]

Another indication of the impact of the Holifield hearings was a letter Weitzel sent to the secretary of defense in August 1965 about a contract with the Lane Construction Company for work at Andrews Air Force Base, Maryland. Payment of the contract balance to the contractor, representing mostly money owed to a subcontractor, had been withheld for two years. There had been considerable discussion of this contract in the Holifield hearings. Weitzel told the secretary of defense that he thought that to hold up the payment any longer would not be fair and that GAO would not object if DOD paid the prime contractor the amount due.[44]

Holifield Report Drafts

Weitzel received a copy of the Holifield subcommittee's draft report on August 27, 1965. The document, issued by the House Government Operations Committee, was quite critical of GAO and contained, in GAO's view, "many deficiencies and inaccuracies." GAO officials, including representatives from AAPS, DAAD, and the Civil Accounting and Auditing Division (CAAD), undertook on Weitzel's orders a detailed analysis of the draft. Weitzel, Keller, and Bailey met with Holifield for a long session to discuss the draft on September 1; Holifield agreed to reconsider it and directed his staff to have further discussions with GAO and study the changes GAO suggested.[45]

In the meantime, a heated disagreement developed between James A. Lanigan, general counsel of the House Committee on Government Operations, and Herbert Roback. Lanigan was very unhappy about the prominent display in the draft report of department and industry criticisms of the comp-

---

[43]Entry for July 2, 1965, ibid. See also Bailey, memorandum for congressional contact file, July 14, 1965, reporting on meeting of Weitzel, Keller, Lawrence J. Powers, and Bailey with Holifield, Horton, Roback, and Dahlin, June 29, 1965, and Bailey, memorandum for congressional contact file, July 14, 1965, reporting on meeting of Weitzel, Keller, Powers, and Bailey with Holifield, Horton, Roback, and Dahlin, July 1, 1965, both in B-155327, #2.

[44]Letter, Weitzel to the secretary of defense, August 18, 1965, ibid.

[45]Entry for September 7, 1965, Morse, *Daily Notes*, 1965-1966. In this entry Morse summarized events between August 27 and September 7, 1965.

troller general. "This approach," he wrote, "runs the danger of encouraging the Executive agencies and industry to resist and disparage the work of . . . [GAO] and could add substantially to the GAO's difficulties in getting information, in looking into agency and industry's records and in making meaningful reports to the Congress." Lanigan stated that it would be more productive to work with GAO toward operational improvements "than to spread upon the public record all sorts of unresolved, partially resolved, and to some extent ill-resolved criticisms . . . with the resultant effect of making . . . [GAO] less rather than more effective." Lanigan's memo dealt specifically with sections of the draft that he considered wrong.[46]

Roback responded in a memo that rejected Lanigan's criticism and charged him with "errors" and "unwarranted characterizations or conclusions." Roback wrote: "Lanigan's position seems to be that the GAO can do no wrong. . . . The fact is that there are many things wrong, and it may seem a little stern to put them in one report, but it is high time this were done."[47] Although copies of the Lanigan and Roback memos exist in GAO records, there is no available evidence that GAO officials saw them at the time they were written. Whatever the case, the memos demonstrated to both Holifield and Dawson that there was serious disagreement between key staff on the contents of the draft report. This situation probably contributed to the months' long redrafting of the report and the delay in its final issuance until March 1966. A more important factor in the delay was GAO's effort to tone down the report before its formal release.

The result of GAO discussions with Holifield and his staff was a revised draft report that Weitzel received on September 15, 1965. Morse noted that the new draft was "sharply cut back" and did not contain about 70 pages of "the most objectionable sections" of the original draft.[48] The draft included an introduction discussing the role of the comptroller general, an overview of GAO defense contract audits, an appendix summarizing 80 contract audit reports, and 23 recommendations. Six of the recommendations did not pertain directly to GAO but rather were recommendations on contract issues to other agencies, including DOD, the Department of Justice, and the Bureau of the Budget.

---

[46]Memorandum, Lanigan, August 25, 1965, Subject: Draft Report entitled "General Accounting Office Audits of Defense Contracts," in GAO History Program Archives. Lanigan's memo is not addressed to anyone in particular, but Holifield and William Dawson, chairman of the House Government Operations Committee, must have seen it. See also Dyke and Gannon, *Chet Hollifield*, 140.

[47]Memorandum, Roback to Holifield, August 30, 1965, Subject: Comments on Lanigan Memorandum of August 25, 1965, GAO History Program Archives.

[48]Entry for September 16, 1965, Morse, *Daily Notes*, 1965-1966.

The other recommendations covered things that the comptroller general should do, including introducing more balance and objectivity in audit reports; seeing that Congress received fewer and better reports; improving procedures for handling draft and final contract reports; preparing instructions or a handbook covering GAO's basic activities, with guidance to agencies and contractors subject to GAO audit; requiring the GAO Office of the General Counsel to review all draft and final reports; taking care in recommending disciplinary action against individuals and giving names of persons involved to agency heads rather than publishing them in reports; cease noting in audit reports that cases had been referred to the Department of Justice and referring to Justice only matters where GAO was convinced prima facie cases existed; maintaining close liaison with Justice on referred cases and helping Justice prepare for prosecution or compromise settlement; developing, in collaboration with DOD and Justice, recommendations on application of statutes of limitations to suits arising from contracts and, with these agencies, take steps to expedite settlement of disputed contracts; studying the present and future relationships between GAO and the new Defense Contract Audit Agency (DCAA, established July 1, 1965); and appointing a GAO internal task force to study the Office's authorizations, functions, activities, and procedures and submitting legislative recommendations to Congress within one year.[49]

Weitzel met with Morse, Keller, and other GAO officials, including representatives of both CAAD and DAAD, on September 16, 1965, to discuss the revised draft. Morse noted later that "the group felt so much had been accomplished in recent but undisclosed negotiations that resulted in elimination of the most objectionable parts of the report that what remained was not too bad." Morse also recorded in his journal that Weitzel had told him that he had been approached by a member of the House Government Operations Committee "who expressed considerable concern about the tenor of the existing draft." Weitzel remarked that this member might try to kill the report.[50] The unidentified congressman was most likely Porter Hardy, Jr. (D—Virginia), who told Holifield at this time that printing a report so critical of GAO was inappropriate. He pointed out that many congressional committees relied on GAO and that releasing such a report could destroy its effectiveness. Hardy informed Holifield that he would oppose the report in the full committee and that if the committee adopted it, he would want to include extensive

---

[49]Draft Report, House Committee on Government Operations, *General Accounting Office Audits of Defense Contracts*, 89th Cong., 1st Sess. (Washington: GPO, 1965), 15-26, copy in GAO History Program Archives.

[50]Entry for September 16, 1965, Morse, *Daily Notes*, 1965-1966.

opposing views. Hardy also mentioned that he had discussed the draft report with Weitzel.[51]

Revised Auditing and Reporting Policies and Procedures

On October 5 and 19, 1965, Weitzel presided over meetings in the GAO Auditorium involving directors and supervisors of the accounting and auditing divisions located in Washington. The meeting speakers were Weitzel, Keller, Powers, and Morse. Weitzel had called the meetings to discuss future audit and reporting practices and related matters; they were a direct result of the Holifield hearings and the contents of the draft subcommittee reports. The remarks of Weitzel and the other speakers demonstrated the impact of the hearings on GAO about three months after their conclusion.[52]

Weitzel said that while the hearings and internal analysis may lead to some revision in auditing and reporting policies and practices, "no lessening of or restrictions on our auditing activities are foreseen."[53]   GAO could cut down the number of reports issued, give them more balance and perspective, and avoid overly broad language. Weitzel suggested more use of transmittal letters to agency heads and congressional committees rather than blue cover reports to handle some matters, such as recommendations for disciplinary action or suggested improvement in agency management. To overcome criticism that GAO reports were only negative, good aspects of performance as well as problems would be noted. Weitzel said that report titles needed to be more constructive and that GAO should state reasons for every report sent to Congress. GAO reports should discover basic causes of problems and recommend corrective action. Reports should be combined "to better bring out the significance and pattern of deficiencies." Weitzel said also that GAO would be paying more attention to agency accounting systems, which he suggested be termed "financial management systems." Finally, he thought that GAO should become more familiar with the programming and systems analysis techniques being introduced in the executive branch "so that we may be in a position to properly evaluate their usefulness and, on occasion, provide advice and assistance."[54]

---

[51]Letter, Hardy to Holifield, September 16, 1965, GAO History Program Archives.

[52]Morse took detailed notes on these meetings. His record, entitled "Notes of Meetings of the Director Groups and Supervisors in the Accounting and Auditing Divisions in Washington," October 5 and 19, 1965, 24 pages, were duplicated and distributed to all staff at the rank of GS-11 and above in the accounting and auditing divisions. A copy of this document is in the GAO History Program Archives.

[53]All quotations are from Morse's notes and are not necessarily the exact words of the speakers at the meetings.

[54]Morse, "Notes of Meetings of the Director Groups and Supervisors," October 5 and 19, 1965, 1-7.

General Counsel Keller discussed several legal issues that had come up in the draft report, including disclosure of proprietary business data. Keller said that such disclosure by GAO was not prohibited by law but that the Office would respect business privacy to the extent possible. He said that GAO was studying the Holifield subcommittee's recommendation that OGC review both draft and final reports for validity as well as legality. He suggested that adopting the recommendation to discontinue seeking voluntary refunds would force an end to GAO efforts to get refunds on contracts dated before December 1962. Keller stated that GAO had agreed that it would not mention referral of cases to the Department of Justice in reports but would inform involved agencies and congressional committees when it made such referrals. He said that he thought that additional legislation might be necessary to clarify GAO's right of access to contractor records.[55]

Morse discussed a number of planned changes in reporting policies and practices. GAO would try to provide greater balance in reports, by including in their text the nature of the audit, the reason it had been made, an explanation not only of GAO's side of the story but other information as well, and a proper and fair description of findings "so the misinterpretation and misunderstanding will be minimized." GAO opinions would be clearly identified, and deficiency titles would be discontinued. As Morse recorded his own words, "The main thrust of our direction of effort will still be on the identification of deficiencies but our emphasis (and the wording of our reports) should be on constructively promoting improvements in operations rather than on reporting criticisms." Morse said that to better inform agencies and contractors about GAO policies and procedures, an existing booklet for agencies would be revised and that AAPS would assume responsibility for preparing a special booklet for contractors. GAO would discontinue naming names in reports but continue to identify individuals responsible for problems; their names would be reported separately as appropriate to agency officials and congressional committees. Morse also reiterated Weitzel's statement that GAO would devote more effort to financial management work—accounting, budgeting, internal auditing, and financial reporting.[56]

Powers devoted his brief remarks to the areas in which GAO was required to render assistance to Congress and the need for increased attention to financial management systems.[57] The comments of Weitzel, Keller, Morse, and Powers constituted mainly positive responses to much of what Holifield's subcommittee had recommended in the revised draft report but were not a

---

[55]Ibid., 8-11.
[56]Ibid., 12-17.
[57]Ibid., 18.

capitulation to congressional, executive agency, and contractor pressures. Since the Holifield subcommittee had not yet settled on the text of its final report—indeed it was not clear in October 1965 that it would even issue a final report—GAO's positive response in part may have been related to the Office's hope that the report would be significantly toned down if not dropped.

In November 1965, Weitzel became concerned about the number of re-ports intended for Congress that had been canceled by the Defense Account-ing and Auditing Division in recent months and asked Morse to review the matter.[58] In March 1966, after receiving data from DAAD and conducting his analysis, Morse reported to Weitzel that DAAD's actions in the cases of 80 reports dropped between July 1 and November 30, 1965, were on the whole reasonable. He mentioned three reports that probably required fur-ther reporting action. In some cases, DAAD consolidated reports with others for more-effective presentation, and some originally intended for Congress went to the secretary of defense instead.[59]

In the meantime, it still was not clear to GAO whether the Holifield sub-committee would issue a final report. Finally, in mid-February 1966, Holifield wrote to Weitzel noting that he had said in the 1965 hearings and follow-up conferences that GAO was making changes and asking him to submit a re-port on developments "which may be related to the issues raised and dis-cussed at those hearings and conferences."[60] Keller and Morse worked on Weitzel's reply to Holifield. The letter, dated March 4, 1966, explained many of the changes that had been discussed by GAO officials and staff in the October 1965 internal meetings. Weitzel pointed out, to put the current changes in context, that GAO had made changes as needed over the two decades since World War II. He noted that traditionally GAO had empha-sized audits of problem areas in agency operations and that thus most reports in recent years had pointed to management problems and recommended improvements. He admitted that some of these reports had not contained enough information about the overall aspects of the areas of operations dis-cussed "to provide an adequate perspective against which the significance of reported weaknesses can be fairly judged." To rectify this problem, GAO would include more information in reports about the activities examined and the nature and the scope of the audits. Also, report titles would "be couched in constructive terms rather than in terms of the deficiencies being reported" and GAO's conclusions and opinions would be clearly identified so that they

---

[58]Entries for November 19 and 23, 1965, Morse, *Daily Notes*, 1965-1966.

[59]Entry for March 4, 1966, ibid.; and memorandum, Weitzel to the director, DAAD, March 11, 1966, B-155327, #2.

[60]Letter, Holifield to Weitzel, February 16, 1966, ibid.

could not be construed as facts. Generally, GAO reports would be broader in scope and fewer in number but more directed to promoting improvement in agency management.

Weitzel indicated that GAO would include comments by agencies, contractors, and others in report appendixes as well as a statement of agency action to correct problems identified in audits. He said that to improve its report distribution system, GAO had adopted procedures to ensure delivery of reports to Congress, agencies, and contractors before distribution to others. He upheld GAO's statutory right to include business proprietary information in reports but noted that since April 1965, the Office had instituted a system of review by senior officials before distribution of draft reports to protect proprietary information "to the maximum extent possible consistent with our reporting responsibilities." In addition, Weitzel stated that GAO had stopped both disclosing in reports the names of persons responsible for actions or operations criticized in the reports and including recommendations for disciplinary action, although such information would be reported to agency officials or Congress as appropriate. However, GAO would continue to identify in reports top responsible agency officials. Similarly, GAO would exclude from reports referrals of alleged violations of law to the Department of Justice but would report them separately to agencies and congressional committees.

Also, Weitzel discussed GAO's previous application of the "due care" test in audits of cost-type defense contracts. The "due care" theory was generally recognized as a criterion for determining reasonable and allowable costs, but authority for determining cost reasonableness belonged to the contracting agency. Weitzel said that in the future when GAO felt that a contractor had not exercised due care, GAO would recommend to the contracting agency that it recover the excess costs "for consideration as a matter of cost allowability under the contract rather than on the basis of a common law right, with the decision thereon to be made by the contracting agency. . . ."

On the matter of voluntary refunds, Weitzel noted that the Truth in Negotiations Act required contractors to certify the basis of cost estimates and provided that contracts negotiated after the law became effective (December 1, 1962) contain clauses for price adjustment for increases resulting from inaccurate or noncurrent cost data certified by the contractor. Weitzel said that for contracts completed before December 1, 1962, GAO would limit its recommendations for voluntary refunds to cases where the contractor had furnished faulty cost data at the time of contract negotiation.

Weitzel reported to Holifield that GAO was preparing a manual explaining audit objectives and policies for contract audits and would distribute it to contractors, agency officials, and congressional members and committees. Finally, he said that GAO was reviewing the organization and the functions of the Defense Contract Audit Agency to determine the agency's effectiveness and to what extent GAO and DCAA could avoid unnecessary duplication of effort.[61]

A letter to Holifield on March 2, 1966, from Paul Ignatius, the DOD official who had presented Defense's position at the Holifield hearings, probably had some effect on the wording of the final Holifield report. Ignatius wrote that there had been noticeable changes in DOD-GAO relationships over the previous six months. "We believe these have resulted from the expressions of interest shown by you and by members of your subcommittee." Ignatius reported that GAO had agreed that DOD was free to release some payments previously withheld from defense contractors. He noted a decrease in the number of final reports on defense matters issued by GAO. "This is not an indication, of course, that the Comptroller is relaxing his examination of defense activities. The Comptroller apparently has concluded that it is not necessary to issue a number of final reports covering the same subject and containing substantially the same findings and recommendations." Report titles had changed so that they indicated the subject matter of GAO audits; the amount of press activity, stimulated by earlier report titles, had decreased.[62]

Final Holifield Report

At the time Weitzel sent his letter to Holifield, it was still not clear whether the House Committee on Government Operations would issue a final report. But on March 16, 1966, the committee voted to approve a report, which it issued formally on March 23. By this time, Elmer B. Staats, nominated in February 1966 by President Johnson to be the new comptroller general, was in office, and Weitzel had resumed his position as assistant comptroller general. Staats, as noted earlier, was about the only non-GAO witness at the Holifield hearings to present generally positive testimony on GAO's work. The final Holifield report, officially titled *Defense Contract Audits*, was only 33 pages long, much shorter than the original draft of August 1965 and the first revised draft in September 1965.

---

[61]Letter, Weitzel to Holifield, March 4, 1966, ibid.

[62]Letter, Ignatius to Holifield, March 2, 1966, reprinted in *Defense Contract Audits*, Twenty-Fourth Report by the Committee on Government Operations, H. Rept. 1344, 89th Cong., 2d Sess., March 23, 1966 (Washington: GPO, 1966), 25-26. This document is the final Holifield report (hereafter cited as *Defense Contract Audits*).

Defense Contract Audits, familiarly known as the Holifield report, began with an introduction stating that in the past GAO had done an outstanding job and that its reports were "an indispensable source of information for the Congress." The report noted the recent dispute between GAO on the one hand and DOD and defense contractors on the other and summarized the subcommittee's examination of more than 80 contract audits. The bulk of the Holifield report discussed 17 major issues raised in the 1965 hearings and described their current status, on the basis of experience over the 8 months since the hearings ended, as well as the statements Weitzel had made in his March 4, 1966, letter to Holifield. *Defense Contract Audits* was critical to a degree of some past GAO activities, but its tone was moderate and much more balanced than the first draft of the document circulated in 1965. Clearly GAO had benefited from the subcommittee's delay in issuing the report, allowing GAO time to make changes, based on its own internal decisions, which went a long way to meet the subcommittee's objections.

The 17 issues dealt with in the report were as follows:

- Style, format, and content of reports;

- frequency and scope of reporting;

- distribution and release of reports;

- handling of confidential business data;

- review by GAO of reports for legal sufficiency;

- naming of officials in reports;

- voluntary refunds from contractors;

- integrity of government contracts;

- theory of contractor exercise of "due care;"

- relationship with DCAA;

- access to contractor books and records;

- referral to the Department of Justice of alleged violations of law in reports;

- disposition of cases by Justice;

- expediting of contract terminations and payments;

- statute of limitations (need for a cutoff date for contractor liability);

- audit procedures manual; and

- the Executive Branch Procurement Policy Board (creation recommended).[63]

The Holifield report explained the subcommittee's position on each of these issues and described changes GAO had made in response to the subcommittee's concerns as expressed in the hearings and later discussions. "Since the subcommittee hearings," the report stated, "the General Accounting Office has made changes in procedures and in other matters which in the committee's opinion have resulted in improvements in reporting practices without in any way circumscribing the GAO from fully and fairly reporting to Congress on matters within its areas of concern which, of course, is a duty Congress expects to be continued." The House Government Operations Committee concluded that the hearings had served useful purposes—GAO had greatly improved reporting practices, established better working relationships with DOD and contractors, reduced the backlog of cases referred to the Department of Justice, and benefited from an internal reexamination of its policies and procedures.[64]

Not all committee members agreed with the majority report. In additional views printed in the report, Jack Brooks (D—Texas) noted Campbell's retirement and Staats's accession to the office of comptroller general. He thought that Staats should have been given time "to determine for himself the propriety and need" for changes. He suggested that many of the recommendations in the Holifield report "will deter rather than encourage improvement in GAO audit procedures." He complained that the report made no reference to DOD or contractor shortcomings "which have resulted in the loss of untold millions in tax funds."[65] Reps. John W. Wydler (R—New York) and Clarence J. Brown, Jr. (R—Ohio), expressed concern that GAO would no longer be naming names in reports or stating that particular cases were being referred to the Justice Department. "Our concern," they wrote, "is one of balancing the fair treatment of companies and individuals against the legitimate right of the press and the public to be fully informed about the public business." Wydler and Brown said that since both GAO and the De-

[63]Ibid., 4-17.
[64]Ibid., 3.
[65]Ibid., 27-28; Dyke and Gannon, *Chet Holifield*, 141.

partment of Justice would state when asked whether a report had been referred, they would approve the Holifield report.[66]

Robert J. Dole (R—Kansas), with the concurrence of Donald H. Rumsfeld (R—Illinois), remarked about "the extent the report appears to place the committee's stamp of approval on decisions in derogation of the people's right to know." He referred specifically to the fact that audit reports would not name names or state that cases were being referred to Justice. He also expressed apprehension that the Holifield report "could tend to place the GAO on the defensive in its future contract operations." Dole concluded, "The GAO is an arm of Congress. Let's not 'disarm' it."[67] Holifield himself inserted additional views in the report, but mainly to refute the views expressed by others. He defended the changes GAO had made on naming names, referring cases to Justice, and the handling of confidential business data. "I believe in a free press and open records of public transactions," Holifield wrote, "and I do not believe that this report or the changed procedures in the GAO transgresses these principles."[68]

The press took considerable notice of the release of the Holifield report and its recommendations. The *Washington Daily News* referred to the "apparently successful attempt by the House Government Operations Committee to limit drastically the powers of the General Accounting Office in auditing defense contracts." James J. Kilpatrick wrote in the *Washington Evening Star*: "The prettiest piece of painless dentistry in quite some time was executed up on the Hill a week or so ago. The House Committee on Government Operations put the General Accounting Office under a gentle anesthetic, and quietly pulled the bulldog's teeth."[69]

The *Sacramento Union* reported that GAO had agreed to issue fewer reports and name fewer names. "If anything," the paper suggested, "we need to beef up the activity and publicity of the GAO to let the public know what's going on in the costly government labyrinth."[70] Charles Nicodemus, a Washington correspondent of the *Chicago Daily News*, reported that Holifield had thrust "a sword . . . into the vitals" of GAO and that Representative Dawson, the chairman of the House Government Operations Committee, had let him get away with it. Nicodemus wrote: "What Holifield has done is to pressure GAO into curbing its investigations in the all-important

---

[66]*Defense Contract Audits*, 28-29.

[67]Ibid., 30-31; Dyke and Gannon, *Chet Holifield*, 141.

[68]*Defense Contract Audits*, 32-33.

[69] Clippings, *Washington Daily News*, March 28, 1966, and *Washington Evening Star*, April 5, 1966, GAO History Program Archives.

[70]Clipping, *Sacramento Union*, May 21, 1966, B-155327, #2.

field of defense procurement, and softening—to marshmallow blandness—
the remaining reports in the field that it does put out."[71]

Sen. Everett M. Dirksen (R—Illinois) sent Comptroller General Staats a
copy of the Nicodemus clipping and wrote: "In response to the inquiries I
have had, I have stated very frankly that it is going to take more than a
couple of Congressmen to pull the teeth of the General Accounting Office. It
can actually be done only by legislation restricting its activities and any such
proposal would not get to first base in the Senate. I favor some additional
money for GAO and for an enlargement of its field staff so that it can do
more work than it has done. You can count on me." In his reply to Dirksen,
Staats said that there was nothing in the Holifield report that would restrict
GAO reviews of DOD. Short of legislative action, Staats added, "we would
not agree to any action which we believe would restrict or otherwise impair
our work."[72]

GAO under Weitzel's leadership as acting comptroller general succeeded
between August 1965 and March 1966 in persuading the House Government Operations Committee to tone down significantly the Holifield
subcommittee's recommendations and the level of criticism of GAO. There
was nothing in the final report that GAO could not live with. Any concessions GAO made because of specific criticisms in the report were based on
long internal discussions and decisions that GAO's top central and divisional
leaders accepted.

GAO's answer to the Holifield report was the responsibility of Elmer
Staats, the new comptroller general, after he entered office on March 8, 1966.
GAO's annual report for fiscal year 1966, issued several months after Staats
arrived, stated that the Office had adopted a number of recommendations
included in the Holifield report "to improve the effectiveness of our reports
. . . ." Staats reported that GAO was broadening its audits "to include a more
extensive inquiry into basic causes of adverse conditions." This approach
would probably result in fewer reports to Congress, but they should be more
significant and have a greater impact on agency management policies and
methods. "In following these reporting procedures, we have not, in our
opinion, lessened our efforts to keep the Congress and appropriate congres-

---

[71]Clipping, *Chicago Daily News*, "Watchdog Unit's Teeth Are Yanked," April 6, 1966, GAO History
Program Archives.

[72]Letter, Dirksen to Staats, April 22, 1966, and letter, Staats to Dirksen, May 12, 1966, both in B-
155327, #2.

sional committees informed on matters of interest to them," Staats concluded.[73]

A change in GAO directly related to the Holifield hearings was a reorganization of DAAD, effective on June 8, 1966. The division dropped its previous structure that included individual groups for DOD and each military service and established eight functional subdivisions—research and development, procurement, supply management, manpower, facilities and construction, support services, management control systems, and program direction and evaluation (placed in the office of the DAAD director). Staats told Holifield that GAO had carefully considered the suggestions and recommendations of the House Government Operations Committee included in the report of March 23, 1966. He also informed Holifield that defense contract audits would continue to be a major activity, that GAO intended to broaden its audit approach, and that the new approach would be evident in reports submitted to Congress.[74]

Although the 1965 Holifield hearings ushered in a rather traumatic period for GAO, bringing the most serious and pointed criticism of the Office's work since the 1930s, the long-range effects were muted. Many contemporary observers, including some GAO officials, concluded that GAO had in effect discontinued defense contract audits. How many of the changes that occurred in 1966 and in the next few years can be attributed to the Holifield hearings is debatable. With a new comptroller general in charge, some change was natural. Staats stated many years later that when he took office, he had told Holifield that he would study the Holifield report recommendations and make up his own mind about them. "I decided very early," Staats said, "that we would restore the level of defense audit work that we had prior to the Holifield hearings." Staats's approach was to try to make certain both that the Truth in Negotiations Act was being enforced and that the DCAA did its job properly. "Some misunderstanding arose later on whether or not GAO had really audited defense contractors [during Staats's term]. We did audit them, but we did it in the context of trying to be sure the Truth in Negotiations Act was enforced and that DCAA was doing its job properly," Staats said.[75]

---

[73]*Annual Report of the Comptroller General of the United States for the Fiscal Year Ended June 30, 1966* (Washington: GPO, 1966), 63-64.

[74]*Defense Contract Audits (Reorganization of the Defense Accounting and Auditing Division of the General Accounting Office)*, 35th Report by the Committee on Government Operations, 89th Cong., 2d Sess., H. Rept. 1796, August 2, 1966 (Washington: GPO, 1966), 1-27. This report includes the committee summary of DAAD changes; Staats's letter to Holifield, July 1, 1966, announcing the DAAD reorganization; and internal GAO documents explaining the reorganization in detail.

[75]GAO, *Elmer B. Staats, Comptroller General of the United States, 1966-1981*, GAO History Program, Oral History Series, GAO/OP-1-OH (Washington: 1987), 10-11.

Conclusions: Defense Audits in the Campbell Period

While GAO operations in other areas, including audits of civil agencies conducted by the Civil Accounting and Auditing Division, continued under Campbell between 1954 and 1965, there was increasing emphasis on defense audits. Expanding and strengthening GAO's defense audit work was a central objective of Campbell's reorganization efforts early in his term. The special attention he gave to the regional offices and particularly to the overseas offices also reflects this orientation. Even though Campbell himself was an accountant, he deemphasized accounting systems and broader financial management work—perhaps because it was more difficult to count up monetary accomplishments ascribable to GAO as a result of such work.

Competition and rivalry between the Defense and Civil Accounting and Auditing Divisions helped to account for report proliferation, provocative report titles, and other changes in reporting practices. Such competition seems to have had more of an impact on DAAD, under the leadership of William Newman, than on CAAD, led less flamboyantly by Adolph Samuelson. But Comptroller General Campbell was the central figure in determining the direction of GAO audit work during his term, especially in regard to defense audits. The mounting criticism of the Office's defense contract audits from defense contractors, the military services, and the Office of the Secretary of Defense should have served as a warning flag to GAO by 1964, but it did not. Even after Holifield began to request information on GAO defense audits in October 1964, Campbell and other top officials did not appear to foresee the extent of the problem. In that sense, the attack on GAO from DOD, the military services, and defense contractors at the Holifield hearings were a shock to these officials. Concurrently Campbell's health problems forced him to resign from office.

Acting Comptroller General Frank Weitzel did a commendable job of leading GAO through the difficult period between the end of the Holifield hearings and issuance of the Holifield report in March 1966. While some observers, both internal and external, felt that Weitzel should have been tougher and done more to resist the Holifield recommendations, such a stance might have influenced Holifield and the House Government Operations Committee to stick to their initial long list of criticisms.[76] As it turned out, the committee softened and shortened its list of recommendations in the final report and GAO had considerable leeway in determining whether and how to imple-

---

[76]See the comments of Gregory Ahart in GAO, *The Civil Division, 1956-1972: Interview with Gregory J. Ahart, Henry Eschwege, and Victor L. Lowe*, GAO History Program, Oral History Series, GAO/OP-22-OH (Washington: 1992), 42-43, and Arthur Schoenhaut in GAO, *Arthur Schoenhaut*, GAO History Program, Oral History Series, GAO/OP-4-OH (Washington: 1988), 42.

ment them. In a very difficult situation, GAO emerged in a better position than might have been expected when the Holifield hearings ended. For this result, Weitzel deserved much credit.

Campbell's departure in July 1965, the issuance of the Holifield subcommittee's final report in March 1966, and the coming of Elmer Staats to the comptroller general's office in the same month ended an era in GAO history and began another. GAO moved beyond the Holifield controversy into another period, which brought fundamental changes to the organization, the personnel, and the work of the Office.

CHAPTER 21

The General Accounting Office, 1921-1966: Conclusions and Observations

During its first forty-five years, the General Accounting Office (GAO) underwent broad and significant change. The GAO of 1966 was very different from the organization that began operations in 1921. GAO's creation in the Budget and Accounting Act, 1921, represented a striking change—the divorce of the federal government's central auditing function from the executive branch, where it had resided since 1789, and its shift to the legislative branch. During the two decades after 1921, change in GAO was slow and limited. But with the coming of an expanding, activist government under the New Deal and then World War II and the vastly increased workload faced by the Office, the stage was set for far-reaching transformations in the organization, the staff, the work programs, and the role of the General Accounting Office in the federal government.

J. R. McCarl, the first comptroller general, laid out GAO's initial approach to its assigned functions, according to his interpretation of the Budget and Accounting Act. He had the difficult task of forging a role for GAO in an environment where the executive branch opposed the Office. In the 1920s, of course, the federal government took few new program initiatives. In the 1930s, GAO added to its agenda the audits of various New Deal programs for relief and recovery from the Depression. McCarl had a strong influence on GAO's culture and work during his 15-year term. Fred Brown, his successor in 1939 after a three-year interim when an acting comptroller general headed GAO, was in office too short a time to have a major impact.

The next two comptrollers general—Lindsay C. Warren and Joseph Campbell—built on the foundations McCarl had established and went on to new challenges and duties. This suggests the first of several themes, all related to change, in understanding the history of the General Accounting Office—the *long statutory term of the comptroller general.*

With one exception—Fred Brown, 1939-1940—the comptrollers general between 1921 and 1965 served long terms—15 years, 13-1/2 years, and over

10-1/2 years. Unlike cabinet-level department secretaries and other federal agency heads, whose average time in office is much less, the comptroller general does not leave his position at the end of a presidential term or at the whim of politics. He has time to develop and implement his own concept of GAO's role, make major organizational changes, lead the Office into new activity areas, and remake the staff along special professional lines if he chooses. An agency head in office for only two or three years, even if he had the experience and the imagination to envision the long-term picture, would not have the time to implement his vision if it meant significant change. To understand the culture and the mission of an organization like GAO takes time. The Budget and Accounting Act gave comptrollers general that time by providing a 15-year term and making it very difficult to remove them from office.

The comptrollers general between 1921 and 1965 differed in professional background and experience, personality, and conception of GAO's role. But each in his own way was a strong personality, willing and able to make internal adjustments that led GAO through significant changes in direction. Centralization of authority in the Office of the Comptroller General, the rule between 1921 and 1965, had a major impact on GAO. McCarl concentrated on carrying on the assigned functions of the Office to a large extent as they had been handled by GAO's predecessor agency, the Office of the Comptroller of the Treasury. He worked diligently to establish and protect the independence of GAO. Some observers thought that he had gone too far in isolating GAO from the executive branch.

Warren led the Office through the rapid growth during World War II and then took GAO in new directions—some statutorily required and some on his own initiative. Particularly notable were his efforts to cooperate with the executive branch, especially in the field of financial management. Campbell built on many of Warren's initiatives and added some of his own—his recruiting and training programs are outstanding examples. He placed greater emphasis than Warren on independence from executive agencies and on reporting deficiencies and cost recovery. The pervasive influence of each comptroller general is a constant in the history of GAO; one does not have to adopt the "great man" theory of history to accept this fact. The small size of the General Accounting Office compared with that of many other federal agencies facilitated the centralization of authority in the person of the comptroller general.

Several other important themes in GAO history through 1966 apply mainly to the period beginning with Lindsay Warren's succession to the office of comptroller general in 1940. One of these themes was the *evolution of functions*. Warren and Campbell both deemphasized some functions that had been important aspects of GAO's work before their terms. Warren virtually discontinued the traditional voucher audits; Campbell assigned lower priority to financial management work and investigative activities. Both Warren and Campbell, on the basis of either personal decision or new laws, led GAO in undertaking new functions. Warren began audits of government corporations, a cooperative financial management program, and comprehensive audits, involving a broadened audit approach that looked at program management, compliance with laws and regulations, and economy and efficiency.

Campbell expanded the comprehensive audit; increased GAO activity in the field, both around the nation and overseas; and stepped up the Office's work in government procurement, especially in the defense area. While many of GAO's traditional statutory functions dating back to 1921—handling government claims, contract work, postal audits, transportation audits, and legal decisions and opinions—continued under Warren and Campbell, they were largely overshadowed by the newer functions and approaches.

A third theme was *organizational change*. Frequently when a new head comes into a government agency, there are organizational changes; often the new executive puts in place a new management team. Sometimes, federal agency reorganization has few positive results that can be identified. Truly effective reorganization requires knowledge and understanding that can come only with lengthy tenure and experience. The comptroller general's long term made this possible. In GAO's case, reorganization usually was based on how the comptroller general conceived of the Office's duties, including audits of new government programs, and how he thought they should be carried out. It was not reorganization for reorganization's sake.

McCarl started with the organization he had inherited from the Office of the Comptroller of the Treasury. Within a few years, he had simplified this structure to five divisions—concentrating all audit work, except that relating to the Post Office, in one division. He placed all staff functions, such as personnel and legal, in the Office of the Comptroller General. Once he had this arrangement in place, it changed very little during the rest of his term.

Both Warren and Campbell undertook major reorganizations keyed to decisions each had made on work areas and approaches. Although there were a few earlier organizational changes under Warren, including establishment of the Corporation Audits Division in 1945, he waited until 1952 to order a major restructuring. He did this after long study and analysis of how GAO did its work and how it ought to be organized to do that work in the future. By 1948, GAO had eight divisions and numerous staff offices. Warren's 1952 reorganization brought the number of divisions down to four, including a Division of Audits that included well over half of GAO's total staff. Warren also established a new regional office system.

Campbell's big reorganization came after he had been in office only about a year and a half. But he did not act hastily or simply in an effort to clean house. Like Warren before him, he carefully considered the existing organization, particularly how it handled defense audits, and took into consideration some early problems in his term, such as the "zinc stink." He then decided on an organizational arrangement designed to improve the scope and the quality of GAO's audits. He devised a structure with five major divisions, including separate groups for civil and defense audits and a new Field Operations Division. He added two new important staff offices, very closely related to the audit effort, for staff management and accounting and auditing policy. The only major addition to this organization came late in his term when he created the International Operations Division.

A fourth theme related to change in GAO was the development of a *broadened legislative base*. The Budget and Accounting Act, 1921, was GAO's original central charter, and it remains so today. A number of other laws expanded the legislative base. The Reorganization Act of 1945, specifying that GAO was a legislative branch agency, was very important. When GAO was under attack from the executive branch in the 1930s, the Office's defenders, including some members of Congress, argued that GAO was a legislative agency and always had been. But the Budget and Accounting Act had not said this and, in fact, had placed in GAO some functions that were arguably of an executive character. In 1945, Congress excluded GAO from the reorganization authority of the president, as it had earlier in 1939, and removed any doubt about the status of the Office as a legislative arm.

Another 1945 law, the Government Corporation Control Act, was the first major statute after 1921 to expand GAO's mandate. This law required the comptroller general to conduct annual audits of government corporations. It extended GAO's statutory duties, making it necessary for the Office to assemble a professional staff to handle the new audits, which went beyond the scope of the voucher audits of the past. Government corporation audits helped pave the way for adoption in 1949 of the comprehensive audit, leading eventually to much more expansive audits in all areas of the government.

The Federal Property and Administrative Services Act (1949) assigned to GAO the duties of prescribing principles and standards of accounting for property and auditing property accounts and transactions. This new function, to some extent the result of Warren's efforts to cooperate in the financial management area with the Treasury Department and the Bureau of the Budget, added important new duties to the GAO agenda.

The Budget and Accounting Procedures Act (1950) reaffirmed some existing GAO functions and added new ones. When he signed this law, President Harry S. Truman described it as "the most important legislation . . . in the budget and accounting field" since the Budget and Accounting Act, 1921. The law gave statutory sanction to the Joint Accounting Improvement Program, which Warren had led in establishing, and reconfirmed GAO's duty to prescribe principles and standards for executive agency accounting. By authorizing the comptroller general and the secretary of the treasury to make changes in the government's financial management system, including modification of the appropriation warrant procedures and discontinuation of GAO's practice of duplicating the accounts of government agencies, the law encouraged modernization. GAO discarded routine voucher checking and other relics of the past. Finally, the Budget and Accounting Procedures Act, by authorizing GAO to audit the financial transactions of government agencies in accordance with principles, procedures, and rules prescribed by the comptroller general, including site audits, gave the comprehensive audit a statutory base. In effect, the law embodied many important aspects of Warren's program of change and modernization.

Another theme that was consistent in GAO's history from 1921 to 1966 was *increased service to Congress*. McCarl, who strove to establish the independence of GAO from all outside influences, pursued the goal of serving Congress indirectly. A very high percentage of GAO's work under McCarl was self-initiated; it was not done at the specific request of Congress, but rather was based on McCarl's interpretation of GAO's functions as spelled out in the Budget and Accounting Act. McCarl considered GAO a legislative branch agent, aiding the Congress in seeing to the financial soundness of the nation. He frequently reminded Congress of this duty. He gradually increased the number of GAO reports sent to Congress, and he detailed staff to congressional committees when requested. When GAO suffered from attacks by the executive branch, McCarl looked to Congress to uphold the independence of the Office.

Warren, a prominent leader in the House of Representatives before he became comptroller general, worked hard to improve and extend GAO's relationships with Congress. He maintained extensive personal contacts with many members of Congress, worked behind the scenes for legislation he considered important to GAO, and constantly emphasized to Congress that GAO was its agent. His support of legislation affecting GAO's work, including the Government Corporation Control Act and the Budget and Accounting Procedures Act, helped get those new laws through Congress. He was much less aloof from Congress than McCarl. As a member of Congress, he had opposed attempts favored by the executive branch in the late 1930s to diminish GAO's role, and he urged Congress to oppose renewed efforts to do the same thing a decade later. Through increasing the number and improving the quality of reports to Congress and by detailing more GAO staff to committees, Warren sought to improve the Office's relations with Congress.

Campbell started off with somewhat shaky relations with some members of Congress who had opposed his nomination as comptroller general. But he understood after he entered office how important smooth relations with Congress were. After the embarrassment early in his term over the zinc stink, Campbell worked to improve congressional contacts. He formalized and expanded GAO's internal structure for dealing with Congress by creating the Office of Legislative Liaison in 1956 and putting it under the supervision of one of his top assistants, Robert Keller, who continued to direct the office after he became general counsel in 1958. Campbell testified occasionally before congressional committees, unlike Warren, who refrained from testimony during the first few years of his term. Given the controversy over his confirmation and notwithstanding his resignation in the midst of difficult hearings over defense contract audits in 1965, Campbell's relationships with Congress were on the whole satisfactory.

Another constant theme in GAO's history after 1940 was the *changing nature of the Office's staff.* Over the 45 years covered in this study, the typical GAO staff member evolved from a low-graded clerk, possibly wearing a green eyeshade, to a professional accountant or auditor, a college graduate with, in some cases, experience in public accounting. During McCarl's term, only the top managers and lawyers in the Office of the General Counsel were in the professional ranks, and there was no perceptible effort under McCarl to improve the educational and experiential levels of the staff. After World War II, Warren began professionalizing the staff, first by bringing in experienced accountants to do corporation audits and a little later auditors to handle the comprehensive audit. Perhaps Campbell's most important accomplishment was his major effort to elevate a larger percentage of the staff to the professional level. The recruitment and training program he fostered, under the direction of Leo Herbert, succeeded. By the time Campbell left office in 1965, the professionalism of the GAO staff had risen significantly. Almost all the new professionals were accountants and auditors, hired to do the audit work that Campbell made the center of GAO's effort.

This study has placed considerable emphasis on the position and the role of the comptroller general. The course of GAO history between 1921 and 1966 supports this approach. Management in GAO was highly centralized; the comptrollers general dealt with all manner of issues, big and small. Campbell's concern about the sick and annual leave records of individual staff being considered for promotion is an extreme example. He required staff to maintain a strictly professional posture in dealing with executive agency personnel. It was the staff, of course—voucher checkers, claims examiners, transportation rate specialists, investigators, accountants, auditors, lawyers, secretaries, and others—laboring in Washington, the field, and overseas—who did the basic work.

Reports to Congress and government agencies, settlement of disbursing officers' accounts, claims settlements, accounting systems work, corporation audits, investigations, recruiting, training, transportation audits, defense contract audits, and other activities—were all done technically in the name of the comptroller general. But they were the result of the efforts of a dedicated staff, a staff that usually responded to pressure, such as during World War II, to get the job done. The gradual professionalization of the staff equipped GAO to undertake more complex audits; to produce reports useful to Congress, executive agencies, and the public; and to recover or save substantial amounts of money for the federal government. Centralization of authority was a fact in GAO. But the success of the comptroller general, and of GAO as a whole, depended on the quantity and the quality of work completed by the staff.

A final theme related to change in GAO was the *effect of national and international developments* on GAO's work programs. As broad changes took place or major events occurred at home or abroad, GAO's work program expanded and evolved to accommodate them. The stock market crash of 1929 ushered in a major depression in the United States—an economic collapse that in time became worldwide. Politically, the depression brought Franklin D. Roosevelt to the presidency in 1933. Roosevelt initiated a New Deal agenda that included major programs of relief and recovery—programs of farm subsidies, public works, support of industry, and many others. GAO had to audit these programs as well as carry on its traditional work.

As war approached in Europe and the Far East in the late 1930s, Roosevelt mounted a national defense effort, again necessitating increased government spending, which GAO had to audit. Once the United States became involved in World War II, GAO faced the massive task of auditing war expenditures, including defense contracts, other military spending, and government transportation bills. While there was massive demobilization of U.S. forces after the war ended in 1945, the Cold War—the competition between the United States and the Soviet Union for economic, political, and military influence around the world—was in full swing by 1947. The Cold War necessitated a large standing military establishment, which grew further after the United States entered the Korean conflict in 1950. A new wave of defense expenditures during the Korean War drew GAO into defense contract auditing again. Even after the war ended in 1953, the rearmament of the United States, with emphasis on nuclear weapons and systems to deliver them, meant a high level of defense procurement that continued through the end of Campbell's term in 1965 and beyond. The environment in which GAO operated—domestic and international—influenced the work programs of the Office substantially.

GAO clearly made progress in many areas between 1921 and 1966. Until 1945, it was engaged mainly in routine voucher checking, making sure that federal agencies spent money only with the proper authorization and according to standing rules, verified by accurate account keeping. By 1965, GAO had moved ahead to look more comprehensively at the activities and the programs of these agencies and to produce substantive reports on them. To be sure, GAO emphasized problems discovered during its audits. The Office rarely praised agencies for their successes. GAO made much of the monetary accomplishments of its work—money actually collected or money GAO calculated the government had saved because of programs discontinued or changed because of reported findings.

GAO was not popular with executive branch agencies anytime between 1921 and 1966. Since GAO's emphasis was on reporting problems and publicly disclosing, through its reports and congressional testimony, errors of omission and commission, there was little basis for popularity. The resentment against the office ballooned in the 1930s, mainly because McCarl chose to stick to the letter of the law and government regulations as he interpreted them. McCarl's disputes with the attorney general of the United States, as well as with other agency heads in Washington, became legend by the end of his term. GAO's reports on such agencies as the Tennessee Valley Authority, the Maritime Commission, and the Reconstruction Finance Corporation generated opposition to as well as support for the Office during Warren's term. And Campbell's term ended with the serious controversy over GAO's audits of defense contracts.

How good was GAO's work during the years between 1921 and 1966? Were the Office's critics right? The answers to these questions depend now and depended then on the position and the perspective of the observer. All the comptrollers general believed that they were operating as required in the public interest and within the permissible bounds of the Budget and Accounting Act and other laws determining GAO's jurisdiction. They generally had the support of Congress, although on occasion, GAO faced severe criticism from some members—in the 1930s, during the mid-1940s when GAO's imperfect transportation audits were disclosed, during the zinc controversy of the 1950s, and particularly during the Holifield hearings on defense contract audits in the 1960s. When President Truman said in September 1951, in a speech dedicating the GAO Building, that GAO was "neither a bugaboo nor a bore," not everyone agreed with him.

One factor that can be looked at in determining the value of GAO's work was the quality of the staff. Clearly the staff improved as the years passed. By the 1950s and 1960s, they were better educated and more experienced and used more sophisticated techniques than their predecessors of the 1930s and the early 1940s. The reports on audits of government corporations that began to appear in the late 1940s and the comprehensive audit reports of the 1950s dug more deeply into the activities of federal agencies and organizations and provided more information to Congress, the executive branch, and the taxpayers about government operations. It is almost impossible to document the substantial deterrent effect of GAO on agency management and in preventing unwise or uneconomical activities. But it is clear, on the basis of the historical record, that GAO made a major contribution to better government in the United States between 1921 and 1966.

But was GAO as good or as effective as it could have been during this period? Was the Office a "sleeping giant" that had not realized its full potential? Perhaps the answer to these questions became clear only in the years after 1966. In 1967, two years after Campbell retired, Congress passed legislation requiring GAO to study and report on the "Great Society" programs—the antipoverty programs—begun in the 1960s under President Lyndon B. Johnson. In just over a year, GAO mounted a nationwide study of these programs, leading to a major report and more than 50 supplementary reports in 1969. Although "program evaluation" was not entirely new to GAO, this was the Office's first major effort in the field. The job required the quick development of new techniques and disciplinary approaches not used previously by GAO and extensive use of consultants and experts. The antipoverty programs work demonstrated GAO's ability to do program evaluation and set the stage for new emphases in GAO's reporting in the 1970s and succeeding decades.[1]

Comptroller General Elmer B. Staats, who entered office in 1966, was also instrumental in leading GAO's movement into program evaluation. As deputy director of the Bureau of the Budget up to 1966, Staats had worked

---

[1]See GAO, *The GAO Evaluation of the Antipoverty Programs, 1967-1969: Interviews with David A. Hanna, Elmer B. Staats, Henry Eschwege, Gregory J. Ahart, and Hyman L. Krieger*, GAO History Program, Oral History Series, GAO/OCG-1-OH (Washington: 1993).

on the federal Planning-Programming-Budgeting System (PPBS), which involved program evaluation. He also believed that the Budget and Accounting Act, 1921, reflected the intention of Congress that GAO would be concerned with program evaluation.[2]

Program evaluation became the heart of GAO's work, sanctioned by Congress in both the Legislative Reorganization Act of 1970[3] and the Congressional Budget and Impoundment Control Act of 1974.[4] To facilitate the new emphasis on program evaluation, GAO diversified its workforce, bringing in staff in business administration, economics, mathematics, engineering, the social sciences, systems analysis, and other fields. The progress of GAO in the three decades from 1966 to 1996 demonstrated that the Office could be more vital and more effective than it had been earlier. But of course after 1965, GAO was responding to new demands from Congress in an era of great change in the nation and the world. To argue that GAO could and should have been doing this work earlier ignores the importance of recognized need and congressional support. It was Congress that initially required the Office to evaluate the antipoverty programs and thus brought GAO into the era of program evaluation.

One area in which GAO showed some insensitivity before 1966 was human relations. Working conditions in the 1920s, 1930s, and 1940s—especially office accommodations—were poor for many GAO staff. GAO's management began an effort to get a new headquarters building large enough to accommodate the Washington staff as early as 1921, but the building was not available until 1951. Even after GAO moved into the new building, the less-favored divisions, such as Claims and Transportation, had quarters that were inferior to those of other units.

Another problem that received little attention during these years—because it was not perceived nationwide as a problem needing attention—was the fact that GAO was managed essentially by white males. There were women and African-Americans on the staff, but they were generally in the lower grades and lesser jobs. There were a few women in the professional ranks—mainly in the Office of the General Counsel. Most of the accountant recruits who came to GAO in the 1950s and the early 1960s under Campbell's recruitment program were white men. Women were mainly in the lower ranks, in clerical jobs for the most part. It was typical for a GAO manager to refer to the "men" he had in his division or to how many "men" he needed for a certain assignment.

---

[2]Ibid.

[3]Public Law 91-510, 84 Stat. 1140, approved October 26, 1970.

[4]Public Law 93-344, 88 Stat. 297, approved July 12, 1974.

GAO was not unique in this regard; professional women were few and far between in public accounting and in the federal government in this period. And there were not many professionally trained African-American and women accountants at this time. The primarily African-American staff in GAO's claims and transportation areas did not receive the kind of treatment, in terms of working conditions, rank, and opportunities for professional advancement, that their white male colleagues did. Not until the late 1960s and beyond, when the civil rights movement made significant gains in the United States, did African-American staff in GAO assert themselves. Class action suits helped to improve the climate. At the same time, GAO moved to broaden staff diversity through special programs to recruit women, African-Americans, and other ethnic minorities.

How effective were the comptrollers general in leading the Office? Fred Brown was in office too short a time to evaluate. J. R. McCarl, the first comptroller general, made a very substantial contribution in getting the Office started, determining its work programs, and establishing its independence from the executive branch. The latter accomplishment was especially important. Whether McCarl chose the right manner to do this is debatable. Perhaps being more cooperative and less combative in his relations with executive agencies would have strengthened GAO's effectiveness. McCarl's actions and attitudes more than anything else stimulated the attacks on GAO in the 1920s and 1930s and led to proposals backed by three of the four presidents of the period to change the Office's status.

To many observers, as demonstrated by the studies of the Brookings Institution and the Brownlow Committee in the late 1930s, the methods and the substance of much of what GAO did at the time, including the meticulous work of voucher checking, were antiquated. McCarl showed little imagination, ignored criticism, and exhibited a high degree of stubbornness. But McCarl did establish GAO's role and reputation as the watchdog of the nation's spending; this was very much to his credit. Through his constant reminding of Congress that it was responsible for the nation's financial well-being, with GAO as its primary agent in that enterprise, McCarl heightened the concerns of the legislative branch and the public to the dangers of fiscal irresponsibility. Perhaps it was fortuitous to have someone like McCarl leading GAO in its initial years.

Lindsay Warren's approach to his duties as comptroller general contrasted in many ways to McCarl's. Instead of being obstinate, confrontational, and picayune in his contacts with executive agencies, he favored cooperation when it was appropriate and consistent with GAO's statutory charter. The prime example was the Joint Accounting Improvement Program involving GAO, the Bureau of the Budget, and the Treasury Department. He was close to the presidents of his era—Franklin D. Roosevelt and Harry S. Truman. He maintained very cordial relations with Congress, where he had served with distinction for many years before he became comptroller general. Most important of all, he saw the need to discard obsolete and unnecessary methods and procedures and move on to work in areas more closely related to the needs of the nation. Audits of government corporations, the cooperative program in financial management, the comprehensive audit, and the extension of audit work at sites around the nation and overseas were the result. He began bringing in new staff and leadership to equip GAO to operate effectively in the new work areas. The contributions of Warren and his staff were very substantial. He led GAO into the modern era.

Campbell's contributions as comptroller general were important, but not as impressive as Warren's. His efforts to raise the professional qualifications of the staff, through extensive recruiting and training programs, were commendable. Perhaps he can be criticized for his almost exclusive concentration on bringing in accountants rather than working toward diversification in discipline and experience. But while he was comptroller general, there was no defined role for such staff. He did not appear to be thinking too much about the future of the Office and what demands might be placed on it at that time. He was dealing with the situation at the moment. That suggested, among other things, especially in the 1960s, an extensive program to audit defense contracts. This effort was necessary and important, but Campbell did not anticipate and deal with some valid criticism from contractors and agencies adversely affected by this work. More consideration of how to present contract audit results in a way that would be most effective in the long run would have been appropriate. He and his top management officials did not foresee the results of the proliferation of reports with titles designed to catch the eye of the public and the press. The Holifield hearings were traumatic in the short run for some people in GAO. The long-term effects were perhaps somewhat beneficial to the Office. The reorganization of the Defense Accounting and Auditing Division and the shift to broader-based reports on defense activities helped lead to more significant contributions by GAO in the years after 1965.

GAO's history between 1921 and 1966 is generally the history of a successful agency that made substantial contributions to the country. There were potentially serious problems along the way; but when they surfaced, GAO responded promptly and positively. The usefulness of the Office to Congress increased over the years, and Congress appreciated GAO's assistance and support. Change in the General Accounting Office was constant, particularly after 1940. While the pace of change may have been slower than desirable at times, change did come and it led to qualitative improvements. When Elmer B. Staats became comptroller general in 1966, he found that his predecessors had created a solid foundation on which to build.

Essay on Sources

This book is based for the most part on original documentary materials, both unpublished and published. These documents come mainly from the legislative branch of the U. S. government—the two houses of Congress and the General Accounting Office. Other important original materials include the records of other government agencies and papers from private collections.

GAO Sources—Unpublished

Unlike most federal government agencies, GAO has not routinely offered its records to the National Archives and Records Administration for accession. Consequently, the National Archives holds very few GAO documents. Almost all existing GAO records are either in GAO offices in Washington and elsewhere or in the Federal Records Center in Suitland, MD. These records, although somewhat spotty and not well-organized by archival standards, provide a substantial documentary basis for preparing the history of GAO.

The A- and B- files are the most important collection of original GAO documents. GAO's Office of the General Counsel (OGC) began to compile this extensive group of case files when the agency began operations in 1921 and has maintained them since that date. The A- files, numbered 1 through 99,999, covered the years 1921 to 1939. Then OGC began the B- files, starting in 1939 with number 1. These files, still being compiled, totaled about 270,000 by 1996. Although not officially a central file of GAO records, the A- and B- files include information on any subject or case that came to the attention of the Office of the General Counsel. For the earlier period, from 1921 to the 1960s, the files contain information, some of it very routine, on most aspects of GAO's work. In more recent years, in the period beyond the scope of this book, the B- files have become less comprehensive. A card index system, providing access by subject, name, and A- or B-number, exists for the period between 1921 and 1978. For the years thereafter, a computerized system captured information about the B- files. Footnote references to documents in the A- and B- files in this book include the appropriate file number, for example, A-13027 or B-155327.

Another large collection compiled by OGC is the series of bound manuscript volumes entitled *Decisions and Letters*, begun in 1921 and continued without interruption to the present. In the early years, OGC prepared one volume of the series each month; in later years, the monthly volumes sometimes contained more than one part. Volume 1 is an exception to this rule--it covers July, August, and September 1921, GAO's first three months of operations. For each succeeding month, beginning with October 1921, the volume number increases by one. Thus, *Decisions and Letters* for October 1921 is volume 2; November 1921 is volume 3. By September 1939, the volume number was 217. The pages within each monthly volume are numbered serially; the first page of the first document in the volume for July 1921 is 1 MS 1. If a document that began, for example, on page 208 of volume 37 had 3 pages, they were numbered 37 MS 208, 37 MS 209, and 37 MS 210. In this book, citations to documents in *Decisions and Letters* give the first page number of the document rather than inclusive page numbers. Thus 217 MS 780 is a reference to a document that begins on page 780 of *Decisions and Letters*, volume 217.

OGC selected the documents for these volumes. They included various materials, such as important decisions and opinions of the comptroller general, internal memorandums, external correspondence, claims cases, and other documents. The documents in *Decisions and Letters* usually were included also in the appropriate A- or B- file. The Legal Support Services Branch of OGC maintains the master set of the *Decisions and Letters* series.

The GAO Room in the GAO Law Library houses various other documents, usually compiled in bound manuscript volumes. Examples include GAO *Intra-Office Memorandums*, ten volumes, covering 1921 through 1979, and GAO *Office Orders*, two volumes. The GAO Room also holds bound volumes of reports issued by the Corporation Audits Division between 1946 and 1953, the annual reports of the Joint Financial Management Improvement Program, and other materials relating to the history of GAO.

The GAO History Program Archives has a miscellaneous collection of documents and other materials that have been used in preparing this book. Particularly valuable are the personal papers of Ellsworth H. Morse, Jr., whose career at GAO spanned the years from 1946 to 1977. Morse, director and later assistant comptroller general for policy between 1956 and 1966, kept subject files relating to GAO activities during his tenure. This very useful collection approximates 22 cubic feet. Morse's speech, article, memorandum, and conference files constitute another 3.5 cubic feet.

Two other sources compiled by Morse are particularly valuable. In 1956, when he became director of the Accounting and Auditing Policy Staff, Morse began a series of *Daily Notes*; they are typewritten and are bound in seven loose-leaf volumes. The first volume covers 1956, and the six subsequent volumes cover two years each, ending with the volume for 1967-1968. Morse's daily notes are particularly useful because of the information they contain about the role of Comptroller General Joseph Campbell between 1956 and 1965 and the first two years of his successor, Elmer B. Staats.

Morse kept another series, entitled *Notes of Meetings of the Accounting and Auditing Division Heads*. There are four typewritten loose-leaf volumes in this set, covering the period from September 1956 through July 1964. They record the deliberations of meetings, which Morse chaired, of the heads of GAO's accounting and auditing divisions and related staff offices. They provide valuable information about the development of accounting and auditing policy and the operations of the Civil and Defense Accounting and Auditing Divisions.

Among other records in the GAO History Program Archives are two boxes of papers documenting the GAO organization survey directed by Ted B. Westfall between 1949 and 1952. The survey reports in this collection reveal much about the operations of GAO divisions and offices during this period and contain recommendations for reorganizing GAO, most of which Comptroller General Lindsay C. Warren adopted in a major restructuring in 1952.

GAO Sources—Published

The annual reports of the comptroller general, beginning with the volume for fiscal year 1922, are rich sources for the history of GAO. Typically these reports review GAO's activities and accomplishments and contain statistics on budgets, staffing, reports issued, and other accomplishments. Usually the annual reports describe the activities of each division and staff office in GAO. The titles vary somewhat over the years. The reports for fiscal years 1922-1925 carry the title *Annual Report of the General Accounting Office*; for fiscal years 1926-1935, 1939-1948, and 1955-1966, *Annual Report of the Comptroller General of the United States for the Fiscal Year Ended June 30, _____*; for fiscal years 1936-1938, *Annual Report of the Acting Comptroller General of the United States for the Fiscal Year Ended June 30, _____*; and for fiscal years 1948-1954, *Comptroller General of the United States: Annual Report for the Fiscal Year Ended June 30, _____*. The Government Printing Office published all the annual reports except those for 1922-1924, which were issued as House documents.

Between 1987 and 1992, the GAO History Program published a series of 24 oral history interviews of former GAO officials, many of whom served during parts of the period covered by this book. Some of the oral histories involved one person; others involved groups of up to four persons. These interviews provide valuable information, insights, and recollections of individuals who played important leadership roles at GAO. The specific oral histories used in preparing this book are listed in appendix II, "Bibliography."

The GAO Review was a monthly journal published by GAO between 1966 and 1986. In addition to carrying many articles, some of them dealing with GAO's history, the *Review* carried notices of major staff appointments, promotions, and retirements. It is a valuable source of information for the history of GAO. Articles from the *Review* cited in this book are listed in appendix II.

Personal Papers

Only one of the four comptrollers general who served during the period covered by this book compiled a collection of personal papers. The Papers of Lindsay C. Warren are housed in the Southern Historical Collection, Wilson Library, University of North Carolina at Chapel Hill, North Carolina. The Warren Papers include voluminous materials for the years of his term as comptroller general between 1940 and 1954. There is a large number of incoming and outgoing letters—to friends and associates in his home state of North Carolina, to family members, to members of Congress, to officials of government agencies, and to Presidents Franklin D. Roosevelt and Harry S. Truman. In these letters, Warren frequently wrote of internal developments at GAO, national affairs, and his personal life, including health and financial matters. The Warren collection also includes a series of scrapbooks for the GAO years, containing clippings and photographs relative to his work as comptroller general. The Warren Papers provide information and insights about Warren's term as comptroller general and GAO's activities that cannot be found elsewhere. They are a rich source.

Lindsay C. Warren, Jr., of Goldsboro, NC, graciously granted to the author permission to use his father's personal papers and to cite from them.

Selected information relating to GAO presented in this book came from the Papers of Franklin D. Roosevelt at the Roosevelt Library, Hyde Park, NY, and the Papers of Harry S. Truman, at the Truman Library, Independence, MO.

Records of Other Government Agencies

The following collections of records, all housed in the National Archives, provided valuable information for chapter 7, "GAO's Quest for a Headquarters Building, 1921-1951."

Record Group (RG) 6, Records of the Department of the Treasury.

RG 66, Records of the Commission of Fine Arts and Minutes of the Commission of Fine Arts (Microfilm).

RG 121, Records of the Public Buildings Service.

RG 328, Records of the National Capital Parks and Planning Commission.

Congressional Sources

Published congressional sources constitute a substantial part of the documentation for this book. Given the unorganized nature of most GAO documents, the difficulty of accessing them, and the gaps in the record for the early years, it would have been difficult to prepare this study without congressional materials. Most valuable were the annual volumes covering GAO's appropriation hearings. Typically at these extensive hearings, GAO officials reviewed the previous fiscal year's activities and accomplishments and presented a justification for the funds requested for the coming fiscal year. In the process, the hearings revealed much information about the ongoing history of GAO. Specifically, the hearings, before a subcommittee of the House Committee on Appropriations, covered the Independent Offices Appropriations Bill for each fiscal year. Congress did not consider GAO's budget as a part of the legislative branch appropriations bill until the mid-1960s. Footnotes in this volume provide complete bibliographical information for each volume of appropriations hearings used.

Other congressional hearings on specific subjects related to GAO activities, in both the House and the Senate, proved to be very valuable, as did selected House and Senate prints, reports, and documents. They are listed separately in appendix II.

The record of debates in the *Congressional Record* also were useful.

Bibliography

This list includes items cited in the text and a few additional books and other materials that provide pertinent information. Sources noted in appendix I, "Essay on Sources," are not included in this list.

I. Bibliographical Aids

Bibliography on Federal Accounting, Auditing, Budgeting, and Reporting, 1900-1970—Annotated. Arlington, VA: Federal Government Accountants Association, 1971.

Hollings, Robert L. *The General Accounting Office: An Annotated Bibliography*. New York and London: Garland Publishing, Inc., 1991.

II. Printed Sources

A. Congressional Documents

1. House Hearings

Committee on Military Affairs. *Authorizing the Secretary of War to Use Funds for Adjustment of Contracts*, pt. 2, 78th Cong., 1st Sess., 1943.

Committee on Expenditures in the Executive Departments. *Budgeting and Accounting Procedures Act of 1950*, 81st Cong., 2d Sess., 1950.

_____, Procurement and Buildings Subcommittee. *Investigation of Procurement and Buildings*, pt. 7, "General Accounting Office Audit of Wartime Freight Vouchers," 80th Cong., 2d Sess., 1948.

Committee on Government Operations, *Comptroller General Reports on Audits of Defense Contracts*, 89th Cong., 1st Sess., 1965.

Committee on Public Buildings and Grounds. *Construction of Public Buildings*, 79th Cong., 1st Sess., 1945.

Committee on Public Works. *GAO Building*, 80th Cong., 1st Sess., 1947.

Select Committee on the Budget. *National Budget System*, 66th Cong., 1st Sess., 1919.

2. House Reports

Amendment of Budget and Accounting Act, 1921, Establishment of Office of Auditor General, 75th Cong., 1st Sess., 1937, H. Rept. 1606.

Defense Contract Audits, Twenty-Fourth Report by the Committee on Government Operations, 89th Cong., 2d Sess., 1966, H. Rept. 1344.

Executive Orders Grouping, Coordinating, and Consolidating Certain Executive and Administrative Agencies of the Government, 72d Cong., 2d Sess., 1933, H. Rept. 1833.

The General Accounting Office: A Study of Its Functions and Operations, Fifth Intermediate Report of the Committee on Expenditures in the Executive Departments, 81st Cong., 1st Sess., 1949, H. Rept. 1441.

The General Accounting Office: A Study of Its Organization and Administration with Recommendations for Increasing Its Effectiveness, Seventeenth Intermediate Report of the Committee on Government Operations, 84th Cong., 2d Sess., 1956, H. Rept. 2264.

Government Organization, 75th Cong., 3d Sess., 1938, H. Rept. 2033.

Investigation of General Accounting Office Audit of Wartime Freight Vouchers, Eighteenth Intermediate Report of the Committee on Expenditures in the Executive Departments, 80th Cong., 2d Sess., 1948, H. Rept. 2457.

Report on Review of General Accounting Office Operations in Europe and the Major Programs Covered by the General Accounting Office in the European Area, Seventeenth Report by the Committee on Government Operations, 85th Cong., 2d Sess., 1958, H. Rept. 1281.

3. House Documents

Audit Report on the Examination of the Commodity Credit Corporation for the period ended June 30, 1945, 81st Cong., 1st Sess., 1949, H. Doc. 148.

Message from the President of the United States Transmitting a Message to Group, Coordinate, and Consolidate Executive and Administrative Agencies of the Government As Nearly as Maybe, According to Major Purposes, 72d Cong., 2d Sess., 1932, H. Doc. 493.

4. House Prints

Constitutionality of the General Accounting Office, A Monograph Submitted to the Select Committee on Government Organization, 75th Cong., 3d Sess., 1938, Revised Committee Print.

5. Senate Hearings

Special Committee on Atomic Energy. *Atomic Energy Act of 1946*, pt. 5, 79th Cong., 2d Sess., 1946.

Committee on Public Works. *GAO Building, Federal Court Building, District of Columbia*, 80th Cong., 2d Sess., 1948.

Committee on Claims. *Losses Sustained by Growers Incident to Federal Campaign for the Eradication of the Mediterranean Fruit Fly in Florida*, 76th Cong., 3d Sess., 1940.

_____. *Mediterranean Fruit Fly*, 76th Cong., 3d Sess., 1940.

Committee on Consideration of a National Budget. *National Budget*, 66th Cong., 2d Sess., 1920.

Committee on Government Operations. *Nomination of Joseph Campbell*, 84th Cong., 1st Sess., 1955.

Select Committee on Government Organization. *Reorganization of the Government Agencies*, 75th Cong., 1st Sess., 1937.

Committee on Expenditures in the Executive Departments. *To Improve Budgeting, Accounting, and Auditing Methods of the Federal Government*, 81st Cong., 2d Sess., 1950.

6. Senate Reports

Government Organization, 75th Cong., 1st Sess., 1937, S. Rept. 1236.

Investigation of Executive Agencies of the Government, Preliminary Report of the Select Committee to Investigate the Executive Agencies of the Government, 75th Cong., 1st Sess., 1937, S. Rept. 1275.

Review of Audit Reports of the Comptroller General, 84th Cong., 2d Sess., 1956, S. Rept. 1572.

7. Senate Documents

Biographical Directory of the United States Congress, 1774-1989, Bicentennial Edition, 100th Cong., 2d Sess., 1989, S. Doc. 100-34.

Committee on Government Operations, *Financial Management in the Federal Government*, 87th Cong., 1st Sess., 1961, S. Doc. 11.

_____, *Financial Management in the Federal Government*, Vol. II, 92d Cong., 1st Sess., 1971, S. Doc. 92-50.

_____, *Functions of the General Accounting Office*, 87th Cong., 2d Sess., 1962, S. Doc. 96.

Reorganization of the Executive Departments, 67th Cong., 4th Sess., 1923, S. Doc. 302.

Reorganization of the Executive Departments, Message from the President of the United States, 75th Cong., 1st Sess., 1937, S. Doc. 8.

8. Joint Hearings

Joint Committee on Defense Production. *Defense Production Act*, 84th Cong., 1st Sess., 1955.

Joint Committee on the Investigation of the Tennessee Valley Authority. *Investigation of the Tennessee Valley Authority*, 75th Cong., 3d Sess., 1938.

Joint Committee on the Organization of Congress. *Organization of Congress*, 79th Cong., 1st Sess., 1945.

B. Documents of the Hoover Commissions

Budgeting and Accounting. Letter from the chairman, Commission on Organization of the Executive Branch of the Government Transmitting Its Report on "Budgeting and Accounting" in the Executive Branch. Washington: GPO, 1949.

Hanes, John W., A. E. Buck, and T. Coleman Andrews. *Fiscal, Budgeting, and Accounting Systems of Federal Government: A Report with Recommendations*. Prepared for the Commission on Organization of the Executive Branch of the Government. Washington: GPO, 1949.

Budget and Accounting. A Report to the Congress by the Commission on Organization of the Executive Branch of the Government. Washington: GPO, 1955.

Report on Budget and Accounting in the United States Government. Prepared by the Hoover Commission Task Force on Budget and Accounting. Washington: GPO, 1955.

C. Oral Histories

1. GAO History Program, Oral History Series

John P. Abbadessa, 1947-1962, GAO/OP-18-OH. Washington: GAO, 1990.

Audit and Legal Services, 1943-1983—a Women's Perspective: Interview with Margaret L. Macfarlane, Geraldine M. Rubar, and Stella B. Shea, GAO/OP-10-OH. Washington: GAO, 1990.

The Civil Division, 1956-1972: Interview with Gregory J. Ahart, Henry Eschwege, and Victor L. Lowe, GAO/OP-22-OH. Washington: GAO, 1992.

Congressional Relations Activities, 1950-1983: Smith Blair, Charles E. Eckert, Martin J. Fitzgerald, and L. Fred Thompson, GAO/OP-14-OH. Washington: GAO, 1990.

Defense-Related Audits, 1937-1975: Interview with Hassell B. Bell, J. Kenneth Fasick, and James H. Hammond, GAO/OP-9-OH. Washington: GAO, 1989.

William L. Ellis: GAO, 1935-1955, GAO/OP-21-OH. Washington: GAO, 1991.

Leo Herbert: GAO, 1956-1974, GAO/OP-7-OH. Washington: GAO, 1988.

Chet Holifield, GAO-OP-5-OH. Washington: GAO, 1988.

International Activities, 1956-1981: Interview with James A. Duff, J. Kenneth Fasick, and Charles D. Hylander, GAO/OP-19-OH. Washington: GAO, 1991.

Policy Guidance, 1963-1986: Interview with Donald J. Horan, Eugene L. Pahl, and Allen R. Voss, GAO/OP-23-OH. Washington: GAO, 1992.

Regional Offices and the Field Operations Division: Interview with Francis X. Fee, Walter H. Henson, and Hyman L. Krieger, GAO/OP-15-OH. Washington: GAO, 1990.

Adolph T. Samuelson, 1946-1965, GAO/OP-11-OH. Washington: GAO, 1989.

The San Francisco Regional Office, 1954-1987: Interview with Harold J. D'Ambrogia, Kenneth A. Pollock, Richard A. Sheldon, and Charles F. Vincent, GAO/OP-20-OH. Washington: GAO, 1991.

Arthur Schoenhaut, GAO/OP-4-OH. Washington: GAO, 1988.

Elmer B. Staats, GAO/OP-1-OH. Washington: GAO, 1987.

John E. Thornton, 1935-1976, GAO/OP-3-OH. Washington: GAO, 1988.

Transportation Activities, 1946-1975: Interview with Joseph P. Normile, Fred J. Shafer, and Thomas E. Sullivan, GAO/OP-24-OH. Washington: GAO, 1992.

Ted B. Westfall, GAO/OP-2-OH. Washington: GAO, 1988.

Charles E. Wolfe, 1935-1988, GAO/OP-8-OH. Washington: GAO, 1988.

2. Other Oral History

Frese, Walter F. *Early History of the Joint Financial Management Improvement Program*, as interviewed by Ellsworth H. Morse, Jr., and Donald C. Kull. Washington: Joint Financial Management Improvement Program, 1980.

III. Secondary Works

A. Books Primarily on the General Accounting Office

Brown, Richard E., ed. *Accounting and Accountability in Public Administration*. Washington: American Society for Public Administration, 1988.

_____. *The GAO: Untapped Source of Congressional Power*. Knoxville, TN: University of Tennessee Press, 1970.

The Government Contractor and the General Accounting Office. Washington: Machinery and Allied Products Institute, 1966.

Havens, Harry S. *The Evolution of the General Accounting Office: From Voucher Audits to Programs Evaluations.* GAO/OP-2-HP. Washington: GAO, 1990.

Improving Management for More Effective Government: 50th Anniversary Lectures of the United States General Accounting Office, 1921-1977. Washington: GPO, 1972.

Klimschot, JoAnn. *Adding Bite to the Bark: A Common Cause Study of the GAO, the Government's Watchdog.* Washington: Common Cause, 1980.

Kloman, Erasmus H., ed. *Cases in Accountability: The Work of the GAO.* Boulder, CO: Westview Press, 1979.

Mansfield, Harvey C., Sr. *The Comptroller General: A Study in the Law and Practice of Financial Administration.* New Haven: Yale University Press, 1939.

Mosher, Frederick C. *The GAO: The Quest for Accountability in American Government.* Boulder, CO: Westview Press, 1979.

_____. *A Tale of Two Agencies: A Comparative Analysis of the General Accounting Office and the Office of Management and Budget.* Baton Rouge: Louisiana State University Press, 1984.

Pois, Joseph. *Watchdog on the Potomac: A Study of the Comptroller General of the United States.* Washington: University Press of America, Inc., 1979.

Schulsinger, Gerald G. *The General Accounting Office: Two Glimpses.* University, AL: University of Alabama Press, 1956.

Smith, Darrell H. *The General Accounting Office: Its History, Activities and Organization.* Baltimore, MD: John Hopkins Press, 1927.

Sperry, Roger L., Timothy D. Desmond, Kathi F. McGraw, and Barbara Schmitt. *GAO 1966-1981: An Administrative History.* Washington: GAO, 1981.

Trask, Roger R. *GAO History, 1921-1991.* GAO/OP-3-HP. Washington: GAO, 1991.

Walker, Wallace E. *Changing Organizational Culture: Strategy, Structure, and Professionalism in the U.S. General Accounting Office.* Knoxville: University of Tennessee Press, 1986.

Wilbur, May Hunter. *An Early History of the General Accounting Office, 1921-1943.* GAO/OP-1-HP. Washington: GAO, 1988.

Willoughby, William F. *The Legal Status and Functions of the General Accounting Office of the National Government.* Baltimore, MD: Johns Hopkins Press, 1927.

B. General Books

Berman, Larry. *The Office of Management and Budget and the Presidency, 1921-1979.* Princeton: Princeton University Press, 1979.

Borchert, James. *Alley Life in Washington: Family, Community, Religion, and Folklife in the City, 1850-1970.* Chicago: University of Illinois Press, 1982.

Chan, James L., and Rowan H. Jones, eds. *Governmental Accounting and Auditing: International Comparisons.* London and New York: Routledge, 1988.

Condit, Doris M. *History of the Office of the Secretary of Defense*, Vol. II, *The Test of War, 1950-1953.* Washington: Historical Office, Office of the Secretary of Defense, 1988.

Cushman, Robert E. *Leading Constitutional Decisions.* 12th ed. New York: Appleton-Century-Crofts, 1963.

Dawes, Charles G. *The First Year of the Budget of the United States.* New York: 1923.

Dyke, Richard W., and Francis X. Gannon. *Chet Holifield: Master Legislator and Nuclear Statesman.* Lanham, MD: University Press of America, 1996.

Falk, Peter H., ed. *Who Was Who in American Art.* Madison, CT: Sound View Press, 1985.

Ferrell, Robert H. *Harry S. Truman: A Life*. Columbia, MO, and London: University of Missouri Press, 1994.

Goldberg, Alfred. *The Pentagon: The First Fifty Years*. Washington: Historical Office, Office of the Secretary of Defense, 1992.

Goode, James M. *The Outdoor Sculpture of Washington, D.C.: A Comprehensive Historical Guide*. Washington: Smithsonian Institution Press, 1974.

Groves, Leslie R. *Now It Can Be Told: The Story of the Manhattan Project*. New York: Harper & Brothers, 1962.

Hamby, Alonzo L. *Man of the People: A Life of Harry S. Truman*. New York: Oxford University Press, 1995.

Jensen, Merrill S. *The Articles of Confederation*. Madison: University of Wisconsin Press, 1940.

_____. *The Founding of A Nation: The History of the American Revolution, 1763-1776*. New York: Oxford University Press, 1968.

_____. *The New Nation: A History of the United States During the Confederation, 1781-1789*. New York: Alfrcd A. Knopf, 1950.

Kelly, Alfred H., and Winfred A. Harbison. *The American Constitution: Its Origins and Development*. New York: W. W. Norton and Company, 1963.

Kohler, Eric L., and Howard W. Wright. *Accounting in the Federal Government*. Englewood Cliffs, NJ: Prentice-Hall, Inc., 1956.

Lilienthal, David E. *The Journals of David E. Lilienthal*, Vol. I, *The TVA Years, 1939-1945*. New York: Harper & Row, 1964.

Lowitt, Richard. *George W. Norris: The Persistence of a Progressive, 1913-1933*. Urbana and Chicago, IL, and London: University of Illinois Press, 1971.

Morris, Richard B. *The Forging of the Union, 1781-1789*. New York: Harper & Row, 1987.

Opitz, Glenn B., ed. *Dictionary of American Sculptors*. Poughkeepsie, NY: Apollo, 1984.

Pritchett, Herman C. *The Tennessee Valley Authority: A Study in Public Administration.* Chapel Hill: University of North Carolina Press, 1943.

Short and Ford, architects. *Historic Structure Report and Preservation Manual for the General Accounting Office, Final Report.* Princeton, NJ: Short and Ford, 1990.

Smith, Kathryn Schneider, ed. *Washington at Home: An Illustrated History of Neighborhoods in the Nation's Capital.* Northridge, CA: Windsor Publications, 1988.

Studenski, Paul. *Financial History of the United States.* New York: McGraw-Hill, 1963.

Wallace, Robert A. *Congressional Control of Federal Spending.* Detroit: Wayne State University Press, 1960.

White, Leonard D. *The Federalists: A Study in Administrative History, 1789-1801.* New York: Macmillan, 1948.

_____. *The Jeffersonians: A Study in Administrative History, 1801-1829.* New York: Macmillan, 1951.

_____. *The Jacksonians: A Study in Administrative History, 1829-1861.* New York: Macmillan, 1954.

_____. *The Republican Era: A Study in Administrative History, 1869-1901.* New York: Macmillan, 1958.

Whitnah, Donald R., ed. *Government Agencies.* Westport, CT: Greenwood Press, 1983.

Wilmerding, Lucius, Jr. *The Spending Power: A History of the Efforts to Control Expenditures.* New Haven: Yale University Press, 1943.

Wood, Gordon S. *The Creation of the American Republic, 1776-1787.* New York: W. W. Norton & Company, 1972.

C. Theses and Dissertations

Pow, Alex S. "The Comptroller General and the General Accounting Office of the United States." Ph.D. dissertation, New York University, 1960.

Rosales, Manuel George, Jr. "An Analysis of the Progress of the Joint Financial Management Improvement Program." M.P.A. [Master of Professional Accounting] thesis, Graduate School of Business, University of Texas, 1969.

D. Articles and Essays

Anderson, Marcia, and Jeff Jacobs. "A History of GAO's Buildings." *GAO Review* (spring 1979): 16-17.

Bethell, Thomas N. "The Best Job in Washington." *Washington Monthly* 12 (1980): 12-22.

Bowsher, Charles A. "Federal Financial Management: Evolution, Challenges, and the Role of the Accounting Profession," in James L. Chan and Rowan H. Jones, eds. *Governmental Accounting and Auditing: International Comparisons*. London and New York: Routledge, 1988: 29-51.

Conkin, Paul K. "Tennessee Valley Authority (TVA), in Donald R. Whitnah, ed. *Government Agencies*. Westport, CT: Greenwood Press, 1983: 497-504.

Fenton, John C. "The Corporation Audits Division—Its Legacy to the Seventies." *GAO Review* (summer 1971): 88-110.

_____. "Irwin S. Decker—A Career of Service." *GAO Review* (summer 1967): 57-62.

Flesher, Dale L., and Tonya K. Flesher. "T. Coleman Andrews and the GAO Corporation Audits Division." *Government Accountants Journal* 38 (1989): 23-28.

Ford, Robert W. "A Look Back at GAO in 1936—and Something About 1976." *GAO Review* (summer 1976), 61-70.

Herbert, Leo. "A Perspective on Accounting." *Accounting Review* 47 (1971): 433-40.

Howard, Jerilynn Brezil. "The Old Red Barn and Other Local Landmarks: A Brief History of GAO's Changing Neighborhood." *GAO Review* (winter 1984): 26-29.

Hughes, Charles E. "The Overseas Offices of the General Accounting Office." *GAO Review* (summer 1971): 136-43.

Hylander, Charles D. "Overseas Activities of the General Accounting Office." *GAO Review* (fall 1966): 15-20.

"J. R. McCarl—Some Glimpses of the First Comptroller General." *GAO Review* (summer 1971): 46-53.

Kendall, Lane C. "Federal Maritime Commission (FMC)," in Donald R. Whitnah, ed. *Government Agencies*. Westport, CT: Greenwood Press, 1983: 229-33.

Kiselewski, Joseph. "From Farmboy to Sculptor: An Autobiography." *National Sculpture Review* 28 (1979-1980): 16-19, 27.

Kraines, Oscar. "The Dockery-Cockrell Commission, 1893-1895." *Western Political Quarterly* 7 (1954): 417-62.

Lodwick, David, and Donald H. Friedman. "The Transportation Division— A Forward Look Over the Past 50 Years." *GAO Review* (summer 1971): 144-48.

Macfarlane, Margaret L. "Birth of the General Accounting Office." *GAO Review* (winter 1968): 77-81.

_____. "The Day President Wilson Vetoed the Budget and Accounting Bill." *GAO Review* (fall 1968): 57-60.

_____ and Judith Hatter. "Personalities Contributing to the Enactment of the Budget and Accounting Act, 1921." *GAO Review* (fall 1971): 57-71.

McGuire, Oliver R. "The Opinions of the Attorney General and the General Accounting Office." *Georgetown Law Journal* 15 (1927): 115-26.

Merrill, C. E. "History of the Field Operations Division." *GAO Review* (Summer 1971): 128-35.

Morse, Ellsworth H., Jr. "The Accounting and Auditing Act of 1950—Its Current Significance to GAO." *GAO Review* (summer 1975): 23-31.

_____. "The Application of Public Funds." *GAO Review* (summer 1971): 20-25.

_____. "The Government Corporation Control Legislation of 1945." *GAO Review* (fall 1975), 11-22.

_____. "How GAO's Audit Standards Evolved." *GAO Review* (summer 1977): 54-58.

_____. "Professional Accountants in Government: Roles and Dilemmas." *Public Administration Review* 38 (1978): 120-25.

_____. "Site Audits of War Contracts in World War II." *GAO Review* (fall 1977): 49-51.

Oelkers, William C. "An Album of GAO Buildings." *GAO Review* (Summer, 1986): 18-23.

Olson, James S. "Reconstruction Finance Corporation (RFC)," in Donald R. Whitnah, ed. *Government Agencies*. Westport, CT: Greenwood Press, 1983: 462-66.

Pemberton, William E. "Truman and the Hoover Commission." *Whistle Stop*, 19 (1991): 2-4.

Poel, Elizabeth. "GAO Remembers President Harry S. Truman." *GAO Review* (fall 1984), 14-18, 44.

Rosapepe, Joseph S. "Works of Art at GAO." *GAO Review* (spring 1978): 28-31.

Smith, Frederic H. "The Joint Financial Management Improvement Program is 20 Years Old." *GAO Review* (winter 1969): 81-88.

Sperry, Roger L., and Jonathan D. Towers. "Expenditure Analyses by GAO: An Idea Whose Time Had Not Arrived." *GAO Review* (fall 1980): 39-42.

"The Accounting Systems Division." *GAO Review* (summer 1971): 111-14.

Voss, Allan R. "Ellsworth H. Morse, Jr., Assistant Comptroller General of the United States." *GAO Review* (winter 1978): 1-12.

Weitzel, Frank H. "Lindsay Carter Warren: Comptroller General of the United States, 1940-1954." *GAO Review* (spring 1977): 1-30.

Williams, Elizabeth M., and Alvin S. Finegold. "Remembering GAO's Field Operations Division." *GAO Review* (Spring 1984): 21-25, 39-40.

APPENDIX III

The Budget and Accounting Act, 1921 (Title III)

Sec. 301.

There is created an establishment of the Government to be known as the General Accounting Office, which shall be independent of the executive departments and under the control and direction of the Comptroller General of the United States. The offices of Comptroller of the Treasury and Assistant Comptroller of the Treasury are abolished, to take effect July 1, 1921. All other officers and employees of the office of the Comptroller of the Treasury shall become officers and employees in the General Accounting Office at their grades and salaries on July 1, 1921, and all books, records, documents, papers, furniture, office equipment and other property of the office of the Comptroller of the Treasury shall become the property of the General Accounting Office. The Comptroller General is authorized to adopt a seal for the General Accounting Office.

Sec. 302.

There shall be in the General Accounting Office a Comptroller General of the United States and an Assistant Comptroller General of the United States, who shall be appointed by the President with the advice and consent of the Senate, and shall receive salaries of $10,000 and $7,500 a year, respectively. The Assistant Comptroller General shall perform such duties as may be assigned to him by the Comptroller General, and during the absence or incapacity of the Comptroller General, or during a vacancy in that office, shall act as Comptroller General.

Sec. 303.

Except as hereinafter provided in this section, the Comptroller General and the Assistant Comptroller General shall hold office for fifteen years. The Comptroller General shall not be eligible for reappointment. The Comptroller General or the Assistant Comptroller General may be removed at any time by joint resolution of Congress after notice and hearing, when, in the judgment of Congress, the Comptroller General or Assistant Comptroller General has become permanently incapacitated or has been inefficient, or guilty of neglect of duty, or of malfeasance in office, or of any felony or conduct involving moral turpitude, and for no other cause and in no other manner except by impeachment. Any Comptroller General or Assistant Comptroller General removed in the manner herein provided shall be ineligible for reappointment to that office. When a Comptroller General or Assistant Comptroller General attains the age of seventy years, he shall be retired from his office.

Sec. 304.

All powers and duties now conferred or imposed by law upon the Comptroller of the Treasury or the six auditors of the Treasury Department, and the duties of the Division of Bookkeeping and Warrants of the Office of the Secretary of the Treasury relating to keeping the personal ledger accounts of disbursing and collecting officers, shall, so far as not inconsistent with the Act, be vested in and imposed upon the General Accounting Office and be exercised without direction from any other officer. The balances certified by the Comptroller General shall be final and conclusive upon the executive branch of the Government. The revision by the Comptroller General of settlements made by the six auditors shall be discontinued, except as to settlements made before July 1, 1921.

The administrative examination of the accounts and vouchers of the Postal Service now imposed by law upon the Auditor for the Post Office Department shall be performed on and after July 1, 1921, by a bureau in the Post Office Department to be known as the Bureau of Accounts, which is hereby established for that purpose. The Bureau of Accounts shall be under the direction of a Comptroller, who shall be appointed by the President with the advice and consent of the Senate, and shall receive a salary of $5,000 a year. The Comptroller shall perform the administrative duties now performed by the Auditor for the Post Office Department and such other duties in relation thereto as the Postmaster General may direct. The appropriation of $5,000 for the salary of the Auditor for the Post Office Department for the fiscal year 1922 is transferred and made available for the salary of the Comptroller, Bureau of Accounts, Post Office Department. The officers and employees of the Office of the Auditor for the Post Office Department engaged in the administrative examination of accounts shall become officers and employees of the Bureau of Accounts at their grades and salaries on July 1, 1921. The appropriations for salaries and for contingent and miscellaneous expenses and tabulating equipment for such office for the fiscal year 1922, and all books, records, documents, papers, furniture, office equipment, and other property shall be apportioned between, transferred to, and made available for the Bureau of Accounts and the General Accounting Office, respectively, on the basis of duties transferred.

Sec. 305.

Section 236 of the Revised Statutes is amended to read as follows:

> "Sec. 236. All claims and demands whatever by the Government of the United States or against it, and all accounts whatever in which the Government of the United States is concerned, either as debtor or creditor, shall be settled and adjusted in the General Accounting Office."

Sec. 306.

All laws relating generally to the administration of the departments and establishments shall, so far as applicable, govern the General Accounting Office. Copies of any books, records, papers, or documents, and transcripts from the books and proceedings of the General Accounting Office, when certified by the Comptroller General or the Assistant Comptroller General under its seal, shall be admitted as evidence with the same effect as the copies and transcripts referred to in sections 882 and 886 of the Revised Statutes.

Sec. 307.

The Comptroller General may provide for the payment of accounts or claims adjusted and settled in the General Accounting Office, through disbursing officers of the several departments and establishments, instead of by warrant.

Sec. 308.

The duties now appertaining to the Division of Public Moneys of the Office of the Secretary of the Treasury, so far as they relate to the covering of revenues and repayments into the Treasury, the issue of duplicate checks and warrants, and the certification of outstanding liabilities for payment, shall be performed by the Division of Bookkeeping and Warrants of the Office of the Secretary of the Treasury.

Sec. 309.

The Comptroller General shall prescribe the forms, systems, and procedure for administrative appropriation and fund accounting in the several departments and establishments, and for the administrative examination of fiscal officers' accounts and claims against the United States.

Sec. 310.

The offices of the six auditors shall be abolished, to take effect July 1, 1921. All other officers and employees of these offices except as otherwise provided herein shall become officers and employees of the General Accounting Office at their grades and salaries on July 1, 1921. All books, records, documents, papers, furniture, office equipment, and other property of these offices, and of the Division of Bookkeeping and Warrants, so far as they relate to the work of such division transferred by section 304, shall become the property of the General Accounting Office. The General Accounting Office shall occupy temporarily the rooms now occupied by the office of the Comptroller of the Treasury and the six auditors.

Sec. 311.

(a) The Comptroller General shall appoint, remove, and fix the compensation of such attorneys and other employees in the General Accounting Office as may from time to time be provided for by law.

(b) All such appointments, except to positions carrying a salary at a rate of more than $5,000 a year, shall be made in accordance with the civil-service laws and regulations.

(c) No person appointed by the Comptroller General shall be paid a salary at a rate of more than $6,000 a year, and not more than four persons shall be paid a salary at a rate of more than $5,000 a year.

(d) All officers and employees of the General Accounting Office, whether transferred thereto or appointed by the Comptroller General, shall perform such duties as may be assigned to them by him.

(e) All official acts performed by such officers or employees specially designated therefor by the Comptroller General shall have the same force and effect as though performed by the Comptroller General in person.

(f) The Comptroller General shall make such rules and regulations as may be necessary for carrying on the work of the General Accounting Office, including rules and regulations concerning the admission of attorneys to practice before such office.

Sec. 312.

(a) The Comptroller General shall investigate, at the seat of government or elsewhere, all matters relating to the receipt, disbursement, and application of public funds, and shall make to the President when requested by him, and to Congress at the beginning of each regular session, a report in writing of the work of the General Accounting Office, containing recommendations concerning the legislation he may deem necessary to facilitate the prompt and accurate rendition and settlement of accounts and concerning such other matters relating to the receipt, disbursement, and application of public funds as he may think advisable. In such regular report, or in special reports at any time when Congress is in session, he shall make recommendations looking to greater economy or efficiency in public expenditures.

(b) He shall make such investigations and reports as shall be ordered by either House of Congress or by any committee of either House having jurisdiction over revenue, appropriations, or expenditures. The Comptroller General shall also, at the request of any such committee, direct assistants from his office to furnish the committee such aid and information as it may request.

(c) The Comptroller General shall specially report to Congress every expenditure or contract made by any department or establishment in any year in violation of law.

(d) He shall submit to Congress reports upon the adequacy and effectiveness of the administrative examination of accounts and claims in the respective departments and establishments and upon the adequacy and effectiveness of departmental inspection of the offices and accounts of fiscal officers.

(e) He shall furnish such information relating to expenditures and accounting to the Bureau of the Budget as it may request from time to time.

Sec. 313.

All departments and establishments shall furnish to the Comptroller General such information regarding the powers, duties, activities, organization, financial transactions, and methods of business of their respective offices as he may from time to time require of them; and the Comptroller General, or any of his assistants or employees, when duly authorized by him, shall, for the purpose of securing such information, have access to and the right to examine any books, documents, papers, or records of any such department or establishment. The authority contained in this section shall not be applicable to expenditures made under the provisions of section 291 of the Revised Statutes.

Sec. 314.

The Civil Service Commission shall establish an eligible register of accountants for the General Accounting Office, and the examinations of applicants for entrance upon such register shall be based upon questions approved by the Comptroller General.

Sec. 315.

(a) All appropriations for the fiscal year ending June 30, 1922, for the offices of the Comptroller of the Treasury and the six auditors, are transferred to and made available for the General Accounting Office, except as otherwise provided herein.

(b) During such fiscal year the Comptroller General, within the limit of the total appropriations available for the General Accounting Office, may make such changes in the number and compensation of officers and employees appointed by him or transferred to the General Accounting Office under this Act as may be necessary.

(c) There shall also be transferred to the General Accounting Office such portions of the appropriations for rent and contingent and miscellaneous expenses, including allotments for printing and binding, made for the Treasury Department for the fiscal year ending June 30, 1922, as are equal to the amounts expended from similar appropriations during the fiscal year ending June 30, 1921, by the Treasury Department for the offices of the Comptroller of the Treasury and the six auditors.

(d) During the fiscal year ending June 30, 1922, the appropriations and portions of appropriations referred to in this section shall be available for salaries and expenses of the General Accounting Office, including payment for rent in the District of Columbia, traveling expenses, the purchase and exchange of law books, books of reference, and for all necessary miscellaneous and contingent expenses.

Sec. 316.

The General Accounting Office and the Bureau of Accounts shall not be construed to be a bureau or office created since January 1, 1916, so as to deprive employees therein of the additional compensation allowed civilian employees under the provisions of section 6 of the Legislative, Executive, and Judicial Appropriation Act for the fiscal year ending June 30, 1922, if otherwise entitled thereto.

Sec. 317.

The provisions of law prohibiting the transfer of employees of executive departments and independent establishments until after service of three years shall not apply during the fiscal year ending June 30, 1922, to the transfer of employees to the General Accounting Office.

Sec. 318.

This Act shall take effect upon its approval by the President: *Provided*, That sections 301 to 317, inclusive, relating to the General Accounting Office and the Bureau of Accounts, shall take effect July 1, 1921.

The Seal of the General Accounting Office

Figure IV.1: GAO Seal

Since the last report, there has been adopted an impression seal for use by the General Accounting Office, as authorized by law, and an impression thereof will be found at the end of this report. The seal comprises a shield segmented by a right angle containing 13 stars, representing the organization of the accounting office when there were but 13 united states. Below the stars is set out in relief the dome of the Capitol and the figure of freedom thereon representing the independence of judgment to be exercised by the General Accounting Office, subject to the control of the legislative branch. Above the right angle of stars, there appears the balance beam and scales symbolizing the justifiable principles on which the activities of the office are based, and to the right thereof is shown an account book and quill on which is crossed the key of the Treasury symbolizing the keeping of books on the accounting and auditing of public moneys. The combination represents an agency of the Congress independent of other authority auditing and checking the expenditures of the government as required by law and subjecting any question arising in that connection to quasi-judicial determination.

Source: *Annual Report of the General Accounting Office, 1924.*

Number of GAO Personnel, 1921-1966

Table V: Number of GAO Personnel, 1921-1966

Date	Number of personnel	Date	Number of personnel
7/01/21	1,708	6/30/44	11,992
6/30/22	2,011	6/30/45	13,836
6/30/23	2,035	6/30/46	14,219[a]
6/30/24	2,042	6/30/47	10,695
6/30/25	1,992	6/30/48	9,234
6/30/26	1,965	6/30/49	8,919
6/30/27	1,968	6/30/50	7,876
6/30/28	1,944	6/30/51	6,906
6/30/29	1,961	6/30/52	6,127
6/30/30	1,970	6/30/53	6,206
6/30/31	1,988	6/30/54	5,913
6/30/32	1,950	6/30/55	5,776
6/30/33	1,943	6/30/56	5,552
6/30/34	2,064	6/30/57	5,523
6/30/35	2,758	6/30/58	5,389
6/30/36	4,401	6/30/59	5,203
6/30/37	4,933	6/30/60	5,074
6/30/38	4,959	6/30/61	4,990
6/30/39	4,915	6/30/62	4,763
6/30/40	5,195	6/30/63	4,659
6/30/41	5,525	6/30/64	4,350
6/30/42	7,218	6/30/65	4,278
6/30/43	8,829	6/30/66	4,148

[a]All-time peak in the midpoint of fiscal year 1946: 14,904.

Sources: GAO *Annual Report*, fiscal years 1922-1966.

GAO Appropriations, 1921-1966

Table VI: GAO Appropriations, 1921-1966

Fiscal Year	Amount	Fiscal Year	Amount	Fiscal Year	Amount
1922	$ 2,019,550	1937	$5,715,840	1952	$ 32,488,832
1923	3,922,418	1938[a]	5,306,540	1953	32,060,000
1924	3,870,801	1939[a]	9,486,540	1954	31,981,000
1925	3,724,612	1940[a]	10,531,540	1955	31,981,000
1926	3,701,960	1941[a]	10,906,540	1956	33,481,000
1927	3,859,960	1942[a]	12,349,627	1957	34,000,000
1928	3,833,000	1943[a]	17,545,285	1958	37,009,546
1929	3,820,000	1944[a]	26,664,645	1959	39,020,500
1930	4,092,000	1945[a]	38,480,225	1960	41,800,000
1931	4,193,500	1946[a]	37,150,780	1961	42,179,000
1932	4,297,620	1947[a]	40,300,000	1962	43,000,000
1933	4,262,620	1948	36,517,000	1963[b]	43,900,000
1934	3,280,000	1949[a]	33,841,000	1964[c]	45,700,000
1935	4,461,920	1950	35,070,000	1965[d]	46,900,000
1936	4,970,600	1951	34,439,500	1966[e]	47,435,000

[a]The following figures represent amounts withheld in the prior fiscal year from contracts for payments of wages due to laborers and mechanics under the Employees of Contractors Act of August 30, 1935 (U.S.C. a-2) to be used in the following year in addition to the annual appropriation for that year:

Fiscal year	Amount	Fiscal year	Amount
1938	$ 4,692	1944	5,552
1939	2,005	1945	1,970
1940	967	1946	766
1941	10,479	1947	1,052
1942	1,475	1949	450
1943	1,446		

[b]$1,000 was transferred to "Operating Expenses, Public Buildings Service," GSA.

[c]$2,000 was transferred to "Operating Expenses, Public Buildings Service," GSA, 1964 (77 Stat. 436).

[d]$265,000 was transferred to "Operating Expenses, National Archives and Records Service," GSA, 1965 (77 Stat. 436).

[e]$23,000 was transferred to "Operating Expenses, Public Buildings Service," GSA, 1966, and $390,000 was transferred to "Operating Expenses, National Archives and Records Service" GSA, 1966 (79 Stat. 531 and 80 Stat. 674).

Source: The Office of Budget, General Services and Controller, GAO, compiled the information in this table.

Reports to the Congress, 1928-1966

Table VII: Reports to the Congress, 1928-1966

The following table indicates the volume of reports GAO submitted to the Congress and its Officers, Members, and Committees between 1928 and 1990. Statistics for fiscal years 1922-1927 are not available. Since GAO presented this information in varying ways over the years, the numbers are not always directly comparable.

Fiscal Year	Number of reports to the Congress	Fiscal Year	Number of reports to the Congress	Fiscal Year	Number of reports to the Congress
1928	231[a]	1947	196[b]	1959	159[c]
1929	255[a]	1948	429[b]		714[e]
1930	288[a]	1949	581[b]	1960	159[c]
1931	190[a]	1950	685[b]		493[e]
1932	320[a]	1951	686[b]	1961	143[c]
1933	122[a]	1952	37[c]		697[e]
1934	100[a]		4,205[d]	1962	152[f]
1935	127[a]	1953	71[c]		119[d]
1936	203[a]		3,783[d]	1963	196[f]
1937	186[a]	1954	41[c]		141[d]
1938	200[a]		3,353[d]	1964	293[f]
1939	188[a]	1955	71[c]		197[d]
1940	180[a]		718[e]	1965	411[f]
1941	143[a]	1956	89[c]		167[d]
1942	151[a]		632[e]	1966	181[f]
1943	138[a]	1957	85[c]		146[d]
1944	233[a]		731[e]		
1945	194[b]	1958	106[c]		
1946	139[b]		651[e]		

[a] Requested or suggested.
[b] Required, requested, or suggested.
[c] To the Congress and its officers.
[d] To the Committees and Members.
[e] To Committees.
[f] To the Congress.

Sources: GAO Annual Report, fiscal years 1928-1966.

Top Officials of the U.S. General Accounting Office, 1921-1966

Comptroller General	John Raymond McCarl, 1921-1936 Fred H. Brown, 1939-1940 Lindsay C. Warren, 1940-1954 Joseph Campbell, 1954-1965
Acting Comptroller General	Richard Nash Elliott, 1936-1939, 1940 Frank H. Weitzel, 1954, 1965-1966
Assistant Comptroller General	Lurtin R. Ginn, 1921-1930 Richard Nash Elliott, 1931-1943 Frank L. Yates, 1943-1953 Frank H. Weitzel, 1953-1969
Solicitor General Counsel (beginning in 1928)	Rudolph L. Golze, 1921-1939 John C. McFarland, 1939-1947 Edwin Lyle Fisher, 1947-1958 Robert F. Keller, 1958-1969
Executive Officer	J. L. Baity, 1921-1944 Dudley W. Bagley, 1944-1946 John F. Feeney, 1946-1953
Director, Office of Administrative Services	John F. Feeney, 1953-1965 Herschel J. Simmons, 1966-1971
Chief Clerk	F. B. Kitterman, 1922- (?) John K. Willis, 1925-1929 Reed Martin, 1930-1950 Ernest C. Bohannon, 1951-1953

Chief, Personnel Division	David Neumann, 1926 Earl Taggart, 1926-1933 W. W. Richardson, 1934-1939 Thomas A. McNamara, 1939-1943 E. Ray Ballinger, 1943-1946 Thomas A. Flynn, Jr., 1947-1968
Director, Office of Staff Management	Leo Herbert, 1956-1966
Director, Office of Personnel Management	Leo Herbert, 1968-1974
Special Investigator	Frank H. Bogardus, 1921-1922
Chief, Office of Investigations	Homer A. A. Smith, c. 1923-1931 Stuart B. Tulloss, 1931-1949 William L. Ellis, 1949-1955
Chief, Treasury Department Division	W. M. Geddes, 1921-1923
Chief, State and Other Departments Division	W. S. Dewhirst, 1921-1923
Chief, Interior Department Division	John K. Willis, 1921-1923
Chief, War Department Division	W. H. Barksdale, 1921-1923
Chief, Navy Department Division	George McInturff, 1921-1923
Chief, Civil Division	Earl Taggart, 1923-1926
Chief, Military Division	W. H. Barksdale, 1923-1926
Chief, Claims Division	W. S. Dewhirst, 1923-1926 Stuart B. Tulloss, 1926-1928 W. S. Dewhirst, 1928-1931 (acting) David Neumann, 1931-1945 A. Banks Thomas, 1946-1956 Lawrence V. Denney, 1957-1968

Chief, Transportation Division	Harrell O. Hoagland, 1948-1959 John P. Abbadessa, 1959 Oye V. Stovall, 1960-1964 Thomas E. Sullivan, 1965-1975
Chief, Post Office Department Division (Postal Accounts Division, 1940)	Charles T. M. Cutcheon, 1921-1930 Charles H. Cooper, 1931-1940 J. C. Nevitt, 1941-1943 Gary Campbell, 1943-1950
Chief, Check Accounting Division	Edward H. Bell, c. 1923-1925
Chief, Bookkeeping Division	Frank H. Bogardus, 1925-1935
Chief, Accounting and Bookkeeping Division	J. Darlington Denit, 1935-1950
Chief, Accounting Systems Division	Walter F. Frese, 1948-1956
Director, Accounting and Auditing Policy Staff	Walter F. Frese, 1956 Ellsworth H. Morse, Jr., 1956-1966
Director, Records Division	Reed F. Martin, 1926-1928 Russell H. Herrell, 1929 William W. Richardson, 1930-1933 Vernon R. Durst, 1934-1940
Director, Reconciliation and Clearance Division	Vernon R. Durst, 1940-1952
Director, Planning Staff	Robert F. Brandt, 1953-1955
Director, Corporation Audits Division	T. Coleman Andrews, 1945-1947 Stephen B. Ives, 1947-1952
Director, Audit Division	David Neumann, 1926-1930 Charles T. M. Cutcheon, 1931-1933 E. W. Bell, 1934-1952
Director of Audits	Ted B. Westfall, 1951-1952

Director, Division of Audits	Ted B. Westfall, 1952 Robert L. Long, 1952-1956 Ellsworth H. Morse, Jr., 1956
Director, Civil Accounting and Auditing Division (later Civil Division)	Ellsworth H. Morse, Jr., 1956 Adolph T. Samuelson, 1956-1972
Director, Defense Accounting and Auditing Division (later Defense Division)	Lawrence J. Powers, 1956-1959 William A. Newman, Jr., 1959-1968
Director, Field Operations Division	John E. Thornton, 1956-1976
Director, International Operations Division (later International Division)	Oye V. Stovall, 1963-1973
Director, European Branch	Henry R. Domers, 1952-1954 Charles M. Bailey, 1954-1956 Smith Blair, Jr., 1956-1959 Robert F. Brandt, 1959-1961 Lloyd G. Smith, 1961-1963 Edward T. Johnson, 1963-1965 Joseph DiGiorgio, 1965-1967
Director, Far East Branch	Robert F. Brandt, 1956-1959 Joseph Lippman, 1959-1963 Charles H. Roman, 1963-1974

Regional Managers:

Albuquerque, NM	P. J. Horman, 1952-1954
Atlanta, GA	Richard J. Madison, 1952-1972
Billings, MT	R. R. Everard, 1952-1954
Boston, MA	O. E. Paquin, 1952-1956 Thomas H. MacDonald, 1957 C. F. Carr, 1957-1962 Joseph Eder, 1963-1975

Regional Managers: (continued)

Chicago, IL	F. J. Pelland, 1952
	D. R. Moysey, 1952
	J. S. Sheridan, 1953-1954
	H. Perrill, 1954-1956
	Hyman L. Krieger, 1956-1959
	Meyer R. Wolfson, 1959-1973
Cincinnati, OH	Kenneth L. Weary, 1958-1966
Cleveland, OH	M. R. Beeman, 1952-1960
Dallas, TX	Harold P. Batchelder, 1952-1959
	Smith Blair, Jr., 1959-1964
	Walter H. Sheley, Jr., 1964-1974
Dayton, OH	Philip Charam, 1952
	H. H. Rubin, 1952-1955
	Stuart D. McElyea, 1955-1958
Denver, CO	H. L. Bushong, 1952-1954
	A. R. Horton, 1954-1962
	Stuart D. McElyea, 1963-1970
Detroit, MI	Kurt W. Krause, 1952-1957
	Charles H. Moore, 1957-1974
Juneau, AK	R. N. Earll, 1952
Kansas City, MO	J. H. Hammond, 1952-1954
	Forrest R. Browne, 1954-1966
	Kenneth L. Weary, 1966-1977
Los Angeles, CA	Harold L. Ryder, 1952-1966
	Hyman L. Krieger, 1966-1970
New Orleans, LA	H. D. Eaton, 1952-1956
	H. C. Barton, 1956-1963
	Walter H. Sheley, Jr., 1963-1964
	Walter H. Henson, 1964-1970

Regional Managers: (continued)

New York, NY

H. B. Bell, 1952-1954
Robert Drakert, 1954-1959
Hyman L. Krieger, 1959-1961
Robert Drakert, 1961-1970

Norfolk, VA

Clyde E. Merrill, 1957-1965
Albert J. Strazzullo, 1965-1970

Philadelphia, PA

J. S. Sheridan, 1952-1953
R. S. Tyree, 1953-1956
James S. Rogers, 1956-1973

Portland, OR

Charles F. Wells, 1952-1960

Richmond, VA

J. P. Glick, 1952
Clyde E. Merrill, 1953-1957

Salt Lake City, UT

A. J. Mouton, 1952
William N. Conrardy, 1953-1954

San Francisco, CA

John E. Thornton, 1952-1953
Alfred M. Clavelli, 1954-1974

Seattle, WA

G. Ray Bandy, 1952-1958
William N. Conrardy, 1958-1972

St. Louis, MO

Collin H. Blick, 1952-1960

St. Paul, MN

Harold H. Rubin, 1952-1953
W. F. Lutz, Jr., 1954-1956
Orlaf B. Hylle, 1957-1960

Washington, DC

Donald L. Scantlebury, 1964-1970

GAO Organization Charts

Figure IX.1: 1923

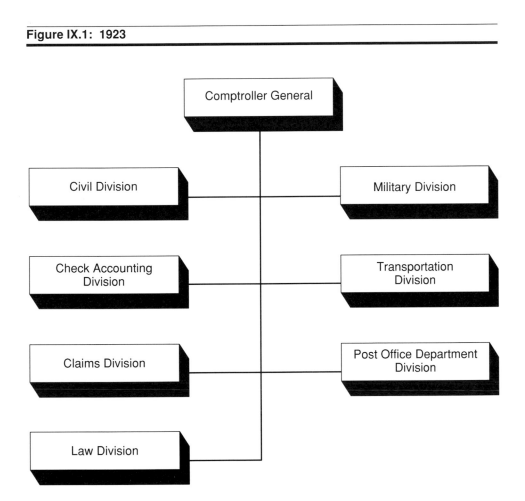

Figure IX.2: 1927

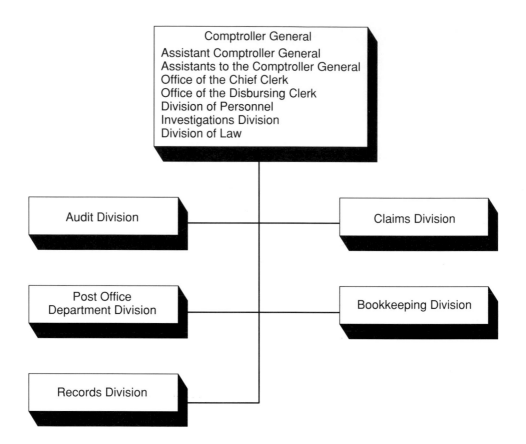

Figure IX.3: 1939

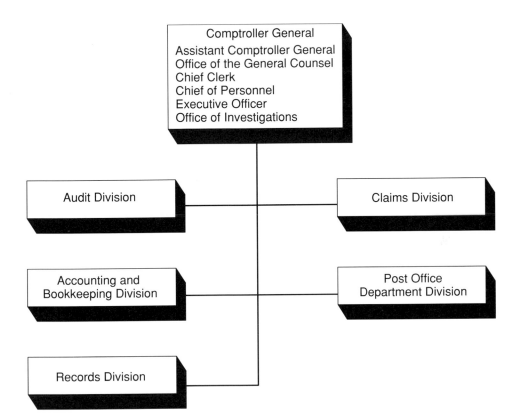

Comptroller General
Assistant Comptroller General
Office of the General Counsel
Chief Clerk
Chief of Personnel
Executive Officer
Office of Investigations

Audit Division

Claims Division

Accounting and Bookkeeping Division

Post Office Department Division

Records Division

Figure IX.4: 1948

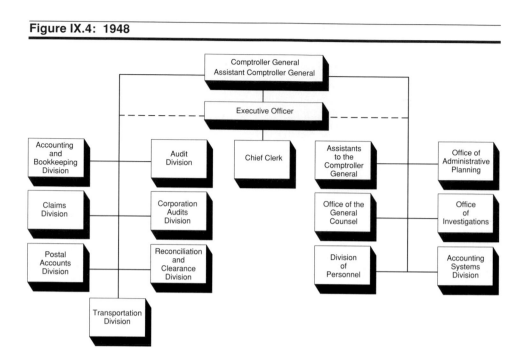

Figure IX.5: 1952

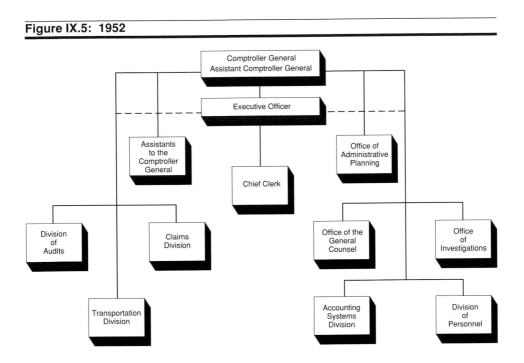

Figure IX.6: 1956

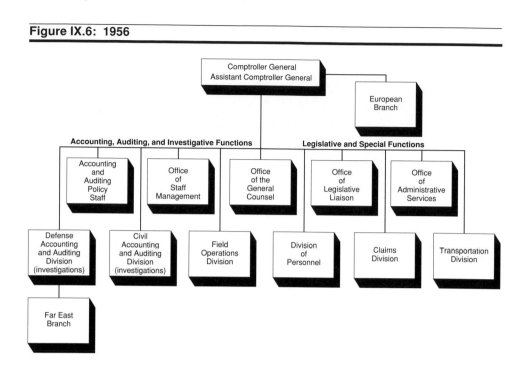

Figure IX.7: 1967

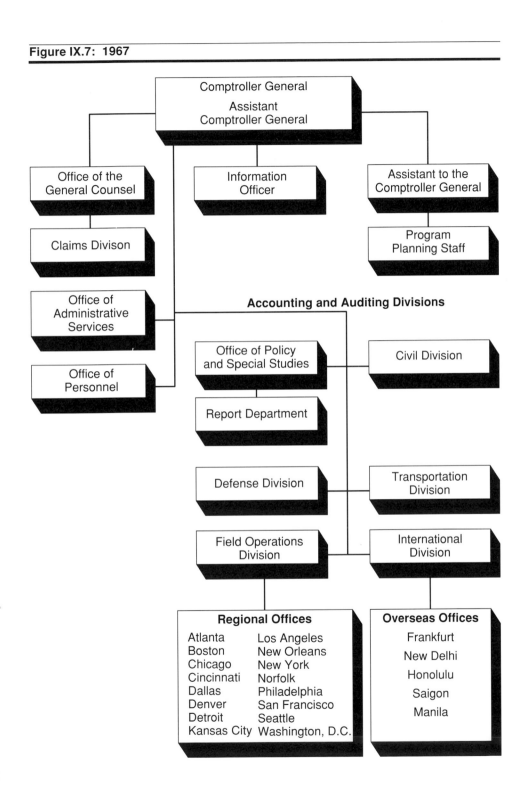

Comptroller General
Assistant Comptroller General

Office of the General Counsel

Information Officer

Assistant to the Comptroller General

Claims Divison

Program Planning Staff

Office of Administrative Services

Accounting and Auditing Divisions

Office of Policy and Special Studies

Civil Division

Office of Personnel

Report Department

Defense Division

Transportation Division

Field Operations Division

International Division

Regional Offices

Atlanta   Los Angeles
Boston   New Orleans
Chicago   New York
Cincinnati   Norfolk
Dallas   Philadelphia
Denver   San Francisco
Detroit   Seattle
Kansas City Washington, D.C.

Overseas Offices

Frankfurt

New Delhi

Honolulu

Saigon

Manila

Index